Throwing off the Cloak

Reclaiming self-reliance in Torres Strait

Elizabeth Osborne

Aboriginal Studies Press

First published in 2009
by Aboriginal Studies Press

© Elizabeth Osborne 2009

All rights reserved. No part of this book may be reproduced or transmitted in any form or by any means, electronic or mechanical, including photocopying, recording or by any information storage and retrieval system, without prior permission in writing from the publisher. The Australian *Copyright Act 1968* (the Act) allows a maximum of one chapter or 10 per cent of this book, whichever is the greater, to be photocopied by any educational institution for its education purposes provided that the educational institution (or body that administers it) has given a remuneration notice to Copyright Agency Limited (CAL) under the Act.

Aboriginal Studies Press
is the publishing arm of the
Australian Institute of Aboriginal
and Torres Strait Islander Studies
GPO Box 553, Canberra, ACT 2601
Phone: (61 2) 6246 1183
Fax: (61 2) 6261 4288
Email: asp@aiatsis.gov.au
Web: www.aiatsis.gov.au/aboriginal_studies_press

National Library of Australia
Cataloguing-In-Publication data:

Author: Osborne, Elizabeth, 1930–

Title: Throwing off the cloak : reclaiming self-reliance in Torres Strait / Elizabeth Osborne.

ISBN: 9780855756628

Notes: Includes index. Bibliography.

Subjects: Torres Strait Islanders — Ethnic identity. Torres Strait Islanders — Politics and government. Torres Strait Islanders — Government relations.

Dewey Number: 323.119912

Printed in Australia by Ligare Pty Ltd

Front cover image: James Akiba dancing at Djarragun College, Cairns. Courtesy Djarragun College

Contents

Illustrations	v
Informants	vi
Clusters of island communities in Torres Strait	vii
Map of Torres Strait and surrounds	viii
Map of islands of the Torres Strait	ix
Shortened forms	x
Acknowledgments	xii
Introduction	xiii
Chapter 1 The early years	1
Chapter 2 Paternalism challenged	21
Chapter 3 The growth of political activism	43
Chapter 4 Political momentum	71
Chapter 5 Ownership of land and sea	88
Chapter 6 Traditional ownership of the sea's resources	117
Chapter 7 Greater autonomy	135
Reflexions	158
References	168
Index	176

Aboriginal and Torres Strait Islander people are respectfully advised that this publication contains names and images of deceased persons. The Australian Institute of Aboriginal and Torres Strait Islander Studies apologises for any distress this may cause.

Illustrations

(between pp. 78–79)

Replicas of women's traditional digging sticks
Native village Murray Island (Mer)
Students at Darnley Island (Erub)
Pearling boats (Thursday Island)
Re-enactment of landing of missionaries (Saibai)
The author with the late Elders Eselina Nawie and Maleta Lota
Island women dancing at festival (Thursday Island)
Wartime hospital (Badu)
Ugarie Nona's house (Badu)
House built by Americans (Badu)
DNA boat *Melbidir IV*
Kuzi, DAIA training trawler.
Landing traders from Sui (PNG) (Mer)
Anglican Mission boat *Stephen Davies*
Island teachers, TSIREC Conference (Badu)
Barry Osborne with Dennis Passi and Dana Ober
The late Ted Loban
John Abednego
Terry Waia
Ron Day with visiting sea claim judge
Pedro Stephen
Bertha Natanielu
George Mye
Ron Day draped in Torres Strait flag
The late Eddie Koiki Mabo
Dancer wearing a Dauan Shark Headress, Saibai festival
Dancing at the Saibai festival
George Mye (Mer)
Japanese diver
Men aboard a lugger (Badu)
Drying trepang (Mer)
Solomon Nona with a dugong (Badu)
Church building (Mer)
Church procession (Badu)
Blessing a new dinghy (Mer)

Informants

Many of the Torres Strait Islanders I interviewed requested anonymity, and so I made the decision to give them all a descriptive title followed by a year date in brackets. As many of the interviews were conducted a long time ago I chose to add the year date to give readers a sense of timing. The perspectives of other Islanders who were named were generally from written sources.

Badu council employee (2006)
Late Badu Elder (1989)
Badu man living on Thursday Island (1990)
Badu nurse (1990)
Female Badu teacher (2006)
Badu man (1989, 1990)
Badu woman (1990)
Boigu man (1990)
Young Boigu nurse (1990)
Eastern island leader (2007)
Erub Elder (1989)
Young Erub fisher (2006, 2008)
Late Keriri Elder (1990)
Kubin woman (1990)
Local fisheries officer (2007)
Mabuiag woman (1989)
'Malay' woman (1989)
Masig woman (1989)
Late Meriam Elder (1990)
Former Meriam Island nurse (1991)
Meriam woman (1990)
Nagir woman (1989)
Two Nagir woman (1989)
Late Saibai Elder (1989)
Saibai woman (1989)

Tamwoy Town woman (1990)
Tanu's niece living on Thursday Island (1991)
Thursday Island female activist (2007)
Thursday Island health expert (2006)
Thursday Island woman (1988, 1990)
Younger Thursday Island woman (2007)
Thursday Island matron (1989)
Islander woman living in Brisbane (1989)
TSLI veteran (1989)
TSLI man (1989)
Ugar man (1990)
Veteran (Early History Workshop, Thursday Island, 1987)
Late Warraber Elder (Early History Workshop, Thursday Island, 1987)
Wartime signaller on Mer (1989, 1990)
Late Yam Island Elder (1989)
Yam Island teacher (2006)

Clusters of communities in Torres Strait

Near Western islands
- Badu (Mulgrave Island)
- Kubin and St Paul's on Moa (Banks Island)
- Mabuiag (Jervis Island)

Top Western islands
- Boigu (Talbot Island)
- Dauan (Mount Cornwallis Island)
- Saibai

Central islands
- Poruma — Purma (Coconut Island)
- Warraber (Sue Island)
- Yam (Turtle Backed Island)
- Masig (Yorke Island)

Eastern islands
- Erub (Darnley Island)
- Mer (Murray Island)
- Ugar (Stephens Island)

Inner communities
- Nurupai (Horn Island)
- Thursday Island
- Muralag (Prince of Wales Island)
- TRAWQ (Tamwoy, Rose Hill, Aplin, Waiben, Quarantine)

Northern Peninsula communities
- Bamaga
- Keriri (Hammond Island)
- Seisia

Torres Strait and surrounds

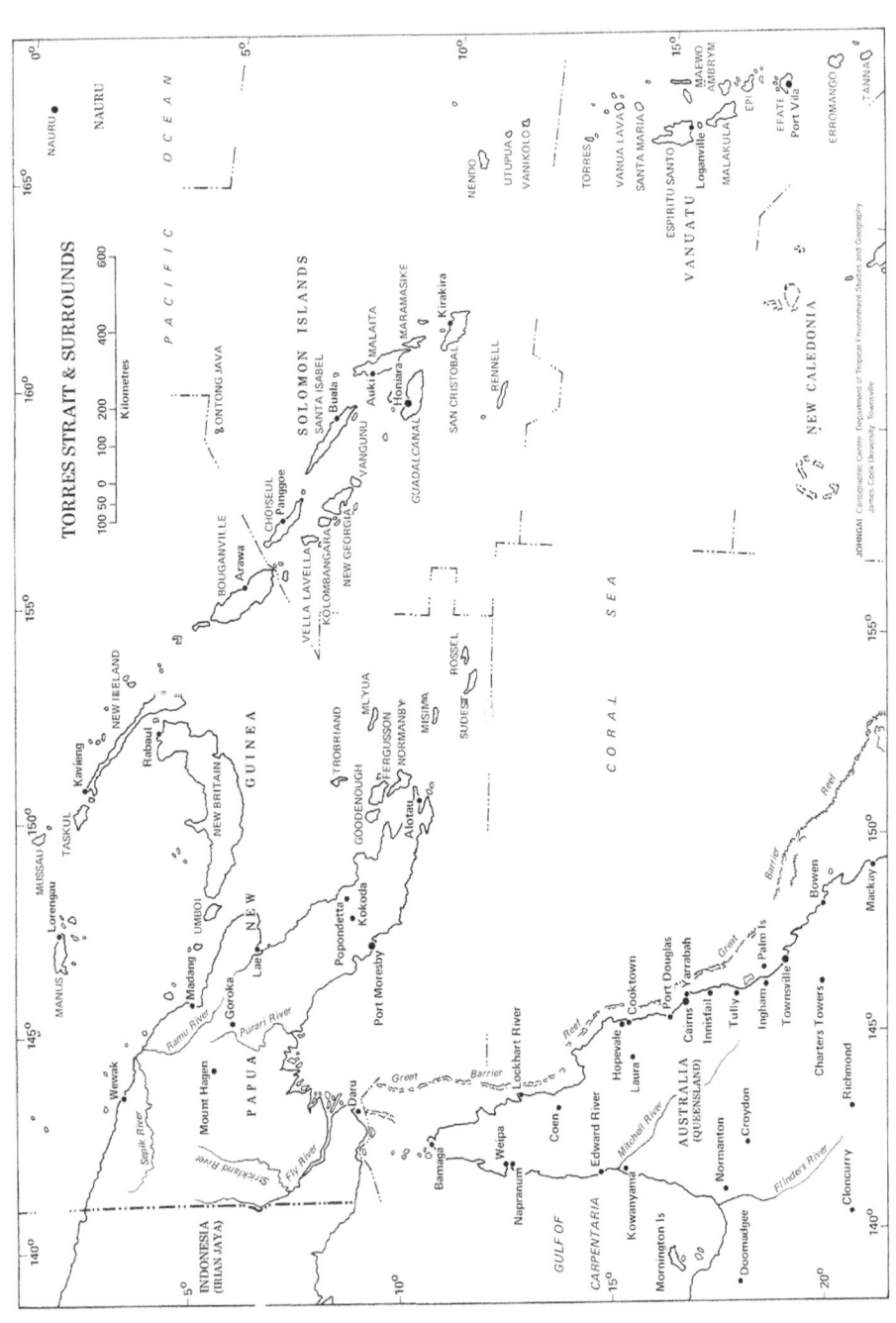

Reproduced with permission from Torres Strait Islander Women and the Pacific War, *Osborne E, 1997, Aboriginal Studies Press.*

Islands of the Torres Strait

Reproduced with permission from Torres Strait Islander Women and the Pacific War, *Osborne E, 1997,* Aboriginal Studies Press.

ix

Shortened forms

AAP	Allocation Advisory Panel
AFMA	Australian Fish Management Authority
AIATSIS	Australian Institute of Aboriginal and Torres Strait Islanders Studies
ATSIA	Aboriginal and Torres Strait Islander Affairs
ATSIC	Aboriginal and Torres Strait Islander Commission
AWM	Australian War Memorial
CDEP	Community Development Employment Program
CPA	Chief Protector of Aborigines
DAA	Department of Aboriginal Affairs (Commonwealth)
DAIA	Department of Aboriginal and Islander Affairs
DATSIP	Department of Aboriginal and Torres Strait Islander Policy
DLGPSR	Department of Local Government, Planning, Sport and Recreation
DNA	Department of Native Affairs
DOGIT	Deed of Grant in Trust
GASC	Greater Autonomy Steering Committee
HRSCATSIA	House of Representatives Standing Committee on Aboriginal and Torres Strait Islander Affairs
IAC	Island Advisory Council
ICC	Island Co-ordinating Council
IIB	Island Industries Board
ITE	Individual Transferable Effort
ITQ	Individual Transferable Quota
LMS	London Missionary Society
MAP	Medical Aid Post
NNTO	National Native Title Office
NTO	Native Title Office
PIL	Papuan Industries Limited
PNG	Papua New Guinea
QFMA	Queensland Fish Management Authority
QLA	Queensland Legislative Assembly

QPD	Queensland Parliamentary Debates
QPP	Queensland Parliamentary Papers
QSA	Queensland State Archives
TI	Thursday Island
TIB	Traditional Inhabitant Boat (licence)
TISHS	Thursday Island State High School
TRAWQ	Tamwoy, Rose Hill, Aplin, Waiben, Quarantine
TSC	Torres Shire Council
TSLI	Torres Strait Light Infantry
TSRA	Torres Strait Regional Authority
TSRC	Torres Strait Regional Council
TUP	Torres United Party
TVH	Transferable Vessel [Licence] Holder

Acknowledgments

This work would not have been possible without the contributions of the voices of Torres Strait Islanders. Many, who remain anonymous, personally shared their stories with me as much as twenty years ago. Sadly, many have died. But to those still on the islands or elsewhere I say 'a very big esso'. To all I am very grateful that I had the opportunity to record those stories. Throughout the book, Torres Strait Islander insights were also drawn from printed material and occasional discussions, and these informants are named — I owe to each one of them a debt of gratitude. The voices of all contributors made possible the weaving of the fabric of this history of the people's struggles to reclaim self-reliance in Torres Strait.

I acknowledge Aboriginal Studies Press, AIATSIS, for their tireless work in publishing this book. My thanks go to the two reviewers of the original manuscript for their valuable inputs.

And to my husband Barry Osborne for his enduring patience and motivating support over the years that it took to complete this work, I add yet another big ESSO.

Introduction

Before I went to Torres Strait, I, like most Australians, knew nothing about the area or its people. So when, in the mid 1960s, my 'missionary zeal' convinced me to go there from Adelaide it was no surprise that my daughter's grade 7 teacher asked, 'Where is Torres Strait? Who are the Torres Strait Islanders?'

I arrived on Thursday Island in December 1967, seven months after the referendum that gave the Commonwealth Government power to legislate for all Indigenous people, a power previously exercised by state governments and, in Queensland, by a government with low expectations for its Indigenous peoples. I knew nothing about Indigenous people being 'under the Act' (a paternalistic piece of nineteenth-century legislation that restricted Islander people's social and economic progress), but it was not long before I realised that the black people on Thursday Island were being treated very differently from white people.

My ignorance deprived me of any real understanding of the people's struggles that were going on at that time, though I did wonder why Ted Loban and his sister Ellie Gaffney, both of whom had Torres Strait Islander and Indonesian heritage, were so vocal about their treatment under the state's laws and by the Director of Native Affairs. However, I can recall that my Islander women friends unobtrusively manifested their concern for their children's futures through their willingness to work for anything in the community that might benefit them: on school committees because they wanted a higher standard of education in the schools; or by raising money for sporting facilities and trips so that their children could have a wider experience of the world. In hindsight I see them as always straining forward in the hope of a better life for their children and an escape from an unresponsive government.

It is now over 40 years since I first arrived on Thursday Island. I am no longer totally ignorant of the history of those past struggles, and of those still being played out today. Hence, the focus of the history I have written is the people of the Torres Strait Islands — the Torres Strait Islanders and the Kaurareg Aborigines — and their determination that their unique and separate identities be recognised and acknowledged in law and governance.

I began writing this history in the late 1980s, and updated it subsequently. There was and continues to be so much going on in Torres Strait with regard to land, sea and fishing rights and the search for a form of governance that would give people greater autonomy that I felt it was a story that needed to be told. I am seriously concerned that so little is known about the people of Torres Strait. Richard Davis, in *Woven histories, dancing lives: Torres Strait Islander identity, culture and history*, expresses concern about 'how little the wider public [know] about Torres Strait' and that there is a need to 'communicate to a broad audience the unique histories, identities and cultures of Torres Strait Islanders' (2004, p. vii). I agree with Davis. I also believe that the more we know about Indigenous history, the better we will understand our own history and indeed ourselves.

My work is grounded in what the philosopher of history Frank Ankersmit calls 'the scraps, the slips of the tongue' (1989, pp. 145–8). He claims that 'the goal [of history] is no longer integration, synthesis, and totality but it is those historical scraps which are the center of attention' (p. 149). In 1988, while I was working on my doctoral dissertation, I looked to the philosophical writings of Ankersmit, Michel Foucault and Jean-François Lyotard as their theories made 'room for all knowledges and afford[ed] greater opportunities for obtaining them' (Osborne E 1995, pp. 32–7). However, it seemed that my determination to write a dissertation grounded in the oral histories of old Torres Strait Islanders was pushing the academic boundaries in the history department of the university at the time. The response I received was that one could not write a doctoral dissertation foregrounding the memories of old people 50 years on — oral histories were considered no more than myth and legend.

However, Thomas Docherty, in an article entitled 'Criticism, history, Foucault', suggests that even the humblest of informants have 'unsuspected knowledges' (1992, p. 365) that should not be devalued, as they have been within the modernist rationalist notion of knowledge. Foucault talked about 'popular knowledges' (1980, p. 82), those of the ordinary people, and claimed there was a 'whole world of discourses' equally valuable whether accepted or excluded, dominant or dominated, that come into play in various ways (see also Ramazanoglu 1993, p. 19). Therefore, in the text that follows I have presented the voices of both the powerful and less powerful as all are valuable for a broader understanding of the diversity that exists in relation to the issues faced in Torres Strait. Moreover, Lyotard calls on us to 'actuate difference' (1991, p. 82); that is, set in motion diverse positions. In the latter chapters, these diverse positions are clearly apparent. Nevertheless, Torres Strait Islander academic Professor Martin Nakata points out that 'lack of a singular perspective' ('difference') in Torres Strait Islander affairs should not suggest that they have 'lost their way' (2007, pp. 211–12). Armed with these philosophical positions, my aim is not only to actuate difference but also to foreground Torres Strait Islander voices, from whatever source, in their articulation for a self-regulatory system in Torres Strait: a form of resistance to internal colonisation (Beckett 1987, pp. 17–21). I want the reader to hear their voices, as only they can tell the story of how it was and is for them.

In foregrounding the people's voices I have used my own interviews and conversations with Torres Strait Islanders and Kaurareg Aborigines. In acknowledgment of many requests for anonymity I have not named the individuals concerned but have used broad descriptive titles (the Eastern island leader, the Young Erub Fisher, the Badu nurse etc.). A list of these titles appears on page vi. I have also used citations from other sources: records of old voyagers in Torres Strait; the *Reports of the Cambridge anthropological expedition to Torres Strait*; and Torres Strait Islander voices cited in the works of researchers and perspectives recorded in journals, publications and newspapers. However, perspectives for about the past 15 years have been substantially drawn from *Torres News* (a weekly newspaper published on Thursday Island in print and on line), and newsletters and releases of the Australian Government's Torres Strait Regional Authority. Although I am aware that the reader may not get 'a sense of the deeper texture of the events and personages' (reviewer's comment) because of the impersonal way I chose to collect some of the data, I doubt that peoples' memories would have recalled much of the detail obtained from the written source.

The identity of the people of the Torres Strait is an important issue. Shnukal contends that there are two twentieth-century Torres Strait Islander identities: one 'pan-Islander'; and one 'national' (2004, p. 107):

> By pan-Islander identity I mean [Torres Strait] Islanders' self-perception of themselves at the macro-level as a unified and unique group of people, different culturally and historically from their northern and southern mainland neighbours.

Introduction

While the Torres Strait Islanders certainly see themselves as different to their northern and southern neighbours, at the micro level they have always identified themselves as belonging to individual islands — for example, Meriam, Saibaian, Baduan — hence the occasional references to their island identities (plural). Shnukal explains that a national identity 'seeks its political expression in what Islander leaders have called variously "autonomy", "sovereignty", "self-determination", "self-management", "self-government" and "independence" '. These various terms are used by the Torres Strait Islanders as 'political manifestations' of their aspirations for self-regulation within Australia (2004, p. 108). However, as I discuss later, the meaning of these terms is not widely understood. Further, I contend that a third, pre-twentieth-century Torres Strait Islander identity exists in addition to Shnukal's two twentieth-century identities; that which identifies them with their individual islands. As I will also show there is of course a fourth identity that relates to the people of the Torres Strait: that of the Kaurareg Aborigines.

The struggles of the Torres Strait Islanders are presented in a broadly chronological order, though the complexity of some subjects (particularly land and sea rights, and control of the sea's resources) demands that they be treated separately. Torres Strait Islander politics is dynamic, proactive and reactive, and so there will inevitably be developments in the years following the publication of this book that bring new perspectives to bear on the topics covered. However, the work that follows sets out much of the context of the political and social debates that Torres Strait Islanders and Kaurareg Aborigines are engaging in with Australian governments.

Notes to the reader

Many of the legal discussions around native title, and land and sea rights, that are covered in this book are complex. Some of the complexity arises from the legal terminology used and from the many organisations involved. I have endeavoured where possible to simplify the arguments surrounding these issues without 'dumbing down' the matter at hand. Similarly, I have avoided overuse of shortened forms for departments and organisations. A few key organisations — such as the Island Co-ordinating Council, the Torres Strait Regional Authority and the Torres Strait Regional Council — occur so frequently in some sections that I have used their shortened forms (ICC, TSRA and TSRC respectively). Should the reader unfamiliar with these shortened forms need to refresh their memory, I direct them to the list of 'Shortened forms' on pages x–xi. Where Torres Strait language words are used they are *italicised*.

Finally, a note on the words 'Aborigine' and 'Aboriginal' to denote Torres Strait Islander people. In several older documents or position titles, such as 'Chief Protector of Aborigines', the word 'Aborigine' is used as a blanket term to describe all Indigenous peoples. However, Torres Strait Islanders have for many decades fought strenuously to protect their distinctiveness.

Elizabeth Osborne
April 2009

CHAPTER 1

The Early Years

In the nineteenth century, two cultures collided in Torres Strait: the culture of the Torres Strait Islander peoples, and that of the European peoples. Each had very different beliefs about how their worlds came into being. The Torres Strait Islanders had passed down their unwritten creation stories from generation to generation for thousands of years. Margaret Lawrie collected many of these stories in *Myths and legends of Torres Strait* (1970); three are reproduced below. The first describes how certain rock and land formations around Mabuiag originated. The second tells how an island woman went to live on the moon, where she is seen to this day. The third explains the formation of the two hills on the island of Dauan.

> *Once upon a time two sisters, Widul and Marte, lived with their brother, Umai, at the northwestern end of Mabuiag. Widul had a daughter named Sarabar, and Marte had a daughter named Iadi. One day Widul and Marte quarrelled. Widul threw a spear at Marte, which split her down the middle, at the same instant as Marte threw several spears at Widul. Marte's spears burst the top of Widul's skull and stuck in it.*
>
> *Umai put a stop to the fight between the two sisters — as their brother, he had a right and duty to do it — by moving them far apart from each other and sending them to places of his choosing on the reef which surrounds Mabuiag. The sisters and their daughters became islands. Umai turned to stone and has ever since stood guard over them at the edge of the passage through the reef between Mabuiag and another island, Aipus. He can be seen at low tide.*

Widul stays south of him and keeps her small daughter Sarabar behind her. Marte's place is north of him and she also keeps her daughter Iadi behind her. For a long time, pandanus trees grew at the top of Marte—they were the spears that were thrown at her by her sister Widul.

(Told by Dakanatai (Dakantai) Kris, Mabuiag, 1967;
reproduced with consent of nephew Bani Lee)

Aukam of Saibai wove mats by the light of the moon. The woman did no other work. When the moon rose at night she took dry coconut leaves and began to weave. When the moon set she laid down her work and slept. It was always her way — Aukam of Saibai wove mats by the light of the moon and at no other time.

The moon saw that she worked only when he was present and, believing the reason to be that she loved him, came down one night and took her up to the sky. Within the circle of the moon's embrace Aukam still weaves her mats, as all may see.

(Told by Wagea Waia, Saibai, 1967;
reproduced with consent of son Terry Waia)

Two sisters, Apinini and Sidipaur, wove the two hills of the island of Dauar [Dowar]. Apinini was the elder sister, Sidipaur was the younger. They sat at opposite ends of the island to do their weaving. After a while Sidipaur felt thirsty and she went to visit her sister. When Sidipaur reached her, Apinini laid down her work and did not take it up again. But because Apinini had worked at her hill longer than Sidipaur had on hers, Apinini's hill was bigger than Sidipaur's.

The two sisters turned to stone and may be seen at Au Dauar, the big hill woven by Apinini. The smaller hill woven by Sidipaur is called Kebi Dauar.

(Told by Robert Pitt, Mer, 1968;
reproduced with consent of grandson Edward Captain)

For many westerners the Bible teaches the creation story. The book of Genesis describes how 'In the beginning God created the heaven and the earth'. But not all westerners believe these teachings — some have no answer as to how the world came into being, for others it had no beginning, and there are those who delve into the origins of the earth's creation and its populations scientifically. Much archaeological work is still to be done in Torres Strait and so speculation continues about its formation and the arrival of the inhabitants. Golson (1972,

p. 379) suggests that the western islands were first occupied 6500 to 8000 years ago after the area was inundated by the post-glacial rise in sea level that submerged much of the land bridge between Australia and New Guinea, thus creating a profusion of islands, cays and reefs (Jennings 1972, p. 29). Moore suggests that people arrived by canoe in the east soon after the archipelago was formed (1979, pp. 310–11), while Golson hypothesised that a later population arrived in outrigger canoes 5000 to 6000 years ago (1972, p. 379). According to anthropologist Maureen Fuary (1991, p. 41), what is certain is that the area was well and truly inundated 4000 years ago, but 'whatever [scientific] speculations are made, there is no doubt that colonial occupation of the area pales in insignificance before the thousands of years of Indigenous occupation' (Osborne E 1995, p. 43).

The people living on the archipelago of islands between Australia's Cape York Peninsula and Western New Guinea were free and independent until European intervention. The Westerners who came to the area saw themselves as a 'civilised' people and they asserted that position. They made laws that failed to recognise the peoples' unique individual island ways and ownership of their islands, surrounding seas and marine resources. This has resulted in the long struggle for recognition of this ownership and a form of governance whereby they can determine their own futures.

The environment and the people

Of the 200 or so islands in Torres Strait, only about 20 were permanently habitable as water supplies were often inadequate or non-existent. The population was thought to be 3000 to 4000 during the early contact years (Beckett 1972, p. 312). The islands fell into four geographical groups with different food sources. The volcanic islands of the eastern group were well suited to horticulture and one observer, the missionary W Wyatt Gill (1876, p. 215), wrote: 'every variety of tropical fruit grows profusely' on Mer (Murray Island). Gardens were less prolific on the coral cays of the central group as they often lacked adequate drinking water; during the dry season water had to be transported in canoes from nearby uninhabited islands. The low-lying swampy islands in the top-western group were suitable for gardening in the dry season: in the wet they obtained produce from the villages along the adjacent New Guinea coast. However, Gill found on Mabuiag that there were a 'few cocoa-palms (coconut)' but the population of 300 was engaged in pearl shelling and had, in his Eurocentric opinion, 'unwisely ceased to cultivate the soil' (1876, p. 201). On Badu, Gill reported that 'they never cultivate anything, living on fruits and roots growing spontaneously'. He observed an absence of 'cocoanut-trees' on Moa and Badu and claimed he planted 'fifty cocoa-nuts on different islets' (p. 200). However, 10 years later (1886), under the influence of a white man known only as Wini, it was reported that the people on Moa and Badu were 'giving considerable attention to the cultivation of yams and bananas' (Haddon 1935, p. 62). (Torres Strait Islander historian Ephrain Bani suggested that Wini (or Weenie) was a Dutch sailor, skilled in shipbuilding, who had escaped from Sydney's penal colony and somehow made his way to Torres Strait and was befriended by the Badulgal (Baduans) with whom he worked as a boat builder (*Torres News* 16–22 January 2004, p. 10). Another opinion is that he was a survivor from a shipwreck (Moore 1979, p. 9).)

Barbara Thompson, a Scottish woman who had been shipwrecked when the cutter *America* went down in Endeavour Strait with all others on board lost, lived for almost five years with the Kaurareg tribe on Muralag (Prince of Wales Island). Following her rescue in 1849, Thompson described food supplies on Muralag where the people were semi-nomadic: 'They find a food which they call *coti*, like a yam ... They dig it out among the stony places. In the rainy season it runs all to water and it is no good. When *coti* is down [out of season], they eat the long pods of the mangroves'. She also talked about the men's and women's roles in food collection (Moore 1979, p. 268):

> *On most days the subsistence group on Muralag (usually the extended family) split into two parties, the men and older boys leaving by canoe to catch turtle and fish and the women and girls to the hills and slopes to get yams, coti, and fruits, or else moving around the shoreline to collect shellfish and crustacean.*

On more fertile islands such as Mer, where a great variety of fruit and vegetables flourished in the volcanic soil, men often cleared the land for gardening with shell hoes and axes while the women worked the soil with their digging sticks and planted and harvested crops. One of anthropologist Nonie Sharp's old informants said his Meriam father was a 'real gardener and taught me too'; he added, 'That's why I love gardening. It's in my veins. I give gardening my first priority' (Sharp 1993, p. 82). Throughout Torres Strait the women were generally responsible for the family's daily supplies of fish, crayfish and shellfish collected from along the shoreline. The men's contributions of turtle and dugong were less reliable on a daily basis, but these highly prized foods were important to feasting in every community. The women were the principal carriers of water and fuel. This was basically the male–female division of labour throughout Torres Strait.

1. The Early Years

All islands were involved in the Torres Strait trade network and the men were the traders as well as participants in raiding parties. For example, from their trading partners in the villages along the adjacent coast of New Guinea, the men of the top-western islands obtained long outrigger canoe hulls. In 1976, Eddie Mabo from Mer told a seminar that 'The Strait is criss-crossed with trade routes and some of our items such as shells found their way deep into the interior of New Guinea and into Cape York Peninsula ... exchange through trade was a highly refined system' (Griffin 1976, p. 34). Goods, including New Guinea bird-of-paradise plumes, were exchanged for pearl shell from Badu and Muralag through Mabuiag. The Kaurareg Aborigines obtained spears, spear throwers and red ochre from the tribes on the mainland (p. 34). As early as 1822 'an active barter ... commenced' between the island people and the outsiders (Haddon 1935, p. 95). However, they refused to relinquish their goods until they were satisfied they were receiving an equivalent exchange, suggesting that they 'must have been cheated in former dealings with Europeans' (pp. 95–6).

Traditionally, religious beliefs and practices permeated all aspects of the lives of the various groups of Melanesian people in the South West Pacific, including those who were located in Torres Strait (Whiteman 1983, p. 64). Ethno-historian Whiteman's research led him to believe that Melanesian people did not live in the same 'compartmentalized world of secular and spiritual domains' associated with Christianity (p. 65). Despite variations in their spiritual practices they relied on the supernatural to maintain the balance of their universe and its continual renewal (pp. 65–6). The rhythm of their lives was 'dictated by the stars, moon, winds, tides and seasons along with supernatural powers upon which they called for good and evil purposes'. They believed 'physical and spiritual realities dovetailed ... Plants, animals, inorganic matter and spirit beings all belonged to an integrated cosmos' (p. 65). The Torres Strait Islanders had no national gods (Haddon 1908, p. 217), but rituals were used to tap into supernatural powers. The god Malo of Mer came from the west in the form of an octopus to unite the eight tribes of Mer, Dauar and Waier. On Badu and Mabuiag warriors gained strength from the shell ornaments worn by Kwoiam who came from the Australian mainland (Haddon 1935, p. 58). The 'sacred light' of the Adhibuya Stone (which came from Kiwai New Guinea to Saibai) gave magical powers to warriors (Walker 1972, p. 322; Beckett 1963, p. 13). Totems and sacred inanimate objects were called upon to ensure good hunting and fishing and to give victory in battle. However, in Torres Strait the various island groups seemed to have adopted or added to their religious systems or practices if they discovered a spiritual order which suited their purposes better. Haddon suggests that in the eastern islands totemism was dealt a 'death blow' but in the western islands he thought hero cults were 'grafted on' to their totems (1901, p. 257). By the time of western intervention, a complex web of religious practices existed throughout Torres Strait, the knowledge of which today is generally reflected to the outsider through the blurred lenses of white researchers (Osborne E 1995, pp. 180–6).

Housing ranged from the long bridge-like houses the Kaurareg built for the wet season to more-permanent, small beehive-shaped grass homes on Mer or the two-storied houses on Dauan. Gill indicated that the people on Badu built no houses and had no fixed place of abode (1876, p. 200), but Haddon recorded that in 1888 there were three types of houses on that island: huts 'little more than sloping walls meeting a roof'; small houses on piles; and large grass houses inhabited by the South Sea Island men (1904, p. 97).

The village was the basis of social organisation and kinship taboos regulated island life (Haddon 1908, p. 99). In the eastern islands marriage was across villages or nearby islands (p. 121). On other islands, marriage was across clan totems. A 'significant ceremonial practice' was the loan of a woman as an 'agent of peace' by a warrior husband to an opposing warrior to 'defuse tension' between the warriors. The loan of a woman might lead to an intermarriage between non-warring clans (Kennedy 1986, p. 38). Polygamy was practised and Gill found the chief of Dauan had six wives (1876, p. 208). Smaller islands that could not support large populations practised birth control and children could be adopted by childless families or by older members of families as security for their old age (Haddon 1908, p. 99, but see a deconstruction by Torres Strait academic Martin Nakata 2007, pp. 124–6). Nonetheless, variations existed in the practices of each of the island groups. The title Torres Strait Islanders, given to them by white outsiders, suggests a homogenous group of people but this is far from reality. Indeed, Nakata claims his people were and still are a 'complex and diverse heterogenous group of people with differing needs' (1990, p. 5). An eastern island leader (2007) said that today the people still see themselves as belonging to individual islands as well as the wider Torres Strait Islander community:

> *I always go back to individuality ... [Eddie] Koiki Mabo was just an individual, but he had his immediate family, and then he had his Mabo clan and then he had the tribal and all the tribal get together comes a community ... Obviously without individuality there would be no society ... so when you ask me where I'm from I just simply say from Murray Island. I am Meriam ... but when you come out and*

1. The Early Years

someone meet you in Australia [mainland], where you from? [I say] Torres Strait, Torres Strait Islander and when you get to TI [Thursday Island] and you say, where you from? I'm from Murray.

These island societies were based on a principle of reciprocity as sharing promoted equality and the assurance that no one would go hungry. A Boigu man (1990) recalled the practice, saying that his forefathers had passed the knowledge down from the 'before-before' time (that is, the time long before white intervention; 'before' time refers to a more recent time before intervention):

Our people were never greedy ... If you share with somebody that person would share with you ... seeing an old bloke there, if I come home from fishing and that old bloke is there, you give him that fish.

Haddon wrote that, in general, the islands of the Torres Strait had 'a simple form of government ... an oligarchy of elders ... their decisions were based on tradition and custom, and that justice and equity resulted from the free discussion of the old men' (1904, p. 264). MacGillivray (1852, p. 27) and the missionary McFarlane (1888, p. 28) both concluded that there were no hereditary chiefs on the islands. However, from about the 1840s strong winds of change began to blow in Torres Strait that impacted on many aspects of island life and, in particular, community self-regulation.

As mentioned above, there are diverse opinions on the origins of the Torres Strait Islanders and this is reflected in their language. There is one western and central islands language — Kala Lagaw Ya. Kalaw Kawaw Ya (Saibai) is one of the four dialects of that language. While including Melanesian elements from Papua, Kala Lagaw Ya, has a structure similar to mainland Aboriginal languages (see Shnukal 1993, p. 154). Beckett, who has created an extensive prehistory of the Torres Strait, notes there may have been a 'merging' of the Papuan and Aboriginal peoples in the past. Meriam Mer, the language of eastern Torres Strait, is a member of the Trans-Fly family (Melanesian) (1987, p. 25).

As to the genetic status of the Kaurareg (and to a lesser extent the Kulkalaig from Nagir), their social system was 'closely allied' with the groups to the north and east of Muralag and were integrated into the Torres Strait trading network while maintaining 'intimate' contact with the mainland Aborigines 'although they were physically and culturally more "Aboriginalised" than the other western Torres Strait groups' (Moore 1979, p. 313).

Whatever the cultural mix, the original inhabitants of the Torres Strait had one thing in common: their belief that the islands and the sea surrounding them were extensions of themselves. In 1976 Getano Lui Snr, then chair of the Yam Island Council, made it clear that the 'islands and seas were given to us by our ancestors. We must pass them on to our children. We do not want them to become strangers in their own land' (Griffin 1976, p. xxv). Nonetheless, with the coming of Europeans, sovereignty over their islands and seas was indeed taken from them.

Early outsider intrusions

The people who settled the islands in Torres Strait formed unique cultures with variations from island to island that they passed down orally from generation to generation. Because of their oral traditions, researchers are mainly reliant on Eurocentric records of contact with these island people. The earliest records are those of European seamen who passed through Torres Strait. The London Missionary Society's missionaries also recorded their perspectives of the lives of the people they were attempting to Christianise. In the late-nineteenth century, the anthropologist Alfred Haddon and his team collected artefacts and compiled an extensive written record from interviews with Torres Strait Islanders of their customs, practices and spirituality (however, for a deconstruction of the team's findings see Martin Nakata 2007, pp. 15–128). Margaret Lawrie published the myths and legends told to her by Torres Strait Islander Elders (cited above) and at about the same time David Moore published an ethnographic reconstruction of the journals of Oswald Brierly, the artist aboard the *Rattlesnake* that sailed through the Strait from 1848 to 1850. The late Ephraim Bani, Mabuiag man, historian, linguist and world-renowned cultural ambassador for Torres Strait, shared much of his traditional knowledge in articles in the *Torres News* and other writings (see Bani 1978; Bani 2004). It is from these written records that insights are gained into the traditional world of the peoples of the Torres Strait islands.

The earliest visitors to the Strait were those on voyages of discovery rather than acquisition. In 1606 two ships of the great maritime powers Holland and Spain found their way through the hazardous seaway between Australia and New Guinea that would eventually take its name from the Spanish captain Luis Vaez de Torres. In 1770 James Cook passed through Torres Strait by way of a channel he named Endeavour Strait. Despite the currents and labyrinths of uncharted reefs, Endeavour Strait came to be used as a regular passage for an increasing number of ships. In 1792 Captain William Bligh was sent by the British government to look for a new deep-sea passage, and on this voyage he discovered a suitable waterway north of Hammond Island that he named Prince of

Wales Channel. Midshipman Matthew Flinders, accompanying Bligh on that expedition, made contact with the inhabitants of Erub (Darnley Island) and described them as 'dextrous sailors and formidable warriours [sic]; and to be much at ease in the water as in their canoes ... They could swim like dolphins, fight with the power of sharks and glide through the shallows with the ease of alligators' (cited in Sharp 1993, p. 20).

Arriving at Tutu (or Warriour (later Warrior) Island, to use Bligh's spelling), Kebisu the 'commander of the canoes' led his men with bows and arrows into battle against Bligh; the story of Kebisu's victorious feat has been passed down orally from generation to generation. In a version of the battle told to researcher Nonie Sharp by the granddaughter of Maino-Kebisu, and great-great-granddaughter of the Tut warrior Kebisu, she said: 'They [the warriors] chase away them warship ... It's true he [Kebisu] been win that war' (Sharp 1993, p. 23). Author John Singe (personal communication 1990), relying on European records, challenges this interpretation, indicating that Kebisu died in the mid 1860s and was therefore unlikely to have participated in a battle that took place in 1792. Bligh's records state that he settled the matter by 'discharging two of the quarter deck guns [and it brought] horrible consternation to [the warriors] and they fled from their canoes ... into the sea and swam to windward like porpoises' (Sharp 1993 p. 22). Whoever the victor matters little now to outsiders, but Bligh's discovery of Prince of Wales Channel mattered greatly to them then as it does now because it gave the outsiders a vital deep-sea passage for ships. More importantly for the Torres Strait Islanders, the ownership of their sea space was being challenged by these outsiders.

Throughout the early 1800s the volume of sea traffic through Torres Strait increased, and by about 1840 steamships were appearing in these waters. The Strait — with its unchartered reefs, cays and strong tides — was a dangerous sea passage and many ships were lost.

During this period the Torres Strait gained a notorious reputation for brutality. In 1836, CM Lewis, captain of the schooner *Isabella,* was commissioned to search for survivors from the wreck of the *Charles Eaton.* On Aurid Island he found the 42 skulls of those who had been shipwrecked. (Haddon wrote that 'It was a meritorious deed to kill foreigners either in fair fight or by treachery, and honour and glory was attached to the bringing home of skulls of the inhabitants of other islands slain in battle' (1908, p. 314), and Gill wrote that skulls were traded and worshipped (1876, pp. 207, 217).) The Torres Strait Islanders became known as formidable sea-warriors, and sailing directions to mariners gave warning of that fact (Sharp 1984, p. 8).

Torres Strait Islanders had gone to battle among themselves for generations, but when the outsiders arrived there were occasions of brutality between them. Langbridge (1977, p. 26) suggests the island population was 'depleted through murder, kidnapping and ... diseases', prompting the British government to act to bring order to the area. Between 1842 and 1850, first Captain Blackwood of the *Fly* and then Captain Owen Stanley of the *Rattlesnake* were commissioned for this purpose. (It was the crew of the *Rattlesnake* who rescued Barbara Thompson and she went on to give MacGillivray, the zoologist on board, valuable information about the people living in the region (Moore 1979, pp. 142–229).)

The ocean's bounty enticed the next wave of visitors to the Strait: fishers of bêche-de-mer (also known as trepang or sea slug) and trochus (a type of marine gastropod), and pearl shellers all arrived throughout the nineteenth century. Malay and possibly even Chinese bêche-de-mer fleets worked in Torres Strait prior to 1868, when a Captain Banner set up a pearl shelling station at Tut following the discovery of commercial quantities of pearl shell (Langbridge 1977, pp. 27–8). Soon a flood of shellers and fishers arrived in Torres Strait but, unlike the earlier Asian fishers and Banner, many had little regard for the islands' inhabitants. Profit-seeking pearlers and bêche-de-mer fishers saw them as a cheap source of labour for their expanding industry. They destroyed food and water supplies, young men were taken from their islands for cheap labour (and were often not returned), and abduction and ill treatment of women was common. On Tut, to protect the women the men buried them in the sand up to their noses whenever a vessel was sighted (Sharp 1984, p. 10) and on Pulu, an island west of Mabuiag, there is a cave 'where women and girls were secreted from white and coloured men in the early days of the fishing for bêche-de-mer and pearl shell' (Haddon 1935, p. 55). In about 1864, the South Sea Islander crew of the bêche-de-mer fishing vessel the *Woodlark*, under a Captain Bruce, went to Mer in quest of women. They met with a level of resistance that resulted in the death of one island man, his killer (one of Bruce's crew), and subsequently brutal acts of reprisal against the people in which Bruce himself was involved (Haddon 1908, pp.190–1).

The colonial government of Queensland realised that lawlessness in the Strait must be controlled. Importantly, too, a port of refuge and a coaling station were needed to service the burgeoning number of ships in the area. Somerset at Port Albany was set up in 1864. It was said that 'everybody down south was talking about Somerset ... the merchants of Brisbane and Sydney made up their minds that [it] must go ahead'

(Douglas 1900, p. 9). A Singapore of Australia was envisaged for this northern location, and a 'good many thousands were taken into the Treasury at Brisbane' as allotments of land were sold (p. 9). John Jardine was appointed the police magistrate but he and two of his successors — his son Frank Jardine, and HM Chester, a former government land agent — had 'derogatory attitude[s] to and a total lack of understanding of either Aborigines or [Torres Strait] Islanders' (Moore 1979, p. 11). Mainland Aboriginal troopers replaced the British marines stationed at Somerset after the British withdrew their protection of the outpost.

It was Chester's notorious Aboriginal troopers who carried out reprisals against the Kulkalgal (Nagir Island people) and were responsible for the infamous attack on the Kaurareg. In 1869 the crew and captain of the *Sperwer* were murdered; Gudangs (a tribe of Cape York Aborigines) identified three Kulkalgal as the culprits and Chester's troopers burnt their camp and shot, without trial, Kulkalgals (Carroll 1969, p. 40). After the attack on the *Sperwer* there was, according to one of Nonie Sharp's informants who got information from Frank Jardine's son, a slaughter at the Kaurareg village by the Aboriginal mounted troopers and the South Sea Islander crew of the *Melanie*: '[They] burnt [it] out ... There was a terrible killing ... No one knows how many were killed' (Sharp 1992, p. 71). Three years later the missionary W Wyatt Gill wrote that he visited that area and described a 'scene of more than ample revenge exacted by whites' (1876, p. 200). While there are those who reject the interpretation that Kaurareg numbers in the Cape York area were drastically reduced by outsiders, Moore contends 'there was a considerably greater slaughter of Prince of Wales Islanders than was mentioned in the official reports ... the Kaurareg were decimated ... and scattered' (Moore 1979, pp. 12–13). Eventually, their traditional lands came under the control of the Queensland Government along with those of the people who lived on the other islands in Torres Strait.

The marine industry and its effects on the people

With the advent of so many ships passing through the Torres Strait from about 1840, the Torres Strait Islanders were introduced by seamen to goods such as sugar, flour, rice, biscuits and iron, the latter exerting a powerful influence on them (Beckett 1987, p. 37). Perhaps the earliest European to live amongst the Torres Strait Islanders was Wini (see above). He was seen by the people as a good man who assisted the Badulgal to repair their boats. According to Barbara Thompson, speaking in 1849, he had been there a long time, probably from circa 1840 until his death in 1864 (Moore 1979, pp. 144–5). Gill met a Badulayg in 1872 who sang an English song learnt possibly from a white man who had lived on a shelling station on the island (1876, p. 201).

From the mid 1860s there was an influx of bêche-de-mer fishers into the Strait. Then from 1870, after commercial quantities of pearl shell were discovered, some notable outsiders arrived: the American Yankee Ned (Mosby), who settled on Masig (Yorke Island); James Morrison, born on New Caledonia to the son of a Scotsman and a local woman whose descendants now live on St Paul's (Moa); Douglas Pitt, a Jamaican who established a bêche-de-mer station on Mer. Each of these men has numerous descendants in modern Torres Strait. South Pacific Islander men, and later South East Asian men, also arrived to work in the pearling industry.

Prior to the arrival of the white pearlers and bêche-de-mer fishers both Torres Strait Islander men and women collected shell while wading in the shallow water around their islands. The newcomers saw the Islanders as a cheap and tractable workforce. However, the locals were opposed to long periods away from home on the boats, and even though they wanted trade goods they were soon 'repelled by dishonest employers and abusive skippers' (Beckett 1987, p. 37). The missionary AW Murray reported in 1874 that the Mabuiag people kept out of the way of 'the pearl shell fishers as they [were] tired of working for them, and they find it difficult to keep from getting entangled with them' (p. 37). Indeed, during the initial years of the maritime industry in Torres Strait the people experienced disruption to their lives and violent treatment from master pearlers ('master' boats were privately owned by outsiders, as opposed to clan-owned 'company' boats) and bêche-de-mer fishers looking for quick profits while operating without government regulations (Mullins 1995, p. 76). Because they were beyond British law, masters commonly used force to intimidate the men into working for them; others were lured into the fisheries by perceived benefits. They crewed boats or worked on bêche-de-mer and pearling stations set up on Tut, Gabba (Brothers), Erub and Mer. They worked for little money and were often not paid and, as indicated above, not repatriated to their home islands at season's end. Masters abducted women to meet the sexual needs of their crews. By 1872 the once fearless and confident island people were 'cowed' by the outsiders (Beckett 1987, p.33).

Crews on shelling boats made up of Pacific Islanders and Torres Strait Islanders were frequently unsupervised by the masters with the result that there were violent clashes between the two groups (Mullins 1995, p. 77). The premier of the young colony of Queensland was advised of these abuses but he was not concerned until about 1872 when regulation of the 'labour trade', the importing of coloured men to work in the cane industry on the mainland, became an issue. Indeed he had no jurisdiction in Torres Strait until 1872 when Queensland Governor Normandy, under Letters Patent of the Imperial Government, annexed the Strait to the 60-mile limit from the Australian shoreline. And, when the home government passed the *Pacific Islanders Protection Act 1872* (UK) (the Kidnapping Act), two controversial issues for the premier were addressed: regulating recruitment of Pacific Islander labour; and easier protection of Torres Strait Islanders from 'abuse and lawless colonial seamen' (p. 89). However, Torres Strait Islanders living on islands beyond the 60-mile limit became 'Pacific Islanders' for the purposes of the Act, and they were prevented from working for the master pearlers. The Act was amended in 1875 to allow these Torres Strait Islanders to again engage in the industry and, in 1879 under Letters Patent of the Imperial Government, the *Queensland Coastal Islands Act 1879* was enacted to extend the Queensland border closer to the Papuan border, thus bringing the top-western islands within Australia's northern border (pp. 76–96, 13–161).

By the mid 1870s, South Pacific Island men were living on practically all of the central and north-eastern islands (Mullins 1989, pp. 10–11). They appeared first in the 1860s aboard Sydney-based bêche-de-mer vessels. (Asian junks had fished for bêche-der-mer around the western islands much earlier, but apparently without making sustained contact with the Torres Strait Islanders.) Many of these South Pacific Island men were good seamen and were in demand but they also knew how to improve their wages and conditions, by strikes if necessary (p. 7). Within a decade of their arrival they were monopolising the better-paid jobs as 'hard hat' divers (divers who used the diving suits and helmets introduced in the late-nineteenth century) and skippers of swimming boats (boats with none of the suit or helmet equipment) (pp. 10–11).

However, their ability to challenge the masters brought responses like that of racist police magistrate Frank Jardine: 'the great grievance and thorn is the South Sea Islander who will not remain the heathen Polynee that he [is], but keeps pace with the time' (p. 9). Their intransigence resulted in Filipino and Indonesian men being brought to the Strait in the late 1870s by masters wanting a 'steadier and more tractable workforce' (p. 16). Masters too wanted more Torres Strait Islanders as they were also expert sailors and divers with 'an intimate knowledge of the region's reef systems' (p. 74).

Within a very short time, all islands were 'affected by the incursion of foreign seamen seeking wives' (Beckett 1987, p. 38). Many of these men could afford to pay high bride prices, and parents were known to save their daughters for the highest bidders (LMS 1796–1906, p. 10). Local men found it hard to match these high bride prices with the result that in 1885 about 30 South Sea Islander families were removed from Mer to Erub as they were 'regarded by the natives as intruders' (QLA 1885, pp. 1083–4). In 1905 the 'half-caste' problem also resulted in the first families of mixed marriages moving from Mabuiag to Moa, and in 1908 St Paul's Anglican Mission was established there. Some women in mixed marriages moved to Thursday Island with their husbands and families, something they could not otherwise do.

Around 1890, masters wanted other foreign seamen who would work for less than the South Pacific men. They had cut wages arguing it was because of low wages paid by producers in the Philippines. White seamen refused to risk their lives for the wages being paid in Torres Strait so, because of the importance of the marine industry to the young colony of Queensland, and despite concern about the labour trade, masters were permitted to import experienced fishers from Malaya and the Philippines, and later Japan (Beckett 1987, pp. 36–7). Arriving in the 1890s, Japanese divers were the first seamen to be indentured — they 'undercut and outworked everyone else' (1987, p. 36) — and soon took a firm hold on the shelling industry, a hold that continued until the outbreak of the Pacific War in 1941. A few of these men married island women and settled on Thursday Island but the men were interned in late 1941.

The London Missionary Society

The missionaries of the London Missionary Society (LMS) arrived on Erub on 1 July 1871 with the aim of evangelising the entire South Pacific. They were not the first to work in the Torres Strait; the Rev FC Jagg and a teacher, WT Kennett, of the Society for the Propagation of the Gospel worked with the Kaurareg in 1867 and 1868 (see Moore 1979, pp. 237–67, the Kennett Report). However, the LMS believed that by establishing a mission in Torres Strait they would have a stepping stone into their area of ultimate focus, New Guinea. It was envisaged that trained Torres Strait Islander teachers would go there in the same way that the Pacific Islander teachers came to work in Torres Strait.

The first white LMS missionaries, Samuel McFarlane and AW Murray, landed on Erub before moving to other islands, where there was a peaceful acceptance of them. The people were by this stage 'cowed and sullen' from contact with the outsiders and welcomed the prospect of some protection from marauding seamen (Langbridge 1977). During this early period the LMS sought to expand its work to all island communities in Torres Strait.

Joe Tonga — or Tongatabut, a Pacific Islander married to a Tut woman and Captain Banner's most experienced overseer pilot (Mullins 1995, p. 127) — was loaned to the missionaries to act as an interpreter, and with his mediacy they were able to explain their presence to the people (Gill 1876, p. 200). Other captains made their boats available to the missionaries, and so they travelled throughout the Strait and eventually won widespread acceptance of their Christian teachings (Mullins 1995, pp. 54, 59, 72, 127).

However, not every island community responded immediately to this latest intrusion. The chief on Ugar (Stephen Island) told Gill, 'I will not have a teacher; it would lessen my authority' (1876, p. 213). In 1872, the missionaries received no response from the leaders on Masig to a suggestion that a teacher be left there (Bayton 1969, p. 18). Within 16 months, however, the white missionaries visiting Erub said that the people there were 'No longer liable to be trampled upon and spoiled by wicked foreigners ... their own countrymen, natives of neighbouring islands. Their plantations [were] safe; their houses not plundered or burned; and their wives and daughters [were] safe' (p. 19).

But as time went on problems arose because the white missionaries seemed to give the Pacific Islander teachers practically no ongoing supervision. After an official visit to the islands, Captain Pennefather of the QGS *Pearl* complained about this to the Queensland Government:

> *It appears to me that these teachers require a great deal more looking after by the head of the London MS ... These 'Native Evangelists' are very fond of a little power, and ... are rarely men to use it wisely. They are left for months without supervision from the heads of the Mission.* (QLA 1880, p. 1158)

Nevertheless, in a remarkably short time the Meriam people had 'received the mission and acceded to its considerable demands'. Murray reported after a few months that (Beckett 1987, p. 40):

> *The entire population of Mer seemed ready to yield to their missionary teacher's guidance. No work is done on the Sabbath and the people come together from the three islands [Mer, Dauar, Waier] to attend the services which, except the hymns and reading of scripture, are conducted in the native tongue.*

Beckett suggests that the people may have seen the new religion as 'simply the latest in a series of cults that came to them from time to time', one that promised 'unprecedented power and wealth' (p. 40). Nonetheless, the missionaries eventually deprived them of their sacred objects and desecrated their shrines. Soon they realised this new 'cult' could demand their whole attention (p. 40) and so they surreptitiously retained some of their old practices, such as totems (Langbridge 1977). On Mer, despite the missionaries' threats to kill anyone who participated in their traditional Malo initiation ceremonies, they continued them in secret (Sharp 1996, p. 64).

'Civilising' their converts was an integral part of LMS teaching. Accordingly, warfare, skull-taking, mummification, initiation, polygamy, nudity and traditional dancing were banned (though Sharp points out that traditional dancing continued to exercise a 'fascination' for the people on Erub until 1907, and that rain-making ceremonies were still practised in the 1910s (1980a, p. 53)). A night curfew was imposed and perceived sexual immorality was punished by head-shaving, flogging and public humiliation. Women could no longer choose their partners (Mullins 1995, p. 84) and could not exercise their traditional right to propose marriage (Beckett 1963, p. 77). In the 'new order' village houses were built around the church and 'adjacent to a good anchorage'. In this way, their missionary teachers kept them to a 'daily routine of religious observance and their conduct subject to close surveillance' (p. 42). In just over a year the missionaries felt pleased with their civilising program on certain islands. It was reported from Erub that:

> *The whole population renounced heathenism as to abstain from work on the Sabbath and attend services conducted in their own language ... all wear some article of clothing when they come together for worship of God and as many as twenty [out of 170] wear clothing all the time.*
> (Bayton 1969, p. 19)

Beckett points out that while the missionaries 'declared war on the "idol gods" ' and claimed the 'complete conversion' of the Meriam people, there was evidence that some lived away from the mission and may have resisted this war on their traditions (1987, p. 116). Haddon recorded the 'chants of the Malu-Bomai ceremonies in 1898' that had not been performed for 20 years, suggesting that they had been secretly preserved (pp. 116–7).

The new church structure allowed for local participation of the men as a reward for 'piety and good character' that led to the deaconate (p. 42). Suitable young male converts were trained for missionary work at the Papuan Gulf Native College established about 1879 on Mer, the mission's headquarters (Williamson 1990, p. 94).

In 1883, an industrial school opened on Mer for male and female students, teaching school subjects, trade skills and sewing. The Annual Mei (May) meeting, or gathering of teachers and Christian leaders, was instituted to inspire everyone in the cause (Langbridge 1977, p. 39). A matter of some contention for the missionaries was the men's participation in the marine industry, working on boats and on the pearling and bêche-de-mer stations. A monetary economy had become essential to the maintenance of the missions, but for the missionaries, work on the boats meant the men came into contact with 'a certain class of foreigner' (Beckett 1987, p. 43) who could undermine the missionaries' authority so the men were encouraged to collect shell around their islands. Murray, in his earlier claim that the Maubiag people wanted to keep out of the way of the shell fishers, may have based this on his own agenda. Nonetheless, many still worked on the master boats until an opportunity arose for them to buy their own boats. This opportunity was in fact made possible through loans from Papuan Industries Limited, a company set up on Badu in 1904 by the Rev Walker, a disenchanted evangelist who left the mission because it was opposed to his entrepreneurial schemes for the people (p. 43).

During the 1870s and 1880s the Queensland Government, due to limited resources, was content to leave the 'civilising' of the Torres Strait Islanders to the missionary teachers. Nevertheless, when former premier of Queensland John Douglas was appointed Government Resident on Thursday Island in 1885 he engendered more interest in the Torres Strait Islanders. Indeed, Douglas was impressed with the work of the LMS. In his report to the colonial government he said that there had been 'great progress in the civilization of the natives ... through the instrumentality of the LMS' (QLA Reports 1885, pp. 1079–84).

In 1876, the Queensland Government's administrative centre at Somerset was officially abandoned. The harbour had proved 'troublesome and even dangerous for large mail steamers' (Austin 1949, p. 226). In addition, with the extension of the Queensland boundary to encompass all of the islands in Torres Strait except Daru, there was a need for a more convenient judicial and administrative system (p. 226). In 1877 HM Chester was appointed police magistrate at Thursday Island to oversee the system. On each island the missionaries had invested as chief, or *mamoose*, the island man named by the local people as the most important (Langbridge 1977, p. 63). Then, on a tour of the islands in 1878, Chester advised these chiefs to 'appoint magistrates and police ... Laws were formally inaugurated ... Mr Chester ... requested [the Polynesian teachers] to guide [these officers] in their administration ... until they themselves were capable' (McFarlane, cited in Beckett 1987, p. 41). This early but very basic form of island governance gave the Torres Strait Islanders a limited say in their own affairs.

In 1879, Captain Pennefather visited the islands to advise the people of their new status as citizens (though without the same rights as white citizens). While on Mer, however, he was informed that one woman:

> had been flogged for quarrelling with her husband, and [another] for quarrelling with her brother ... The [Polynesian] teacher ... denied [they] were flogged by his orders, but [by] the chief, and the ... policeman ... The natives told [Pennefather] ... the chief was not to blame [but was] merely a tool in the [teacher's] hands. (QLA report 1880, p. 1158)

Pennefather told the people that the South Sea Islander teacher's power did not extend to settling serious disputes: only the police magistrate on Thursday Island could do that. On Mabuiag, his attention was drawn to unrest as a result of the South Sea Islanders taking women away from the island (p. 1158). Such concerns, and the growing economic importance of the area, prompted the government to appoint John Douglas as Government Resident for Torres Strait. Douglas remained in this position until his death in 1904; for a colonial representative of the time he showed remarkable empathy for the people. In 1886 the acting Government Resident, Hugh Milman, drew up a code of penalties for the guidance of magistrates on Mer. This was in response to discovering one magistrate fined a man according to his means and not the gravity of the offence. Subsequently, other island chiefs asked for the code to assist them in their new roles in the communities.

Formal education began to take a more prominent role in people's lives. The LMS brought to the Strait schooling based on the western model, and their teachers 'taught vernacular literacy, catechism and bible stories, and secular subjects such as arithmetic and geography ... On Murray and Darnley Islands, some English literacy was taught, particularly at the Papuan Gulf College' (Williamson 1987, p. 1). The most viable schools were on Mer and Erub from 1873 to 1892, but there was no evidence of schooling on the western islands until the late 1880s (p. 1). However, by 1892 the LMS had begun to wind down its operations in the Strait because of financial problems, problems with the government and because of its main focus on New Guinea.

As the LMS wound back, Douglas was concerned to raise the Torres Strait Islanders to their 'rightful place' in the scale of 'civilisation'. He believed the only solution was a good education for the children and for the people to have the 'authoritative guidance of a white resident' on their islands (QLA Reports 1889, p. 171). Thus in 1892 a new phase in island administration commenced on Mer. John Bruce, on the recommendation of Douglas, was appointed to Mer as the first government magistrate–teacher in Torres Strait. From then on the activities of the LMS were confined to spiritual matters, but its presence lingered on until 1914 when it passed its flocks over to the Anglican Diocese of Carpentaria and permanently left Torres Strait.

Paternalistic government control begins

Within 20 years, the LMS's Polynesian teachers had established a 'stern theocracy' (Beckett 1978, p. 215), but with Bruce's appointment in 1892 erosion of their school teaching roles began. Ever forward-looking for the Torres Strait Islanders, Douglas instigated the institution of elected councils on all islands in 1899 that gave the people 'limited but important rights of self-management' (Sharp 1987, p. 18). In 1900, Douglas spoke of the worth of the Torres Strait Islanders who, he believed, had embraced the outsiders' teachings with some success, and he proposed that they be given full citizenship rights:

> They are a civilized people. They marry and are given in marriage; they live in good houses. They are human beings; they are our flesh and blood. They are born under our jurisdiction and they are entitled to the privileges we enjoy. The natives of the Torres Strait are capable of exercising all the rights of British citizens, and they ought to be regarded as such. (Douglas 1900, p. 35)

Former missionary Walker encouraged industriousness and economic independence among the Torres Strait Islanders and a new sense of self-regulation was evidenced when, by the turn of the century, clans were buying boats and working neighbouring reefs for shell and trepang (bêche-der-mer) (Beckett 1977, p. 86). Along with Douglas's belief in the people and Walker's scheme for them to become more economically viable through Papuan Industries Limited, their acceptance as British citizens might have been validly foreshadowed.

In 1897, however, Queensland enacted legislation to control the lives of Aborigines (see next chapter). Soon after, with the passing of the *Immigration Restriction Act 1901* by the newly created Commonwealth Government, it became apparent that Australia was set on a path to keep Australia white. Douglas resisted until his death any attempt to bring the Torres Strait Islanders under the Queensland Government's 1897 Act because of his belief in their worth as 'civilised' people, but following his death in 1904 the term 'Aboriginal' was informally reinterpreted to include Torres Strait Islanders, resulting in the loss of their pan-identity and any right to full citizenship. They were now Aborigines for the purposes of legislation that segregated and controlled Queensland's Indigenous peoples.

Prior to 1871, while the Torres Strait Islanders were adversely affected by marauding master fishers, they maintained the political, social and religious institutions that served their needs as small individual autonomous societies with unique maritime cultures. However, many of the people's traditional structures were rapidly dismantled by the missionary teachers. Their aim was to Christianise and 'civilise' the people. By the turn of the century, there had been a remarkable transformation in the island societies toward this goal. Nonetheless, without official explanation, after 1904 these people found themselves increasingly controlled by restrictive and segregationist Queensland legislation. It was a retrograde step for the Torres Strait Islanders, whom Douglas regarded as rightfully entitled to British citizenship.

CHAPTER 2

Paternalism challenged

When the Aboriginals Protection and Restriction of the Sale of Opium Bill was debated in the Queensland Parliament in 1897, it was decided that the Torres Strait Islanders 'did not need the protection of the Crown, because they were capable of doing their own business' (CPA report 1902). In a reflection of this self-reliance, by 1907, 18 Islander-owned and operated 'clan' or 'company' boats (as opposed to the privately owned 'master' boats) were working in the bêche-de-mer and pearl shell industries. Clan boats were purchased with loans jointly allocated from two sources: the Aboriginal Property Protection Account, an account maintained by the Chief Protector of Aborigines; and Papuan Industries Limited, an account established by the London Missionary Society's Rev. FW Walker (Austin 1972, pp. 32–68). In 1905, the then Chief Protector commented on the speed with which these boats were being paid off, as in the case of the Purma/Poruma (Coconut) Islanders: '[They] brought in produce which realised £97 [A$194] and of this amount they took only £6 [A$12] in cash, leaving the balance to pay off the boat and purchases of stores, etc'. He anticipated that by the end of 1906 all boats would be 'the sole property of the natives' (CPA report 1905, p. 29).

In 1905, an average monthly earning on a company boat was about £12, while seamen on other boats received £2. However, incomes were reduced by 'exorbitant charges per medium of the notorious "slop chest"', a system of credit through which seamen bought goods at the government store on Thursday Island and had the amount deducted from wages (CPA report 1905, p. 29). The balance in cash was sent in a sealed package to their respective islands and, at a public meeting, distributed among the people. The schoolteacher, or a 'competent younger person', made the balance sheet intelligible for the community (CPA report 1904, p. 21). The people were told to be thrifty with whatever moneys they had, and savings accounts were opened for them (CPA report 1907, p. 8). The Protector subsequently reported that a 'very tangible benefit' from the earnings of the company-boat men was that people were able to be self-reliant when their crops failed, whereas on other islands without boats flour had to be issued to avert potential famine (CPA report 1905, p. 29).

In 1899, Government Resident John Douglas instituted an elected council on Mer (Muray Island), with one member appointed by himself to advise the white teacher and, as Beckett suggests, 'to counter the influence of the church courts' (1987, p 45). Subsequently, elected councils were set up on all communities. In his report of 1907 the Chief Protector described the structure of the council:

> *a native chief or mamoose [is] assisted and advised by the councillors or elders of the village with a staff of native police to uphold this authority and to keep order ... [The mamoose] acts as a police magistrate and governor with power to deal summarily with offences and breaches of local regulations and is directly responsible for the behaviour and cleanliness of his village to the government resident and police magistrate at Thursday Island.* (CPA report 1907, p. 8)

The local police upheld by-laws (formulated by the councils) with powers of arrest. The moneys collected from fines and dog taxes were expended on public improvements. The white teacher taught 'the three Rs, agricultural and domestic subjects'. In addition he was the medico, the clerk of court and official registrar (CPA report 1905, p. 8). Douglas's initiative gave the people a measure of self-regulation.

By 1904 Christianity was universally practised: young men were being trained as missionaries, older men acted as deacons, and churches were being built and supported by the people. Thus, people rapidly adjusted to certain economic, political and spiritual institutions of the dominant society resulting in a commonly held view that they were more 'intelligent' and better able to care for themselves than their 'brother[s] on the mainland' (QPD 1939). Nonetheless, attitudes changed after Douglas's death in 1904, and Torres Strait Islanders were placed under the protection of the *Aboriginals Protection and Restriction of the Sale of Opium Act 1897* (shortened simply to 'the Act') — originally enacted for the protection and segregation of mainland Aborigines — resulting in the erosion of self-regulation on the island communities.

'Under the Act'

The Boigu man (1990) suggested that Islanders were put under the Act because there was 'fighting ... Mabuiag and South Sea men on pearl shell and trochus [boats] fight'. He said there were 'many big fights' because the local people did not want their women to marry South Sea Island men. An official interpretation was the government's concern regarding the sale of liquor to the island seamen when they came to Thursday Island to discharge pearl shell. By 1900 there were seven hotels on an island with a population of just 2000:

> It was open and unrestricted ... licensed victuallers make no secret that all of them could not make a living if deprived of the custom of the South Sea Islanders and Straits Islanders and Binghis (i.e., mainland aborigines), and have come really to consider themselves as having a vested interest in the paltry earnings of these poor creatures. (CPA report 1902, p. 7)

Moreover, commercial interests on Thursday Island were 'robbing' island seamen: one family that owned their own boat lost £500, another boat crew lost £3000 over two years. They were, in many cases, underpaid and overcharged for goods purchased in the government store. Labour problems on master boats were solved in many cases by 'seeing the aboriginals [Torres Strait Islanders] were charged prices that would keep them a little in debt until the end of the season' (QPD 1939, p. 498). Complaints were made against master pearlers: on Nagir, a South Sea Islander was 'high handed' with his men (CPA report 1905, p. 33); on Mabuiag there were accusations that employers ordered island police to handcuff, arrest and imprison 'natives' without warrants or authority (p. 28).

But there were two possible further reasons why the Torres Strait Islanders were placed under the Act. First, a large and cheap labour pool was needed for the burgeoning and lucrative marine industry that economically benefited the young state. It was in jeopardy at the turn of the century because coloured labourers were being returned to their homelands, in keeping with the 'White Australia' policy (Beckett 1987, p. 47). Second, Australia's obsession with the 'threat of colour' justified segregation of the Torres Strait Islanders in the eyes of people indoctrinated with the racist notion of white supremacy. When they came under the Act in 1904, purportedly to protect them from the sort of exploitation mentioned above, both the requirements of labour for the capitalist maritime industry and the preservation of a 'white monoculture' were safeguarded (Sharp 1980a, p. 73).

Protectors criticised but seldom praised Torres Strait Islanders during the first decade of the era of protection, despite their rapid embracement of the 'civilising' influences around them. The official interpretation of the Islander work ethic was that the 'predominating characteristic of the aboriginal [Torres Strait Islander] race asserts itself, and immediately they know the vessel is no longer in debt, all incentive to work is gone, the catch of fish decreases and the vessel is neglected' (CPA report 1907, p. 8). There were objections to people giving coconuts to neighbours when copra prices were high (CPA report 1910, p. 20) and it was suggested that 'The majority have little or no idea of the value of money and are quite satisfied as long as their immediate wants are supplied' (CPA report 1914, p. 20). In his 1922 report, the Protector labelled the people as 'thriftless' (p. 23). Government officials were unwilling to concede that the people's system of reciprocity had worked for them for generations. Thus, they were unwilling to adopt, in totality and immediately, all the principles of commerce of the dominant society. The Islanders' world had always been a world of mutuality: 'We do not want to buy and sell — we give and take; that's our watchword' (Sharp 1980a, p. 46). In their quiet way they were demonstrating that they would embrace the new society on their own terms.

The 1897 Act created 'reserves' and made provision for the appointment of Local Protectors and superintendents (ss. 6, 7) with powers over the employment of 'inmates' (s. 3) who lived on them. Once under the Act, a series of amendments gradually stripped Islander people's rights over their income, their property and even where they might live. Amendments passed in 1901 widened the Protector's powers (ss. 7, 12), with section 12(2) impacting upon Islanders' ability to manage their own money:

> *Payment of wages to responsible person* — *a Protector may direct employers or any employer to pay the wages of aboriginals [Torres Strait Islanders] or female half-castes to himself or some officer of police named by him* ... *The protector or officer of police who receives such wages shall expend the same solely on behalf of the aboriginal or female half-caste to whom they are due and shall keep an account of such expenditure.*

Further, the Protector now had the power '[to] take possession, retain, sell or dispose of real or personal property, and sue for recovery ... exercise in the name of the aboriginal any power which the aboriginal might exercise for his own benefit' (s. 13). Thus, once their vessels were paid for, an assignment to the Protector that was 'properly drawn up and registered in the Supreme Court at Townsville' could be validated (CPA report 1905, p. 29). Not only had Islander people lost absolute control of their money but also their property.

In 1911, the Protector complained that clan boats were not being worked regularly or kept in good repair (CPA report 1911, p. 21). He claimed 'stringent regulations' with penalties for offenders would ensure 'a fair amount of work by every able-bodied man' (CPA report 1912, pp. 21–2). Moreover, in 1912 an Island Fund supervised by the Protector was instituted, and each seaman was required to pay a percentage of his wages into the fund. Its stated objective was 'to promote a spirit of independence ... and generally make provision for the welfare of their relatives and villages without asking monetary assistance from the Government' (CPA report 1913, p. 14), but this was a blatant denial of their system of reciprocity. Government policy, purported to make them self-reliant, denied them the opportunity to manage their own economic and commercial interests.

Control of the people's commercial interests was only one aspect of the Protector's power. He could also remove and relocate any Torres Strait Islander (s. 9); segregation was codified in the provision for control over who could visit any island (s. 11); and only with permission could a woman marry a man other than a Torres Strait Islander (s. 9). Exemption from the Act (s. 33) was dependent upon the Protector's permission, but he could revoke it at any time. A Thursday Island woman (1990) spoke about a young island woman who married a Malay man by arrangement and subsequently separated from him because she was unhappy. She had her exemption revoked and was 'removed' to Palm Island.

People surreptitiously thwarted regulations — continuing to use bush medicines when it was an offence to do so (Meriam woman, 1990) and refusing to abandon their system of reciprocity (Late Badu Elder, 1989) — but more and more they came to realise their powerlessness.

Keeping the level of education low

The London Missionary Society promoted education as a 'civilising' agent, and later Douglas saw it as the way for Torres Strait Islanders to gain rights of British citizenship. He used his influence with home secretary Foxton to agree to provide a white teacher for Mer, and subsequently for other large schools, because he believed a greater mastery of English would set them on this path (QLA report 1891, 4, p. 1422). However, in 1903 Murray Island School No. 774 was removed from the Department of Public Instruction's list. This meant that the Protector became responsible for Torres Strait Islander education, a move that not only widened his control but eventually lowered the standard of education. It was claimed that 'The simple village life of the natives did not call for a standard of education required in schools for white people' (Bleakley

1961, p. 289). The objective was 'In general to fit the pupils for the future so that they will be useful citizens when the time arrives for them to leave the school and take their place among the men and women of the village' (QSA Education, 1936–38, A/15996). With this narrow vision for the education of island children, the standard was deliberately kept low by the application of 'the mark' — the level of attainment a child could attain (Williamson 1989, pp. 124–98). This frustrated the people:

> *The government put a mark for our school. The teaching went up to grade four and then back to teaching them babies and go up to grade four again and stop. How you going to realise something when you only go half way in the teaching then you come back and go through the same procedure again? Going to the mark and then come back and start we again. That's too bad!* (cited in Williamson 1989, p. 79)

The island communities were remote from Brisbane's decision makers. These bureaucrats had 'no expertise in selecting teachers [and] well-qualified teachers rarely opted to teach on the islands'. As well, the Protector's department ran on an 'inadequate budget' so that 'teacher wages were low and bi-annual leave was minimally funded', giving no incentive to more-qualified white teachers to come to the islands (Osborne E 1995, p. 242). Thus a combination of remoteness, very basic teacher qualifications and inadequate money ensured the maintenance of a low standard of education. On the one hand the government wanted the people to be more 'civilised'; on the other, it withheld the level of education required to assist in this process.

There was a growing need for teachers in island schools, but a lack of teachers with the desire or qualifications to fill these posts. Hence, white teachers picked school leavers from the island schools, those who had only achieved 'the mark', to fill these positions. Some were given extra help. Macintosh Murray was respected as one of the good white teachers of the time: 'Getano Lui Snr, Murray Lui and Sam Passi were taught like that. Getano Lui was said to be Macintosh Murray's boy and everyone was saying, "Go learn proper so you can be like Getano Lui"' (Erub Elder, 1989). The people made it known that they wanted an education:

> *[to] the stage at which they could check over their earnings and accounts with their employer [because] although they are not able to prevent themselves from being robbed, they are conscious of being robbed, because they realised they were not getting value for their money.* (QPD 1939, p. 499)

The people wanted a 'proper' education, and their dissatisfaction eventually forced the government to lift the standard of the untrained monitors and teachers. In 1935 a Native Teacher Training School was set up on Mabuiag and promising young students might be chosen to receive a year's training there under the tutelage of PR Frith. A Mabuiag woman (1989) who went to that school said they were shown how 'to get knowledge' because 'We don't realise that much at that time'. Even though they were pressing for an education whereby they could not be 'cheated by DNA [Department of Native Affairs]' (Late Yam Island Elder, 1989), in reality nothing less than equality with the dominant society was their ultimate aim.

Controls, controls, controls

After the death of John Douglas and his successor HM Milman's demise, WM Lee-Bryce became Local Protector, and he brought his negative views of Indigenous people to the job. In 1911, whatever local autonomy existed was lost under more stringent government controls. The power of the *mamoose* and the council was transferred to the government teacher. On a visit to Erub (Darnley Island) as Chief Protector in 1914, JW Bleakley told the people: '"Me bigfeller government", introducing himself to the people in the court-house and "this man, Mr Guillemot [government teacher] ... him smallfeller government"'; from that point on 'no notice was taken of *mamus* (*mamoose*)' (Sharp 1984, p. 181). The people were demeaned by Bleakley's paternalism: ' "Oh, I'm your big *mamus*, here are two sticks of tobacco here are two blankets". Oh, so we bend the knee and bow down to him because he's the big *mamus*. I get one stick tobacco; that's my pay for Chief Councillor' (cited pp. 189–90). The Boigu man (1990) recalled that there was minimal supervision of the white teachers and they became 'the law, terrible law'.

During the period of economic stringency of the late 1920s and early 1930s, further regulations and by-laws adversely affecting the people were enacted. Authorised visits to Thursday Island continued to be confined to daylight hours. The people were not free to travel to the mainland just as Marou, an old Meriam leader, had done when he was a young man. He learnt not to fear whites and he set an example for one young man who subsequently became an island leader: ' "Remember son", he said, "you don't go to jail because you argue against white, you only go if you break the law" ' (Erub Elder, 1989). Moreover, visits to other islands could only be made with the white teacher's permission, and a curfew ensured that people were in their houses by nine o'clock. A Badu woman (1990) remembered that 'they blow whistle, that's bedtime ... Everyone got to stay in, nobody walk about from house to house'. Meeting a boyfriend could result in harsh punishments for both parties, such as being sent to jail or having the head shaved on one side to shame the person. A 14-year-old boy was given three months' hard labour for walking, in daylight hours, with a white woman — at her invitation (Sharp 1984, p. 191). Willie Thaiday was removed from his island at 17 because another fellow he was with 'put his arm around the girl and kiss her' (Thaiday 1981, p. 10). The 1934 amendments to the Act extended the Protector's powers to adjudicate on offences such as carnal knowledge (s. 9) and soliciting (ss. 11, 19). Other provisions provided for medical examination of seamen when their contracts expired (s. 14), cancellation of employment agreements (s. 15), will-making (s. 16), and dealing with 'uncontrollable aborigines' (s. 21).

For three decades, legislators with a 'mania' for paternalistic control (Sharp 1984, p. 74) extended the Protector's powers and frustrated the people's aspirations for self-regulation. Increasingly, white people administered island affairs with a racist mentality of their own supremacy (p. 74), and with no respect for the culture of those they administered. Tatz argues that a requirement necessary for the successful 'administration and development of indigenous people' is that 'ideally you should love the people that you are administering ... at least that you respect them' (1967, p. 20). The Protectors showed no love for the people nor did they respect them. The bottom line for government was control.

In 1930, Papuan Industries Limited was transferred to the government and renamed the Aboriginal Industries Board, and branch stores were set up on four of the larger islands in 1932 and 1933. By this time recruitment of crews, sale of produce, and distribution of earnings were under the absolute control of the Protector (Beckett 1987, pp. 47–9). Company boats were confiscated if not worked 'satisfactorily' in the opinion of the Protector (Sharp 1980b, p. 14). The people resented these controls. A Masig woman (1989) explained: 'Before time if we wanted to save little bit we put it in a tin. Might put the tin — bury it, keep it for emergency. Only few people were wasting money — waste it on drinking'. At that time 'DNA [Department of Native Affairs, though the informant may have meant the earlier title of Protector's Office], you know, has power and every money going through the account. So any money you want you go there and then you ask for money, "How much you want?" they say'. The people resented this question. They had always battled for their money and most knew how to look after it. Now it was entered into a passbook and to spend it they had to 'crawl on [their knees]' and say, '"Please, please, I would like more" ... If [the teacher] said, "No", that was it' (Sharp 1981–2, p. 116). The Masig woman also said that 'If we spent the money in the wrong way, well that was up to the people themselves.

We wanted to take care of it ourselves'. It was control by 'outsiders' and that was wrong:

> We feel funny when government take over. It was not right. Too long ... still control over us. Why didn't they appoint someone to care for their own people, good sensible people. Lot of them were trained by Mr. Bruce [a respected white teacher on Mer]. It was okay if council control, but not DNA.

This old woman was recalling things that happened a long time ago, but it is clear from her words that she still resented the control that was exercised over their lives then.

In 1933, focus was once again on the white teachers when the governor of Queensland, on a visit to Torres Strait, expressed his concern that their authority was being undermined. He told the people that the teachers were the government's representatives responsible for the schools, administration, store sales, native law and their welfare. The governor recommended that the teachers be called 'superintendents' so that their authority would be respected (QSA Governor's Office 1933, A/3664). Every aspect of people's lives was under the control of government regulations strictly administered by the white teachers. In this oppressive environment, the people reached breaking point.

Rumblings of discontent

Following JD McLean's appointment as Local Protector in 1932, rumblings of discontent were relayed to the Chief Protector in Brisbane. And, in an anonymous article in a Brisbane newspaper, the question was asked: 'What can one do to assist people who at least think they are being wronged by their legal Protectors when the latter turn continually a deaf ear?' (QSA, Aborigines gen. 1930–35, A/3598). After the governor of Queensland's visit to Torres Strait he told the Chief Protector: 'I found the natives happy, well cared for', but he suggested there was a 'feeling growing, more among the younger men, that they are desirous of being freed from some of the regulations with which they are surrounded' (QSA, Aborigines gen., A/3598). Island men visited mainland towns and were aware that there were 'natives or half-castes' there who had gained some rights of citizenship. The Chief Protector responded that his official policy was for 'improved native lives, fostering native village life, arts, crafts and music and avoiding Europeanisation' (QSA, Governor's Office, A/3664). Administered under this philosophy, fulfilment of the people's vision of gaining the rights that white Australians enjoyed was unlikely.

Between 1933 and 1935 the Bishop of Carpentaria, the Rev Dr Stephen Davies, became increasingly critical of Local Protector McLean's dictatorial methods. He was so concerned that he told synod in 1935 that Indigenous control should pass to the Commonwealth. The bishop's proposal spread from island to island via the 'bush telegraph', with messages being passed around by the seamen on the government-controlled boats (see Sharp 1993, pp. 184–5) igniting people's hopes. On 9 January 1936, the bishop wrote to the governor:

> *The Torres Strait Islanders are setting up a passive resistance in one matter only, that is the manning of their own company boats. This passive resistance may become something much worse unless a person of a different temperament to the present protector at Thursday Island takes it in hand. I think that persuasive methods may overcome the native objections in many cases though not in all, bluff and anger have in the past years been used freely by former protectors, but the native will not be driven again.* (QSA, Governor's correspondence 1936, A/12228)

He added: 'It is unfortunate that the Aboriginal Department is getting a very poor quality of man as junior officials' (QSA A/12228). Nevertheless, the department was satisfied with its administration based on its own officers' interpretations of the unrest as the 'cupidity' of the people that had been played upon by 'people with axes to grind, who resent the department's control of their money'; 'injudicious discussion of fancied grievances with certain minor elements'; and that 'these ignorant natives ... have jumped to the conclusion ... that [if control was vested in the Commonwealth] they would be free to work their own boats as they pleased, sell their produce where they like and spend the money as it suited them' (QSA A/12228). A day before the bishop wrote to the governor, the *Brisbane Telegraph* reported a speech by the minister to the effect that 'Already the natives of Torres Strait were self supporting and in addition were contributing something towards the support of aboriginals on the mainland' (Beckett 1987, p. 51). Was the minister aware of the negativity in his department?

The shell market was recovering after the depression and the industry was once again lucrative. Nevertheless, while outsiders were debating the situation, around Torres Strait leaders were plotting to demonstrate their refusal to bow any longer to the white teachers' and Local Protector McLean's paternalistic authority.

The Maritime Strike

Notwithstanding the government's confidence in its own administration, the island men thought and talked about how they could regain their freedom and dignity. According to the Masig woman (1989), Erub, Mer and Ugar (Stephen Island) leaders met surreptitiously on the beach at Erub to discuss issues and devise tactics to enable them once again to 'manage their own affairs'. She remembered that for a long time her father had 'sat by himself thinking of ways to help'. She said the way they saw it was that Torres Strait Islanders were 'only boss for the wood just for the timber [of their boats], but somebody else had all that takings'. So:

> *they had meeting and talked it over because of how this government treat them as natives ... they decide to contact Hankin [a man born on Samoa to a Cornish father and Samoan mother, married to a Mabuiag woman] on Mabuiag ... contact all this people to come, talk over that thing ... they have to make strike, send word around every island. Letter too slow, and send [by] boat and send that message round.*

They 'outwitted and out-organised' the Protector by using invisible island networks to secretly pass their message along and 'Old M' (a Badu man), captain of the Protector's cargo boat the *Darton* (renamed *Mulgrave*), carried the messages around Torres Strait (Sharp 1993, p. 188). Marou from Mer was one island leader who helped plan the strike. The Erub Elder recalled in 1989 that Marou was an impressive, independent man whom he admired. He had been elected to the Meriam council in 1928; in 1931 he was chairman and a churchwarden, in 1933 he lost office on the council but by 1936 he was returned and was an intrepid leader in the strike, after which the Protector dismissed him.

The Torres Strait Islanders had nothing apart from their labour with which to demonstrate their refusal to accept a cultural death under the outsiders' law. But use it they did. Seamen from all around Torres Strait stood unified and refused to 'sign on' with their own company boats in January 1936. They told Local Protector McLean: '"You take 'em ... we live before the boats come here"' (Sharp 1993, p. 183). Thus began the events that came to be known as the Maritime Strike.

Nine months after negotiations with the government were completed, the boats resumed operations, with the exception of the Meriam seamen. These men re-established their strong commitment to gardening. Newspapers initially carried reports of the strike, and there was some public sympathy, but the local feeling that provoked such a bold act was, and still remains, a very poignant memory for the few people still living whose lives were caught up in the event.

In October 1936, Cornelius (Con) O'Leary, a former Local Protector at Thursday Island and now the Deputy Chief Protector at Brisbane, reported to the Chief Protector in Brisbane that:

> Meetings [with boat crews] were held when the general scheme of reorganisation, as it will apply to the boats and social life of the people, was outlined briefly ... proposals with amendments will come into operation after they have been accepted by the Councillors in conference, but in the meantime the people are being educated to the suggestions which will be submitted to the Councillors. (Sharp 1981–2, p. 113)

O'Leary's paternalism is obvious in these words, so whether things would be different in the future remained to be seen.

Nevertheless, the strike had been a victory in terms of demands concerning some aspects of the management of their boats, although Beckett (1987, p. 55) points out that the government did not relinquish total control over their lives — and certainly not their earnings. However, some unpopular by-laws were rescinded, including the nine o'clock curfew; there was to be freedom of movement around the islands; and McLean, the 'abrasive and authoritarian' Local Protector left Torres Strait. The first edition of *The Islander*, printed quarterly by the Aboriginal Industries Board with the intention of keeping people informed, was circulated free in December 1936. The Aboriginal Industries Board was renamed Island Industries Board and control of local affairs was wrested from the teacher/supervisors. When McLean left his position as Local Protector in 1936, O'Leary who had negotiated with the seamen reported to Chief Protector Bleakley in Brisbane: 'A greater measure of responsibility has been given to the councillors and they will now control a considerable portion of the domestic life of their communities which previously were the responsibility of the government teachers' (Beckett 1987, pp. 54–5). He 'established mechanisms for regular consultation with elected island representatives, and gave the island councils a degree of local autonomy, including control over the island police and courts' (p. 55). Local control was returned to island councils under Section 18 of the *Torres Strait Islanders Act 1939* which stated that 'The Island Council shall have delegated to it the functions of local government of the reserve and shall be charged with the good rule and government of the reserve in accordance with island customs and practices'. Under this Act, which became known as the 'New Law', a Department of Native Affairs was established in lieu of the Office of the Chief Protector, and the title Director of Native Affairs replaced that of Chief Protector. Probably the people had reason to feel some satisfaction although their aspirations were, as yet, far from met.

Perhaps the most important outcome of the strike was the holding of the first Inter-Island Councillors' Conference in August 1937. Thirty-four elected councillors from 14 communities attended, and a chairperson was elected by secret ballot. Issues discussed included fishing grounds, councillors' wages, outer-island stores, higher wages, a scout jamboree, competition for the best catch by a company boat, and training divers. Traditional land rights were reaffirmed on the basis that all land used by their forefathers was 'boundaried up by them' (Sharp 1993, pp. 213–14). Island leaders made it known to O'Leary that they wanted an end to his department's paternalism: they wanted 'equality with Australian society' and they would work their boats for nothing less (Sharp 1981–2, p. 120). While O'Leary's perception was that the conference had resulted in the people's 'greater confidence in the [government's] administration than existed previously' (Sharp 1993, p. 214), the Torres Strait Islanders wanted to believe the outcomes from the strike augured well for their own future self-regulation.

The New Law was in fact based on indirect rule. Moreover, whatever self-determination became possible stood on shaky ground as the government proved that it was not yet ready to totally release its paternalistic hold, evidenced by its determination to continue to control seamen's earnings, the boats and who skippered them. It would be a Department of Native Affairs fleet with the keynote of efficiency and productivity (Sharp 1981–2, p. 120).

Indeed many of the old protectionist/segregationist policies were retained and were implemented in more subtle ways. Island councils were given certain powers, but the government retained overriding powers, such as the power to suspend a council's resolution or order; to prohibit expenditure of moneys from the Island Fund; or to vet island policy. With the advent of radio contact in the mid 1930s the director was able to continue to keep his finger on the pulse of each island. He was well informed by men who were willing to ignore the fact that the principles that united Torres Strait Islanders in 1936 remained imperative (Sharp 1993, pp. 181–202). Nonetheless, an important gain was that, for the first time, legislation acknowledged Torres Strait Islanders as distinct from Aborigines.

For three decades the Torres Strait Islanders had smarted under the unbridled paternalism of the Queensland Government. In the mid

1930s, the individual island communities that had not previously acted as a cohesive group challenged that administration in a unified show of strength (see Sharp 1980b; 1981–82 for full account of the strike). However, in 1941 the gains of the strike were overshadowed by a total focus on the Pacific War.

'Army time': looking for 'the new light'

Despite the New Law, Torres Strait Islanders were hoping for even wider freedom; in fact they wanted no less than equality with white Australians. But following Japan's attack on the American naval base of Pearl Harbor in Hawaii in December 1941, and the Japanese military's rapid move south, northern Australia became vulnerable to attack. A Late Meriam Elder (1990) said old Marou called a meeting on Mer. He told the young men, 'If you want freedom now is the time. You are going to fight for your country'. Looking back, the Masig woman (1989) said: 'God sent World War Two to put us in right position with the [Commonwealth] government'. The men, she said, went to war 'to help themselves: they were looking for "the new light"'. She continued: many believed that 'enlistment was a good thing — we might get help from the army'. So they 'quick join' because the feeling was that after their war service they would get help from the Commonwealth to gain freedom from their state overlords.

Recruitment commenced on the outer islands in mid 1941, but as the war came closer to home the islands were swept clean of able-bodied men. The Masig woman (1989) recalled how 'army men with guns' came: 'You got to go, you got to go', they said, and women working in their gardens a distance away returned to the village to find the men gone. It was a 'frightening' experience: 'The men never been talk with their wives. They just sign. They take them straight away. Never warn them. Them poor women cry, they be left. They might have nothing in the house'. A Male Late Badu Elder (1989) recalled that seamen on their boats as far south as Mackay were ordered to return immediately to Thursday Island. Their boats were impressed or beached and they enlisted unbeknown to their families: 'We can't tell them, we got no phone'. A late Warraber Elder said the boats were intercepted a 'long way from home ... They never seen their parents and families. They reported straight from the working area to TI [Thursday Island]' (Early History Workshop, TI, 1987). Thomas Lowah from St Paul's wrote that 'they were more scared than willing' by the tactics used for recruitment (1988, p. 75). The Masig woman (1989) said, 'The sergeant fired a pistol in the middle of the street and frightened the boys to join'. This was the reality that the men had not envisaged when they thought about the gains from enlistment.

2. Paternalism challenged

A white soldier remembered their arrival late at night at the camp on Thursday Island:

> *I could just hear the thump, thump, thump of feet in the night. I felt sorry for them because half of them didn't know where the hell they were; just marched into camp dead of night ... didn't know whether they were going to be slaughtered or not.* (Sharp 1984, p. 244)

In 1943, the top-western, central-western, central and eastern island groups were formed into four Torres Strait Islander military companies known as the Torres Strait Light Infantry (TSLI) Battalion. State segregationist policies enabled the army to discriminate against them: their pay was less than that of white soldiers; there was no advancement beyond the rank of corporal; there was no family allowance; and the men could not wear the slouch hat. They were not permitted to drink alcohol or gamble. Some discriminatory practices were subsequently modified, such as the wearing of the slouch hat, but as Hall pointed out: 'it was segregation which made [the practices] possible in the first place' (1989, p. 34).

A Late Saibai Elder (1989) thought about his army life and said that it was a strange new life:

> *When we be join army we not know anything. When [they] give command, we don't know about left hand, right hand. No savvy anything from A to Z — about turn, right turn, left turn, right incline, left incline. Strange because we not savvy anything. That was very hard for us. We don't think anything about army. Army teach us discipline. Our culture, white people different culture. First we join army we learn something about Europeans.*

A veteran telling his story at the Early History Workshop on Thursday Island (1987) said 'army time', as it was called, gave the men new experiences:

> *[We] begin to learn something as we train to be a soldier, and a carpenter, and any such work which we were given to do even to do what engineers do and what soldiers do, but most of us were very thankful because we never learnt anything about it before, then we started to learn about patrolling ... and all these things.*

White diggers provided knowledge of things previously denied them: 'It was the first time Islanders were allowed to touch knobs on the radio ... The Department people didn't trust [them] to do these things' (Sharp 1984, p. 244). Many white soldiers recognised their potential. One said that with proper training the island soldiers would have been 'the equal

... of any soldier in the world ... I had nothing but respect for them; I loved them' (p. 244). As the enlisted men saw it, army training was preparing them for the new life they believed they would be entitled to after the war, and they were proving, contrary to wide-spread opinion, that they could work alongside whites.

In his report for 1947, the director acknowledged that the men of the TSLI had 'performed excellent war service for the nation' (QPP 1948, p. 2). Despite these words the irony had been the long controversy over the TSLI men's pay. Because of their status as wards of the state of Queensland, the Commonwealth Government had consulted the director regarding rates of pay for enlisted island men. The director's stand was that 'if they received a much greater income than they [were] likely to earn after the War, they may be spoilt from the State point of view in time of peace' (AWM Coast Artillery 1939–45, AWM54 6228/1/1). A private's rate of pay was set at £3/10/- a month (QSA Aboriginals 1941, A/4218, 5601–5800), which meant that he received less than half the normal rate to which he was legally entitled (Beckett 1987, p. 64). Despite segregation, 'coloured and white soldiers [became] great mates ... just like brothers' and the white soldiers told the island men 'their rights', and that they 'should have got more' (TISHSS 1987, p.10). The TSLI men also resented restrictions on their gambling and drinking, while their white counterparts could do both freely. Again the director's paternalism and the injustices they were experiencing with the collaboration of the army, in other words the Commonwealth Government, fuelled a fire of resistance among them.

In December 1943, despite a warning that they would be shot if they went on strike, the TSLI refused to attend parade. As in 1936, the men's grievances, this time about their unequal treatment alongside white soldiers, led them to form a cohesive group to force change. A TSLI veteran (1989) explained that although the four island groups of Torres Strait Islander soldiers were in their 'own battalions,' they had 'no feeling of hate [toward one another] no growl now' (that is, inter-island rivalries were suspended). The outcome was a pay increase to two-thirds of the white soldiers', plus dependants' allowance (rates just as illegal as the initial rates that were once again determined on Bleakley's advice). His reason for the soldiers' low pay remained the same: 'they may be spoilt from the State point of view for times of peace' (AWM 54, 6228/1/1). The army's acquiescence in this, however, was not unrelated to the greater sum involved if these men received the proper rates of pay (Osborne E 1995, pp. 127–9). The illegality of their underpayment as members of the Australian Army was at the time known to the army, and in the 1980s they finally received back pay for their wartime service (Seekee n.d.).

When Marou called the young men to go to war they had high expectations for the future. However, they had no idea that again they would be treated as lesser beings, and this time by the Commonwealth Government to whom they were looking for equality. Their eventual rejection of this status was the second occasion when men from different islands acted cohesively to resist injustice.

'Hard times': women in a war zone

Once the men were established in the army camps on Thursday Island they had no contact with their families for long periods of time and the women had no way to contact their men. In early 1942 all women and children on Thursday Island and Keriri (Hammond Island) were ordered to evacuate but no such order was made for the outer island women. They remained on the doorstep of a potential invasion of Australian soil. The Torres Strait fixed defences, centred on the Prince of Wales group, lay south behind them: the advancing Japanese forces were to the north in New Guinea. The Late Yam Island Elder (1989) described the women as 'meat in the sandwich'. A rifle and 150 rounds of ammunition issued to each of the 12 signallers (Wartime signaller on Mer, 1990) on the bigger island communities constituted their protection. Only two white people volunteered to remain in Torres Strait: Charlie Turner, a teacher who came to the Strait in 1935 (and continued to teach there until 1964; he died on Thursday Island in 1982 (Osborne 1998)); and WC Curtis, manager of the Island Industries Board store on Badu, who during that time was de facto Local Protector.

By August 1942 the majority of able-bodied men had been recruited, which one TSLI veteran (1989) described as a 'cruel act — leave all those women' there. He said, 'The government they run away, on all island white teacher, they all run away, fright from dead and leave us. They leave women nobody to protect them only old men'. Old women who lived through that time told me that there was great apprehension and fear among them: 'We frightened because we got no man. We don't know what enemy like come destroy your life … We didn't understand what was going to happen to us'. It was 'the blind lead the blind [because] we didn't know nothing about [the war]'. These women, who had never left their small communities, saw themselves as 'innocent, we don't know what [is] going on in the outside world. We were sort of trusting in God. We got to pray for stop this war … every night' (Osborne E 1995). At the Early History Workshop (1987) on Thursday Island, the Late Warraber Elder recalled how the women felt when the men were enlisted:

> *When all that was going on it brought a lot of sadness, sorrow and even brought tears to the Torres Strait Islanders' eyes on that day because they had never seen anything like that before, seeing all the men and young boys taken away from their homes to go and defend their country and their islands, their homes, their families.*

When the Japanese bombed Nurupai (Horn Island) on 14 March 1942, the army instructed the women on civil defence. On the large hilly island of Moa, the women at Poid were ordered by soldiers to move into the bush and build houses. A Female Kubin Elder (1990) remembered how hard it was:

> *Some of them [made] bush houses [out of] grass and bark skins, some of them irons. We went a long way in the bush. Terrible. We had to carry everything. Terrible time, and all the plane flies on top make [us] fright. Children cry — 'This way, this way'. [We were] frightened.*

When the war became 'very, very strong' these women were again ordered by the army: 'All right. Tell chairman go more in [the bush]. We have to carry things more inside … and [sergeant] tell us not to make one camp, make different camp so if anything happen they might only destroy one village and another small camp they save'. This was yet another move in a long history of relocations.[1]

Saibai is a flat swampy island and a Saibai woman (1989) recalled their civil defence strategy: 'Everybody go underground [into trenches], everybody grab children and grandchildren and go underground … when the plane go past everybody come back home. Everybody must be ready like cyclone. As soon as plane come everybody move [quickly]'. On Mer the people stayed in the village, but when planes were sighted a Female Merian Elder (1990) explained how mothers told their children, 'Come quick, let's go, plane come'. They ran with bundles of clothes and hid in the creek. The Late Yam Island Elder (1989) said that on the small flat coral cays when the women heard the bombing on nearby Nurupai there was little they could do but run into the low scrub and hope they

---

1. Following the decimation of the Kaurareg people of Muralag, the remnant relocated to Keriri (Hammond Island). In 1922, the government moved them at gunpoint (late Keriri Elder, 1990) to Adam (later named Poid) on Moa because, according to Chief Protector Bleakley, 'Thursday Island, with its drink and other attractions, was too easily accessible from Hammond' (1961, p. 294). In 1944, the army told the women hiding in the bush on Poid that they had to relocate to Kubin. A Female Kubin Elder (1990) told me that they camped on the beach while they began to build their new village, Kubin, 'another big struggle'. Some of the Kaurareg from Kubin have now moved back to Nurupai (Moore 1979, p. 19).

2. Paternalism challenged

were not visible to enemy airmen flying over their islands. On Badu, the Female Thursday Island Elder (1990) said the women were dispersed into eight bush villages and they dragged iron from their village houses long distances into the bush to make shelters.

The people on Yam, the Elder (1989) recalled, were terrified when the village was strafed, and on Mer and Erub they witnessed the frightening flash and the sounds of gunfire during the Battle of the Coral Sea (Wartime signaller on Mer, 1989). The boys on Saibai thought it was exciting to see '36–45 bombers, fighters' fly daily over Saibai on the way to New Guinea, but the Saibai woman (1989) remembered that their mothers were in great fear of what might happen to them if they were spotted by the planes. Fifty years on a Nagir woman (1989) said she still had vivid recollections of Japanese and Allied planes over their islands: 'Like white birds everywhere on top and we can see the smoke when they fire them guns'. A Tamwoy Town woman (1990) spoke about how she and other Ugar women ferried the pilots who were essential for the navigation of the Great North Eastern Channel in small rowboats out from their island to meet cargo vessels traversing to and from New Guinea. She recalled the shock and fear they experienced when the sea boiled and a submarine surfaced to take on a pilot. In many ways, no island community was spared the realities of this mechanised war about which the people had no understanding.

Despite their fears, the wartime signaller (1989) remembered that the Meriam women were good at disguising their true feelings. They went about their work singing and laughing as though there was no war. Work included, among other things, tending their gardens. That was hard work, the Meriam woman (1990) said: 'We speared the ground for planting bananas, paw paws, watermelons, sweet potatoes, cassava, yams ... everything was fresh ... we had no refrigerator. We went out each day. It was a long way'. She said that they had to collect wood every day: 'We come from the hills and carry down loads of wood on our backs'. This work was vital but they never knew if enemy planes would suddenly appear while they were out in the open, something the army told them to avoid.

Two Nagir woman (1989) recalled that their grandmother who, with no understanding of mechanised warfare, thought she was safe by crouching in her garden with a towel over her head when planes flew over. Although the granddaughters laughed when they recalled what their grandmother did, they too did not understand the extent of what airmen could see below them. They said that when they were fishing in the lagoon and they heard the planes: 'we floated under the water with only our noses out. We didn't know they could see us under the water'. Women all around Torres Strait continued to work in their gardens and to fish the lagoons as they had always done as, irrespective of the dangers, wartime shortages of basic store goods made their work all the more imperative.

With the withdrawal of the white teachers and their wives, who administered western medicine on the communities, young island women — with no formal training — diagnosed sicknesses, dispersed minimal supplies of western medicines and applied their own bush medicines. There had always been difficulties in getting patients to the hospital on Thursday Island on their sailing boats because of the winds and tides, but now there was the added danger of sailing in a war zone. The one old local midwife travelled in these dangerous waters to deliver babies. A Male Ugar Elder (1990) said he rowed his dinghy to Masig about a month before his wife was due to have her baby and returned with the midwife. Another mother was taken to Badu in a dinghy but died, although the baby survived on milk collected from other nursing mothers. The Late Yam Island Elder (1989) talked about his brother's wife: 'She gave birth ... and the women were there trying to do what they could to help her. She was just there all day, until four or five in the afternoon. The baby was delivered and the mother died'. These were not isolated stories of women paying a high price for what they hoped would be a better future (see Osborne E 1995).

One revolutionary event in the women's lives at this time was that for the first time they received money from the government. Segregation policies were being questioned in the late 1930s with the result that the Commonwealth Government, for 'reasons of justice and practicality' (Beckett 1987, p. 64), extended the benefits of social services legislation to Torres Strait Islanders. Hence, in 1941 the women received child endowment for the first time. For most women, having their own money was a new experience. Their men generally handled what little money the Protector did not control. The Late Yam Island Elder, a former storekeeper (1989), recalled, 'That was the first time they had to use money. They don't know nothing about money. Ladies would sit out there [the store] and call people, ask people who understand about money, "Would you do shopping for me?"' They were excited, the Meriam woman (1990) remembered, 'Look at all I got'. The feeling was good: 'We bought little bit tea, sugar ... They don't know about money, just keep it and spend just a little bit. It was good just having money, and food in the garden'. For a short time these women familiarised themselves with the outsiders' monetary system. Soon, however, because the government believed the money was being wasted, the women no longer received cash payments.

A passbook system was established because, like the men, the women were seen as incapable of managing money wisely. With the passbook system controlled by the storekeeper, who more often than not had no training in bookkeeping, the women — and indeed the storekeeper — rarely knew how much money was in the accounts to enable the women to buy much-needed store goods when they did become available.

As the war progressed, supplies of store goods became intermittent because of shipping difficulties and prices soared. To help meet the cost of living, the women took whatever opportunities there were to make extra money. For instance, the women who rowed their dinghies out to ferry pilots received a small remuneration. Elsewhere they dived for trochus; on Moa they gathered and carried wolfram (tungsten) long distances from the mine to sell at the store. The Female Kubin Elder (1990) remembered, 'Some might be kept in Sunshine Milk tins to be sold later'. Domestic tasks were performed for the signallers and army personnel who came to the islands, and in the latter part of the war when some schools re-opened teaching gave a few young women an income. Others received a basic training in nursing and staffed the hospitals set up on Badu and Masig in late 1943. However, long delays in crediting these wages to their accounts, and the non-payment of the full amount, added to families' financial hardships (Osborne E, 1995).

Like their men, Torres Strait Islander women were thrown into a situation totally alien to them and all had their own poignant stories of isolation and fear. Almost all of their white teachers and administrators had abandoned them, but their resourcefulness cannot be underestimated, nor can their belief that it would all be worthwhile after the war.

High aspirations

After 40 years of paternalistic rule, Torres Strait Islander men and women had been drawn into an incomprehensible war. A Islander woman living in Brisbane in 1989 told me how she believed island women felt about it:

> That war was a new thing for our people ... it was an experience of real fear ... probably all of them did not even understand the war ... They know the war ... between Papua New Guinea and Torres Strait Islands ... with bow and arrow, nothing like planes. Those wars were scary but this came in the middle of their Christianity ... why this happening? ... The wars that we experience were heathen!

Despite this lack of understanding, what the people wanted was equality with other Australians, and they lived with the belief that if this incomprehensible war was to set them on this path, the hard times would be worth it. A year before the war ended, the Governor of Queensland was presented with a petition which expressed what most Torres Strait Islanders believed would be their rightful entitlements at the end of the war.

> *To his excellency — Sir*
>
> *Torres Strait Islanders be self-controlled by the people with the aid of the Commonwealth Government. When Japan declared war against Australia all our European leaders of Torres Strait were escaped for their lives leave us helpless there was no word of evacuation, we were left as a precious bait to the enemy. And the Governor is now asked that Torres Strait be self-controlled by the aid of the Commonwealth Government for that purpose. Torres Strait had volunteered in this present war therefore its people must be on the same position as the European. That is to say to have full Citizen Rights. To have full Trade of Union. To have full European wages for all employment and Labour condition and to have a higher standard of University Education.* (QSA Governor's correspondence 1944, 12257)

Beckett (1987, p. 61) suggests Marou from Mer may have been the author, while George Mye believes that it may have been James Idagi (James Williams). Whoever it was who wrote them, these were bold words from men whose war experience had strengthened their resolve to be free from the oppressive Queensland legislation, the Department of Native Affairs and its paternalistic director.

CHAPTER 3

The growth of political activism

The men of the Torres Strait Light Infantry (TSLI) returned to their islands in 1946 satisfied that they were worthy of Australian citizenship and the freedoms enjoyed by white Australians. They wanted the Commonwealth Government to assume responsibility for their affairs. However, the Queensland Government jealously guarded its state rights, and the Liberal Coalition government in Canberra was reticent to interfere. Indeed, the road to freedom was to prove long and frustrating.

In 1946, re-establishment of the shelling industry was vital for Torres Strait Islander economic self-reliance. The rested seabeds were well stocked and shell prices were high. With their savings and deferred pay, many ex-servicemen 'rushed to buy boats of all sizes' (Beckett 1987, p 68) and the Boigu man (1990) said skippers made 'good money' working their own boats:

> The only thing we get more money after war ... We get our own little boat ... from Mackay. We buy that with our soldier money, me and my mate. That my boat, government cannot do anything ... We work one week, come back eleven hundredweights, two hundred pounds trip. That was good money. That was big change.

They were glad to be independent of government, but, he said, they maintained their custom of reciprocity:

> When big money we try to help countrymen ... three families we tried to feed everybody ... We had two boat, my brother and we got another one for him. We got eight brother and we work with [them]. We got more boats so more could get work, and income without government assistance.

The marine industry was re-established rapidly as the director of the Department of Native Affairs reported:

> Practically every available Torres Strait Islander, totalling 700, is now employed in the marine industry gathering pearl-shell and trochus shell. Of this number, approximately 100 are employed on boats owned by registered pearling companies, the balance are engaged gathering marine produce on their own boats. (DNA report 1946, p. 2)

In 1942 the Torres Strait Islanders' boats were beached or impressed by the army, and by war's end many were no longer in existence or fit for use (Mendis 2007). However, he acknowledged the island men's financial contributions to re-establishing the marine industry:

> Torres Strait Islanders now possess 32 pearling vessels. During the year it has built up from five vessels to its present number through the efforts of Islanders, who from their war savings have been able to purchase luggers and cutters for cash. The expenditure by these men of the sum of fifteen thousand pounds [A$30 000] cash in rehabilitating themselves in the marine industry constitutes a record that can be favourably compared with any community in Australia. (DNA report 1946, p. 2)

Prior to the war, Japanese skippers and divers monopolised the better-paid jobs, but once this monopoly was broken island men filled many of these positions. A new wage scale was introduced by government regulation ranging from a monthly minimum of £6 (A$12) for an ordinary seaman to a maximum of £20 (A$40) for skippers. There was provision for bonus payments when the catch exceeded certain tonnages (Bleakley 1961, p. 273). Notwithstanding, the Boigu man (1990) said that for the ordinary seaman who did not own his own boat the 'money was a bit better than before the war, still not very good … it's a real hard life … everything was more [money]'.

Island seamen were permitted to visit Thursday Island during daylight hours only in the years before the war, though the Protector saw fit to relocate a handful of women to Thursday Island to do domestic work for whites. The Badu woman (1990) said, 'I worked in the Grand Hotel … Mr O'Leary bring us in … I was a house girl, look after the children and housework. My mother used to work for the sergeant. She was a widow'. The Late Badu Elder (1989) recalled that as a very young man he was permitted to go to Thursday Island to help his uncle cut wood: 'I cut wood and we sell it in the town'. After the war, the restriction was lifted and as many men were needed to rebuild Thursday Island outer-island men were recruited. To house them, Island Industries Board purchased 'a complete block of buildings that [became] known as the

Labour Pool Barracks ... Approximately sixty Islanders [were] resident in these buildings, from which [was] drawn all labour required' (DNA report 1946, p. 13).

The Torres Strait Islanders were excluded from the Australian census until 1967, but Beckett suggests that from available post-war Queensland Government figures the 'population was increasing rapidly' (1987, p. 69). Simultaneously, state government operations expanded and more positions became available for island teachers and medical aides on the outer-island communities as well as assistants in the Board's 16 branch stores (DNA report 1946, p. 13). Of the 'native' branch managers, whose responsibilities were extended during the war to include management of all social service payments, the director observed, 'It is gratifying that this increased work has been carried out in a manner that pays tribute to the ability and necessary adaptability of the present-day Torres Strait Islanders' (p. 13). Island men were employed to establish a new settlement (Tamwoy Town) on Thursday Island to house outer-island families. Although other employment beyond the fishing industry became available, it was generally in the public sector because Torres Strait Islanders lacked formal qualifications for positions in the private sector. However, even if they performed the same work as white employees, their pay was much lower (Beckett 1987, p. 70).

The standard of housing improved somewhat on the outer islands. Houses and building materials left by the military on Nurupai (Horn Island), Gialag (Friday Island) and Thursday Island were purchased by the Island Industries Board and sold to the people at a figure 'that just covered handling expenses' (DNA report 1946, p. 15). This enabled replacement of pre-war homes with more substantial housing, as well as providing housing for newlyweds or those about to wed, as explained by the Boigu man (1990): 'That was our custom to build house before we got married. I got this galvanised iron from army. Cost me £52 for iron. [DNA] bought from army when finish'. His brother got a boat and purchased and transported his own house from Gialag: 'I go with him and buy that house. My brother and me build dinghy to come back here'. For the first time, houses with glass louvres appeared on the outer islands.

White military officers suggested in 1943 that the women had become dependent on 'European foods' to the detriment of their families' health (QSA Native Affairs 1942–44, TR1227, Bundle 140). The women contradicted this outsider perspective and were adamant that, even when store goods were available, they frequently lacked money to buy them (Osborne E 1995, pp. 276–81). However, in 1946, the director's interpretation was that this situation was brought about as a result of the long absence of the men (who were not in fact the principal gardeners) but he added that the 'leeway of the war years' had picked up and on some islands 'fruit and gardens are more prolific than they were pre-war' (DNA report 1946, p. 13). Even so, the people's dependence on store goods increased after the war, perhaps because of easier availability as there were now stores on all communities, or their slightly better financial circumstances.

People's aspirations for a better life intensified after the war and, as they were no longer confined to their island communities, many moved away in the hope of finding something better. Water shortages on both Purma (Coconut Island) and Saibai prompted some families from both islands to relocate to Warraber and Bamaga respectively. Poid, on Moa, was abandoned for health reasons and a new community was established at Kubin. While the Meriam men pressed for 'proper wages' many realised their only hope of equality with whites was to go to the mainland. In 1947 the director allowed 80 men to go to the cane fields to alleviate labour shortages (DNA report 1948, p. 2). At season's end some men found other employment on the mainland and their families joined them. The men could earn 'five or six times what [they] got at home, and the money was [their] own to spend as [they] pleased' (Beckett 1987, p. 72). The awareness of a new freedom of movement, work opportunities, total control of their money and better education for their children resulted in a relocation of entire families to the mainland.

Post-war politics

Although the servicemen's white 'army mates' had expressed some concern for their treatment, at the war's end few people on the mainland were aware of, or concerned about, the aspirations of this group of Indigenous Australians. The communist journalist Gerald Peel visited the Strait and published the *Isles of Torres Strait* (1946) in which he sympathetically aired the people's position. Indeed, Peel advocated autonomy for Torres Strait under the Commonwealth with 'marine and other natural wealth reserved for the exclusive use of the Islanders' (Beckett 1987, p. 77; Peel 1946, p. 134), issues to be discussed in later chapters. Another communist, J Devaney, wrote about island conditions in the *Tribune*, the party's newspaper. However, the people did not embrace communism and in 1949 many turned to the Australian Legion of Ex-Servicemen and Women to promote their cause, but several island councils banned membership as it was seen as opposing the Department of Native Affairs' rule on the islands. Nonetheless, some Torres Strait Islanders, smarting from a strong sense of injustice, continued to look for help from southern whites who came to Torres Strait after the war. Conversely, there were those who chose to work within the state system.

On Badu, the early, strongly anti-administration council of elected ex-servicemen was ousted and Tanu Nona assumed the position of chairman for life. Until the pearling industry's decline, Badu retained its pre-war record of 'top island for pearling' with the Nona boats taking more than half the earnings of the remaining DNA fleet from 1946 to 1958 (Sharp 1984, p. 247). Tanu's father, the Samoan Tipoti Nona, married Ugarie, a woman from Saibai, and moved to Badu around the turn of the twentieth century, and there they reared nine boys and five girls. He was a hard man who brooked no opposition to his authority. According to the Badu woman (1990), one of his children, 'If you give him cheek he take a knife out and throw and you got to run for save your life'. He demanded hard work of his children: 'He learned us how to do work so we weren't hungry', she said. One of his granddaughters, and Tanu's niece living on Thursday Island (1991), remembered Ugarie as 'an influence on all the sons'. They sat with her under the almond tree and 'yarned about everything and political things ... things about law, and why they made this law' when it was not the traditional role of women to engage with politics. There were other outstanding Badu women, according to Tanu's niece, and she saw them as all 'quite wise'. For instance, at a time when racism was prevalent, her mother counselled her: 'If people say things about you, that's their problem', counsel that she says stood her in good stead for her own political career.

Ugarie's eldest son, Tanu, was born in 1902. Prior to the war he skippered the *Waikaid* with 'all the best men' (Beckett 1987, p. 154). He too was a hard master and was known as the man who 'taught Badu how to work' (p. 148). One of Sharp's informants explained:

> *Competition on, under Tanu Nona, and we Western [island] ones won the competition, but it was very bad. Before sun-up you had your one piece of damper ... And God knows when you going to get your second bite ... We eat now clamshell meat to keep ourself alive ... Who gonna complain 'gainst Tanu? Anyway, we were the people which obey the orders given to us whether it's right or wrong.* (Sharp 1984, p. 215)

Tanu introduced new council by-laws that forbad desertion from boats and emigration to the mainland, and he abolished traditional land tenure (Sharp 1980a, p. 82). The Nona men knew how to socialise with whites and they brought master pearlers home for a drink. As Tanu's niece (1991) saw it, his example was not as it was widely suggested — 'toadying to the DNA line [but] just getting on with their life'. In 1949, when Tanu became chairman of Badu for life, his reputation was a talking point. The Erub Elder (1989) remembered when he was a young man: 'I feel in my head that time the older men were talking about Tanu Nona. What's this superman! I kept getting messages — Tanu, Tanu, Tanu — and I heard someone say Tanu is a Badu man'. By 1959 he had entrenched his power and unified it 'through kinship ties' (Beckett 1987, pp. 162–3). Tanu, without a doubt, was for a long time a leader who enhanced his clout through his relationship with the Queensland Government. Other leaders only wanted to get out from under that government.

After the war, the government was forced to recognise that fact: 'The rehabilitation of these people embodied not a return to pre-war conditions, but a return to conditions forever changed by the wave of unprecedented prosperity that had swept over the area' (DNA report 1947, p. 25). The director further stated that a 'complete conversion to the life of the white races must come,' but that 'a carefully thought out plan of education must be instituted' (p. 25). In 1949, the Queensland parliament was made aware of the unanimous decision of the Island Councillors' Conference that 'civil rights as applicable to white citizens should be granted them' as they had 'not yet attained their desire for the franchise' (DNA report 1949, p. 23). Nevertheless, the people continued to be denied enfranchisement and Beckett (1987, p. 74) suggests the retired Bleakley's paternalistic stand on the civilising of the people had been an influential factor. He had administered Indigenous affairs for many years and was seen by those in government as an authority. But Bleakley's attitude never changed, and long after his retirement he wrote, 'It would be a sorry day for their happiness as a race if the franchise were extended to them and they were subjected to the disturbing influence of political partisanship, which actually could have little meaning and interest for them' (1961, p. 299). These protective and segregationist attitudes died hard in state government administration of Indigenous people, even after Bleakley's retirement. The attitudes of his successors — Con O'Leary and later Pat Killoran — were also set in the same paternalistic mould.

In a contradiction of their unanimous decision nine years earlier, however, some island councillors declared in 1958 that they were 'not ready for the vote' (Beckett 1987, p. 74). While it is hard to understand this turnaround it suited the government. Thus, even with the eyes of a new anti-colonial post-war world upon Australia, the Department of Native Affairs was able to continue to see the people as incapable of looking after their own affairs, so they were not yet ready for the vote.

3. The growth of political activism

The department's position was probably made possible because of its veto control over island council decisions and the men's fears that they would lose their jobs if they opposed the administration. Moreover, in the Cold War era dissent could be construed as having communist sympathies. Simultaneously, the federal and other state governments were moving toward a policy of assimilation (Reynolds 1989, p. 209).

Gradually, island leaders began to communicate their grievances to the government through their triennial inter-island conferences, first held in 1937 after the Maritime Strike. However, without access to the media their grievances were kept from the wider Australian society that, in any case, was scarcely aware of Torres Strait let alone this Indigenous group of Australians (Beckett 1987, p. 185). From 1949, the strongest voices in post-war Islander politics were those of the entrenched Tanu (representing the western islands), Jim Mosby (central islands) and, until 1956, the 'intransigent' Marou (eastern islands). The former two took the 'official line' (p. 75), but Marou valued his independence and was admired by those who rejected the official line: he was a man who did not cow to O'Leary. As a young man, the Erub Elder (1989) listened to Marou when he explained how he related to O'Leary on an equal footing: 'He [O'Leary] used "bloody" first [when talking to me] so I give him back "bloody" and we come out square'. Marou was the man who told the younger man that he was going to fill his place. The younger man's admiration of the older man's independence and wisdom had a lasting effect on him. He said he was humbled: 'It's a blessing that is rare that one can get from an elderly Torres Strait man. I feel that I am not worthy'. He followed Marou on trips 'for nothing, to do secretarial work without money. I wanted to know how the bugger ticked'.

The value of work was impressed upon the young men by priests and parents as their earnings helped to support the older generation and the church. They were aware that a seaman's life was hard and dangerous but its rigours proved their manhood, gave them opportunities to visit mainland towns, and there was the hope that one day they might win the approval of prospective parents-in-law. Beckett (1987, p. 106) quotes an Erub man as saying, 'Trochus work was something you wanted to do, boys took a pride in it'. The Boigu man (1990) proffered his point of view when he said that for a young man to remain on the island all year long there was the problem of the strictness with which morality by-laws were applied:

> *It was bad thing to stay on island. That's why [I] got out. Life on island bit terrible, boring, and, you know, too many go around [with] girls. They were very, very, very strict DNA, they were the law ... Very strict,*

one false move and you get about with girls, if girl's parents disagree and girl's father and mother said 'out' and the council will agree.

By the mid 1950s the people's post-war aspirations were not dead, but it was a difficult time to express them. The Local Protector and the director made it their business to have a personal knowledge of individuals so they had to be careful. A Badu man living on Thursday Island (1990) described it thus:

You are isolated in those days, no communication, no transport, no means of anything. If you are under fire from the top, you had no one else to go with. Only means to get to outside world and it has to go through office here [Thursday Island], and it was under their control and you had nothing only a smoke signal and it could not be seen by the outside world. All messages were checked, I am sure. If you picture a time a person in a community ... try to come up against chief on TI. Even if you leave island to come to TI and you had no place to stay there was even the police here to say 'removal order'. They could remove you back to your home islands. They had powers to do it. What can one do under these circumstances? In those days it was the by-laws and whatever the Act said.

They felt they had no alternative but to overtly conform while covertly resenting the administration and the Torres Strait Islander Acts that gave it the final say in their affairs.

Searching for an economic base for future independence

The post-war boom in the pearling industry peaked in 1951 with almost all able-bodied men in employment: 1957 was a good year, but by 1961 only one-third of these men were still in the industry (Beckett 1987, p. 70). By the time the Commonwealth gained constitutional rights to intervene in Indigenous affairs in 1967 the economic high in the pearl shell industry was well and truly over. With the introduction of plastics, world demand for pearl shell dropped. This was partially offset by the setting up of Japanese–Australian pearl culture stations in Torres Strait. However, this industry also declined in the 1970s as a result of a disease affecting the oysters and the damage done to the pearl-shell beds by an oil spill from the shipwrecked *Oceanic Grandeur* in 1970. Badu, which had always prided itself on its successful operations in the shell industries, provides an example of the decline:

The year 1960 saw Badu at its high point, with fourteen boats at work. In 1961 ... only eleven boats were at work ... the decline continued to eight for 1967 and, after a suspension of pearl culture [which had kept some boats at work] in the early 1970s, to two. (Beckett 1987, p. 168)

However, another viable source of economic independence was being investigated in the 1950s.

Prior to the war, individual Torres Strait Islanders were digging for wolfram on Moa and selling it to the Island Industries Board on Badu. The Female Kubin Elder (1990) said families came from as far away as Mer, Boigu and Saibai to dig. It was, she said, a three- or four-hour walk from the village on Moa with women and children also working at the mine, and at the end of the day they carried the heavy metal down the hill 'on the backside, like a horse' (Osborne E 1995, p. 71). However, disputes arose amongst the miners and in order to fall into line with Queensland mining laws and good mining practices, the following motion was passed at the Masig Island Councillors' Conference in 1944:

> *As wolfram mining on Moa Island failed through there being too many bosses and disputes between Poid and St Paul's people on the question of boundaries and ownership, the Director be requested to arrange for the Govt. to declare the wolfram area on Moa Island a mining field and that it be worked and developed in accordance with State mining laws. Also that a competent European miner be engaged to supervise labour and production and to advise on the necessary material required to develop the field.* (QSA TR1227, bundle 140)

After the war, the call went around Torres Strait to 'come dig' (Sharp 1993, p. 169) in the hope that the mine would become a viable enterprise. And, in December 1953, the Inspector of Mines reported on the open-cut wolfram mines on Moa. He indicated a need to blast deeper to ensure the industry's profitability and stated that more men would need to be trained to use explosives as only two or three island men were authorised to do so. Indeed, the inspector indicated that 'little, if any, progress [could] be expected until ... local miners [became] sufficiently familiar with mining methods to carry out developmental work' and that 'within 3 years or so, most of the miners would [need to be] authorised' to use explosives. Moreover, 'a considerable number of men' had left the mines because they saw their futures as insecure 'owing to their lack of being able to develop the field' (Fleischman 1953, pp. 935–6). Meanwhile, families from a number of islands continued to work the mines hoping to make a good living. The Badu woman (1990) recalled that her mother and father worked there during the week: 'My father used to send the dinghy [to Badu] for us kids to come in on Friday afternoon. We used to work in the mine. He needed us to carry the drums [of wolfram] and pack them. After the war the mining was good'. However, problems arose with this attempt to achieve a viable mining enterprise, such as the lack of mining skills, transport difficulties and the remoteness of the site. To counter the problems a move was made to mine the wolfram on a cooperative basis, something the director did not want.

In 1956 an Anglican priest, Rev. Alf Clint, came to Torres Strait. He believed that cooperatives would enable the people to gain their independence and a Christian cooperative was established in 1958 that offered an alternative to both the pearling industry and to the government's Island Industries Board, which did not benefit the people economically (Beckett 1987, p. 79). A supporter said, 'Most wanted freedom. They thought this society would give them freedom so they joined ... So anyhow we worked. Lots and lots of people outside Moa joined because they thought this was the answer' (Sharp 1993, p. 171). A Christian cooperative on Moa based on wolfram was mooted (Loos & Keast 1992, pp. 286–301). A wider vision was to 'incorporate cray-fishing and agricultural operations as well as a bakery' (Sharp 1993, p. 170). A bakery was subsequently set up on St Paul's and the supporter explained (p. 170):

> *The Melbidir, DNA boat, took all that machinery over put on Island at St Paul's Moa. We do that building, we put that motor in the machine, we put that lighting plant down. build everything. Kubin people all for it, Badu, Saibai, all the Torres Strait islands and the Cooperative was coming good for all people.*

To ensure the success of the bakery operation, Jacob Abednego was sent to Sydney to learn the baker's trade.

Clint taught the people cooperative business methods and told them, 'It doesn't matter whatsoever you do — if you go out in boats and pick up shell — you must know how to sell it: that's part of book-keeping' (p 172). Bread was delivered three times a week by boat to other islands, but the boat was small and 'if the wind blew really hard [they] can't make it' (p. 172). The bakery was 'alright' until problems arose with deliveries of flour and yeast on the only available transport, the government boat, and the payment for it: 'When yeast's supposed to come over to the bakery they say there's no yeast on the boat. That's the DNA! Then ... they change over the manager [of DNA] ... He asked we to pay cash. In business they give you thirty days. Well, that was on purpose too'. Then the people were told they could not use the Anglican mission boat to transport the flour because 'it might dirty the boat' (p. 172). This was a

3. The growth of political activism

tame excuse because the boat was there to service the mission. Finally, the scheme was labelled 'communist'— according to one island man, a word the people did not understand: '[I]t's a European word. We haven't got it in the Torres Strait; we've only got our own custom, working together, live happy, share things together' (Sharp 1984, B166). Clint was expelled by the government from Torres Strait in 1962 and refused permission to enter any mission station in Queensland (Kelly 1980–1, p. 2), and the cooperative enterprise in Torres Strait failed. Wolfram mining also ceased. Moreover, the people were denied any opportunity to market for themselves the plentiful fish in the seas around their islands because they did not have the boats and freezers to make commercial fishing viable. As they saw it, 'Other people take all the fish from Torres Strait to Cairns ... we'd have [had] boats out there and be fishing for ourselves. But they washed the brains of my people: they paint we red' (Sharp 1984, B163–6).

In the late 1960s the Moa–Adai–Waiben housing cooperative ('the MAW') was established with Ted Loban, a returned serviceman and Thursday Island leader, as a prime motivator. One of Sharp's informants explained the operation of the building of much-needed housing in Torres Strait: 'When a house is complete it no more belongs to the MAW, it belongs to Moa Island Investment Company. Same with Adai ones. We in the community choose this person to be in that house and that same person pays rent, $15 every week' (Sharp 1993, p. 172). Then, at some point, the director instructed that unless the money was paid to the island councils the housing cooperative could not build more houses (TSIMA newsletter 1990, p. 3). In the 1970s, an EMU (Erub–Mer–Ugar) cooperative was set up in the eastern islands but it too was unable to survive the political climate of the time.

Disappointment and disillusionment at the failure of these attempts to begin to break the people's dependence on the government was partially compensated for by the increase in government jobs, or as the Badu man (1990) remarked, 'In those days [the 1960s] everyone was looking to go down south, the life was to get away', and there was certainly an exodus of Torres Strait Islanders to the mainland. Those who remained continued to do battle with governments unsympathetic to their aspirations for self-reliance.

Freedom of worship: equality in education and health services

Almost the entire outer Torres Strait Islander population until the early 1950s followed the Anglican faith, the exception being the Catholic family on Nagir. The former catered to the people's distinctive likes, such as the singing of island hymns, using drums instead of organ music, and feasting and dancing on religious holidays. Senior clergy were whites but there were ordained island priests and one archdeacon, though Beckett suggests he 'served a very limited purpose' as training at the theological college on St Paul's was seen as lower than mainland standards. Beckett also cites the instance of an island priest being treated as an inferior when he was offered lemonade while two white priests drank wine (1987, p. 81). However, island men who worked on the mainland soon discovered that southern Anglican congregations were 'unwelcoming' (p. 81). Not surprisingly, when they saw that the Pentecostals (Assemblies of God) were 'ready not just to receive them, but also to seek them out on the streets and the remote railway sidings where they worked' (p. 82), they responded. The lively services and freedom of expression appealed to them. Its requirement of European dress and prohibition on drinking and dancing gave them a sense of moral superiority over Anglicans. Moreover, when their newfound 'brothers and sisters' invited them into their homes they experienced an unprecedented sense of equality with people other than Torres Strait Islanders (p. 82). In 1950 Marou, the Meriam chairman who had earlier suppressed the 'sect' on Mer, gave consent for it to be established as an Assembly. Beckett suggests Marou had a 'change of heart' in line with his campaign for citizen rights (p. 129). The Meriam people were experiencing, to a greater degree than the more commercially successful islands like Badu, 'economic impoverishment and political frustration' (p. 209) that drove some, particularly veterans and their wives and widows, to think about a new deal and they looked to the Pentecostals for this.

The Anglican synod responded by increasing the number of minor church positions for island men that gave them a small income. By 1960, 70 per cent of men over 30 held some title in the Anglican church (Beckett 1978, pp. 209–29). But the operations of the new church caused a furore throughout Torres Strait and resulted in the director removing Marou from elected office. Marou's belief that all citizens had rights also led to his ex-communication by the bishop from the Anglican Church because he condoned religious dissent (p. 83). This, for a time, prompted the stifling of dissent on other islands even though it contravened an earlier unanimous resolution of the councillors at their conference on Masig on 19 August 1944: 'Moved James Williams [Mer], seconded Anau Mau [Dauan] that there should be no objection to any religious persuasion entering upon religious work in the Torres Strait Islands' (QSA TR1227, bundle 140). Nonetheless, the denomination eventually spread to other islands 'attracting some who had not been on the mainland but liked the form of service and the emphasis on faith healing' (Beckett 1987, p. 83).

3. The growth of political activism

Frustrations with government increasingly drove the people to believe that a higher level of education was the key to their long-held aspirations for the freedoms enjoyed by white people. The level of education their children received was not based on John Douglas's vision but on a level deliberately set by Chief Protector Bleakley that suited his paternalistic vision.

In the 1944 petition to the governor of Queensland it was requested, among other things, that a 'higher standard of University education' be instituted to put them 'on the same position as the European' (QSA, A/12257). The wording of the request indicates that people had no realistic understanding of what level of education most white children achieved or what a university education entailed and yet, believing education held the key to their freedom, they wanted people who could 'talk to white people', people who had an effective grasp of English (Beckett 1987, p. 76). In 1947 the director acknowledged that there was a need for a 'carefully thought out plan of education' to avoid 'disillusionment' amongst them (DNA report, 1947), but undoubtedly he did not want to raise the bar too high if they were to be kept in Torres Strait, which was his aim. The Late Yam Island Elder (1989) recalled:

> *After the war everybody hungry. That's what they have seen of the Whites during the war. There was a kind of pioneer looking into the future. They realise then that the education don't stop at just merely get your child to learn how your father did, you get that level that you cannot be cheated by DNA. Education stretch much further than what's been taught in the school in the islands.*

Whatever changes were made to post-war education were unsatisfactory. In fact, an answer to the question 'What changes were there after the war?' was cynically voiced by the Badu man (1990) living on Thursday Island who was a former teacher: 'I would call changes after the war nil'. Education remained under the umbrella of the DNA with an inadequate budget and less expertise than the Department of Public Instruction. Larger islands had white principals, usually assisted by island teachers or monitors with little or no training, although after a while some of these unqualified teachers were given the opportunity to do a basic training. A Mabuiag woman (1989) recounted her experiences:

> *I was thirteen. I just finished school up to grade five or six. Mr Frith asked me to come and teach. I like the idea of teaching. I would like to learn more. 1957 I start. In 1965, I come in [to Thursday Island] in school holidays to seminars [for outer-island teachers conducted by Margaret Lawrie and Noel Finch, educators from Brisbane] ... there*

was subjects that some of us don't quite pass and don't understand them and go over that. You don't go enjoying that school break, you come up here. I had six or seven years with Mr Frith. Others only had one year. Young ones had nothing. In 1966 and 1971 I went to Kedron Park [training facility at Brisbane].

On smaller communities, untrained island teachers were in charge. More-gifted children might be sent to the Badu 'secondary school' set up by Mr Frith that went to grade seven. On St Paul's the church offered two years beyond the low primary level but it was difficult for parents from other communities to access this for their children if they did not have a relative willing to house them.

Although the Councillors' Conference on Masig in 1944 was attended by the then deputy director when a motion was carried recommending 'a higher standard of education than applied previously [and] that children suitable for higher education be recommended for admission to a high school in the south for an advanced education', this did not eventuate (QSA TR1227, bundle 140). 'If we'd had that proper education', a Female Thursday Island Elder (1988) said wistfully, 'we'd have had our own doctors and solicitors now'. She was expressing the disillusionment she still felt that more had not been done after the war to raise the level of education so that they could reap benefits for the future of Torres Strait.

Pre-war Torres Strait Islanders often surreptitiously treated sicknesses with their outlawed traditional medicines, and minimally trained white teachers or their wives administered western medicines and diagnosed patients' complaints. Anyone who needed hospital care on Thursday Island was transported on a sail-powered boat with all the dangers that presented. The Late Yam Island Elder (1989) remembered people lost their lives.

> *Sometimes you steadied the patient and got there all right. Sometimes they get worse and when the wind dropped you had to float along, follow the tide. When the tide going to that island because you follow it, okay, but when it come from that island you have to anchor and wait for the tide to turn.*

And the Boigu man (1990) said, 'We travelled by sail and it was one and one-half days [to the Thursday Island hospital]. If there's no wind, you don't go. It was very sad, people died'. Some changes in health care late in the war augured well for a better post-war health care system.

At the 1944 Masig councillors' meeting a comprehensive health scheme prepared by Major GR Beattie, an army physician, was adopted

3. The growth of political activism

to meet what he saw as the desperate medical needs in Torres Strait. Beattie's scheme included 50-bed fully equipped hospitals on Badu and Masig, medical aid centres on all islands under the supervision of 'fully qualified native nurses'; dental and optical services; and nursing training in the island hospitals. Beattie had faith in the island women's suitability for this work as he had seen them working in the two rudimentary hospitals set up on Badu and Masig in 1943. He claimed: 'I can readily conceive strong characters developing who would be quite satisfactory as Matron ... Some individuals [will] attain high qualities of leadership' (QSA TR1227, bundle 140). These nurses received a very basic training in hospital procedures from Mrs Curtis (wife of the wartime de facto Local Protector and Island Industries Board store manager on Badu) and Mrs Frith (wife of the returned school teacher on Masig), both nursing sisters. In the last months of the war a few young women were sent for brief periods to Thursday Island. Beattie's scheme was formulated in response to army officers' perceptions of the wartime situation: 'The health of the people, excluding Service personnel, has deteriorated to a dangerous point over the War years necessitating urgent and extensive action to remedy the drift' (QSA TR1227, bundle 140). Health issues did arise during the war but were made worse during the two years when the conflict was at its height and no proper medical care reached the outer islands.

A former Thursday Island matron (1989) recalled that, when she took up her position there in 1952, there were no trained island nurses on the outer islands, so:

> *some poor [white] woman, if your husband was a teacher and you were given about forty-eight hours' training at the hospital on TI, shown how to give injections ... put bandages on. We decided it was stupid and they [the white teachers] were asked to pick out [island] nurses that they would employ at medical aid posts and we had them in for training for a month or two.*

These nurses, it was anticipated, would return to their islands. The matron continued: 'We cleared out the MAPs [Medical Aid Posts] of [out-of-date] drugs and sent a letter to DNA recommending that [the island nurses] have certain drugs kept in MAP refrigerators and take blood pressure'. She added that by the 1950s a senior certificate was required for nursing and the outer-island school leavers had no way of achieving that level. Some white sisters were posted to the larger communities but it was not easy to get these nurses to go to such remote islands that lacked everything a city girl was used to.

A former Meriam Island nurse (1991) recalled that in the early 1960s she and two or three minimally qualified young women were given highly responsible positions at the Thursday Island hospital because 'they had trouble with getting them [white staff] to stay'. White sisters taught them how to give injections and other hospital procedures. At times they were required to 'scrub up for theatre', they might be given the keys to the operating theatre or 'act as charge nurses, even in the white ward' of this segregated hospital. Another former island nurse from Badu (1990) spoke of the extent of their hospital training:

> *I was fifteen years when I went nursing at the TB [tuberculosis] hospital. There was no real training. When I went nursing they just showed us the anatomy, the body structure, and how to take temperatures, how to make beds, that was all we were allowed to do. I remember just a couple of times Dr Holt talked to us about TB.*

She said she wanted to go to Innisfail for more training but 'DNA didn't want me to do it'. Years later she was wistful about this decision that had denied her an opportunity to make a worthwhile career. There would have been opportunities for young women to become qualified nurses if Beattie's recommendation for health services in Torres Strait had been implemented. It was not until air services and telephones, introduced in the 1970s and 1989 respectively, that medical help was closer in emergencies, and medical teams visited the outer islands at intervals.

In keeping with their vision to have equality with white mainlanders, the Torres Strait Islanders wanted freedom of worship, a higher standard of education and better health facilities but they were constantly reminded that the wheels of government change do not turn quickly, if at all.

Assimilation/integration

In 1956 the DNA committed itself on paper to a national policy of assimilation, with the qualification that there would be no 'impetuous' forcing of Indigenous people to 'change their environment while they were unwilling to accept the responsibility of full citizenship' (DNA report 1958, p. 2), but this was hardly an issue because they had no encouragement to believe they would be given full voting rights any time soon. As already suggested, for a few Torres Strait Islanders the glow of their post-war aspirations had faded, perhaps because they had lost faith in any government's ability or desire to help them. In any event, from 1962 they did become eligible to vote in federal elections and in 1964 they were finally enfranchised for state elections (though, as Beckett points out (1987, p. 73), ex-servicemen already had the federal vote but 'no one had intervened to give them their rights'). Enfranchisement, they had always believed, was an important step toward their goal of greater freedom in Australian society. However, future state government legislation did not fall into line with the national assimilation policy to which it had agreed. In reality, assimilation of Indigenous people would have seen them absorbed into the larger Australian society and erosion of their unique identity, something they would have vigorously opposed. In any event, their vote seemed to them to count for nothing as they continued to be denied freedoms enjoyed by white Australians. Then from about 1962:

> *the assimilation policy came under increasing criticism in Australia because it did not recognise the strength of resilience of Aboriginal [and Torres Strait Islander] culture, which seemed to make the aim of assimilation unattainable. It ignored the natural right [of the people] to make their own choice about their manner of life. Critics of official Government policy argued that a policy of 'integration', based on recognition of the value of [their] culture and their right to retain their language and customs and to maintain their own distinctive communities, was more practicable, more acceptable to [them] and more readily justified.* (Nettheim 1981, p. 170)

Then in 1967 the Commonwealth called a referendum with the aim of gaining the Australian people's consent to legislate for Indigenous people. On 27 May a 'yes' vote was returned. Twenty years after island servicemen called for the Commonwealth to take over their affairs their aspirations were partially met, but it also meant that Torres Strait Islanders would now have to work with two governments and their laws.

In July 1967, a conference of state and federal ministers and officers responsible for Indigenous welfare 'reaffirmed a new definition of assimilation … a modification of what had been announced as the assimilation policy in 1951':

> *No longer, said all Australian governments (including the Queensland government), will we try to force Aborigines and Islanders to become white Australians and to share the same hopes, loyalties and beliefs and so on, and to behave in the same way as white Australians or to become white Australians. Governments said we will give Aborigines and Islanders a choice as to whether they wish to live this way or live some different way.* (Tatz 1967, p. 21)

Governments had moved on from the original concept of assimilation to make Indigenous people 'white' to a model of assimilation/integration incorporating Indigenous choice, but in the case of the Queensland Government on its terms (Nettheim 1981, p. 2).

There were those who were sceptical, such as Joe McGinness, the Aboriginal president of the Federal Council for Advancement of Aborigines and Torres Strait Islanders. He claimed that:

> To begin with, the report [the Hansard Report of the first conference of Commonwealth and state ministers responsible for Aboriginal welfare, where Indigenous policy was discussed] is a reaffirmation of the policy of assimilation formulated by the government during the early 1950s. In spite of assertions to the contrary this policy can only result in the absorption of Aborigines and Island people into the white community, which will result in the loss of our identity as people. (McGinness 1967, p. 26)

However, using its new power to legislate for Indigenous people the Commonwealth established a Department of Aboriginal Affairs (DAA) with the aim of achieving a 'more unified approach' in Indigenous governance. Queensland was the only state that refused to hand to the Commonwealth 'administrative responsibility for policy planning and co-ordination' of its Indigenous people (Nettheim 1981, p. 161).

The Queensland DNA was redesignated the Department of Aboriginal and Islander Affairs (DAIA) by the *Aborigines' and Torres Strait Islanders' Affairs Act 1965*. It was purportedly a 'transitional' measure to 'promote the well-being and progressive development of Aboriginal inhabitants of the State and of the Torres Strait Islands' (p. 161). The official reading of the Act was that it 'aimed at, and has achieved, the abandonment of protection as a policy. It has placed much more emphasis on the process of development ... of resources, both human and material' (p. 6). Nonetheless, despite government protestations to the contrary, Queensland's 1965 legislation was still seen as protective. McGinness pointed out that 'Aborigines and Islanders living in their homelands are automatically declared assisted and so are children if declared by the Director whose powers are almost unlimited' (1967, p. 27). In addition, Nettheim's analysis of the later Queensland *Aborigines Act 1971* found 'apparent violations of some eleven articles' of the Universal Declaration of Human Rights (1981, pp. 7–8).

As late as 1978, the director of DAIA, PJ Killoran, was fulfilling Joe McGinness's prophecy of 1967 that the policy, as formulated by the states and the Commonwealth, would 'result in the loss of our [Islanders'] identity as people' (McGinness 1967). Killoran wanted no part of any progressive ideas about Indigenous people. He claimed (DAIA report 1978, p. 10):

> *it allows for land rights, customary law and tribal language to be developed as goals in themselves. It is ... a policy based on differences and yet states the policy objective is to build a united nation. More alarming, however, is the philosophy being enthusiastically promoted that Aboriginals [and Torres Strait Islanders] are different, are a separate race, and must be encouraged to retain a separate total identity.*

Killoran's words sum up the history of the ideology of the department. Until the Torres Strait Islanders proved their total identification with the dominant society, they would remain children in his administration's eyes and only by patient, paternalistic rule would ultimate conformity be realised.

As Beckett pointed out, when the Commonwealth came onto the scene in 1973 the Torres Strait Islanders had 'representatives seasoned through years of dealing with the Queensland government' and they were 'quick to respond to the approaches of the Commonwealth to take advantage of the rivalry between the two' (1987, p. 177). The Commonwealth had in fact broken Queensland's monopoly of power in Torres Strait, with a new direction in policy. It would 'provide material assistance in the welfare mode, but progress towards integration would no longer be the touchstone ... The goal was now community development, with the community itself as the final arbiter of its needs' (p. 174). Beckett suggests a 'new politics' was ushered in that he labelled 'welfare colonialism' and defined it as a political ideology that 'requires consultation with, and the consent of, its subjects' (p. 185). While Queensland's Island Advisory Council (formed in the late 1930s and made up of members of the island councils) gave the Torres Strait Islanders limited advisory powers, its rival government's entry into Torres Strait 'decisively altered the balance of power' (p. 185). Torres Strait's seasoned political leaders now set themselves to negotiate their way between two governments to progress their desire for greater powers of decision-making.

The border issue: 'Border Not Change' [2]

The call by the Torres Strait Light Infantry men in 1944 for 'Torres Strait be self-controlled by the aid of the Commonwealth' was realised in a limited way after the 1967 referendum. However, Torres Strait Islanders were soon disillusioned with that government. In 1972, Labor Prime Minister Gough Whitlam gave support to a proposal during the New Guinea independence negotiations for the relocation of Australia's only

---

2. Also referred to as 'Border No Change'

international border to the tenth parallel. This would mean that nine islands in Torres Strait would be forfeited to the forthcoming independent nation of Papua New Guinea. It was not the first time a proposal had been made to move the border. In 1879, Queensland's boundary was extended north to bound Saibai, Dauan and Boigu. Then in 1885, Government Resident John Douglas on Thursday Island, along with Queensland Premier Sir Samuel Griffith and Administrator of British New Guinea Sir William McGregor, put forward a proposal to move the boundary further south. Douglas saw 'a readjustment of the maritime boundary had been rendered desirable [with] the establishment of the protectorate over New Guinea' (van der Veur 1966, pp. 25–6). Moreover, he was sceptical about the importance of the area to the people of Queensland (p. 26):

> *They regard them, if I am not mistaken, rather as sources of probable future expenditure than as sources of revenue. It must be admitted also, that this is a region in which the native or coloured races will, in all human probability, preponderate. Such a condition of society is not in accordance with the genus of the people of Queensland.*

Douglas subsequently saw the Meriam people as civilised and deserving of the rights of British citizenship (Douglas 1900, p. 35; see Griffin 1976, pp. xv–xx, for a fuller history of border change).

Aspects of the 1972 border issue concerned competition for oil, New Guinea's claim that the Torres Strait Islanders on those islands were ethnically and historically New Guineans, and Whitlam's belief that these top-western islands were stepping-stones on a 'walk into and through Queensland' (Sharp 1993, p. 226–7). For the people to lose them meant losing much more. Old people were often buried in their families' yards and one of Sharp's informants explained what the loss of the islands would mean to them: 'You see how we think of our dead; for us they're still alive and nobody would be looking after them' (p. 227).

Conversely, at a seminar in Port Moresby in June 1972, Ebia Olewale, member for the Western Province of Papua, said he did not believe that the inhabitants of the Torres Strait were opposed to belonging to Papua New Guinea. He asserted however that his concern was 'not the people — people can move south of the border if they still want to reap the benefits of the Commonwealth social services and other benefits which come out of it' (Griffin 1976, p. xxi). There is no doubt that Torres Strait Islanders on islands in close proximity to the Papuan coast where they have traded for generations knew the poor conditions of the village people and would not voluntarily opt for that life. But Yam Island Elder Getano Lui Snr, at a seminar held in Townsville on the border issue in 1976, was quick to put the record straight (p. 32):

> *[Olewale] has said that we want to become Australians because we are getting Australia money. We were in Torres Strait ... long before there were social services. We survived in our own way. And it is only right that we get social services because we have paid our taxes to the Australian Government and, as Australians, we are entitled to a fair return. This is not our reason for wanting to remain Australians ... Our children were born here, were educated here, our men have come to work on the railways here. We have done our part for Australia: trochus shell, bêche-de-mer. There are no handouts from Australia for us. Our men have worked for every penny they get.*

Key federal and state government players were noticeably absent from the Townsville seminar and Griffin, its convenor, suggested that they may have thought that if they did not attend it 'might prove ephemeral for lack of support' (p. ix), but this was not the case.

Getano Lui Snr reminded seminar participants that onYam in September 1973 Torres Strait Islanders sat down with their Papuan neighbours, Killoran (Queensland director of Native Affairs) and Dr HC 'Nugget' Coombs on behalf of the federal government, when an agreement was arrived at between Torres Strait Islanders and Papuan New Guineans — 'we are the people involved', he said (p. xxiv). The outcome of that meeting was the passing of a resolution that Queensland premier Joh Bjelke-Petersen, who Lui said had 'supported us and respected our wishes from the start', agreed to put through parliament. It read (p. xxiv):

- There would be no change in our border.
- That our Torres Straits would be declared a Marine National Park to safeguard our fishing grounds.
- That the Torres Strait Islanders and the people of the nearby Papuan coast share their traditional fishing rights.

Lui expressed his people's determination that: 'We will never agree to giving away one grain of sand or one cup of water. Our islands and our seas were given to us by our ancestors. We must pass them on to our children. We do not want them to become strangers in their own land' (p. xxv).

Island leader George Mye, in his closing address at the Townsville seminar, explained how difficult it had been in the past to reach the outside world with the truth (p. x):

> *We can only speak on our feelings and traditions, the two fields in which we are experts ... In remote Torres Strait communication between the Islands and mainland Australia are virtually non-existent. We have no newspapers, no television and our only news contact with the outside*

> world is through the DNA radio network, and this is usually limited to official business. Things can get distorted and out of shape.

He added that this is a 'democratic state which [claims] to protect minority rights' and yet it was now forcing the people to prove their right to retain all their islands within the Australian border (p. x).

Whitlam's support for the proposal to move the border triggered a swift reaction in Torres Strait. For the third time (after the 1936 Maritime Strike and the 1944 Army Strike) the Torres Strait Islanders, now with the support of their mainland brothers and sisters, were united. They lobbied state and federal governments through a Border Action Committee, chaired by their vigorous and articulate leader George Mye. Generally, island women had not taken political roles in village life and Meriam woman Etta Passi told me in 1989 that it was a 'momentous' occasion when she became the first woman elected to an island council and was then selected as a member of the committee to go to Canberra on the border issue. The committee members realised they needed to be heard beyond Torres Strait if their campaign were to be successful, and they used the Australian media and international arenas as political tools. Passi recalled that '[We were] controlling [the border issue]. [We] travelled around Australia looking for support and advice. [We] went to Fiji, New Zealand and Tonga ... where [we] met Somari ... and made friends with him and came back and reported here. We signed the agreement'. Thus in the 1970s, unlike in 1885, the Torres Strait Islanders did not rest their case with the Commonwealth. Indeed, every possible avenue of support was solicited. Sharp concluded: 'They had won a significant victory; they had strengthened their will, just what they needed in the 1980s' (1993, p. 227).

The Torres Strait Islanders were thrown into the real world of the outsiders 'without the luxury of learning experiences, natural adjustments and gradual knowledge that everyone else [took] for granted' (Kehoe-Forutan 1988, p. 11). And, despite their elation when the treaty between Australia and Papua New Guinea was ratified in 1985, leaving the islands as they were, there was also a sense of disappointment about its terms that they interpreted as again putting their interests 'in a subordinate position to others' (p. 10). For them, later events supported their interpretation.

How can we lease back what is already ours?

The border issue reinforced for the Torres Strait Islanders the fact that they had few, if any, rights under Queensland law to the lands that had belonged to their ancestors for centuries, and it seemed they could be given away at the whim of a government. They had not forgotten that the Queensland Government had denied them their land rights when returning servicemen were unable to access loans to build war service homes because the government said they did not own the land. Then, in 1981, the Queensland Government announced its intention to revise legislation related to land tenure (see Nettheim 1981 on Queensland's legislative changes 1972 to 1980). The responsible minister wanted perpetual leasehold: the premier favoured 50-year leasehold. The people interpreted this latest move as a total denial of ownership of their islands. Infuriated, the eastern, western and central island leaders bypassed DAIA and went directly to the premier to put their case for inalienable freehold. On his undertaking that no precipitate action would be taken, the leaders returned to the islands 'to test the feeling in the Strait' (Beckett 1987, p. 190). A majority was in favour of inalienable freehold and the Torres Strait Advisory Council relayed to the premier what they wanted (p. 191):

- *Inalienable freehold title to all land presently designated Reserve Land.*
- *Establishment of a Land Trust with elected Islanders to oversee the transfer of the land.*
- *A Statutory Body of elected Islanders to gradually assume the DAIA's role and functions and its statutory bodies.*

In July 1982, the island councillors at their conference 'reaffirmed [their] preference for inalienable freehold by a vote of 35 to 1' (p. 191).

In 1984 the Queensland Government responded with the establishment of a 'system of community level land trusts to own and administer former reserves under a special form of title called a Deed of Grant in Trust (DOGIT)' with island councils as trustees of the lands (Brennan 1984). Earlier in December 1983, while debating the Bill introducing DOGIT, Bob Katter Jnr, minister for Aboriginal and Islander Affairs, explained:

> *The bill is designed to further secure the legal tenure of the Aboriginal and Islander people who will hold in trust under a deed of grant those areas presently reserved for Aboriginal/Islander community purposes ... The proposals embodied in this bill will bring into the area of Aboriginal land rights a tenure not only adequate to the real long-term needs of people on Aboriginal reserves in Queensland, but a refreshingly precise and forthright method of transferring control into the hands of the local people ... The purpose of the bill is to give Aborigines and Islanders a stronger tenure over land which they and their predecessors have occupied for thousands of years.* (Brennan 1984)

With certain amendments, Katter said:

> [The proposals are] superior to any other because they give a perpetual title absolutely inalienable unless the parliament for some reason wants to decide otherwise by a special Act. Nobody except the parliament can alter the size of the area covered by the deed or take the deed away from the Aboriginal or Islander trustees ... Aboriginal land subject to a deed of grant in trust cannot be resumed, acquired or forfeited except by Act of the Queensland parliament. However, the Governor in Council is empowered upon the making of the grant to reserve from the grant a specified area, with or without specifying a particular purpose or purposes (s. 334D, Land Act). (Queensland Land Rights 1984)

Thus, the *Aboriginal and Torres Strait Islanders (Land Holding) Act 1985*, which set up DOGITs, ignored Torres Strait Islander 'customary tenure systems' (Sharp 1987, p. 2), and did not give them the unqualified inalienable rights that they believed belonged to them.

The government took a further step in land rights when it enacted the *Queensland Coast Islands Declaratory Act 1985* to nullify any sovereign rights of Torres Strait Islanders that had survived the annexation by Queensland of their islands in 1879 (see Brennan 1992, p. 69; also Nettheim 1981). By the passing of this Act the government attempted to once and for all block the people's desire for total recognition of their inherited right to inalienable freehold of their lands. The Act had particular relevance to the Mabo Meriam land claim which was at that time pending in the High Court. However, in December 1988 the High Court ruled the Act inconsistent with the Commonwealth *Racial Discrimination Act 1975* enacted to uphold the right to equality before the law for all people (Sharp 1993, p. 232).

The outcome was that on 17 October 1985, 15 island councils took up DOGITs and the Island Coordinating Council, comprising elected chairpersons of each island community, received DOGITs for the uninhabited islands (Brennan 1992, p. 84). Mer was the exception. The Meriam people saw this land tenure as inconsistent with what they perceived as their traditional rights. They said, 'How can we lease back what is already ours?' (Sharp 1987, p. 3). Moreover, a land claim for Mer, lodged by Mabo and others, was pending in the High Court. Meanwhile, the DOGIT communities remained 'fairly independent on their views ... as they let it be known that they [DOGIT] did not fulfil as much as they had hoped for'. But they were determined to 'try to make them work' (Kehoe-Forutan 1988, p. 12).

Eddie Koiki Mabo and four other Meriam felt so strongly about native title to their lands that they commenced legal proceedings in the Queensland Supreme Court in 1982 'to establish their traditional ownership of land on Murray Island' (Beckett 1987, p. 191). In November 1990, that court found that these plaintiffs 'had claims to some lands in accordance with Murray Island law' (*Torres News* 18–24 January 1991, p. 18). The question remained whether the High Court would decide that the 'system of land law operating at Murray Islands is capable of recognition by the Common Law of Australia' (p. 18). By their actions, the Meriam plaintiffs forcefully demonstrated their rejection of any overriding by the government of their customary ownership of their lands.

Governments and the people from 1970

In 1973 the Commonwealth Government established the Department of Aboriginal Affairs (DAA) on Thursday Island. As discussed earlier, this led to a directional change, with the two governments (state and federal) purportedly giving Torres Strait Islanders wider consultative and/or advisory powers. Islanders gained representation by appointment or election to various bodies, such as the National Aboriginal Consultative Committee, its successor the National Aboriginal Conference, the Aboriginal Development Commission, the National Aboriginal Education Committee, and the Queensland Aboriginal and Torres Strait Island Consultative Committee (see Beckett 1987, p. 176). This was in line with the Commonwealth policy favouring community input and development, which the Queensland Government was obliged to follow in an 'uneasy condominium' (p. 171). Nevertheless, the people were constantly frustrated when they perceived that their inputs were more often than not being modified or ignored.

After the state elections in 1983, the National Party's Robert Katter Jnr was appointed minister responsible for Indigenous Affairs. Katter was a 'keen advocate of self-management and immediately instigated Phase I of [a] self-management process' (Kehoe-Forutan 1988, p. 13). In 1984 the initial intention of the state Department of Community Services, the body that administered island affairs, was to hand over some of its functions to the outer-island councils to be 'co-ordinated and assisted by the newly formed ICC [Island Coordinating Council]' (p. 13). The ICC's responsibility was to administer regional projects and to 'keep abreast of the rapid changes occurring within the region' (p. 15). However, increased services brought about 'a polyglot of agencies at all levels of government, all with a variety of functions and responsibilities', and while duplication was common, unity was more difficult to achieve. One of Kehoe-Forutan's informants remarked, 'If someone doesn't agree, instead of trying to go halfway, maybe find a solution, they just go off and form another group. Then nothing gets done because they work against each other instead of with each other to find the answer for all Islanders' (p. 20).

Even so, island leaders did not waver in their desire for the sort of life mainland Australians enjoyed, one example being a legal aid service. In the early 1970s an office was established on Thursday Island thus giving people for the first time the 'unqualified right to legal representation before the Courts' (Nettheim 1981, p. 166). In the past their counsel may have been their accuser as there was generally no independent solicitor on the islands to assist them. This was an important gain, and while some of their aspirations had been refined after years of disillusionment and frustration, resentment was still felt toward the state government. And although the federal government's policies resulted in a more 'liberal and solicitous' form of internal colonialism (Beckett's 'welfare colonialism' (1987, pp. 17–21)) it did not meet the people's long-held aspirations for freedom — even though its outcome was intended 'to transform indigenous people into citizens'. However, the irony was that it rehabilitated the old colonial structure in new form (p. 16):

> *Indigenous status takes on new ideological significance and the old administrative apparatus is retooled for new tasks. The formation ... is found only in wealthy states with small indigenous populations ... Continuous with classic colonialism, it is solicitous rather than exploitive, and liberal rather than repressive.*

Beckett's definition is clear (p. 17):

> *Welfare colonialism, then, is the state's attempt to manage the political problems posed by the presence of a depressed and disenfranchised indigenous population in an affluent, liberal democratic society. At the practical level it meets the problem by economic expenditure well in excess of what the minority produces. At the ideological level the 'native', who once stood in opposition to the 'settler' and outside the pale of society, undergoes an apotheosis to emerge as its original citizen.*

Hence, welfare colonialism is political in that it gives the recipients a voice, even if that input can be modified to suit the government or to gain acceptance in the dominant society.

While the state government was unhappy about the Commonwealth's 'infringement of State rights' and its 'slight on [State government] achievements', the two governments continued to 'share responsibility for Torres Strait in [that] uneasy condominium'. In practice, their policies differed little, 'consisting primarily of programmes designed to improve the living standards of Torres Strait Islanders' (p. 17). The Queensland Government, in many instances, provided the structures through which Commonwealth funds were distributed. Apart from social benefits and certain community amenities, some commercial projects were funded in anticipation of providing much-needed employment. In the early 1970s the government equipped a freezer boat to enable Torres Strait Islanders to find a foothold in the prawning and fishing industries, and a turtle farm was set up in 1982. Unfortunately, these ventures failed. The question was asked by outsiders whether the Torres Strait Islanders had the business acumen needed for their success, and they also questioned whether there had been effective training and support of personnel for these ventures. Later, in the 1990s, the Commonwealth Government sought to encourage private enterprise by providing loans from the newly established Aboriginal and Torres Strait Islander Commission funds.

Nevertheless, frustrations culminated in 1987 when the state cabinet froze Katter's second phase of the self-management process for Indigenous people while a 'stocktake' was taken. The government wanted time to review, obtain feedback, do audits and make adjustments in the communities that had 'undergone significant changes in a short period of time'. The people interpreted this as 'A stalling tactic ... lack of faith on the government's part or another example of where the Islanders suffer for being included with the Aboriginal communities as a whole, instead of being judged on their own merits' (Kehoe-Forutan 1988, pp. 19–20). This process of stalling and neglect concerned island leaders and George Mye, ICC chair, cabled the Pacific Forum listing the people's grievances: 'continuing colonial treatment and neglect of the Torres Strait people: poverty; [lack of] basic government services; widespread abuse of regional fishing agreements ... European and Asian control of Thursday Island' (*Sydney Morning Herald* 9 June 1987, p. 4). Government neglect extended to all the important institutions in a society wanting to move toward greater self-sufficiency.

Aboriginal Study Grants, financed by the Commonwealth in the early 1970s, opened the way for higher education for island children, but the standard of primary education on the outer islands continued to work against their success until at least 1985. In health, the government was slow to improve facilities and training of local people, and it remained within the director's department far too long, until 1990. Thirty enrolled nurses graduated from the Thursday Island Hospital between 1981 and 1991 but they did not rush to work on the outer islands, due mainly to the still inadequate facilities and low salaries. Health care on remote communities was frequently in the hands of unqualified people. A young Boigu nurse (1990), who received minimal training, told me: 'I have to use my head if [someone is] really sick, tell doctor symptoms and [get] reaction on phone and that's it'. She also pointed out that the one phone on the island in 1990 was often out of order. Adequate and better housing was still very much on community agendas.

Torres Strait Islander frustration with governments was leading the call from island leaders (the main players in the late 1980s being George Mye (Mer), Getano Lui Jnr (Yam), James Akee (a Torres Strait Islander living on the mainland)), for greater control of their own affairs. Some wanted secession. Some wanted self-government. From the mid 1980s there began an era fraught with struggles for independence in one form or another.

CHAPTER 4

Political momentum

Throughout the 1970s and 1980s Torres Strait Islanders sought to establish their own enterprises in the hope of becoming economically independent and to counter the economic dependency of welfare colonialism (see Beckett 1987, pp. 12–21, previous chapter). Sadly, their success was limited. The Commonwealth Government shied away from integration and continued toward community development, but island leaders were constantly frustrated as they believed that both state and Commonwealth bodies ignored or modified their inputs. And even though bureaucracies and services proliferated, island leaders' continued dissatisfaction resulted in a greater push for self-reliance.

For many years the people had associated education with success in the outsiders' world, and finally in the 1980s their concerted efforts achieved change. Fr Frank Brennan, a Catholic priest and barrister who was concerned about the laws relating to Indigenous Australians, stated that 'I think the time has come to entrust the delivery of some specialist services to the various specialist departments … All government-run educational institutions in [Torres Strait] should now be conducted by the Education Department' (1992, p. 47).

As mentioned in the previous chapter, the Commonwealth had introduced Aboriginal Secondary Education Grants enabling some students to go to the mainland for their education. Then in 1975 a process of policy development for schooling Torres Strait Islander children began when George Mye (Mer) and Ted Loban (Thursday Island) recommended to the Aboriginal Consultative Group that 'The Queensland Government consider transferring schools in the Torres Strait Islands from the administration of the Queensland Department of

Aboriginal and Island Affairs (DAIA) to the Queensland Department of Education as quickly as possible' (TSIRECC 1992, p. i). Mye and Loban were convinced that a higher level of education for students and island teachers with full qualifications to teach them were imperative to the future of an independent Torres Strait.

In 1983, the Queensland Government formed the Torres Strait Islander Regional Education Committee (TSIREC, 1985). Inaugural members were representatives from all outer islands, including George Mye, Ted Loban and Badu Elder Walter Nona, who retained a strong connection to education into his eighties. TSIRECC (1992) lobbied the Queensland Government for improved education in Torres Strait and the upgrading of community teachers to fully qualified teachers. This process, together with recommendations to the Commonwealth Government from the Goulburn Conference held in 1983 (pp. i–ii), was the forerunner to education being removed in 1985 from the Department of Community Services (successor to the Department of Aboriginal and Islander Advancement) and handed over to the Queensland Department of Education. The Commonwealth Government provided financial assistance to replace run-down school buildings. TSIRECC was an example of the strong resolve of the people to end the struggle for a service that was well below the standard set for white children. Indeed, in the foreword to *Ngampula Yawadhan Ziawali: educational policy for Torres Strait* (TSIRECC 1992) Barry Osborne, workshop facilitator with a long history of association with education in Torres Strait, highlighted the people's resolve:

> *The voice of Torres Strait Islanders is strong in matters to do with education. More and more Torres Strait Islanders are gaining academic qualifications and promotions — their skills in negotiating academia, departments, bureaucracies and politics while maintaining distinctive Islander identities and ways make them the emerging spokespersons ... All these people see the gains that have been made where once there was hopelessness. And, importantly, they support the articulate younger leadership who are building on the strong foundation of earlier Torres Strait Islanders who have spoken out and played their part in starting the process of change.* (TSIRECC 1992, pp. ii–iii)

In 1995, TSIRECC held a conference on Badu attended by about 40 Torres Strait Islander teachers from various island communities. Barry Osborne, editor of the guidebook produced after the conference, was moved to say:

> *I reflect back on 28 years of involvement in educating Torres Strait Islanders and I believe substantial steps forward have been taken. When*

> *I started teaching [in 1968] we worked in an assimilatory way. We discouraged Torres Strait languages. We deprecated Torres Strait Islander knowledge and ways. We knew nothing of Torres Strait Islander history. We could not, did not, link education to culture. Many of us tried hard and many of our good students tried hard but we did not know how to work together. Some of those good students have done well and some of them are here today, but they had to work against the odds.* (Osborne E 1995, p. 26)

Gausa Dau, a teacher on Badu, expressed how he felt about the conference (p. 2):

> *[It] was very very helpful to me. Some of the words and things we discussed remind me of how I feel from my heart, but I sometimes forget to use them. I hope I will never forget the importance of the children, the people of the Torres Strait and their future.*

A presenter at the conference, Martin Nakata, started his schooling under the repressive assimilatory education referred to by Barry Osborne and, as a mature-age student, became the first Torres Strait Islander to earn a doctorate and go on to become a professor. His concluding remarks give an insight into his deep thinking on education (pp. 22–3):

> *I think Torres Strait Islanders need to re-view Western education not just as an end in itself but as a tool for understanding our position at this interface. At the outset we need to see education as connected to our economic and social position and in every way that is political. English language and literacy cannot continue to be viewed as if there is no connection between its acquisition and our economic, social and political position. It is not a separate entity that runs apart from and different to traditional knowledges, ways, and realities. There is no easy translation between the two, rather there is a slipping in and out of them using each where appropriate and most effective. The relationship is one of complementarity rather than separateness. The English language and Western knowledges play an integral part in shaping our lives, they intersect with our own languages and knowledges. Our relationship and agency with them are all important. Far from assimilating us or destroying our uniqueness they may well be a fundamental key to our survival.*

TSIRECC made it possible for Torres Strait Islanders, for the first time, to have positive inputs into the education of their children.

Brennan also claimed that the 'three-year-old state cabinet resolution that all health services gradually be handed over to the Queensland

Health Department should have run its course' and he called for the responsibility to be transferred forthwith (1992, p. 47). However, improved health services on the outer islands took longer to implement.

The Island Coordinating Council and early independence movements

In an atmosphere of change, there was growing unrest among Torres Strait Islander leaders. The Queensland Government's response was the passing in 1984 of the *Community Services (Torres Strait) Act* (the 1984 Act). The 1984 Act established the Island Coordinating Council (ICC) comprising the chairs of the 17 island councils and reputedly giving the people, for the first time, 'formal local government-type status [in a] new overarching regional body' (Sanders 1994, p. 8). The 17 chairpersons included 14 from the outer-island councils and one each from Bamaga, Seisia (on Cape York) and Keriri (Hammond Island). Subsequently a single 'directly elected representative' from Tamwoy was admitted making a total of 18 members. (Tamwoy fell within the area serviced by the Torres Shire on Thursday Island, hence there was no separate council. However, because it was a Torres Strait Islander community a representative on the ICC was seen as appropriate and important.)

The 1984 Act provided for councillors and chairpersons to be elected from among Indigenous people who had resided continuously in the area for not less than 24 months prior to their nomination for election, and voters must have resided on a community for three months (s. 17). However, the people living on these island communities still considered themselves disenfranchised at the local government level as the Torres Shire Council (the TSC, which was incorporated under Queensland's *Local Government Act 1993*) on Thursday Island subsequently incorporated the land areas of the island councils. Moreover, the Queensland Government supervised these island councils more closely than conventional councils, and people believed that their local island councils were not equal in status with mainland Queensland local government councils, or the TSC itself (Sanders 1994, p. 8).

With the Commonwealth's entry into Torres Strait, Islanders had a representative with an advisory role on the National Aboriginal Consultative Committee, and two representatives on its successor the National Aboriginal Conference. Nonetheless, there was still dissatisfaction in Torres Strait and on the mainland because their inputs into the management of their affairs were limited. In 1976, two dissatisfied mainland Torres Strait Islanders, Carlemo Wacando (from Erub) and James Akee (from Mer) formed the Townsville-based Torres United Party

(TUP) and called for independence for Torres Strait under the title of 'Sacred Island Nation'. Roland Cantley, a white Australian born in New South Wales and a journalist with many years' association with Torres Strait, a man with a 'flair for flamboyant promotion', was appointed as the TUP's adviser and public relations officer (Sharp 1993, p. 228). The TUP put forward plans for a viable nation: 'Hydro-power, fishing, tourism and, significantly, oil and gas, were to form the basis' (p. 228). Cantley named companies such as Essington Investments Pty Ltd and Oil Company of Australia NL as expressing interest. In the same year, Wacando challenged in the High Court of Australia Queensland's annexation of the islands in Torres Strait in 1879 and submitted a 'request to the United Nations to make "independent inquiries" into the case for [Torres Strait] sovereign status as a separate nation' (p. 228). The High Court rejected Wacando's challenge in 1981, the appeal to the United Nations 'languished ... and TUP disintegrated' (Beckett 1987, pp. 204–5).

In 1987 after a seven-year silence, Wacando and Akee moved their operations to Torres Strait. They saw, to the outrage of the traditional owners of Muralag (Prince of Wales Island), the potential for the development of a 'Torres Strait Island City' there, and in 1988 established a consortium, the Torres United Prince of Wales Party. This party proposed low-priced blocks for housing for Torres Strait Islanders, major development interests focused on tourism and, it was suggested once again, some interest in oil and gas exploration. However, the project was dependent on the encroachment onto the Aboriginal Kaurareg people's land, and it was unlikely that these people would sit by and let it be developed by other Islanders, let alone outsiders, particularly as a proposal was put forward to construct a dam at one of their sacred sites. The party's business support weakened and the project did not come to fruition (Sharp 1993, pp. 228–230).

That same year ICC chair George Mye (supported by Roland Cantley, now the 'unofficial information officer or adviser' to the ICC, and so representing 8000 Torres Strait Islanders), declared that he wanted no less than 'sovereign independence' for Torres Strait (Sharp 1993, p. 229). For at least three decades Mye had struggled to achieve justice and equality for his people: now he intended to take more drastic action. He called a meeting of the people. On 20 January 1988, a 400-strong meeting on Thursday Island voted unanimously for 'sovereign independence from the State of Queensland and the Commonwealth of Australia' (*Sydney Morning Herald* 21 January 1988, p. 1) with the intention to send a delegation to Geneva and New York to lobby the United Nations for independent status. Mye claimed 'There is no turning back ... the government will have to take notice of us this time' (p. 1). The meeting gave the island leaders a mandate to negotiate with banks and businesses about ways to ensure the new nation's economic viability and a call was made for Prime Minister Hawke to meet with them (p. 1). There was consensus that the people had experienced 'decades of neglect by Federal Government' (*Townsville Bulletin* 21 January 1988, p. 3). Mye said living in Torres Strait was like 'living in a backwater and the Islanders needed independence to improve their lot' (p. 3). The Thursday Island meeting resulted in a call for recognition of Torres Strait Islanders as a separate people and an Independence Working Party was established to further this aim.

Interviewed on radio on 29 January 1988 about government opposition to calls for independence, Getano Lui Jnr — the son of the Yam Island Elder — a fledgling politician and deputy chair of the ICC, said:

> *Well we're pretty sure that commonsense will prevail and we hope that we can make the Premier ... and the Prime Minister see the light that we're talking about that independence is very crucial to us simply because first of all ... our identity is very critical at the moment because we're being invaded ... from people from the north and from people in the south and if we're not careful, I'd say within ten years, islanders will be strangers in their own land.* (Radio broadcast, January 1988)

Subsequently, the federal Labor government acknowledged that there were 'some huge resources' in Torres Strait and that the government must 'look at the possibilities of helping the people to be more independent in the use of those resources' (*TB* 24 February 1988, p. 4). John Howard, Leader of the Opposition, favoured 'moves for more devolution of responsibility, especially in financial matters' (p. 4). However, with the people's history of dealings with governments they may have doubted that their aspirations for full control of their resources and financial affairs would result from such responses.

By the latter part of the 1980s, many leaders declared they were no longer interested in talk and the findings of inter-departmental committees, which they described as 'imbued with a "welfare" mentality'. It was no longer a matter of government 'creating more jobs and better co-ordination of services'. The people were anguishing over their loss of control of their land, over their sea and their lives (p. 4). Getano Lui Jnr described the situation thus:

> *Our whole future depends on development and unless we control it, we are going to have an invasion of outside developers. My main concern is about the identity of Islanders. We are going to lose that. It is a matter of*

showing the people that we survived before without the welfare system.
(*Times on Sunday* 21 February 1988, p. 6)

He stood firm and declared: 'There will be no compromise. We will not back down. If it takes ten years or twenty years we will fight for what is rightfully ours' (*TB* 29 January 1988, p. 1).

One ICC member who did not jump immediately onto the independence bandwagon was Joe Mosby from Masig (Yorke Island), then seen by some Islanders as an 'unabashed conservative' (*Australian* 21 January 1988, p. 16). He said that he had no 'grouses' about administration of island affairs: 'What I say is slowly, slowly, slowly — take it steady, no rush. What the islands need is education. Australia has always treat us fairly. I think we get a fair deal' (p. 16). Nonetheless, both Lui and Mosby seem to have been in agreement that timing was important and that independence was not something that could be rushed into. Other leaders however believed the time was right for further progress toward their goal of greater independence, and the federal government was forced to address these people's dissatisfactions.

Aboriginal and Torres Strait Islander Commission

During 1987 and 1988 the ICC was concerned about two issues related to the Commonwealth Government. On the first issue, it:

> *reconfirmed a 'long-standing resolution' ... to 'claim sovereignty over the land, sea and air in Torres Strait' and had called for the ICC to be given power over matters such as revenue-raising, trade, fishing, mining, land, broadcasting and the staff and funds of the Commonwealth Aboriginal Affairs portfolio agencies in Torres Strait.* (Sanders 1994, p. 10)

The second issue, coming within days of the bicentenary of British colonisation of Australia in 1988, related to consultation with the Commonwealth on the setting up of an Australia-wide Aboriginal and Torres Strait Islander Commission (ATSIC).

The federal Labor government's relations with Indigenous people were not good at the time as it had backed away from an election commitment to uniform national land rights and had disbanded the National Aboriginal Conference in 1985. In 1986 it was casting around for a new representative structure for Indigenous Australians with which to replace the National Aboriginal Conference; that new structure was ATSIC, created under the *Aboriginal and Torres Strait Islander Commission Act 1989* (Sanders 1994, pp. 9–10). It was to be an Australia-wide elected Indigenous people's commission with significant powers (Sanders & Arthur 2001, p. 5) built from 60 elected regional councils. Torres Strait was to have its own Torres Strait Regional Council (TSRC). While the proposal was met with antipathy in Torres Strait, the ICC called for ' "recognition" of the institutions, culture and territories of the Torres Strait Islander people and the "right to control and develop" their own "resources and economy" ' (Sanders 1994, p. 11). The ICC also made it very clear that they did not want another structure of political representation imposed upon them. Indeed, they wanted the ICC to assume greater importance and to become a government in its own right (p. 11).

Accordingly, an Interdepartmental Committee on Torres Strait was formed and it recommended changes to the proposed ATSIC legislation. These changes led to special provisions relating to the TSRC being incorporated into the ATSIC Act. They were (p. 10):

> 1. *No elections would be held for the ATSIC regional council in Torres Strait (the TSRC).*
> 2. *The 17 elected chairpersons and one elected Tamwoy representative on the ICC would automatically become members of the TSRC.*
> 3. *Two additional positions on the TSRC would be created, one for the Port Kennedy area of Thursday Island and one for Horn [Nurapai] and Prince of Wales [Muralag] islands combined.*

These changes meant that the TSRC would have a total of 20 members while membership of the ICC remained at 18. The TSRC had no executive powers or functions but, like other ATSIC councils, played an important role in regional planning and budgeting. All executive powers were exercised by ATSIC's 20 commissioners, of which TSRC (unlike other regional councils) elected its own national commissioner. The ATSIC legislation was passed in 1989, and the TSRC came into operation in March 1991.

In a Commonwealth Government review of the ATSIC legislation in 1992 and 1993, a case was made for greater autonomy in Torres Strait (p. 11):

> *Aspirations for a 'form of self-government' in the Strait were ... persistent and seemed to require more than the regional council structure could provide. The review recommended the development of a Torres Strait authority that would exist within the framework of the ATSIC legislation but would have a 'single line appropriation' of its own.*

The review resulted in the overall number of ATSIC regions being decreased from 60 to 36, with some of its powers delegated to the regional councils, but no change was made to the region covered by the TSRC. The main change to concern the Torres Strait council region was an upgrade of the TSRC to an independent statutory body, the Torres

*Replicas of women's traditional digging sticks.
(Barry Osborne collection)*

Native village Murray Island (Mer), circa 1917–1920. (National Library of Australia)

Students at Darnley Island (Erub), circa 1908. (State Library of Queensland)

Pearling boats, Thursday Island, circa 1917–1920. (National Library of Australia)

Re-enactment of landing of missionaries on Saibai, 1987. (Barry Osborne collection)

The author with the late Elders Eselina Nawie and Maleta Lota, Kaurareg women who spent the war years in the bush on Moa Island and returned to their tribal area on Nurupai after the war, 1990. (Barry Osborne collection)

Island women dancing at festival to celebrate their culture, Thursday Island, 1994. (Barry Osborne collection)

Wartime hospital on Badu, 1990. (Barry Osborne collection)

Ugarie Nona's house on Badu, 1990. (Barry Osborne collection)

House built by Americans and transported to Badu post-war, 1990. (Barry Osborne collection)

DNA boat Melbidir IV, *circa 1976. (Chris De Vine collection)*

Kuzi, *DAIA training trawler*, circa 1976 *(Chris De Vine collection)*

Landing of traders from Sui (PNG), Mer Island, 1958. (Beckett collection, AIATSIS)

Anglican Mission boat Stephen Davies, *circa 1976. (Chris De Vine collection)*

Island teachers attending TSIREC Conference, Badu, 1971. (Barry Osborne collection)

Teacher Barry Osborne (middle) with Dennis Passi (left) and Dana Ober, students 'who worked against the odds'. (Barry Osborne collection)

The late Ted Loban, war veteran and fighter for his people's rights. (Lillian Perry)

John Abednego former chair TSRA. (Torres News)

Terry Waia, Saibai leader and former chair TSRA. (Torres News)

Ron Day (Mer) with visiting sea claim Judge. (Torres News)

Thursday Island Mayor Pedro Stephen.
(Torres News)

Bertha Natanielu, member of six-person GASC. (B Natanielu)

Veteran island politician George Mye.
(Torres News)

Ron Day (Mer) draped in Torres Strait flag. (Brian Cassey collection)

The late Eddie Koiki Mabo. (Noel Loos collection)

Dancer wearing a Dauan Shark Headress, Saibai festival, Saibai Island, 1961. (Beckett collection, AIATSIS)

Dancing at the Saibai festival, Saibai Island, 1961. (Beckett collection, AIATSIS)

George Mye campaigning, Mer Island, 1958. (Beckett collection, AIATSIS)

Japanese pearl diver. (State Library of Queensland)

Men aboard a lugger, Badu Island, 1961. (Beckett collection, AIATSIS)

Drying trepang, Mer Island, 1960. (Beckett collection, AIATSIS)

The late Solomon Nona with a dugong, Badu Island, 1959. (Beckett collection, AIATSIS)

Church building on Mer Island, 1959. (Beckett collection, AIATSIS)

Church procession on Badu Island, 1959. (Beckett collection, AIATSIS)

Blessing a new dinghy, Mer Island, 1959. (Beckett collection, AIATSIS)

Strait Regional Authority (TSRA), with an appropriation of its own. It came into being in 1994, had powers similar to ATSIC, and it took over the functions and staff of the regional office.

A new framework for Torres Strait

In his 1993 Boyer Lecture Getano Lui Jnr, chair of both the ICC and TSRC, looked into a future when he said it was time to build a new framework for Torres Strait (Lui 1994a, p. 63). While he could not then foretell its actual constitution he did state that he would use existing government institutions to advance his people's greater independence. He saw negotiation, not consultation, as the key and he was ready to go to the negotiating table (p. 63):

> We've done our homework ... there's only limited potential in Torres Strait for ... economic development ... it would be ludicrous to cut ties with Australia. Australia would be in charge of Defence and Foreign Affairs and National Security ... but all we're talking about is the essential services would be controlled by local people themselves.

Moreover, he indicated a desire for transparency: 'I've got between now and the year 2001 to consult with people and really get people aware of what the situation would be by the year 2001' (ABC Radio 19 November 1993). Then, in mid-June 1994, Lui outlined the principles for Torres Strait constitutional renewal on which his vision of self-government was based:

> We need to be able to make decisions about social, cultural, economic and environmental matters in our region, not just have the right to attend advisory meetings which may, or may not, pass our ideas up the line. We need a clear legally enforceable regime of land and sea rights. We need real control of staff and office budgets, not the appearance of control as through ATSIC. We need the means and facilities to secure and develop our culture. (Lui 1994b, p. 17)

He was prepared to 'sit down and work out the details with government'. He went as far as to say: 'That is when we can talk about Australian "reconciliation and Australian unity"' (p. 17).

The new status of the TSRA was heralded as 'a brand new day' for Torres Strait and Getano Lui Jnr, its first chair, said, 'the Authority would have significantly enhanced powers compared to the first Torres Strait Regional Council' (TSRA press release 1 July 1994). It was seen as a 'unique body committed to the principles of self-determination, self-management and empowerment ... devolving decision making to its elected representatives and Torres Strait ... organisations' (TSRA press release 1 July 1994). At a Thursday Island meeting held on 17 and 18 May 1993, Lui — in anticipation of this new day — had pointed out that if the TSRA fulfilled these aspirations then Torres Strait Islanders, who for almost a century had aspired to control their lives, would indeed be taking charge of their own destinies instead of being controlled by no less than 35 government departments.

In an address to the ATSIC commissioners and regional council chairpersons in August 1994, Lui acknowledged that the institution of the TSRA had been a 'significant milestone' in the move toward self-determination by the year 2001, but that there would be no 'overnight achievement' of that goal. Through an ongoing negotiation process, Lui believed development would occur in a coherent, 'consistent and coordinated way' (Sanders 1994, p. 10). He pointed to the TSRA as a stepping-stone: 'The Aboriginal and Torres Strait Islander Commission saw [TSRA's] creation as a transitional arrangement providing a basis for progressive negotiated movement towards greater regional authority in the delivery of programs and services for Torres Strait Islanders' (p. 10). To that end the TSRA made a detailed submission to the Social Justice Task Force outlining a framework for achieving the aspirations of the people of the Torres Strait that emphasised devolution as an important step toward 'greater local control and authority over decision making' (p.14).

By now there was no doubt about the aspirations for a self-governing body in Torres Strait being nurtured by Getano Lui Jnr and his supporters. By September 1995, Prime Minister Keating was prepared to make concessions for any 'push for more autonomy', but ruled out 'self-government' by 2000. He rejected any suggestion of the Norfolk Island form of self-government favoured by many until a stronger economy was developed (*Cairns Post* 15 September 1995, p. 8). Nevertheless, the government's next hurdle was to consider removing responsibility for Torres Strait from ATSIC and to possibly 'set up a separate Torres Strait Authority to deal with island funding and spending programs'. The rationale was that 'the move would allay Islander concerns that their culture was being swamped by the larger Aboriginal culture within the ATSIC structure' (*CP* 13 September 1995, p. 7), something that had been a concern since ATSIC's inception. The possibility that these hurdles would soon be behind them might reasonably have been interpreted as another 'jump forward towards the self-government target' and the greater independence it would give Torres Strait Islanders after a century of bidding for it in one form or another (*CP* 15 September 1995, p. 8).

The Republic of Mer

The earlier move to gain sovereign independence for the people of Torres Strait made by James Akee's Torres United Party had failed. However, Akee — unlike Lui and Mosby — was unwilling to be patient. Moreover, his goal was not greater autonomy within the state and federal structures but secession and the setting up of a sovereign nation. In 1989 he declared that 'Torres Strait Islanders should strive towards and commit ourselves so that we can eventually "think and do for ourselves" as a sovereign nation within our own inherited region' (*Torres News* 29 January–4 February 1989, p. 2).

Meanwhile, on Thursday Island many residents were expressing grave concerns about talk of secession. This led to the setting up in 1985 of the Port Kennedy Association by Ted Loban (a Thursday Island World War Two veteran and activist who claimed to be in 'constant contact with Islanders'). He held that 'up to 80% of Islanders did not want secession because they were concerned about life after independence' (*Australian* 21 January 1988, p. 16). A 'Malay' woman (1989) on Thursday Island whose grandmother came from Kubin said: 'They [the secessionists] are saying that once independence comes everyone without "cooried" [tight curly] hair will be kicked off the Island. What about our kids? Some are married to Islanders. What happens to them and their kids?' However, those in favour of secession stated that any concern about loss of social security would be counteracted by the resources in Torres Strait and the potential for industry which could be achieved with 'capital investment, whether it is from overseas or mainland sources' (*Australian* 21 January 1988, p. 16). Akee's position was that:

> Our 'half-caste' islander brothers and sisters or non-Torres Strait Islanders living here [Thursday Island] should not be fearful of sovereignty ... To those sceptics of sovereignty and I direct that to the minority who are living in the Port Kennedy area ... you better get real and support the majority of us 'native' Torres Strait Islanders because you are living in a traditional area. (TN 4–10 January 1991, pp. 4, 9)

Moreover, he indicated that his plan would be based on the best advice (p. 4):

> The question of Torres Strait sovereignty, its associated issues and how to go about achieving that goal will become much clearer as I am about to attend a month-long forum in Sydney being briefed on the decolonisation process and the right of sovereignty (self-determination, self-government or independence) by experts in this field who have affiliation with the United Nations.

Roland Cantley had first suggested that the Torres Strait Islanders put their case for independence before the United Nations Committee on Decolonisation (*Australian* 21 January 1988, p. 16), and Akee was now anxious to gain all the support he could from outside the Strait. But Akee's confidence in his scheme was of little comfort to the 80 per cent of people who may not have been totally satisfied with their political status but who could not conceive of a life cut off from Australia.

On 17 September 1993, Akee released a Declaration of Sovereignty addressed to the 'Prime Minister and Peoples of Australia, Her Majesty the Queen of the British Commonwealth and the Secretary General of the United Nations'. Subsequently reproduced in the *Torres News*, its essence was:

> We the tribal Elders of Mer, Erub, Ugar, Warraber and Kaurareg of the Torres Strait are happy to announce after a unanimous decision of our people and much consultation, our declaration of sovereignty which allows our other brothers and sisters of adjacent islands to join us. The appointment of a provisional government embodying our traditional island customs inherited by Birth Right from our ancestors.
> (*TN* 24–30 September 1993, p. 7)

Members of the ICC and the TSRC (at that time still to become the Torres Strait Regional Authority) totally 'disassociated themselves from the sovereignty declaration' (*CP* 23 September 1993, p. 7). Getano Lui Jnr saw these bodies as the only legitimate political institutions because they were democratically elected. Meanwhile, Akee was claiming the 'backing of five islands' and expected more to follow. For his part, Akee saw ICC and ATSIC as 'puppets of governments while his group was listening to the elders and landowners' (p. 7). Lui's response was that control of each island was by the local council and not the Elders. If they wanted to go that way, he concluded, there was little that could be done, but his assurance was that they 'didn't speak for all Torres Strait' (ABC Radio 24 September 1993). By October 1993 there was considerable disquiet amongst the various groups of people living in Torres Strait, particularly on cosmopolitan Thursday Island.

The fear that power would be concentrated in a 'few people of only one racial background' was being fed to the people by conflicting and confusing talk of independence, autonomy, sovereignty and secession for Torres Strait (*TN* 24–30 September 1993, p. 3). Allan Mosby from Masig, living on Thursday Island, called a public meeting for 7 October 1993 at which all parties to the debate and the public were given opportunity to express their views.

At the meeting, attended by 500 people, Mosby stressed that there was a 'need for reconciliation in Torres Strait … it's about time that we stand and speak in the one voice for the future of Torres Strait' (*TN* 15–21 October 1993, p. 4). Dana Oba (Ober) attended to represent mainland Islanders whom he said wished to be considered when 'Torres Strait becomes an autonomy in 2001 and beyond' (p. 3). Akee reiterated his claim that he had the backing of five communities. He also claimed that his authority for the declaration was a proclamation signed in 1872 by Queen Victoria, and never repealed, which stated 'To the Australasian governments of that time, you are to protect, you are to nurture, the tribes toward their sovereignty' (p. 4). Thus, he claimed his party could validly set up a provisional government with himself as provisional prime minister, and he would ask the Australian Government to withdraw their officers from Torres Strait within 21 days. He further claimed Queensland's boundaries would be re-gazetted. However, his new nation, the Commonwealth of Torres Strait, would remain loyal to the British monarchy.

The meeting was broadcast live throughout Torres Strait and the Northern Peninsula Area. While there was no unity on the issues discussed, the great interest in the meeting confirmed that the people wanted to be informed rather than rely on hearsay. Furthermore, it became apparent that mainland Torres Strait Islanders believed that they too had a stake in what was happening in their home region. Dana Ober, a Saibai Islander living on the mainland, emphasised that Torres Strait Islanders, wherever they lived, are 'one nation of people' and are concerned to maintain 'unity for all' (*TN* 15–21 October 1993, p. 4).

While Lui worked within the established political bodies, Akee and his supporters moved ahead with their plans. It is difficult to know what percentage of support Akee really had. However, subsequent to the Thursday Island meeting a Torres Strait Islander Media Association telephone poll purported to show 48 per cent of people supported the concept of self-government put forward by Lui; 34 per cent were undecided or unclear on the issue; and no figure was given for Akee support (p. 3). In an article in the *Koori Mail* on 1 November 1995 it was claimed by Torres Strait Islander Victor Mabo that Akee's secession bid had 'little support', only 10 per cent — it was no more than 'a pie in the sky'. The thinking of many, Mabo claimed, was that 'The community council was elected by the island people. They represent us and are doing a pretty good job … most people would be reluctant to change their lifestyle' (p. 2).

Akee called for the Australian Government to remove its services from all islands, but his focus was on Mer (Win Television News 8 October 1993) and he subsequently flew in the face of his objectors on that island. He set about to make plans for an interim government and declare it the Republic of Mer, with himself as president for five years. He claimed primary industries and an airline would be in operation within two months. Moreover, he was confident that overseas interests would establish eco-tourism and oil drilling which would give the people employment and thus an economic base for his scheme (*Courier Mail* 9 November 1995, p. 3).

The announcement caused unease on Mer. It was reported that state police were being rushed to the island 'amid fears of violence between activist Jim Akee supporters and those opposing secession' (*CP* 11 November 1995, p. 13). Subsequently, Akee's now personal assistant, Joe Guivarra, announced 'The community is united at last ... We've come a long way since last week when local shopkeepers wouldn't even serve us and we were afraid to walk through the village alone' (p. 5). Despite this opposition, Akee indicated he had the backing of Meriam leaders. Their differences, he claimed, were buried when an agreement was made with the council when Akee gave his assurance that proposed oil drilling would not proceed without a full environmental and economic impact assessment. The date for secession was set for 20 November 1995 and Akee's intention was to implement his 'economic package' immediately. One hundred and twenty mainland supporters waited in Townsville and 80 in Cairns to be transported to Mer by means to be supplied by Akee. Simultaneously, he claimed he was negotiating international investments (p. 5). However, the logistics involved in Akee's plan were enormous: there was the removal from the mainland of about 200 people and provision of accommodation for them; there was the transportation of machinery and other commodities necessary for constructing the infrastructure associated with the commercialisation of this small, technically unsophisticated island community; and there was the demand for skilled people to carry out the work.

The Republic of Mer did not come into existence on 20 November 1995. The logistics of the operation were obviously a factor. Did Akee's optimism about overseas financial backing also fall short? Meanwhile self-government was still on the agenda in the wider Torres Strait community.

Self-government

Slowly, slowly, the determined Getano Lui Jnr continued to pressure the Commonwealth Government for the freedom he and his followers wanted for the people of Torres Strait. In line with his policy of negotiation, talks began with the newly elected Liberal–National Party Coalition government. During the election campaign in 1996, the Coalition had supported the concept of the handing back of 'the economic reins' to the people. Then Senator John Heron, the new minister for Aboriginal and Torres Strait Islander Affairs, intimated that 'he favoured more power being devolved to the TSRA' (*CM* 18 March 1996, p. 7). Moreover, he publicly stated that the Torres Strait Islanders were 'culturally distinct and have different problems from remote Aboriginal communities' and he acknowledged the 'belated recognition' by his government of the two Indigenous groups of people living in Australia. And, although the government was opposed to total independence for Torres Strait or a Cocos Island-type independence, Heron intimated he was 'a great believer in the devolution of power to the lowest level of decision making' (p. 7). At a pending meeting with the minister, Lui said he would raise the matter of the Coalition's policies on Torres Strait Islander affairs, including the feasibility of a separate commission for Torres Strait (*TN* 19–25 April 1996, p. 1). Lui might have felt some optimism about this new beginning with the Coalition but he had to ask himself would the people gain the greatest control possible over their lands, seas, resources and economy under this government? This was certainly his bottom line.

Meanwhile, Torres Strait Islanders living on the mainland were speaking out. Their spokesperson Belzah Lowah, chair of the IINA Torres Strait Islander Corporation in Brisbane (*iina* is a word meaning 'we are here'), said they were 'being left out in the cold' while plans were afoot to give those in Torres Strait greater autonomy (*CM* 17 July 1996, p. 6). Lui's response was that while this concern was important, it needed to be addressed as a separate issue (p. 6).

In August 1996, the federal Coalition government was looking at cut backs of A$400 million over four years to ATSIC's overall funding, and this furthered Lui's resolve to obtain financial independence. TSRA's funding was determined by ATSIC, a system Lui labelled 'unfair' (*CP* 20 August 1996, p. 5), and he claimed any cuts to funding for Torres Strait would mean greater suffering for people who already lived with health and housing standards well below those on the mainland. Lui wanted not only freedom by way of self-government but also the meeting of the people's long-held aspirations for more equality of living conditions with those of the dominant society. With loss of funds, these aspirations would of necessity be put on the back burner. Lui was disappointed when, subsequently, an overall cut of 14.3 per cent was made to the TSRA budget (*TSRA Newsletter* September 1996, p. 1). However, the Coalition government took the next step. It called for submissions to an inquiry into greater autonomy for Torres Strait. The TSRA made its submission in October 1996.

In the interim, at the Sixth National Torres Strait Islander Seminar/Workshop in Brisbane in 1996, George Mye put the case for the islands to have their own administrative body:

> *There must be an exact replica of what is for Aboriginal people that should be the same for Torres Strait Islanders ... Whatever it takes it's got to allow for the two distinct cultures of our people ... When the first ATSIC legislation was first drawn up the differences between the two cultures weren't considered which had caused a lot of bad feeling ... It failed the Islander people from the word go in the provisions in the Act ... The relationship between our two people suffered particularly in the case of our people on the mainland. It's not the fault of the Aboriginal people and it's no fault of the Islander people, it's just the circumstances we find ourselves in as a result of that legislation ... The way it was structured meant Islander people have to stand in line for services after Aboriginal people.* (*Land Rights Queensland* October/November 1996, p. 15)

He concluded by stating what had been an ongoing problem for Torres Strait Islanders since 1904 when they first went 'under the Act': 'We know we are a minority within a minority' (p. 19). Mye, like Lui, wanted no less than a Torres Strait Islander authority to put this difference in status at rest forever. The chairperson of the seminar, a Victorian member of parliament who seemed to have little grasp of the history of Torres Strait Islander status and aspirations, concluded that 'secession seemed to be a dead issue' and yet, without pre-empting the inquiry's recommendations, 'suggested a separate Torres Strait authority was a possibility' (p. 15). Meanwhile, the TSRA was admitted to the Ministerial Council for Aboriginal and Torres Strait Islander Affairs as a non-voting member, acknowledged by Commonwealth Senator Heron as 'another step toward greater autonomy' (*TN* 29 November–5 December 1996, p. 1). However, while Lui saw it as a 'significant step' it was still only a 'first step': 'we are now aiming to become a voting full participant member, the same level ATSIC is now on' (p. 1).

Time has been a factor in the Torres Strait Islanders' moves toward recognition of their unique identity and independence, and changes of actors were inevitable. In April 1997 John Abednego was elected chair of the TSRA, and he immediately stated his support for:

> *A move away from the control of the Aboriginal and Torres Strait Islander Commission so decisions affecting almost 7000 people in the region could be made from Thursday Island, the administrative capital ... within six years ... Torres Strait would fall under the jurisdiction of its own Act ... a move from ATSIC also would give the Torres Strait a single line of funding and direct access to the Federal Government.* (*CP* 24 April 1997, p. 5)

And in July 1997 a Commonwealth Bill was drawn allowing for a separate budget for the TSRA in line with the goal of a separate Act (*TN* 4–10 July 1997, p. 3), and the establishment of a Torres Strait authority separate from ATSIC by 2000 (*TN* 11–17 July 1997, p. 1).

Some people may have thought that these developments augured well for Torres Strait Islander aspirations for the freedoms for which they had been struggling for so long. However, during the next 10 years the reality was that the struggles were ongoing to gain recognition of their traditional rights to lands, seas, fish resources and to formulate a model of governance for greater autonomy in Torres Strait.

CHAPTER 5

Ownership of land and sea

Traditional ownership of the land

The people of the Torres Strait islands knew self-reliance was dependent upon common law recognition of their traditional rights of ownership of lands and seas passed down to them for generations. The first step toward achieving this was their claim to their lands. In August 1981, a public meeting was held at Tamwoy Town, Thursday Island, at which Torres Strait island Elder Flo Kennedy made a call to 'take them to court' (Sharp 1996, p. 23) to gain recognition of their law and ownership of their islands. On 20 May 1982, five Meriam plaintiffs — Eddie Koiki Mabo, Celuia Salee, Sam Passi, Rev Dave Passi and James Rice — lodged their statement of claim in the High Court of Australia: *Eddie Mabo and Others v. the State of Queensland and the Commonwealth of Australia* (B12 of 1982) (see Sharp 1996, pp. xi–xv). The plaintiffs in what became known as the Murray Island Case or the Mabo Land Case asked the High Court to declare:

1. That the Meriam people are entitled to the Murray Islands
   (a) as owners; or
   (b) as possessors; or
   (c) as occupiers; or
   (d) as persons entitled to use and enjoy the Islands; and
2. That the State of Queensland has no power to extinguish the Meriam people's title.

On 3 June 1992, the High Court of Australia's decision was handed down. It ruled (Butt et al. 2001, pp. 8–9):

1. That the Meriam people are entitled to possess, occupy, use and enjoy the Murray Islands. *(The Court left open the position regarding certain land that had been leased, and other land used for government administrative purposes.)*
2. That the State of Queensland has the power to extinguish the Meriam people's title, as long as it exercises that power validly and in a manner consistent with Commonwealth laws.

Of the seven judges on the bench, six recognised native title at Murray Islands. (Murray Islands refers to the islands of Mer, Dauar and Waier, but as will be shown determinations were not made for Dauar and Waier concurrently with the Mer decision.) In his leading judgement Justice Brennan concluded that, with the exception of certain validly appropriated lands for administrative purposes, 'the Meriam people are entitled as against the whole world to possession, occupation, use and enjoyment of the lands of the Murray Islands' (Butt et al. 2001, p. 92). The High Court, however, 'left a number of fundamental issues unresolved' (p. 95). These were met in future claims for native title under the Commonwealth *Native Title Act 1993*. Nevertheless, the Mabo Land Case boosted all Torres Strait Islanders' aspirations for independence and, as Jull pointed out, it 'jolted the whole of Australia into action, and created a new atmosphere for indigenous rights in Australia' (1994, p. 4). In 1992, too, the Torres Strait flag (designed by the late Bernard Namok) was unveiled as a symbol of a self-governing nation of Torres Strait peoples within the nation of Australia. In this environment, island leader Getano Lui Jnr's vision that all Australians would accept his people as equals in a 'reformed constitution and social community' by 2001 (Lui 1994b, p. 20) could be seen as more than just a pipe dream.

The history of the Torres Strait Islanders' struggles for recognition of native title is peppered with uncertainties. Historian Henry Reynolds recorded Eddie Mabo's 'astonishment and horror when he learnt in the late 1970s that, in Queensland law, Mer was regarded as Crown land' since the 1879 annexation of the islands (Sharp 1996, p. 38). Islander people remembered only too well how governments had challenged the traditional ownership of their lands, such as when some islands were put under threat of excision; when the state moved to de-gazette island reserves; and when the government made an offer of 50-year leases to island communities (p. 38). The offer of Deeds of Grant in Trust raised the question 'How can we lease back what is already ours?' and angered the Meriam people who refused to trade their birthright. They wanted what was rightfully theirs, inalienable freehold of their islands. One of researcher Nonie Sharp's old informants said in 1980:

> Torres Strait is ours and we want our lands returned to us. My great-grandfathers and great-grandmothers and my grandfathers and grandmothers and my father and mother before me were here in these Islands before white people came. It is my wish and the wish of all the people of the whole of Torres Strait for us to own all these islands ourselves. (Sharp 1993, p. 23)

However, the Queensland Government, in line with its long history of ignoring or underestimating rumblings in Torres Strait, sought to end the Meriam plaintiffs' audacious court action and rushed a Bill through parliament with the intention of retrospectively extinguishing any remaining rights of the Meriam to land. It would have ended the Mabo Land Case but for the plaintiffs' successful court challenge.

Even after jumping this hurdle, another presented itself when the Queensland Government objected to oral testimony given in evidence, which was of necessity basic to the plaintiffs' case. The ownership of their lands had for centuries been passed down orally, not by written agreements. Mabo told the court how his grandfather explained to him about boundary markers, such as a '"clump of stones" with a stone in the middle larger than the rest ... that can be aligned with another stone marker further on' (Sharp 1996, p. 64). The court ruled such evidence was admissible. In May 1989, Supreme Court Justice Moynihan inspected land boundaries on Mer and heard oral evidence from the land claimants before concluding: 'I have little difficulty in accepting that the people of the Murray Islands perceive themselves as having an enduring relationship with the land on the [Murray] Islands and the seas and reefs surrounding them' (p. 152). He listened to explanations of traditional law, Malo ra Gelar (Malo's Law, see Sharp 1996, pp. 63–4), that the missionaries had failed to eradicate and concluded that this law was a 'manifestation of social attitudes ... deeply imbued in the culture of the Murray Islanders' (p. 153). This evidence, and the court's acceptance of it, were basic to recognition by the High Court that there were valid native laws among Indigenous people that could not be overridden by the laws of the dominant culture. This was what Mabo was all about: Was there such a law as native title on Murray Islands recognisable at common law? On 3 June 1992, the High Court majority judgement confirmed that at common law the Meriam people, by virtue of their long and enduring association with their islands, were the rightful owners of them. (For the comprehensive story see Sharp 1996.)

The judgement shattered the whole structure of the subordinate status of Indigenous Australians to which they had been relegated by their colonisers. *Terra nullius*, literally meaning 'land of no-one' and the

5. Ownership of land and sea

common law principle which held that Australia was unoccupied at the time of white settlement, 'took for granted that the Meriam people were primitive and uncivilised, without recognised laws or social organisation and hence lower in the scale of humanity than the newcomers' (Sharp 1996, p. 153). Terra nullius was the colonisers' legal invention that enabled governments to claim sovereignty over the lands of traditional people without any obligation to make treaties and/or pay compensation. Indeed, the Mabo Land Case finally established common law recognition of the law of native title. Unlike any previous event in their history, the Mabo decision brought Torres Strait and its people into the bright lights of the widest possible public arena in Australia.

For almost a century the Torres Strait Islanders had clung tenaciously to their aspirations for full recognition as a separate Indigenous people in Australia and the freedom to enjoy what they believed were their rights and what belonged to them. The people had not forgotten a time when, apart from the Meriam people, they saw no alternative but to compromise their claim to inalienable freehold. With the Mabo decision they were able to think about what recognition of native title might mean for their progress toward self-regulation. Nonetheless, Getano Lui Jnr added a sobering thought with the claim that while acknowledging the great impetus that the Mabo decision had given them toward their goal of freedom, they should realise that the fullest freedom possible may take until at least the end of the century to achieve (Lui 1994b, p. 12). And the people still had to ask: Where are we now, where are we heading, how do we get there, and how does it benefit all the people of the region? The answers would be the keys to greater freedom for all Torres Strait Islanders, but they would not be easy to find.

The subsequent passing of the Commonwealth *Native Title Act 1993* did not resolve Torres Strait Islanders' concerns about what governments could or might do if the people were not ready to meet all contingencies arising from native title claims. Thus, any proposed amendments to the Act were of great importance to them, and when changes were mooted in 1996 the first of many native title workshops was held on Erub. The aim was to ensure that people became better informed about the complex issues relating to land rights, and legal counsel was brought in to advise on 63 native title claims already lodged. They had been encouraged by the court's decision in the Mabo Land Case to allow oral history in evidence, and later anthropological research was accepted as a vehicle to establish the first claim to native title on Saibai (*TSRA newsletter* 1996 (6), p. 3). Perhaps what the Torres Strait Islanders could not conceive of at that time was that they would again be plunged into the outsiders' legal system with all its twists and turns and in the next decade it would, at times, stall and frustrate the people's hopes.

The Native Title Act 1993

The Mabo ruling remains 'one of the most significant court decisions in Australia's history' and it is the basis upon which all native title claims are judged or determined (Butt et al. 2001, p. 95). Nevertheless, it fell short of the plaintiffs' aspirations in that it did not rule on Waier and Dauar islands and it allowed for the possibility of state government extinguishment of native title. More generally, it also left unresolved other fundamental issues (p. 95):

- *the possibility that titles granted by both the Federal and State governments since the Racial Discrimination Act was passed in 1975 could be invalid because of their effects on Native Title*
- *handling future Native Title claims with regard to the time factor, complexity and expense of law suits*
- *treatment of Native Title if developers or governments wished to carry out development or public works where Native Title might exist*
- *compensation for loss or impairment of Native Title rights.*

Thus, there was clearly a need for legislation, but when no agreement between the federal and state governments (particularly the Queensland Government, which had more at stake as it had made most of the land grants that affected native title) could be arrived at about its form, the federal government proceeded to negotiate directly with Aboriginal and industry groups. The Native Title Act defined native title as 'the communal, group, or individual rights and interests over land or waters held under traditional law by Aboriginal people or Torres Strait Islanders' (pp. 96–7). It allowed for validation of Commonwealth land grants and gave the states a similar right. Where validated, the effects on native title were to be spelled out, such as: some freehold grants extinguished native title completely; grants of non-exclusive interests extinguished native title 'only to the extent that the interest conflicted with [native title]'; and mining and other leases that prevented the exercise of rights, suppressed native title for the period of the grant 'rather than extinguishing it forever' (p. 97). Importantly, the Native Title Act subjected all acts by governments to the 'requirement that native title holders be treated no less favourably than holders of other interests in land' (p. 97). Native title holders were given a right to compensation if prior land grants were validated and for future impairment of native title. An Indigenous Land Fund was set up to compensate for native title that had already been extinguished, and in 1996 a TSRA Native Title Office was set up to provide culturally appropriate services for land rights' claimants.

Processes were put in place when applying for recognition of native title, and a TSRA representative body was established to research and assist presentation of claims and represent claimants. Initially, all applications were lodged with a National Native Title Tribunal set up under the Native Title Act to:

> [mediate] between indigenous parties, governments and other interests to see whether an agreement can be reached about the existence of Native Title. The tribunal also has power to arbitrate when parties can't agree about whether an act which might impair or affect Native Title should go ahead under the 'right to negotiate' process. (Butt et al. 2001, p. 117)

Once their claims were lodged, claimants had a right to negotiate with other parties that had interests in the land.

There were the sceptics who doubted that native title and the operation of the Native Title Act would result in harmonious relations between native title holders and other interested parties in the land. Lois O'Donoghue, chair of ATSIC, remained positive:

> Native Title and the Native Title Act are now irrevocably part of the Australian landscape — embodied in its legal, social and political systems. Despite political attacks and the proliferation of negative uninformed and misleading comment, we have seen the emergence of a pragmatic view among certain State governments and industry groups which accept the viability of negotiating with indigenous people who are armed with Native Title rights. At the same time Aboriginal and Torres Strait Islander people have shown willingness to work with the strategic potential of the Act. They are already negotiating private agreements with resource developers and governments which will be mutually satisfactory and beneficial. It is representative bodies which are best placed to facilitate development of these. (TN 16–12 October 1995, p. 5)

It was early days, and only time would tell if native title holders could work side by side with governments and with those who had acquired interests in native title land or who were potential users.

Wik Peoples v The State of Queensland

In 1996 the High Court handed down the Wik decision, a case involving pastoral leases on two cattle stations granted under Queensland land legislation. By a slender majority the justices held that 'Native Title was not, as a matter of legal necessity, extinguished by the grant of pastoral leases' over the parcels of land covered by the leases (Butt et al. 2001, pp. 99–100). The majority justices were not 'unduly troubled by the reference in Mabo to Native Title being extinguished by the grant of a "lease"' (p. 103). In the justices' opinion, it was more important to consider in each case 'the nature of the rights granted' under any 'so-called' lease and because in the Wik decision the two leases were granted under Queensland legislation their 'characteristics had to be deduced from the intention of the statutes' (p. 102) relating to each lease: Was it the intention of the lease to give exclusive possession? In this case, upon a close examination of the facts, the justices found that this was not the case (p. 102) and the Wik decision made it clear that not all pastoral leases extinguish native title. However, a subsequent call from pastoral and industry interests to have the Native Title Act amended in their favour concerned Indigenous people.

The pastoral and industry groups wanted clarification of the type of grant that extinguished native title and stricter rules for 'gaining the "right to negotiate"' (p. 109). The Commonwealth Government's response was to put forward a Ten Point Plan to resolve uncertainties. Its essence can be summarised within four groupings (pp. 111–13):

- *extinguishment and exercise of Native Title rights (points 1, 2, 4, 5)*
- *a modified right to negotiate (points 3, 6, 7, 8)*
- *agreements encouraged (point 10)*
- *changed procedure for applications (point 9).*

The first grouping focused on validation of certain leases; the requirement that the type of grants that extinguish native title be spelled out in a schedule to the Native Title Act; an upgrade of certain activities; and protection of a native title holder's right to go onto pastoral leases. The second provided for a 'stricter test for Native Title holders to get the "right to negotiate"'; a native title holder's right to negotiate with government about certain acts of government, such as granting permits, would be replaced by a 'right to be consulted' (p. 121). The third encouraged registered Indigenous Land Use Agreements (pp. 111–13) between native title holders and other interested parties over a range of matters. The fourth concerned future native title applications being initially made to the Federal Court instead of to the National Native Title Tribunal (p. 113).

The plan generated intense debate. Indigenous groups protested that the Wik decision had not created uncertainty as others claimed. Some

5. Ownership of land and sea

Aboriginal interests feared their rights would be impaired contrary to the Commonwealth *Racial Discrimination Act 1975* and they went to the United Nations with the claim that 'the amendments treated indigenous property rights less favourably than non-indigenous rights' (p. 110). It was found that the amendments did breach Australia's human rights obligations regarding racial discrimination but the UN's advice 'to re-open discu-ssion with indigenous representatives' was ignored (p. 110). The debate over the Ten Point Plan ended in a compromise in the Senate that involved (p. 113):

- the States being able to *'set up their own schemes'* to determine Native Title claims consistent with the Act;
- where Native Titleholders occupied the land on which they claimed Native Title, extinguishment was *'not taken to have occurred'*;
- there was no presumption of extinguishment on Crown held land, even in freehold, unless *'Native Title had been extinguished under common law'*;
- a proposed six-year limit on making Native Title claims was abandoned;
- Native Title claims could proceed even where current physical connection could not be shown if they had been *'locked out of their traditional country'*.

These amendments were probably less controversial than the Torres Strait Islanders may have expected.

When the justices in the Mabo Land Case handed down their ruling that common law recognised a form of native title defined by the laws and customs of the Meriam people and the enjoyment of their traditional lands where there had been no extinguishment of native title, there was jubilation around Torres Strait. However, at that time other island groups had no way of knowing that their claims would be subject to a complex act of parliament, amendments to it, lengthy time restraints and considerable expense. The interpretation and intent of the numerous provisions of the Native Title Act and any amendments were beyond all but the most skilled legal minds, as were the processes of preparation and lodgement of native title claims in the Federal Court. Moreover, while the Wik decision on pastoral leases had little relevance for native title in Torres Strait, extinguishment of native title did become an issue for Torres Strait Islander claimants.

Following the amendments to the Native Title Act, the Torres Strait Islanders were faced with alien processes of legal validation of their rights.

The Native Title Act in practice

'How does the Native Title Act work?' was the focus of a conference held in Townsville in May 1995 for people involved in land claims who realised the complexity of the Act and were unaware of their rights and obligations. For example, there was confusion regarding the presentation of the anthropological research considered important in the submission of claims. Moreover, claimants indicated they did not want to be bogged down with 'ideologies, academic language, "authorities and experts" ' (*TN* 12–18 May 1995, p. 5). In November, representatives from the National Native Title Office, Department of Lands, the Land Tribunal and the Indigenous Land Corporation Commission explained to members of the TSRA and the public the processes necessary to proceed to native title determination (*TN* 24–30 May 1995, p. 11).

Torres Strait Islander native title claimants were made aware that there would be no simple or speedy way to reach a determination, or even how they would manage native title in the future. Despite their aversion to 'authorities and experts', lawyers, judges, government agencies, anthropologists, historians and mediators were essential to appropriately present their cases. Time, too, proved to be an inescapable factor. Saibai Island Council lodged its community's claim in 1995 and a determination was celebrated in February 1999. At this early stage, Meriam councillors found it necessary to liaise with Melbourne-based former Mabo Land Case barrister Brian Keon-Cohen regarding the unique position on land rights to that island (unique because their claim to native title was settled by the Mabo decision, whereas other island claimants had to make application to the High Court for a determination of their rights). They sought advice on the:

> *development of a new system of community administration to account for native title ... to discuss future funding, to obtain legal advisers and the employment of a local Murray Islander as a resident Native Title Development Officer to work with lawyers to adjust and develop community and government administration.* (*TN* 15–21 December 1995, p. 7)

The aim, too, was to protect and account for the interests of the entire 'Meriam community (approximately 4000) most of whom lived on the mainland' in line with the High Court stipulation to 'consider the community as a whole' (p. 7).

The local representative bodies, set up to assist native title claimants work through the claim processes, became the 'keys to land negotiations' (*TN* 5–11 April 1996, p. 5) and were used as parties saw appropriate. For

5. Ownership of land and sea

instance, the TSRA representative body for Torres Strait assisted but did not represent the native title claim lodged by the Mualgal people on Moa. The Kaurareg people claimed native title in 1996 over parts of Nurupai (Horn Island), Muralag (Prince of Wales Island), Zuna (Entrance Island), Tarilag (Packe Island), Yeta (Port Lihou Island), Damaralag (Dumuralug Islet), and Mipa (Pipa Islet, also known as Turtle Island) (see NNTT 2001 for details on Kaurareg claims). They were represented by the Cape York Land Council, the Aboriginal representative body for Cape York Peninsula (though they received funds from the TSRA), and its representative body assisted them to comply with the necessary statutory procedures in the presentation of their unique claim. The reason for using the Cape York Land Council may have been because some Kaurareg had become impatient with perceived TSRA delays in progressing claims or that some Kaurareg related more strongly to an Aboriginal connection. Despite the Kaurareg people's history of forced removal from their homelands they claimed they had 'maintained their traditions and their attachment to these islands. They have survived as a culturally distinct and viable group of people who ... know their territory' (Butt et al. 2001, p. 113). In some instances, they were not able to show actual physical connection to lands for the reason that they were 'locked out' of those areas of their 'traditional country' (p. 113). However, their stated aim was to settle their land claims by mediation with other parties rather than 'costly court action' (*TN* 14–20 June 1996, p. 16).

When Justice French, the president of the National Native Title Tribunal, visited Saibai in 1997 he aimed to mediate with the community council on issues of negotiations with other parties. He had already had a number of teleconferences involving state and Commonwealth governments. Other negotiations were held with the Far North Queensland Electricity Board and Telstra. He also visited Mer to 'get a sense' of any problems that may arise there because they then lacked a mediation process. He warned that:

> There are a lot of individual landholders on Murray Island and the risk is that when they don't get some cooperative approach between land owners to making land available for community facilities, vital community facilities will not be available so there will have to be compulsory acquisition. (*TN* 14–20 November 1997, pp. 1, 3)

Because of the complex processes related to land rights claims, communities soon realised that their representative bodies were indispensable. Moreover, mediation was vital because the Federal Court was adamant that all parties had to agree if a consent determination was being sought.

Community councillors were concerned that their people should not be kept in the dark about the progress of their native title claims. Reflecting their '*Ailan Kastom*' (Island custom) of showing '*gud pasin*' (respect and kindness) toward those who need help, the Erub Community Council convened and hosted a three-day native title workshop in December 1996. The aim was to 'provide information about the Native Title Act, the ... claim process, the present stage of the claims, future issues with the granting of Native Title' to ease the minds of the claimants (*TN* 20–26 December 1996, p. 15). In June 1998, after meetings on several islands, the TSRA representatives attended meetings with Torres Strait Islanders at Cairns and Townsville to discuss native title issues: 'The meetings provided an excellent opportunity for mainland Islanders to ask questions and ensure their interests were being served correctly by the TSRA Native Title Office' (*TN* 26 June–2 July 1998, pp. 3, 5). The TSRA and island councils cast their nets of consultation as widely and as often as possible to assist the people in their understanding of the workings of the Native Title Act and to inform them what progress had been made toward resolution of their claims. An issue raised by Justice French on his visit to Torres Strait was the considerable cost involved in processing the many claims for Torres Strait, 'there being currently [1997] 63' (*TN* 14–20 November 1997, pp. 1). He said, 'People have a right to follow their own claims ... but there is not going to be enough money', as funding from the Commonwealth Attorney-General under Legal Aid was becoming more difficult to access. He urged the communities to use a 'cooperative-collective approach' when dealing with their claims. If this approach was adopted, he assured them, funding could flow from ATSIC to the TSRA representative body (pp. 1, 3). In various ways the people were kept abreast of requirements and progress related to their claims.

Consent determinations

In February 1999 the Federal Court made a formal finding that native title existed on Saibai Island. It was the first claim to reach a successful conclusion in Torres Strait through the representation of the TSRA. A formal finding of native title was also made in favour of the Mualgal people of Moa Island. John Abednego, chair of the TSRA, concluded:

> For the second time in Torres Strait and the first time for the region under the amended Native Title Act, an Australian court has formally acknowledged what we have known for thousands of years — that Native Title exists on Saibai Island and Moa Island. Prior to last week's hearing, theoretically the land was owned by the Crown or by the island council under Deed of Grant in Trust, but now another form

of ownership has been recognised—traditional ownership. First since
Mabo 1993. (*TN* 19–25 February 1999, pp. 1–2)

Abednego's words resounded with satisfaction and on the islands the
people were jubilant and feasted to celebrate these great victories.

Of special interest on Mer was the Federal Court's consent
determination over the small neighbouring islands of Waier and Dauar,
handed down in July 2001 after three years of consultation with the
Queensland Government. The High Court in the Mabo decision left
undecided the native title rights to these islands even though the decision
referred to 'Murray Islands', covering the three islands. Lloyd Maza, chair
of Mer *Gedkem Le*, the Prescribed Body Corporate (the organisation set
up on each community to deal with native title issues) saw the Mabo
decision as 'a dream come true for the whole country and now our
community is looking forward to this determination. It will be a great day
for us' (*TSRA News* May 2001, p. 1). Also successful in achieving native
title rights in May 2001 were the Kaurareg people on Nurupai in the
inner-island group (i.e. those situated in proximity to Thursday Island).
Chief Elder Bill Wasaga said it was an emotional day of celebration:

> It captured the heart of the struggle that all indigenous people go through
> ... The land and the sea are the heart and soul of indigenous people so
> to get something back that has been lost for 79 years can only make the
> Kaurareg people feel good. (*TSRA News* May 2001, p. 1)

The Federal Court had recognised native title over their seven inner
islands. At this point, seven separate island group consent determinations
had been finalised.

Extinguishment of native title

With these victories, the remaining native title claimants must have been
optimistic. They could not have foreseen the Queensland Premier Peter
Beattie's backflip when determinations for Boigu, Badu, Iama, Erub
and Ugar were cancelled at the last minute. Premier Beattie had given
'in-principle support' for these determinations to proceed but went
'back on his word' after the Federal Court ruled that 'a question still
existed whether public works land was exempt from Native Title' (*TN*
28 February–6 March 2002, pp. 1, 3). Terry Waia, chair of the TSRA, made
it clear that the people would not agree to extinguishment of native title
on land supporting any government or other infrastructure. He wanted
the government to recognise that 'under that infrastructure is land
that belongs to us'. He went on, 'My people are saying, "Who the hell
are those people, never seen the Torres Strait before and making a

decision about it? This is our land, our people's, this is our birth right'" (*TN* 20–26 September 2002, pp. 1, 3). In defence, he spoke forcefully: they would fight Beattie and his government.

The Torres Strait Islanders' greatest fear was that if native title was extinguished over any part of their land, once the land was no longer needed for public or other works it could be sold and be 'lost by our people forever' (*TN* 28 February–6 March 2003, pp. 1, 3). What was difficult to understand was that previous determinations had allowed native title to remain over these areas of their lands. The minister for Natural Resources, Stephen Robertson, pointed out (pp. 1, 3):

> *The issue is not about a position the State government is taking 'but is a legal question as to what is permitted under the Commonwealth Native Title Act'. Native Title over public works is legally impossible under current circumstances and, without amendment to the Native Title Act, it does not exist and cannot occur. In those circumstances it cannot be fudged or 'ignored'.*

He added that the state would be happy to reinterpret the section if the court ruled differently. Terry Waia, TSRA chair, expressed regret that the dispute had to go back to court and added: 'This course of action is necessary to find a solution. At the start of the year we really hoped that negotiations between the Queensland Government and TSRA would resolve this matter', but they did not (*TN* 11–17 April 2003, p. 3). So, the *Erubam Le* (Darnley Islanders) 'took matters to the full Federal Court for separate determination as to the legal effect of the establishment of certain public works by or on behalf of, and on land owned by, the Erub Island Council under a Deed of Grant in Trust' (*AIATSIS newsletter* no. 6, 2003, pp. 6–7). The case was set down before the full Federal Court, an indication of its importance.

Premier Beattie's backflip produced angry responses from Torres Strait leaders. The voice of the intransigent elder statesman George Mye, 'seething with anger', was loud and clear. On ABC's *Big Country* (Connolly 2003), using his own style of political brinkmanship, he called for 'civil disobedience' against Beattie's government: refusal to collect rents; rejection of funding for public works; withdrawal of cooperation on surveillance in Torres Strait. As in 1988, when he and other leaders called for sovereign independence, he again called for the 'full loaf of bread' — full control of Torres Strait 'because the place belongs to us lock, stock and barrel' (Connolly 2003). He described his action as taking the bullet between the teeth because 'that's the way to go ... We have been confronted with extinguishment of land belong you me'. That, he said, 'hit us well under the belt and no-one ... is going to take it sitting down'. On Erub there was the belief that they had their 'backs toward the wall' but there would be no lying down and crying, only 'fight with all your might' (Connolly 2003).

At the eleventh Mabo Day Celebrations in June 2003 the Torres Shire Mayor Pedro Stephen told the people: 'processes and processes are being put forward to water down Native Title ... More processes mean more lies. The land and the seas belong to us' (*TN* 6–12 June 2003, p. 1). Henry Garnier from Keriri, and chair of the ICC, expressed his frustration: 'governments are placing obstacles in our way. If we find public works do not extinguish native title, they will find something else' (p. 1). John Abednego, chair of TRAWQ (an incorporated body covering the Tamwoy, Rose Hill, Aplin, Waiben and Quarantine residential areas on Thursday Island), added his feelings: 'Native Title was ... complex and far-reaching but at the end of the day, the onus of proof still rests with the traditional owners and the government should come here and prove we are not the traditional owners' (p. 1). TSRA deputy chair Margaret Mau believed the people were at a 'crossroads, because our right to traditional lands is currently under dispute ... [it] is the most significant issue facing Native Title since the *Native Title Act* was introduced in 1993 and it has the potential to "make" or "break" Native Title in our region' (p. 1). Mau warned that all 14 island communities could be faced with uncertainty about the strength of their native title if the Federal Court decided public works *did* extinguish native title (p. 1). TSRA chair Terry Waia said the 'community is rebelling against the State government's inaction ... [it] has not listened ... What do we have to do to get these people [federal and state governments] to talk to us?' (*TN* 15–21 August 2003, p. 15).

Finally, at a land summit held in October, the traditional owners and state and Commonwealth bodies sat together and discussed full recognition of native title, but the owners were left believing the situation was 'tragically unfair': they were being 'forced to choose between a new school or health clinic, or the preservation of their Native Title rights' (*TN* 3–9 October 2003, p. 11). There was consensus among the traditional owners that it was difficult to understand the link between their rights and legislation when they knew the land belonged to them. Disappointment, frustration and anger were the reactions of those attending the summit. They could only hope that the court would rule in their favour.

Federal Court of Australia upholds extinguishment

The Erub Community applied to the High Court on behalf all communities that had their determinations cancelled in 2002, and in October 2003 the Federal Court brought down its ruling in *Erubam Le (Darnley Islanders) v. State of Queensland*. After considering whether s. 47A of the

Native Title Act could be applied to enable the court to disregard certain extinguishing acts, it found that works constructed prior to 1996 'were previous exclusive possession acts ... which specifically includes public works' and these acts were deemed to extinguish native title. Under s. 23D, grants or vesting for the benefit of Torres Strait Islander peoples were considered exceptions to extinguishment, but the court ruled this was not the case because 'the creation of a public work is not a grant or vesting' (*AIATSIS newsletter* no. 6, 2003). This decision set a precedent for native title claims Australia-wide. On Erub, extensive government-funded infrastructure had been put in place, including residential housing. One resident complained: 'our crabs will have more land than me' (*TN* 12–18 December 2003, p. 4). People looked to place blame somewhere for what they saw as the 'biggest bureaucratic bungle in indigenous affairs in 200 years' (p. 14). Fingers pointed at Beattie, the Queensland Department of Aboriginal and Torres Strait Islander Policy (DATSIP), and the TSRA. The irony, traditional owners Peter Stephen and Robert Sagigi said, was that DATSIP and TSRA 'are charged with the broader responsibility by law to manage our affairs and have allowed for the extinguishment of the right of those very clients they have a statutory obligation to protect'; the demand was for 'those responsible [to] fix what they broke' (p. 1).

The editor of the *Torres News* entered the debate, suggesting that the key groups — the traditional owners; TSRA; DATSIP; and Stephen Robertson, the Queensland Government minister responsible for Native Title — get together and 'to talk to each other' (*TN* 12–18 December 2003, p. 17). But Getano Lui Jnr believed they had been consulted to death and responded: 'What are we seeing after all those determinations and consultations ... look at what we have achieved?' (Author's notes, Senate Inquiry Meeting August 2004, p. 1). Torres Shire Council mayor Pedro Stephen was cautious of more talk: 'It could have been solved if everyone knew where people were coming from and talk to each other ... The frustration and legal costs and jargon used has confused our people' (p. 1). Elder Flo Kennedy told the senate inquiry in August 2004 that she believed it all came back to this: 'You don't know what we feel in our hearts about our lands and sea. We know exactly what we own and when it comes to our boundary it's when we see the enemy we come out. So the boundary is known ... You don't know what we understand' (p. 2).

Government solutions to extinguishment

In late January 2004, state Labor member Jason O'Brien announced that his government was 'committed to returning land to its traditional

5. Ownership of land and sea

owners'. He added: 'The State still may require certain land for community purposes but if that is not the case we will certainly support transferring the land back to traditional owners' (*TN* 23–29 January 2004, p. 1). O'Brien said this was an opportunity for them to claim back certain lands. He gave as an example the old health-care centre on Yam that was no longer required because a new one had been built. The land would be returned as Torres Strait Islander freehold and not in recognition of native title. Mayor Stephen hailed the decision as a 'very positive way for the affected traditional owners to sit down with the State government and conduct negotiations clear of all doubts and fears ... The commitment would help remove all obstacles to government funded construction on ... islands that had been delayed' because of the court's ruling on extinguishment. Some Torres Strait Islanders saw this as an initial way out of the bind: others did not (p. 1).

The battle over native title was not over. The TSRA, while seeing the government's offer as a start to resolving the issue, rejected as inadequate its offer to give back unwanted land to traditional owners. Chair Terry Waia, in similar vein to Flo Kennedy, said, 'The offer ... simply demonstrates that [the government has] never understood the issue at hand and don't respect Torres Strait people's Native Title rights'. He emphasised that 'the traditional owners ... want full recognition of Native Title *and* strong freehold tenure'. Pedro Stephen reiterated that 'it is frustrating to continuously be forced through new legal processes in pursuit of this goal ... It has always been about keeping the lawyers in business ... Frustration from the community is from one process to another' (*TN* 6–12 February 2004, p. 3).

In April 2004 the Queensland Government put forward a further proposal to fix the ongoing dispute over native title on five islands. It proposed to 'recognise Native Title over all land outside the townships on the affected islands, in addition to concluding Indigenous Land Use Agreements for the townships' (*TN* 14–20 April 2004, p. 1). Ugar leader Brian Williams said he wanted full land ownership and, as Australian citizens, Torres Strait Islanders were entitled to their rights as citizens. O'Brien replied that (p. 1):

> *The Federal Court decision was not helpful to anyone and that is why we are trying to find a way to avoid going to court again and trying to get a win/win for everyone. This proposal is a step in the right direction but it is really up to the traditional owners to decide if they think this is the way forward or if they go back to court.*

In early May Stephen Robertson, state minister for the Department of Natural Resources, together with O'Brien, visited Torres Strait and declared that he wanted to 'come back with the pieces of paper that would give the Traditional Owners what they want'. He said, 'I passionately believe in repairing the mistakes of the past and one of the most powerful ways to do this is to facilitate the absolute recognition of the rights of Traditional Owners' (*TN* 12–18 May 2004, p. 1). Don Banu, Boigu Island Council chair, replied (p. 1):

> *It's easy for the politicians to say at the time of the meetings [that they want to resolve the Native Title issue], but this is completely different from making that happen and that is why we've lost faith in Queensland government with the cancellation of Native Title determinations back in 2002.*

O'Brien said the government's position was that the traditional owners' goal was not achievable under the current Commonwealth Native Title Act and urged each group of claimants to remove the townships from their claims as an interim measure and (p. 1):

> until we can get either the Federal Government to change the Native Title Act or we receive better legal direction, we would form Indigenous Land Use Agreements over the township, which would effectively give Traditional Owners rights over that land ... [that] can offer ... advantages over Native Title in terms of what they can do with their land.

The traditional owners neither 'agreed [nor] said no' (p. 1) to the proposal. Nonetheless, the minister said, 'following further consultation with Traditional Owners, the state government will return with a full proposal on how to resolve the ongoing issue' (*TN* 12–18 May 2004, p. 1). A strong reaction came from Patrick Thaiday, chair of Magni Lagougal Torres Strait Islander Corporation (the Native Title Prescribed Body on Yam Island): The land is 'our family and any proposal that did not grant ... full rights as owners of the land was unacceptable ... I find [the proposal] downright insulting' (*TN* 19–25 May 2004, p. 1). He intimated that if the present discussions failed to resolve the issue, the native title lawyers would commence preparations to take the matter back to court. The people were once again playing the waiting game with the government.

By June 2004, dissatisfaction with TSRA's handling of this native title issue led to a call for the native title Office to be 'removed from the TSRA and placed under the control of an independent tribunal' (*TN* 9–15 June 2004, p. 2). The ICC and TRAWQ chair Robert Sagigi's 'passionate' address on this position at the Mabo Day celebration drew applause from a large crowd (p. 2):

The [Native Title] Office is answerable to the Federal Government and the TSRA, and every time we seek assistance it is not given. They protect the interests of the TSRA and the Government, and [this] doesn't give us much of a hearing ... The system is controlling the Traditional Owners ... We're not being represented under the present system; the land is ours. They can't even advise us because they would bite the hand that feeds them ... It is our God-given right and they can't take that away from us; we want respect; we want to see where we are with our land claims.

John Toshie Kris, newly elected chair of the TSRA, spoke on the issue of the time factor (p. 2):

Although it is a time to celebrate the achievements of Eddie 'Koiki' Mabo and the Meriam people, it is hard to ignore the fact that Native Title in the region is under real threat ... Last year we said that we are at a crossroads, and unfortunately twelve months down the track we are still here. I want the Queensland Government to make a commitment that this public works matter will be resolved once and for all before Christmas 2004 ... Let this be the measure of how committed Premier Beattie is to protecting our traditional rights as the people of the Torres Strait.

These leaders' frustrations were being felt on all communities: Would their land inheritance ever be recognised in its entirety?

Finally: recognition of native title

Finally, in late October 2004, the Queensland Government agreed to recognise the exclusive native title rights of traditional owners on Badu, Boigu, Iama, Erub and Ugar that had been cancelled. The TSRA portfolio member for native title, Don Banu, said, 'this significant move comes after substantial negotiations, court action and anguish over possible extinguishment of Native Title rights to these traditional lands' (*TN* 27 October–3 November 2004, p. 1). He pointed out that direct negotiations with the state minister, Stephen Robertson, aided this positive outcome. When the minister visited Torres Strait in May he was reported as saying, 'Personally, I was moved by the passion shown by the many members of the communities as they spoke about their aspiration for their communities, which will remain with me and strengthen my resolve to fix these matters and get a solution' (*TN* 12–18 May 2004, p. 1). At last John Abednego's call to politicians, made in June 2003, to come to the islands and prove that the Torres Strait Islanders are *not* the traditional owners, had been heeded. The people's special connection to their land was at last recognised by one politician — one who made a difference. The people set about preparing for the special sittings of the High Court on each of the five islands in late December 2004. On Badu, where celebrations would be held, traditional owner William Bowie expressed the feelings of the Baduans: 'It has taken the State Government many long years to recognise our Native Title but we never lost track of our struggle' (*TN* 22–28 December 2004, p. 22). Robert Sagigi pointed to the future when he said the determinations for these remaining inhabited islands were 'part of the broader struggle for autonomy ... we have started to build a nation ... but autonomy won't fall into our laps' (p. 22). Traditional owner Maluwap Nona claimed that 'We have broken the cycles, not just physically, mentally and spiritually, but today is a benchmark for the next generation to see the fruits of our labour' (p. 22).

At the end of 2006, while determinations were awaited for a number of uninhabited islands and there were residual issues on some islands about people's direct rights and how they should be expressed, the finalisation of the five delayed determinations meant that native title was recognised over all inhabited islands in Torres Strait.

During the mediation process the native title claimants, governments and others with interests in the land met and agreed on practical ways to co-exist that were subsequently incorporated into and registered as Indigenous Land Use Agreements. Land agreements can 'help resolve Native Title claims by setting out the practical matters involved in the co-existence of Native Title and other rights' (Butt et al. 2001, p. 131) and are drawn 'according to a process [the parties] develop for themselves and which meets their own particular needs' (p. 131).

In May 2004, when the Queensland Government offered native title recognition over all land outside the island townships, the offer contained an option to draw up land agreements over certain lands in the townships to give traditional owners some rights (*TN* 12–18 May 2004, p. 1). Understandably, no agreements were signed. Conversely, in the same year traditional owners on Badu and Dauan signed agreements to co-exist with the Commonwealth Government to pave the way for the construction of a radar system to improve border protection by providing more effective surveillance of aircraft, ships and boats travelling in Torres Strait (*TSRA News* 2004, p. 4). While this was an example of a practical agreement beneficial to both parties, the installation failed and was removed.

Governments can affect native title by granting interests in and rights over land from 'freehold grants, to leases, to large open-cut mining ventures' (Butt et al. 2001, p. 122). They may want to build roads, declare national parks, or make laws to protect the environment over native title land. Described as 'future acts' they are graded on a sliding scale with 'a right to negotiate' acts that have the most impact on native title to cases of lesser impact where the native title claimants are notified and are given an opportunity to comment only (p. 122). It is anticipated that land agreements will be negotiated extensively in the future to settle coexistence arrangements where they are deemed appropriate and practical.

As has been shown, much time and energy was spent to reach final resolutions on all land claims on the inhabited islands in Torres Strait. Traditional owner Ned David said, 'Now focus is on the sea claim. It does not take a rocket scientist to recognise that as a people there is no way we could have survived just on the land itself. Our ties are just as strong with the sea as with the land' (*TN* 22–28 December 2004, p. 15). On 23 November 2001, a joint claim for recognition of native title over the seas in Torres Strait was lodged with the Federal Court.

Traditional ownership of the sea

While the Mabo Land Case set a precedent for native title to land of the Torres Strait Islanders, the court did not settle another question of great importance to them — traditional ownership of the sea that surrounded their islands. In the statement of claim in Mabo, the plaintiffs sought to establish ownership of the surrounding seas, seabeds, fringing reef and adjacent islands, but the court was unwilling to proceed with this issue at that time even though the inseparability of sea and land and island custom was stressed. Nonetheless, island leaders were determined to do whatever it took to bring about a satisfactory legal conclusion to their sea right claims. Meanwhile, island leaders continued to be faced with issues associated with their sea areas.

The Meriam leaders pressed for the declaration of a 10 nautical mile economic zone around their islands based on the understanding that their rights to fish in the area were 'given to them and their forefathers in "Birth" ' (Sharp 1996, p. 189). This led in 1993 to disagreement between the Meriam people and commercial fishers fishing around their islands. The Commercial Fishermen's Organisation agreed to a voluntary moratorium awaiting a government report (*TN* 31 December 1993–6 January 1994, p. 1). However, encroachment by non-Islander fishers continued to be a concern. In October 1996, when Walter Waia of the Torres Strait Regional Authority Native Title Office attended a meeting in Canberra dealing with proposed changes to the Commonwealth *Native Title Act 1993*, he raised the issue of an impending amendment 'to include the area between the low-water and high-water marks as "seas"' (*TSRA newsletter* (6) 1996, p. 3). If adopted, he feared, prospective native title holders were unlikely to win their claims to the seas around their islands and thus would be excluded from dealing with these areas. The people never doubted ownership of their sea areas — it had been drummed into them that 'This is our boundaries, this is our land, this is our reef' (Sharp 1996, p. 19).

A parallel issue of concern was the mining activities taking place in neighbouring Papua New Guinea. Island leaders had reason to think the interests of others were being put ahead of theirs in the government negotiations that were taking place in preparation of a treaty between Australia and Papua New Guinea. Island leaders were concerned that pollution from BHP's Ok Tedi copper mine was entering the Torres Strait via the Fly River, and while the TSRA subsequently repeatedly requested that the Commonwealth Government conduct ongoing monitoring of the area, little had been done. It appeared that BHP's interests were being safeguarded. In 1996 TSRA chair Getano Lui Jnr said that 'this issue will be treated like any other in Torres Strait, which is to ignore it until it goes away or kills someone' (*TSRA newsletter* July 1996, p. 1). A protected zone to be set up under the treaty stipulated that mining and drilling of the seabed would be prohibited for 10 years, but 'without prejudice to right of either party to undertake seismic exploration of the subsoil ... under their jurisdiction' (Kaye 2002, p. 15). This clause caused obvious nervousness as any interference with the seabed would drastically affect fish stocks and people's livelihoods.

People of the top-western islands were particularly concerned that the treaty would not be policed tightly enough. These people have a tradition of trade with their Papuan neighbours and, while the treaty protects this trade, there was the possibility that people other than traders or those visiting relatives might use the area as a way into Australia with all the dangers that entails: imported diseases; animal and vegetable products entering without inspection; drug smuggling and associated crime; and the illegal entry of people from other parts of the world. Islander leaders continue to call for more support from the Australian Government: 'The

Torres Strait is used as a buffer zone and not enough resources are put into it' (*TSRA newsletter* 1996 (6), p. 1).

If Torres Strait Islanders were to go along Lui's road of self-government as a nation within Australia, there would be many issues of responsibility to resolve relating to the seas. Lui said that the 'bottom line is recognition by government of a greater control of our land and our own resources by our own people'. However, this would take time, as he was well aware. His target date was 2001, but he was willing to concede that 'if it doesn't happen then at least there is a goal for the younger people to carry on from there' (*CP* 15 July 1996, p. 7).

Recognition of sea rights

Traditional owner Ned David's claim that the ties of the people of the Torres Strait to the sea are just as strong as those to the land leaves no doubt that sea rights must also be recognised at common law. Meyers et al. (1996, p. 1) point out that:

> *On a practical level, identification of indigenous sea rights is necessary for the interaction of these rights with the rights of other users of Australia's coastal waters. At a cultural level, indigenous peoples have the opportunity to explain and identify the nature and scope of their cultural heritage. At the legal level, constitutional and international law ramifications need to be identified, questions of extinguishment examined and the nature of evidence for proof of sea rights considered.*

The Torres Strait Islanders knew that to validate their native title claim to particular areas of the ocean they must once again use the judicial process, with the Native Title Act as the framework for that action (Tsamenyi & Mfodowo 2000, p. 13). By 23 November 2001, when the Torres Strait regional sea claim was lodged, the claimants were fully aware that these legal processes would test not only the practical, cultural and constitutional issues described by Myers et al. above, but also their determination to see it through, just as they had been tested in their ongoing struggle for recognition of native title to their lands.

Section 223 of the Native Title Act provides for native title rights to 'land or waters', indicating that the government acknowledges the 'possibility that the common law recognises marine Native Title' (Meyers et al. 1996, p. 30). While there is domestic and international law to support this conclusion (p. iii), Meyers et al. add that any argument against this possibility imposes a narrow interpretation of Mabo and restricts common law recognition to *land* only. In Mabo, two justices spoke of ' "retreating" from the "past injustices [of] the dispossession of Aboriginal peoples of most of their traditional lands" ', so it was probable that the High Court would be cautious about handing down a narrow view of native sea title (pp. 30–1).

The Torres Strait Islanders themselves do not accept the artificial distinction between the aquatic and the terrestrial created in western law. They regard the sea as a 'watery extension of estates on land' (Meyers et al. 1996, p. 3). However, under western law (based on the 1876 English case *R v. Keyn*) it was held that the common law ended at the low-water mark: 'Simply put, if NO common law — then NO Native Title' (Cain 2006a, p. 22). Guided by this legal precedent, the Commonwealth Government's policy position from 1992 to 2001 was that native title could not be recognised beyond the low-water mark because the common law did not extend offshore (that is, to sea areas beyond the low-water mark) (p. 22).

This position was challenged in the first native title claim to sea country, which was brought by the Yarmirr Croker Island people (in *Yarmirr v. Northern Territory* (1998), 156 ALR 370, 428) from the Coburg Peninsula near Arnhem Land, Northern Territory. In this landmark case the Federal Court of Australia held that native title 'could exist over territorial seas extending to the twelve nautical miles zone', a decision that was upheld in 2001, on appeal, by the High Court (*Commonwealth v. Yarmirr* (2001–02), 208 CLR). Thus, the Commonwealth courts rejected the Commonwealth Government's own policy position. Indeed, the majority justices in the High Court stated pointedly that the 'territorial sea was not a "lawless province" ' (Cain 2006a, p. 23). It would now be difficult for the Commonwealth to apply the *R v. Keyn* ruling.

In the Croker Island Case (*Commonwealth v. Yarmirr* (2001–02), 208 CLR), the High Court's ruling was that the people's sea rights were:

1. *subject to the group's traditional laws,*
2. *subject to all valid Commonwealth and Northern Territory laws,*
3. *a non-exclusive Native Title right to have free access to the sea and seabed,*
4. *for the purposes of travel, non-commercial fishing and hunting, visiting and protecting places of cultural and spiritual importance and safeguarding cultural and spiritual knowledge.* (Cain 2006b, p. 19)

Cain points out that in this context 'Despite the achievements of the "Native Title" revolution, ultimately the rights recognised, valued and protected by "Native Title" is a smaller subset of the content of customary

5. Ownership of land and sea

rights recognised under an Indigenous legal system'. He suggests this does not 'unduly diminish the achievements of Native Title. It is a measure of the maturity of the current debate' (p. 20), which suggests that the application of the law could be broadened in future claims.

Nonetheless, claimants are aware of the problems associated with claiming the broadest possible sea rights because of 'myriad of constitutional and international law concepts at work in offshore areas' (Meyers et al. 1996, p. 2). Torres Strait is a major sea route between the Pacific and Indian oceans and is subject to the 1982 United Nations Convention on the Law of the Sea relating to international straits, to which Australia is committed. The convention does not recognise Indigenous rights (Kaye 2002, pp. 3–9). To maintain its international obligations, Australia '*cannot* include a right to exclude vessels from transiting their waters, or to impede transit in any way' in any sea claim decision (p. 6). In the Croker Island Case (2001–02), the majority justices of the High Court found that there was a 'fundamental inconsistency between the continued existence of the exclusive Native Title rights claimed; and the common law public rights to navigate and to fish and the international right of innocent passage' (Cain 2006a, p. 25). In 2002 the High Court 'confirmed its view … about the non-exclusive nature of Native Title in maritime areas' in a Western Australia case (*Western Australia v. Ward* (2002), 191 ALR 1) (p. 29). Thus there is a common law right of navigation, and native title rights are subject to the rules as settled in the Croker Island Case on appeal in 2002. Indeed, island claimants knew that 'exclusive possession' was not a viable option, but they sought the broadest possible application of the law.

Meyers et al. point out that the burden of proof of any argument that native title had been extinguished lies with those asserting extinguishment (1996, p. 3). Native title claimants, however, have the burden of proving:

- *the existence of traditional practices or connection to the area prior to the Commonwealth assuming sovereignty over territorial waters, arguably, prior to 1 January 1901*
- *[that] Native Title rights belong to a system of rules of an identifiable indigenous group*[3]

---

3. Cain describes two very different species of legal systems: the Australian Legal System, an amalgam of law introduced into Australia in 1788 and heavily evolved in the years hence, with different systems depending on geographical location, but condensed into one overall species of legal system; and the Australian Indigenous Legal Systems, fractured and undervalued, but underpinning the customary usage of [traditional lands and seas] and living marine resources by Aboriginal and Torres Strait Islander people (Cain 2006b, pp. 12–13).

- *[that] the claimants are biological descendants of that group*
- *[that] they have continued to exercise these rights in the intervening period.* (Meyers et al. 1996, p. i)

These criteria, however, must be presented with 'realism and reason' to avoid rendering recognition of native title illusory by 'standards of proof impossible to achieve' (p. iii). Moreover, the High Court in Mabo explained that 'Native Title is not a title "created" by common law but one "recognised" by common law' and has 'its origins in and is given its content by the traditional laws' of the Indigenous inhabitants (Butt et al. 2001, p. 40). Terry Waia, a Saibai leader with a strong traditional focus, listed his people's cultural connections to the sea:

1. *There are many traditional owners and stories that tell of voyages, battles and trade on our waters, all illustrating respect [for our seas] that formed a large part of our natural environment.*
2. *Individual island territories were identified by well-known seascape margins that all people of the Torres Strait knew and respected as boundaries of each island's territorial waters.*
3. *To this day many of our communities identify with these markers and boundaries and can point out where their territorial waters begin and end.*
4. *In our traditional communities, the sea not only provided a right of passage for young Torres Strait men, it was also the main provider of food and wealth for our people and survival as self-sufficient communities.*
5. *Our ancestors were seafaring people who relied on the maritime environment for their food resources to trade and transport.*
6. *Geographically the sea continues to link our islands and until modern air travel was accessible it was the main means of transport.* (*TN* 21–27 June 2002, p. 14)

Waia's list leaves no doubt that the Torres Strait Islanders have always had strong cultural connections to their seas. Meyers et al. (1996, p. 40) point out that:

Indigenous sea rights exist as a matter of fact, and their 'origins' are not founded on any concept of English land law, or indeed on notions of international law, as they depend entirely for their existence on observance by indigenous people of their traditional laws and customs. Some of these laws and customs have been evident for thousands of years, and possibly tens of thousands of years. They pre-date international or municipal law notions of sovereignty, coming to the fore only when international law recognises sovereign rights.

In the early 1990s Justice Owen, in the Supreme Court of Western Australia, suggested that Indigenous people's 'best evidence ... lies in the hearts and minds of the people most intimately connected to aboriginal culture, namely the aboriginal people themselves'. Justice Owens went on to say (p. 55):

> Expert evidence from anthropologists and others is of significance and due regard must, and will, be afforded to it. However, it seems to me that the full story lies in the hearts and minds of the people. It is from here that it must be extracted. This is not always easy, particularly from people whose primary language might not be English and who historically, have depended on oral rather than written recording of tradition.

In New South Wales in 1994 Justice Kirby too recognised the special circumstances of Indigenous parties in litigation (p. 55):

> [Because of] the nature of Aboriginal society ... it is next to impossible to expect that Aboriginal Australians will ever be able to prove, by recorded details, their precise genealogy back to the time before 1788. In these circumstances it would be unreasonable and unrealistic for the common law of Australia to demand such proof for the establishment of a claim to Native Title.

These broader approaches to the presentation of evidence like Waia's permit evolution over time and are preferred (p. iv).

Lodging the sea claim

In 1998, TSRA chair John Abednego welcomed the Federal Court's decision in the Croker Island Case as having 'major implications for sea rights in Torres Strait: [It] will provide a legal basis for the Torres Strait Islanders to claim and protect their cultural attachment to the sea' (*TN* 17–23 July 1998, p. 3). However, he also expressed disappointment that the decision did not 'recognise exclusive rights' as was the case in the Mabo decision. In the light of this decision he warned island claimants that they should be realistic as their gains 'may not be as extensive as some people [were] hoping', though he did feel that 'in a number of areas, the evidence of Islander connections with their sea culture could be stronger than [that] presented in the *Croker Island Case*' (*TN* 31 July–6 August 1998, p. 5).

During 1996, Torres Strait Islanders lodged numerous sea claims 'without community consultation or strategic thought' (*TSRA News* October 2000, p. 4). In 1998, in an attempt to coordinate claims, the TSRA moved to develop a united sea claim encompassing the whole of Torres Strait that '[would] have a greater chance of achieving recognition of rights [and] speed up the claims process [without] the problem of overlapping claims' (*TSRA News* September 1999, p. 4). After community consultation to gain support for its move the TSRA Native Title Office began preparations for a united legal sea claim.

Two years after the Federal Court decision in the Croker Island Case, the TSRA had not filed its application. Both parties in the Croker Island Case had filed appeals in the High Court and the TSRA waited to see if that court would affirm the Federal Court's ruling. When the affirmative decision was known, the TSRA settled upon a 'strategy to progress' the people's claim (*TSRA News* October 2000, p. 4).

In 2001 a maritime summit was held in Torres Strait at which Maluwap Nona was appointed organiser of a working committee to 'work towards a blanket sea claim of the whole of Torres Strait' (*TN* 30 March–5 April 2001, pp. 1, 3), and on 23 November of that year the claim was lodged with the Federal Court (*TN* 30 November–6 December 2001, pp. 3, 5). The claim was lodged with the prior assurance of Terry Waia that it would 'pursue sea rights to the very highest extent ... and attempt to broaden the application of the law' (*TN* 26 October–1 November 2001, p. 1). The TSRA's blanket claim covered the sea, the seabed, subsoil, reefs, shoals, sandbanks and waters within Torres Strait but excluded waters surrounding the inner island group. It included the geographical areas of all groups of islands — eastern, central, top-western and near-western — and covered an area of 42 000 square kilometres (TSRA press release c. October 2007).

The regional sea claim was brought by veteran island leader George Mye (representing the eastern islands), along with Talitiai Joseph (near-western islands) and Fr Napoleon Warria (central islands) on behalf of Torres Strait Islander claimants from 14 island communities. They not only saw it as 'a significant step by our people in their struggle for recognition of Native Title rights over the sea' but also believed that 'By achieving the legal recognition of [these] title rights ... we will move closer to our political aspirations of creating a territory-style government within Torres Strait' (*TN* 30 November–6 December 2001, pp. 3, 5). The people viewed sea rights as absolutely vital to a territory-style government because, without control of the sea, it would be difficult for them to achieve a much-needed strong economic base.

5. Ownership of land and sea

Concerning registration of the claim, TSRA chair Terry Waia warned claimants that 'this process is a long and complex one and is likely to take several years' (*TN* 30 November–6 December 2001, pp. 3, 5). The application took seven months to pass the registration process then entered the next stage, mediation. Finally, in March 2005, after almost three years, Justice Cooper of the Federal Court fixed December 2006 for a consent determination; he warned that if the matter had to go to trial it would be mid 2007 before it could be set down for a hearing.

Once again the plaintiffs were enmeshed in the complex processes of western law. It was now four years since their claim was lodged, and it had not progressed far. As they saw it, they were again only asking this legal system for common law recognition of what belonged to them under their laws. Understandably, some leaders became frustrated with the processes. Robert Sagigi, chair of both the Island Coordinating Council (ICC) and TRAWQ (the organisation representing Tamwoy, Rose Hill, Aplin, Waiben and Quarantine), spoke out (*TN* 8–14 June 2005, p. 5):

> Go to court over sea rights if they [continue] to drag on ... Follow the example of Mabo ... We have to make it happen. Sea rights are important ... The sea is our livelihood; we have not got a big parcel of land for farming; we have lived off the sea for 20 000 years before bully beef came here 200 years ago. If we have to go to court, we go to court.

This statement reflected the belief of many leaders: that with sea rights they would no longer be economically 'compressed by a system where we are dependent on welfare' (p. 5). The stakes were high for everyone.

The feelings of frustration felt by many people were articulated by Jim Akee when, in a letter to the *Torres News*, he described the sea claim as 'farcical and a waste of resources' (*TN* 24–30 August 2005, p. 8). Akee was responding to a brief, drafted by the TSRA Native Title Office and presented at a public meeting on Thursday Island, which stated that there were public rights to the sea that were inconsistent with island people being able to claim 'exclusive possession' (p. 8). Akee understood the UN convention, described earlier, and had no problem with navigation through Torres Strait. However, he opposed protection of commercial fishers who 'legally steal' (p. 8) fish products by using government-approved licences in areas of the sea that should be reserved for Torres Strait Islanders. Akee believed that if under Australian law they lost their right to exclude others then 'our efforts should be directed to the international court to question the validity of the Crown's sovereignty ... Torres Strait has got to go to the United Nations'. Why then, he asked, with the evidence Torres Strait Islanders have of prior ownership of land and sea, 'present that to a court to get only "half a loaf of bread"?' (p. 8). Erub chair Bully Hayes Saylor responded by backing the recently appointed regional sea-claim negotiating team. While realising the legal system 'may not give us the "full loaf of bread"', he suggested that there may be other ways to achieve their aspirations. Meanwhile, the newly appointed negotiating team of island representatives, including George Mye, Leo Akiba (Boigu) and Donald Banu (responsible for native title policy), anticipated negotiating with the two governments (*TN* 7–13 September 2005, p. 3).

In a newsletter dated 3 July 2006, the TSRA presented an update:

> *The Regional Sea Claim remains in mediation. The NTO [Native Title Office], with the assistance of Counsel Robert Blowes, QC, will be travelling to the western and central islands over the next couple of months to prepare witness statements in support of the claim. Anthropological research continues and due to the complex nature of the issues involved in preparing connection materials, the NTO anticipates forwarding connection material to the State and Commonwealth by the end of June [2006].* (*TSRA* News July 2006, pp. 1–2)

There was no encouraging news here for those who were already frustrated by long delays.

CHAPTER 6

Traditional ownership of the sea's resources

The development and lodgement of land claims consumed a great deal of political and intellectual energy during the 1990s, but the parallel issue of the sea and its bounty was debated and fought over with equal intensity. Though perhaps less glamorous than the headline-grabbing issues of land and sea claims, the rights of the Torres Strait fishermen to their traditional resources needs to be understood as an important and unifying strand that brings land and sea claims together.

This particular phase in the Strait's political history has its roots in New Guinea achieving independence in 1975. In 1978, Australia and the new Papua New Guinea (PNG) signed the Torres Strait Treaty, though the treaty did not come into operation until it was ratified in 1985. Its principal purpose was 'to acknowledge and protect the traditional way of life and livelihood of the traditional inhabitants including their traditional fish and traditional movement' (Article 10.3 cited in AAP 2006a, p. 6). When the Commonwealth Government enacted the *Torres Strait Fisheries Act 1984* it became the law for fisheries in Torres Strait, although the treaty is 'basic to the legislative process' (Altman et al. 1994, p. 6). Prior to the Act both Torres Strait Islander and non-Islander fishers held Queensland Transferable Vessel Holder (TVH) fishing licences, which allowed them to work the east coast of Australia and the Torres Strait. Then, under the Act, the following commercial fishing licences came into use:

- *Traditional Inhabitant Boat (TIB) licences, also known as 'community licences', were open to Torres Strait Islanders only; there was no limit on the issue of TIB licences.*

Throwing off the Cloak

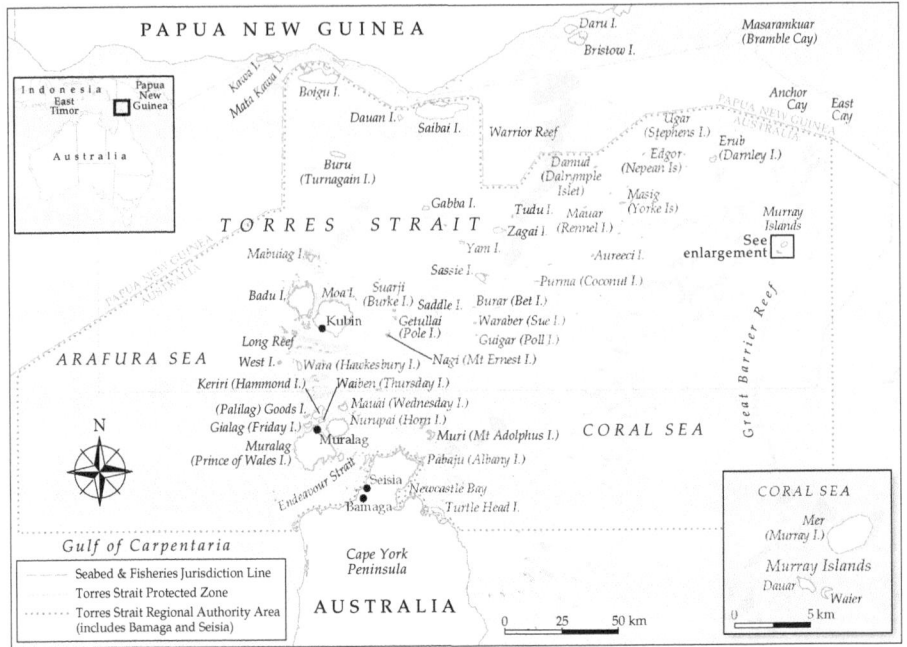

Torres Strait Region showing the Torres Strait Protected Zone, Fisheries Jurisdiction Lines and Torres Strait Regional Authority Area.

- *The TVH licences were now open only to non-traditional fishers who could demonstrate a history of operating in the fisheries. No new licences were granted after 1988, and non-traditional fishers wishing to fish in Torres Strait had to purchase a TVH licence from an existing operator.*

Islander fishers could retain their old TVH licences, allowing them to fish the east coast as well as Torres Strait, or they could sell those licences and take up a Torres Strait-only TIB licence. All but two fishermen sold their original TVH licences to non-Islander fishers (*TN* 1–7 February 2002, p. 4). Thus, almost all traditional fishers operated under the new TIB community licences.

Under the treaty a Torres Strait Protected Zone ('the Zone') was established and the two nations agreed on the extent of fishing effort (in respect to vessels and fishing technology) allowed in their respective areas of the zone. However, Torres Strait Islander lawyer Heron Loban argues that 'Torres Strait Islanders [were] not a party to this treaty, and protecting and preserving Torres Strait culture [was] not a primary concern' for its designers (Loban 2002, p. 1).

An obligation of the Australia–PNG treaty was to monitor 'the impact of commercial fisheries on the marine environment and species traditionally utilised [by] customary fishers' (Altman et al. 1994, p. 1). It, and associated legislation, established a 'regulatory regime' on the basis of 'commercial catch-sharing between Australia and PNG', and this regime included the setting up of the Torres Strait Protected Zone Joint Authority (the 'Joint Authority') in 1988 — a Commonwealth–state body 'responsible for monitoring ... the jointly managed fisheries and ... formulation of policies and plans for their management' (p. 3). The sole members of the Joint Authority, and so responsible for the Zone's management, were the Commonwealth and Queensland ministers for fisheries. Adding to the layers of complexity, both Commonwealth and state governments had their own statutory bodies: the Commonwealth, its Australian Fish Management Authority (AFMA) and Queensland, the Queensland Fish Management Authority (QFMA). Queensland enacted its own *Torres Strait Fisheries Act* in 1984, though it could not contravene the Commonwealth provisions.

The Joint Authority managed the prawn, tropical rock lobster, Spanish mackerel, pearl shell, dugong, turtle and barramundi fisheries. Prior to 1999, when a single jurisdiction was put in place, the QFMA managed trochus, mud crab, bêche-de-mer, shark and line fishing (except Spanish mackerel). The Joint Authority had a structure of consultative and advisory bodies with non-voting Torres Strait Islander representation nominated by the ICC but, while they were set up as advisory and consultative bodies, there was concern over whether the island fishers' recommendations would ever be implemented.

For a decade, island fishers had struggled to have their decision-making inputs into fisheries management strengthened. Simultaneously, island leaders were calling for recognition of their property rights in their seas. Mer chairperson Ron Day vehemently claimed:

> Our traditional law says that our boundary runs from the top of the hill under the sea where the bed of the resources are. The water can be common ground but not the bed and the resources — that's what we claim ... Our area should be left alone for us. (TN 18–25 June 1998, p. 5)

Single jurisdiction management

Clearly this situation was ineffective, and in 1996 the Joint Authority asked Indigenous and non-Indigenous fishers in Torres Strait to give their views on a proposal to establish a 'single jurisdiction management system' for the Zone, with Commonwealth law having sole jurisdiction. The new single jurisdiction would also incorporate a 'streamlined fisheries licensing system' (*TN* 17–23 July 1998, p. 9) which it was anticipated would reduce the number of licences held by non-Islander commercial fishers and '75 Islander fishermen' would benefit from the reduction (*TN* 18–25 June 1998, p. 5). A target date of July 1998 was announced for its commencement. With the one Commonwealth body managing all fisheries, the Joint Authority claimed, it would be 'simpler, clearer and fairer for fishermen [and] help safeguard the future of the Torres Strait fishers'; moreover, it would 'ensure expansion of the fishing fleet as a reserve of the traditional inhabitants' (*TN* 15–21 May 1998, p. 1).

But some leaders were sceptical. They doubted that system would ensure any more local input and control or address Torres Strait fishers' concerns about overfishing. Their immediate concerns were about fish stocks and they wanted, as a priority, the authorities to check on current fishing practices. It was suggested that the Joint Authority did not even know how many unlicensed line fishers were operating in Torres Strait and what the effect was on marine resources (*TN* 27 March–2 April 1998, p. 3). In his Boyer Lecture in 1993, Getano Lui Jnr spoke about the effects of the management of the fisheries: '[We have] high unemployment, but very little control over our fisheries which have sustained our people throughout our history. We ... face governments and fishermen outside our region who deny our rights and who claim that our resources are for them to control' (1994a, p. 63). And, in line with his thinking on Torres Strait Islander control of this region, Lui said, 'It is totally out of our hands and we want a say in who gets the licences. What is self-government and self-management if we cannot have the controls?' (*TN* 27 March–2 April 1998, p. 3).

Two Islander fishers concerned about non-Islander encroachment and overfishing in traditional areas were Ben Ali Nona (son of the politically active Ben Nona) from Badu, and George Gesa, from Mer. They took matters into their own hands and, in June 1998, they were charged with armed robbery and dishonestly obtaining property when they intercepted a commercial non-Islander fisher and confiscated the catch of trout caught in what they asserted was their sea area. A jury acquitted them after a three-day trial when it was ruled that they had 'an honest claim' to the trout (*Australian Magazine* 26–27 May 2001, p. 30). Following this victory, Ben Ali Nona — who was deeply influenced by Eddie Mabo — changed his name to Maluwap, 'ocean fish' (*Weekend Australian* 2–3 March 2002, p. 25). Nona explained his and Gesa's use of such a strong measure thus (p. 30):

> To stand against the might of government in this country and the might of the commercial fishing, you are fighting a losing battle. But my ancestors are with me to do something about what has happened over the past 100 years. Our things, our rightful things have been taken away, which is why I had to take this stand.

Ron Day, Meriam Council chair, pointed out that they were defending their traditional rights to resources that had:

> ensured their survival through centuries ... The government must recognise that we are prior occupiers of areas not only for the land but the sea also. It is time we had control and management ... so that fishing can be a sustainable industry. People are coming in and wrecking the area and if the resources are over-harvested they will pack up and leave us with nothing. (*TN* 18–25 June 1998, p. 3)

He went on to explain what the sea and its resources meant for his people (p. 3):

> From our culture we deal with the land and the sea; we touch the sea and then leave for replenishment; we go to the land and its our tribal estate ... the sea contributes, supports the land. If we didn't have it [the sea] the land would suffer ... The white fishermen they only look at the dollars.

For its part, the Commonwealth AFMA persisted in its claim that the single jurisdiction would result in a 'reduction in [non-Islander] commercial fishing boats ... and prove a great benefit to Torres Strait Island fishermen' (p. 5).

Islander fishers had a long-held view that the non-Islander fishers were given more consideration than Islander fishers received from government. A young Erub fisher (2006) pointed out that with their freezer boats and seven or eight dinghies the non-Islander fishers 'take all the produce from the reef and stock it in their freezers and take it to the mother ship'. He said they came to the 'local boundary and fish on the neap tide in our area'. These boundaries were fixed, he said, but the government favours these commercial fishers because of their boat capacity (*TN* 3–9 July 1998, p. 6).

A group of non-Islander mackerel fishers, acknowledging the prospect of Torres Strait Islanders gaining recognition of their sea rights, proposed a voluntary government-compensated selling back of their licences to island communities. They reasoned that 'even the mildest form of sea rights would affect them [by] reducing their area by half ... making their fishing uneconomical' (p. 6). These fishers proposed that a scheme be implemented by 2001 to co-exist with the Torres Strait Islanders' then anticipated shift to greater autonomy. The mackerel fishers' proposal pre-empted a later government buy-back initiative.

The single jurisdiction continued to be discussed but was not implemented in July 1988. In December of that year, to the surprise of many fishers, ICC chair Getano Lui Jnr called a boycott of fisheries meetings and declared his opposition to a single jurisdiction with its new licensing arrangements, a system that he had actually 'helped to create and [had] signed off for implementation' (*TN* 4–10 December 1998, p. 1). Shire mayor Pedro Stephen thought a boycott was tantamount to 'throwing the baby out with the bathwater' (p. 5). Nevertheless, while the new management plan under Commonwealth law with its new licensing structures was expected to remove 99 per cent of non-Islander commercial fishing boats from the Torres Strait, enabling traditional fishers to reap the benefits, Lui was not satisfied (p. 5):

> *How can we have to get licences to fish our own waters? Let's be in control of our own fisheries, let's be in control of our own lives instead of other people controlling our lives ... We are not talking about management any more, we are talking about ownership of control.*

Finally, after a nine-month delay, the single jurisdiction for all commercial fishers in Torres Strait was set to come into effect on 1 April 1999 with the Commonwealth Minister for Agriculture, Fisheries and Forestry Mark Vaile's assurance that the move would ensure the 'long-term sustainability of the fisheries' (*TN* 2–8 April 1999, p. 11). Moreover, he reiterated that there would be more opportunities for traditional fishers, and that they would have greater input into the decision-making process. Under the single jurisdiction, state-managed fisheries would come under the Joint Authority; community licences for reef-line fishing, Spanish mackerel and tropical rock lobster would be replaced by a system of individual vessel licensing, and *only* licensed vessels would be able to operate in the fisheries for which they were endorsed. The Torres Strait Islander-only TIB licences would be issued to and transferable amongst Islander fishers for any or all of the commercial fisheries (with limitations in the prawn fishery), thus allowing for future expansion reserved for traditional fishers (AAP 2006a, p. 10). Traditional fishing for turtle, dugong and other forms of non-commercial fishing would be unaffected (p. 11).

Yet these assurances did not dissuade Lui. When the Joint Authority announced 1 April 1999 as the date for the introduction of the single jurisdiction, he stood firm. Fishers at a Badu meeting in April passed a motion rejecting the new system due to lack of consultation and opted to remain under community licences until 'such time where total control is recognised' over their sea areas (*TN* 28 May–3 June 1999, p. 1). Lui remained defiant and told the AFMA that 'Our people will still go out and fish as if under community licence and if they get caught, not only will they go to court but you will be taking the whole community to court'. Nevertheless, he indicated that he and his supporters did not 'write out' the single jurisdiction; they simply did not want to regret later something they had put in place earlier (p. 3).

The implementation deadline was extended to early July and then to late July as there was concern about new changes and decision-making processes (*TN* 25 June–1 July 1999, pp. 3–5). Islander leaders and fishers, at a meeting on Yam in late July 1999, confirmed their continued dissatisfaction with the single jurisdiction management plan and reaffirmed that they would continue to operate under community licences. They called for its suspension until Torres Strait Islanders had 'achieved a regional agreement for seas, reefs and resources' (*TN* 23–29 July 1999, p. 1).

Lui said that he would have 'taken a different tack' (*TN* 30 July–5 August 1999, p. 3) if he knew there was bipartisan support for autonomy in Torres Strait: 'We want to suspend it until we talk about the bigger picture of autonomy'. In turn, the Commonwealth fisheries minister replied that his department could not talk about autonomy; that matter, he suggested, rested with 'heads of government' (p. 3). At that meeting, a new consultative and advisory structure, with representation from each community to replace the existing 'unworkable and unsatisfactory' structure, was also considered along with a review into current licensing because of the effects of catch on people's livelihoods. As yet it had not been conducted (*TN* 23–29 July 1999, p. 1).

Then, in April 2000, a meeting was held on Thursday Island of all interested parties — including the two fisheries ministers — to once again discuss the new licensing arrangements in the hope of coming to a satisfactory position on the issue. At the conclusion, TSRA chair Terry Waia reported: 'We have achieved an understanding among ourselves and came to an agreement. I am confident that the new community licensing arrangements, which allow Islanders to maintain ... traditional fishing rights, will work for the benefit of our people' (*TN* 19–25 May 2000, p. 3). Waia added that AFMA had reiterated its support 'for the continuation of traditional fishing without licensing requirements' (p. 5), an issue of great concern. Those present agreed to trial the new licensing arrangements for one year and, if it proved unsatisfactory, further discussion would be held; otherwise, it could be endorsed for another five years (p. 3). And, in response to concerns about the consultative structure raised at the Yam meeting in July 1999, a fisheries taskforce was set up comprising 10 people six of whom were Torres Strait Islanders (*TN* 19–25 May 2000, p. 3) in anticipation of achieving greater input into decision-making in the fishery bodies. In addition, state cabinet announced the formation of a Queensland Fisheries Service and the appointment of a Fishery Advisory Board to advise the minister (*TN* 30 June–6 July 2000, p. 21).

In order to allay the fishers' ongoing concerns about their inputs into Torres Strait fisheries, the TSRA appointed Toshio Nakata as its Fisheries Project Officer in October 2000. Nakata aimed to set up incorporated fishers' organisations on each community and to seek their views on various fisheries' policies in order to present the Torres Strait Islander position to the AFMA (*TSRA News* December 2000, p. 3). In December 2000, as a result of Nakata's consultations, the TSRA endorsed recommendations put to it on behalf of all Torres Strait fishers for presentation to the AFMA. They were:

- *The development of a community and regional fisheries consultative and management structure within the Torres Strait Fisheries.*
- *The establishment of a full-time position in the proposed regional fishermen's body.*
- *The incorporation of the aspirations of community fishers in their respective Community Development Plans.*
- *The strengthening of relationships between fisher groups, TSRA, Island Co-ordinating Council (ICC) and the individual community councils.* (*TN* 5–11 January 2001, p. 21)

These recommendations were seen as belonging to a 'moment in time for Torres Strait Islander fishermen who have pushed many years to include them in the management of the Torres Strait Fisheries'. Some fishers thought that when implemented these recommendations would 'put to rest … their crucial concerns' (p. 21).

Torres Strait Islander frustrations

While their concerns about the fisheries continued, Torres Strait Islanders were also anxious about their native title rights to the sea. The tension of the ongoing fisheries and sea rights issues came to a head at a Maritime Summit to discuss sea rights, held in March 2001 on Thursday Island. The summit ended with a declaration 'giving the commercial [non-Islander] fishing fleet in the region a week to get out' (*TN* 30 March–5 April 2001, p. 1). They hoped that this action would move both governments on all issues to do with their seas.

While some Torres Strait Islanders disagreed with the earlier illegal actions of Nona and Gesa, there was widespread support for warning the commercial fishing boats away from around their islands (*Australian Magazine* 26–27 May 2001, p. 30). The Queensland acting premier responded firmly, asserting that the state government would 'not tolerate people taking the law into their own hands', and that Nona and Gesa's acquittal did not set a precedent for lawlessness (*TN* 30 March–5 April 2001, p. 3). He pointed out that Commonwealth legislation entrenched commercial fishing rights; that the National Native Title Tribunal was dealing with their sea claim (though in fact the claim was not lodged until November 2001); and that Queensland criminal law 'applies to the sea up to 320 km off the coast'. The fishers were reminded that there was a lot of support for autonomy from the Commonwealth government and it was suggested that 'this move is a huge step backwards' (p. 3).

Within days, the Commonwealth and state ministers arrived in the Torres Strait to listen to the concerns of the fishers. TSRA chair Terry Waia told them: 'This declaration is the result of my people's frustration that their rights to the sea are not being recognised. There are growing concerns amongst my people over the sustainability of our sea resources and we want to ensure that positive action is taken immediately' (*TN* 6–12 April 2001, p. 5). Time was a concern for long-time Meriam fisher Dennis Passi. He believed that fish stocks were diminishing and that the reefs were 'no longer plentiful': the non-Islander commercial fishers had 'wiped out the fish stocks surrounding Mer ... and within five or ten years there will be little left for the Islanders' (*Australian Magazine* 26–27 May 2001, p. 30).

When the Torres Strait Fisheries Taskforce met with Wilson Tuckey, the federal minister for Fisheries, in April 2001 he was told that the taskforce was moving toward completion of an 'improved fisheries management structure' (*TN* 13–19 April 2001, p. 10), started in mid 1999, that would alleviate some of the fishers' frustrations. Then, in the same month, Tuckey met on Badu with the Member for Leichhardt, Warren Entsch, officers from related Commonwealth agencies, TSRA members and representatives from most island communities. There was agreement on the following recommendations:

- *Islander fishers to have a direct line to management*
- *there be a review of the Torres Strait Fisheries Act and possible amendments*
- *it be stipulated in the Act that traditional fishing comes before commercial fishing in Torres Strait*

- *there be changes to the [Joint Authority] representation giving indigenous presence equal status*
- *as an ultimate goal there would be complete management and control of fisheries by indigenous people in the region*
- *evidence of the impact of commercial fishing in the region to be documented*
- *that there was concern for environmental damage from present commercial fishing.* (*TN* 20–26 April 2001, p. 3)

A major outcome of the meeting was the achievement of full voting rights for a Torres Strait Islander on the Joint Authority council, with TSRA chair Terry Waia subsequently endorsed for this position (p. 3).

It is important to remember that these recommendations resulted from many meetings, negotiations and discussions over a lengthy period of time. The federal minister presented to the meeting the possibility of a buyback of licences from the commercial fishers but his impression at this time was that it was not 'very favourably met' (p. 15) — an issue that became pivotal to greater traditional participation in commercial fishing. Meanwhile the people, accustomed to the slow turning of the wheels of government when it came to changes for their benefit, may have had reason for some optimism after this meeting.

Concern for resources

Early in 2002 there was particular concern amongst Islander fishers about the tropical rock lobster industry, and they lobbied the state government to further regulate the industry and impose a four-month closure 'to go some way to protect the breeding stock' (*TN* 1–7 February 2002, p. 4). They also wanted to prevent non-Islanders with large, well-equipped boats from 'pulse fishing' — in which operators extend the season by moving from one area to another — and to restrict the rock lobster fishery to local fishers to prevent exhausting stocks that provided the necessities for many island families. One fisher said the outsiders were 'feathering their own nests' and keeping his people in poverty by bringing in big boats with large crews. Another fisher claimed that fishing was their bread and butter and he wanted all commercial fishing done by Islander fishers 'so that the economy is brought in, and kept in, Torres Strait' (*TN* 8–14 February 2002, p. 2).

In March of that year, TSRA chair Terry Waia and taskforce chair Maluwap Nona agreed that the fishing industry was approaching a 'crossroads in its management structure and negotiations are needed for a smooth transition process' (*TN* 8–14 March 2002, p. 28). Simultaneously, Commonwealth and state agencies were warning non-Islander fishers in the rock lobster, line and mackerel fisheries about long-term management developments and possible effects upon them; indeed, warnings were mailed out by the Joint Authority and placed in local newspapers explaining that 'any expansion of fishing ... after today's date' would not be recognised under the new licensing arrangements (AAP 2006a, p. 21). This raised non-Islanders' concerns about future licensing and catch allocation. But this seemingly positive development failed to dissuade Islander fishers from wanting further negotiations to ensure a 'management structure that recognises traditional inhabitants' rights' (*TN* 8–14 March 2002, p. 28), and Nona warned that the industry was entering a crucial stage: 'We want negotiations to continue at the highest level and for communication lines to remain open to facilitate the creation of a system that will empower Torres Strait fishermen' (p. 28).

The application of the cut-off date in the warning notice resulted in tensions between the groups that became the focus of a meeting on Mer in April 2002 when Islander fishers sought exclusive access to the region's fish and non-Islander fishers their right to fish in the region (*TN* 26 April – 2 May 2002, p. 5). Islander fishers developed options designed to reduce the tension in the reef-line fishery. While most participants thought it was a productive meeting, non-Islander boats were sighted around reefs west of Mer less than 24 hours later, and they were given warning to stay away from reefs 'on which Island fishers are most dependent' (p. 5). Toshio Nakata of the inner islands' fishermen's association said Indigenous and non-Indigenous fishers in the rock lobster industry were 'enjoying good relations' (*TN* 28 February–6 March 2003, p. 4). Nevertheless, in 2003 it was reported that non-Islander fishers were still fishing close to Nurupai (Horn Island), Mawain (Wednesday Island) and Dollar Reef. Nakata questioned why these ocean going freezer boats come to island communities when they are aware that the 'indigenous fishermen are limited in their capacity and distance they can work' (p. 4). A Badu council employee (2006) explained that 'Commercial fishermen can fish in Torres Strait. There is a gentleman's agreement not to come near the communities'. He continued vehemently 'I know for sure the government wants to protect the commercial, so it's ...still a big fight going on with government over commercial mob. We want what is ours'. It is difficult to know how many non-Islander fishers breached this oral agreement but any breach greatly concerned island fishers.

Revolutionary new consultative structure

When two years' work by the Fisheries Taskforce ended it had completed a proposal, developed from input from the fishers and endorsed by the

TSRA, for a management and consultative structure for the Torres Strait fisheries. Then, with the demise of the taskforce on 30 June 2002, the TSRA announced that it would strengthen its internal portfolio representation in the fisheries by the creation of a Fisheries Committee comprising representatives from the six island clusters with Terry Waia, as its first chair (*TN* 5–11 July 2002, p. 5). It would advise the Joint Authority on regional management issues. It was revolutionary as it dramatically increased Indigenous representation in fishery management to 24. Waia was convinced that 'The struggle for equal representation … will come to an end and a new era of cooperatively addressing outstanding issues will begin' (*TN* 13–19 December 2002, pp. 3-4).

Douglas Jacob from Nurupai questioned TSRA's claim that 'fishing control has been revolutionised' while it was also claiming the accolades for the new fisheries initiatives (*TN* 31 January–6 February 2003, p. 10). Jacob suggested that the taskforce, with Maluwap Nona as the driving force, had done the hard work. He criticised the AFMA and the ICC for their inaction. Moreover, low Islander representation suited the non-Islander fishers who did not want to give Indigenous fishers a 'fair go'. Island fishers, he said, were asking for greater control and decision-making input 15 to 20 years ago and calls for a new management structure became 'especially relevant beginning with meetings held in 1999, firstly at Badu and then Yam Island' (p. 10). Furthermore, island fishers were still not making decisions even though TSRA said the inclusion of its chair on the Joint Authority as an 'equal' member would remedy this. So, he asked, 'What has changed? Instead of ICC we now have TSRA running the show … AFMA is still, or may be even more, involved than before … it's still in the hands of government and not Indigenous fishermen' (p. 10). Of course there were those who claimed that active representation in the Joint Authority structure, quadrupled to 24, was resulting in a real impact on the decision-making process (*TN* 13–19 June 2003, p. 23).

Addressing sustainability of stocks

Logbooks recording the catch in the commercial finfish fishery comprising the reef line and Spanish mackerel fisheries had been mandatory from 1988. These logbooks recorded effort and indicated the related impact on resources. Unfortunately, logbook catch and effort data had been collected from only a 'handful of fishers operating larger vessels … [and] from over 400 fishers operating under TIB licences … few data have been collected'. The Torres Strait Fisheries Manager explained that 'running the "traditional" logbook programmes had been almost impossible because TIB fishers generally operate from dinghies' (*TN* 12–18 December 2003, p. 31). A Yam Island teacher (2006) working on Badu explained:

> These outboard motor-powered dinghies are usually smaller than six metres in length and fishing trips are generally completed in a day but if longer the fishers camp overnight on isolated islands. As an example, Badu fishers travel fifteen miles from their island to Warraber in these dinghies with no freezers. It takes two to three trips to take what they need to set up on sand banks and they work from there for three weeks with the neap tide. They fill up the dinghy and come in to Badu and unload into the freezers there and go back.

Islander fishers' activities were restricted by the size of their boats, making them vulnerable to bad weather and limiting the distance they could travel from the home community (Fairhead & Hohnen 2007, p. 1). Their marketable catch was usually sold to a 'community freezer' or privately owned freezers, then processed and freighted. Non-marketable catch was generally retained for food (AAP 2006a, p. 15). The informality of processing made it difficult to calculate catches (and, by inference, remaining stocks) and so in 2003 catch books were issued to Torres Strait seafood buyers to 'fill in [any] gap by collecting basic catch and effort information when fish are sold' (*TN* 12–18 December 2003, p. 31).

During 2004, in an effort to reduce TVH fishing licences in the rock lobster fishery and thus pressure on resources and related to the investment warning in 2002, the Joint Authority, by a reduction process, removed three primary vessels (a primary vessel in this context generally described a freezer boat), 13 tenders (that is, dories or dinghies), and six non-transferable dinghies (dinghies under 6 metres that cannot be freely transferred) from that fishery. To further reduce fishing effort a 30 per cent reduction in tenders was applied for the 2003 to 2006 seasons. Rock lobsters can be caught by fishers free-diving on shallow reef tops but others use a 'hookah' (surface-supplied air) to dive to deeper, open-bottom areas; in 2005, a spring tide closure prevented all fishers from working with these hookahs for seven days each month from February to September inclusive (AAP 2006b, p. 13). This closure was expected to reduce the effort by 15 per cent and would adversely impact on both TVH and TIB operators (p. 13).

A new round of talks was held on Thursday Island in early 2005, during which the management arrangements for the rock lobster fishery were discussed. Senator Ian Macdonald, the Commonwealth fisheries minister, exhorted 'everyone to fish sensibly and in harmony' because the rock lobster fishery 'is paramount to the economic development of Torres Strait' (*TN* 2–8 February 2005, p. 3). An assessment made by the Australian Government's Bureau of Rural Sciences indicated that, following two seasons of above-average lobster haul, the fishery was now over-fished necessitating 'longer-term arrangements' (p. 3). The Bureau looked to the Joint Authority, as the body tasked to manage rock lobster and finfish fisheries, and so in November the Joint Authority announced a 'raft of landmark reforms' in both (*TN* 16–22 November 2005, p. 14). These reforms, based on a public consultation paper released by Senator Macdonald and circulated to Islander fishers, were subsequently confirmed by both state and federal governments.

Under its treaty with PNG, Australia was entitled to 75 per cent of the resource haul in these waters, with PNG entitled to the remaining 25 per cent. The Joint Authority's reforms were intended to move toward greater allocation of that 75 per cent of the rock lobster and finfish fisheries to traditional inhabitants, from a 30:70 split between traditional and non-traditional fishers to a 50:50 split (PNG was entitled to 25 per cent of the Spanish mackerel but no entitlement in the reef-line fishery) by the beginning of the 2007 season. This movement of concessions was to be achieved through a voluntary open tender of non-Islander licences. In the longer term the Joint Authority anticipated a 70:30 allocation of Australia's entitlement in favour of traditional fishers (*TN* 16–22 November 2005, p. 14). The belief was that this overall shift in fishery management would provide greater economic and employment opportunities for island communities. It was also anticipated that a voluntary buyback of non-Islander licences would give these fishers an avenue to leave the fisheries with dignity and fair compensation (p. 14). Donald Mosby, TSRA portfolio member for fisheries, stated that the Authority's target was to 'gain exclusive rights to the total allowable catch (TAC) in both fisheries for traditional fishers' (*TSRA News* December 2005–January 2006, p. 2).

Not all Torres Strait Islander fishers embraced the changes. One fisher, quoted in the *Torres News*, was concerned that lobster licences could be lost:

> All sorts of rules are being talked about. They are talking about a 6 month season and quotas. They give us quotas and the PNG fishermen do what they like [while] we are shut down for four months … The quota system will force some fishermen out of the system next year. (*TN* 16–22 November 2005, p. 14)

Moreover, he said that boat numbers had doubled after the investment warning was issued because of a buy-out of dormant licences from non-Islander fishers. Other fishers believed at least five years of research was essential to more accurately gauge crayfish movements (p. 14).

The Torres Strait fishing industry was awash with rumours about the suggested lobster quota, the allocation to PNG's fishers and the proportion of the remaining catch between traditional and non-Islander fishers. Some Island lobster fishers believed that, even if they were to achieve the proposed 70:30 in their favour in 2008, financially they would 'be crucified' as the quota and restrictions would only allow for two months' work: 'and then what: "play with our thumbs" for the rest of the year? [Or] Tell our workers to come back in 9 months and leave a million dollars fishing vessel idle' (*TN* 23–29 November 2005, p. 6). There were similar concerns about the new structure for the finfish industry. The young Erub fisher (2006) was sceptical: 'Without big freezer boats it will be impossible for [Islander] fishers to take full advantage of even the 50 per cent split'. Non-Islander fishers, he pointed out, were able to use their individual quotas as collateral with lending institutions while Islander fishers, whose quotas were community related, could not.

The Joint Authority announced new restrictions for the prawn industry for the 2006 season, but this decision would have no effect on traditional fishers as they were not equipped to work in the area. Bluey Bedford, long-time fishery adviser to the ICC, expressed his concern that in 'thirty years that the prawn industry has operated the Islanders have not benefited'. Bedford believed this was a 'SHAMEFUL legacy of the past' and should not continue. He spoke of three prawning licences 'held in trust by the ICC' (*TN* 13–19 July 2005, p. 8) and recalled it had been intended that at least one licence would be used as a training vessel for those Indigenous fishers wanting to enter the industry (in the 1970s a government cray vessel operated for a short time with trainee Islander fishers). They had not been used, and Altman et al. suggest it was mainly because of a 'major financial commitment' (1994, p. 11). Nevertheless, Bedford's concern was that TSRA and ICC took 'the lead in disposing of these assets' (*TN* 13–19 July 2005, p. 8) even though, in 1997, a recommendation of the new deal (to be discussed) recommended allocating certain moneys to commence a prawn training program to enable the prawn entitlements to be used (*TN* 16–22 November 2005, p. 14). The upside is that using the proceeds of the licences, 'a buy-back of non-Islander finfish licences would result in fin fishing becoming a totally Torres Strait Islander enterprise' (young Erub fisher (2006)).

In July 2005, the Joint Authority ruled that it would implement 'a ten nautical mile commercial exclusion zone for Finfish for non-traditional ... fishers' around the islands of Mer, Erub, Masig and Ugar (*TSRA News*, December 2005–January 2006, p. 2). The exclusion zone would disallow non-traditional fishers from commercially catching finfish species, including Spanish mackerel, in those zones. Fishers from other island groups soon demanded that similar exclusion zones be applied to their areas and wanted the Joint Authority precedent to include them in legislation. Maluwap Nona said the fishers were calling on Prime Minister John Howard and new federal minister for Fisheries, Forestry and Conservation Eric Abetz to increase the exclusion zones to include 'all inhabited and uninhabited islands and cays ... throughout Torres Strait' (*TN* 8–14 March 2006, p. 11). Nona continued by expressing concern that health and employment were associated with their welfare dependency: '[Our] people need an industry that can take us off the welfare ... We want full-time work in the fishing industry, not this on-and-off welfare situation' (p. 11). Not surprisingly, the proposal for the exclusion zones raised at a fisheries working group meeting in March 2006, was not supported by non-Islander members and was deliberately neglected, arousing fears that it would be 'negated, diluted or put on the back burner' (p. 11). Indeed, an Allocation Advisory Panel appointed by the Joint Authority advised that the 10 nautical mile exclusion zone 'would be reconsidered' after it had completed its report on the fisheries (AAP 2006a, p. 24).

Independent Allocation Advisory Panel

In June 2006 Senator Eric Abetz, the Commonwealth's fisheries minister and chair of the Joint Authority, announced the establishment of an independent panel to report to the Joint Authority on the allocation of finfish and rock lobster concessions in the non-Indigenous sectors of the fisheries industry. The members of the Independent Allocation Advisory Panel were Federal Court judge Jeffrey Miles; fisheries economist Sevaly Sen; and the Pearls Producers Association's Bret McCallum. Senator Abetz confirmed that 'They have skills and experience to provide [the Joint Authority] with independent advice on the most appropriate ways of allocating the transferable quota and effort units in these fisheries that form part of the new management measures that will be introduced in 2007' (*TN* 22–27 June 2006, p. 4).

An earlier specialist group within the Joint Authority had already adopted a hierarchy of principles relating to finfish resources. These principles were:

- *protection of the fishery resources*
- *protection of the traditional way of life and livelihood of Traditional inhabitants*
- *enhancement of economic opportunities for Traditional inhabitants*
- *enhancement of economic opportunities for non-Traditional inhabitants and in a more general sense enhancing economic and employment opportunities within the Torres Strait region.* (AAP 2006a, p. 7)

The advisory panel acknowledged these principles, as well as remaining cognisant of the Australia–PNG treaty and the *Torres Strait Fisheries Act 1984*. The panel noted that the finfish fishery should 'proceed to greater Traditional inhabitant allocation' on the following basis and reaffirmed the transition, described earlier, from a 30:70 split between traditional to non-traditional fishers to 50:50 and, in the longer term, to a 70:30 split in favour of traditional fishers. The process should be achieved through the purchase of non-Islander licences by a self-funded, open-tender process.

The advisory panel was asked to make two recommendations relating to the non-Islander commercial finfish fishery. The first recommendation was on a method to determine who should be eligible for individual transferable effort (ITE) fishing concessions. An ITE is a 'right to one of a number of equal portions analogous to shares in a fishery' (AAP 2006a, p. 5); the value of each ITE would depend on the annual total allowable effort determined in accordance with the Torres Strait Finfish Management Plan. The second recommendation was to be on a method of determining the allocation of the concessions between eligible fishers.

In considering eligibility, the panel's recommendation was based on material provided by the Joint Authority, collected and verified data, and consultations with interested individuals, traditional inhabitants and other stakeholders (pp. 21–23). It recommended that those in the fishery who should be granted ITE concessions were 'persons to whom the PZJA has granted a TVH licence under the Act where that licence is current… [in] October 2006' (p. 26).

In formulating a method to determine the allocation of ITE concessions, the panel examined the economic impacts on individuals, their economic position, catch history, use of licence, and effort history (pp. 29–30). A series of public meetings was held to seek fishers' inputs into the development of the formula. Following a lengthy and comprehensive inquiry the panel recommended that the allocation should be made on the basis of either the best of 'a fixed 2 per cent per fishing platform or the average annual catch of the best of three out of five years from 1 January 1997 to 31 December 2001 catch history scaled down to equal the remaining total allowable catch after allowing for base allocations' (p. 33).

The advisory panel carried out similar consultations for the rock lobster fishery, with corresponding recommendations to determine eligibility for a new Individual Transferable Quota (ITQ) concession and a method for the allocation of these licences. Like an ITE, an ITQ licence is 'a right to an equal portion analogous to shares in the fishery' and depends upon the total allowable catch (AAP 2006b, p. 5).

In considering eligibility the panel considered issues such as catch history, market values of licences and tenders (the dories or dinghies), residency in Torres Strait, longevity in the fishery, and Master Fishermen's Licences (pp. 16–20). It recommended that those who should be granted ITQ concessions were persons 'to whom a licence has been granted under the Act ... where that licence is current ... [in] October 2006' (p. 22).

To determine a method of allocation, the panel endeavoured to minimise the adverse effects on licence holders, applied Joint Authority advice on catch history prior to 2002, and took into account incomplete data from 1997 to 2005 (p. 27). It recommended that 30 per cent of total allowable catch be allocated among existing licence holders (including first tender) as a base allocation, with the remaining 70 per cent being allocated equally among remaining tenders attached to a licence in 2002 (p. 29).

The AAP's draft reports on both fisheries were submitted to the Joint Authority in August 2006 to be presented to its meeting in October. At the Joint Authority's meeting in March 2007 it was agreed that the way had been cleared for a voluntary Islander buyback of licences from non-Islander fishers in both industries.

The preceding description of licence and catch allocations, distribution of access to the ocean's resources, and the fine detail of percentages available to Australian versus PNG or commercial versus Islander fishermen may appear overwhelming to anyone not directly involved. However, an understanding of the seemingly endless rounds of talks, inquiries and negotiations over these fundamental rights are vital if one is to appreciate the Torres Strait Islander people's viewpoint of how these issues influence their aspirations for a form of government that allows greater autonomy or self-regulation based on their major potential economic resource: a viable fishing industry. From a distance the minutiae of changes in licensing and allocation of sea resources may appear as a sideline to 'real' history, but the outcomes of these events will not only regulate non-Islander commercial fishing in the Strait but also slow down the rate at which fish resources — seen by Islanders as a key to their autonomy — are being depleted.

For two decades the people of Torres Strait struggled with governments and those who take mercilessly from their seabed resources. Perhaps the most articulate expression of what all this means to a Torres Strait Islander was delivered by the Eastern island leader (2007) when he was asked, at a sea claim conference, 'What are you claiming, are you claiming the sea, the beach or the resources?' He replied, 'If an oil tanker ran aground it kills the bed, kills the fish and it kills me. So this is what we are claiming the bed and the fish because it's our first priority as far as our survival'.

CHAPTER 7

Greater autonomy

When the Torres Strait Regional Authority (TSRA) came into operation in 1994 it was foreshadowed as a 'transitional arrangement', a basis for a 'progressive negotiated movement towards greater regional autonomy' in Torres Strait (Sanders 1994, p.1). With the agreement of the people of Torres Strait and the Commonwealth and Queensland governments, it was tasked to 'develop proposals to achieve self-determination in stages' (p. 1). This final chapter traces that development.

On 15 July 1996, TSRA chair Getano Lui Jnr met with the prime minister John Howard to discuss autonomy for Torres Strait and, in August, the Commonwealth minister for Aboriginal and Torres Strait Islander Affairs requested the House of Representatives Standing Committee on Aboriginal and Torres Strait Islander Affairs (the Committee) to inquire into and report on 'greater autonomy for the people of the Torres Strait' (Sanders 1999, p. 1). The Committee's terms of reference were to inquire into and report on:

1. *Whether the people of the Torres Strait would benefit from a greater degree of autonomy*
2. *If so, what forms should a greater degree of autonomy take*
3. *What implications would greater autonomy have for Torres Strait Islanders outside the Torres Strait region including whether the Aboriginal and Torres Strait Islander Commission (ATSIC) or the Torres Strait Regional Authority should represent the interests of such residents.* (HRSCATSIA 1997, p. xii)

The Committee visited Torres Strait in October 1996 to gain people's views on the benefits, form and implications of greater autonomy.

Public hearings were held on Thursday Island and in Townsville and Cairns. Meanwhile, the TSRA gained feedback through community consultations. In August 1997, the Committee tabled its report to parliament: *Torres Strait Islanders: A new deal (a report on greater autonomy for Torres Strait Islanders)*. The report, sometimes referred to as 'the New Deal report', contained 25 recommendations. The tabling of the report augured well for Lui's proposed timeline of 2001 for greater autonomy in Torres Strait.

The Committee proposed a new governance structure that incorporated a parliamentary-style body titled the Torres Strait Regional Assembly, open to *all* residents of Torres Strait as both electors and elected officeholders. The revolutionary aspect of this new body was that it would replace the TSRA, the Island Coordinating Council (ICC) and the Torres Shire Council, but the 17 island community councils were to maintain their separate identities.

Local federal member Warren Entsch saw the proposal as 'a positive step toward autonomy ... where the resources of the region will once again be in the control of the Islanders' (*TN* 12–18 September 1997, p. 3). There were, nonetheless, a number of difficulties with the proposal: clarification of the relationship between island councils and the Queensland Government; the need for Torres Strait Islanders to feel confident that their interests would be effectively represented by an assembly that also represented non-Islanders; and assurance that any government departments and agencies that consulted with the assembly would ensure 'consistency with the integrated service delivery approaches developed by [state] departments' when allocating funds (p. 7).

The Commonwealth 'backed away, somewhat half-heartedly' (Sanders 1999, p. 7) from the abolition of the Torres Shire Council, stating it was premature to consider its incorporation into the proposed new body and favouring a staged approach. Similarly, the Queensland Government asserted strongly that it would find it difficult to support the recommendation regarding the council as it was a state government initiative. Sanders suggests that Queensland was either being 'unnecessarily negative' about change in Torres Strait or it had a 'better feel than [the Committee] for the complexities and uncertainties of change in Torres Strait governance structures and the need to negotiate those changes carefully and thoroughly' (p. 7). The Commonwealth also reacted negatively to the Committee's recommendations on the issue of mainland Torres Strait Islanders, and Queensland failed to respond at all, seeing this as a Commonwealth issue. Nevertheless, TSRA chair John Abednego pointed out that the 'future structure of greater autonomy must be designed by our people' (*TN* 3–9 October 1997, p. 3) and that it was 'now up to us to look at the recommendations' (*TN*, 24–30 October 1997, p. 5).

Not surprisingly, one island leader who was totally opposed to the proposal to abolish the Torres Shire Council was its mayor, Pedro Stephen. Stephen reacted strongly to the recommendations dealing with council's constituency and the potential loss of representation, pointing out that 'This part of the report shows complete lack of understanding by the Canberra bureaucrats about the works of local government and the pivotal role it plays in delivering services to its residents' (*TN* 5–11 September 1997, p. 1). He expressed disappointment that Entsch was in favour of the report's recommendations and called on shire residents to make it known that they 'do not want their local government service delivery delivered to them ... by some large bureaucracy ... but want their own democratically elected representative Torres Shire Council' (p. 1). His constituents gave him strong support (*TN* 12–18 September 1997, p. 5).

In October the chair of the Committee, Lou Lieberman, visited Torres Strait 'to gauge people's thoughts on the recommendations' with an emphasis on the need to 'reflect the true feelings of the people living in the region' to any change to their governance (*TN* 24–30 October 1997, p. 5). Lieberman, in response to Stephen's opposition to the abolition of the council, explained his three-point rationale thus: because there was a 'geographic proximity' between the council's operations and the 'probable physical location' of the regional assembly, it would be more efficient to have the one governing body; the shire council did not represent a traditionally based and homogeneous Torres Strait Islander community in the way that the island councils did; and shire residents would not lose political representation (Sanders 1999, p. 5).

Mayor Stephen demanded to know where the 'huge administration cost savings' would be made, and in relation to the second point claimed that there was a 'hidden political agenda to neuter the rights of non-indigenous residents' (*TN* 19–25 September 1997, p. 3). He claimed that the recommendations were undemocratic because people on the inner islands wanted to elect their own local council just as did those on the outer islands. This Torres Strait Islander mayor was defending the rights of non-Indigenous residents, something that would not have happened even five years previously; until 1994 the shire council was an 'enclave ... of non-Islander interests', and it was only after this time that Torres Strait Islanders began to gain a foothold, resulting in a greater balance of interests (Sanders 1999, p. 4).

Apart from the sticking point over the abolition of the shire council, Stephen did conclude that the report made 'good sense' and was a step forward toward regional autonomy (*TN* 5–11 September 1997, p. 1). The next step was to use the recommendations as a basis for a form of governance in Torres Strait to give people greater autonomy in determining their own affairs.

The Committee was also asked to investigate the implications of greater autonomy for Torres Strait Islanders living on the mainland. These people were represented on ATSIC through the Torres Strait Islander Advisory Board and the Office of Torres Strait Islander Affairs, a situation they described as 'unsatisfactory' (Sanders 1999, p. 6). The mainland Islanders' solution was an Australia-wide Torres Strait Islander authority entirely separate from ATSIC, but the Committee dismissed this possibility as 'impractically expensive and a duplication of ATSIC' (p. 5). Moreover, in considering a united representative structure for the two groups it concluded their needs were different: the focus was on services in Torres Strait while on the mainland it was culture. Sanders suggests that the Committee had failed to 'come to grips with the strength of the depth of Islanders' feelings of distinctiveness and separateness from [mainland] Aboriginal Australians and their dissatisfaction with being placed in a combined Aboriginal and Torres Strait Islander representative structure' (p. 6). Nonetheless, the Committee concluded that the mainlanders should remain under ATSIC.

TSRA chair John Abednego described the New Deal report as 'comprehensive, proposing some radical changes and deserving of careful consideration' as well as a need for 'dialoguing with all levels of government' (*TN* 3–9 October 1997, p. 4). However, he also looked beyond the political structure to practical issues related to greater autonomy, such as infrastructure and health: 'How can autonomy exist and be relevant if you live in substandard conditions?' he asked. He was far-sighted enough to realise that 'greater autonomy without the financial assistance to improve the level of basic infrastructure ... is not worth having' (p. 5) and called on state and federal governments to jointly fund major infrastructure development over 10 years. Each government responded in October 1998 by pledging A$15 million as the first phase of a A$60 million infrastructure program to be implemented over three years.

Greater Autonomy Taskforces

A community meeting attended by the chairs of the three main local governing bodies — John Abednego (TSRA), Getano Lui Jnr (ICC) and Pedro Stephen (Torres Shire Council) — was held in March 1998. The meeting resulted in two outcomes. One was the formation of a seven-person Greater Autonomy Taskforce comprising the three chairs, plus George Mye (Erub), Bakoi Bon (Mer), Margaret Mau (Dauan) and Pearson Wigness (Kaurareg). The other was a 'vote in favour of the establishment of a Torres Strait regional government body to represent all residents in Torres Strait' (*TN* 13–19 March 1998, p. 1). The meeting agreed that there was urgency for more community consultation and that the taskforce would travel to all communities to explain the 25 recommendations from the Committee's report.

But divergent views were soon to become apparent. Veteran politician George Mye agreed with mayor Stephen that the Torres Shire Council, being an autonomous entity, should not be abolished; however, he also asserted that the shire council should 'move into the line-up' with island councils for a share of the spoils resulting from the abolition of the TSRA and ICC. Mye also rejected as inappropriate the title Torres Strait Regional Assembly on the grounds that (*TN* 22–28 May 1998, p. 28):

- *the implication is that people other than indigenous can be elected*
- *it subjects ailan [Islander] people to a delineated area of space, unable to represent their cause nationally*
- *the title must be one asserting the ethnic sovereign status of the islands and people as a separate indigenous nation.*

Mye suggested the title Federal Assembly of Islands as being more appropriate. The federation would better reflect core *ailan* feelings of control of their own island and territorial waters and their loathing of outside interference in their affairs (p. 28).

After 12 months of relative inactivity the taskforce convened a three-day public meeting on Thursday Island with the objective of arriving at a majority position on a model of governance that would receive both state and federal endorsement (Sanders 1999, p. 8). Francis Tapim, a mainland Torres Strait Islander, had been added to the taskforce and he and other mainlanders attended the meeting. The meeting developed three key positions: first, it supported the formation of a central, culturally appropriate governing structure to cover all permanent residents of the Torres Strait and Torres Strait Islanders on the mainland; second, it intended working towards territory status through negotiating for increased control over existing federal and state functions; and third, it intended maintaining all existing local government structures and their responsibilities (p. 8). In other words, mainland Torres Strait Islanders would be included in the proposed body and the Torres Shire Council would continue to exist, both positions being contrary to the Committee's recommendations.

The goal of territory status was not a position entirely ruled out by the Committee, but its report had indicated that this status could only be achieved 'when the region secures a greater degree of economic self-sufficiency' (HRSCATSIA 1997, p. 39). Getano Lui Jnr was aware of this fact and reminded the meeting that TSRA had to manage and control the fisheries in Torres Strait because that was vital to their economic independence (*TN* 12–18 March 1999, p. 17; and see previous chapter). Henry Garnier held a similar position: 'It is important that Torres Strait Islander people fully participate in the management of the fisheries, because they will ensure the economic benefits come back into the region and provide an opportunity for the traditional ways to be maintained' (HRSCATSIA 1997, p. 74). Commonwealth and state government participation was not ruled out: the former would have a continuing involvement through defence, customs and quarantine and would be the principal funding body; while the latter would continue to provide services (p. 39).

In April 1999, TSRA chair John Abednego briefed Prime Minister John Howard and Queensland Premier Peter Beattie on the outcome of the March meeting. Both politicians confirmed their support for autonomy, but Premier Beattie added the proviso that the Torres Strait remain a part of Queensland. Abednego stressed that both Indigenous and non-Indigenous residents were involved and explained that Torres Strait Islanders wanted 'more direct say and control' over the policies that affected them: 'Currently these decisions are made in Canberra and Brisbane and very often contradict the view of our people. This system is therefore unsuitable' (*TSRA News* April 1999, p. 1). Meanwhile, the taskforce continued to visit communities to 'gain a regional view of autonomy and provide every individual ... with the opportunity to state their case, thereby arriving at a position to present to the state and federal governments' (*TSRA News* September 1999, p. 1).

While there was much talk about autonomy, a large number of people were unsure about what it really meant. The Committee reported that 'Autonomy is a multifaceted concept and different users ... tend to emphasise different interpretations of its meaning ... When distilled, the meanings have tended to focus on political/structural, economic and cultural interpretations' (HRSCATSIA 1997, pp. 34–5). Getano Lui Jnr agreed that people had 'different perceptions of what autonomy was' (*TN* 12–18 March 1999, p. 17), and this fact was not lost on others. In a TSRA video, *Greater autonomy*, an island leader said, 'If you spoke to ten different people about the meaning of Torres Strait autonomy, you would have ten different answers' (TSRA 2001). Some saw economic independence as essential, others did not. Mayor Stephen believed that the basis was 'how to empower' people, others thought autonomy was 'just not a word' our people understand (TSRA 2001). A female Badu teacher (2006) said, 'Autonomy. I heard someone talking about it once but ordinary people don't talk about it. If you have mines you can have autonomy, but we have nothing behind us. We have not got that economic base to help us'. And Labor senator Jan McLucas (2006), who has followed the autonomy debate for 20 years, said she did not know 'whether there is a clarity of understanding of what the term means in Torres Strait'. Despite this confusing bag of perceptions, leaders continued to stress that there was a need for the widest possible consultation and input into the debate.

At a meeting on Saibai on 18 September 2000, the three leaders of the main governing bodies — now Terry Waia (TSRA), Henry Garnier (ICC) and Pedro Stephen (Torres Shire Council) — formed a new taskforce as the original taskforce had made 'very little headway' (*TN* 22–28 September 2000, p. 13). Their plan was to collect information to develop a discussion paper to present to the TSRA board in December and, once endorsed by the board, the three leaders intended to return to the communities to gain feedback. From this feedback they hoped to 'develop a model for autonomy to present to the government in June 2001' (*TSRA News* October 2000, p. 1).

By this stage Getano Lui Jnr's vision for new governance in Torres Strait by 2001 was unachievable. Sanders suggests that opportunities may have been missed but 'in the final analysis it would seem … [it] was just bad timing' (1999, p. 11). Sanders and Arthur pointed out in 2001 that 'Islanders have a number of issues to sort out among themselves. They need to become much clearer about what it is they are seeking' (2001, p. 16). That said, it must be remembered that the TSRA, ICC and island leaders had for some years been occupied with complex planning and negotiations on issues closely related to autonomy — particularly land and sea rights and the struggle to gain more control over the Torres Strait fisheries. Throughout all this the various TSRA chairpersons had stressed recognition of Torres Strait Islanders' rights over these areas was essential to greater autonomy.

The preparation of the new taskforce's discussion paper proceeded, and in January 2001 the TSRA board members took it back to their communities for discussion and comment. The paper was explained over Torres Strait Islander Media Association radio and TSRA chair Terry Waia subsequently explained, 'Through this process we are not responding to a government report, we are building our own regional framework' and that an established position would be taken to government 'as a basis for negotiation' (*TSRA News* March 2001, p. 1).

It was a staged process that Waia knew would not be completed quickly. Meanwhile, other perspectives on greater autonomy were emerging.

Creative thinking on greater autonomy

The TRAWQ Community Council Inc. represented Thursday Island residents living at Tamwoy, Rose Hill, Aplin, Waiben and Quaratine. This organisation presented a model of governance drawn from the 'people's views of greater autonomy' that would create the opportunity for them 'to demonstrate their creativity in determining, managing and delivering services and programs that are consistent with local needs, appropriate and affordable education, and unique *Ailan Kastom*' (*TN* 23 February–1 March 2001, 'yellow pages' supplement). TRAWQ prepared and circulated a suggested framework for the re-organisation of both state and federal departments and community controlled organisations. Its emphasis was on improved social and economic status, something it was argued governments had failed to provide: people 'continue to suffer the great burden of ill-health and are relatively less able to participate actively in the social and economic developments of the region' (*TN* 23 February–1 March 2001, 'yellow pages' supplement.). In another move the residents of the Port Kennedy area of Thursday Island met to discuss what the autonomy model would look like and, importantly, to whom it would apply. There was concern that there would be a loss of Torres Strait Islander identity, and Romina Fujii — president of the Port Kennedy Association — commented that there were still 'a lot of different ideas about people's understanding of autonomy, and a lot of confusion on the issue' as a result of wrong feedback, but she stressed autonomy was 'for *all* people' in Torres Strait (*TN* 16–22 March 2001, p. 10).

In a letter in the *Torres News,* Michaelangelo Newie, a young St Paul's man, spoke of a governance where non-Islanders 'would pay tax and rates' to a Torres Strait Island Government — including on vessels in 'our territorial waters, aircraft in our airspace, and [on] all natural resources within our territorial waters' (*TN* 30 March–5 April 2001, p. 2). Under an economy at 'its highest level', this Torres Strait Island government would pay for all the region's infrastructure, ferries and helicopters. Newie was concerned about people's health, referring back to Community Development Employment Program (CDEP) gardening programs proposed in 1984 that had not been implemented, resulting in 'a Torres Strait nation grossly affected by diabetes, obesity and renal disease' (p. 2).

There was a flurry of meetings and expressions of ideas on greater autonomy during early 2001; accordingly, in October the taskforce called a meeting to draw together the various views on greater autonomy.

A people's movement: the Bamaga Accord

The taskforce urged all elected leaders to attend a special meeting at Bamaga from 10 to 12 October 2001 to discuss a number of models for greater autonomy. TSRA chair and taskforce member Terry Waia said there had been public recommendations for a regional referendum, holding forums, and more community consultation and these issues were to be discussed. People were also urged to submit their suggestions and ideas for discussion: 'the process will continue to be driven by the people through their elected leaders. This is a people's movement', he reiterated (*TN* 5–11 October 2001, p. 9). During four years of consultation and reporting, leaders had emphasised that greater autonomy for Torres Strait was a people's movement.

After a comprehensive nine-month consultation covering all communities and consideration of the people's views presented at the Bamaga meeting, TSRA put forward a new regional governance model (a regional assembly). Its vision was for:

> *A Territory Government responsible for the good governance and wellbeing of all people in the Torres Strait, at all times maintaining Ailan Kastom and promoting the development of the Torres Strait and community wellbeing through control of the region and its resources.*
> (*TSRA News* October 2001, p. 2)

The TSRA stated that the ultimate aim of the model was 'for a territory government, elected by all residents of the Torres Strait (Indigenous and non-Indigenous)' and that members elected from the island communities would 'decide on policies, priorities and direction for a portfolio or executive group' (p. 3). Made up of 21 members from Torres Strait Island communities, with an executive of six portfolio members and a chair elected directly by the members of the assembly, this new territory government would build on existing regional governance arrangements (that is, the ICC and the TSRA). Arrangements would be made through a proposed new Torres Strait Regional Authority Act, separating it from the ATSIC Act and allowing for direct election of members of the TSRA from island communities (p. 1). The government's key electoral features would be direct elections by all Islander communities, the election of a chair by the elected members and the election of a governing body with portfolio responsibilities by the people voting in clusters (p. 1).

This model foreshadowed the introduction of 'transitional arrangements through a new TSRA Act by March/April 2003' (*TSRA News* October (40) 2001, p 1). Whether the model, referred to as the Bamaga Accord, had arrived at a position in tune with all the people's thoughts and a basis for firmer negotiations with the two governments became a moot point.

A few letters of criticism of the Bamaga Accord were published in the *Torres News*. Percy Misi from Mabuiag was opposed to following the *Kole* (whiteman's) system of government and demanded that people be elected 'to represent the different tribes or clans ... to go to important meetings' (*TN* 19–25 October 2001, p. 2). Meriam man Nai Tapim asked 'Is the territory government yet another set-up system [like] DNA [and] DAIA ... [a] new high-tech system and dressed up program?' (*TN* 26 October–1 November 2001, p. 4). He queried whether Torres Strait people would 'again for the umpteenth time' be dictated to by 'party-governments and their associates' and called for a 'totally all Torres Strait people's government ... by Torres Strait Islander people, for Torres Strait Islander people' (p. 4).

However representative Misi's and Tapim's views were is difficult to tell, but they did indicate a nervousness that western influences may overwhelm Torres Strait Islander perceptions of the type of governance they wanted. For many people their memories, or the stories of outsiders' methods of governance told to them by their fathers and grandfathers, were not easily forgotten.

James Akee, unlike Misi and Tapim, believed their leaders were taking a 'momentous step for the future of our people' (*TN* 23–29 November 2001, p. 4). He supported the move towards territory status: 'The Torres Strait territory will fit into the Commonwealth of Australia like a hand fits into a glove', and he believed the 'political will from Canberra and Brisbane has to be formed but that will come if the direction from Torres Strait is unwavering' (p. 4). Daniel Reuben from Bamaga, who believed the people had freedom of choice, remarked that 'I sincerely feel that most of us are reluctant to change and the majority is ... complacent, apathetic and lethargic towards changing their political prowess and social order'. He warned 'once we make that choice we become servant to that choice' (*TN* 22–28 March 2002, p. 10).

The autonomy movement had been an on/off issue since 1997 but it was not an easy task to find an appropriate people's model with so many divergent opinions. But irrespective of these diverse views, the TSRA moved on by producing a video, titled the *Bamaga Accord*, and a pamphlet to explain what it saw as an historic decision on its preferred model for regional governance (*TN* 19–25 April 2002, p. 1).

The Greater Autonomy Steering Committee

On 24 May 2002, the second taskforce stepped down after completing its task of consulting all communities and facilitating the development of the Bamaga Accord. However, following public criticism of the Bamaga model the TSRA announced a public forum to be held on Thursday Island in order to 'bring the various views that exist to the table and discuss as a people how we want this process to develop and what our goals are in terms of creating a form of governance for Torres Strait'. There was a 'high level of enthusiasm ... for the forum' (*TN* 24–30 May 2002, p. 3). At the 200-strong forum, a six-person Greater Autonomy Steering Committee (GASC) was endorsed, comprising Pedro Stephen (Thursday Island), Getano Lui Jnr (Yam), George Mye (Erub), Emmanuel Namoa (Badu), Gabriel Bani (Mabuiag) and Bertha Natanielu (Thursday Island). GASC's task was to 'evaluate alternative models, consult with the general public and make its own recommendations' (Submission to the Minister 2003, p. 8). It was also directed to establish a secretariat and provide guidance to the secretariat to 'ensure its activities at all times reflect the aspirations of the Torres Strait people' (*TN* 31 May–6 June 2002, p. 5). However, to draw together the various models being put forward would not be an easy task.

At the forum, Adrian Bon from Mer followed up on his address at the Bamaga forum with his views on a proposed structure Mer *Ira Per* (governance of Mer) to benefit Torres Strait and the Northern Peninsula area. A Federation of Torres Strait would be formed from an 'amalgamation of indigenous landowners', including the Kaurareg people (*TN* 7–13 June 2002, p. 4). He reminded his fellow Torres Strait Islanders of the respect afforded elders in the communities before colonisation and saw the representation of elders from every community as an important element in his model. Bon did not want to 'mark time any longer ... We need to move forward with the grace of God' (p. 6). TSRA chair Terry Waia put another spin on the autonomy debate at a treaty conference in Canberra in September 2002:

> *[It] does not start with government systems and flags, it starts with each and every one of us as individuals because if we can control our own life, then we have a fundamental level of freedom that nobody can ever take away from us — that's where our sovereignty starts.* (*TN* 30 August–5 September 2002, p. 7)

Waia said his people were proud of their Torres Strait Islander and Australian identities and of what they had achieved, but modern Torres Strait leaders, he believed, must 'define a level of realistic sovereignty that our people want and that can be achieved ... [remembering] as our forefathers did that we share a region with others and we must co-exist' (p. 7). Bon and Waia put spiritual and psychological faces respectively onto the greater autonomy debate, indicating the people's deep and divergent feelings, but Joseph Elu, chair of Seisia, talked about the 'divided voice of island autonomy':

> While autonomy is the word on everybody's lips there are differences on how to achieve it ... [For some] it starts with the creation of a separate entity to ATSIC and a greater focus on economic development. To others it means creating a new territory style government separate from Queensland. Ultimately, the rift has had the effect of slowing the pace of change. (*Weekend Australian* 6 July 2002, p. 35)

Elu's last words were indeed prophetic.

Dissatisfaction with TSRA and the role of United Nations

The Kaurareg Aborigines living on Nurupai (Horn Island) were represented on the TSRA by a directly elected member, but felt that TSRA and the ICC treated them poorly, resulting in 'fourth-world living conditions'. Isaac Savage, a traditional owner claiming to represent them, declared that (*TN* 8–14 November 2002, p. 1):

> the people are reverting to traditional boundaries ... [We] have reclaimed half of Torres Strait [through land rights] from corrupt civil unrest streaming from years of neglect and misrepresentation by Australian governments and indigenous organisations.

The Kaurareg Tribal Council of Elders, however, made it known that Savage was not 'a spokesman for the council' and categorically refuted his assertion that there was any sort of civil unrest in Torres Strait or that the 'Kaurareg tribe has declared itself separate from the rest of Australia'. Indeed, the Council of Elders stated its belief that 'unity with other Indigenous groups and the government' would enable them to build a better future for their people (*Koori Mail* 13 November 2002, p. 16). The TSRA and ICC joined forces to dismiss the accusations against them, the TSRA claiming it had responded to Kaurareg community issues as they related to their wellbeing since 1994 (*TN* 8–14 November 2002, p. 1). Nevertheless, Savage's dissatisfaction over what he saw as 'moves to declare Torres Strait autonomy over their lands' led him to declare that 'Aboriginal traditional owners should not be represented by Islander people' (*Townsville Bulletin* 20 December 2003, p. 36).

The records of non-Indigenous researchers suggest that the Kaurareg people belong to the Torres Strait, though they have a long history of contact with their Aboriginal neighbours on Cape York (Moore 1979, pp. 259–60; Laade 1968, p. 145). But, in a conversation with the author (May 2008), Savage was adamant that the Kaurareg are Aborigines belonging to seven islands reaching from the tip of Cape York into Torres Strait. Indeed, the Cape York Land Council — not the TSRA Land Council — represented the Kaurareg people in their successful native title land claim to these islands, and Savage subsequently became chair of the Cape York Boundary Interim Committee that included members from the Kaurareg and Injinoo peoples, and Aborigines from tribes on the Cape.

Savage was not alone in his criticism of the TSRA. In January 2003, at a meeting of regional elders, frustrations caused a group of 10 to talk about the alleged failures that had occurred in the fight for self-government. They were scathing of the TSRA, of Philip Ruddock (the federal minister for Aboriginal and Torres Strait Islander affairs) and, to a lesser extent, the ICC. Veteran Elder statesman George Mye expressed his frustrations:

> It's been going on for too long. No one can come to our rescue; no organisation can take on the government, not even the TSRA can take on the government. Who is going to stand up to protect our rights? We are in a God-forsaken wilderness where the government hears nothing and sees nothing. (*TN* 24–30 January 2003, p. 1)

Mye claimed that Torres Strait was already a sovereign nation in its own right and that the elders 'were the most appropriate people to lead the way ... Give us self-government. We must force the Minister to listen to the people. Why does he listen to the TSRA which is appointed by the government and not the people?' (p. 13).

A further issue on his mind was what he termed an abuse of their hard-fought electoral franchise by Ruddock's decision to postpone TSRA elections from 2003 until 2004 so that they would coincide with local government elections. The postponement of the TSRA elections developed into a touchstone issue. Elder Flo Kennedy believed Torres Strait had been betrayed by its own people and that no government had been any good for black people: 'We have to get our own government ... they don't really understand us' (*TN* 24–30 January 2003, p. 1). TSRA board member Phillip Bowie relinquished his position on the TSRA Board as representative for Nurupai and Muralag in protest. He claimed that the federal government does not 'listen to the people' and pointed out that his term of office was for three years and that was all he intended to serve without a further franchise. He wanted people to believe they had power over the federal minister, not the other way around. Mye accused Ruddock of depriving Indigenous people of their democratic rights; when Ruddock responded by saying that he had acted on the advice of TSRA, Mye countered by stating that since the minister appointed the majority of its members 'their allegiance will be to him, not to the people'. The chairperson replied that the TSRA did all it could, but deferring the elections was 'the most cost effective way of doing it' (*TN* 28 February–6 March 2003, p. 3).

Again the letters pages of the *Torres News* became the forum for argument and counter-argument over the autonomy issue. Thursday Island's Kevin Savage said that Torres Strait Islander people had been:

> *trying for generations to get greater decision-making power ... since the region was annexed in 1879 to Queensland. Today we call it greater autonomy. But how do we get this greater autonomy? All of the ways we have tried has led us to a place that only looks like we make the decisions, or to places where we argue for years in the courts over the definition of 'rights' in Australian law.* (*TN* 13–19 June 2003, p. 20)

Savage pointed out Australia's obligation under the United Nations Declaration of Human Rights 'to help us achieve our rights to self-determination' (p. 20). The best way for the people to choose the form of self-government they want, he claimed, was through the United Nations' process on decolonisation. Ken Dun, a tutor for the Remote Area Teacher Education Program who had lived at Kubin for some time, added to the debate by suggesting that — as full citizens of Australia 'with the same access to democratic processes of government as other Australians' — decolonisation was not the way to go. Instead, he urged people to look at:

> *the situation of some UN trust territories and non-self-government territories that have taken the road suggested by Mr Savage ... How many Torres Strait Islanders look with envy at the lifestyle in the Western Province of our nearest neighbour PNG, a country that achieved self-determination in 1975?* (*TN* 26–30 June 2003, p. 2)

Those people living on the top-western islands did indeed have first-hand knowledge of this area from their visits to the villages along the Papuan coastline and would undoubtedly relate to Dun's reading of that situation.

Some weeks later, Dun described what he, as an outsider, perceived as a greater challenge on the road to autonomy: an indifference and apathy among people resulting from the long periods of delay, a theme already taken up by Reuben in March 2002 after the negative response to the Bamaga Accord. Dun claimed:

> Six years have now passed since the New Deal Report ... These years have been marked by flurries of great activity and long periods of silence. After the work was finished on the Bamaga Accord, the TSRA published its paper on Torres Strait Territory Government (October 2001), a good deal of importance was expressed by some at delays in implementing the steps towards autonomy. Now more than a year has passed since the special community steering committee took over the Taskforce from TSRA. Again there was silence, only two weeks ago when suddenly we read of a proposal for several changes to TSRA being placed before the Federal Minister, Ruddock. The only details provided in the press were that the number of TSRA representatives would be reduced from 20 to 6, that separate elections would be held, and that the Minister asked for a full submission. (TN 1–7 August 2003, p. 25)

He further suggested that the long delays may have caused many to become 'indifferent and apathetic' about autonomy (p. 25).

In September 2003, George Mye replaced Pedro Stephen as chair of GASC. At the sixty-sixth anniversary of the first Torres Strait Councillors' Conference he called for Torres Strait to become 'a territory of Australia — immediately' (TN 5–11 September 2003, p. 1). Mye continued: 'We are looking for a territory that will not be precisely the same as Norfolk Island, Northern Territory or ACT but something in the middle that will be a creation of Torres Strait'. He said he intended to meet with governments to formulate a 'tripartite negotiating table', and Father Dalton Bon echoed this with a demand for territorial status 'immediately' (p. 1). Ken Dun, by now a seemingly self-appointed watchdog on the progress of autonomy, pointed out that Mye — who had signed off on the TSRA policy statement on improved governance in February 2003 — was now 'ready to negotiate at a moment's notice with government' on a vaguely worded concept for territorial status (TN 12–18 September 2003, p. 14). Dun wondered how people could be expected to 'wade through the misinformation and confusion surrounding this vital issue and come to an informed decision', and asked how could anyone expect governments to take seriously the 'mixed signals coming from Torres Strait leaders' (p. 14).

For some Islanders, education is higher on the agenda than autonomy. An analysis of TSRA's performance by a Yam Islander teaching on Badu (2006) was that 'it gives the grassroots people some incentive to improve', but needed to apply objectives that would raise people's expectations, education and standard of living. A Thursday Island health expert (2006) believed that a bigger issue than autonomy was education: 'I think the way forward is education. We have tried to solve bigger issues of inequality and social problems but the only way real change will come about is through education. Even after all our struggles 80 per cent of children are still below state average.'

In all the circumstances it is understandable that there were questions about TSRA's performance and a loss of interest in the autonomy movement. Practically speaking, there was still no clear sense of what greater autonomy entailed, particularly as any genuine autonomy was dependent on final determinations of ongoing land, sea and fisheries rights.

The TSRA's proposal on improved governance

In February 2003 a proposal, developed by TSRA in consultation with GASC on improved governance for Torres Strait, was signed off by both parties. While an August edition of the *Torres News* carried a brief article on TSRA's next step toward the autonomy movement, the reality was that TSRA had already submitted to government its proposal to 'Improve regional governance in Torres Strait: Proposed TSRA Bill' (TSRA 2003, p. 8) in July 2003. The Bill was introduced thus (p. 3):

> As a step towards giving more prominent recognition of the aspirations of the people of the Torres Strait, the Commonwealth Government has previously agreed to establish the Torres Strait Regional Authority under its own legislation. This would separate it from the ATSIC Act. A draft Torres Strait Regional Authority Bill has been prepared for presentation to the Parliament.

In other words, the TSRA had resolved not to wait for GASC's work to be completed and proffered to government its own 'incremental adjustments' to the existing governance arrangements. The proposed Bill delineated the structure and operations of an improved regional government in Torres Strait, its members and their accountability.

The key element of the Bill was to have more democratically elected members on the TSRA board. Other reforms included:

- *separation of regional governance, administration and funding from community and local governance and have direct input into how members are elected*
- *a Torres Strait Regional Authority Act that would take TSRA out of the ATSIC Act but still perform the functions prescribed in the ATSIC Act, with the Commonwealth providing direct funding to TSRA*

- *the establishment of a Torres Strait Islander Forum bringing together Island community councils, the Torres Shire Council, relevant organizations and the TSRA to ensure full participation and accountability in decision-making in the Torres Strait.*

The TSRA waited for the government's reaction.

In December 2003, Getano Lui Jnr voiced his frustration with the TSRA for failing to implement reforms originally agreed upon by board members. Some of these, such as the resolution that the 20-member board be reduced to six members representing their respective island clusters, with all community members voting for the chair, were covered in the proposed Bill yet remained unacted upon. These reforms, Lui said, were intended to result in democratic elections; only two positions (Tamwoy and Port Kennedy) out of 20 were democratically elected at that time, with the federal minister appointing the 18 ICC chairpersons. Lui saw TSRA's failure to reform as a 'backflip of monumental proportions' giving government the impression that Torres Strait Islanders were not serious about self-government. 'It makes you look like we are indecisive, not unified, and frightened of change ... We are sending conflicting messages to the government' (*TN* 19–25 December 2003, p. 4).

However, according to the newly appointed federal minister, Amanda Vanstone, the TSRA was unable to unilaterally make the reforms. In a letter to Mye she justified her refusal to implement the reforms and referred him to former minister Ruddock's advice to the TSRA that there would need to be a thorough consultation process with all stakeholders, including the Electoral Commission (*TN* 23–29 January 2004, p. 14).

Mye was concerned that a newly elected TSRA would fail to push for the reforms; likewise, Lui had no confidence in TSRA's support for the reforms. Then, confirming their fears, less than six months after submitting its Bill to the minister, and to Lui's 'shock and dismay', the TSRA passed a resolution 'supporting the "status quo" ... to retain the present structure of TSRA' (*TN* 19–25 December 2003, p. 4). All this despite chairperson Waia's previous assurances. Mye fumed: 'We have had a gut full. What can we do?' and using his position as a 'senior leader' and Elder on GASC he called for a 'boycott of the upcoming elections' (*TN* 2–8 January 2004, p. 2).

The protest over the forthcoming 'non-democratic' March 2004 elections of TSRA board members built in momentum. A number of council chairpersons indicated that they 'may not accept automatic appointment to the TSRA if re-elected'. Masig chair Donald Mosby and Purma chair Francis Pearson confirmed they would boycott the elections if that were the wish of the communities. Torres Shire Council mayor Pedro Stephen, one of the two democratically elected members of the Board, supported the boycott as 'It is hard to stand ... when you know what the community wants and what the TSRA board represents are two different things' (*TN* 16–22 January 2004, p. 1). He opted out of re-election, saying that 'After looking at the internal processes in the ways TSRA operates I can see that there is no real commitment given to enhancing the aspirations of the people to establish a body that reflects true representation of everyone living in the region' (p. 8). Citing the failure of the Bamaga Accord and the TSRA's failure to enact the reforms (such as the reduction of board members to six), Stephen concluded: 'It is beyond me why these decisions are not being implemented' (*TN* 26 March–1 April 2004, p. 8).

In defence of the TSRA, Waia said that in 2001 the TSRA had moved to create a Torres Strait Regional Authority Act and reforms to the make-up of the board, the Bamaga Accord (which it endorsed), but Stephen and Lui themselves had led a forum to endorse GASC in order to develop new models of regional government. 'They killed off the Bamaga Accord', he said. 'This is 2004 and we are still waiting for Mr Stephen's steering committee to propose [an alternative] model' (*TN* 19–25 March 2004, p. 5). ICC chair Henry Garnier added his voice to Waia's, pointing out that GASC was empowered to develop a range of options for the future of Torres Strait but, he claimed, 'I have not seen any outcomes ... no feedback, no public meeting, nothing. This is what is holding up greater autonomy for Torres Strait' (*TN* 26 March–1 April 2004, p. 4).

In the middle of this debate came an ultimatum from Isaac Savage, a tireless advocate for the Kaurareg Aborigines, calling for the boundary of his people's land to be moved north to Bramble Channel as their recognised traditional islands reached from Cape York to north of Keriri. He believed his people were being 'dictated to by a shire council' and were 'treated like garbage'. He wanted Torres Strait Islander elders to 'sit at the table ... to discuss the boundary and other high profile and sensitive issues' (*TN* 21–27 April 2004, p. 1). In July 2004, the Cape York Boundary Interim Committee chaired by Savage met with newly elected TSRA chair John Toshie Kris, who described the meeting as a 'landmark step' and that there was a 'common desire among all parties ... to resolve some of the outstanding issues' (TSRA media release, 7 July 2004). These first few months of 2004 saw leaders struggle at every step as one obstacle after another was presented that delayed even a staged progress toward greater autonomy.

7. Greater autonomy

ATSIC abolished: what future for the TSRA?

In late April 2004 the Commonwealth Government announced that it would abolish ATSIC and that mainstream government departments would deliver most Indigenous-specific services. However, Torres Strait Islanders in Torres Strait were to 'retain control of an organisation [TSRA] that both represents them and delivers services' (Senate Select Committee 2005, p. 75). Conversely, Torres Strait Islanders throughout the mainland and other Indigenous people were to 'lose everything' (p. 75). The abolition of ATSIC meant that, unlike their brothers and sisters on the island communities, mainland Torres Strait Islanders would effectively be disenfranchised and unrepresented in any Indigenous body, and they doubted that there would be sensitivity to their needs in the mainstream delivery of services. Francis Tapim called for 'representation and respect' to be given to his people living on the mainland by addressing their need for finances and human resources (p. 75).

Mainland Torres Strait Islanders may have looked with envy at those in Torres Strait with their own representation via TSRA. In the Strait itself, however, there were still groups calling for the scrapping of TSRA. GASC, in a nationally distributed press statement, called for TSRA's abolition and the creation of a body called *Zenadth Kes*, a phrase derived from the languages of eastern and western Torres Strait to describe the place or area between Australia and Papua New Guinea. The GASC statement led retiring TSRA chair Terry Waia to question the reporting credibility of Corey Bousen, editor of the *Torres News*, claiming Bousen's bias towards his 'bed mates' in GASC (*TN* 12–18 May 2004, p. 16). Bousen rebutted this by detailing its not insignificant reporting for TSRA (against one article on GASC), and he compared TSRA's A$50 million budget with GASC's budget of 'nil dollars'. GASC chair Pedro Stephen gave his perspective on the issue: 'With the planned abolition of ATSIC the people of the Torres Strait believe now is the time to also abolish the TSRA and deliver self-government at the grass-roots through a proposed federation of island councils' (*TN* 5–11 May 2004, p. 1).

Isaac Savage also called for TSRA's dismemberment: 'The Aboriginal and Islander people need to be reunited and drawn outside of the racist separation brought about by a regional government administration [TSRA] which lacks the understanding of us blackfellas' (p. 1). Savage had already lodged an application with the Commonwealth to disband the TSRA as a 'racist and discriminatory organisation duplicating the services of ATSIC and gobbling up huge amounts of taxpayer funds for no practical purpose' (p. 3). George Mye declared 'The time is now for absolute change', and Getano Lui Jnr emphasised the need for 'swift progress with this issue' (p. 3). Robert Sagigi, the democratically elected chair of TRAWQ, added to the debate his strong and passionate beliefs (p. 9):

> *I do not see any reason for the existence of the TSRA once ATSIC is abolished and believe that the administration should be devolved or transferred to ICC or an appropriate regional structure established to reflect the wishes of the people. Funding should also be directly channelled to each of our local councils and the regional body to only provide technical support.*

It was clear, Sagigi said, that the TSRA did not represent the wishes of the people; instead it had developed a 'huge empire unto itself ... [and] I am boycotting any efforts by TSRA to justify its existence' (p. 9).

On the eve of his retirement, Terry Waia expressed amazement that GASC was calling for change when it was actually set up to develop models for public discussion. He asked if anyone on GASC was 'able to justify where this new mandate has come from' and pointed out that: 'GASC does not represent the Torres Strait people because it was set up to do a task, not bring about reform. The membership ... has lost the plot' (*TN* 12–18 May 2004, p. 16). If the TSRA were abolished, he said, programs would be mainstreamed and the A$50 million that the TSRA provided directly to the region would be spread among many providers. Federal member for Leichhardt Warren Entsch also expressed surprise at GASC's call for the abolition of TSRA and claimed TSRA was a credible organisation. Furthermore, he pointed out, no proposal for future governance was forthcoming (p. 16):

> *Even to the point where on the eve of the introduction of the Bill [for a proposed TSRA Act] myself and the then Minister Philip Ruddock received a deputation from the Torres Strait Island community leaders, including a current member on the GASC, where they pleaded not to introduce the legislation, as they required further deliberations.*

The request was acceded to: the Bill was withdrawn and no other proposal has emerged.

Three months after the debate over the future of the TSRA, ICC chair Robert Sagigi called for action 'now' to finalise a model for greater autonomy: 'There has been a history of too much talking and marking time and not enough action' (*TN* 4–10 August 2004, p. 1). He saw no justification for further inactivity and maintained that it was time to 'take a stand to develop once and for all a plan which will drive autonomy into reality' (p. 1). Sagigi spoke on the eve of the all-Island councillors' forum

7. Greater autonomy

on Badu on 23 August 2004. He stressed that 'decisions should be made by consensus,' and he urged grassroots people to contribute as they had been 'left out in the cold for far too long' (p. 1).

A united approach was essential and at the *Kuiku Mabaigal* Forum (KMF) on Badu, 11 decisions were unanimously endorsed. Among these resolutions were:

- *a demand that Torres Strait people be allowed to retain Island councils*
- *that a federation of island councils, Zenadth Kes, be developed to absorb responsibility of the state departments of Aboriginal and Torres Strait Islander Policy and Local Government and Planning and the federally funded TSRA*
- *that the Torres Strait achieve territory status by 2008 in accordance with the 1997 'New Deal' Commonwealth parliamentary report*
- *that there be a full and independent review of the TSRA*
- *a vote of no confidence be passed in the draft TSRA Native Title Strategic Plan and its endorsements and implementations be strongly refuted and rejected*
- *that the forum establish an independent Torres Strait Islander authority to control and manage fisheries in the Torres Strait on behalf of Torres Strait Islanders.* (*TN* 25–31 August 2004, p. 2)

John Toshie Kris stated: 'Where we are going from here is up to … the elders and the people of Torres Strait' (p. 1). At last it seemed some measure of consensus had been arrived at to give impetus and direction for a model of greater autonomy for Torres Strait. In the same month as the Badu forum, a senate committee held a forum on Thursday Island at which many Islander voices expressed their pent up feelings about the progress of autonomy and the hostility some held towards the TSRA.

The future governance of island communities and their relevance to the autonomy debate continued to be of great importance for Torres Strait Islanders. Twenty years after its enactment the Queensland Government finally realised that the 1984 Community Services (Torres Strait) Act was 'out of date and inadequate' for a people wanting greater control of their own affairs (*TN* 25 May–1 June 2004, p. 4). As a consequence, from 1 July 2004 the responsibility for working with island councils on local government matters was moved from the Department of Aboriginal and Torres Strait Islander Policy to the then Department of Local Government and Planning, Sports and Recreation (now the Department of Infrastructure and Planning). The proposal incorporated a councillor-training program designed to give councils and their communities 'a leading role in developing new community governance arrangements for Torres Strait' (*TN* 25 May–1 June 2004, p. 4). The Green Paper went on line in October 2005, with three basic options for local councils put forward for comment: retain the existing model; move to the Local Government Act model; or move to the Local Government Act model but with special provision for Island councils (DLGPSR 2005, p. 4).

Meanwhile, the TSRA and the Torres Shire Council put their differences to rest when they signed a memorandum of understanding declaring their intention to 'strengthen and familiarise an ongoing working relationship' (*TN* 1–7 March 2006, p. 3). Island councils were assured of their continued existence, but the exact model of local governance to be adopted when island communities came under the full control of the state Department of Local Government was still to be determined.

When ATSIC was abolished the TSRA was left intact, the Commonwealth Government passed the *Aboriginal and Torres Strait Islander Act 2005* — not the separate Act requested by the TSRA in its submission. The ATSI Act also failed to incorporate electoral changes along the lines requested in the TSRA submission: the minister was empowered to fix the eligible number of board members at 'at least 20 and not more than 23' (not the six stipulated in the submission); there was no provision for the chair to be democratically elected; and while there was provision for the division of the Torres Strait area into 'specified wards' it did not specifically state their number whereas the submission delineated six divisions with one democratically elected member from each. It is reasonable to conclude that the 2005 ATSI Act did not sit well with leaders who wanted a people's model of governance in Torres Strait.

In early 2006, Patrick Mills described 2005 as 'a year of political turmoil ... due to a leadership coup' in the ICC when its chair, Robert Sagigi, was ousted (*TN* 18–24 January 2006, p. 12). He believed Sagigi gave 'transparency' to the ICC and 'high hopes' for the people's dreams. Percy Misi questioned the ousting: 'Zenadth Kes people did not ... democratically ask for [Sagigi] to step down' (*TN* 26 October–1 November 2005, p. 8). Misi saw the obstacle to progress as coming from within the leadership. Even so, in early 2006 moves were afoot to revive the autonomy debate.

In March 2006, a group of Meriam elders, members of an organisation called the Mer *Zogo Le* ('sacred power') Association, called for 'the autonomy team ... to be revived vigorously from the current inertia to ensure the region achieves autonomy as soon as possible'. The whole debate, they said, had 'stalled and gone quiet for whatever reason' (*TN*

1–7 March 2006, p. 1). They saw more consultation with the people as essential to reignite 'the flame of autonomy' (p. 2).

Autonomy deadlines have been set and been missed, but not for lack of passion, commitment and desire on the part of Torres Strait Islanders and their leaders. As Sanders pointed out, the deadline of 2001 that Getano Lui set in 1993, although ambitious, was simply the victim of bad timing (Sanders 1999, p. 11). The Bamaga deadline of 2003 was also ambitious considering the complexities that entered the debate along the way. A further deadline of 2008, foreshadowed at Badu in 2004, has suffered the same fate as Lui's as there are still many issues to be resolved — not least of which is a majority consensus on a form of self-government for Torres Strait.

But, as Torres Strait Islander academic Martin Nakata points out, this lack of 'a singular perspective' should not be construed to suggest his people have 'lost their way'. He observes that gaining consensus is elusive 'when Islanders reflect or discuss within the collective the details of designs for the future and the ways to change practices in their own interests', much more so than in the face of external threats (Nakata 2007, pp. 211–12) such as the Maritime Strike, the sit-down strike and the Border Not Change issue. Thus, Nakata signals hope for a majority consensus in due course.

Reflexions

Ma nole ogog nazir siridge etakerwa, ma kei batimed bidbidem poipikak le pe taraisir.

Do not pick up shells from the shallow areas of the reef for they are considered dirty, go to the deep part and dive on the ledge of the reef where the shells are clean.

Extract from presentation by Ron Day (Mer) at the Rehoboth: Torres Strait Free Thinking Symposium, Thursday Island, 13 December 2007.

In this history I sought to open a window, however slightly, on the struggles of the people of the Torres Strait islands for recognition of their unique separate island identities, their pan-identity, and an emerging national identity under a form of regional self-regulating governance. These struggles are recorded with emphasis on the voices of the people. My reflexions in the following pages are a form of self-awareness — a turning back on myself to look at the text I produced (Sarup 1988, p. 49).

For over 130 years outsiders have imposed their beliefs and laws without understanding or respecting Torres Strait ways of being. The people who have lived on this archipelago for thousands of years claimed beyond any doubt that their islands and seas had been passed down to them for generations. With the coming of the outsiders these claims and their self-reliance were eroded so that resentment, frustration, resistance and disillusionment increasingly became factors as they struggled to have their voices heard.

There was resistance to the earliest interventions, resistance that built with the increasing oppression laid upon them by a racist and paternalistic government. Their resentment of that body and its administrators led to a cohesion of the individual island groups and a refusal to work their pearling luggers that were virtually owned by their masters, the government. When war broke out, people had high hopes that enlistment would be the catalyst to free them from state control: soon, however, disillusionment with their conditions of service led them to refuse to attend military parades.

In 1944 their call was for self-control with the aid of the Commonwealth and full citizen rights, and the enlisted men returned home with expectations of improved economic circumstances and a lifestyle more in tune with that enjoyed by white Australians. This did not eventuate. However, in the early 1970s, the Commonwealth Government now empowered to legislate for Indigenous Australians, enacted a form of liberal (welfare) colonialism as an attempted antidote to internal colonialism that gave Torres Strait Islanders a voice but one that could be muted and a far cry from self-control. They were again disillusioned when the Commonwealth proposed giving nine of their islands and surrounding sea to Papua New Guinea. They responded by expressing opposition in state, national and international arenas. A decade later the Queensland Government introduced new land tenure for their islands and they asked: 'How can we lease back what is already ours?'

In the 1980s a group of more politically seasoned leaders resisted governments by challenging discursive boundaries. Eddie Koiki Mabo and others began what most people thought was an impossible court action to gain common law recognition of native title to their islands. Other forward-looking leaders resorted to group pressure on the government to end the struggle for 'proper education'. Growing unrest resulted in the institution of a state government 'overarching regional body' with 'formal local government-type status', the Island Coordinating Council (ICC), while the Commonwealth Government cast around for a 'new representative structure for Indigenous Australians, the Aboriginal and Torres Strait Islander Commission', with its Torres Strait Islander arm, the Torres Strait Regional Authority (TSRA).

Nonetheless, frustrated leaders declared they were no longer interested in talk that was 'imbued with a welfare mentality'; they said their people were anguishing over 'loss of control of their land, their sea and their lives'. Their future depended on economic development. Initially, the TSRA was generally welcomed as a unique body with decision-making powers 'committed to the principles of self-determination, self-management and empowerment'. However, dissatisfaction with progress toward self-reliance escalated from about 1976 resulting in the late 1980s in frustration and plans for a secessionist movement; negotiations with and pressure on governments; and the call for a regional administrative body with emphasis on their unique identity. There were, nevertheless, early signs in the 1990s that augured well for Torres Strait Islander aspirations for self-reliance.

A major boost to the people's aspirations came in 1992 when, after 10 years of struggle in an alien law system, the High Court in the Mabo Land Case ruled that native title existed at common law — finally giving recognition that native title to their islands had been passed down orally for generations. Lengthy, expensive and frequently frustrating legal processes followed in order to achieve final determinations until, to their amazement, the state government extinguished native title on land that supported government infrastructure. Another struggle ensued until the government relented.

The Torres Strait Islanders are fully aware that self-reliance is dependent upon their sea resources for a solid economic base, and that common law does not recognise native title over their sea areas. With financial and legal support from the TSRA, the Torres Striat Islanders lodged a united sea claim in the outsiders' court system, and it is committed to fight for the broadest possible native title rights.

Traditional fishers were concerned about encroachments into their sea areas and the depletion of resources due to overfishing and abuse of licensing regulations by non-Islander fishers. They, too, were continually disillusioned when their inputs into fishery management were not taken into account. The Protected Zone Joint Authority introduced a single jurisdiction management plan, purported to give island fishers a greater share in resources. In November 2005, that Joint Authority announced a 'raft of landmark reforms' related to non-Islander licensing and catch in the fisheries that would result in a buyback of non-Islander licences, and the TSRA committed itself to gain 'exclusive rights to the total allowable catch' for island fishers.

Greater autonomy was the focus of a government report tabled in August 1997, *Torres Strait Islanders: A new deal*. However, its recommendations did not receive majority support and an acceptable people's model of regional governance was sought. Two successive taskforces were set up with this aim, followed by creative thinking about possible models, including the Bamaga Accord, but all lacked consensus. Dissatisfaction with progress resulted in the endorsement of a steering committee to 'evaluate alternative models, consult with the general public and make its own submissions'. In 2003, the TSRA presented government with its proposal on improved governance for Torres Strait. Meanwhile, island leaders called for more-democratic elections; the Kaurareg Aborigines wanted resolution of 'long-standing issues'; and the TSRA defended its handling of the autonomy issues and accused the steering committee of holding up greater autonomy. A year later, the Aboriginal and Torres Strait Islander Commission was abolished, leaving the TSRA intact.

Governance of island councils was to be moved to the state Department of Local Government, and people were asked to comment on options for the future of their local councils. Torres Strait Islanders were once again frustrated when the Commonwealth Government enacted a combined Aboriginal and Torres Strait Islander Act that did not provide for more democratic elections in line with TSRA's 2003 submission.

The TSRA was foreshadowed as a transitional arrangement and a basis for a progressive negotiated movement towards greater regional autonomy, although at the time of publication an acceptable model for regional governance is still to be formulated. However, the politically seasoned Elder George Mye is not defeated. He sees his 'style is being adopted' by younger leaders: 'I content myself to see younger ones come up and get hold of it like we did'. For him, the struggle for identity and self-reliance continues: 'The place belongs to us ... and when we have full control again that's the promised land and we are heading back there and we can see it but we are not just there yet'. Ultimate self-reliance means for him that the Torres Strait will be a 'Territory of the Commonwealth of Australia ... because I personally have no qualms about being an Australian. I have travelled around the world and I feel Australia is the right place for Torres Strait Islanders, it's a right country for the freedom we enjoy here'. His one reservation is the 'effects of colonialism that is still upon the people. They feel they have been pressured so we want to throw that cloak away and be Torres Strait Islander Australians' (Connolly 2003).

The voices of the people recorded in this history did not occur in a vacuum but in the context of the government policies of the time. In 1936 the Maritime Strike forced the paternalistic Queensland Government to introduce major legislative and administrative changes, but the advent of World War Two stalled any real progress toward self-reliance. The referendum of 1967 ultimately led to the Commonwealth Government making space for the people's voices without necessarily funding their aspirations. Sometimes the voices challenged and reframed the status quo, as in the case of the 'Border Not Change' and the Mabo Land

Case, but both state and federal governments were not averse to watering down gains. The ICC and the TSRA gave island leaders new spaces to voice their concerns for greater control over their own affairs, and more recently the people have found space in the *Torres News* where many diverse positions are presented by all manner of people with and without positions of leadership within the communities. Maybe politicians do not listen to these edited voices in newspapers, voices that may not portray the 'deeper texture of the events' that are gained by researchers' probing interviews, but for those who want to listen this history presents a collation of voices that certainly belong to a bigger picture that may eventually be drawn by an Indigenous historian from Torres Strait.

After 2006

The people's struggles are ongoing, and to open the window on their struggles a little wider I shall discuss briefly some of the issues that were concerning people during 2007.

By October 2007 determinations had been finalised for all but three native title land claims in the Torres Strait region, and one outside (TSRA News Column 2007, p. 2). A Thursday Island woman (2007) gave her perspective on native title rights:

> *Traditional landowners are jumping up and down, the councils [trustees of their lands] own nothing. The traditional owners don't want native title because they say it's their land anyway and not the councils' — no such thing. We don't have that thing white people have, it's oral, it's by mouth, by stones, trees and we know it's ours.*

An eastern island leader (2007) says it is 'still a very complicated situation'.

Queensland law requires that all communities set up Prescribed Body Corporates to make certain decisions and to be trustees for the traditional landowners, but there are some landowners who say: 'No one, not even a Meriam, could be a trustee for my land'. There can also be difficulties in negotiating Indigenous Land Use Agreements between traditional landowners and non-Islander bodies or individuals when infrastructure is needed. The Eastern island leader (2007) concluded:

> *That's the bottom line of it, but very slowly people are starting to realise that, okay, it must be a two-way thing. Importantly, though, landowners question the idea that the government has given them back their land to be held in trust and they say 'What are you doing giving me something that I already own? ... We own the land, we go generations back of*

ownership of the land and we have something spiritual with the land and the government don't understand the spiritual affiliation'. So that's where the land issue is. It's not over.

The late Fr Edward Rocky Nai went as far as to say that 'land issues, which we thought would be a blessing, are dividing us' (*TN* 21–27 February 2007).

The Torres Strait sea claim was filed in 2001, and in October 2007 the TSRA reported that a judge was coming to the islands to hear 'first-hand traditional evidence [that] will be preserved and become part of the Court record ... to assist parties to either reach agreement or narrow down some of the issues to be contested'. The local Native Title Office warned that 'more work was needed to progress the claim' because anthropological research had proved to be more complex than first thought and 'a number of complex legal issues and factual matters', including Australia's international obligations relating to the sea, had to be negotiated (*TSRA News* 9–16 October 2007, p. 1). However, traditional owners were reassured that their local Native Title Office would continue to work to secure the best possible outcome for all, adding that if the claim cannot be settled by consent, it is likely that it will have to proceed to trial, a daunting prospect when the ten-year struggle over land rights followed by long delays in reaching determinations is recalled (p. 1).

John Toshie Kris (chair of the TSRA at the time of publication) confirmed the TSRA's long-term objective to progress management and ownership of the region's fisheries toward securing a greater share of the catch for traditional fishers, with a boost of A$300 000 to the fisheries' budget and assurance that community fishery representatives would have a voice in consultative forums. The tender process for the voluntary buyback of non-Islander tropical rock lobster fishing licences had been implemented and Kris indicated that when complete traditional fishers 'will enjoy an increase in the share of the future lobster quota'. The next step will be a buyback of finfish fishing licences. Kris concluded: 'Our fisheries are the primary natural resource from which a real economy can be based and it is important that our people are adequately equipped to sustainably manage this asset' (*TN* 4–10 July 2007, p. 5).

Buyback of fishing licences in Torres Strait became a political football during the 2007 federal election campaign. A local fisheries officer (2007) indicated that the policy of the Joint Authority, the body responsible for administering the buyback, was to 'purchase enough effort in the tropical rock lobster fishery from the non-Islander sector to provide 25 per cent for Papua New Guinea and to spend the rest of the funds to buy out as much effort as possible from the private sector for the Islander sector'. As far as the finfish and mackerel fisheries are concerned, ABC Radio Cairns announced in December 2007 that a 100 per cent buyback was complete. John Toshie Kris saw the buyback as 'another step towards ... achieving greater ownership and an increased role in the management of the region's fisheries' (*TN* 26 December 2007–1 January 2008, p. 1). A long-time non-Islander who had fished the Torres Strait was quoted as saying: 'It was hard to walk away but I want to go back to Torres Strait with some arrangement with the Islanders' (ABC Radio).

As regards both fisheries, a Queensland Seafood Industry Association representative concluded 'This has been a tortuous process with many a twist and a turn along the way' (*TN* 26 December 2007–1 January 2008, p. 3). However, while there was 100 per cent buyback of finfish licences, in the rock lobster industry there was no total buyback because of limited funds. Of the licences bought, Papua New Guinea receives 25 per cent of the buyback and, of the remaining 75 per cent, the split between the Torres Strait Islanders and the non-Islanders is 53 per cent and 47 per cent respectively. The next step was to consider the leasing back of finfish licences to non-Islander boat owners to ensure the maximum quotas will be met (p. 1). Islander fishers do not have the boat capacity, as yet, to do this (Young Erub fisher, 2008).

As the seafood industry representative said, to arrive at these mutually acceptable outcomes in fisheries effort was a tortuous exercise for those involved, and the same can be said for the lay reader attempting to take in its content and context. Nevertheless, what was finally achieved is critical for any future self-regulatory governance in Torres Strait.

A very long-standing issue for the Torres Strait Islanders is greater autonomy based on a model of self-governance that ensures control of their own futures. A diversity of opinions was clearly stated in the section of the book that covered this major topic. However, as shown, autonomy must be a people's movement and in my coverage it is the individual people's voices that resound the loudest, some hopeful of change, others not so.

The Thursday Island female activist (2007) pointed out:

> *It's getting harder to get that recognition of unity ... people want to do their own thing ... they don't need the group ... theirs is the right vision.*

She continued:

> *They are still waiting for autonomy to happen but with the new state government laws they are still fighting for recognition which is getting*

harder, being diffused every day. I think that was a time back then in 80/90s in the new millennium it has not happened. The Bamaga Accord killed it off. After the Accord it never got up.

Patrick Mills points out that the 'idea of independence has been around for a long time', citing Akee's and Wacando's move for it in the 1980s (*TN* 8–14 August 2007, p. 7). The late Father Nai saw a problem with unity and caring for one another: 'We need to appreciate each other; we need solidarity and then we can go to the government to tell them what we want and need ... We talk about *gud pasin* but are we showing it?' (*TN* 21–27 February 2007).

The Mer Zogo Le Association called for a revival of the autonomy taskforce as a matter of priority, but the Eastern island leader (2007) commented: 'It's from my honest understanding of situations like this it is just born out of frustrations, people are just creating, establishing all sorts of recommendations ... and I am only hoping in doing all that we are not going to confuse ourselves'. Nonetheless he suggests: 'Autonomy is at the forefront, that's the way we're going, but it's difficult to make logic out of what is illogical. It's developing [but] people are still confused, and that's the bottom line'. When I asked him to say where he thinks autonomy is at in 2007, he used traditional symbolism to show the need for all-important unity:

We have a cultural [thing]. I always wear a necklace my brother carved it for me and it's an old paddle they used to row canoes and we have this saying, the old traditional [men] when they had the ceremonies they always say look at our war canoes, warriors, the spears, the clubs and everything and look at the paddle. If you put one paddle [up] it falls down, you put two or three they wobble, but if you put them [four] paddles together then they will stand. So before unity, divided we fall [but if] Torres Strait get together like that then we go for autonomy.

Of grave importance to the Torres Strait Islanders was the Queensland Government's sudden announcement on 27 July 2007 that: 'Excluding TSRA represented Bamaga and Seisa the remaining fifteen Torres Strait Island communities will come together to form a Torres Strait Island Regional Council' (*TSRA News* 14–21 August 2007, p. 1). Twelve months previously, island councils were in the process of transition from the state Department of Aboriginal and Torres Strait Islander Policy to the Department of Local Government, when all Torres Strait Islanders were being urged by minister Desley Boyle to 'get involved and tell us how you think your island councils should operate' (*TN* 7–13 July 2004, p. 8). Moreover, there was assurance that the community councils would continue to exist. Now these councils are to be amalgamated despite the TSRA's call to the government to 'work in partnership ... to ensure that changes imposed do not threaten community culture and identity, authority within our communities, land tenure arrangements and the overall work of past and present leaders towards autonomy and empowerment of our people' (*TSRA News* 14–21 August 2007, p. 1). Thus, suddenly the Torres Strait Islanders are faced with the loss of their individual island councils. But, Getano Lui Jnr remains adamant that: 'Each council is a sovereign entity in its own right and should remain as such regardless of how small they are' (*TN* 9–15 May 2007, p. 6).

Lui added his concern about the media's focus on accountability and transparency of Torres Strait Island councils and says that, if this is the case, 'we need to tidy up our back yard so that we are confident in moving forward'. He continued:

> *We don't agree with amalgamation and we would have preferred the current system to stay as we were. But if we are to have amalgamation, we need to spell out clearly what we stand for and what we want ... At the moment it's all about emotion and there's no real substance to it. There's nothing about what we want to do. We have been blaming the government; and that's well and good but we need to get past it. There's something that's stopping us ... but once we clear that up we can move forward. That's the responsibility of being a leader, and we need to accept that and move on.* (*TN*, 26 September–2 October 2007, p. 5)

On the ABC TV program *Message Stick* on 19 November 2007 Lui also stressed: 'It is about Torres Strait Islanders coming together and deciding what is best for the region'. He asked: 'Whatever happened to this self-determination and self-management doctrine which Peter Beattie championed when he was elected?' and he called for the federal government to intervene and overrule amalgamation. Matthew Bon from Mer said, 'Amalgamation was dumped on us', and John Toshie Kris was concerned about the lack of consultation. Chair of the newly formed Torres Strait Island Regional Council Local Transition Committee, Fred Gela, saw funding advantages, but disadvantages in land management.

A younger Thursday Island woman (2007), who has deep concerns about autonomy and what amalgamation means to the people, believes:

> *With this amalgamation our culture will be a problem ... Government has created something that takes our whole identity away ... the Australian government doesn't know us, east and west don't get on, all have different way of doing things and now government's going to stick their noses in.*

An issue related to amalgamation is the future of the Commonwealth's Community Development Employment Program that pumps money into the communities and is managed by the island councils.

There is serious concern that in the future, particularly with the increasing mainstreaming of Indigenous services, Torres Strait Islander people's voices will not be heeded — and indeed may be totally excluded. However, unlike in the period before the 1980s, there is now an articulate and highly vocal cohort of leaders in many departments and across many locations in Torres Strait and outside of it who will speak up and do speak up to build on the gains made by the seasoned campaigners who came before them, people such as Mimi Marou, Tanu Nona, George Mye MBE OAM, Ephraim Bani, Getano Lui Jnr OAM, Koiki Mabo, Etta Passi, Flo Kennedy OAM, Ted Loban and Ellie Gaffney. Nevertheless, this new cohort could be at risk of 'whitealisation', a term coined by the late Koiki Mabo while a student at James Cook University (Henderson 1994); that is buying into the dominant society's discourses to the exclusion of traditional ways. The Eastern island leader's opinion (2007) is that today 'it's not possible to rely solely on our traditional ways'. But, he assured me, it is still important to look to traditional symbolism and as an example he reminded me of the symbolism of the multiple paddles providing unity.

References

Published sources

AAP *see* Allocation Advisory Panel.

Abetz, E, Mulherin, T & Kris, T 2006, 'Media release: Revised plan for Torres Strait fisheries', released 20 December, URL viewed 2 March 2007, <http://www.mffc.gov.au/releases/2006/06151aj.html>.

Allocation Advisory Panel 2006a, 'Advice on the appropriate basis for the allocation of fishing concessions in the non-community commercial sector of the Torres Strait finfish fishery', draft report to the Torres Strait Protected Zone Joint Authority, 21 August.

—— 2006b, 'Advice on the appropriate basis for the allocation of fishing concessions in the non-community commercial sector of the Torres Strait rock lobster fishery', draft report to the Torres Strait Protected Zone Joint Authority, 21 August.

Altman, JC, Arthur, WS & Bek, HJ 1994, *Indigenous participation in commercial fisheries in Torres Strait: a preliminary discussion*, CAEPR, Australian National University, Canberra.

Ankersmit, FR 1989, 'Historiography and postmodernism', *History and Theory*, vol. 28 no. 2, pp. 137–53.

Austin, CG 1949, 'Early history of Somerset and Thursday Island', paper presented to The Historical Society of Queensland Inc, Brisbane.

Austin, T 1972, 'FW Walker and Papuan Industries Ltd', *Journal of the Papua New Guinea Society*, vol. 6 no. 1, pp. 38–62.

Australian Institute of Aboriginal and Torres Strait Islander Studies 2003, *Native Title Newsletter* no. 6, November/December, AIATSIS, Canberra.

AWM *see* Australian War Memorial (Archival sources)

Bani, E 1978, 'These are my islands', *Australian Natural History*, vol. 19 no. 6, pp. 214–6.

Bani, E 2004a, 'Hunterskills: the dugong, the hunter and the talking sea grass', in R Davis (ed.) *Woven histories, dancing lives: Torres Strait Islander identity, culture and history*, Aboriginal Studies Press, Canberra.

Bani, E 2004b, 'What is a totem?', in R Davis (ed.) *Woven histories, dancing lives: Torres Strait Islander identity, culture and history*, Aboriginal Studies Press, Canberra.

Barham, AM, Budworth, S, Ghaleb, B, Harris, DR, Head, L, Smith, P, Stevenson, AC & Williams, E 1987, *Archaeological and palaeoenvironmental investigation in Western Torres Strait: Northern Australia*, University College, London.

Bayton, Rev J 1969, 'Missionaries and Islanders: a chronicle of events associated with the introduction of the Christian mission of the people of Torres Strait during the period 1866-1873', *Queensland Heritage*, vol. 1 no. 10, pp. 16–20.

Beckett, JR 1963, 'Politics in the Torres Strait islands', PhD thesis, Australian National University, Canberra.

—— 1972, 'The Torres Strait Islanders', in D Walker (ed.), *Bridge and barrier: the natural and cultural history of Torres Strait* (pp. 207–26), Australian National University, Canberra.

—— 1977, 'The Torres Strait Islanders in the pearling industry: a case for internal colonialism', *Aboriginal History*, vol. 1 no. 1, pp. 77–104.

—— 1978, 'Mission, church, and sect: three types of religious commitment in Torres Strait islands', in J Boutilier, DT Hughes & SW Tiffany (eds), *Mission, church, and sect in Oceania* (pp. 209–29), University of Michigan Press.

—— 1987, *Torres Strait Islanders: custom and colonialism*, Cambridge University Press.

Bleakley, JW 1961, *The Aborigines of Australia: their history, their habits, their assimilation*, Jacaranda, Brisbane.

Brennan, F 1992, *Land rights Queensland style: the struggle for aboriginal self-management*, University of Queensland Press, St Lucia.

—— 1984, Queensland land rights: a comparison of deeds of grant in trust (amended) with *Aboriginal Land Rights (NT) Act* 1976, *Aboriginal Law Bulletin* 2, 1 (10), p. 4, URL viewed 29 November 2007 <http://www.austlii.edu.au/journals/AboriginalLB/1984/2.html#Heading>.

Butt, P, Eagleson, R & Lane, P 2001, *Mabo, Wik and native title* (4th ed.), The Federation Press, Leichhardt, NSW.

Cain, P 2006a, 'A critical appraisal of Australian legal responses to customary rights of use of living marine resources – Part 1 – native title', presented at NTSC Seminar, Townsville.

—— 2006b, 'A critical appraisal of Australian legal responses to customary rights of use of living marine resources — Part 2 — customary rights', presented at NTSC Seminar, Townsville.

Carroll, JM (ed.) 1969, 'Journey into Torres Strait', *Queensland Heritage*, vol. 1 no. 1, pp. 35–42.

Connolly, B (producer, director) 2003, *A Big Country Revisited — The Islander 1977*, ABC Video.

Davis, R (ed.) 2004, *Woven histories dancing lives: Torres Strait Islander identity, culture and history*, Aboriginal Studies Press, Canberra.

Department of Local Government, Planning, Sport and Recreation 2005, 'Torres Strait community government review', Green Paper summary booklet, Queensland Government, Brisbane.

Docherty, T 1992, 'Criticism, history, Foucault', *History of European Ideas*, vol. 14 no. 3, pp. 365–78.

Douglas, J 1886, 'The islands of the Torres Strait', *Queensland Geographical Journal*, no. 1, pp. 70–83.

References

—— 1900, *Past and present of Thursday Island*, The Outridge Printing Co, Brisbane.

Fairhead, L & Hohnen, L 2007, 'Torres Strait Islanders: improving their economic benefits from fishing', ABARE Research Report 07.21.

Fleischman, KR 1953, 'Inspection of Lockerbie (Cape York) area and wolfram workings on Moa, Torres Strait', *Queensland Government Mining Journal*, no. 54, pp. 933–7.

Foucault, M 1980, *Power/knowledge: selected interviews and other writings 1972–1977* (ed. C Gordon; trans C Gordon, L Marshall, J Mepham, K Soper), Harvester Wheatsheaf, New York.

Fuary, MM 1991, 'In so many words: an ethnography of life and identity on Yam Island, Torres Strait', PhD thesis, James Cook University, Townsville.

Gill, WW 1876, *Life in the southern isles: or, scenes and incidents in the South Pacific and New Guinea*, The Religious Tract Society, London.

Golson, J 1972, 'Land connections, sea barriers and the relationship of Australia and New Guinea prehistory', in D Walker (ed.), *Bridge and barrier: the natural and cultural history of Torres Strait* (pp. 375–97), Australian National University, Canberra.

Griffin, J 1976, 'Introduction: a background paper to Torres Strait Border Issue', in J Griffin (ed.), *The Torres Strait border issue: consolidation, conflict or compromise?* (pp. xiii–xxxiv), College of Advanced Education, Townsville.

Haddon, AC 1890, 'Ethnography of the western tribes of Torres Strait', *Journal of the Anthropological Institute*, no. 9, pp. 297–437.

—— (ed.) 1901–1935, *Reports of the Cambridge anthropological expedition to Torres Strait* (vols 1–6), Cambridge University Press.

—— n.d., *Head-hunters, black, white and brown*, Watts & Co, London.

Hall, RA 1989, *The black diggers: Aborigines and Torres Strait Islanders in the second world war*, Allen & Unwin, Sydney.

Henderson, L 1994, 'Reeves' pedagogic model of interactive learning systems and cultural contextuality', in L McBeath & R Atkinson (eds), *Proceedings of the second international interactive multi-media symposium*, Perth (pp. 189–98).

House of Representatives Standing Committee on Aboriginal & Torres Strait Islander Affairs 1997, *Torres Strait Islanders: a new deal. A report on greater autonomy for Torres Strait Islanders*, The Parliament of the Commonwealth of Australia, Canberra.

Jennings, JN 1972, 'Some attributes of Torres Strait', in D Walker (ed.), *Bridge and barrier: the natural and cultural history of Torres Strait* (pp. 29–38), Australian National University, Canberra.

Jull, P 1994, *Changing political contexts for Torres Strait: new realities and necessary technique*, TAFE, Cairns.

Kaye, S 2002, 'Torres Strait native title sea claim: legal issues paper (National Native Title Tribunal Occasional Papers Series)', URL viewed 22 November 2007 <http://www.nnt.gov.au/research/reports.html#occasionalpaperseries>.

References

Kehoe-Forutan, S 1988, *Torres Strait independence: a chronicle of events*, University of Queensland Press, St Lucia.

Kelly, L (ed.) 1980–1, 'Salute to Alf Clint', *Goorialla*, Summer, no. 2.

Kennedy, R 1986, 'Ladies who gave all to bring peace and prosperity to their people', in R & J Kennedy (eds), *Adha Gar Tidi: cultural sensitivity topics for workers in western Torres Strait* (pp. 38–41), James Cook University, Townsville.

Laade, W 1968, 'The Torres Strait Islanders' own tradition about their origin', *Ethnos*, no. 33, pp. 141–58.

Land Rights Queensland 1996, newspaper of the Queensland Federation of Land Councils, October/November.

Langbridge, JW 1977, 'From enculturation to evangelisation: an account of missionary education in the islands of Torres Strait to 1915', BEd (Hons) thesis, James Cook University, Townsville.

Lawrie, M 1970, *Myths and legends of Torres Strait*, University of Queensland Press, St Lucia.

Loban, H 2002, 'Reflections on the Treaty from a Torres Strait Islander lawyer', *Indigenous Law Bulletin*, URL viewed 22 November 2007 <http://www.austlii.edu.au/au/journals/ILB/2002/80.html>.

London Missionary Society 1796–1906, 'Records relating to South Seas', Microfilm Reel 11M, James Cook University, Townsville.

Loos, N & Keast, R 1992, 'The radical promise: the Aboriginal Christian Cooperative Movement', *Australian Historical Studies*, pp. 286–301.

Lowah, T 1988, *Eded Mer (my life)*, The Rams Skull Press, Kuranda, Qld.

Lui, G Snr 1976, 'A perspective from Torres Strait', in J Griffin (ed.), *The Torres Strait border issue: consolidation, conflict or compromise?* (pp. 31–3), College of Advanced Education, Townsville.

Lui, G Jnr 1994a, 'A Torres Strait perspective', in M Yunupinga, D West, I Anderson, J Bell, G Lui Jnr, H Corbett & N Pearson (eds), *Voices from the land: 1993* (pp. 62–75), ABC Books, Sydney.

—— 1994b, 'Torres Strait: towards 2001', *Race and Class*, vol. 35 no. 4, April/June, pp. 11–20.

Lyotard, J-F 1991, *The postmodern condition* (trans G Bennington, B Massumi), University Press, Minneapolis.

MacGillivray, J 1852, *Narrative of the voyage of HMS Rattlesnake*, vol. 2, T & H Boone, London.

McFarlane, Rev S 1888, *Among the cannibals of New Guinea*, LMS, London.

McGinness, J 1967, 'Legislation and government policy as applied to Aborigines and Torres Strait Islanders', in *We the Australians. What is to follow the referendum?* (pp. 26–8), Proceedings of Inter-Racial Citizens' Committee, Townsville.

Mendis, P 2007, *Australian Dictionary of Biography*, URL viewed 9 December 2007 <http://www.adb.online.anu.edu.au/As10336b.htm>.

Meyers, GD, O'Dell, M, Wright, G & Muller SD 1996, *A sea change in land rights law: the extension of native title to Australia's offshore areas*, AIATSIS, Canberra.

References

Moore, DR 1979, *Islanders and Aborigines at Cape York*, Institute of Aboriginal Studies, Canberra.

Mullins, S 1987, 'On the frontier of history: Torres Strait 1864–1884', paper presented at the 57th Australian & New Zealand Association for the Advancement of Science (ANZAAS) Conference, Townsville.

—— 1989, '"heathen polynee" and "nigger teachers": Torres Strait and Pacific Islander ascendancy', paper presented at Peripheral Visions Conference, Townsville.

—— 1995, *Torres Strait: a history of colonial occupation and culture contact 1864–1897*, Central Queensland University Press, Rockhampton.

Nakata, M 1990, 'Constituting the Torres Strait Islanders: a Foucauldian discourse analysis of the 1989 National Aboriginal and Torres Strait Islander Education Policy: joint policy statement', paper present at AARE Conference, Sydney.

—— 1993, 'Culture in education: for us or for them?' in N Loos & T Osanai (eds), *Indigenous minorities and education: Australian and Japanese perspectives of their indigenous peoples, the Ainu, Aborigines and Torres Strait Islanders* (pp. 334–49), Sanyusha Publishing Co Ltd, Tokyo.

—— 2007, *Disciplining the savages: savaging the disciplines*, Aboriginal Studies Press, Canberra.

National Native Title Tribunal 2001, *The Kaurareg people's native title determinations: questions and answers*, National Native Title Tribunal, Perth.

Nettheim, G 1981, *Victims of the law: black Queensland today*, George Allen & Unwin, Sydney.

Osborne, Barry (ed.) 1995, *Ibupeoydhay Ziauxali Pu Tisa Ngalpun Omasker: a guidebook for teachers of our children*, James Cook University, Cairns.

Osborne, E 1993, 'Looking for the new light: Torres Strait Islanders and the Pacific war, 1942–1945', in N Loos & T Osanai (eds), *Indigenous minorities and education: Australian and Japanese perspectives of their indigenous peoples, the Ainu, Aborigines and Torres Strait Islanders* (pp. 55–66), Sanyusha Publishing, Tokyo.

—— 1995, 'Our voices: Torres Strait Islander women in a war zone, 1942–1945', PhD thesis, James Cook University, Townsville.

—— 1997, *Torres Strait Islander women and the Pacific war*, Aboriginal Studies Press, Canberra.

—— 1998, 'In the midst of war: a lone teacher in Torres Strait', *The Educational Historian*, vol. 3 no. 3, pp. 1, 7.

Peel, G 1946, *Isles of the Torres Strait*, Current Book Distributors, Sydney.

Ramazanoglu, C (ed.) 1993, *Up against Foucault: explorations of some tensions between Foucault and feminism*, Routledge, London.

Reynolds, H 1989, *Dispossession: black Australians and white invaders*, Allen & Unwin, Sydney.

Sanders, W 1994, *Discussion paper. Reshaping governance in Torres Strait: the Torres Strait Regional Authority and beyond*, CAEPR, Australian National University, Canberra.

—— 1999, *Torres Strait governance structures and the Centenary of Australian Federation: a missed opportunity?* CAEPR, Australian National University, Canberra.

Sanders, WG & Arthur, WS 2001, *Autonomy rights in Torres Strait: from whom, for whom, for or over what?* CAEPR, Australian National University, Canberra.

Sarup, M 1988, *An introductory guide to post-structuralism and post-modernism*, Harvester Wheatsheaf, New York.

Seekee, V n.d., '"One ilan man": the Torres Strait Light Infantry', URL viewed 22 January 2007 <http://www.awm.gov.au/wartime/12/article.asp>.

Senate Select Committee on the Administration of Indigenous Affairs 2005, *After ATSIC – life in the mainstream?* Senate Printing Unit, Canberra.

Sharp, N 1980a, *Torres Strait Islands 1879–1979: theme of an overview*, Latrobe University, Bundoora, Vic.

—— 1980b, *Torres Strait islands: a great cultural refusal. The meaning of the maritime strike of 1936*, Latrobe University, Bundoora, Vic.

—— 1981–2, 'Culture clash in the Torres Strait islands: the Maritime Strike of 1936', *The Royal Historical Society of Queensland Journal*, vol. XI no. 3, pp. 107–26, Brisbane.

—— 1984, 'Springs of originality among the Torres Strait Islanders', PhD thesis, Latrobe University, Bundoora, Vic.

—— 1987, 'Faces of power in the Torres Strait islands: The 1908s and the 1930s', paper present at 57th Australian & New Zealand Association for the Advancement of Science (ANZAAS) Conference, Townsville.

—— 1992, *Footprints along the Cape York sandbeaches*, Aboriginal Studies Press, Canberra.

—— 1993, *Stars of Tagai: The Torres Strait Islanders*, Aboriginal Studies Press, Canberra.

—— 1996, *No ordinary judgment: Mabo, the Murray Islanders' land case*, Aboriginal Studies Press, Canberra.

Shnukal, A 1993, 'Torres Strait Island Languages Past and Present', in N Loos & T Osonai (eds), *Indigenous minorities and education: Australian and Japanese perspectives of their indigenous peoples, the Oinu, Aborigines and Torres Strait Islanders* (pp. 152–64), Sanyusha Publishing, Tokyo.

——, 'Language diversity, pan-Islander identity and "national" identity in Torres Strait', in R Davis (ed.), *Woven histories, dancing lives: Torres Strait Islander identity, culture and history*, Aboriginal Studies Press, Canberra.

Submission to Minister for Immigration, Multicultural and Indigenous Affairs 2003, 'A proposal to improve regional governance in Torres Strait', Proposed TSRA Bill, TSRA, Thursday Island.

Tatz, C 1967, 'The politics of Aboriginal administration', in Inter-Racial Citizens' Committee (ed.), *We the Australians. What is to follow the referendum?* (pp. 20–5), Proceedings of Inter-Racial Citizens' Committee, Townsville.

Thaiday, W 1981, *Under the Act*, The NQ Black Publishing, Townsville.

Thursday Island State High School Students 1987, *Torres Strait at war: a recollection of wartime experiences*, State High School, Thursday Island.

Torres Strait Islander Regional Education Committee 1985, 'Policy Statement on Education in Torres Strait' (mimeo).

Torres Strait Islander Regional Education Consultative Committee 1992, '*Ngampula Yawadhan Ziawali*: educational policy for Torres Strait' (mimeo).

References

Torres Strait Regional Authority n.d. (c.Oct 2007), 'Torres Strait regional sea claim', URL viewed 22 November 2007 <http://www.tsra.gv.au/the-tsra/native-title.aspx>.

Tsamenyi, M & Mfodwo, K 2000, 'Towards greater indigenous participation in Australian commercial fisheries: some policy issues (ATSIC policy seminar series)', URL viewed 21 November 2007 <http://www.atsic.gov.au>.

van der Veur, P 1966, *Search for New Guinea boundaries: from Torres Strait to the Pacific*, ANU Press, Canberra.

Walker, D (ed.) 1972, *Bridge and barrier: the natural and cultural history of Torres Strait*, Australian National University, Canberra.

Whiteman, DL 1983, *Melanesians and missionaries: an ethnological study of social and religious change in southwest Pacific*, W Carey Library, Pasadena, Cal.

Williamson, A 1987, 'White and Islander teachers in outer islands' schools of Torres Strait 1892–1941', paper presented at 57th Australian & New Zealand Association for the Advancement of Science (ANZAAS) Conference, Townsville.

—— 1989, 'Educational exchanges in a colonial context: the Torres Strait Islands', in A Williamson (ed.), *Educational exchanges and their implications: challenge and response* (pp. 72–86), University of Queensland, Brisbane.

—— 1990, 'Schooling the Torres Strait Islander 1873–1941', PhD thesis, The University of Sydney.

Archival sources

Australian War Memorial, Coast artillery Torres Strait written records, 1939–1945 war, AWM54, 6228/1/1.

Queensland State Archives, Aboriginals, Torres Strait infantry, 1941, A/4218, 5601-5800.

——, Aborigines gen., Health and Home Office affairs, 1930-1935, A/3598.

——, Chief Protector of Aborigines, reports, 1902-1914.

——, Department of Aboriginal and Islander Affairs, report, 1987.

——, Department of Native Affairs, reports, 1946-1958.

——, Education, mission schools, inspection, reports, etc., 1936-1938, A/15996.

——, Governor's correspondence, islands of Torres Strait, 1936, A/12228.

——, Governor's correspondence, islands of Torres Strait, 1944, A/12257.

——, Governor's office, islands of Torres Strait, 1933, A/3664.

——, Native affairs, Thursday Island, 1942-1944, TR1227, bundle 140.

——, Protector of Aborigines, report, 1947.

——, Queensland Government Legislative Assembly, reports, 1880-1889.

——, Queensland Government Legislative Assembly, votes and proceedings, 1891.

——, Queensland Government, parliamentary debates, 1939

——, Queensland Government, parliamentary papers, 1948.

——, Staffing DNA, 1942, A/4291.

Acts of Parliament

Aboriginal and Torres Strait Islander Act 2005
Aboriginal and Torres Strait Islander Affairs Act 1965
Aboriginal and Torres Strait Islander (Land Holding) Act 1985
Aboriginal and Torres Strait Islander Commission Act 1989
Aboriginal Land Rights (NT) Act 1996
Aborigines Act 1971
Aborigines Protection and Restriction of the Sale of Opium Act 1897
Community Services (Torres Strait) Act 1984
Immigration Act 1901
Local Government Act 1993
Native Title Act 1993
Pacific Islanders Protection Act 1872 (Kidnapping Act)
Queensland Coast Islands Act 1879
Queensland Coast Islands Declaratory Act 1985
Racial Discrimination Act 1975
Torres Strait Fisheries Act 1984 (Commonwealth)
Torres Strait Fisheries Act 1984 (Queensland)
Torres Strait Islanders Act 1939

Newspapers, periodicals and other media

The following were consulted or cited; dates given in text.
ABC Radio
The Australian and the *Australian Weekend Magazine*
Cairns Post
Courier Mail (Brisbane)
Koori Mail
Sydney Morning Herald
Times on Sunday
Torres News
Townsville Bulletin
Tribune
WIN Television News

Other sources

Author's notes, Senate Inquiry Meeting Thursday Island, August 2004.
Early history workshop, videotape made by Pro-Octa Production P/L, Thursday Island, March 1987.
TSRA advice, community development, employment and training, c. October 2007, URL viewed 22 November 2007 <http://www.tsra.gov.au/the-tsra/community-development-employment>.
TSRA 2001, *Greater autonomy for Torres Strait*, video.

Index

Abednego, John, 87, 99, 114, 136–7, 138–9, 140
   TRAWQ chair, 101
Abetz, Eric, 132
Aboriginal and Torres Strait Islander Act 2005, 156
Aboriginal and Torres Strait Islander Commission (ATSIC), 69, 85–7, 135
   abolition, 153–4, 156
   Akee's opinion of, 82
   establishment, 77–9
   Lui's 1994 address to, 80
   mainland Torres Strait Islander representation, 138, 139
   O'Donoghue, Lois, 93
   see also Torres Strait Regional Authority
Aboriginal and Torres Strait Islander Commission Act 1989, 77–9, 86
   TSRA Act separate from, 87, 143, 150–1, 152, 154
Aboriginal and Torres Strait Islanders (Land Holding) Act 1985, 65–6
Aboriginal Consultative Group, 71
Aboriginal Industries Board, 28, 32
Aboriginal languages, 7
Aboriginal Property Protection Account, 21
Aboriginal Study Grants, 69
Aboriginal troopers, 11
Aborigines Protection and Restriction of the Sale of Opium Act 1897, 19–20, 21, 22–32
Adai, 53
Adhibuya Stone, 5
AFMA, 119, 121, 122, 123, 124, 128
Akee, James, 74–5, 81–4, 115–16, 144
Akiba, Leo, 116
Altman et al., 131
America, 4

Anglican faith, 30, 52–4
   Clint, Rev. Alf, 52–3
Ankersmit, Frank, xiv
army enlistment, WWII, 34–7
   ex-servicemen, 58–9, 65, 81
Assemblies of God, 54
assimilation/integration, 58–61
ATSIC, *see* Aboriginal and Torres Strait Islander Commission
Aurid Island, 9
Australian Fish Management Authority, 119, 121, 122, 123, 124, 128
Australian Legion of Ex-Servicemen and Women, 46
autonomy, 79–87, 106, 135–57, 164–7
   case made to ATSIC legislation review in 1992 and 1993, 78
   fisheries management arrangements in anticipation, 122, 123, 125
   independence movements, 74–7, 81–4, 165
   maritime strike outcomes, 32–3
   Peel's advocacy for, 46
   see also territory status

Badu, 50–2, 53, 141
   education, 56, 72, 149
   Greater Autonomy Steering Committee representative, 145
   horticulture, 3–4
   hospital, 40, 41, 57, 58
   housing, 6
   Kuiku Mabaigal Forum, 154–5, 157
   native title claim, 99–106
   Nona, Tanu, 47–8, 49
   protection policy, 25, 27
   radar installation agreement, 106–7
   residents relocated to Thursday Island, 44, 55
   TSIRECC conference (1995), 72–3

Wini (Weenie), 4, 11–12
World War II, 34, 39, 40, 41; white people volunteering to stay, 37
Badu maritime industry, 11–12, 17, 31, 47, 50–1, 128–9
  fisheries management, 120–1; meetings, 122–3, 125, 128
  shell trade, 5
bakery, St Paul's, 52–3
  Jacob Abednego, 52
Bamaga, 46, 74, 143, 144, 165
Bamaga Accord, 143–6, 149, 152, 157, 165
Bani, Ephraim, 4, 8
Bani, Gabriel, 145
Banks Island, *see* Moa
Banner, Captain, 10, 15
Banu, Don, 104, 105, 116
barter system, 5
Beattie, Major GR, 56–7
Beattie government, 99–106, 140, 166
bêche-de-mer, *see* maritime industry
Beckett, JR, 7, 32, 45, 49, 58
  on Anglican faith, 15, 16, 22, 54
  author of 1944 petition to governor of Queensland suggested by, 42
  on Bleakley's influence, 48
  'welfare colonialism', 61, 68
Bedford, Bluey, 131
BHP, 108
birth control, 6
Bjelke-Petersen, Joh, 63
Blackwood, Captain, 10
Bleakley, JW, 32, 36–7, 38*n*, 48
  visit to Erub (Darnley Island), 27
Bligh, William, 8–9
boats, 12–14, 45, 52–3
  canoes, 3, 5, 9
  fishing licences, 117–34, 163–4
  freezers, 69, 121, 127, 129, 131
  World War II, 39, 40, 41
  see also company (clan) boats and boatmen
Boigu, 7, 49–50, 51, 62
  health services, 56, 70
  housing, 45
  maritime industry, 43, 44
  native title claim, 99–106
  regional sea claim, 116
  white teachers, 27

Bon, Adrian, 145–6
Bon, Bakoi, 139
Bon, Fr Dalton, 149
Bon, Matthew, 166
Border Action Committee, 64
borders, 13, 17, 61–4
Bousen, Corey, 153
Bowie, Phillip, 147
Bowie, William, 106
Boyle, Desley, 165
Brennan, Justice F, 89
Brennan, Fr Frank, 71, 73–4
Brierly, Oswald, 8
Brisbane Telegraph, 30
Brothers, 12
Bruce, Captain, 10
Bruce, John, 19, 29
Bureau of Rural Sciences, 129–30

Cain, P, 110–11
canoes, 3, 5, 9
Cantley, Roland, 75, 82
Cape York Boundary Interim Committee, 147, 152
Cape York Land Council, 97
Cape York Peninsula, 5, 11, 146–7
  Bamaga, 46, 74, 143, 165
  Seisia, 74, 146, 165
  Somerset, 10–11, 17
Carpentaria, Diocese of, 19, 30
Catholic faith, 53
CDEP, 142, 167
Charles Eaton, 9
Chester, HM, 11, 17
Chief Protector of Aborigines, 21–33, 38*n*
child endowment, 40–1
Christianity, *see* Anglican faith, Pentecostals, Assemblies of God
clan boats, *see* company boats
Clint, Rev. Alf, 52–3
Coconut Island (Purma/Poruma), 21, 46, 151–2
commercial fishermen, *see* maritime industry
Commonwealth government control of Indigenous affairs, 59–61, 67, 76
  Bishop Davies' proposal, 30
  Peel's advocacy for, 46
communism, 46, 49, 53

177

Index

community councils, *see* councils
Community Development Employment Program, 142, 167
Community Services (Torres Strait) Act 1984, 74, 155
community (TIB) licences, 117, 118, 122–4, 128–9
company (clan) boats and boatmen, 21–2, 24–5, 28
   loans to buy, 17, 19, 21; assignment to Protector, 24
   New Law, 33
   resistance to Protector McLean, 30; Maritime Strike, 31–2
   World War II, 34, 44; post-war re-establishment of industry, 43–4, 47
consent determinations, 97, 98–9
consultative and advisory mechanisms, 67–8, 74–5, 86
   ATSIC establishment, 77–9
   Beckett's 'welfare colonialism' label, 61, 68
   in education, 71–2
   Island Advisory Council, 61, 65
   Torres Strait fisheries, 63, 119, 122–4, 127–8
   see also Island Coordinating Council
Cook, James, 8
Coombs, Dr HC 'Nugget', 63
Cooper, Justice RE, 115
cooperatives, 52–3
council conferences, 49
   1937, 33, 48; Mye's speech at sixty-sixth anniversary, 149
   1944 (Masig Island), 51, 54, 56–7
   1982, 65
   2004, 154–5
councils, 8, 19, 27, 74, 151–6, 165–7
   1930s, 32; New Law, 33
   Deeds of Grant in Trust (DOGITs), 65–7
   first woman elected to, 64
   independence movements and, 82, 83
   Island Advisory Council, 61, 65
   native title claims lodged by, 91–116
   New Deal report recommendation, 136–8
   post-war years, 46–9
   Torres Strait Regional Council

   membership, 78
   see also Island Coordinating Council; Meriam Council; Torres Shire Council
creation stories, 1–2, 5
Croker Island Case, 110–11, 113, 114
cultivation, 3–4, 39, 46, 142
curfews, 16, 27–8, 32
Curtis, WC, 37
Curtis, Mrs WC, 57

dancing, 16, 54
Darnley Island, *see* Erub
Darton, 31
Dau, Gausa, 73
Dauan, 6, 54, 62, 106–7, 139
Dauar, 5, 15, 89, 99
David, Ned, 107, 109
Davies, Rev Dr Stephen, 30
Davis, Richard, xiv
Day, Ron, 119, 121
Deeds of Grant in Trust (DOGITs), 65–7
Department of Aboriginal Affairs, 60, 67
Department of Aboriginal and Islander Affairs (DAIA), 60–1, 63, 65, 71–2
Department of Aboriginal and Torres Strait Islander Policy (DATSIP), 102, 155, 165
Department of Community Services, 67, 72
Department of Education, 71–2
Department of Lands, 96
Department of Local Government and Planning, Sports and Recreation, 155, 165
Department of Native Affairs (DNA), 27, 28, 48–50, 51, 58, 60
   Bishop Davies' criticisms, 30
   education responsibilities, 55
   establishment, 32–3
   see also Director of Native Affairs
Devaney, J, 46
Director of Native Affairs, 33, 46, 50, 52
   1946 report, 44, 45–6
   1947 report, 48, 55
   army pay, 36–7
   Killoran, Pat, 60–1, 63
divers, *see* maritime industry
Docherty, Thomas, xiv
DOGITs, 65–7

Index

domestic work, Thursday Island, 44
Douglas, John, 17, 18–20, 22, 25, 62
Dun, Ken, 148–9

earnings, *see* wages and earnings
economic independence, 50–3, 54, 69, 76–7
  independence movements' plans, 75, 84
  Lui's 1993 Boyer Lecture, 79
  see also employment; land ownership
education, xiii, 71–3, 142, 149–50
  Aboriginal Study Grants, 69
  army training, 35–6
  councillor-training program proposal, 155–6
  fishers' training, 131
  London Missionary Society, 16–17, 18–19
  nurse training, 41, 57–8, 69–70
  protection–control/segregation policy, 25–7; 1944 petition to Queensland governor, 42, 55; New Law, 46, 55–6
  teacher training, 26–7, 55–6
  theological training, 16, 54
  see also teachers
elections, *see* franchise
Elu, Joseph, 146
employment, 50–3, 69
  World War II, 34–7; women, 41
  after World War II, 44–5, 46
  see also maritime industry; wages and earnings
EMU, 53
Endeavour Strait, 4, 8
enlistment, *see* Army enlistment
Entsch, Warren, 125, 136, 137, 154
Erub (Darnley Island), 48, 49, 82
  Bleakley's visit, 27
  Flinders' description of inhabitants, 9
  London Missionary Society, 14, 15, 16, 18
  maritime industry, 31, 49, 121, 131
  native title claim, 99–106
  native title workshop 1966, 91, 98
  regional sea claim, 116
  South Sea Islander families removed to, 14
  Wacando, Carlemo, 74–5
  World War II, 39

  see also Mye, George
Erub–Mer–Ugar cooperative, 53
ex-servicemen, 58–9, 65, 81

Federal Court, 132
  native title claims, 94, 95, 97, 98–102;
  sea claims, 107, 110, 113–16, 163
females, *see* women
Finch, Noel, 55
Fisheries Committee, 128
fisheries management and ownership, 63, 117–34, 140, 163–4
  Kuiku Mabaigal Forum resolution, 155
  Peel's advocacy in 1940s, 46
  see also maritime industry
Fisheries Taskforce, 124, 125–6, 127–8
Fishermen's Association, 127
flag, 89
Flinders, Matthew, 9
food, 3–4, 7, 22, 24
  World War II, 39–40, 45–6
Foucault, Michel, xiv
franchise, 48–9, 58–9
  council elections, 19, 74
  TSRA elections, 143, 147–8, 151–2, 156
freezer boats, 69, 121, 127, 129, 131
French, Justice RS, 97, 98
Friday Island (Gialag), 45
Frith, PR, 27, 55–6
Frith, Mrs PR, 57
Fuary, Maureen, 3
Fujii, Romina, 142

Gabba, 12
Gaffney, Ellie, xiii
gardening, 3–4, 39, 46, 142
Garnier, Henry, 101, 140, 141, 152
gas and oil drilling, 62, 75, 84, 108
Gela, Fred, 166
genetic status, 7
Gesa, George, 120–1, 125
Gialag, 45
Gill, W Wyatt, 3–4, 6, 9, 11–12, 15
Golson, J, 2–3
Greater Autonomy Steering Committee (GASC), 144–6, 149, 150, 151, 152, 153–4, 156
  Zenadth Kes proposal, 153, 155

179

Index

Greater Autonomy Taskforces, 138–45
Greater autonomy video, 140
Griffin, J, 63
Griffith, Sir Samuel, 62
Gudangs, 11
Guivarra, Joe, 84

Haddon, Alfred, 6–7, 8, 9, 16
Hall, RA, 35
Hammond Island, *see* Keriri
Hankin (Mabuiag), 31
Hawke, Bob, 76
health conditions, 85, 138, 142
  World War II, 45–6, 57
health services, 40, 45, 56–8, 103
  nurse training, 41, 57–8, 69–70
  transfer to Health Department, 73–4
Heron, John, 85, 86
High Court, 106
  Croker Island Case, 110–11, 113, 114
  Queensland annexation challenge, 75
  Queensland Coast Islands Declaratory Act ruling, 66
  Wik decision, 93–5
  see also Mabo decision
Holland, 8
Horn Island, *see* Nurupai
horticulture, 3–4, 39, 46, 142
hospitals, 40, 41, 56–8, 69–70
House of Representatives Standing Committee on Aboriginal and Torres Strait Islander Affairs, 135–40
housing, 6, 75, 85, 102
  cooperatives, 53
  London Mission Society period, 16
  Thursday Island Labor Pool Barracks, 44–5
  war service homes, 65
  World War II, 38
  after World War II, 45
Howard, John, 76, 132, 135, 140

Iama native title claim, 99–106
Idagi (Williams), James, 42, 54
identity, xv–xvi, 6–7, 142, 161
  under 1897 Act, 19–20
  assimilation/integration policy, 58–61
  Heron's recognition, 85
  Lui Jnr's concerns, 76–7
  mainlander Torres Strait Islanders, 138

Mye's address to National Torres Strait Islander Seminar/Workshop, 86
  under New Law, 33
  Torres Strait flag, 89
IIAN Torres Strait Islander Corporation, 85
immigration policy, 19, 23
income, *see* wages and earnings
independence movements, 74–7, 81–4, 165
Independence Working Party, 76
Independent Allocation Advisory Panel, 132–4
Indigenous Land Corporation Commission, 96
Indigenous Land Use Agreements, 94, 103, 107, 162–3
individual transferable effort concessions, 133
Individual Transferable Quota concessions, 133–4
integration/assimilation, 58–61
Inter-Island Councillors Conferences, 33, 48
  Mye's speech at sixty-sixth anniversary, 149
Interdepartmental Committee on Torres Strait, 78
Isabella, 9
Island Advisory Council, 61, 65
Island Coordinating Council (ICC), 67, 74–80, 151
  Bedford, Bluey, 131
  DOGITs, 66
  establishment of TSRA, 77–80
  fisheries management, 122–3, 124, 128, 131; Joint Authority consultative mechanism, 118
  Garnier, Henry, 101, 141, 152
  Greater Autonomy Taskforces, 138–9, 141
  independence movements, 74–7, 82
  Lui, Getano (Jnr), 122–3, 138–9
  native title, 101, 104–5; regional sea claim, 115
  New Deal report recommendation, 136, 139
  Nurupai accusations against, 146
  Sagigi, Robert, 104–5, 115, 154–5, 156
island councils, *see* councils

180

Index

Island Fund, 25, 33
Island Industries Board, 32, 44, 52
   Badu, 37, 51
   Thursday Island, 44–5
The Islander, 32
ITE fishing concessions, 133
ITQ concessions, 133–4

Jacob, Douglas, 128
Jagg, FC, 14
Japanese, 14, 50
   see also World War II
Jardine, Frank, 11, 13
Jardine, John, 11
Joseph, Talitiai, 114

Kala Lagaw Ya, 7
Katter, Bob (Jnr), 65–6, 67, 69
Kaurareg Aborigines (Muralag/Prince of Wales Island), 37, 38*n*, 78, 82, 145
   Aboriginal troopers reprisal attack, 11
   food collection practices, 4
   genetic status, 7
   Greater Autonomy Taskforce member, 139
   housing, 6
   missionaries, 14
   Moa (Poid), 38, 46, 51
   native title claim, 97, 99
   Savage's call for lands boundary to be extended, 152
   'Torres Strait Island City' proposal, 75
   trade, 5
   TSRA Board position, 147
   see also Nurupai
Kaurareg Tribal Council of Elders, 146
Keating, Paul, 80
Kebisu, 9
Kennedy, Flo, 88, 102, 147
Kennett, WT, 14
Keon-Cohen, Brian, 96
Keriri, 37, 38*n*, 74
   Garnier, Henry, 101, 140, 141, 152
Kidnapping Act, 13
Killoran, Pat, 60–1, 63
Kirby, Justice M, 113
Kiwai, 5
Koori Mail, 83
Kris, John Toshie, 105, 152, 155, 163, 164, 166

Kubin, *see* Moa
Kuiku Mabaigal Forum (Badu, 2004), 154–5, 157
Kulkalaig (Nagir Island people), 7, 11, 23, 39–40, 53
Kwoiam, 5

land ownership (land rights, native title), 64–7, 88–116, 162–3
   ALP election commitment, 77
   Inter-Island Councillors' Conference (1937) reaffirmation, 33
   Kuiku Mabaigal Forum resolution, 155
Land Tribunal, 96
Langbridge, JW, 10
languages, 7
Law of the Sea Convention, 111, 115
Lawrie, Margaret, 1, 55
Lee-Bryce, WM, 27
legal aid services, 68, 98
legends and myths, 1–2, 3
legislation, 13, 19–33, 60, 74, 155, 156
   ATSIC, 77–9, 86
   fisheries management, 117–19, 125, 132
   land, 65–6, 89–107, 108, 109–10, 162
   racial discrimination, 66, 92, 95
   social services, 40–1
   TSRA separate from ATSIC, 87, 143, 150–1, 152, 154
Lewis, CM, 9
Lieberman, Lou, 137
loans, 69
   to buy boats, 17, 19, 21; assignment to Protector, 24
   war service homes, 65
Loban, Heron, 118
Loban, Ted, xiii, 53, 71–2, 81
lobsters, *see* rock lobster industry
Local Protectors of Aborigines, 24, 37, 44, 50
   Lee-Bryce, WM, 27
   McLean, JD, 29–32
London Missionary Society, 8, 14–19
Lowah, Belzah, 85
Lowah, Thomas, 34
Lui, Getano (Jnr), 140, 151, 153–4, 166
   fisheries management, 120, 122–3
   Greater Autonomy Steering Committee (GASC), 145, 152

Index

ICC chair, 122–3, 138–9
independence movements, 76, 82
meeting with Howard, 135
mining, 108
native title, 102; Mabo decision observation, 91
proposed timeline for greater autonomy, 79, 80, 109, 136, 141, 157
public support for self-government concept, 83
TSRA chair, 79–80, 82, 85–7, 108, 135;
Greater Autonomy Taskforces, 138–9
Lui, Getano (Jnr), speeches by, 76–7
  to ATSIC, 80
  Boyer Lecture, 79, 120
Lui, Getano (Snr), 8, 26, 62–3
Lui, Murray, 26
Lyotard, Jean-François, xiv, xv

Mabo, Eddie Koiki, 5, 88, 89, 90
Mabo, Victor, 83
Mabo Day celebration addresses, 101, 104–5
Mabo decision (Meriam land claim), 66–7, 88–92, 96, 97
  influence on Wik decision, 94
  sea claims, 107–8, 109–10, 112
Mabuiag, 3, 5, 8, 144, 145
  creation story, 1–2
  Murray's report on pearl-shell fishers, 12, 17
  Native Teacher Training School, 27, 55–6
  South Sea Islander families, 18, 23, 31; move to Moa, 14
McCallum, Bret, 132
Macdonald, Ian, 129, 130
McFarlane, Samuel, 7, 14
MacGillivray, J, 7, 10
McGinness, Joe, 60
McGregor, Sir William, 62
McLean, JD, 29–32
McLucas, Jan, 141
magistrates, 11, 13, 17, 18, 19, 22
mainland, Torres Strait Islanders living on, 64, 83, 85, 86
  abolition of ATSIC, 153
  emigration to, 46, 47, 53

Greater Autonomy Taskforce, 139
ICC representation, 74
independence movements, 74–5, 84
from Mer, 43, 97
native title issue meetings, 98
New Deal report recommendation, 136, 137, 138, 139
Malays, 10, 14, 25, 81
Malo, 5
  initiation ceremonies, 16
mamoose, 17, 22, 27
maritime boundaries, 13, 17, 61–4
maritime industry, 10, 11–14, 50–1
  freezer boat equipment, 69
  Gill's observations about Mabuiag (1876), 3
  LMS opposition to men's participation, 17
  New Law, 33
  protection policy, 23–4, 28; resistance to, 30–2
  sea claims, 107–8, 115
  shell trade, 5
  South Sea Islanders, 10, 23
  World War II, 41; re-establishment after, 43–4, 47
  see also boats; fisheries management and ownership
Maritime Strike, 31–4
Marou, 27, 31, 34, 42, 49, 54
marriage, 6, 16, 25
  to South Sea Islander men, 13–14, 18, 23, 31, 47
Masig, 15, 28–9, 31, 34, 131
  health services, 40, 41, 57
Mosby, Allan, 82–3
Mosby, Donald, 130, 151–2
Mosby, Joe, 77
Mosby, Ned, 12
Masig Island Councillors' Conference (1944), 51, 54, 56–7
Mau, Anau, 54
Mau, Margaret, 101, 139
MAW, 53
Maza, Lloyd, 99
medical services, *see* health services
Melanie, 11
Mer (Murray Island), 51, 58, 74, 144, 145, 166

182

cultivation, 3, 4, 39
education, 16, 18, 22, 25; teachers, 19, 29
fisheries management, 120–1, 125, 127, 131
Justice French's visit, 97
Greater Autonomy Taskforce representative, 139
housing, 6, 53
island identity, 6–7
London Missionary Society, 15–19; South Pacific Islander teachers, 15, 18
Mabo, Eddie Koiki, 5, 88, 89, 90; *see also* Mabo decision
Malo, 5; initiation ceremonies, 16
maritime strike, 31–2
Marou, 27, 31, 34, 42, 49, 54
Pentecostals, 54
petition to governor of Queensland, 42, 55
Pitt, Douglas, 12
under protection policy, 25, 27
Republic of Mer, 84
sea rights, 107–8, 119
South Sea Islander families, 14
travel to mainland, 27, 46
Woodlark's visit (1864), 10
World War II, 34, 38, 39, 40
see also Mye, George
Mer *Gedkem Le,* 99
Mer *Zogo Le* Association, 156, 165
Meriam Council, 22
  advice sought on Mabo decision, 96
  Day, Ron, 119, 121
  Marou, 31, 54
  Passi, Etta, 64
  religious freedom issue, 54
  Republic of Mer issue, 84
Meriam Mer, 7
Message Stick program, 166
Meyers et al., 109–10, 111–12, 112–13
Miles, Justice Jeffrey, 132
Mills, Patrick, 156, 165
Milman, Hugh, 18
mining, 62, 75, 84, 108
  wolfram, 41, 51–2, 53
Ministerial Council for Aboriginal and Torres Strait Islander Affairs, 86

Misi, Percy, 144, 156
missionaries, 7, 8, 12, 14–19, 51–2
Moa (Kubin and St Paul's), 4, 12, 14, 81, 142, 148
  cooperatives, 52–3
  Mualgal people's native title claim, 97, 98–9
  Poid, 38, 46, 51
  school education, 56
  theological training, 54
  wolfram mining, 41, 51–2, 53
  World War II, 34, 38, 41
Moa–Adai–Waiben housing cooperative, 53
money, 21–2, 23–5, 28–9, 45
  TSRA funding, 85–6, 87, 98
  see also loans; wages and earnings; welfare payments
Moore, David, 3, 8, 11
Morrison, James, 12
Mosby, Allan, 82–3
Mosby, Donald, 130, 151–2
Mosby, Jim, 49
Mosby, Joe, 77
Mosby, Ned, 12
Moynihan, Justice M, 90
Mualgal people, 97, 98–9
Mulgrave Island, *see* Badu
Muralag, *see* Kaurareg Aborigines
Murray, AW, 12, 14, 15, 17
Murray, Macintosh, 26
Murray Island, *see* Mer
Murray Island Case (Mabo decision), 66–7, 88–92, 94, 96
Mye, George, 147–8, 153, 161
  author of 1944 petition to Queensland governor suggested by, 42
  Big Country interview, 100–1
  border issue, 63–4
  cable to Pacific Forum, 69
  education issues, 71–2
  Greater Autonomy Steering Committee (GASC), 145, 149
  Greater Autonomy Taskforce, 139
  National Torres Strait Islander Seminar/Workshop (Brisbane, 1996) address, 86
  regional sea claim, 114, 116

Index

sovereign independence declaration (1993), 75–6
Vanstone's letter to, 151
myths and legends, 1–2, 5

Nagir, 7, 11, 23, 39–40, 53
Nai, Fr Edward Rocky, 163, 165
Nakata, Martin, 6, 73, 157
Nakata, Toshio, 124, 127
Namoa, Emmanuel, 145
Natanielu, Bertha, 145
National Aboriginal Consultative Committee/Conference, 74, 77
National Native Title Office, 96
National Native Title Tribunal, 93, 94, 97, 125
National Torres Strait Islander Seminar/Workshop (Brisbane, 1996), 85
Native Teacher Training School, 27, 55–6
native title, *see* land ownership
Native Title Act 1993, 91–107, 108, 109–10
New Deal report, 135–40
New Guinea, *see* Papua New Guinea
New Law, 32–4
Newie, Michaelangelo, 142
Ngampula Yawadhan Ziawali, 72
night curfews, 16, 27–8, 32
Nona, Maluwap (Ben Ali), 106, 114, 126, 127, 128, 132
    armed robbery charge, 120–1, 125
Nona, Tanu, 47–8, 49
Nona, Tipoti, 47
Nona, Ugarie, 47
Nona, Walter, 72
nurse training, 41, 57–8, 69–70
Nurupai (Horn Island), 38*n,* 78, 127, 146–7
    native title claim, 97, 99
    World War II, 38; building material left after, 45

Ober, Dana, 83
O'Brien, Jason, 102–3, 104
occupation of islands, 2–3
O'Donoghue, Lois, 93
oil, 62, 75, 84, 108
    Oceanic Grandeur spill, 50
'Old M', 31

O'Leary, Cornelius (Con), 32, 33, 44, 49
Olewale, Ebia, 62–3
oral histories, xiv–xv, 90, 91
Osborne, Barry, 72–3
outrigger canoes, 3, 5, 9
Owen, Justice NJ, 113

Pacific Forum, 69
Pacific Islanders Protection Act 1872, 13
Pacific War, *see* World War II
Papua New Guinea, 14, 18, 148
    border, 13, 17, 61–4
    fishing, 118, 130–1, 133, 163, 164
    mining activities, 108
    Torres Strait Treaty, 64, 108, 117–19, 130–1, 133
    trade with, 3, 5, 108
Papuan Gulf Native College, 16, 18
Papuan Industries Limited, 17, 19, 28
passbook system, 28–9, 41
Passi, Rev. Dave, 88
Passi, Dennis, 125
Passi, Etta, 64
Passi, Sam, 26, 88
pastoral leases, 93–5
pay, *see* wages and earnings
Pearl, 15
pearl shelling, *see* maritime industry
Pearls Producers Association, 132
Pearson, Francis, 151–2
Peel, Gerald, 46
Pennefather, Captain, 15, 18
Pentecostals, 54
petition to governor of Queensland, 42, 55
Philippines, 14
phones, 58, 70
Pitt, Douglas, 12
Poid, 38, 46, 51
police, 17, 18, 32
    Mabuiag, 23
    Mer, 22, 84
    Thursday Island magistrates, 11, 13, 17, 18, 22
polygamy, 6, 16
population, 3, 10, 45
    birth control, 6
    Thursday Island, 23
Port Kennedy, 78, 81, 142, 151

184

Index

Poruma (Purma), 21, 46, 151–2
Prince of Wales Channel, 8–9
Prince of Wales Island, *see* Kaurareg Aborigines
protection/segregation policy, 19–58
Protectors of Aborigines, 21–32, 37, 38*n*, 44, 50
public works land, 100–1
Pulu, 10
punishments, 16, 27–8
Purma, 21, 46, 151–2

QGS *Pearl*, 15
Queensland Coast Islands Declaratory Act 1985, 66
Queensland Coast Islands Act 1879, 13
Queensland governor, 29, 30
   1944 petition presented to, 42, 55
Queensland Seafood Industry Association, 164

R v. Keyn, 110
Racial Discrimination Act 1975, 66, 92, 95
Rattlesnake, 8, 10
referendum (1967), 59
regional sea claim, 109, 113–16, 163
religious beliefs and practices, 5–6, 53–4
   creation stories, 1–2, 3
   under London Missionary Society, 15–16
   see also Anglican faith, Pentecostals, Assemblies of God
Republic of Mer, 84
residential housing, *see* housing
returned servicemen, 58–9, 65, 81
Reuben, Daniel, 144
Reynolds, Henry, 89
Rice, James, 88
Robertson, Stephen, 100, 102, 103–4, 105–6
rock lobster industry, 119, 122, 126–7, 129–31
   AAP draft report, 133–4
   voluntary buy-back of licences, 134, 163, 164
Ruddock, Philip, 147–8, 149, 151, 154

'Sacred Island Nation', 75
sacred objects and totems, 5–6, 9, 15–16

Sagigi, Robert, 102, 104–5, 106, 115, 154–5, 156
Saibai, 46, 47, 51, 62, 141
   connections to sea, 112
   creation story, 2
   language, 7
   native title claims, 91, 96, 97, 98–9
   Ober, Dana, 83
   trade with New Guinea, 5
   World War II, 35, 38, 39
   see also Waia, Terry
St Paul's, *see* Moa
Salee, Celuia, 88
Sanders, W, 136, 138, 141, 157
Sanders and Arthur, 141
Savage, Isaac, 146–7, 148, 152, 153
Savage, Kevin, 148
Saylor, Bully Hayes, 116
schooling, *see* education; teachers
sea boundaries, 13, 17, 61–4
sea industry, *see* maritime industry
sea resources, *see* fisheries management and ownership
sea rights, 107–16, 119, 124–5, 163
   mackerel fishers' compensation proposal, 121–2
sea slug, *see* maritime industry
secession movements, 74–7, 81–4
segregation/protection policy, 19–58
Seisia, 74, 146, 165
self-government, *see* autonomy
Sen, Sevaly, 132
sexual division of labour, 4
Sharp, Noni, 16, 64
   informants' observations, 4, 9, 11, 47, 53, 62, 89–90
shelling, *see* maritime industry
ships and shipping, 8–10, 17, 39
   see also boats
shipwrecks, 9, 50
   Thompson, Barbara, 4, 10
Shnukal, A, xv–xvi
Singe, John, 9
skulls, 9, 16
social services benefits, *see* welfare payments
Society for the Propagation of the Gospel, 14
Somerset, 10–11, 17

Index

South Sea Island men, 10, 11, 12–14
  housing on Badu, 6
  LMS teachers, 14–19
  marriage to Torres Strait women, 13–14, 18, 23, 31, 47
sovereignty, *see* autonomy
Spain, 8
Sperwer, 11
St Paul's, *see* Moa
Stanley, Captain Owen, 10
Stephen, Pedro, 122, 140–1
  Greater Autonomy Steering Committee (GASC), 145, 149, 152, 153
  Greater Autonomy Taskforces, 139, 141
  native title, 102, 103; Mabo Day Celebrations address (2003), 101
  New Deal report, 137–8
Stephen, Peter, 102
Stephen Island, *see* Ugar
strikes, 64
  in army, 36
  maritime industry, 31–4

Tamwoy Town, 45, 74, 78, 88, 151
  see also TRAWQ
Tapim, Francis, 139, 153
Tapim, Nai, 144
Tatz, C, 28
teachers, 41, 45, 128–9, 141, 148–9
  South Sea Islander missionaries, 14–19
  trainees, 26–7, 55–6
  TSIRECC conference (1995), 72–3
  white, 21–2, 25, 37, 55, 57; protection policy, 26–9, 32
telephones, 58, 70
Ten Point Plan, 94–5
territory status, 80, 85, 139–40, 149, 161
  Bamaga Accord, 143, 144
  Kuiku Mabaigal Forum endorsement, 155
Thaiday, Patrick, 104
Thaiday, Willie, 28
theological training, 16, 54
Thompson, Barbara, 4, 10, 11
Thursday Island, xiii, 69, 148
  Department of Aboriginal Affairs established on, 67
  Douglas, John (government resident), 17, 18–20, 22, 25, 62

government store, 21, 23
Greater Autonomy Steering Committee representatives, 145
hospital, 40, 56, 57–8, 69
hotels, 23, 44
Labour Barracks Pool, 44–5
legal aid office, 68
Loban, Ted, xiii, 53, 71–2, 81
Local Protectors of Aborigines, 24, 37, 44, 50; Lee-Bryce, WM, 27; McLean, JD, 29–32
police magistrates, 11, 13, 17, 18, 22
Port Kennedy, 78, 81, 142, 151
secession movement, 81–3
travel to, 14, 27, 44–5; for teacher education seminars, 55–6
TSRA (May 1993), 80
Waiben, 53
World War II, 14, 34–7; building materials left after, 45
see also Tamwoy Town; TRAWQ
Thursday Island, meetings held on, 88
  about autonomy, 82–3, 136, 139–40, 145, 155; ICC 'sovereign independence' declaration, 75–6
  fishing licensing arrangements, 123–5, 129
  sea rights: regional claim, 115, 124–5
TIB licences, 117, 118, 122–4, 128–9
Tonga, Joe (Tongatbut), 15
Torres, Luis Vaez de, 8
Torres News, xv, 8, 130, 150, 162
  Akee's sovereignty declaration, 82
  editor, 102, 153
  letters to editor, 115, 142, 148; on Bamaga Accord, 144
Torres Shire Council, 74, 151, 156
  New Deal report recommendation to abolish, 136, 137, 139
  see also Stephen, Pedro
Torres Strait Advisory Council, 61, 65
Torres Strait Fisheries Act 1984, 117–19, 125, 133
Torres Strait flag, 89
Torres Strait Island City, 75
Torres Strait Island Regional Council, 165–6
Torres Strait Islander Regional Education Committee, 72–3

Index

Torres Strait Islanders Act 1939 (New Law), 32–4
Torres Strait Light Infantry (TSLI) Battalion, *see* Army enlistment
Torres Strait Media Association, 83
Torres Strait Protected Zone, 117–34
Torres Strait Protected Zone Joint Authority, 119–20, 122, 126–34, 163
  Independent Allocation Advisory Panel, 132–4
Torres Strait Regional Assembly proposal, 136, 139
Torres Strait Regional Authority (Council) (TSRA/TSRC), 85–7, 135–56, 165–6
  Abednego, John, 87, 99, 114, 136–7, 138–9, 140
  abolition of ATSIC, 153–4, 156
  Akee's sovereignty declaration, 82
  Bamaga Accord, 143–6, 149, 152, 157, 165
  Banu, Don, 105, 116
  establishment, 77–80
  fisheries management, 123–8, 130, 131, 140
  funding, 85–6, 87, 98
  Great Autonomy Taskforces, 138–9, 140, 141–2
  Kris, John Toshie, 105, 152, 155, 163, 164, 166
  Lui, Getano (Jnr), 79–80, 82, 85–7, 108, 135, 138–9, 140
  Mau, Margaret, 101
  Mosby, Donald, 130
  Mye's criticisms, 147–8, 151
  Nakata, Toshio, 124
  native title, 93, 97, 98–105; sea claims, 108, 114–16, 163
  New Deal report, 135–8, 139
  Nurupai accusations against, 146–7
  see also Waia, Terry
Torres Strait Regional Authority Act, 87, 143, 150–1, 152, 154
Torres Strait Regional Authority Native Title Office, 98, 108, 163
  dissatisfaction with performance, 104–5
  establishment, 93
  regional sea claim, 114, 115
Torres Strait Treaty, 64, 108, 117–19, 130–1, 133

Torres United Party, 74–5
Torres United Prince Of Wales Party, 75
totems and sacred objects, 5–6, 9, 15–16
Townsville native title conferences (1995), 96
Townsville seminar on border issue (1976), 62–4
trade, 3, 5, 7, 16, 108
  in skulls, 9
Traditional Inhabitant Boat (TIB) licences, 117, 118, 122–4, 128–9
Trans-Fly language family, 7
Transferable Vessel Holder (TVH) licences, 117, 118, 129
  concessions, 133–4
  voluntary buy-backs, 121–2, 126, 130, 131, 133, 134, 163–4
travel restrictions, 25, 27, 32, 44–5, 46
  Badu, 47
TRAWQ, 101, 104, 115, 142, 154
treaties and international agreements, 111, 115
  with PNG, 64, 108, 117–19, 130–1, 133
trepang, *see* maritime industry
Tribune, 46
trochus, *see* maritime industry
Tuckey, Wilson, 125–6
Turner, Charlie, 37
Tut (Tutu), 9, 10, 12, 15
TVH licences, *see* Transferable Vessel Holder (TVH) licences

Ugar, 15, 31, 82, 131
  EMU cooperative, 53
  native title claim, 99–106
  World War II, 39, 40
United Nations, 75, 81–2, 95, 115, 148
  Convention on the Law of the Sea, 111, 115

Vaile, Mark (Commonwealth Fisheries Minister), 122, 123
Vanstone, Amanda, 151
violence, 9–11
  see also warriors and warfare
voting rights, *see* franchise

Wacando, Carlemo, 74–5
wages and earnings, 24, 45, 46

187

Index

in Army, 36–7
for church positions, 54
petition to governor of Queensland, 42
seamen, 14; Torres Strait Islander, 12, 21–2, 25, 28, 33, 44
teachers, 26
women, during World War II, 41
Waia, Terry, 145–6, 151, 152, 153, 154
fisheries management, 123, 126, 128
Greater Autonomy Taskforce, 141–2, 143
native title, 99–100, 101, 103; regional sea claim, 114, 115
Saibai people's connections to sea, 112
Waia, Walter, 108
Waiben, 53
see also TRAWQ
Waier, 5, 15, 89, 99
Waikaid, 47
Walker, Rev. F W, 17, 19
Warraber, 34, 37–8, 46, 82
Warria, Fr Napoleon, 114
Warrior Island, 9
warriors and warfare, 5, 9–10, 16
women as 'agents of peace', 6
see also World War II
Wasaga, Bill, 99
'welfare colonialism', 61, 68
welfare payments, 40–1, 45, 62–3
dependency, 76–7, 132
'White Australia' policy, 19, 23
Whiteman, DL, 5
Whitlam government, 61–4
Wigness, Pearson, 139

Wik decision, 93–5
Williams, Brian, 103
Williams, James, 42, 54
Wini (Weenie), 4, 11–12
wolfram, 41, 51–2, 53
women, 18
abduction by ships' crews, 10, 12
as 'agents of peace', 6
food collection role, 4
nurse training, 41
Thursday Island work, 44
World War II, 34, 37–41
see also marriage
Woodlark, 10
World War II, 14, 34–42
boats and boating, 34, 39, 40, 44
building materials left after, 45
ex-servicemen, 58–9, 65, 81
health services, 40, 41, 57

Yam Island, 55, 104, 128, 149
health services, 40, 56, 103
meetings held on, 63; about single jurisdiction fisheries management (July 1999), 123, 124, 128
World War II, 37, 38–9, 40
see also Lui, Getano
Yam Island Council, 8
Yarmirr Croker Island people, 110–11, 114
Yorke Island, *see* Masig

Zenadth Kes, 153, 155, 156

IN THE TIME OF KIAROSTAMI: WRITINGS ON IRANIAN CINEMA

BY GODFREY CHESHIRE

edited by
JIM COLVILL

introduction by
MATT ZOLLER SEITZ

Woodville Press · New York

in collaboration with
KIAROSTAMI FOUNDATION

ISBN: 979-8-9864463-0-1
Library of Congress Control Number: 2022944739

Published by Woodville Press, New York.
woodvillepress@gmail.com

First printing of 1,000 copies, 2022
Printed in Spencer, Indiana by World Arts

Introduction © Matt Zoller Seitz
All other text © Godfrey Cheshire

*Dedicated to the memory of three men who
gave me more than I could ever repay.*

*Godfrey ("Buddy") Cheshire Jr., wonderful father
and true Southern gentleman.*

*R.B. ("Bernie") Reeves, extraordinary mentor and patron,
"the Citizen Kane of North Carolina."*

*Abbas Kiarostami, phenomenal artist, inspiration
and ever-generous friend.*

CONTENTS

Introduction by Matt Zoller Seitz   9
Author's Preface   13

1. My Journey with Iranian Cinema   18

2. Iran Up Close: Inside the Islamic Republic   70
    Nights in Tehran   71
    Axis of Cinema   85
    Return to Tehran 2017   89

3. Abbas Kiarostami, Cinemaster   102
    Remembering Abbas Kiarostami   103
    A Cinema of Questions   115
    Seeking a Home: On Koker, Cannes and *Taste of Cherry*   125
    How to Read Kiarostami   143
    Of Experiments and Women: Two Post-Millenium Features   162
    Certified Copy: At Home and Abroad   175
    Desire's End: *Like Someone in Love*   181
    24 Frames   188

4. Iranian Filmmakers   194
    Dariush Mehrjui:
        Revealing an Iran Where the Chadors Are Most Chic   195
    Mohsen Makhmalbaf:
        Gabbeh, Gabbeh, Hey   199
        Film in the Mirror: *A Moment of Innocence*   208
    Samira Makhmalbaf:
        The Apple   215
    Bahman Ghobadi:
        Crossing the Border: *A Time for Drunken Horses*   221
    Jafar Panahi:
        Persian Crack-Up: *Crimson Gold*   225
        Closed Curtain   230

Asghar Farhadi:
   About Elly   233
   The Salesman   237
Mahmoud Kalari:
   Interview with Mahmoud Kalari   241
Mohammad Rasoulof:
   Manuscripts Don't Burn   255

Endnotes   259
Author's Writings on Iranian Cinema   261
Acknowledgments   267
Index   269
About the Author   309

INTRODUCTION

When I first met Godfrey Cheshire in October, 1995, at a pastry shop not far from his West Village apartment, I had no idea what an important figure he'd be in my life. I had just moved to New York from Dallas to take a job as a pop culture columnist for the *Star-Ledger* of Newark, New Jersey. Even though Godfrey was authoritative in every way, he didn't carry himself like an authority figure. He was more like one of those beloved, film-loving friends that every cinephile has in their lives—someone who is not content to treat special insights and unique experiences as signifiers of developed taste, but instead projects his intellect and curiosity outward, hoping to create more moviegoers whose tastes are as broad as his own.

The man sitting across from me smoking a cigarette and letting his coffee get cold was the lead movie critic for the weekly *New York Press*, and would become its assigning film editor. The paper had picked my clips out of a pile of submissions answering an in-house wanted ad for additional film writers and asked Godfrey to to meet me for a job interview. He had recently turned 44, but had a youthful energy and seemed wise beyond his years. Godfrey had an encyclopedic knowledge of American film history and style and had been all over the world and reported from festivals, archives, and movie sets of every size and type. One of the first things he asked me during that first meeting was whether I was familiar with what was happening in current Iranian cinema. He was pleased with the writing I'd submitted on international films, in particular those from Hong Kong and mainland China, but was concerned that I hadn't included any writing on Iranian film. I said I had never had occasion to review one. Dallas, I explained, may have been a major American city with a reasonably healthy art-house scene, but to my knowledge it had never shown an Iranian film in any of its cinemas, outside of one-off festival showings—and even those were few and far between. Godfrey said no apology was necessary because at that point, Iranian cinema had only just begun to gain a serious foothold in the United States, even in New York. Until that point, it had been largely shut out of exhibition spaces, due to a combination of reactionary politics, racism, xenophobia, and garden-variety American aversion to any film that had subtitles or asked audiences to pay attention to subtext. "If you're going to be a film critic in New York, you'll need to be conversant with what's happening in the two most vital film scenes in the world right now,

China and Iran," he told me. "Iran is making the best films in the world right now, as far as I'm concerned."

Over the next few years, Godfrey would introduce me and many other New Yorkers to the works of major Iranian filmmakers. Their ranks included Abbas Kiarostami, Jafar Panahi, and Mohsen Makhmalbaf, whose works are considered at length in this volume, as well as Majid Majidi, whose crystalline drama *Children of Heaven* ended up being the first Iranian film I ever reviewed for the *Press*. Godfrey was also responsible for one of the greatest moviegoing experiences of my life, a showing of Kiarostami's *Close-Up* at the Tribeca Screening Room. Godfrey was the primary driver of that theater booking *Close-Up*, and devoted thousands of words to promoting it in his newspaper column. Afterward, he stayed in the lobby discussing the film with audience members who wanted to learn more about Kiarostami's masterpiece and invited them to continue the conversation over drinks at a nearby bar. He was filled with stories he'd gained through in-person visits with filmmakers and film programmers and arts figureheads in Iran, where he was one of a handful of American critics, including Jonathan Rosenbaum, who were welcomed and trusted. Many of the tidbits were gleaned through his burgeoning friendship with Kiarostami, including the decision to switch between dramatic re-enactments of a film buff insinuating himself into the life of a family by claiming to be Mohsen Makhmalbaf, and the same man's subsequent trial for impersonation, which Kiarostami covered documentary style with 16mm cameras. Originally the story was to be told linearly, starting with the re-enactments and moving on to the trial. But when a film festival showed the reels out of order, Kiarostami decided the story was more interesting that way, and re-edited the movie to alternate the impersonation and the trail. At the time, this was perhaps the most astonishing story I'd ever heard about a major filmmaker embracing a "mistake" and using it to deepen his art. As it turned out, it was far from the only such story Godfrey had to tell about the legends of Iranian cinema, artists whose existence as artists was predicated on their ability to roll with whatever punches life threw at them.

What's most remarkable about this volume is its transparency. Throughout, in new, rewritten and republished pieces, you can see Godfrey's questing and questioning mind latching onto a subject for which he has a deep affinity, learning as much as he can about it—by pondering the works themselves, talking to their creators, and absorbing the culture that birthed the scene—and then figuring out a way to transmit his enthusiasm to the widest American audience possible. Though now recognized as the leading authority on Iranian cinema among American film critics, Godfrey does not write for his colleagues, although of course he's delighted when they read him. Rather than wear his erudition like a suit of armor, he writes in a direct, approachable way. That makes his work accessible to audiences who might not know a single thing about the topic he's chosen. Godfrey is a great teacher, one of the best I've had. The quality that unites all great teachers is that they never stop being students.

Matt Zoller Seitz
2022

AUTHOR'S PREFACE

THIS BOOK IS A RECORD of one American critic's encounter with Iranian cinema over a period of nearly 30 years, beginning in the early 1990s. It contains two kinds of pieces. While most of the book comprises reviews and articles written for various publications during that period, other pieces (including all of Section 1 and parts of Section 3) were written specifically for this book.

Readers are invited to note the various dates and venues of the pieces, for two reasons. One is to make clear the editorial provenances of the articles, which have a lot to do with which films are covered and the audiences for both the films and the articles. Quite clearly, the writings here don't reflect coverage of Iranian cinema as a whole but rather a specific slice of it, occupying a particular cultural space: art films—which Iranians often call "artistic films"—that are aimed at cinephile audiences around the world, which they reach via a chain of entities that include film festivals, film distributors, cultural institutions such as museums, and individual exhibitors (art houses). These organizations in turn inhabit a world where the opinions and attention generated by critics, journalists, curators, award-giving groups, etc., influence the ways that films are perceived, discussed and disseminated.

The time that my coverage began was an opportune one. Iranian cinema, which had enjoyed a fevered decade of activity and accomplishments in the 1970s ("the Iranian New Wave") and then nearly been destroyed during the Iranian Revolution of 1979, came back to life in the mid-1980s, thanks in large part to a government initiative aimed not only at rebuilding an entertainment industry but also at producing Iranian art films that could reach international audiences. By the late 1980s the first fruits of this renaissance began trickling into European festivals and catching critics' and programmers' eyes. In the early 1990s it reached North America. There followed a near-miraculous decade during which Iranian films won hundreds of awards at film festivals around the world, and cinephiles from Tokyo to Toledo came to know the names of auteurs such as Kiarostami, Makhmalbaf, Majidi and Panahi.

The second reason to note these pieces' dates and places of publication is to perceive my trajectory as a critic-journalist covering films emerging from a culture about which initially I knew very little. While I was quickly taken by many of the movies I saw, I only gradually began to learn about the political, social and cultural context they emerged from—a context I was fortunate enough to encounter directly when I began visiting Iran in the late 1990s. Even at the time, I realized I owed a great deal to the many genial, enthusiastic Iranians—bemused, in many cases, to meet the rare American able to enter their country—who kindly took it upon themselves to educate me on many fascinating aspects of their culture, cinematic and otherwise. While many urged me to investigate the pre-revolutionary cinema to understand the roots of the recent renaissance, others steered me toward ancient and modern Iranian poetry, literature and art, as well as numerous political and philosophical thinkers.

In trying to understand the earlier period of Iranian cinema, I was fortunate to meet some of its key figures. In Paris, I interviewed Farrokh Gaffary, who had worked with Henri Langlois at the Cinémathèque Française, was credited with writing the first serious film criticism in Iran, and made some of the nation's first art films. In New York, I talked with Gaffary's friend and collaborator Fereydoun Hoveyda, who wrote alongside Truffaut and Godard in *Cahiers du Cinéma* and later represented the Shah's government at the United Nations. At his palatial digs in rural England, I interviewed the formidable Ebrahim Golestan, auteur of *The Brick and the Mirror* and other important pre-revolutionary films, about "The House Is Black," the enormously influential documentary short he produced for the legendary poet-filmmaker Forough Farrokhzad. In Iran, the pre-revolutionary filmmakers whose remarks proved especially enlightening included Parviz Kimiavi, whose satiric *Mongols* was often cited by cinephiles; Bahman Farmanara, a prodigiously talented director and producer; and Kamran Shirdel, who showed me his "The Night It Rained," an innovative short that prefigured certain currents in post-revolutionary cinema.

These conversations, and those with filmmakers who gained global attention in the 1990s and after, proved invaluable in my attempts to better understand Iran and its cinema, as did the input I received from various Iranian critics and cinephiles and numerous Iranian-American friends. I learned a great deal from certain New York–based writers, teachers and filmmakers who are mentioned in the text, including Jamsheed Akrami, Hamid Dabashi and Bahman Maghsoudlou. Books that were crucial in the enlightenment and guidance they provided included Hamid Naficy's magisterial four-volume *A Social History of Iranian Cinema* as well as his *An Accented Cinema: Exilic and Diasporic Filmmaking*. I should also note the pleasure and insights I derived from books by critic friends, including Jonathan Rosenbaum and Mehrnaz Saeed-vafa's *Abbas Kiarostami*, Tina Hassania's *Asghar Farhadi* and Geoff Andrew's monograph on the Kiarostami film *Ten*.

Recently, one critic friend remarked to me on his surprise at how few books about Iranian cinema by Western film critics have been published since it began to gain international attention. Certainly, there have been far fewer than those that resulted from the successes of the French New Wave in the 1960s and the New German Cinema in the 1970s. No doubt there are numerous reasons for the difference, including changes in moviegoing that have made foreign-language films an ever-smaller portion of yearly box-office earnings, and a trend away from auteur-focused cinema in academic studies and other forums for commentary.

Yet it's also undeniable that Anglophone film criticism has historically been Eurocentric from its earliest days, and though many film festivals the world over welcome distinctive films from the most far-flung countries—and indeed, take pride in doing so—the individual artworks and their creators meet the public in a context where the surrounding media and educational institutions do little to examine and explain their cultures of origin. In the case of Iran, this lack of information and understanding is perhaps at its most extreme. Arguably, during the last half century, no country with a potent indigenous cinema has been as isolated from the world as the Islamic Republic of Iran. In part, this has been a deliberate strategy on the part of the IRI's government to keep out foreign (especially Western) cultural "toxins," which have been held in suspicion since before the Iranian Revolution of 1979. Yet while the same government, somewhat paradoxically, has encouraged and facilitated the making and export of art films in hopes that they might help improve Iran's image internationally, Iranian filmmakers have had to face a situation in which appreciation of their work has faced silent, rarely acknowledged barriers of hostility and misunderstanding that stretch back not just decades but millennia—barriers that I had the occasion to observe and ponder beginning with my first visit to Iran (see Section 2's "Nights in Tehran").

The vast, bilaterally created and maintained chasm separating Iran and the West, the United States especially, since the Iranian Revolution is a geopolitical tragedy that also constitutes an ongoing danger to world peace. In this fraught situation, culture has been a small but vital lifeline across that chasm capable of connecting individuals as well as disparate, interlinked artistic traditions. And of all the arts that have come to the West from Iran, cinema has surely reached the greatest number of people. From the first appearances of Iranian films at Western film festivals in the late 1980s to the two Oscars won by Asghar Farhadi films in 2012 and 2017, the visibility of and acclaim for Iranian films has steadily increased, giving non-Iranians around the world a set of complex, artistically distinctive and often compellingly humanistic images to put against the reductive and militant images of Iran purveyed by Western news media.

This book's account of my interactions with Iran's movies and moviemakers is organized thematically. In Section 1, "My Journey with Iranian Cinema," I recount my professional and personal experiences from the time of my first exposure to Iranian films to the present. Section 2, "Inside the Islamic Republic" preserves my impressions of Iran in reports I wrote on visits there beginning in the late 1990s. Section 3, "Abbas Kiarostami, Cinemaster," collects a number of my pieces about the past era's most lauded filmmaker, along with some recent reflections on the man himself and certain of his films I'd not previously gotten to write about. (It should be noted that these are only a portion of my writings on the director; others can be found in different sources: see Author's Writings on Iranian Cinema.) Section 4, "Iranian Filmmakers," includes reviews—and one interview—of the work of filmmakers whom I consider among the era's most significant.

In following and reporting on the development of Iranian cinema, and in getting to know many of its leading artists, I have continually been impressed not only by their inexhaustible creativity but also by the courage and tenacity they have displayed when faced with the harassment, obstruction and even prison sentences visited upon some of them by antagonistic officials. Filmmakers in the West can barely imagine working under such conditions, and some Iranian filmmakers have understandably elected to move or work abroad to escape these difficulties. In observing the choices these conditions militate, I have had the unusual, privileged position of being able to witness the Iranian cinema's evolution from both within Iran and without: at film festivals around the world, including my home city of New York. While this book contains only a fraction of the articles I've written about that cinema over three decades (and is focused on films and filmmakers based in Iran rather than the Iranian diaspora), it does offer a personal view of an artistic phenomenon of extraordinary power and resilience, and I hope its perspectives will interest and inform the innumerable admirers of Iran's cinema.

Godfrey Cheshire
New York City
August 2022

1.

MY JOURNEY WITH IRANIAN CINEMA

It started with a phone call from Gavin Smith, an editor at *Film Comment*, sometime in mid-1992. I had moved to New York City from North Carolina the previous year and begun writing for the alternative weekly *New York Press*, as well as contributing to other publications. Since international film had long been a primary focus of my writing as a film critic, and I'd become particularly interested in Chinese-language cinemas after encountering Hou Hsiao-hsien's *A Time to Live and a Time to Die* and Zhang Yimou's *Red Sorghum* at the New York Film Festival in the late 1980s, my first assignment for *Film Comment* was a fortuitous one: It involved visiting Beijing to observe the filming of Chen Kaige's *Farewell, My Concubine* in early 1992. The resulting article pleased the magazine's editors, I was told, so Gavin was calling to offer another assignment: Would I attend the upcoming Lincoln Center festival of post-revolutionary Iranian cinema—the first one in New York—and see if it was "worth an article"?

I almost said no, because I had no idea that it would be. I had been hoping to delve further into another cinema I was already interested in, and had no inkling that anything noteworthy was happening in Iran. In fact, Iran's government-backed film revival had begun to produce its first fruits in the mid-1980s, right around the same time Taiwan's and mainland China's did, but the latter had been more quickly embraced by the West's cinema gatekeepers. Still, because I wanted to continue writing for *Film Comment*, I said yes to Gavin's offer.

Though a non-cinematic trip to Egypt meant that I returned to New York after the Lincoln Center event had started, I plunged in right away... and soon found myself immersed in one of the most astonishing and personally consequential film experiences I'd ever had. I told friends I was amazed at what I'd encountered—I thought I knew the basic map of world cinema fairly well, but this festival showed me something as imposing as it was entirely unexpected. I felt like I'd stumbled upon a lost continent of cinema, improbably located between East and West in a country that had been calling mine "the Great Satan" since 1979.

This was an auteur cinema, clearly, and a major one. If I had discovered one or two extraordinary directors in the sixteen films the festival included, I would have been sufficiently impressed. But in first seeing works by Abbas

Kiarostami (*Close-Up*, *Where Is the Friend's House?*), Mohsen Makhmalbaf (*Once Upon a Time, Cinema*), Dariush Mehrjui (*Hamoon*), Bahram Beyzai (*Bashu, the Little Stranger*) and Amir Naderi (*Water, Wind, Dust*) all together, I felt I was encountering a fecund national film scene comparable to Italy in the late 1940s and 1950s, France in the 1960s or Germany in the 1970s. Not only were the individual voices and styles extraordinarily distinctive, but the sophisticated uses of the medium seemed to bespeak a cinematic culture of great depth and complexity.

It turned out these great auteurs, all of whom had enjoyed substantial careers by the time I encountered their work, were only the tip of a formidable iceberg. The festival also included films by directors such as Ebrahim Forouzesh (*The Key*, scripted by Kiarostami), Khosro Sinaie (*In the Alleys of Love*), Alireza Davudnezhad (*The Need*) and Sa'ied Ebrahimifar (*Pomegranate and Cane*) whose work suggested a second level of auteur cinema populated by filmmakers of considerable accomplishment and promise. And yet there was still more to consider. Works such as Azizollah Hamid-Nezhad's compassionate Iran-Iraq War film *Hoor on Fire*, Varuzh Karim-Masihi's intricate crime drama *The Last Act* and Behrouz Afkami's tragic romance *The Bride* gave proof of a more commercial, genre-based cinema that evidently shared certain qualities with Iran's most striking "artistic" films.

As I put it in the article I wrote for *Film Comment*, "What's most striking about these new Iranian films is a profound, pervasive humanism which, in asking the most searching questions about countless aspects of Iranian life, makes them political in the best and broadest sense."[1] If anything, I had been expecting films that were political in a much narrower and more obvious manner. What I found was, first and foremost, a sense of compassion that extended to all levels of society and every manner of individual: from intellectuals with troubled marriages in upper-class Tehran to ragtag school children in impoverished villages, to women constrained by social strictures, and adolescents damaged by war's ravages. At a time when American movies were increasingly characterized by big-budget fantasy and special effects extravaganzas at the high end, and cleverly mounted displays of irony and idiosyncrasy in the newly burgeoning independent sector, the Iranian insistence on not only the importance of social realities and individual lives, but also the artist's probing, sympathetic views of these subjects, gave their cinema a collective identity that was striking in its differences.

That this cinema emerged under the auspices of an authoritarian Islamic government, during a decade when Iran was an international pariah and engaged in a ferocious, hugely destructive war with neighboring Iraq, made it all the more remarkable. These conditions had obvious effects on the ways films were produced in Iran, and thus on some of the qualities that came to be associated with the post-revolutionary cinema. Virtually all of the films were made with budgets that would have been considered small for American or European independent films, yet if this made shooting on location far more common than studio productions, it didn't entail a sense of financially determined constraints. Indeed, Iranian directors seemed spurred toward greater inventiveness by the limitations imposed on them. And many of their solutions resulted in a greater degree of realism. While a few of the films I saw at Lincoln Center included brilliant performances by established actors (e.g., Susan Taslimi in *Bashu, the Little Stranger* and Khosro Shakibai in *Hamoon*), many others exemplified the Iranian method of using non-actors as performers, a practice so widely and successfully employed as to suggest that every Iranian might be a movie actor just waiting to be discovered.

Just as financial limitations sparked different creative strategies, so did the content restrictions imposed by the Islamic Republic. In a sense, the relationship between Iran's government and its filmmakers was paradoxical from the aftermath of the Revolution, and it remained so. On one hand, the government created a new infrastructure for the country's film industry, encouraged production and even funded a good bit of it; besides commercial films and propagandistic Iran-Iraq War movies, it even supported the creation of artistic films and helped submit them to international festivals, with an eye toward improving Iran's global image. On the other hand, the cinema officials under the Ministry of Culture and Islamic Guidance (Ershad) closely monitored filmmakers' activities, requiring scripts to be submitted in advance of production and sometimes censoring or banning the completed films. They also enforced a new production code that proscribed most of the sexual and violent content then common in cinemas globally, as well as blasphemy, disrespect for Iran's government and leaders, and so on.

The restrictions regarding the depiction of women and relations between the sexes were especially problematic, and provoked a range of responses from filmmakers. The rules said that women must always be shown in head covering and loose, shape-disguising clothing; these requirements were enforced in public, but a great many Iranian women doffed the head scarves and billowing chadors as soon as they were behind closed doors. Men and women also could not touch unless the actors were married in real life, and all physical expressions of love, affection or passion among adults were strictly forbidden. Kiarostami, Naderi and other directors decided these restrictions made it impossible to depict adult characters honestly or realistically, so they largely avoided showing grown-ups in private situations. This set of limits also prompted some filmmakers to sideline adults and focus on children as lead characters, a trend that informed some of the post-revolutionary cinema's earliest successes and became one of that cinema's calling cards at international festivals. Nevertheless, directors including Mehrjui and Beyzai went ahead and made films by the rules, showing women with headscarves when they wouldn't have worn them in real life—a decision also underlying Asghar Farhadi's more recent *A Separation* and *The Salesman*.

The sense that most of these films, even the more commercial or genre-bound ones, gave of engaging strongly with Iranian social realities seemed to signal a country undergoing a period of intensive self-examination. As happened in Italy and France in the years after World War II, the aftermath of the Iranian Revolution's traumas and the Iran-Iraq War's devastation gave artists a new set of possibilities as well as the impetus to probe past and ongoing problems, failings and injustices. In the films generally, there's a positive energy that conveys the hopefulness and determination of a nation that is consciously reinventing itself, looking toward a future freed of the impediments of the past. Yet at the same time, filmmakers were impelled to examine those impediments and problems, especially ones that might have been expected to have been overcome by the Revolution but weren't.

Such examinations were what I called "political in the best and broadest sense," but it increasingly became clear to me why they weren't political in the way I had expected. In interviews I did later with Kiarostami, Makhmalbaf, Mehrjui and Beyzai, all were very explicit about their lack of interest in engaging with nominally political issues and subjects; these were transitory and superficial, they said. The real subjects of interest lay beneath them: cultural factors and complexes, aspects of Iranian character, experience and psychology that reached far back in history and that in many cases had barely been touched by the changes wrought by the Revolution. Yet many of these issues were tricky to address under the strict eyes of the censors. So filmmakers frequently followed the example of Iranian poets and artists of centuries past by couching their meanings in metaphor, symbolism and suggestion—creating a form of cinema often richer, more complex and nuanced than those in other parts of the world.

This cinema also entailed an excitement about *cinema itself* that had several evident causes. First, the Islamic Republic prohibited various forms of art and expression, especially those involving public performance, which left movies in a position of greater cultural centrality than they had previously enjoyed. Second, at a time when many national cinemas around the world were being decimated by the impact of Hollywood movies as trade and culture were increasingly globalized, Iran effectively sealed itself off from this inundation: Very few foreign movies were permitted to play cinemas in Iran, affording Iranian films a privileged position that translated as cultural cachet. Moreover, while the discussion of ideas grew difficult or impossible in many public forums and areas of the media, cinema became a rallying point for educated Iranians looking for the kind of serious, challenging ruminations that novelists, poets and intellectuals had supplied in earlier times. Finally, the mystical currents present in much of traditional Iranian thought and artistry seemed to find a modern vehicle in the cinema's imaginary transformations, which concurrently served to elevate both the viewer and the filmmaker.

Indeed, the Iranian films I saw at Lincoln Center suggested a kind of cinephilia more profound and catalytic than any I knew of in the West, and no film illustrated that more potently than Kiarostami's *Close-Up*, a documentary—admittedly a dubious term for a film that contains so many elements of fictionalization—about a poor young man named Hossein Sabzian who is arrested for impersonating the director Mohsen Makhmalbaf to an upper-middle-class Tehrani family. Because the family suspected Sabzian was out to rob them he was arrested and, during the trial that Kiarostami films, it emerges that the accused and his accusers were drawn together by a single thing: a "love of cinema."

Surely it was not incidental that the events of *Close-Up* took place in 1989: a decade after the Revolution, in the year following the bitter, non-victorious end of the Iran-Iraq War, and just months after the death of Ayatollah Khomeini. In various subtle ways, the film conveys the sense of a deflated, somewhat disoriented society, one still attached to the ideals that its renewal had promised, but also unsure of its future course. And if this entailed a lessening of belief in religion, revolution, military and political leaders, it also opened the way for increased devotion to secular faiths, such as cinema.

Has there ever been a film that conveyed so many dimensions of the social roles of cinema, or that showed a society so captivated by the medium? Everything about the tale hints at film as a vehicle for displaced religious feeling and the yearning for social and economic justice. Doubtless Sabzian revered directors in general, as many cinephiles do, but Makhmalbaf was clearly a special case in his personal pantheon, as he was in Iranian cinema. As the first director to establish himself in the front ranks of that cinema who emerged after the Revolution, a former Islamic fundamentalist who at first embraced the new government but then made a trio of films—*The Peddler, The Cyclist, Marriage of the Blessed*—that damned its failure to deliver on many of the Revolution's promises, he was, for many Iranians, a filmmaker whose courageous speaking-truth-to-power on behalf of the powerless made him a peerless artistic hero.

In the film's final scene Sabzian embraces Makhmalbaf with an expression of serene rapture: the rapture of a true believer united with his ultimate hero, or a sinner touching his redeemer, or even a mortal soul encountering what some Iranian mystics would call the "angel of one's being." Kiarostami has said the film is about "the power of dreams." Which it certainly is. But the context here is a society in which cinema's dreams have a unique, historic and multifaceted potency, one that allows filmmakers to shape the reality they are addressing.

In several senses, my journey with Iranian cinema began with *Close-Up*. It was the film that struck me most strongly in the 1992 Lincoln Center festival, and it was more than just a personal favorite. Later in the decade, polls of Iranian and international film critics named it the best Iranian film ever made, an opinion that would endure. As my fascination with Iranian cinema grew after this initial encounter, *Close-Up* came to seem even more important in retrospect, in large part because of the way it put filmmaking and filmmakers in the frame. As I would later write in describing its international impact, in the first five years of the Iranian cinema's post-revolutionary revival, 1985–90, its films, in beginning to draw attention at European festivals, evoked comparisons to the two great paradigms of post–World War II "new" cinemas: Its humanism, low-budget ingenuity and focus on social hardships and injustices brought to mind Italian neorealism, while its intellectual deftness and preponderance of distinctive auteur voices suggested a kinship to the French New Wave. Such comparisons, especially the citation of neorealism, however, were often made regarding "new" cinemas arising in disparate parts of the world, especially those torn by historical crisis. *Close-Up* changed the description of Iranian cinema by adding something new: the contemplation of cinema itself.

It is my contention—one supported only by circumstantial and anecdotal evidence—that *Close-Up* was the pivotal film that set Iranian cinema on the road to the great successes it would enjoy in the 1990s. But that didn't happen in the usual way. The film puzzled audiences and critics and drew mostly negative reviews when it opened at Iran's Fajr Film Festival (much debate centered on whether it was meant to glorify or demean Makhmalbaf, when Kiarostami was clearly much more interested in Sabzian). The most prominent international festivals, including Cannes, Berlin, Venice and New York, passed on it.

But then something happened: Critics began discovering and talking about the film, especially about the novel self-reflexive element and Kiarostami's wry, thoughtfully complex point of view. These laudatory appraisals had their most important impact in France. Kiarostami's next film, *And Life Goes On*, was included in the Un Certain Regard section of the 1992 Cannes Film Festival. As the world's preeminent film festival, Cannes has enormous influence on global perceptions of film art, so by making *And Life Goes On* the first post-Revolutionary Iranian film shown in one of its main sections, its programmers instantly gave Iran's cinema an enormous boost in visibility and prestige. It also elevated Kiarostami to the ranks of world auteurs, something that baffled the many Iranian critics and cinephiles who considered him a lesser talent than certain other directors.

If any of the French admirers of *Close-Up* hoped that the film's self-reflexive dimension would be continued in his subsequent work, they were not to be disappointed. *And Life Goes On* concerns a film director modeled on Kiarostami himself who drives into an earthquake-stricken area trying to discover if the child actors of an earlier film of his (*Where Is the Friend's House?*) survived the devastation; the film fictionalizes a journey that Kiarostami made in 1990. And in his next film, *Through the Olive Trees*, which was included in Cannes 1994's Official Competition, Kiarostami fictionalized the making of *And Life Goes On* with the story of a film director trying to deal with a bit actor's romantic frustrations. With their Möbius-strip intertwining of documentary and drama, autobiography and philosophical fiction, the two films cemented Kiarostami's place as the most acclaimed director to have recently emerged on the world stage. The magazine *Cahiers du Cinéma* celebrated him with a cover story titled "Kiarostami le magnifique!"

Although it may have seemed that the powers-that-be at Cannes were grooming Kiarostami to become the first Iranian filmmaker to win one of the festival's major prizes, that was not to be. Ironically, the honor went to his erstwhile assistant Jafar Panahi, who directed his *The White Balloon* from a Kiarostami script. The film won the important Camera d'Or prize for best first film at Cannes in 1995 and went on to become the post-revolutionary cinema's first worldwide art-house hit (it was the first Iranian film to receive a serious release in the U.S.). And its Cannes success anticipated that of Kiarostami's next directorial effort, *Taste of Cherry*, which won the festival's top prize, the Palme d'Or, in 1997. If *Close-Up* was the film that lit the fuse, *The White Balloon* and *Taste of Cherry* were the works that confirmed the Iranian cinema's launch into global prominence, a position that would see other Iranian filmmakers winning numerous festival awards and admiring reviews in the late 1990s and beyond.

Given the astonishments I encountered at Lincoln Center in 1992, my fascination with Iranian cinema could only grow. After my article in *Film Comment* was published in early 1993, I met my first Iranian filmmakers in the flesh during the spring of that year when Amir Naderi's *Manhattan by Numbers* played in the annual New Directors/New Films Festival, co-presented by the Museum of Modern Art and the Film Society of Lincoln Center. Naderi had moved to New York since *Water, Wind, Dust*, his last film made in Iran, and *Manhattan by Numbers* made a fascinating transposition of the previous film's hyper-kinetic visual style from a desert setting to the convoluted urban spaces of the city. Amir himself was an ebullient, gregarious, charismatic guy and a fanatical cinephile whose legend included the tale that he drove a Volkswagen bug from Tehran to London to be first in line to see Kubrick's *2001: A Space Odyssey* when it opened in 1968. *Manhattan by Numbers* was produced by another genial immigrant to New York, Ramin Niami, a gifted filmmaker in his own right.

Abbas Kiarostami was the next Iranian filmmaker I met, when he accompanied *Through the Olive Trees* to the 1994 New York Film Festival. Though we were in the formal situation of journalist and interview subject, Kiarostami immediately put me at ease and impressed me with his warmth and good humor. I told him *Close-Up* was my favorite of his films and he said it was his own favorite, adding that he'd just talked with someone who compared it to *Citizen Kane* (a startling juxtaposition that made more sense the more *Close-Up*'s renown grew). I was very curious about the culture of Iran and how it produced the remarkable films I'd seen so far, and he responded generously, beginning an exchange of ideas as well as a friendship that continued in future years. Nor was this the only friendship born that day. Our translator was Prof. Jamsheed Akrami, a former Iranian film critic and early Kiarostami champion who now lived and taught in New Jersey and later made several documentaries about Iranian cinema.

These contacts helped amplify and render more personal the sense of Iranian character and culture I had perceived in the films. I began to seek out and get to know various Iranians and Iranian-Americans in the U.S., and some of these proved crucial to my understanding of Iranian culture. Bahman Maghsoudlou, a pre-revolutionary critic, who now lived in New Jersey and went on to make notable documentaries about Iranian cinema, was kind enough to share his knowledge and tapes of pre-revolutionary films with me. And I well remember a lunch in the early 1990s when the renowned Columbia University professor Hamid Dabashi, who would later serve as translator when I interviewed Makhmalbaf in Iran, advised me to read Roy Mottahedeh's *The Mantle of the Prophet: Religion and Politics in Iran*. That terrific book was the beginning of a deep dive into reading about Iran, a preoccupation that has continued to the present day.

In 1980 I began attending and writing about the New York Film Festival, reporting for North Carolina's *Spectator* magazine. During my early years of visiting the NYFF, its director was the cosmopolitan, erudite Richard Roud, who co-founded it in 1963. In 1987, Roud was succeeded by Richard Peña, who liked my reports in *Spectator* and reached out to me even before I moved to New York.

In shifting away from Roud's essentially Eurocentric approach to programming, Peña gave the NYFF a more global focus, which included showcasing films from previously ignored countries such as Iran. Very interested in and knowledgeable about Iranian cinema, Peña was a key actor in introducing its films and filmmakers to New York and American audiences and critics.

When I moved to New York in 1991, Richard Peña was one of the few people I knew in the film community there. But that soon changed. I quickly discovered New York's film world to be a hyper-sociable realm. Film critics love to talk, and I did a lot of talking about my newest passion, Iranian cinema. My colleagues, I found, were interested and curious. Although none to my knowledge had attended that 1992 festival at Lincoln Center, word started getting out at international festivals of growing heat around Iranian cinema. Kiarostami's elevation to Cannes and his visit to New York in 1994 helped increase that awareness. If other critics wanted to discuss any of this, I was ready. In fact, it seemed I acquired something of a reputation for it. I became "the Iran guy." One wag even dubbed me "the Iranian ambassador to New York."

Being a film critic in New York entailed a kind of power that writing in North Carolina never had, so my activist impulses transferred to interacting with the business in ways I hadn't attempted before. One example involves Miramax Films, which had become the powerhouse indie distributor whose chairman, Harvey Weinstein, was lionized in the press as a kind of latter-day Medici cum Irving Thalberg. In 1994, Miramax acquired the U.S. distribution rights to *Through the Olive Trees*. I and other critics were excited about this, since it seemed poised to become the first Kiarostami film to get a real American release, backed by the company which then had unparalleled clout at U.S. art houses.

But those expectations were disappointed when Miramax released *Through the Olive Trees* into a single downtown theater with only one press screening. I reviewed Kiarostami's latest in *New York Press*, calling it the best film of the year to date.[2] Then two weeks later I wrote a column[3] in which I scrutinized Miramax's way of trying to scoop up every film with any arthouse potential, then releasing them in kind of a three-tier structure: Those at the top level (e.g., *Pulp Fiction* or *The Piano*) got months of build-up, publicity and promotion; those with real but more modest commercial potential (e.g., *Bullets Over Broadway*) received more specialized handling; while films on level three, like *Through the Olive Trees*, were released with minimal support and left to fend for themselves. I could not find a single ad in any New York newspaper for Kiarostami's film.

Frankly, this surprised me. I thought Weinstein was cannier, understood the great and mounting critical esteem Kiarostami enjoyed, and would release the film in a way that provided a solid launching pad for a director who was likely to produce much important work in the future. (I later heard that Weinstein bought the film in order to get other films in a package a French sales company was offering.) Such missteps, I wrote, "raise questions about Miramax's ability to juggle major-studio ambitions and indie credibility. What happens if critics, who've been instrumental in the company's success to date, come to see its imprimatur as a red flag rather than a mark of distinction? And when tales like the handling of *Olive Trees* start to hit home with filmmakers, how long can it be before another distributor steps in to fill the breach...?"

The article had an impact. I later read that an up-and-coming indie director backed away from a Miramax deal after reading it. A critic friend told me that, as the first piece to criticize Miramax in detail, it gave other critics and journalists the okay to start looking at the company in a more skeptical and questioning way. Evidently, and not surprisingly, it did not please Harvey Weinstein (this of course was more than two decades before the scandals that would end his career and send him to prison). But he responded diplomatically, having his head of publicity take me to lunch at Nobu, then TriBeCa's trendiest restaurant, and make nice.

Two months after the Miramax piece, my engagement with Iranian cinema entered a new phase when I began five years of covering the Cannes Film Festival for *Variety*. *Variety*'s operation at Cannes was something to behold. On the first day of the festival, the magazine's team of critics—from London,

Paris, Rome, Sydney, L.A., etc.—met at a restaurant on the beach where, after lunch, reviews editor Todd McCarthy divided up the large number of films in the festival's main sections and many from its huge market, with each critic getting a full complement to review. Thus began a week and a half of nonstop film viewing and writing, along with intensive socializing and partying, that made the festival alternately grueling and exhilarating.

Cannes' glamor and excitement were undeniable, and for me as a devotee of international cinema, it was an incredible smorgasbord of fascinations from around the world. Which is not to say that the majority of films were great. On the contrary, when I reported on my first year at Cannes, I noted how many highly touted films got divided or negative reactions. Even Emir Kusturica's sprawling Yugoslav history phantasmagoria, *Underground*, which provoked fisticuffs after its Palme d'Or win was announced, seemed to have as many detractors as supporters. The exception to this rule, happily enough, was Panahi's *The White Balloon*. I wrote afterwards that the Iranian Camera d'Or winner was the one film at Cannes '95 that seemed universally liked.[4] It was acquired for U.S. distribution by October Films, founded by Bingham Ray and Jeff Lipsky, who gave the film the kind of smart, successful release that Miramax bungled for *Through the Olive Trees*.

The year 1995 was the centenary of cinema, a fact that was ballyhooed especially in France, and among the films there advertised as paying tribute to this, easily the most striking to me was Mohsen Makhmalbaf's *Salaam Cinema*, which played in the Un Certain Regard section. Another Iranian feature that mixes the real and the artfully contrived, the film presents itself as a documentary about the overwhelming response Mahkmalbaf gets when he advertises an open casting call for his next film. Thousands of Iranians storm his studio, where they profess their love for cinema and audition by obeying any command he gives them, even the most ridiculous. Writing about the film, a portrait of Iranian cinemania equal to that of *Close-Up*, I said that while much of it is hilarious, it "also telegraphs a spiky if discreet commentary on authoritarianism."[5]

The authoritarian in this case—the film director as ayatollah—was Makhmalbaf, who came across as increasingly tyrannical and unsympathetic in the demands he places on his would-be movie stars. But the Makhmalbaf here is a made-up character, a figure in an allegory (if *Close-Up* presents cinema as a means of escape from life's confinements, *Salaam Cinema* reveals its potential as an instrument of social control), something I didn't fully grasp until I met the man himself at Cannes. In person, Makhmalbaf was genial, outgoing and continually engaging. The more I got to know him, the more I saw him as a noble, even heroic figure—much closer to the gallant rescuer of Sabzian in *Close-Up* than the mini-despot of *Salaam Cinema*.[i]

The following year, Cannes again hosted a full complement of auteur cinema, with new films by the likes of Robert Altman, Mike Leigh, Hou Hsiao-hsien, Steven Soderbergh and others. But to me the best film there was unquestionably Makhmalbaf's *Gabbeh*, a visually ravishing, dreamlike fable about the lives of nomads in central Iran who weave *gabbehs*, rugs that are far simpler (but still richly symbolic) than the elaborate Persian carpets for which Iran is known. I wrote a rave review in *Variety* of the film, which went on to an appearance at the New York Film Festival and U.S. distribution via New Yorker Films (both firsts for Makhmalbaf).

Somewhere around this time I got an idea—a purely intuitive notion—that I've never written about till now. It was that Makhmalbaf was engaged in a fierce race to beat Kiarostami to cinema's coveted mountaintop, the Palme d'Or at Cannes. Of course the younger director was behind. Cannes had anointed Kiarostami its chosen Iranian; I had the distinct impression that the programmers didn't invite other Iranian giants such as Mehrjui and Beyzai because they didn't want to give him any competition. It's arguable that Panahi and Makhmalbaf got their films into Cannes sections due to their connections to Kiarostami, though they were obviously his juniors. The only way Makhmalbaf could reach the mountaintop first would be if the older director stumbled and didn't deliver a prize-winning film. That didn't happen of course. When *Taste of Cherry* took the Palme the following year, the race—if race it was—was over.

But my main point here is to note the extraordinary creative peak Makhmalbaf reached during this time. *Salaam Cinema*, *Gabbeh*, and another film, the autobiographical meditation *A Moment of Innocence* (premiered at the 1996 Locarno Film Festival), comprise a de facto trilogy that stands as one of the most brilliant achievements of the New Iranian Cinema. To

---

i. Cinematographer Mahmoud Kalari discusses this in the interview on p. 241.

my mind, they equal Kiarostami's celebrated Koker Trilogy in ambition and accomplishment and deserve to be as well known.

Beyond Cannes, I got to know Makhmalbaf better as I saw him in New York and at other film festivals. At the Montreal World Film Festival, he told me that one of his Iranian associates worried when he saw me waiting for him in a hotel lobby, thinking I might be an Iranian agent, maybe even an assassin. (I knew Makhmalbaf had been threatened due to his anti-regime stances.) I laughed at this, saying how could I be mistaken for an Iranian anything given my blond hair and blue eyes. He replied, seriously, that when Alexander the Great conquered Persia, he had his officers marry aristocratic women and that there are still blond and blue-eyed Iranians due to these unions. (Note to my biographer: This was the only time I was ever mistaken for an Iranian secret agent or a descendant of Macedonians.)

At Italy's Turin Film Festival in November 1996, where Makhmalbaf served on the main jury and I on the international critics (FIPRESCI) jury, several prizes went to the Iranian contender, Majid Majidi's *The Father*. Turin proved more significant, though, as the place where Makhmalbaf and I saw Mamhoud Chokrallahi and Moslem Mansouri's "Close-Up Long Shot," a 45-minute documentary portrait of Hossein Sabzian that reveals him to be a far more complex and troubled figure than *Close-Up* depicted. As I wrote, Sabzian "talks about his love of movies but also about feeling betrayed by them—which Makhmalbaf, speaking after first seeing the new film, said left Sabzian standing anew as symbol of an unfulfilled people."[6] (Kiarostami would later tell me that "Close-Up Long Shot" was "not a good film" but that he couldn't sleep for three days after watching it.)

Around the same time, I received an invitation that left me very excited, and perhaps just a bit nervous. The cinema authorities in Iran, I was told, liked the writing I had been doing about Iranian cinema and wanted to invite me to the Fajr Film Festival, an annual event where new Iranian films premiere. When, in February 1997, I landed at Tehran's Mehrabad Airport and walked into its cavernous entrance hall, where stern-looking soldiers examined arriving passengers under huge portraits of Ayatollahs Khomeini and Khamenei, I was as wonderstruck as if I'd landed on Mars. And the wonderment only increased from there. Everything I saw fascinated me, and the more I saw, the more I wanted to see. Other international guests at Fajr left after the weeklong festival ended. I stayed for a month.

Perhaps the simplest way to sum up this visit, the first of seven I would make to Iran in the next twenty-one years, is to say that while the Lincoln Center festival of 1992 left me enamored with Iranian cinema, being in Iran left me smitten with Iranian people and their culture. Some of those people of course were famous. As my report on that visit indicates,[ii] I spent time with Kiarostami and Makhmalbaf and met other filmmakers, perhaps most importantly the great Dariush Mehrjui, who told me of accompanying the Ayatollah Khomeini on his flight from Paris to Tehran at the beginning of February 1979. But I also met and conversed with a whole range of people, and many in the film community were generous in providing me with insights and information that would help me begin to answer the primary question I brought with me: How did Iran engender such an amazing film culture?

Cinema came to Iran, I learned, in the year 1900. Muzzafer al-Din Shah, the fifth monarch in the Qajar dynasty, which ruled Iran from 1789 to 1925, was on a tour of Europe that summer when, outside of Paris, he saw a display of the cinematograph, which had been introduced to the world only five years before. Impressed with the device, he recorded in his diary, "We instructed [court photographer Mirza Ebrahim Khan] Akkasbashi to purchase all kinds of it and bring it to Tehran so that God willing he can make some [motion pictures] and show them to our servants." The first films shot in Iran, then, were essentially home movies for the royal family, its friends, and their households.

The new medium remained an aristocratic diversion until Tehran got its first movie house, in 1904. This was two years before the outbreak of Iran's Constitutional Revolution (1906–11), which saw the overthrow of the Qajars and the establishment of a republican government before that was deposed and the nation's final dynasty, the Pahlavis, was later introduced by the machinations of the Russian and British empires (few realize that Iran had not one but two democratic governments in the 20th century undermined by the West, the second being the CIA/MI6 coup that overthrew Prime Minister Mohammad Mossadegh and reinstalled the last Pahlavi Shah in 1953).

---

ii. See "Nights in Tehran," p. 71

Fittingly for a democratic entertainment medium, Iran's first cinema was founded by a liberal Constitutionalist (i.e., anti-monarchist) named Mirza Ebrahim Sahhafbashi. It showed comedy shorts and newsreels, but features soon followed, and the city's exhibition scene grew exponentially over the next decade—although, as happened in many countries, religious authorities inveighed against the movies' supposed incitements to immorality (this resulted in cinema audiences being segregated by gender). And there was no indigenous production; for a full quarter-century, the movies shown in Iran typically hailed from Hollywood or Europe.

The making of Iranian feature films got off to an important if limited start in the 1930s, which saw a total of nine features made by three directors. Of the films, two are remarkable enough to be of continuing interest, and not only because Makhmalbaf delightfully spoofed them in *Once Upon a Time, Cinema*. In 1930 in Tehran, Ovanes Ohanian, an Armenian who had studied cinema in Russia, opened the Film Actors School for male and female students, and soon after began making feature films to give them employment. The second of these, *Haji Agha, Cinema Actor*, concerns a film director and two romantically involved students who use surreptitious cinematography to convince the girl's conservative religious father that both acting and cinema are socially beneficent. Made with confident verve and full of fascinating views of Tehran in the early 1930s, the comedy-melodrama strikingly anticipates subjects and themes—directors, identity, transgression, performance, pedagogy, class divisions, cinematic self-reflexiveness—that would become identified with Iranian cinema with the arrival of *Close-Up*.

The film did well enough, but because it was silent, it was eclipsed by a film that opened shortly before it in 1933. Iranian cinema's first talkie, and its biggest hit of this era, *The Lor Girl* was made by Abdolhossein Sepanta, a dashing young journalist/poet who wrote, directed and starred in the film as well as penning its songs. Sepanta plays Jafar, a government agent sent to capture a bandit chieftain in the lawless Khuzestan region, where he meets and falls in love with Golnar, a dancing girl whose parents the bandit had killed. Expertly made (and shot in India), the film has elements that would later factor into Iran's commercial cinema: attractive performers, exciting action and suspense scenes, an intriguing cultural and political backdrop, and a love story, as well as dancing and musical numbers. Seen today, it retains a charm and freshness similar to comparable Hollywood and European movies of the 1930s.

Following World War II, the commercial cinema that *The Lor Girl* anticipated got underway in earnest. In 1947, Ismail Kushan, an Iranian working at the UFA studios in Berlin, purchased the rights to several European movies and had them dubbed in Farsi in Istanbul. These were successful enough in Iran to convince Kushan to go into production himself. Released in 1948, his first two features weren't hits at the box office, but they were followed by ones that were, and they launched an industry that grew by leaps and bounds in subsequent years. Between Kushan's first films and the Revolution in 1979, Iran produced approximately 1,200 features. The industry had its own star system, which regularly intersected with the pop-music galaxy, but most educated Iranians still looked to America and Europe for serious cinema. The indigenous product, which came to be known by the derogatory term *filmfarsi*, was regarded as vulgar and third-rate.

The artistic cinema that Iran would produce in future decades also had its roots in this era, however, and its connections to the postwar developments in France and Italy are represented by two young Iranian friends who found themselves sharing the excitement over cinema in Paris after the war. Fereydoun Hoveyda became acquainted with Francois Truffaut and Jean-Luc Godard and began writing alongside them in *Cahiers du Cinéma*; he had a keen interest in the Italian neorealists, especially Roberto Rossellini (Hoveyda later served as Iran's Ambassador to the United Nations). His pal Farrokh Gaffary, who wrote for *Positif*, returned to Iran in 1949 and began publishing what is regarded as the nation's first serious film criticism, as well as launching cine-clubs and researching the history of Iranian cinema. After another stint in Paris, where he worked with Henri Langlois at the Cinémathèque Française, he returned to Iran again in 1956 bent on making films, ones different from the prevailing commercial fare.

Like many of the Italian neorealist films that influenced it, Gaffary's *The South of the City* had a narrative core that was melodramatic rather than radically anti-conventional. A woman who has lost her husband is forced by desperate circumstances to take a job in rough, poor southern Tehran, where she becomes the object of an emotional contest between two men who have been bitter rivals for years. Gaffary aimed to use this tale to explore harsh social realities that other films ignored, and as his friends Truffaut and Godard would do not long after his own filming, he took his cameras out of the studio and shot in the unvarnished, sometimes seedy areas where the story took place. He later recalled to me that filmmaker friends would drop by the set and say, "If this film succeeds, it will change Iranian cinema. We won't be confined to studio sets and silly comedies anymore."

It was not to be. *The South of the City* opened at three cinemas in November 1958. According to Gaffary, it did good business but after five days it was seized by government officials and never seen in its original form again (he assumed that the film's elements and script are lost and unrecoverable). Since the film had been cleared by government censors prior to its release, the reasons for its suppression are murky and remain in dispute. Whatever the reasons, Iran would have to wait another decade for its cinematic revolution.[iii]

During that decade, its most significant cinematic advances came in the area of documentaries, especially short ones. Thanks to generous funding from the government's Ministry of Fine Arts, and later the Ministry of Culture and Art and National Iranian Radio and Television, documentaries were produced in abundance and served as a training ground for numerous directors who would establish themselves as feature makers later. While the Shah's censors maintained strict oversight, some of these films offered views of Iranian life not unlike what Gaffary had hoped to achieve fictionally in *The South of the City,* and incurred official displeasure in doing so: e.g., Kamran Shirdel's "The Women's Prison" (1965) and "The Castle" (1966) about prostitution in south Tehran, overstepped content restrictions regarding women.

Other short documentaries that were among the first Iranian films to win international prizes represented a storied convergence of cinema and Iran's literary culture. Ebrahim Golestan was a noted fiction writer when he founded Golestan Film Studio in Tehran in 1952. Forough Farrokhzad, a passionate young poet who became and remains the most renowned female literary figure in all of Iranian history, went to work for Golestan in 1958 and a year later he sent her to England to study film editing and English. The two began a love affair that was scandalous (he resolutely refused to divorce

---

iii. Gaffary's comments from an interview by the author in Paris, 1998.

his wife) but legendarily creative. In the early 1960s, three Golestan-directed short documentaries won awards at festivals in San Francisco, Pesaro and Venice, Italy. But the couple's most famous collaboration was directed by her and produced by him.

In late 1962, Golestan was approached by a charitable foundation about making a documentary to benefit a leprosarium in Tabriz. He turned the assignment over to Farrokhzad, who went to the leper colony and shot for 12 days in 35mm black-and-white with a crew of three. The resulting 21-minute film, "The House Is Black," which she also edited, is arguably the Iranian cinema's first unequivocal masterpiece. Intercutting observational documentary sequences with staged scenes that illustrate the harshness and occasional felicities of life in the leper colony, Farrokhzad employs frequent repetitions and visual rhymes, together with a soundtrack that makes dramatic use of silence, musical effects and her own recitation of plangent biblical verses, for a cumulative effect that resonates on many levels: as a personal lament of the filmmaker's inner pain, as a veiled sociopolitical allegory about life in the shah's Iran, and as an uncompromising look at some of the country's true unfortunates. The film was Iran's first great example of a poetic cinema, and its enormous influence has been amply attested to by Kiarostami, Makhmalbaf and others. (Farrokhzad died in a car accident in 1967 at the age of 32. Kiarostami's film *The Wind Will Carry Us* bears the title of one of her poems.)

Of the dramatic films made in the 1960s, Iranian critics usually cite two 1965 titles as of particular significance. Both are by directors already mentioned, whose B&W films suggest the influence of film noir. In *Night of the Hunchback*, his third feature, Farrokh Gaffary turned to black comedy with the tale of a hunchback theater performer who chokes to death at a party, after which his body is passed from one group of people to another (Gaffary himself plays a hairdresser); with obvious parallels to Hitchcock's *The Trouble with Harry*, the film's surrealism also evokes Buñuel. Though it also narrates a single night's misadventures and offers an odyssey of images of nocturnal Tehran, Ebrahim Golestan's first feature, *The Brick and the Mirror*, is a more somber film and a more formidable accomplishment. It starts with a cab driver finding a baby left in his cab and then going around the city trying to get help and advice, most poignantly from his sympathetic girlfriend.

Beautifully directed, the drama's depiction of romantic disquiet and urban anomie recalls the films of Michelangelo Antonioni. It was the first feature shot in Iran using direct sound.

The explosion came at the decade's end. Much as the French New Wave legendarily burst onto the world with the 1959 debuts of Truffaut's *The 400 Blows* and Godard's *Breathless*, Iran's new-cinema renaissance kicked off with the appearance in 1969 of two groundbreaking films. Both were second features made by directors then aged twenty-seven. Dariush Mehrjui's *The Cow*, set in a village where the death of the community's lone bovine sends its owner (a brilliant performance by Ezatollah Entezami) spiraling into madness, offers a tragic view of the kind of traditional villages idealized to a ridiculous degree by earlier Iranian films. Its opposite number in many respects, Masoud Kimiai's *Qeysar* follows its title character (incarnated by iconic tough-guy star Behrouz Vossoughi) as he hunts down and kills the villains responsible for his sister's rape and brother's murder; one particularly striking death takes place in a bath house and involves a mirror and a straight razor. (Makhmalbaf paid comedic tribute to both films in *Once Upon a Time, Cinema*.)

As the films that launched the Iranian New Wave (a term designating the Iranian auteur cinema of the 1970s, while New Iranian Cinema designates the post-revolutionary cinema), *The Cow* and *Qeysar* established a paradigm that would endure, with one pole tilting toward the artistic and the other toward the commercial—as indicated by their very different fates. A film most suited to a small, intellectual audience, *The Cow* had been backed by the government, but when officials saw the result, with its depiction of a poor, backwards Iran so at odds with the Shah's efforts to project an image of modernization, it was banned and had to be smuggled out of the country to reach the 1971 Venice Film Festival, where it became the first Iranian feature to win an international award (the FIPRESCI prize). With its skewed camera angles, propulsive editing and stirring score, *Qeysar* combined the stylistic sizzle of Hollywood crime films with a uniquely Iranian thematic thrust; some later saw its politicization of culture and class as laying the groundwork for the Shah's overthrow (Makhmalbaf said "it gave lumpenism an ideology"). Though it received mixed reviews, Kimiai's film was a huge box-office hit.

The two films opened the floodgates on a decade of hyperactive creativity and a raft of new and promising young auteurs. The two orientations indicated above were, of course, not airtight categories, but rather points on a spectrum, bordering a continuous gradation across a wide sweep of possibilities. At one side, represented by *The Cow*, was Iran's new breed of art film, serious, intellectual, European-influenced and, more often than not, funded by the government. At the other side, inspired by *Qeysar* and an earlier hit, *Qarun's Treasure*, was a new generation of commercial films which often aimed to replace (or at least update) the old-fashioned formulas of *filmfarsi* with Hollywood-style production values and excitement (including increased doses of sex and violence). Between the two poles came numerous admixtures, films that, each in their own way, hoped to combine artistry and audience appeal.

The art-film side of the spectrum produced the richest yield, and judging by critical appraisals both inside and outside Iran, the most enduring reputations. Besides Mehrjui, who made four more acclaimed films during the decade (his *The Mina Cycle* became the rare Iranian film to get a U.S. art-house release in the 1970s, titled *The Cycle*), and certain veterans of the previous decade—including Gaffary and Golestan—the leading lights here included Sohrab Shahid-Saless, Bahram Beyzai, Parviz Kimiavi, Abbas Kiarostami, Bahman Farmanara, Mohammad Reza Aslani, Hajir Dariush, Arbi Ovanesian, Marva Nabili and Arsalan Saasani.

The common thread uniting these filmmakers was a fascination with Iranian culture. Whether the approach was contemporary or historical, satiric or tragic, sociological or poetic, the films seemed absorbed, sometimes even obsessed, with penetrating the outward surfaces of Iranian life. Shahid-Saless' *Still Life* (1974)—which Makhmalbaf once ranked with "The House Is Black" as the two most important prototypes for the mature Iranian art film—is an almost microscopic examination of the daily life of a railroad worker on the edge of retirement. With its slow rhythms and classical framing, the film distills both the dignity and the melancholy of an Iran that seems at once eternal and rapidly passing away.

To the project of probing Iranian culture, no director brought a deeper knowledge of its historical and literary roots than Bahram Beyzai, a playwright and expert on ancient Iranian theater. With his eclectic visual sense, a mixture of theatrical suggestiveness and Hitchcockian precision, Beyzai explored the undercurrent of myth in Iranian life, whether in an offbeat social drama such as *Downpour* (1971), his feature debut, or in the archetypal romances *The Stranger and the Fog* (1975) and *The Ballad of Tara* (1978), which take place in far-flung locales that seem to merge history and dream, personal destiny and collective passion.

Two other directors offered very different takes on the Iranian past. Parviz Kimiavi, who was dubbed "Iran's Godard," in *Mongols* (1973) used an ironic, surrealistic style to compare television's invasion of Iran to the devastating onslaught of Genghis Khan's hordes seven centuries earlier. His next feature, *Okay Mister* (1978), satirized the Shah's modernizing efforts via a story in which William Knox D'Arcy (the first foreigner granted oil exploration rights in Iran) lands a balloon in a remote village and tries to teach the ways of the West to the mystified villagers. In his masterpiece, *Prince Ehtejab* (1974), adapted from Houshang Golshiri's acclaimed novel, Bahman Farmanara explored the decadence of the Qajar dynasty with a chilly, distanced style that could be compared to the work of R. W. Fassbinder or Straub-Huillet. In his other pre-revolutionary film, *Tall Shadows of the Wind* (1978), Farmanara depicted a remote village where giant scarecrows were used to cow the population. Though evidently aimed at the Shah's regime, the film's indictment was so all-purpose that the Islamic Republic banned it.

In 1970, Abbas Kiarostami, a young artist who had directed some successful TV commercials, was brought in to head up a filmmaking division at the government's Center for the Intellectual Development of Children and Young Adults (which Iranians call Kanoon), a position he retained for over two decades. "Bread and Alley" (1970), the first of his numerous short films "about, but not necessarily for, children," observed the encounters of a boy wending his way home carrying a loaf of bread. *The Traveler* (1974), his first feature, told of a provincial boy so avid to get to Tehran to see a soccer match that he would lie and cheat his fellows. *The Report* (1978), Kiarostami's one "adult" feature of the pre-revolutionary period, was produced outside of Kanoon (by Bahman Farmanara); it offered a searing portrait of a collapsing marriage, a tale that reflected Kiarostami's own life. (Kanoon also produced films for other directors including Beyzai and Amir Naderi.)

On the Iranian New Wave's more commercial side, Masoud Kimiai remained the pace-setter, directing seven more features in the 1970s, while there was a remarkable diversity of output from directors including Amir Naderi, Naser Taghvai, Khosrow Haritash, Ali Hatami, Parviz Sayyad, Jalal Moghadam, Fereydoun Goleh, Kamran Shirdel, Shapour Gharib and Alireza Davudnezhad.

In this area of filmmaking, as in many of the films noted above, there were frequent signs of discontent with life in the Shah's Iran. One of the decade's most influential and critically lauded films, Taghvai's *Tranquility in the Presence of Others* (1969) concerns a retired colonel who moves to Tehran to be near his two daughters, but their disastrous lives—one commits suicide, the other has a terrible marriage—drive him ultimately into an insane asylum. Like Shahid-Saless' *Still Life*, the film, which was adapted from a novel by Gholam Hossein Saedi, the originator of *The Cow*, offers a quietly devastating depiction of the darkness in ordinary Iranian lives.

A versatile director who was one of the pre-revolutionary period's most distinctive voices, Amir Naderi began his career with two gritty, noirish crime dramas, *Goodbye, Friend* (1971) and *Impasse* (1972). His next feature, *Tangsir* (1973), was a large-scale period tale of revenge that seemed to integrate influences as diverse as Richard Brooks' *The Professionals* and Akira Kurosawa's *Seven Samurai*; it starred *Qeysar*'s Behrouz Vossoughi.

Naderi wasn't the only director to assimilate or adapt an eclectic blend of foreign influences. Kamran Shirdel remade Godard's *Breathless* in *The Morning of the Fourth Day* (1972). And Jalal Moghadam interpreted Theodore Dreiser's *An American Tragedy* in his *The Window* (1970).

Perhaps no career better illustrates the ability of some artists to span pure entertainment fare and the most serious subjects than that of Parviz Sayyad. With a lifelong background in traditional theater, Sayyad turned to movies with the precedent-setting romantic melodrama *In the Course of the Night* (1967), a commercial hit that starred the musical superstar Gogoosh. In the 1970s he made nine movies (and numerous TV shows) centered on a character called Samad, a lovable but bumbling peasant. Yet Sayyad also mounted *Dead End* (1977), one of the most powerful and incisive dramas evoking the mood of Iran in the period leading up to the overthrow of the Shah. Loosely based on a Chekhov story, the film concerns a romantic young woman who imagines that the man standing outside her house is a shy suitor, only to discover too late that he is an agent of SAVAK, the Shah's brutal secret police, pursuing her fugitive brother, a political dissident.

I went to Iran in 1997 knowing almost nothing about the country's pre-1979 cinema. When I asked people how to explain the extraordinary display of artistry I saw at Lincoln Center and at film festivals subsequently, the answers often boiled down to four words: the Iranian New Wave. The more I saw the films of this period and learned about its filmmakers, the more I understood that reaction. Like the "new waves" in countries such as Poland, Great Britain, Czechoslovakia, Brazil and others inspired by the French breakthrough, Iran's was a remarkable efflorescence of film culture (including critics, cine-clubs, festivals, etc.) that laid the groundwork for what would come later. Yet the anti-regime sentiment I often felt in the Islamic Republic meant that, for some people, the complete answer to my question seemed to be: "Give all credit for today's cinema to the Iranian New Wave, none to our present government."

However, that government clearly did deserve a significant share of credit. Iranian cinema had approached the Revolution not only in an economic crisis but, in certain senses, in an identity crisis, under suspicion from both the left and the right. In the 1960s the influential writer Jalal Al-e Ahmad coined the term *gharbzadegi*, often translated as "Westoxication," which lamented the extent to which educated Iranians were intoxicated with the West's technological culture, including cinema; the analysis seemed to underlie the uncertainty and sense of alienation that some felt in the film culture. Despite the many strides made in the 1970s, critics Jamsheed Akrami and Bahman Maghsouldlou both thought the New Wave era ended with much of its promise unfulfilled.

Meanwhile, hardline Islamists made cinema a symbol of the Western moral corruption they saw as undermining traditional Iranian life. On August 10, 1978, the Rex Cinema in Abadan was torched by perpetrators who doused its locked doors in airplane fuel. Over three hundred spectators, who had been watching a Kimiai film, died in the inferno. By mid-1979, up to 180 cinemas, roughly a third of the country's total, had been burned down or otherwise put out of business.

Given the strong antipathy of many religious conservatives to cinema, film production might never have resumed in a country suddenly run by them. But the Ayatollah Khomeini reportedly was an admirer of *The Cow* and its sympathetic view of the rural poor. In a speech made just after he returned to Tehran from Paris on February 1, 1979, with an entourage that included Dariush Mehrjui, the Imam specifically approved the continued existence of cinema when used for proper social purposes such as education rather than corruption and exploitation.

Khomeini's crucial words came at a moment when Iran's cinema essentially lay in ruins. Some sources say that as few as four movies were produced in the year after the Revolution, and there was an average of fifteen in the years 1979–82, a drastic fall-off from the annual peak of over seventy in the 1970s. During this period many filmmakers, including Gaffary and Golestan, left Iran, and the outbreak of the Iran-Iraq War in September 1980 heightened the social and economic disarray left by the Revolution.

The movement to revive the cinema began even amidst that disarray. After a group of New Wave veterans including Mehrjui, Beyzai, Kiarostami and Naderi published an open letter in May 1981, urging the regime to look for a way to "organically and comprehensively" reconstruct the film industry, the Cabinet approved a set of regulations that empowered the Ministry of Culture and Islamic Guidance to execute a wholesale reorganization of the nation's cinema. This led, in 1983, to the creation of the Farabi Cinema Foundation (named for the important medieval philosopher al-Farabi), a semi-autonomous agency under the Ministry of Culture and Islamic Guidance charged with coordinating public and private efforts in the reconstruction and revitalization of Iranian cinema.

Under its brilliant managing director, Seyyed Mohammad Beheshti, the Farabi leadership were essentially bright young Muslim intellectuals who saw their task as two-fold: economic-industrial and cultural. In the former area, they recreated Iran's moviemaking infrastructure by overseeing everything from ticket prices to managing government financial assistance to producers. The cultural component meanwhile involved fostering the values of the Revolution and the society it created, and beyond that, nurturing an art-form that would find original ways of employing Iran's vast heritage as it forged a new cultural identity for Iranians. While the cinema that emerged following the resumption of production after 1983 encompassed a revived commercial branch that included comedies, war films and the like—though minus the vulgarity of *filmfarsi*, thanks to new content restrictions—Beheshti and company clearly wanted to encourage a new kind of Iranian art film, one that could go abroad and win acclaim internationally. To that end, they invited prominent pre-revolutionary directors including Mehrjui, Kiarostami and Beyzai to resume working. (Beheshti himself persuaded a reluctant Kiarostami to direct *Where Is the Friend's House?*)[iv]

The success of this effort, a brilliant exception to the rule that government-managed artistic enterprises seldom produce anything but mediocrity, was everywhere apparent in the films I had encountered. And it was only partly due to the resurrected careers of directors from the Iranian New Wave, because the New Iranian Cinema also included a burgeoning complement of important post-revolutionary filmmakers such as Makhmalbaf, Panahi, Majid Majidi and two prominent women directors, Rakhshan Bani-Etemad and Tahmineh Milani.

"Nights in Tehran," my report on that first visit to Iran, left a few things unmentioned. One was the suggestion that Dariush Mehrjui, who had been educated at UCLA, majoring in philosophy, and spoke fluent English, gave me: "Read Henry Corbin." I had never heard of the eminent French Iranologist, a translator of Heidegger and associate of Carl Jung. But once I started reading Corbin, I was hooked. At once scholarly and deeply, performatively mystical (I said it was like Carlos Castaneda as written by Jean-Paul Sartre), his in-depth explorations of Iranian thought from pre-Islamic times to the modern era not only illuminated the culture I was studying, but also led me into investigating other branches of mystical philosophy (especially Neoplatonism) and influenced how I saw some Iranian films; combined with a disciplined practice of meditation, they also led me on an inner journey that in some ways paralleled the outward one with Iranian cinema.

Another thing not registered in that piece was the difficulty Abbas Kiarostami faced in trying to complete *Taste of Cherry* in time for Cannes. I don't now recall my thinking at the time, but because some of his troubles

---

iv. Kiarostami had written the film's script but was hoping another filmmaker would direct it.

had to do with the government, I assume I didn't write about them fearing that might increase his difficulties. In my book *Conversations with Kiarostami*, I recall that when I saw him in February of 1997, "he was clearly in a period of stress." The closer Cannes got, the more the stress mounted, much of it due to the fact that his film concerns suicide, a taboo under Islam. There was opposition within the government to letting the film go to Cannes. When a Kiarostami associate asked if I could get something into the U.S. press that would give his allies some ammunition by suggesting that his troubles could damage Iran's image internationally, my activist instincts kicked in and I instigated and contributed to a front-page article in *Daily Variety* that discussed his situation.

As I recalled in my book, the weeks leading up to Cannes "were a time of nerve-wracking high drama… Discussions about the film's fate reportedly went to the top of the Iranian government, yet when I left New York for Cannes, it was still unclear if it would make it to France.

"That the film made it to Paris in time to be subtitled and then to Cannes for its screening seemed well-nigh miraculous. But these events only paved the way for the real miracle: its win of the Palme d'Or (shared with Shohei Imamura's *The Eel*)." After his press conference he and I had a drink on the Croisette, then I walked with him toward the festival's formal banquet. No one seemed to recognize him until we got close to the banquet hall and he was suddenly engulfed in a swarm of paparazzi. I didn't have an invitation to the dinner or any idea of attending it, and was wearing a T-shirt. But when my friends Amir and Vahid Esfandiari from the Farabi Cinema Foundation saw me, they laughingly grabbed a jacket from someone, handed it to me and pulled me into the hall.

From Cannes I went to Paris. I had been planning to get a visa for Iran there and then spend the summer based in Tehran researching Iranian cinema. I hadn't realized that in April, after a German court convicted Iranian officials of ordering the 1992 Berlin assassinations of four Kurdish leaders, Iran had withdrawn its ambassadors from European capitals. As I discovered when I went to the Iranian embassy, no ambassador meant no visas. I went back every week but the answer remained the same.

Being stranded in one of my favorite cities ordinarily wouldn't be a cause for consternation. But I didn't want to be in Paris; I wanted to be in Tehran. Naturally the stay wasn't exactly a hardship. I whiled away the glorious spring days with young French actors, including actor-acrobat James Thiérrée, grandson of Charlie Chaplin. He put me up at his apartment where I watched him learning to play the violin while riding a unicycle. Some days I would ride with him on his motorcycle (shades of Sabzian and Makhmalbaf) as he roared across Paris to the French Circus School.

I continued to try to figure out how to get to Iran. One day, after James went off to England to perform for the Queen, an Iranian contact relayed Mohsen Makhmalbaf's instruction for me to FedEx my passport to someone at the Iranian mission to the United Nations in New York, who would send it to the Iranian Interests Section at the Pakistani embassy in Washington, D.C., which issues visas. I did as I was told, though being in Paris with no passport was a uniquely weird feeling. But the plan worked. A few days later I got a FedEx envelope containing my passport with an Iranian visa inside.

I arrived in Iran in time to attend Kiarostami's 57th birthday party on June 22. Early on, a friend helped me find an apartment to rent in a neighborhood I'd noted earlier that seemed especially nice, conveniently located just south of the central Vanak Square. (I think I may have been the first American journalist to rent an apartment in Tehran since the Revolution.) The place was an ideal base from which to move around Tehran conducting interviews and, later, to venture out to the cities of Isfahan and Shiraz. I learned enough Farsi to get meals, taxis and other necessities. (My lack of fluency has of course meant that I've depended on an array of translators and subtitlers over the years.)

The neighborhood was a congenial one. It included a laundry run by an elderly man who, after learning that I was a film critic, would regale me with the names of his favorite 1950s Hollywood stars. "Hey, mister!" he would shout. "Kirk Douglas! Susan Hayward! Victor Mature!" My presence also sparked the curiosity of some I encountered. One day I came out and was spotted by a guy in a large SUV. We started talking and I learned he had attended the School of Dentistry at UNC–Chapel Hill, my alma mater. He asked what I was doing there and when I told him I had rented an apartment and was living here, he exploded in laughter. "You must be very brave or very crazy!" he said. (I appreciated the remark but told him I didn't think I was either.)

I saw a fair amount of Kiarostami and his sons Ahmad and Bahman, whom I'd met on my previous visit. The interviews I did prior to and during the excursion to the village of Koker that Abbas took me on comprise *Conversations with Kiarostami*. Our other interactions and my thoughts on his work during the summer are recorded in "Abbas Kiarostami, Cinemaster" and "Seeking a Home."

I also spent time with Makhmalbaf, who seemed to have turned from his own work to producing a new generation of filmmakers. He was homeschooling his three kids and some of their friends as a way of avoiding the lamentable Iranian educational system that Kiarostami interrogated in his documentaries *First Graders* and *Homework*. Both of Makhmalbaf's daughters, Samira and Hana, wanted to be directors, while son Maysam was interested in photography (perhaps to avoid competing with Dad). The way the girls started out in filmmaking was funny. Hana, who was eight, made a short called "The Day My Aunt Was Ill," which went to the Locarno Film Festival and won a prize. I gathered this sparked a bit of competitiveness in 17-year-old Samira.

One day I got a call from a friend who said that Makhmalbaf was making a new film. I was surprised as I'd been talking with Mohsen almost daily and hadn't heard anything about a new film. It turned out the film was being directed by Samira with Mohsen serving as screenwriter and editor. Not unlike *Close-Up*, the movie stemmed from a news item, a TV report Samira saw just two or three days before about a family the authorities had found in which the father had imprisoned his two teenage daughters since birth. The Makhmalbafs contacted the family and persuaded them to play themselves in a film that would be shot documentary-style. *The Apple* went from idea to "wrap" in under two weeks, and launched Samira's career when it was released internationally the following year.

I got to know more about Makhmalbaf's history as I spent time with him. I knew he was captured after a terrorist action as a teenager and imprisoned under torture for four years until released by the Revolution. One night, when he, Prof. Hamid Dabashi and I were driving north on Valiasr Street, he recalled that when Jimmy Carter wanted to press Iran on human rights and the Red Cross sent a team to investigate torture allegations, the Shah's prison officials had two prisons and would shift the tortured prisoners from one to the other depending on which one the Red Cross was inspecting. But there were ten prisoners who had been so badly tortured they were afraid lest there was any slip-up. So they executed eight of them; Makhmalbaf and another boy were spared due to their youth.

Another night, Mohsen invited Prof. Dabashi and me to have tea at his house. When we sat down on the floor and he took off his socks, I almost gasped. The skin of his feet was entirely covered in scar tissue. Seeing a similar pattern in the neck opening of his shirt, I deduced that his whole body must be covered in scars. The kind of courage it takes to withstand the horrors that produce such wounds is quite beyond my capacity to imagine, but I came to regard Makhmalbaf as one of the rare people I've ever met who was completely without fear.

That courage manifested in various ways. At one point during the summer it was announced that one or two of Makhmalbaf's films would play in Israel. The right-wing press was outraged and there was a big hue and cry about the news. It was expected that Makhmalbaf would denounce the showings or at least keep silent, but I was with him when he called one news outlet and shouted emphatically, "I want the Israeli people to see my films!"

Yet while such gutsiness was striking and admirable, Makhmalbaf was increasingly hemmed in. The threats against him and the regime's antipathy were real. Though he wouldn't permanently move abroad until 2005, he had already made his last film in Iran. (The next phase of his career would include films made in Tajikistan and Afghanistan, Persianate cultures beyond the authority of Tehran.)

Makhmalbaf and Kiarostami each had several films banned by the Islamic Republic. The difficulties Kiarostami faced in trying to complete and export *Taste of Cherry*, like the numerous obstacles thrown in front of Makhmalbaf once his anti-regime stance became evident, illustrate the strange paradoxicality of moviemaking under a government that both supports and suppresses cinematic art, a situation in which a never-ending series of behind-the-scenes battles among liberals, moderates and hardliners keep changing the rules and conditions of creative expression. And it was not a situation that was born with Iran's Revolution. Starting with *The Cow* and continuing under the Islamic Republic, Dariush Mehrjui had films banned both by the Shah's government and its successor, some of them films funded by the same government. "The governments change, the people change," Mehrjui said to me with a wry shrug, "but the problems remain the same."

After I returned to New York in late summer, 1997's emerging status as a breakthrough year for the Iranian cinema became more and more apparent to me, although much of the media still hadn't gotten the news. That fall the *New York Times* published an op-ed piece by writer Philip Taubman, who reported on a trip to Iran by comparing it to the unrelieved bleakness of the Soviet Union (a well-worn trope), saying that the authorities had "all but obliterated" the arts including film. I wrote a letter in reply noting that, on the contrary, the extraordinary vitality of Iran's cinema was indicated by the more than 200 awards Iranian films had won since the mid-1980s, including three big ones since the spring: After *Taste of Cherry* won the Palme d'Or, Panahi's *The Mirror* took the Golden Leopard at Locarno, and Majid Majidi's *Children of Heaven* swept the top honors in Montreal. These events laid the groundwork for a busy fall during which the New York Film Festival hosted Kiarostami with *Taste of Cherry* and Makhmalbaf with *Gabbeh*. Both films were acquired by American distributors so that the following year their directors received their first real U.S. art-house launches, a time that also saw the successful releases of *Children of Heaven* and Mehrjui's *Leila*.

The following February I returned to Tehran for the 1998 edition of Fajr, where Mehrjui's lyrical, autobiographical *The Pear Tree* won awards including Best Picture and Best Actress for debuting Golshifteh Farahani, who would go on to international stardom. Winner of a special jury award, Rakhshan Bani-Etemad's critically lauded *The May Lady* brought a feminist slant to the story of a female documentary director in conflict with her son. And I got my first look at Samira Makhmalbaf's *The Apple*, which combined true filmmaking smarts with a sharp and original view of traditional Iran's patriarchal power structures.[v] The film spurred debate at Fajr, some of it centered on whether it was all directed by Samira or partly by Mohsen. That controversy, however, didn't follow the film out of Iran, but I did; I witnessed its acclaimed debut at Cannes in May and its American bow at that fall's New York Film Festival,

---

v. See review, p. 215

where I escorted Samira to the Opening Night party. (*The Apple* also went on to a successful U.S. art-house release.)

My reports on Fajr 1998 did not mention one development that proved significant for me. During the trip I met *Newsweek*'s Paris-based Middle East bureau chief, Christopher Dickey (son of poet-novelist James Dickey of *Deliverance* fame), who in turn introduced me to John Marks and other representatives of Search for Common Ground, a Washington and Brussels-based NGO that takes very creative approaches to building bridges between divided peoples and countries. These include using science, radio, journalism, medicine, and, in the case of their first venture into Iran, sports. Learning that Iranians were especially avid about wrestling, Search managed to get an American team into a big international tournament in Tehran. It was the first time since the Revolution that any public event involving Americans had been staged, and it was a roaring success for Search: Images of Iranians cheering the American wrestlers and the Stars and Stripes went around the world.

Marks and his colleagues had no idea anything important was happening cinematically in Iran, but when they told Chris Dickey they thought movies might be another way to build some bridges, he referred them to me. Given how bothered I was by the dangerous chasm separating the U.S. and Iran, I was ready when Search recruited me to assist in its "track two" diplomacy In two succeeding years, I organized and Search staged meetings between Iranian and American film people at the Cannes Film Festival. To the first of these I invited Lincoln Center's Richard Peña, Geoffrey Gilmore and Nicole Guillemet of the Sundance Film Festival, and others; the Iranian side included members of Khaneh Cinema, Iran's equivalent of the Academy of Motion Picture Arts and Sciences.

That first meeting was aimed at formulating future projects that could bring the Iranian and American film communities together, including filmmaker exchanges. One, for example, brought female Iranian filmmakers to New York to talk to the Council for Foreign Relations. In another, I took filmmaker Michael Almereyda to Tehran to show his Ethan Hawke–starring film of Shakespeare's *Hamlet*, a trip that had some unintended seriocomic consequences.[vi] Also during the years I worked with Search, I testified before

---

vi. After Almereyda took photos of a site near our hotel that he didn't realize had recently been

a subcommittee of the U.S. Congress about the importance of Iran's film renaissance.

In the fall of 1998 I wrote an article for the *New York Times* in connection with another Lincoln Center festival of Iranian films, this one spotlighting Dariush Mehrjui. For unintended seriocomic consequences, it equaled my and Almereyda's later brush with the law in Tehran. In the article I dubbed Mehrjui "the most interesting and accomplished filmmaker the United States has never heard of," and noted that he "almost surely is the only filmmaker raised as a devout Muslim who counts the novelists J. D. Salinger and Saul Bellow as major influences on his work. He's even made a film of Mr. Salinger's *Franny and Zooey*, called *Pari*, set in contemporary Iran." (Such a film was possible because there are no copyright agreements between Iran and the U.S.)

Following the festival's opening weekend, with Mehrjui in attendance, the Film Society of Lincoln Center was contacted by Salinger's lawyers who threatened legal action, resulting in all the showings of *Pari* being canceled and the print of the film spirited out of Lincoln Center lest marshals show up to seize and destroy it. I felt a little guilty about having probably set all this in motion, but mainly I was dismayed by *Pari* not being seen. Using a fax number for Salinger's agent, I sent the novelist a long and passionate letter in which I argued that, while he was surely within his rights in keeping the film from being shown, I wished that, since Franny's invocation of the Jesus Prayer touches on a tradition shared by the Jewish, Christian and Muslim faiths, he might consider making an exception in the name of ecumenical bridge building. Niki Karimi, the film's luminous star, a huge Salinger fan who translated *Franny and Zooey* into Farsi, and two colleagues also wrote him a letter. None of us heard back, nor did I ever learn if he watched *Pari*. If he did, I can't imagine he wouldn't have found it fascinating.

As the following summer got underway, Iranian cinema was not uppermost in my thoughts. After seeing the first commercial digital movie

---

hit by a terrorist bomb, he and I were hauled into a police station for questioning. Fortunately we were released when three Iranian film producers intervened. The incident is recounted in "Iran 2000, Part 1" (*New York Press*, October 18-24, 2000) and has been reprinted in *The Press Gang* (Seven Stories Press, 2020).

projection in New York, I pondered the ramifications of digital cinema in a pair of articles for *New York Press*, "The Death of Film" and "The Decay of Cinema."[7] Soon after, I arrived in Italy for the Venice Film Festival, to serve on the FIPRESCI jury and see the premiere of Kiarostami's *The Wind Will Carry Us*. The film, which is full of poetry and gorgeous views of Kurdish landscapes and village life, puzzled me at first; it took repeated viewings and a lot of thought before I decided it was one of his greatest works. It was, in any case, another success for him, winning Venice's Special Grand Jury Prize and our FIPRESCI prize in the Competition category. Not incidentally, it also converged with my digitization articles in a certain way, for *The Wind Will Carry Us* proved to be the last celluloid feature Kiarostami made in Iran. With his next film, he would wholeheartedly join the digital revolution.

As the 1990s drew to a close, I had one lingering frustration. Though I had talked to distributors endlessly about the importance of *Close-Up*—which I would name the best film of the decade—since first encountering it in 1992, it had not been picked up. But that changed as the year went on. Thanks to Zeitgeist Films, the film opened theatrically in New York the last week of 1999. I couldn't help but view the event as a very pleasing capstone to a remarkable decade.

The next decade began with auspicious developments on several fronts. Looking back at the year in an article ("Iran's High Water Mark") for the *Village Voice*,[8] I said the successes of Iranian films at international festivals made 2000 "another banner year for a cinema that a decade ago was barely a blip on programmers' screens. At Cannes, the Camera d'Or (for best first film) was shared by Bahman Ghobadi's *A Time for Drunken Horses* and Hassan Yektapanah's *Djomeh*, while the Jury Prize went to *Blackboards*, the sophomore feature by Samira Makhmalbaf. At Venice, Jafar Panahi's *The Circle* became the first Iranian film to capture the Golden Lion, and Marziyeh Meshkini's *The Day I Became a Woman* took the Future Cinema prize. And at Fajr, Iran's own international festival, top honors were claimed by *Smell of Camphor, Fragrance of Jasmine*, the first film in over twenty years by veteran moviemaker Bahman Farmanara." These indeed looked like boom times for Iranian cinema.

I described those films as belonging to what I called "the Khatami wave." The former Minister of Culture and Islamic Guidance under whom the Iranian cinema was resuscitated in the early 1980s, the liberal cleric Mohammad Khatami was elected President of Iran the same week in 1997 that *Taste of Cherry* won the Palme d'Or. The effects of his administration's cultural liberalization were still being felt three years later. I also noted that the festival successes mentioned above all had connections to the two filmmakers who dominated the previous decade: "The directors of *Djomeh* and *The Circle* are former Kiarostami assistants; *Smell of Camphor*'s Farmanara is a longtime friend who produced Kiarostami's second feature. *Blackboards* and *The Day I Became a Woman* were made, respectively, by Makhmalbaf's daughter and wife. *A Time for Drunken Horses*' Ghobadi spans the two streams, having worked as an assistant to both Kiarostami and Makhmalbaf."

The year 2000 also brought two of the most unexpectedly moving experiences I ever had with Iranian films. In the spring, the critic Roger Ebert invited me to join him and his wife, Chaz, for a screening of Majidi's *Children of Heaven* at what was then called the Overlooked Film Festival. Majidi had acted in an early Makhmalbaf film and was a religiously oriented man who had good relations with conservatives in the regime. While Kiarostami and others at Kanoon had pioneered what I called the "kid-centered film" that became important to Iranian cinema after the Revolution, these movies were still mainly art films for adults. Majidi's films were more broadly accessible with an appeal that extended even to kids.

I got a potent demonstration of that when the Eberts screened *Children of Heaven* for 1,500 grade-schoolers, aged roughly eight to fourteen. Watching what for most was undoubtedly their first subtitled film, the kids, I wrote, "were enraptured throughout… erupting in cheers at the end when the film's poor young hero wins the foot race that he hopes will bring him a pair of shoes that he can give to his sister." After the screening, Roger invited kids from the audience to come on stage and ask questions of us and Chaz. I was amazed at their seriousness and astuteness. When one girl asked why the film's last shot showed the hero's feet surrounded by goldfish in a pond, Chaz replied, "Someone said to me, it's like God is kissing the boy's feet through the goldfish"—an answer Majidi would undoubtedly have applauded.[9]

The other experience came at the Telluride Film Festival in Colorado, where I saw the U.S. premiere of Bahman Ghobadi's *A Time for Drunken Horses*.[vii] I had met Ghobadi three years earlier at a party in Tehran that Makhmalbaf took me to. He was a shy, bearded, extremely polite young Kurd who Makhmalbaf and others considered among Iran's most promising young filmmakers. He had a fierce dedication, I learned, to telling the stories of his people, and *A Time for Drunken Horses*, his feature debut, is a very moving drama about poor Kurdish teenagers forced by desperate circumstances to smuggle articles across the Iran-Iraq border.

"In Telluride," I wrote in my review, "I watched Ghobadi speak to a group of high school kids, including Navahos, who had just seen the film. He told about how his whole family had worked on the production (his mother's tasks included praying for the right weather), about how they hauled the cameras up the mountains by mule, and how he used the prize money he got at Cannes to build a school for his village.

"One of these American kids suddenly said, 'Mr. Ghobadi, you are such a wonderful person, I think I am going to cry.' At that point, pretty much everyone in the room was misty-eyed...."

For New Yorkers the year 2001 has a grim reputation due to one terrible event. The attacks of September 11 had many repercussions, one of which was the cancellation of Lincoln Center's latest Iranian festival, scheduled to open September 14. The festival was to include a salute to Amir Naderi, by then a long-established resident of New York City.

But my main memory of 2001 was a much happier one from earlier in the year. In April, Kiarostami arrived in the U.S., having accepted my invitation to have the American premiere of his latest film, the documentary *ABC Africa*, at the Double Take Documentary Film Festival in North Carolina. He brought with him his sons Ahmad and Bahman. In New York, I recall accompanying Abbas when he shopped for camera equipment at B&H Photo, and all of us enjoying the spring weather at the New Jersey home of Kiarostami's longtime friend, Prof. Jamsheed Akrami.

In Durham, Kiarostami showed *ABC Africa* and discussed it with the

---

vii. See review, p. 221

audience (with Akrami translating) on the stage of the Carolina Theatre. Kiarostami was his usual charming and eloquent self and the film was very well received. Double Take also showed some short documentaries by Bahman Kiarostami. Outside the festival, we went to Raleigh for a lunch given by my parents, who took an instant liking to Kiarostami. And on the last night of his first and only visit to the American South, the local Iranian-American community honored him with a lavish banquet full of great Persian food and Persian-Southern hospitality. As I say, happy memories.

Far less happy was what happened the following January as I prepared to return to Iran. I was packing in my living room and the TV was on, broadcasting George W. Bush's State of the Union address, when I heard him use the phrase "axis of evil" to describe Iran, Iraq and North Korea. The expression was as idiotic as many things that came out of Bush's mouth, but it obviously served the purposes of his neoconservative advisors, who were in the early stages of a campaign of lies and propaganda that would result in America's disastrous invasion of Iraq. I had a sinking feeling that the expression was not going to help me in the least.[viii]

At the 2002 edition of Fajr, there seemed to be a metaphorical chill in the air. Though our Farabi and Fajr hosts were as genial and hospitable as ever, they also advised us not to take solo walks across the park that separated our hotel and the screening facilities. There were no untoward incidents, but this was the first time I had the slightest trepidation about being an American in Iran.

After the Fajr of 2002, I didn't return to Iran for fifteen years.[ix] During this

---

viii. Bush's election had deleterious effects on Iranian filmmakers seeking to enter or transit the U.S. and on cultural institutions hoping to sponsor or help them. Among those affected: In April 2001, Jafar Panahi was "viciously man-handled" when he tried to transit through JFK Airport en route from Hong Kong to South America; rather than being allowed to continue his trip, he was taken in chains to a plane returning to Hong Kong. In 2002, Abbas Kiarostami, after seven uneventful trips to the U.S. in the previous decade, was denied a visa to accompany his film *Ten* to the New York Film Festival and to lecture at Harvard and Ohio State universities.

ix. In late 2009 I was invited to serve on a jury at the 2010 Fajr Film Festival. When filmmakers including Jafar Panahi urged foreign guests to boycott the festival in protest of the "stolen election" and its cultural effects, including the imprisonment of filmmakers, I was torn, thinking I might be able to help the filmmakers more if I went to Fajr and wrote a report for a prominent U.S. outlet about the current situation for artists in Iran. Ultimately, I asked the opinion of my friend journalist-filmmaker Maziar Bahari, who had just recently been released from prison (and Iran) after a grueling ordeal. He advised me to boycott the festival and I did.

period, my life circumstances changed. At the end of 2000, I parted company with *New York Press* and stopped covering international festivals for *Variety*. I was looking for new and different horizons, and from 2003 through 2008 the main focus of my energies was making and then releasing my documentary about my family's Southern plantation, *Moving Midway* (which I was pleased to screen for Kiarostami later in New York). I kept in touch with Iranian friends and continued seeing and writing about Iranian films, but in a more occasional and distanced way than before.

The cultural tenor of this time was inevitably influenced by the fact that both countries elected dim right-wing presidents. The reelection of the feckless George W. Bush in 2004, despite the disaster he had unleashed in Iraq, fortunately didn't result in a war with Iran, though Bush's most hawkish advisors kept pushing for exactly that. In Iran, the optimism of the Khatami era was left behind with the election of the clownish Mahmoud Ahmadinejad in 2005. The new president was no friend of artists and the conditions for filmmakers grew harsher during his rule. It was said that his election was what spurred Makhmalbaf to leave Iran for France.

As the decade progressed, a range of new films reflected the unfolding social and political events in both the region and Iran itself. Mohsen Makhmalbaf's *Kandahar* (2001) and Samira Makhmalbaf's *At Five in the Afternoon* (2003) were among the first films shot in Afghanistan following the American invasion and overthrow of the Taliban; the latter concerned a young woman's pursuit of education. Bahman Ghobadi continued to explore the hardships and hopes of Kurdistan in *Marooned in Iraq* (2001) and *Turtles Can Fly* (2004), the first film made in Iraq following the fall of Saddam Hussein; he returned to Iran for *No One Knows about Persian Cats* (2008), his delightful documentary portrait of Tehran's underground music scene. Majid Majidi probed the plight of poor Afghan immigrants working in Tehran in *Baran* (2001), while Mohammad Rasoulof looked at Arab maritime squatters in the allegorical *Iron Island* (2006). And feminist themes informed Rakhshan Bani-Etemad's family drama *Under the Skin of the City* (2001) and *Ten* (2002), the first of Kiarostami's low-budget digital dramas.

There was an oppositional tone to many of these films that seemed to lay the groundwork for the kind of more directly political filmmaking that I had expected to find but didn't in the Iranian films I saw in 1992. In this regard, the decade's most important director to me was unquestionably Jafar Panahi. With Makhmalbaf working and then living abroad, and Kiarostami concentrating on photography, art installations and low-budget or foreign-made films, Panahi dominated the decade by making a trio of bold, ambitious, brilliantly mounted dramas that directly challenged several Iranian ills and reached a wide international audience in doing so.

From this perspective, his *The Circle* looks like the most significant of 2000's prize-winners. While Panahi's first two features, *The White Balloon* and *The Mirror* were gentle, humanistic child-centered comedy-dramas very much in the Kiarostami mold, his third outing marked a sharp departure (I later speculated that the dark turn Kiarostami took in *Taste of Cherry* might have influenced the change). The film, I wrote, "follows the miseries of several women in succession, observing the ways that prostitutes or women who've been let out of prison, say, are constantly dogged by the police and the vigilantes known as the *komiteh*, until every street corner and glance seems like a potential trap. Life for women in Iran, the film's central metaphor unsubtly suggests, is a veritable noose of oppression."[10]

I went on, however, to say that while it was unquestionably audacious and beautifully directed, "*The Circle* left me more ambivalent than impressed. That's because its overtly political tone seems decidedly opportunistic, as if Panahi suddenly hit on a new hook for wowing foreign audiences: appeal to their anti-Iranian prejudices and self-righteous sense of cultural superiority." Curiously for a work that appeared to champion Iranian women, *The Circle* was the rare film that seemed intended to be banned (it was). Of the Iranian women who did see it, not all were impressed. Two writing in the Montreal Gazette worried that it would "feed racism in the name of feminism."

Panahi's next film, *Crimson Gold* (2003)[x] inspired no such reservations. Working from a script by Kiarostami, he turned out one of his greatest works, a darkly elegant film that recalled some of the bleakest crime dramas of the New Wave era. It was based on a true story that Kiarostami had heard. Opening with a robbery that results in a murder and (apparently) a suicide, the film then flashes back to see what led its protagonist, heavyset pizza-delivery man Hossein, to commit the crime. The tale, in which the stark gap

---

x. See review, p. 227

between rich and poor touches on the failure of Iran to reach some of its revolution's key ideals (a thematic undercurrent in some Kiarostami films), beautifully exemplifies, as I put it, the Iranian cinema's "reputation for linking artistic vision to social and moral vision."

In *Offside* (2006), Panahi returned to the subject of women's concerns, but with a wittier, more spirited approach than that of *The Circle*. His story focuses on a group of girls who disguise themselves as boys to sneak into Azadi Stadium to see a World Cup playoff match between Iran and Bahrain. Shot in part documentary-style during the game it depicts, the film displays all of Panahi's usual stylistic energy and intelligence while registering the righteous resentment that women soccer fans feel over having been barred by religious authorities from attending games since the Revolution.

The film was supposed to be distributed but the government banned it at the last minute. Shortly after, unlicensed DVD copies of the film appeared all over Iran, resulting in *Offside* becoming the Panahi film that has probably been most seen by Iranians. It also enjoyed success outside Iran, winning the Silver Bear at the Berlin Film Festival, an honor that seemed to take Panahi to a new career peak.

And then came the events of 2009 and 2010. On June 12, 2009, the Iranian presidential election was held and the incumbent Mahmoud Ahmadinejad won by a quickly announced and suspiciously large majority. Irregularities were suspected and anti-regime demonstrations began that eventually involved millions of Iranians, both in Iran and in numerous other countries, and led to the creation of the Green Movement. In late July, Panahi was reported to have been arrested in a cemetery near the grave of Neda Agha-Soltan, the student protester whose slaying was witnessed on video around the world. Filmmakers and the news media pressured the government to release him and he was let go after eight hours.

After he continued to publicly support the Green Movement both in Iran and in international forums, Panahi was arrested again the following March. Police took him, his wife, their daughter and fifteen of his friends including filmmaker Mohammad Rasoulof to Evin Prison. Most were released within forty-eight hours, but Panahi was not.

News of his captivity spread around the world. In New York, Panahi's friend Jamsheed Akrami and I joined with film-community friends Ted Hope,

Kent Jones, Jem Cohen and Anthony Kaufman in an ad hoc committee to ask prominent American filmmakers to sign a petition calling on the Iranian government to release Panahi. Published in mid-March, the letter contained the names of Martin Scorsese, Francis Ford Coppola, Robert Redford, Oliver Stone, Steven Spielberg, Ang Lee, Robert De Niro, Terrence Malick, Jonathan Demme, Michael Moore and others.

Having seen how sensitive the Iranian regime sometimes is to its international image, I thought this and similar appeals had at least a chance of working. So when Panahi was released in May, I wasn't surprised (though I later learned that the many petitions and protests probably had less to do with this than the hunger strike Panahi embarked on the week before). But if I assumed the regime's image sensitivity would lead it to quietly drop the case against him, I was shockingly wrong.

In December, the Islamic Revolutionary Court convicted Panahi of "colluding with the intention to commit crimes against the country's national security and propaganda against the Islamic Republic" and sentenced him to six years in prison and a twenty-year ban from making films, writing screenplays, giving interviews or leaving Iran except for religious pilgrimages or medical treatment. Rasoulof was sentenced to six years in prison but that was reduced to one year on appeal. Panahi's appeal wasn't as successful: The following October, his sentence was upheld. But here the dark tale enters the realm of the absurd, a uniquely Iranian form of absurdity. Apparently the regime wanted to make an example but not a martyr out of Panahi. So he was not sent to prison, even though the sentence remained in effect. For a while he supposedly was under house arrest, but then that was relaxed. Cinematographer Mahmoud Kalari laughingly told me, "Kiarostami said, 'I thought Panahi was supposed to be in prison, but every time I go to a party—there's Panahi!'"[xi]

Besides partying, he kept making films while simply not asking the government's permission. If Panahi had dominated the previous decade with three large-scale, politically minded features, he gained a unique place in the

---

xi. In July of 2022, Panahi was arrested when he went to Evin Prison to inquire about the recent arrests of filmmakers Mohammad Rasoulof and Mostafa Al-Ahmad. A spokesman for the judiciary said Panahi would be obliged to serve the six-year sentence he received in 2010, which had not previously been enforced. The arrests were seen as part of a crackdown on filmmakers that had begun in the spring. Numerous international organizations protested the arrests.

next decade's cinema with his illicitly made films, all of which were smuggled out of the country and earned wide acclaim at international festivals and via art-house distribution in many countries.

The first of these, *This Is Not a Film* (2011), begun even while his sentence was being appealed, showed how much technology had changed cinema since Kiarostami converted to digital in 2000. Made in collaboration with Mojtaba Mirtahmasb, it was shot in four days in Panahi's apartment with a digital camcorder and an iPhone. Add in his computerized editing suite and it's clear that Panahi enjoyed, in effect, a full movie production studio without leaving home. If Kiarostami said he felt digital cinema liberated him from expensive productions with big crews, it helped liberate Panahi from something else: government control.

The film shows Panahi at home making phone calls about his legal appeal, watching TV news stories, interacting with neighbors, and talking about his past work and the film he was working on when he was arrested. The tone is light and some of the film is very funny, as if Panahi's ultimate revenge on the regime was to remain good-humored. (Not incidentally, the film takes place on the popular pre-Islamic holiday Fireworks Wednesday, which, as Jamsheed Akrami said, "is a slap in the face of the Islamic Republic's authorities who despise this day and have called it a paganist ritual.") *This Is Not a Film* was reportedly smuggled on a USB drive inside a cake to the Cannes Film Festival, where it premiered. It was later shortlisted for Best Documentary Feature for the 85th Academy Awards.

Panahi appears in all four of the movies he made in this decade, which gives them a strong autobiographical dimension as well as extending the Kiarostamian tradition of films about filmmakers and filmmaking. All also refer to the activism that got him into trouble with the government, thus keeping politics front and center in their concerns. Yet their shifting geographic purview seems to indicate the increasing creative freedom he felt. In *This Is Not a Film*, he's in his Tehran apartment, presumably under house arrest. *Closed Curtain* (2013), which is melancholic where its predecessor had been witty, takes place in his Caspian Sea vacation home.[xii] In *Taxi* (2015), which won the Golden Bear at the Berlin Film Festival, a smiling Panahi is

---

xii. See review, p. 230

a cabbie driving all over Tehran listening to his passengers talk about politics, cinema and city life. And in *3 Faces* (2018), winner of the Best Screenplay prize at Cannes, he pays tribute to the women of Iranian cinema—past, present and future—with a sharp comedy-melodrama that involves a road trip to distant Turkish-Azeri villages in northwestern Iran.

Mohammad Rasoulof also doubled down on making highly political films, turning out three that got him into further trouble. In *Goodbye* (2011), a prize winner at Cannes, he limned the repressive situation in Iran with a dark drama about a woman lawyer whose license has been revoked, whose husband has gone underground and who seeks an abortion as part of a scheme to escape the country. His next film, the riveting *Manuscripts Don't Burn* (2013), I called "easily the most daring and politically provocative film yet to emerge from Iran" for evoking a subject that was virtually radioactive: the so-called "chain murders" of roughly eighty intellectuals and dissidents by government agents between 1988 and 1998.[xiii] And in *A Man of Integrity* (2017), Rasoulof depicted endemic small-town corruption with the story of a farmer who gets involved in a lawsuit and then gets in deeper trouble by refusing the advice he's given at every turn: Bribe everyone involved, including the police and bank officials.

In March of 2020, Rasoulof was sentenced to one year in prison for the three movies, which were judged "propaganda against the system." The sentence also includes a ban on making films for two years; he had already been barred from leaving the country. He announced that he would appeal and would not turn himself in due to the Coronavirus epidemic.[xiv] Instead, he went on working. His next film, *There Is No Evil*, a four-part drama meditating on the practice of execution in Iran which I called "a powerful work of moral courage and urgency," won the Golden Bear at the Berlin Film Festival.[11]

Some outside observers have speculated that the repression Iranian filmmakers have had to endure for decades is not entirely a bad thing, that it has effectively served to stimulate their creativity and ingenuity. I've

---

xiii. See review, p. 255.

xiv. In July of 2022, Rasoulof and filmmakers Mostafa Al-Ahmad were arrested for social media posts criticizing police violence against protestors in the city of Abadan. A judiciary spokesman indicated Rasoulof would be obliged to serve his one-year sentence of 2020.

heard Iranians, including filmmakers, say the same. Yet that repression also *is* a bad thing, and the ways filmmakers have reacted to it can be charted on a spectrum that has two poles. At one pole are filmmakers including Naderi, the Makhmalbafs, Ghobadi and Beyzai who, finding conditions in Iran intolerable, have moved abroad. Yet it has been observed that none of these directors have found success outside Iran equal to that which they enjoyed while inside it. Which may help explain the stubborn intransigence of the filmmakers at the other pole, like Panahi and Rasoulof, who seem to illustrate the belief that Iranian artists are at their best when rooted in their own culture.

Of course, most Iranian filmmakers living in Iran exist between the two poles, and thus have been obliged to devise various strategies to continue working while trying not to run afoul of the country's repressive authorities. The long career of Dariush Mehrjui who, apart from a four-year sojourn in France in the early 1980s, has remained in Iran making often-daring, sometimes-banned films for a half-century, offers a textbook example of the tricky balancing act many Iranian filmmakers are obliged to perform.

Some survive by avoiding direct political statements in their films or their lives. Which can have its own perils. Kiarostami, for example, was criticized for not speaking out more forcefully regarding the persecution of Panahi and Rasoulof that followed the "stolen election" and protests of 2009. (He did speak out, just not loudly enough for some.) But I always found his discretion entirely understandable, even wise, especially given what a big target for hardliners his prominence made him. It also was thoroughly in accord with the personality of an artist who generally employed nuance and metaphor rather than direct statements about anything. And Kiarostami in effect did make a statement by shooting his only two major dramatic features of Ahmadinejad's second term outside Iran: *Certified Copy* (2010) in Italy and *Like Someone in Love* (2012) in Japan.

On Saturday, July 5, 2016, I was at the Queens home of my friend Rodrigo Brandão working on a documentary when my phone rang. It was my friend Dorna Khazeni calling from California to tell me that Abbas Kiarostami had died the previous day in Paris. I was stunned. Since I was in regular touch with his son Ahmad (who had relocated to the U.S. after his 2001 visit and now lived in the Bay Area), I knew that Kiarostami had been in a Tehran hospital for a long while, but the most recent reports had suggested he was on the mend. Post-mortem investigations indicated that malpractice by the medical team in Iran was responsible for his sudden downturn, which was too severe to be remedied by his transfer to a Paris hospital.

The news sent shock waves around the world, and filmmakers everywhere began speaking out about the meaning and importance of his work. "Kiarostami gave the Iranian cinema the international credibility it has today," Mohsen Makhmalbaf told *The Guardian*. "He changed the world's cinema; he freshened it and humanized it in contrast to Hollywood's rough version." In cities across the globe, tributes to Kiarostami began. At one I attended in New York, I talked with directors Jim Jarmusch and Jem Cohen, independent filmmakers whose work Kiarostami had praised, and numerous speeches were made; the most moving ones to me came from Iranian-American artist Shirin Neshat and director Martin Scorsese, who recalled his long friendship with Kiarostami.

Within days of Kiarostami's death, I conceived the idea of this book, which is intended not only as a tribute but also as a corrective. I had long been bothered by non-Iranian cinephiles and critics who seemed to regard Kiarostami as a kind of super-auteur who might have come from anywhere. But he didn't come from just anywhere, and this book is meant to point up his connection to the millennia-long civilization of Iran, its distinctive artistic traditions and especially to a rich, vibrant film culture that produced many other important auteurs. It is a book not just about Kiarostami, but also about the cultural context he emerged from and the cinematic era he defined.

In other ways too, his passing spurred me to a renewed engagement with Iranian cinema. Later in the summer, I joined Ahmad Kiarostami and filmmaker Ramin Bahrani in speaking at a tribute to Kiarostami in Toronto, staged under the auspices of the Toronto International Film Festival. The venue where the event was held, the Bell Lightbox, is a large one, but it was completely filled and many were turned away.

And the following April, I returned to Iran to take part in a tribute there. When Kiarostami's body had been returned to Iran the previous summer, there was a massive public outpouring of grief and reverence, and tributes came from many quarters. But some felt that the cinema authorities had not done enough and there was pressure to do more, so this tribute was organized to be held in conjunction with the 2017 Fajr International Film Festival.

Beautifully organized by Seifollah Samadian, a cinematographer who worked with Kiarostami, the four-day event included a photo exhibit, films and talks by Kiarostami friends, associates, collaborators and students, as well as a few foreign guests; I was the one American invited to speak at the tribute.

This trip was very meaningful to me on many levels. I enjoyed reconnecting with friends from previous visits, filmmakers, actors, cinematographers, critics, other journalists and folks in the film business. I made some new friends too. The current heads of Fajr and some of my friends from the Farabi Cinema Foundation seemed particularly appreciative of my presence and eager to see our renewed association continue. I felt the same. (In succeeding years, I encouraged filmmakers Oliver Stone and Paul Schrader to accept invitations to Fajr; both seemed to enjoy their visits to Iran enormously.)

Also during this visit I learned more about what must be considered the most significant developments in Iranian cinema during that decade, developments that made me recall something that had happened in 2009.

One day in the spring of that year, I was walking down a street in New York and ran into the always-ebullient Amir Naderi, who introduced me to the pleasant-seeming, goateed Iranian he was with. Asghar Farhadi was in town to present his fourth feature, *About Elly* (still my favorite of his films), at the Tribeca Film Festival.[xv] I had seen Farhadi's second feature, *The Beautiful City* (2004), at New York's Film Forum and was intrigued. But I had no idea in 2009 what would happen with the release of his next feature.

A Separation (2011), Farhadi's incisive, brilliantly mounted drama about a well-off Tehran couple who are spiraling toward divorce and fall into a conflict with a working-class couple, literally stormed across the world beginning at the Berlin International Film Festival, where it won the Golden Bear and its male ensemble was awarded the Best Actor prize and the female ensemble won Best Actress. In the months following it opened in country after country, won rave reviews and broke all previous box office records for Iranian films. The same thing happened in the United States after it made its American debut at the fall's New York Film Festival.

---

xv. See review, p. 233.

The pinnacle of the movie's world conquest came the following February when it became the first Iranian film to win an Oscar by taking the Best Foreign-Language Film prize (Farhadi was also nominated for Best Original Screenplay) at the 84th Academy Awards. In addition to being the most acclaimed and commercially successful Iranian film of all time, *A Separation* thus achieved a victory that was witnessed by the Oscarcast's billions of viewers. All the film festivals in the world couldn't equal that. Amazingly enough, Farhadi would repeat the feat five years later when his seventh feature, *The Salesman* (2016), another acclaimed drama about a marriage under stress, also won the foreign-language film Oscar.[xvi]

After seeing *A Separation* it occurred to me that one reason it was viewed as so fresh and different was that it veered from conventions established by certain Iranian films and filmmakers that critics were most familiar with. In the post-revolutionary period, Kiarostami, Makhmalbaf and Panahi all made a big point of saying they would not make films that showed women at home wearing veils, which wouldn't be realistic. The result was that their films very seldom depicted middle-or upper-class adults. Farhadi simply tossed out that convention. In deciding to show women veiled in private environments, he sacrificed a literal kind of realism for a psychological and sociological realism that made his dramas both intellectually engaging and emotionally powerful.

He wasn't the first great director to make that decision. Films including Beyzai's masterpiece *The Travelers* and great Mehrjui movies such as *Hamoon*, *Pari* and *Leila*, among many others, reflected the same decision. But those directors had not been championed and boosted to wide attention by major festivals like Cannes—perhaps because their work deviated from what foreigners had come to regard as the "Iranian" cinema aesthetic. When I interviewed Farhadi about *A Separation*, I told him I thought it perhaps reflected the influence of Beyzai and Mehrjui. He agreed and, as I reported in *Film Comment*, said he "feels they are less well-known outside Iran because their work remains rooted in Iranian social reality rather than 'trying to explain Iran to the world.'"[12]

As recounted in "Return to Tehran 2017," at Fajr 2017 I ran into Mani Haghighi, a grandson of Ebrahim Golestan whom I'd known since before

---

xvi. See review, p. 237.

he began making films with 2003's *Abadan*. He told me that in thinking, circa 2005, about why his and Farhadi's first two films had flopped, he decided it was because both filmmakers were still following the "Kiarostami-Makhmalbaf" model of making low-key, non-dramatic art films about poor or rural people using non-actors. Looking to jettison that model (which Kiarostami and Makhmalbaf themselves had long since left behind), he went to Farhadi and suggested they collaborate on a film that would 1) concern middle-class urbanites, 2) be well-scripted and tightly plotted, and 3) use movie stars.

Fireworks Wednesday (2006), which they co-wrote and Farhadi directed, was a huge hit in Iran (it starred the formidable Hedieh Tehrani and up-and-coming Taraneh Alidoosti). Suddenly Iranian cinema had a new model, one that led directly to the brilliance of *About Elly* (which co-starred Haghighi) and the global triumphs of *A Separation* and *The Salesman*. While I was told that Farhadi's success had spawned a raft of imitators, much as Kiarostami's had two decades earlier, what I sensed at Fajr in 2017 and when I returned the following year was that the Farhadi phenomenon had mainly served to liberate young filmmakers from the overbearing burden of their cinematic heritage, suggesting new creative possibilities and avenues toward attention both in Iran and abroad. Quite simply, I saw films at both editions of Fajr that seemed strikingly fresh and original and that got me excited about Iran's cinema all over again.

Back home, the Iranian Film Festival New York, held at Greenwich Village's IFC Center in January 2019, which I co-founded and programmed with distributor Armin Miladi, aimed to introduce New Yorkers to new cinema from Iran with a program which placed that work in the context of what had come before. So, from a historical perspective, the program had three levels. Representing the generation of the Iranian New Wave was our Guest of Honor, the genial and eloquent Bahman Farmanara, who showed his most recent film, the autobiographical *Tale of the Sea* (2018), and its predecessor, the spirited satiric comedy *I Want to Dance* (2016). The same generation was also evoked by the New York premiere of one of Kiarostami's last shorts, "Take Me Home," and two fine documentaries about the departed master, Seifollah Samadian's *76 Minutes and 15 Seconds with Abbas Kiarostami* and Jamsheed Akrami's "A Walk with Kiarostami."

The first generation of the post-revolutionary New Iranian Cinema, meanwhile, was represented by Panahi's *3 Faces* and Kamal Tabrizi's *Sly*, a daring and hilarious satire of Iranian politics. (When I watched this film with Oliver Stone in Tehran, he called it "an Iranian *A Face in the Crowd*.")

The films named above framed a quartet of exceptional new films by younger directors: the film that won our jury's grand prize, Houman Seyyedi's violent, machine gun-paced crime drama *Sheeple*; Mani Haghighi's equally energetic if somewhat less manic *Pig*, which concerns a serial killer who's targeting filmmakers, and opens with the discovery of Haghighi's own severed head lying in a gutter; Asghar Yousefinejad's *The Home*, a complex tale of a family's hidden agendas with tight plotting and expert acting and direction;. and *Hendi and Hormoz*, a sophomore feature by Abbas Amini that continues Iran's tradition of perceptive movies about youngsters.

The festival was a hit and I was asked if there was any political dimension to that success or the films the festival screened. I said yes to both. For Americans, the festival was not only an aesthetic adventure and opportunity to learn about a fascinating culture; it was also, let's face it, a way to give the finger to the execrable, ignorant, destructive president who issued the so-called "Muslim travel ban." Like George W. Bush before him, Trump was surrounded by rabid hardliners who'd love to go to war with Iran.

Even though they replaced Ahmadinejad with the moderate Hassan Rouhani in 2013, Iranians had their own hardliners to contend with, and it's a never-ending battle. Before I arrived in April of 2018, the country had been gripped by widespread riots, and while I was there, two of Iran's leading filmmakers told me they thought the regime would topple before year's end. That didn't happen, of course, and unfortunately mounting American hostility and pressure almost surely served to strengthen the hardliners' grip on power. In this situation, cinema remains both a refuge and a redoubt for artists yearning for a more humane and internationally accepted Iran. Look at almost any important Iranian film and you'll find a political message or dimension, whether expressed with the bluntness of a Panahi, Rasoulof, Farmanara, Tabrizi or Haghighi, or the subtlety and metaphorical nuance of a Kiarostami or Farhadi.

The excited reactions to our 2019 festival made me think back to a question that I heard several times during visits to Iran in the late 1990s. How long, I was asked by cinephiles and critics, did I think Iran's current cinematic renaissance would last? I put on my best thoughtful scholarly expression and said that, having studied the likes of Italian neorealism, the French New Wave and New German Cinema, I had concluded such movements generally lasted between seven and fourteen years before fading out.

If that's a fairly serviceable general rule, then at this point in history Iran's cinema must be regarded as a magnificent exception. Though it experienced lulls or downturns around the time of the Revolution and the early Ahmadinejad era, it has continued to turn out exceptional talents and acclaimed films that gain attention around the world. From "The House Is Black" and *The Brick and the Mirror* to *The Cow* to *Bashu, the Little Stranger* and *The Runner* to *Close-Up* and *Taste of Cherry* to *Gabbeh* and *The Apple* to *Children of Heaven* to *A Time for Drunken Horses* to *Crimson Gold* and *This Is Not a Film* to *About Elly*, *A Separation* and *The Salesman*, the Iranian cinema has shown a remarkable capacity to continue renewing itself, arising phoenix-like out of its own ashes time and again. It is a phenomenon I feel privileged to have witnessed, chronicled and, in some small way, participated in.

2.

IRAN UP CLOSE: INSIDE THE ISLAMIC REPUBLIC

Nights in Tehran
First published April 1997 in New York Press

MY FIRST DAY IN IRAN they took me to the big "Death to America" march. I was the only American. It's no tribute to my paltry reserves of courage to say that I was never scared, but I wasn't. I was simply too giddy with amazement, too inoculated by a rush of adrenaline that outlasted the experience by an hour. I was, in a word, tripping. It took a while before I calmed down enough to muse that this startling cultural baptism may have reflected a deliberate, and even shrewdly benign, strategy on the part of my Iranian hosts—show him the cliché first since everything to come will explode it.

I'm not sure how many people were at this event, since I have a hard time telling the difference between 50,000 and 100,000. But there are enough to fill one of Tehran's grandest boulevards, Azadi Street, as far as the eye could see. I was with a group of foreign visitors to Iran's annual film festival being led on a short, escorted visit to the massive outdoor celebration, which was, in fact, in honor of Islamic Revolution Day, Iran's holiday honoring its birth as an Islamic Republic in 1979. "Death to America" actually was no more than a prominent sub-theme, though one that easily caught my notice.

"I'm glad you don't understand the language," said my translator with an embarrassed laugh after a truck rumbled by filled with young men shouting slogans, their fists in the air. No, I don't speak the language, but I understood perfectly. The gist was the same as in those various murals and mobile art displays that, for example, showed a crippled Iranian veteran riding his wheelchair over the Stars and Stripes, or Uncle Sam being strafed by jet fighters.

I had only begun to digest this—I mean, to gape at such images and feel my heart start to thump double-time—when a short, intense but generally unthreatening-looking guy ran up to me, greeted me in English and asked, "Where you from?" It was sheer reflexes combined with a stubborn disinclination to go on the defensive, I guess, that made me say immediately, "America."

I'm not sure his mouth fell open, but he was clearly thunderstruck—for two, maybe three seconds. Then he grinned a big, welcoming grin to beat the band. I thought he was going to hug me.

No doubt it was because of the setting, but this was merely the most dramatic instance of something that happened to me over and over in Iran.

The question naturally arose a lot because I stood out like an Eskimo at a clambake. Being blond and blue eyed, I felt like I was on stage every moment that I was in public, and it never took long before someone got around to asking where I was from. The truth, it turned out, virtually assured a warmer, more interested response than I would have gotten if I'd claimed to be Czech or Canadian, say.

"Iranians adore Americans," said an Iranian friend who lives in the U.S. Apparently they do, even when enjoying a big "Death to America" street shindig. The guy I met at the Islamic Revolution Day march fell in step with me—people were strolling purposefully, patriotically, in both directions along the boulevard; it reminded me of the North Carolina State Fair back home—and I made cautious reference to the ambient, colorful diatribes against my homeland. He waved his arm as if to say, "Oh, that—pooh! Silly stuff, pay no attention."

I got more elaborately apologetic dismissals of the official anti-Americanism from educated, upper-class Iranians, but this guy was blue-collar, an ordinary Tehrani Joe. He was very proud of being Iranian and of the Revolution this holiday commemorated. He spoke in tones of passionate reverence about "the Imam," as Iranians call the late Ayatollah Khomeini. As regards the apparent differences between our countries, he was equally fervent in voicing an opinion that I would hear a lot in Iran: "Iranian people like American people. *People* have no problem. Problem is with *governments*."

A couple of days later, I heard the opposite view when a Dutch journalist told me of being at a press conference where a reporter from *Time* asked Iran's president, the genial and media-savvy Hashemi Rafsanjani, what was up with this "Death to America" stuff that's still part of Iran's celebration of its Revolution. Reportedly, Rafsanjani smiled regretfully and said the government had nothing to do with it, it was simply the spontaneous emotion of the people.

My own impression was that public anti-Americanism at this point is basically pro forma, and that the forma is increasingly outdated. Certainly, it was current 18 years ago when the U.S. was seen as backing a Shah that a huge number of Iranians wanted deposed, just as it was current 12 years ago when we were viewed as supporting Saddam Hussein (you remember our good friend Saddam) in the grueling, hugely destructive eight-year war that Iraq and Iran fought. But much has changed in the last decade, even in the last two or three years, and today there are signs that official thinking in Iran is swinging closer to the friendly views of the man in the street—a change that won't make much difference, of course, unless our policy makers are sharp enough to take advantage of it.

One obvious reason for this turn of events is that the Islamic Republic is no longer struggling to come into being, or to beat back the onslaught of a massively armed neighbor. It is at peace, increasingly prosperous and full of the kind of buoyant self-confidence that comes with surviving a protracted ordeal. In its government, nuanced pragmatism has rapidly overtaken the ideological purism that used to determine everything. One Iranian acquaintance, however, offered me the view that not all of the recent changes are traceable solely to Iran's own experience.

"The collapse of the Soviet Union really made them look at things differently," he said of Iran's leaders. "They were really surprised. They saw that the Soviet Union didn't lose a military war, it lost culturally. So they started to see that that's what Iran is in with the U.S.—not a war but a contest that will come down to culture."

Which is one angle on why this regime takes movies very seriously indeed, and why being the lone American film critic here at the moment entails a surprising amount of local celebrity (one night I'm interviewed so many times that I tell someone I feel like Sharon Stone) as well as a constant sense of fascination with the surroundings. Movies, after all, are only the tip of the cultural iceberg. When we got back on the bus after leaving the Islamic Revolution Day march, my adrenaline still surging, I started noticing the graffiti on Tehran's walls. Besides the scrawls in Persian script, there were some in English, mainly the names of rock bands: MEGADETH and METALLIKA [sic], and, my favorite of all, IRAN MAIDEN.

Tehran reminds me of L.A., and not just because both are movie capitals, the former to the international art film right now, arguably, what the latter is, perennially, to the global biz. Both cities are also sprawling urban arrivistes in countries harboring older and more elegant metropolises, and both are jammed with serpentine freeways and roads thanks to their addiction to the automobile. Since the Revolution, many, many thousands of displaced Iranians have understandably migrated to L.A. They call it Tehrangeles.

Tehran, though, seems to be winning the race to choke itself to death on air pollution. Like L.A., it's situated in a natural bowl that produces smog-trapping temperature inversions. Most days the air makes the city look as if a gray-brown scrim covers it. On the rare clear day, the effect is startling; the snow-blanketed Alborz Mountains skirting the city's northern edge appear as present, sharp and luminous as a diorama. Higher than the Alps, their near reaches contain three world-class ski resorts that, during my visit in February and March, are magnets for Tehran's wealthy and athletic on the Thursday-Friday weekend.

A grandly tree-shaded and extremely long avenue called Valiasr, Tehran's own, dustier Champs-Élysées, bisects the city, dividing east from west. A more striking cultural divide, however, cuts in the opposite direction. Like the world itself, Tehran is composed of a rich north and a poor south. And in that fact lies a defining irony: While Iran's Revolution was powered by the lower classes (though amply supported by the others) and had a decided socialist component wedged into its intellectual framework alongside the dominant Islamic fundamentalism, it didn't result in anything like a classless society. One encompassing look at the city tells you that.

While the city center contains all the business and government stuff you would expect, Tehran is most striking at its extremes. The southern sections are by no means squalid, and some signs—like a recent upsurge in small, clean parks backed by the city's aggressively innovative and forward-looking mayor—suggest that things are improving rapidly. But the south still has a struggling, Third World air; you could be in Cairo. In the north, you could be in Bel Air. There are Mercedes and mansions and movie producers.

My own experience of the city changes as familiarity increases. On first arriving I am with a largish group of foreign visitors (from places including Bosnia, Lebanon, Korea and Japan) to the Fajr Film Festival. We are put up at the Azadi Grand, a posh enclave in the swanky north; its stationery bears the ingenuous legend "ex-Hyatt," advertising its pre-revolutionary identity. Initially I like the security of the place and the group setting. Then restlessness sets in, and I begin peeling off at lunch-time and exploring the city center on foot. Eventually I move myself downtown to a hotel near Ferdowsi Square that costs about a third of what the Azadi costs. But I decide that this place is still too insulated, so I move to an establishment I discover that is, in a word, aces. I dub it the Chelsea Hotel of Tehran. The Hotel Naderi.

One of the most popular films in the international section of Fajr is Jim Jarmusch's *Dead Man*. Seeing that Jarmusch seems to have a sizable following in Tehran, I suggest that he make his next episode of "Coffee and Cigarettes" at the Naderi. The hotel's coffee shop has been a hangout for bohemians and intellectuals for a half century, and you couldn't find a movie set that fits that role more perfectly. I am so awed by this place's cool that I sometimes just sit and gaze at it long after my coffee is finished.

Granted, the hotel's elegance is several decades in the past, and cleanliness isn't a by-word. But I met a German woman who'd been there for six months while negotiating to sell a mansion she owns in the north, and she put it well in saying, "The staff are the nicest people, and the *atmosphere* is just unbelievable." The Naderi costs about $8.50 a night. But then, everything in Iran is incredibly cheap if you have dollars. It is a tourist mecca just waiting to happen.

I find it easy enough to get around by having people write directions, in Persian, which I give to the taxi drivers. (Taxis are a culture unto themselves in Tehran, and the traffic is completely insane; work has just begun on a desperately needed subway system.) Luckily for me, English is now the standard second language for educated Iranians. I go to parties where Portishead is on the stereo and people are discussing Noam Chomsky or Laurie Anderson. You look around and think you could be in Stockholm or San Francisco. Occasionally, when I remark on how surprising this would be to most Americans, I am obliged to explain why this is so. Iranians, bless their hearts, harbor an impression that Americans are informed and worldly.

I generally sigh and say that the view most Americans have of Iran would fit on a postage stamp, and it wouldn't be a very pretty or subtle postage stamp. You can, alas, surprise even educated Americans with the news that Iranians aren't Arabs, and that even within the world of Islam, they comprise a separate culture (Shiite rather than Sunni: The philosophical breach between the two is a millennium old). In fact, the anti-American propaganda that Iranians encounter is readily identifiable as such; our own prejudices, I'm afraid, are not nearly so transparent, or so recently coined.

It strikes me that the cartoon picture we have of Iran compounds three widely separated epochs of reductive hysteria. Eighteen years ago there was the daily psychodrama called the Hostage Crisis, which launched the TV show *Nightline*; like the trauma of Vietnam in a more concentrated dose, it seared a scary, hostile image into the national imagination, and I'm not talking about Ted Koppel.

Eight hundred years before, the West was given a similar, if much more protracted, negative impression of the entire Islamic world in something called the Crusades. We were the aggressors but we made them the heavies. And even that wasn't the bad PR's beginning.

I'm not sure if they teach ancient history in American schools anymore, but they did when I was a kid, and the story of who "we" are effectively started with the valiant, outnumbered Greeks holding off the dastardly Persians—Iranians!—at Thermopylae. Because this was presented as the endangered infancy of democracy itself, in the Cold War it conjured up fragile America being overwhelmed by communism's dark legions. The prevailing nightmare thus acquired a potent genealogy and an inevitable progeny all at once.

Tallied up, that's almost 2,500 years of bad press, starting with Herodotus: surely some kind of record. When you begin to ponder the facts behind these emotional scenarios, however, impressions change drastically, sometimes to the point of reversal.

The Thermopylae legend, for example, conveniently disguises the reality that Greece, led by Alexander the Great, actually did to Persia what Persia only threatened to do to Greece: invade and conquer. As a Southerner I'm naturally sympathetic to cultures defined by a memory or fear of invasion's trauma, and examining Iran's history makes its defensiveness entirely understandable. It has been overrun repeatedly, and not always by folks as diplomatic as Alexander. During one medieval swoop into the beautiful city of Isfahan, the Mongols methodically decapitated 70,000 people.

Yet, remarkably, defensiveness hasn't meant an exclusionary animus. America and Iran have one strong common element in the assimilationist ethos they share. The multi-ethnic Iranian melting pot includes Armenians, Baktiaris, Turks, Afghanis, Azerbaijanis and others. As for religions, there are Christian, Jewish and various minority faiths that are not only legal but very visible; I see both churches and synagogues on my solo perambulations. (Admittedly, there's anything but tolerance for the poor Bahais, who are regarded as a subversive heresy rather than a religion, just as the melting pot can and does get medieval on Kurds with separatist aims.)

But the main revelation awaiting anyone who peels away the bumper sticker that covers Iran can be summarized in a single word—Persia. Oh yeah, you realize when you come face-to-face with the cultural reality: This place wasn't always just radical students hurling taunts at *Nightline* cameras, and before that a gilded Shah perched on his precarious Peacock Throne. There was also Zoroaster and Ahura Mazda. Cyrus the Great, Darius and Persepolis. A civilization that was already ancient at the time of Julius Caesar.

In the Middle Ages, Islamic Persia produced scientists and philosophers of epochal brilliance, and a spate of mystical poets whose influence has continued down the centuries: In the 1800s, Edward FitzGerald's translation of *The Rubaiyat of Omar Khayyam* became the most popular poem ever printed in English. At the moment, there are voices even in America calling 13th-century Persia's Jelaluddin Rumi the greatest poet ever, in any language. A new collection titled *The Essential Rumi* is prominently displayed at the bookstore across the street from where I live.

I'm not about to suggest that it's a short step from "A Flask of Wine, a book of Verse—and Thou" to "lights, camera, action." But when an Iranian critic, interviewing me in Italy last fall, asked why I thought Iranian cinema had experienced such a surge in the last dozen years, I found myself musing that every collective, localized surge in "artistic" cinema (Italian neorealism, Nouvelle Vague, New German Cinema, China in the 1980s, etc.) could be seen as the result of an older, established *literary* culture suddenly having the impetus and opportunity to transfer its energies to film.

This notion received some support in Iran, where I was told that serious filmmaking now enjoys the sort of prestige and influence typically reserved for fiction and poetry two decades ago. But such has been the pattern for "author's cinema" since D. W. Griffith took his cues from Dickens and the Victorian melodramatists back when. The question now is, with traditional literary cultures increasingly being mulched into the global cybersphere, where does that leave the moviemaking forms that descend from them?

While I'm in Tehran, an Iranian friend tells me he's heard by fax from Europe that Jean-Luc Godard has recently offered this definition: "The cinema is Griffith to Kiarostami." I have no idea if the quote is accurate, but the elegiac edge to the implied alpha-omega sure sounds Godardian. So does the irony that the line of auteurs that began with an American ends with an Iranian.

Persia, as Iran was called until the 1930s, gave birth to Zoroastrianism and Manicheism, faiths that divide the universe into light and dark, good and evil: cosmic extremes. There are some who say that Iran itself remains likewise divided. In her recent book *The Iranians* Sandra Mackey analyzes the culture's historical mood swings, including the extraordinary turbulence of the last two decades, in terms of an ongoing conflict between its most essential components—Persia and Islam.

That sort of analysis carries one a certain distance. Yet its implications can play into the tendency toward rhetorical extremes, including those faced by Iranian filmmakers who in recent years have been repeatedly edged into the uncomfortable position of choosing between various nominal opposites, especially East-West, that effectively boil down to variations of Us-vs.-Them.

The past decade's cinematic achievements may well have their roots in Iran's literary culture, and in a 1970s "new wave" inspired, as many others at the time were, by the French and Italian models of the previous two decades. But it was the Iranian Revolution that produced two sets of necessary, and highly unusual, preconditions for the artistic upsurge.

The first was that, in effect, the regime erected an invisible cultural wall around Iran aimed at keeping out most foreign cultural intrusions, especially the audiovisual sort. Thus, at a time when Hollywood was making like Godzilla in most of the world, stomping national cinemas into the ground left and right, its heavy tread and powerful leveling influence were unknown in Iran. (Apart from a few exceptions: Kevin Costner's *Dances with Wolves* and Oliver Stone's *JFK* were among the American movies deemed ideologically agreeable enough to play Tehran. Ironically, the brisk and very up-to-date rental trade in bootleg videocassettes means that Iranians get to see the likes of *Independence Day* and *Twister* at home. But not in theaters.)

Meanwhile, beginning in the mid-1980s, the government put the task of revitalizing the national cinema in the hands of some remarkably progressive and shrewd individuals who were allowed to decide everything from how much advertising a movie could have to which foreign festivals it would be submitted to. Naturally, they devoted appropriate attention to the fortunes of the action films, melodramas, war movies and such that make up the "commercial" majority of Iranian film production. Yet these officials were especially effective in nurturing the development of the "artistic" minority, which in the late 1980s began attracting wide notice and regularly winning major prizes at international festivals.

That lunge into the global limelight was not an uncomplicated boon, however. Almost as soon as it began, there were voices—including some among Iranian film critics, who are numerous and who span the ideological spectrum—charging that indigenous values were being undercut and manipulated by Western mindsets. When is an Iranian film not Iranian enough? It was up to each filmmaker to answer such aspersions in his or her own way.

Abbas Kiarostami, who in France and other parts of the world is considered not just the greatest of the Iranian cinema's masters, but chief among the world's, lives in a pleasant, unostentatious house in northern Tehran. When I go there for dinner one night late in the month I spend in Iran, I notice that the living room is decorated with lithographs by Akira Kurosawa. These, in a way, represent one Iranian's defense against charges of ideological impurity.

When I asked Kiarostami, on first meeting him in New York a couple years ago, if he had come under suspicion for being so acclaimed in Europe, he said he had, and that it had made things uncomfortable for a while. Ironically, relief came from the most eminent of Japanese directors. When Kiarostami's films were shown in Tokyo, Kurosawa issued a statement that said. "I believe the films of Iranian filmmaker Abbas Kiarostami are extraordinary. Words cannot relate my feelings… Satyajit Ray passed away and I got very upset. But having watched Kiarostami's films, I thank God because now we have a good substitute for him."

Kurosawa had spoken out similarly, it was reported, only for three other filmmakers—Ray, John Cassavetes and Andrei Tarkovsky. The endorsement from the East, Kiarostami told me, stopped the charges that he was a tool of the West.

A filmmaker facing similar problems that have yet to end, Mohsen Makhmalbaf may be second to Kiarostami in international regard, but on home turf it's another story: He is a celebrity whose renown, as I have noted before, is comparable to that of John Lennon's. How he got to that position is a story that could only happen in Iran.

A product of Tehran's poor southern district, Makhmalbaf started out as an Islamic fundamentalist terrorist. Captured, at age 17, after an assault on a policeman, he was locked up by the Shah's security apparatus and tortured for four years. When he was released by the Revolution, he still had never seen a movie, but that soon changed. An autodidact who became a prolific writer (he has now some 20 books to his credit), he fashioned himself as an Islamic fundamentalist auteur; his earliest films were shown in mosques.

Then, as his own beliefs began to shift away from orthodoxy, Makhmalbaf made a series of films (*The Peddler, The Cyclist, Marriage of the Blessed*) that lashed out at injustices in Iranian society and culture while championing the poor, the scorned, the disenfranchised and war damaged. It was these movies that established him as a passionately revered national icon.

Yet the fact that Makhmalbaf converted from fundamentalism to stinging social criticism to, more recently, a kind of ecstatic cinematic poetry that brings to mind Rumi has not endeared him to his former brethren among the true believers, including those in the cinema establishment. On the contrary, he has been the target of ideological campaigns, and five of his films have been banned. His most recent, *Gabbeh*, was recently released in Iran only after getting a personal thumbs up, I'm told, from the nation's current spiritual leader, Ayatollah Ali Khamenei.

Makhmalbaf has not taken the attacks against him lying down. Gritty and unapologetic, he has returned the metaphorical fire without hesitation, and has recently announced that he's so fed up with the obstructions Iran puts in front of its artists that he will make his next film in India. In a conversation with German director Werner Herzog that was printed in an Iranian film magazine, Makhmalbaf seemed to sum up his entire career in a single aphorism. "It is easier to attack an armed policeman with your bare hands than to attack ignorance with culture," he declared.

The warmest, most down-to-earth and charismatic of Iranian directors, he takes me one day to see a famous mosque in southern Tehran, where he still lives. For once, I'm not the one that everyone is staring at. Women in chadors shyly approach him and ask for autographs. Another day a fax arrives from the head of the Singapore Film Festival saying, "*Gabbeh* is the most beautiful film I have ever seen." This and the eye toward India make sense: Makhmalbaf is as opposed to Hollywood's mechanical brutality as he is to orthodox intolerance. His spirituality, like his cinema, belongs to the East.

Iran is not an open society, make no mistake. It is a theocracy, which here means a gamble on the proposition that clerics—mullahs—can run worldly affairs without ultimately being corrupted by them. History will judge the success of that experiment. In the meantime, the Islamic Republic operates according to very strict rules that include proscriptions against bars, dancing, satellite dishes and most forms of Western pop culture and entertainment.

That doesn't equate with boring, however. When I return home and tell my friend Wendy that the ban on alcohol means that the illegal hooch people have tends to be vodka rather than beer, which is bulkier to transport, she thinks for a moment, and then says, "Oh, you mean it's like boarding school." Precisely—Iran in a nutshell. And here's an analogy for the cultural atmosphere: It's like the mullahs have succeeded in turning the clock back to the 1950s.

If that doesn't sound intriguing, we're not on the same page. I've come to the point of regarding about 95 percent of American pop culture as toxic waste that's rapidly eroding the entire social context. Who's to say the West won't perish of the mental and spiritual poisons unleashed in the heedless pursuit of the "phantom of liberty"? In Iran, meanwhile, because the restrictions on them are so tight, pop music and movies still seem to *matter*, to hum with idealism, to point toward enlightenment rather than stupefaction.

This is not an argument for repression, even if it does point up some of its advantages. For years Iranian filmmakers have operated under the severest of limits, especially regarding the depiction of women and relations between the sexes. As a result, they have been unusually creative, resorting to symbols and suggestion, finding new avenues of expression as ways around the censor's inspections. Yet there's obviously a limit to the positive value of limits: Just the right number and artists get stimulated. Too many, they suffocate.

Someone remarks to me that there was a time a few years back when the rules were relaxed a bit, and the effect was oddly baneful: Filmmakers began censoring themselves mentally. Something similar seems to be happening right now, but for the opposite reason. The rules and the people setting and administering them have grown more conservative of late, and many filmmakers seem to be reacting by playing it safe, sticking to the tried and true. At the 1997 Fajr Film Festival, Iran's annual display of its new movies, the result is a mediocrity that seems at once calculated and defensive.

The closing night of Fajr for me is an experience to place alongside the Islamic Revolution Day march. This is Iran's version of the Academy Awards, and to an American newcomer it represents the oddest collision of cultures—it's half Oscar, half Ayatollah.

Staged in Tehran's opera house, the event follows the format of the American Oscars, with all the glitz that can be mustered and TV cameras constantly sweeping the room and broadcasting their images on a huge screen onstage (a version of the ceremony is also telecast nationally). At the same time, it kicks off with a recitation from the Koran and later detours dramatically into such things as a salute to the Iranian soldiers in the war with Iraq and a video showing prominent film people visiting Ayatollah Khomeini's tomb a few days before. When the latter featurette commences, I sit up, remembering that my visit to the tomb was filmed by a TV crew, for reasons I couldn't imagine. But no image of the American critic paying his respects to the Imam appears on the giant video monitor.

I've seen the four films up for Best Picture, and most seem overly familiar. One's a war drama (about Iran-Iraq, a burgeoning genre) that's got plenty of visual punch but little dramatic development. Two others belong to a genre I call "kid-quest" films. Tales of young people on some sort of journey or search, these seem to be making a formula out of the concept that helped win Jafar Panahi's *The White Balloon* the Camera D'Or at Cannes two years ago.

One of them, *Children of the Heaven* by Majid Majidi, sweeps Fajr's top awards, winning Best Picture, Director and Screenplay. It's a polished comedy, albeit rather soft-edged and conventional. I doubt it will make much of a splash on the festival circuit.[i]

The fourth film, the one I root for to no avail, is as dark, mannered and question-laden as Jane Campion's *Portrait of a Lady*. Written and directed by veteran director Dariush Mehrjui, *Leila* tells of a young upper-class woman

---

i. My prediction turned out to be completely wrong. Majidi's film enjoyed worldwide success, including an Oscar-aimed Miramax release in the U.S.

who, because she can't have children, gives in to her in-laws' demands that she let her husband take a second wife (not a very common Iranian practice but one that's legal). Even though it doesn't end despairingly, the narrative traces a vertiginous descent into a social and psychological hell.

I don't think various things about this fascinating film work as well as they might (not including the fine acting and polished look) but then, every Iranian guy I talk with registers the same logical objections, while virtually every woman claims to have been moved to tears. One guy says that *Leila*, like a recent Mehrjui film derived from Ibsen's *A Doll's House*, is the worst date movie imaginable: Couples leave the theater fighting. Even so, I hear that the mostly teenage filmgoers that jammed its festival premiere nearly started a riot, so anxious were they to witness the unveiling of Mehrjui's latest foray into sexual politics.

And consider Mehrjui himself, as an emblem of the cosmopolitan culture Americans know so little of. He's now arguably the leading cinematic interpreter of J. D. Salinger, having recently made a striking film of *Franny and Zooey* (it's called *Pari* and owes its existence to the absence of copyright agreements between the U.S. and Iran). Besides Salinger, Mehrjui, who looks uncannily like Lou Reed, says his other big influence is Saul Bellow. And in addition to the adaptations already noted, he recently made his own version of Buñuel's *Viridiana*; it was quickly banned and remains so.

"Of course it was banned!" a Tehrani friend exclaimed to me, laughing uproariously. "Is Mehrjui crazy? A movie in which the nice big Iranian house is overrun by a bunch of lazy, freeloading, ill-mannered poor people! How could he ever get away with *that*?"

Whenever it seems that the Iranian film renaissance is a deliberate flower liable to be uprooted by the next shift in the political winds, Mehrjui stands as a great counterexample. He is credited with starting the whole shebang with *The Cow* (1969), a film he made as a twentysomething freshly returned from majoring in philosophy at UCLA. He has had films banned under the Shah and under the present regime. When I ask him about the difference in censorship hassles between the two, he smiles and says, "Not much. Different people, same problems." Yet he has enjoyed a certain cachet in the Islamic Republic, because the Ayatollah Khomeini made a big deal about his great admiration for *The Cow*.

Mehrjui, though, is the sort to look forward rather than back, and this spring should be rife with anticipation for many Iranians. In May, the presidential election will decide Rafsanjani's successor; one of the two leading candidates was instrumental in launching the film movement as Minister of Culture and Islamic Guidance in the 1980s (alas, this contest looks like Adlai Stevenson versus Lyndon Johnson, and the professorial intellectual is not favored).[ii] And of course, May also brings the Cannes Film Festival, where Iran may again vote for its dreams rather than its—and our—fears.

---

ii. Another erroneous prediction by me: The professorial Mohammad Khatami won by a landslide.

Axis of Cinema
First published February 2002 in the Independent Weekly

I CAN'T SAY MUCH for George W. Bush's timing. Just three days before I was to leave for Iran's annual Fajr Film Festival, he all but declared war on my second-favorite country. Nor were the terms he used any less idiotic than the declaration itself. Axis of evil? Give me a break. Did the president think he was writing videogame copy for testosterone-addled 13-year-olds? No doubt, though, it would be hard to set the nation's sabers rattling by identifying Iran, along with Taiwan and Denmark, as, say, part of an "axis of cool cinema."

But so it is. Since the late 1980s, Iran has produced what even a staid establishment publication like *Time* calls the world's most vital national cinema. During a period when American movies have grown ever more brainless and puerile, addicted to mammoth budgets and saturation TV advertising, Iran's micro-budgeted films have been hailed for retaining what much of the cinematic world seems to have lost: intelligence, poetry, and a profound sense of humanity and compassion.

Indeed, the image of Iran conveyed by films like *The White Balloon*, *Through the Olive Trees* and *Children of Heaven* is so at variance with the familiar U.S. news image (fist-shaking, flag-burning fanatics) as to reveal the essentially propagandistic nature of the latter. Still, no single image comes close to capturing the daunting, protean whole. Iran, as I was reminded again in February, is a country and a culture undergoing the sort of convulsive flux that gives both friends and enemies reasons for concern.

This was my third visit to Fajr—and my fifth stay in Iran—since 1997, and the setting was at once comfortingly familiar and oddly changed. The festival is a citywide event that draws huge crowds of Iranians to an array of mostly foreign films; the top attractions this year included Steven Soderbergh's *Traffic*, Alejandro Amenábar's *The Others* and Takeshi "Beat" Kitano's *Brother*. Fajr, though, also plays host to a few dozen "foreign guests" (as we are invariably called), who include mainly European festival programmers along with a few journalists, all here to sample the latest crop of Iranian cinema.

Due perhaps to Bush's remarks, it seemed to me that there was an undercurrent of uneasiness in the foreign contingent this year. Housed at a large midtown hotel, we spend most of our days going to screenings at the Tehran Museum of Contemporary Art, which is a 10-minute walk away. Most of us usually take the pleasant route, through spacious, well-manicured Laleh Park. It's the way I've gone in past years. This time, a couple of days into the festival, the Fajr staff instructs us seriously to take the street and avoid the park, and to move in groups whenever possible. Since I'm accustomed to moving unescorted across Tehran and Iran, I ignore the advice, but it makes me wonder: Is there something wrong here?

One day, there clearly was. A film that had been a likely candidate for Fajr, *Women's Prison*, was banned shortly before the festival. On the quiet, its makers arranged for a handful of foreign guests to see it in a private screening. A few minutes before we were to leave the hotel, though, the film's director, Manijeh Hekmat, ran across the lobby weeping. We soon learned that she'd just received a call from the Ministry of Culture and Islamic Guidance warning that she would immediately be arrested and sent to women's prison if she screened the film. No one was sure how the authorities learned of the showing, but some foreign guests automatically assume that most phones are tapped.

Such heavy-handed authoritarianism stands in sharp contrast to the quiet revolution that seems to be underway in Laleh Park and Tehran's streets. An enormous amount about Iran has changed in the five years I've been coming here. Cell phones and the Internet, rarities in 1997, are now ubiquitous, and young Tehranis seem far more connected to outside fashions and attitudes than they are to their revolutionary forebears of 1979. Waiting in line for movies or lounging in the park, couples have their arms around each other, the women with their head scarves pushed back far enough to reveal chic, insouciant hairstyles.

Even a couple of years ago, the morality police would have put a halt to such scenes instantly. Today, though these Islamic enforcers still shut down loud parties in well-to-do suburbs, their public, daylight presence has largely evaporated. The lovers of Laleh Park radiate a casual defiance that signifies in many areas of Iranian society. As a friend observes, "The women of Tehran could rip off their scarves and chadors and march down Azadi Avenue—what could the regime do?"

Yet such loosening, even playful attitudes ride atop a huge wave of frustration and anger. When the courtly, erudite reformist cleric Mohammad

Khatami was elected president by an overwhelming majority in 1997, many Iranians gave him the benefit of the doubt, hoping he could recast and save Iran's entire Islamic system. After five years of obstruction by the conservative clerical establishment, however, Iran is in a dire economic and social mess, systemic corruption threatens to strangle the country from the top, and most educated Iranians are beyond fed up—they're furious.

Indeed, having experienced some of the lingering idealism associated with Iran's Islamic Revolution, I wouldn't have believed the extent of the current anger if I hadn't heard its expressions myself. But I heard them everywhere. I could hardly say a bad word about Bush. With a kind of desperate glee, people would shout, "We love Boosh! He is wonderful! His State of the Union was genius! Tell him to come bomb us now! Don't wait! Please, don't start with Iraq! Start here!"

On Farsi call-in shows (the calls come from Iran, the shows are beamed in from outside), caller after caller would say things like, "Let the American bombs start falling! I don't care if they kill millions, if they kill me and my whole family, as long as they get those bastards"—one of the more printable epithets now being applied to the country's beturbaned rulers.

Even the most fervent bomb-us-now enthusiasts, though, realize that Bush's rhetoric is almost surely just that. Sadly for them, Iran's rulers are not likely to be suddenly dislodged by saviors from the skies. The current quagmire can only grow worse in the near term, and the actions of the country's seething, disenfranchised under-30 generation will continue to bolster a statistic recently reported by the International Monetary Fund: With its future scientists, professors and engineers fleeing en masse to places like Southern California and Canada, Iran now has the worst case of "brain drain" in the world.

Most of the pro-U.S., anti-regime talk one hears comes either from the educated young or the business class, Iran's equivalent of conservative Republicans. It's only among the equivalent of liberal progressives, over-40 writers and intellectuals who supported the revolution in their youth, that one hears kind words for the benevolent, well-intentioned President Khatami, and hopes that reforming the current system, though glacially slow, might still work. Yet such people are now faced with the cruel irony that, in mid-February, one branch of the country's extralegal security forces began questioning artists and journalists; the same thing happened three years ago just prior to what are called the "serial murders" of intellectuals by shadowy government operatives.

Those crimes were referenced in several films on display at the 2002 Fajr Film Festival, which showed Iran's filmmakers pondering their society's woes through variations on a dominant theme: hopelessness. Indeed, Bahman Farmanara's *A House Built on Water*, which concerns a disaffected doctor facing such hot-button issues as AIDS and heroin addiction, takes its title from the saying "a life without hope is like a house built on water." It won the Iranian competition's Best Film prize.

The festival's big audience favorite, meanwhile, was Ebrahim Hatamikia's *Low Heights*, a wild, extravagantly stylized comedy-drama about a man so desperate for work that he takes his extended family and hijacks a plane out of Iran.[iii] As the family leaves to board their ill-starred flight, the terminal's TVs erupt with CNN images of the September 11 disasters. And when the protagonist, having learned that Iran's Arabic neighbors would extradite him, considers steering the plane to Israel instead, he's told, "Lots of Iranians would like to be with you on this trip!"

Watching *Low Heights* with the other foreign guests, I could only imagine the cheers and whoops that line would evoke from an Iranian audience. And I could only wonder how much longer the winter of Iran's discontent can possibly last.

---

iii. Asghar Farhadi was credited along with Hatamikia for the film's screenplay.

Return to Tehran 2017
A version of this piece was first published under the title "City of Abbas," November–December 2017 in Film Comment

AT THE 2017 FAJR International Film Festival, Tehran hosted visitors from around the globe, as well as many of its own veteran and up-and-coming film professionals. But it was also a festival defined by certain significant absences. Abbas Kiarostami, who died last July, was memorialized throughout the festival in ways that suggested how deeply many Iranians miss him. Asghar Farhadi, two months after his historic second Oscar win, was away making a film in Spain,[iv] though certain of his key collaborators were in attendance. And Jafar Panahi, still making films while still being banned from doing so, avoided the festival but hosted foreign guests and Iranian friends at his north Tehran digs.

For this visitor, returning to Fajr after an absence of 15 years meant encountering a changed festival and a different Tehran. Until three years ago, the event took place in February and was primarily a showcase for new Iranian films; foreign guests, mainly festival programmers and writers, spent their days in a screening room watching the latest crop. Then, the festival was split in two. The "national" Fajr still occurs in February coincident with Iran's celebration of its 1979 Revolution. Its new "international" offshoot takes place in April and includes films from around the world as well as supposedly the best of the new Iranian films, and, most notably, a film market, housed in a sleek temporary structure that serves as the festival's social and business heart.

The April festival's primary location, a complex called Charsou, is bound to astonish any visitor who hasn't seen Tehran in years. It's essentially an ultra-modern, eight-story shopping mall in which all the stores sell electronics (Samsung, Sony, Apple etc.). The top three floors contain, in ascending order, a food court and media space; the film market and adjacent café; and a four-screen multiplex where many of the festival's films are screened. Above this floor is an open-air space that affords glorious views of Tehran and the snow-capped Alborz Mountains at its northern edge. If alcohol wasn't banned in the Islamic Republic, this could be a world-class rooftop bar.

---

iv. *Everybody Knows* (2018).

Having previously seen this city only in the frigid grays of winter and the sun-baked browns of summer, I'm intoxicated by April's luxuriant green parks, temperate breezes and occasional showers. While the traffic is as terrible as ever (I write a friend that I'd "forgotten the exhilaration of feeling like you risk your life every time you cross a street"), the city's prosperous northern sections have vast new freeways and sleek high-rise apartment buildings interspersed with upscale boutiques, art galleries, car dealerships and trendy restaurants. One thing that's missing: I see no signs of the "morality police" trolling streets and parks telling women to cover more hair or couples to separate. When I ask why, I'm told, "It's the young people—they won't stand for it."

When I first came here two decades ago, giant portraits of the Ayatollahs Khomeini and Khamenei greeted one at the old Mehrabad Airport and seemed to dominate most public spaces thereafter. Now the portraits are still evident, but are so much smaller and discreetly placed as to be almost unnoticeable. In years past, I saw that the rare American visitors tended to be greeted everywhere with effusive friendliness and told "American, Iranian people good—governments bad!" I heard the same sentiment this time, while also noticing that the once-ubiquitous "Down with USA" signs have mostly disappeared. One exception, a famous building-size mural on Karim Khan Street that shows the Stars and Stripes festooned with falling bombs and death's heads, reportedly has been maintained as a tourist attraction. Revolutionary kitsch.

Which is not to say that geopolitical tensions didn't intrude on Fajr. Iran was one of the seven Muslim countries included on President Trump's initial travel ban, prompting President Rouhani to declare that Iran would not issue visas to Americans—although this was quickly amended to say that they would be granted only on a case-by-case basis, which was effectively the policy already. Regarding the film festival, the Trumpian crusade had effects beyond the two nations most directly involved; reportedly, people from other countries were leery of attending Fajr for fear of being unable to enter the U.S. if they had Iranian stamps in their passports.

Another complicating factor was the approach of Iran's presidential elections. While much of Iran's film industry and the Fajr festival itself are controlled by the government, they fall under the auspices of the Ministry of Culture and Islamic Guidance, which must appeal to the Ministry of Foreign

Affairs for visas for its festival guests. When an election is imminent, it seems officials are wary of granting permissions to foreigners, for fear of incurring the wrath of the next regime. This situation is perhaps trickiest regarding citizens of the U.S. and Great Britain, who must acquire their visa stamps before arriving in Iran (other nationals can get them upon arrival). This year, I was told no visas were granted to British subjects (Iranians traditionally have harbored their most serious suspicions regarding the British). I was one of two Americans to receive a visa, and the only one to get it in time to attend the festival's opening and Kiarostami tribute.

Once there, I found Iran's film culture as hyperactive and cosmopolitan as ever, and in some ways boosted by new circumstances. Several state-of-the-art multiplexes have opened, and there's a chain called Art and Experimental Cinema that specializes in showing animation, foreign and experimental films and documentaries. Theater attendance was significantly up last year. Most non-Iranian content, however, comes via video on demand, and there's great interest in TV series such as *Game of Thrones*. As for American cinema, a current film magazine has a big spread on Jordan Peele and *Get Out*, and one name that comes up frequently is Damien Chazelle ("Is *La La Land* good or not?"). David Lynch and Tarantino remain cinephile favorites, as do exemplars of "slow cinema" such as Béla Tarr and Angelopolous.

As in most countries, Iran's commercial cinema dwarfs its art cinema. Last year, I'm told, roughly 100 feature films were released; of these, ten or fewer were of the sort that might look for and find cinephile audiences beyond Iran. As for which younger directors are likely to carry the banner of Iranian cinema into its next phase, the names I hear most often are Shahram Mokri and Reza Dormishian; both are in their thirties and have already begun gaining attention in foreign festivals. Yet in discussions of Iranian cinema the names that occur most often are the three who are absent from Fajr this year, yet who have been among those most responsible for carrying Iranian cinema to the world—Kiarostami, Farhadi and Panahi.

Remembering Kiarostami

As the escalator reaches the multiplex level of the Charsou complex, the first thing you see, hanging by invisible wires from the ceiling, is a large copy of Kiarostami's trademark sunglasses, decorated with images of trees taken from his celebrated nature photography (images which also adorn Fajr's 2017 poster). This striking emblem serves as a gateway to a whole floor decorated with dozens of Kiarostami posters and artworks contributed by Iranian artists, as well as photographs concerning the filmmaker. Of these, the most striking to me are photos of his huge funeral procession, which clogged Tehran's streets with thousands of Iranians, many of them young.

"Did you see what I did?" Dariush Mehrjui asks with a rueful laugh when we speak on the phone during the festival. The eminent auteur whose 1969 feature *The Cow* not only launched the Iranian New Wave of the 1970s but also reportedly convinced Khomeini to give his blessing to the continuance of cinema after the Revolution, Mehrjui was outraged like other Iranians by news that Kiarostami's death was avoidable, the result of medical malfeasance and carelessness. At the funeral, speaking in front of filmmakers including Asghar Farhadi and some of Kiarostami's doctors, he broke down weeping and shouted, "The murderers are here among us!"

While some of that anger and bitterness linger, the shock of Kiarostami's death seems to have given way to something else: a growing appreciation of his importance to Iranian and world culture. When I first visited Iran before *Taste of Cherry* won the Palme d'Or at Cannes in 1997, admiration of his growing international renown was mixed with envy and bafflement that Western taste-makers had chosen to elevate him above the likes of Mehrjui and Bahram Beyzai, whom many Iranians considered greater. Today in Iran, recognition of his eminence is near-universal and extends far beyond cinephiles, the film community and the literati. Telegram, a messaging app popular with young Tehranis, is, I'm told, full of groups discussing and hailing Kiarostami's achievements.

The government, it seems, so far has not known how to deal with this upsurge of emotion. Reportedly, anger at the lack of a Kiarostami tribute at the national Fajr in February drove the decision to stage the one that dominates the first three days of the April festival. Mounted by Seifollah

Samadian, the brilliant filmmaker who served as cinematographer on Kiarostami's *ABC Africa*, *Five* and *Roads of Kiarostami*, it features screenings of two late Kiarostami shorts (the last, "Take Me Home," about a soccer ball on the loose in an Italian town, was almost entirely computer generated) as well as Samadian's own *76 Minutes and 15 Seconds with Abbas Kiarostami*, a lovely documentary portrait that captures Kiarostami's wit, warmth and near-constant artistic activity.

Given that ceaseless work, there are naturally questions over what will become of his abundant output. The numerous decisions to be made on such matters will be handled by his sons Ahmad, a California resident, and Bahman, who lives in Tehran. Unable to attend the Fajr tribute at the last minute, Ahmad Kiarostami sent a video in which he announced the establishment of a Kiarostami Foundation to be chaired by Telluride Film Festival head Tom Luddy. He also noted that French distributor mk2 will restore Kiarostami's earlier films.

As for the future, a question I heard early on—"Is Kiarostami more a world artist or an Iranian artist?"—suggests the wide interest in his legacy. To this native of the American South, it's not dissimilar to asking if Faulkner is more a Southern or a universal artist. Obviously each side of the equation is true and cannot be disconnected from the other: Iranians' appreciation of Kiarostami includes an awareness of his world reputation, just as foreigners' encompasses an interest in the Iranian-ness of his art. His death, which was reported all over the planet, seems to have both deepened and broadened his renown. Mohammad Atebbai, a film sales agent and longtime friend of the director, tells me that since 1989 there have been 231 tributes to Kiarostami, 123 posthumously. The two countries that hosted the most were the United States and India. France, a hotbed of Kiarostami appreciation, held surprisingly few, he says.

At the Fajr event, there's an initial emphasis on his international fame. Filmed tributes are shown from numerous foreign filmmakers as well as stars such as Juliette Binoche and critics including Jonathan Rosenbaum and Geoff Andrew. Three of the first day's four speakers—Iceland's Fridrik Thor Fridricksson, Spain's Victor Erice and Turkey's Semih Kaplanoglu—are filmmakers who recall Kiarostami the man as well as the artist. As the other speaker, I start out observing that perhaps no American critic even knew the name of Kiarostami when the 1990s began, yet 10 years later U.S. critics polled by *Film Comment* named him the most important filmmaker of the 1990s. That ascent surely has few equals in cinema history.

Remarkably, after that decade Kiarostami seemed uninterested in maintaining his status as the elevated auteur of celluloid Iranian masterpieces. He embraced low-budget digital feature-making (*Ten* and the documentary *ABC Africa*), made experimental films (*Five*, *Shirin* and his final feature, *24 Frames*) and dramatic features in foreign countries and languages (*Certified Copy* in Italy, *Like Someone in Love* in Japan; at his death he was preparing a feature to be made in China). Even so, filmmaking was just the tip of his activity. He created video and art installations at institutions around the world (*Seven Trees*, on view since 2005 at the Iranian Artists Forum, is a grove of life-sized trees he made out of photographs). His photography resulted in gallery shows and books. And he published several books of poetry, both original and translations.

Then there was the teaching. Over two decades, Kiarostami devoted considerable time and energy to giving workshops for young filmmakers in locales as diverse as London, Marrakech, Oslo, New York, Havana and Potenza. Writer-filmmaker Paul Cronin sat in on many of these classes, recorded Kiarostami's comments and compiled them into a book, the invaluable *Lessons with Kiarostami* (Sticking Place Books). At once concrete and philosophical, and suffused with Kiarostami's generosity and acute perceptions, the talks, Cronin writes, comprise "a poetics, a treatise on the creation and meaning of cinema that expresses aspects of Kiarostami's aesthetic sensibility."

Kiarostami also taught in Iran, and the last day of the Fajr tribute featured a number of his students on stage talking about him and showing short films they made in his classes. His skills in mentorship, at providing both practical instruction and general inspiration, are evident in their comments, but there's something else as well. If the next stage of assaying Kiarostami internationally is likely to involve comprehending the varied facets of his protean creativity, for young Iranians—in both Iran and its far-flung diaspora—his emerging importance may be as a cultural singularity, within Iranian culture and linking it to the world. As the rare Iranian artist of the modern era who has attained a truly global eminence, he is now not just an artist but a symbol: of his culture's age-old richness, surely, but also of its ability to survive and transcend its encounters with the West and modernity—as well as a government that has alternately supported and restrained it.

For that perception of Kiarostami to truly take hold—for him to approach the status of a latter-day Hafez or Rumi—the affection would have to reach beyond the young and the educated to other strata of Iranian society. At Fajr, I encounter one sign that this may already be happening. Attending the festival are various people who worked with Kiarostami on his films; the actors include the two village boys, now men in their late thirties, who starred in 1987's *Where Is the Friend's House?* One of them, Babak Ahmadpour, hands out copies of his own handwritten, one-page tribute. Addressing Kiarostami, he starts out saying how much he misses the lunches they would have in Tehran, and then says that, after noticing a hole in his sock while on his way to work recently, he saw a man on the street selling socks. "Then, right as I was about to ask, 'Excuse me sir, how much are these socks?', the street peddler, looking quite upset, asked me where you are buried. My eyes filled with tears. I felt ill. I left that place without buying anything. When you were here, everyone, smiling, would ask, 'Where is the friend's house?' But today they ask me where you are buried."

From Kiarostami/Makhmalbaf to Farhadi, According to Mani

"We love it!" says Mani Haghighi when I ask about current Iranian filmmakers' feelings regarding the global success of Asghar Farhadi, who recently became one of only six directors in history (along with Fellini, Bergman, Kurosawa and De Sica) to win the Best Foreign-Language Film Oscar more than once. I'm a little surprised at this very upbeat appraisal, since a few days earlier I'd heard him describe working with Farhadi on *About Elly* as "sheer hell."

I've known Mani since well before he made his first feature, 2003's *Abadan*, which Mohammad Atebbai regards as one of three films that launched the current era of Iranian filmmaking (the others being Farhadi's debut, *Dancing in the Dust*, and Mohammad Shirvani's *Navel*). He's a member of one of Iranian cinema's royal families as the grandson of Ebrahim Golestan, the auteur of *The Brick and the Mirror* and producer of Iran's most acclaimed short, Forough Farrokhzad's "The House Is Black." I hadn't had an extended conversation with Mani, though, in many years, so when I ran into him one afternoon on the Charsou roof and heard his comment about Farhadi, I was intrigued enough to set up an interview in his office for later in the week.

Now with six features to his credit, Mani has a perspective on Iranian cinema that spans generations and includes creative and personal relationships with many of its principals. As I discover, he has definite opinions on how the generation of Kiarostami and his main creative rival of the 1990s, Mohsen Makhmalbaf, led to the emergence and eventual triumph of Asghar Farhadi. He even claims credit for what many critics would regard as the decisive creative shift in Farhadi's career.

"There are a couple of things you need to understand about [Farhadi], if you want to understand why he is like he is," he says. "First, he came out of Makhmalbaf. When he was a kid in Isfahan, he watched Makhmalbaf shooting *The Cyclist* and that's when he knew—'I'm going to be doing that when I grow up.' So that's where his social realism and concern for the pain of the working class comes from.

"Let me tell you what happened. He made his first two films and the second, *The Beautiful City*, I thought was just fantastic, and I went and sought him out and said, 'You're a god.' We had a meeting. At the time I had made one film and he had made two, both of which did terribly at the box office. I said, 'Look'—and this is the only contribution I've ever made to his oeuvre—'you are middle class, it's this ideological hang-up you have that you're dealing with the lower classes, peasants, or people who are living on the margins of the cosmopolitan city. You know so much more about apartment dwelling than these people you're making films about. You're just doing it because you want to be Makhmalbaf. So let's discuss doing something about the middle class.' And he said, 'It's interesting that you say that, because I do have a little story that has to do with the problems that come out of living in an apartment building.' At the time he was actually living in an apartment building and having issues with neighbors on his floor. So we started developing that, it turned into *Fireworks Wednesday* and became a huge hit."

Overcoming the Makhmalbaf influence was only half the battle, though. The other half had to do with the "crisis" that Mani says Kiarostami caused filmmakers of his generation.

"I've known him since I was born; he was a family friend," he says of Kiarostami. "I've been on his film sets, I've been in his editing bays many, many times. I have this long-term awareness of his style and his thinking." Kiarostami's turn toward more experimental and minimalist films in the aughts, though, led to "a point where what he was doing had just kind of stopped working, for us. We were all thinking, 'What's going to happen now?' So what happened was—and this is all in retrospect, looking back on it—we thought, this guy is anti-narrative, anti-drama and we think it's boring now. We want some fun, and we want to tell stories, and we want some tension and conflict.

"Two things changed," he says of his and Farhadi's collaboration on *Fireworks Wednesday*. "One was the class shift. The other—and again it was my suggestion—was that he should use movie stars, instead of this Kiarostami/Makhmalbaf thing of not using [professional] actors. He got Hedieh Tehrani. It seemed like a sell-out at the time, but it worked really well because she was extremely good in it." (The cast also included young rising star Taraneh Alidoosti, who would appear in subsequent Farhadi films.)

"So this is when he realized, 'Okay, so this is where I'm gonna go.' This was not totally going against Kiarostami, though. In fact, when we started writing it, we watched [Kiarostami's pre-revolutionary drama] *The Report* over and over again, just to see how an Iranian director we admire deals with marital conflict. *Fireworks Wednesday* is basically a remake of *The Report*, plus some Hercule Poirot thrown in," he says with a laugh.

"That's what all [Farhadi's] films are, if you see it from this perspective. Every one has a very simple kind of detective story at its heart. Around that is this aura of social-realist Kiarostami-slash-Makhmalbaf everyday banality turned into beauty. This is the combination that always works, because it looks like an art film, but if you boil it down to the basics, it's a detective story. It's a whodunit, always.

"This is the story: There's a couple, and then a third person shows up, disrupts their everydayness, then leaves. Then they have to deal with that disruption, and that leads to some repressed secret being discovered. That's *Fireworks Wednesday*, that's *About Elly*, *A Separation*, *The Past* and *The Salesman*. It's the same story over and over. It's a formula that's working extremely well. And he has this amazing talent to each time bring something excellent to it to make it feel like a new thing."

Kiarostami bred a host of imitators, he notes, most of whom failed because they lacked his genius. The same thing has happened with Farhadi, he adds, and the failures this time are owed not just to a lack of talent but also to a misunderstanding of Farhadi's cinema. It's a point I hear made a few days later by Hossein Eidizadeh, a young film critic, who tells me, "When *A Separation* won Berlinale and then was submitted to the Oscars, people said, 'We can do this kind of film—it's a melodrama where every ten minutes there's some twist.' Actually Farhadi's films are not melodramas, they're thrillers made like Hitchcock made his films, but with ordinary people. And some filmmakers didn't understand this: It's not the twists that are important, it's how the characters are built."

Farhadi and Mani also co-wrote *Canaan*, which Mani directed and was a success. Then Mani acted in *About Elly*, part of an ensemble that also included future Farhadi stars Peyman Moadi (*A Separation*) and Shahab Hosseini (*The Salesman*). He never does tell me why making the film was "sheer hell."

But he says his working relationship with Farhadi "was fraught. Because we're both strong characters. Personal issues aside—and there are so many of those—the good stuff is, I'm a structure guy and he's a narrative guy. He comes up with these brilliant plot points that move things forward, and I'm good at saying, 'That's a little too early, let's wait for it.'

"We're both selfish and opportunistic, and it doesn't help when two people like that work together." Are they on good terms now? "Not really. We see each other and say hello."

Panahi's Party

"This party is in honor of you," Jafar Panahi says as I enter his apartment. "Without you, I might be in prison." Since I know that he doesn't speak English, and must have learned these words just to greet me, I am doubly honored.

The greeting reflects legal difficulties he is still enduring but that go back to the so-called "stolen election" that returned Mahmoud Ahmadinejad to Iran's presidency in 2009. A supporter of Iran's Green Movement and backer of opposition candidate Mirhossein Mousavi, Panahi was arrested in July of

2009 in a Tehran cemetery near the grave of Neda Agha-Soltan, who was slain during the post-election protests. He was released a few hours later, but the following spring he was arrested again along with his wife, daughter and 15 friends, who were all taken to Tehran's notorious Evin prison. Most of the party were soon released, but not Panahi.

In New York, I joined with friends in the film community in an ad hoc committee to help Panahi by inviting prominent American filmmakers to sign a petition calling for his release. Published on April 30, 2009, the petition was signed by, among others, Martin Scorsese, Steven Spielberg, Jonathan Demme, Robert Redford, Francis Coppola, Ang Lee, Robert De Niro, Oliver Stone and Michael Moore.

Having observed the Iranian government's sensitivity to negative PR over the years—especially concerning cinema, one of its few international image-boosters—I was happy but not surprised when he was released on bail in late May. What was surprising, even shocking, was the draconian sentence he received on going to trial the following December: six years in prison, a 20-year ban on any filmmaking activity, as well as bans on giving interviews to the press or leaving the country.

He never went back to prison. That sentence morphed into house arrest, although he's not confined to his house but can move about Tehran freely and throw parties for his friends in the film community and foreign visitors. As for the filmmaking ban, though he has made no films officially (i.e., with the permission of government censors who vet all dramatic films before they go into production), he immediately commenced making them unofficially and having them smuggled out of the country. The first was *This Is Not a Film*, set entirely in the apartment I'm now visiting. It was followed by *Closed Curtain* and *Taxi*, the latter of which won the Golden Bear at Berlin.

As for the ban on giving interviews… well, this is not an interview. But when Panahi and I sit down in his kitchen prior to the arrival of the bulk of the party guests, we begin a conversation that's translated by our mutual friend Mahmoud Kalari, the great cinematographer of *The Wind Will Carry Us*, *A Separation* and Panahi's *Offside*.

When I ask how he's doing, he replies, "I can say I have five screenplays now, and I want to make all of them—with freedom, without stress and [government] reviewing and control." (His ban on filmmaking includes screenwriting.) "I think a filmmaker can only be alive by making movies. In recent years, I tried to show that in any situation I can work. I will continue in this way—making movies like I have before.

"Every day, I get up and say, 'Is this a day I can do something?' Every day I have hope for other days.

"One of my scripts I've been working on for three years, and if I can get out of my current situation, that's the one I want to make. This movie is completely different from the other movies I've made. There's just one problem. The movie requires a star, a famous actress. And if any actress agreed to be in my movie, it could cause some problems for her. So I'm not sure if I can get her. It's a difficult situation."ᵛ

I half-jokingly suggest he cast Golshifteh Farahani, who reportedly has been barred from working in Iran since posing nude in a French magazine. Might a banned actress not be a logical casting choice for a banned director?

While Panahi finds himself currently in a strange situation, his career has been unusual from the first. Of all the Iranian directors who have become known internationally, he is the only one whose films were not released in Iran before they went abroad; rather, his career has been played out on the world stage since it started. His debut, *The White Balloon*, premiered in 1995 at Cannes, where it was awarded the Camera d'Or. It also made Panahi wealthy, gaining distribution around the world and becoming the first post-revolutionary Iranian film to receive a serious art-house release in the U.S.

If the 1990s were dominated by Kiarostami and Makhmalbaf, and the present decade by Farhadi, Panahi might be considered the leading filmmaker of the decade between, prior to his arrest. While *The White Balloon* and his second film, *The Mirror* (1997), were Kiarostami-like in their focus on children, he seemed to come into his own with 2000's *The Circle*, which, like *Crimson Gold* (2003) and *Offside* (2006), evidenced something that Iranian cinema hadn't really seen before: a dissident stance toward the Islamic Republic.

That dissidence of course led him into the Green Movement and the cemetery where he was arrested, and eventually to his current in-between status. How can Panahi be banned from making films but still go on making them and seeing them distributed all over the world? That question comes

---

v. The film became *3 Faces* (2018), starring Behnaz Jafari.

up a lot, and the shortest answer perhaps is one that observes that Iran is a place of great contradictions and many competing power centers. If it had only one, he would either be in prison forever or free as a bird. As it is, there's a tension—a stand-off, as it were—between the hardline forces who would just as soon see him completely suppressed and the more moderate powers who, aware of his global fame, don't want Iran to suffer the black eye such a suppression surely would entail.

In the weird limbo he now inhabits, Panahi can't do many things, but one thing he can do is befriend and advise younger filmmakers. The guests at this party include the two directors I've heard mentioned so often as Iran's most promising up-and-coming auteurs, Reza Dormishian and Shahram Mokri. In some ways, the filmmakers seem to represent two sides of Panahi's artistic concerns, the thematic and the formal. Dormishian films such as *I'm Not Angry* (2014) are strongly political and critical of the Iranian regime. Mokri's *Fish & Cat* (2013), meanwhile, is a formalistic tour de force in which an elaborate story with many characters is rendered in a single shot (à la Sokurov's *Russian Ark*).

It's clear that both directors admire Panahi, but like most of his filmmaker friends, they surely wish he could be free to make the films he wants to make, rather than the ones he can make. As our not-an-interview concludes, he says, "I've shown I don't care [about the government's restrictions] by just going ahead and working. I do think about the things I can't do, but it makes no difference to me. They make a rule that I can't make a film for 20 years. They might as well say 150 years."

3.
ABBAS KIAROSTAMI, CINEMASTER

Remembering Abbas Kiarostami

WHEN THE SUDDEN, SHOCKING news of Abbas Kiarostami's unexpected death reached me in July of 2016, the memories started flooding back. Among them:

One day in the late 1990s when I visited him at his home in north Tehran, he told me he wanted to give me a present before I left Iran. He knew I greatly admired his still photographs and said he wanted to offer me a print of one. He asked me to choose it.

As we sat across a card table from each other in his basement office, he held a stack of maybe 75 large prints, showing each one for ten or 15 seconds before lowering it to reveal the next. He kept his eyes on me. Though I was intently interested in everything he showed me, I don't recall revealing any particular feelings. At the end of the display, I told him which photo I liked best. He smiled as if he agreed with my choice.

When I came back to his house a few days later, he said he had to apologize. The negative of the photo I'd chosen had been damaged in the lab, so he couldn't give me that one. But he had another print, he said—of the photo I liked second best.

I was astonished, but he was right: The print he gave me was just that. He knew it was my second favorite from having watched my face while he showed me the photos.

That print is signed, framed and on the wall of my living room now.

I recall this episode because it captures several things that are central to my memories of him: the extraordinary visual acuity that characterizes both his photographs and his films; his sometimes almost uncanny sensitivity to other people; and his mixture of dry wit and unaffected generosity toward those lucky enough to become his friends.

Is it a good thing for a critic to be friends with filmmakers? In my early years as a critic in North Carolina I felt that not knowing any of the celebrated directors whose movies I reviewed was a definite asset; it assured me that my reviews were not complicated by personal acquaintance or biases.

After I moved to New York, things changed. I had regular access to filmmakers and enjoyed getting to know them, even becoming close friends with some. This of course put me in a tricky, potentially compromised situation. I dealt with it through the most practical policy I could devise: If I couldn't review a film forthrightly (that is, register a negative opinion honestly for fear of damaging a friendship), I would recuse myself from reviewing the film. This has remained my policy ever since.

I can't claim that getting to know filmmakers didn't give me greater sympathy for their work. But I don't think that liking a director ever induced me to like a film that I otherwise would have disliked. Overall, I came to think, a certain trade-off was involved. If some of the objectivity I'd had was sacrificed, I gained a greater understanding of filmmakers' work and outlook in getting to know them personally.

There were additional benefits when the artist came from a culture other than my own. In visiting the director Edward Yang in Taipei after being swept away by his *A Brighter Summer Day* in the early 1990s, I listened with deep fascination and pleasure to his engaged, probing commentary about not just his own work and Taiwan's film culture (of which he was frequently very critical) but also the country's complex history and connections to both Chinese and Japanese cultures. Edward's friendship, learning and generosity greatly informed the writing I did about Chinese cinemas in that era.

Getting to know Kiarostami offered similar pleasures and benefits. Interviewing him the first time, in New York in 1994, I was eager to ask not just about his films but about Iran and its film culture. The Iranian films I'd seen till that point, I told him, almost suggested a place that was simultaneously rustic and cosmopolitan, medieval and postmodern, without much of the connecting cultural tissue one would expect. Was this a misimpression? He smiled, and said, in effect: No, that's how it is.

Visiting him in Iran later in the decade extended that discussion, helping illuminate not only contemporary Iran's vibrant intellectual and cinema culture but also its connections to the West's. Kiarostami famously gave interlocutors the impression that he was a dedicated non-cinephile with little interest in the work of other directors apart from a few favorites like Kurosawa and Buster Keaton, but when I interviewed him for a post-Cannes 1997 *New York Times* profile, he noted his interest in New York directors Jim Jarmusch and Jem Cohen, whose work verges toward the experimental and avant-garde. After I remarked that the imagistic quality of his films reminded me of the

Imagism movement in modern poetry, we discussed poets including William Carlos Williams, Marianne Moore and Ezra Pound, which both showed me the breadth of his reading and pointed me toward a consideration of the importance of poetic models to his cinema (and this was well before I knew how prolific his own writing of poetry was).

Kiarostami's warmth was infectious, his wit droll, quick and near-constant. And while his hospitality was offered to many foreign visitors, perhaps because I enjoyed several extended visits to Iran, he made me feel like a member of his close friendship circle. I became friends with his sons Ahmad and Bahman, who were so important to him, as well as friends of his from the Tehran literary and film communities. Although his rapid rise in world renown during the 1990s inspired measures of puzzlement and jealousy from some fellow filmmakers, I never saw Kiarostami react to such expressions with anything other than poised aplomb. He often avoided discussing the work of his colleagues, but when he did, his comments were generally appreciative and perceptive.

As many have noted in various contexts, he always gave the impression of great sensitivity. While this surely accounts for the observational acuteness of his work, it also made him especially vulnerable to external pressures of various sorts, which he faced in ever-greater profusion as his fame increased. It was only after I saw him in Tehran during the editing of *Taste of Cherry* that I came to understand how fierce the winds facing him were during this time. His home was a necessary refuge, solid and impregnable, yet he was buffeted nonetheless.

Like other Iranian filmmakers, he seemed to understand that Iran was essential to his art. I never heard him mention the possibility of moving to another country, even though he made his final two dramatic features (and was planning a third) outside Iran. His determination and fortitude allowed him to survive on home turf, if not always to thrive. Politically, he kept his head down, but still occupied the position of a soccer ball in a heated match between Iran's two political poles: Moderates loved him for presenting the nation's liberal, cultured face to the world, hardliners despised him for the same thing. While Kiarostami never intentionally baited the latter, the violent, hardliner-encouraged furor after he inadvertently accepted a televised kiss from Catherine Deneuve on winning the Palme d'Or suggested the wisdom—

or necessity—of his attempting to maintain an apolitical stance. Naturally, he was criticized for that, especially after the post–"stolen election" protests and crackdown of 2009, but I always felt his caution and circumspection in this regard were his best defenses against being swept away by the political tempests that frequently roil Iran. (At the same time, I reject the contention that political concerns don't factor into his films at all; they do very much, I believe, on a metaphorical level—for example, the Iranian Revolution's failure to produce a classless society looms large in the subtexts of *Close-Up*, *And Life Goes On* and *Through the Olive Trees*.)

Respecting his discretion, I seldom asked him direct questions about politics, but one night when we were talking after dinner at his home and the name of a moderate Iranian political leader came up, he clenched his hand as if about to pull a pistol's trigger and said, "Godfrey, if he were sitting here and I had a gun, I would blow his brains out!" The statement was so uncharacteristically vehement that it left me sensing the very strong feelings behind the political ideas he declined to articulate—a level of emotion and of darker moods, concerning many subjects in fact, that might not have been readily evident to friends or sympathetic critics.

In over 20 years of knowing Kiarostami, the year I saw the most of him was 1997. I talked with him about the editing of the still-unfinished *Taste of Cherry* when visiting Tehran in February. Was with him in Cannes after he won the Palme d'Or in May. Followed him back to Tehran and interviewed him extensively over the summer, when he drove me up to visit the ruins of Koker, the setting of his great (de facto) Koker Trilogy.[i]

As for how getting to know him and our conversations affected my understanding of his work, I would say the most important factor was the way it revealed and sensitized me to the autobiographical dimension of his films. The turning point here was when I asked him if the main characters in his first two features, *The Traveler* and *The Report*, were intended as critiques of a certain kind of Iranian male, and he replied that they were critiques of no one but himself. From then on, I looked for the autobiographical thread in each new film, and I believe that certain of my reviews reflect this interest or

---

i. This journey is described in "Seeking a Home," see p. 125 and Cheshire, *Conversations with Kiarostami* (Woodville Press, 2019).

perspective more than those of other critics that I've read. Looking back on his work, it seems to me that that the two most traumatic events registered in his movies were the collapse of his marriage, which is fictionalized in *The Report* and I believe meditated on from a distance of decades in *Certified Copy*, and the shock of the devastating earthquake of 1990, which prompted the journey dramatized in *And Life Goes On* and inaugurated the theme of the struggle of life against death that runs through several subsequent films.

Pondering Kiarostami's filmmaking career after his death, I mused that it can be divided into three main periods, each spanning 15 or so years. The first, which I call the Kanoon period, extends from his first short, "Bread and Alley" (1970), through the documentary *First Graders* (1984) (most of the short films of this period as well as *The Traveler* and other features through *And Life Goes On* were produced under the auspices of Kanoon). The second, the Masterworks period, encompasses the six features that made him world famous in the last years of the 20th century, from his first post-revolutionary feature, *Where Is the Friend's House?* (1987), through *Close-Up* (1990), *And Life Goes On* (1992), *Through the Olive Trees* (1994) and *Taste of Cherry* (1997) to his last celluloid dramatic feature made in Iran, *The Wind Will Carry Us* (1999) (this period also includes the documentary feature *Homework*, some shorts and screenplays for other filmmakers such as Panahi's *The White Balloon*). The third period, which I call the Experimental period and which was heavily influenced by his embrace of digital technology, begins with the documentary *ABC Africa* (2001) and includes the features *Ten* (2002), *Five* (2003), *Shirin* (2008), *Certified Copy* (2012), *Like Someone in Love* (2012) and the posthumously released computer-animated feature *24 Frames* (2017), as well as documentary, dramatic and animated/experimental shorts and screenplays including Panahi's *Crimson Gold* (2002).

While all three periods have their fascinations and treasures, the Masterworks period obviously looms over the other two for the renown it brought Kiarostami. Its accomplishments can hardly be overstated. When that period began, Kiarostami was essentially unknown outside Iran and even inside Iran was considered of secondary importance. The period ended with Kiarostami's prize-winning ascent through the realm of international festivals (Locarno, Rimini, Cannes, Venice). That rise, especially by a filmmaker from a country isolated from much of the world and global cinema culture, has few parallels in film history. Whether or not Kiarostami consciously set out to conquer festival programmers and critics worldwide—and I rather doubt that he did—he succeeded as if he had. And thereafter, it seemed, he ceased to care much about such acclaim and success. Following what I've called his millennial pivot, he turned to pleasing himself, first and foremost. In a way, his Experimental period was a return to his Kanoon period, when he could work playfully, idiosyncratically, without having to worry about big budgets or grandiose expectations.

Naturally, the writing in the following section is most engaged with the Masterworks period, which is when I first encountered Kiarostami's films and when I saw the most of him personally, not only in New York, Tehran and Cannes but at festivals in other parts of the world. I've always considered it fortunate that the first of his films I saw were the first four of that period: *Where Is the Friend's House?*, *Homework*, *Close-Up* and *And Life Goes On*. These films are all very accessible and because of that, they formed an ideal introduction to Kiarostami's work (I still recommend them as such, although with the documentary *Homework* replaced by *Through the Olive Trees*, which completes the Koker Trilogy and joins it with *Close-Up* in an extraordinary quartet).

While this section contains some pieces (e.g., those on *Ten*, *Shirin* and *Like Someone in Love*) that I've written recently to fill out its consideration of Kiarostami's major movies, many of the remaining essays reflect my coverage of his career as it happened, and therefore record my evolving understanding of his work. My first piece about him, "A Cinema of Questions," has a title that would continue to prove apposite even as it also conveyed my own questioning of the different meanings Kiarostami had for people in Iran, Europe and the West.[ii] This remained a subject of fascination, all the more so as I myself shuttled between these different locations.

Without question, Kiarostami's films—several of which were banned by the government—never won widespread audience favor in Iran, and there's no small irony that he attained his moment of greatest popularity there in death, as a symbol of various qualities that young Iranians especially prize in Iranian art rather than as the maker of specific films. Listening to these discussions in the different locales, especially during the 1990s, I found plenty

---

ii. See p. 115.

to disagree with everywhere. I told Iranians they were right to be suspicious of Western festivals, not because they sought to propagate negative images of Iran (Kiarostami's films didn't do that anyway) but because they cared more for building their own brands than presenting an accurate picture of Iranian cinema (I once appealed to a Cannes programmer on behalf of Mehrjui's work, and got the clear impression that Cannes felt it didn't need more than one Iranian genius). With Western interlocutors, I argued that Kiarostami should be seen as the product of Persian artistic tradition and a vital indigenous cinema which he shared with artists of kindred brilliance, but there was little inclination to investigate that crucial dual context amid the rush to acclaim the singularity of a new world auteur.

To my mind, the lure of the exotic was definitely a factor in the exaltation awarded Kiarostami, just as it was in the adulation Taiwan's Hou Hsiao-hsien received during the same period. (As one of the few U.S. critics who visited both Taipei and Tehran during this time, I observed the similarities in their film scenes, and how each benefited from their distance from the most fervent of their foreign admirers.) That's not to say Kiarostami deliberately cultivated an image of Iran as exotic, but that, for Westerners, coming into contact with long isolated, sophisticated literary/artistic cultures such as Iran's and China's via cinema held various sorts of appeal, especially as nearer countries had produced few catalyzing "new waves" after the 1980s. Of course, for some of the Iranian cultural officials who helped revive Iran's cinema after the Revolution, winning attention internationally was a clear, stated goal, and Iranian directors had obvious incentives to cultivate global audiences. Yet both factors combined to produce not calculatedly formulaic "festival films" but rather various efforts to generate a Persian vernacular within the language of the international art film.

Kiarostami's success at this had a lot to do with timing as well as his own unique artistic inclinations. When he broke away from the pack with *Close-Up*, *And Life Goes On* and *Through the Olive Trees*, introducing the element of self-reflexivity by focusing on cinema itself, he galvanized critics and art-house audiences in the West.

But, at this point, the story suddenly grew more complicated—it certainly did for me. Having written about all of Kiarostami's post-revolutionary work, I thought I understood its basic elements and direction. Yet *Taste of Cherry* initially left me surprised and completely stumped, as would some of the work that followed it. (Despite that film's great success at Cannes, the impression that it drew universal critical approbation is incorrect. In fact, as some of the following pieces record, it sharply divided critics both at Cannes and on its later theatrical release.) Though the benefit of hindsight makes it easier to perceive qualities that connect *Taste of Cherry* to Kiarostami's previous work, at the time the film struck me as a radical break, certainly from the shorthand understanding "Kiarostami = humanism + reflexivity." If neorealist-style humanism essentially means concern for others, here was a film in which compassion seemed to be replaced by morbid self-concern. And apart from its very controversial coda, it was the first feature since *Where Is the Friend's House?* in which cinema wasn't directly referenced.

Was *Taste of Cherry*'s triumph at Cannes assured by its audaciousness and surface brilliance? I think not, and this is important. Its turn from lyrical humanism to suicidal despair could have produced a festival dud; those critical naysayers could have won the day. For me, understanding the film in retrospect involves the autobiographical dimension that I began pondering more and more in the summer of 1997. And by that I don't mean only that the protagonist's attraction to suicide reflected Kiarostami's own (something he admitted) and this in turn made it his most bleak and personal film so far. I also mean that making such a film at this time, when the Cannes programmers had groomed and positioned him to win their top honor, could well have been suicidal from a career perspective. Kiarostami made a daring bet, and it paid off; but it might not have. Before the film's first screening at Cannes, and even up until the awards were announced, Kiarostami's fate was as uncertain as his protagonist's in the film's penultimate scene. This intertwining of the personal and the artistic eventually came to seem to me a core quality of his work that separated him from other Iranian filmmakers.

Although the gamble that *Taste of Cherry* represented was perhaps more pronounced and striking than those of other films, it was not uncharacteristic. His career is full of nervy leaps in new directions, and his daring in this regard—even when the results didn't produce a masterpiece—I find one of the most distinctive and admirable qualities of his work. Yet it also entailed challenges even for sympathetic critics wanting to keep up with him, and temporal distance didn't always guarantee greater critical clarity.

For me, the challenges presented by his next film were no less formidable. Just as I had been with Kiarostami at Cannes when *Taste of Cherry* won the Palme, I was with him when *The Wind Will Carry Us* premiered at the Venice Film Festival in 1999. I interviewed him shortly afterwards but in truth I had little idea of what to ask him because the film left me mystified. I found it strangely abstract, more than any previous film; I couldn't figure out what Kiarostami meant to say by it. Though I later came to see an autobiographical dimension in its story (with the protagonist's dilemma symbolizing the frustrations of a filmmaker unable to attain his highest goals), and the importance of poetry to Kiarostami's conception became clearer the more I studied it, I eventually became most intrigued with something I'd sensed in some of his previous films but which here ended up being central to my reading of the film: the aura of Persian mysticism.

Thinking back on the interviews I did with Kiarostami over the years, the questions I most regret *not* asking him concern Sufism and its influence on him. Though I've never seen this written about, I knew he grew up in a family some of whose members were Sufis. Moreover, much of the traditional Persian poetry that Kiarostami claimed to know by heart is suffused with Sufi thought. So it was part of his cultural framework, but was it a conscious element in the creation of *The Wind Will Carry Us*? Here, consideration of his autobiography gives way to my own. In the years before seeing *The Wind Will Carry Us*, I had immersed myself in the study of Islamic and especially Persian philosophical and religious thought, including Sufism. In thinking about the film, I came to see it more and more as full of Sufi literary/philosophical/mystical elements, a perspective explored and elaborated in "How to Read Kiarostami," which perhaps represents the apogee of my attempt to understand Kiarostami in terms of his cultural context.[iii]

Do the mystical elements I see in the film reflect Kiarostami's actual intent, or unconscious influences from his upbringing and reading? Or neither? I eventually came to think that such questions were irrelevant to the results of my search for meaning, an imaginative journey for which the film provided a more inspiring and effective launching pad than any previous Kiarostami film. For me, *The Wind Will Carry Us* was transformative. Whether

---

iii. See p. 143.

it transformed me more than I transformed it, the film I saw in my mind after months and years of reflecting on it was very different than the one I saw in Venice. And it has, in that way, continued to stand apart from any film I've ever seen. I don't ask any critic or viewer to share my perspective—that would require familiarity with some of the texts I cite—but I do hope it may stimulate others to explore that literature and embark on their own voyages of interpretation and transformation.

At the time of *The Wind Will Carry Us*, I was tempted to think of Kiarostami as a conscious, intentional mystic, as some of his family were. I soon retreated from that view. Indeed, his next dramatic feature, *Ten* (2002), almost seemed designed to purge his vision of any mystical and literary associations; rather than being set in gorgeous remote landscapes as several of his Masterworks were, it was confined to a car in the hustle and bustle of contemporary Tehran; and as his first film centered on women, it also seemed to contain the fewest autobiographical resonances of any of his features. It was, in various ways, a turning point. Due to his work of the previous decade, "Kiarostami" was now a brand name that guaranteed him an audience in many parts of the globe. But that very success also meant that he could quit building the audience and enjoy the freedom it brought him. Which is what he did, making low-budget, generally experimental films. Critics continued to respect and pay attention to his work, but he never again was the central, catalytic figure he had been in the 1990s. However, he clearly had lost interest in pursuing festival and box-office glory, and much of his restless, constant creative energy thereafter went into photography, art projects, poetry, teaching and other outlets.

In revisiting my writings on Kiarostami, I find several ideas that have remained important to my understanding of his work, including three that appear in "Seeking a Home." One is the autobiographical element that has been discussed above and that I came to perceive more acutely in coming to know him and interviewing him at length; this is something that no doubt will become clearer generally when biographers delve into the details of his life and relate those to his creative activity. The second idea concerns the *integrality* of his work, the sense that his films—and other artworks too—are connected by strands of meaning and thematic and formal associations that his admirers will be contemplating and scholars examining for decades to come; this quality is undoubtedly present in the work of other great filmmakers but often in a way that is less pronounced and dazzlingly complex than it is in Kiarostami. The third idea is my statement that poetry, especially modern poetry, offers the best analogy for what Kiarostami was up to in cinema.

Taken together, these three factors I think help account not only for much of what attracted the world to Kiarostami initially, and why he garnered critical and festival favor so rapidly, but also why his work will endure, as I believe it will. The poetic angle concerns both the form and the content of his films. As Kiarostami became known in the West, there was frequent discussion about the meaning of each film, which was no doubt inevitable because those meanings were not at all obvious or simple. In fact, most films seemed to suggest multiple meanings or potential meanings, hence the word often applied to them: multi-leveled. At one point Kiarostami began to use the term "half-made films" to explain that he intended viewers to complete each film with their own minds, which neatly accords with both aspects of his poetic method: Stylistically many of the films are disjunctive, eccentric in their use of cinematic language, involving internal visual rhymes and symmetries that require the viewer's attention and imaginative engagement; meanwhile his narratives contain elisions, omissions, ambiguities and mysteries that oblige a similar engagement. The fact that some of the resulting meanings are culturally determined aligns with the idea of different Iranian, European and (potential) American Kiarostamis that I bruit in "A Cinema of Questions": Just as Westerners were sure that he offered an astute representation of Iranian reality, many Iranians assumed that it was the Western influences on his work that explained his success abroad. The questions these cultural affiliations and viewpoints entailed meant that the films provoked a conversation among critics and cinephiles that is still going on.

The poetic influence—whether from William Carlos Williams and Marianne Moore or Forough Farrokhzad and Sohrab Sepehri—connects with the integrality of Kiarostami's work in the sense that so much of modernist literature is personal and exploratory. From the wry, variegated lyricism of his early shorts, through the constantly evolving stylistic and narrative strategies of the Masterworks, to the adventurous ploys of *Shirin* and *24 Frames*, there is the underlying sense of a singular creative project taking different forms, asking questions that are all intricately related. All of which also conveys a life as lived, a sensibility observing itself, and the sometimes harsh self-criticism that a confessional approach to cinema produces. Without question, the caustic view of his own nature that was already present in *The Traveler* and *The Report*, and that surely informed the suicidal meditation of *Taste of Cherry*, by the latter part of his career had solidified into a deep, steadfast, unavailing bleakness. In films such as *Certified Copy* and *Like Someone in Love*, what's missing is any hope of transcendence. Love and art might offer temporary simulations but those are fleeting, illusory. As in much modern confessional literature, what his work could offer ultimately was an unflinchingly honest account of his life's limits.

It might be said that the bleakness of view here was Kiarostami's philosophical outlook, one that seemed to grow stronger and sharper as his career progressed. Like the protagonist of *Taste of Cherry*, he could not accept religion's promise of a life after death granted by an omnipotent deity, which made death the final limit of any life. Yet philosophy and poetry are often linked in Iranian tradition, and Kiarostami said in interviews that he preferred the vision of poets, which emphasizes the transient, sensory glories of life. For that reason, while his work's philosophical implications may be dour and dark, the man was anything but. Though his moods could be mercurial and some of his relationships (both personal and professional) difficult, I always think of Kiarostami as full of energy, intelligence, warmth and infectious good humor. And his acts of generosity and friendship, like that photograph he gave me in the late 1990s, could be startling. When he was in New York for the American debut of *Like Someone in Love*, we were seated across from each other at a dinner when, as if addressing the whole table, he said, "Godfrey, I consider you a member of my family." I was touched but not surprised; he had always made me feel that way. I had no way of knowing this would be the last time I ever saw him.

A Cinema of Questions
First published July–August 1996 in Film Comment

IN *HOMEWORK*, A FILM MADE in 1989, Abbas Kiarostami goes to a Tehran grammar school to investigate how newly instated practices regarding homework are affecting the educational climate. The mission, he notes in voiceover, was prompted by problems one of his own sons had with homework. Most of the film consists of interviews with first- and second-grade boys. The kids' sunny, open faces offer a wonderfully concrete catalog of unaffected innocence. But their words describe a system in which homework is used more as a flail than a tool, locking teachers, parents and students in a bitter cycle of coercion and resentment. Virtually all of the boys can tell Kiarostami the meaning of "punishment"; relatively few are able to define "encouragement."

A man who seems to be at the school by chance is interviewed. He says he's a father who has lived abroad and studied the educational systems of other countries. The Iranian tendency to punish rather than to engage the child's imagination, he warns, will produce "an indignant, cheerless generation susceptible to any mental problem." Another concern: "Every subject of study including literature has been mixed with religion." Then, just before the final round of interviews, the film, as it were, takes a break: joins the kids outdoors, where teachers lead the sometimes-unruly students in religious chants that have a fervent, martial air. Kiarostami says (voiceover): "In spite of all the attention of the responsible persons to arrange the ceremony properly, it was not performed appropriately. So to observe the reverence, we preferred to delete the sound from the filmstrip." *And the sound goes off.*

The viewer is left with the sight of boisterous youthful faces mouthing inaudible exhortations, and with the impression of a precise, astonishingly Godardian formal coup, one that reverberates in several directions at once. Picture without sound: For a moment we're back at the medium's infancy, recalling how freely images "spoke" before sound came along to control them. Faces without voices: a fleeting glimpse of beauty (natural and thus tinged with anarchy: see *Zéro de conduite*) minus imposed "meaning," the exact opposite of an educational system that subjugates with language. Of course, the bit about "observing the reverence" is pure hooey, a wily end run round the censors. But as soon as you sense who this passage is not aimed at, you have to wonder who its intended audience is. Non-fundamentalist Iranians? Other filmmakers? Cinephiles in the West? Future generations?

Kiarostami's is a cinema of questions. In the documentaries, including *Homework*, the Q&A format attains an almost liturgical sublimity. In the fiction films, questions of place are as emblematic and ubiquitous as the question of time is in *La Ronde*. A little boy asks everyone he encounters directions to a schoolmate's house, sometimes getting helpful replies, sometimes not. A film director trying to drive through an earthquake-devastated region must stop repeatedly to assess his whereabouts and the possibility of reaching his destination. Where am I? What is this place? Where are we headed? Such questions are stressed in ways that push their meanings well beyond the dramatic, into a symbolic realm that unites the social, the moral, the philosophical and the personal. Yet their aim is not the usual one: to get answers. Rather, left to hang in the air like an endless series of echoes, the questions pointedly forestall hard answers, final certainties, "fundamental" truths.

In so doing, they identify Kiarostami not so much with any particular mode of understanding, but as one forever in transit (much as his characters are always in motion) between various modes, which might be expressed as figurative compass points. Indeed, it could be said there's not just one Kiarostami but several, based on perspective and perception: the Iranian, a lightning rod of cultural attention und controversy; the European, lion of film festivals and embodiment of the beleaguered term "auteur"; and the American, a shadow yet to gain the limelight but inevitably, too, a projection screen for our fears and hopes regarding the culture that labeled us the "Great Satan." And if we turn this diagram around to view it from the angle of history rather than geography, we get another trio of Kiarostamis: the pre-revolutionary filmmaker (1970–78), the post-revolutionary (1978–89), and the "international" (1989 on). The unity in this multiplicity may be surprising, but it's the multiplicity itself—the complex interlock of event and event, perception and perception—that deserves closest scrutiny.

Americans, we needn't hesitate to fear, will lead with the wrong question. Are the films "political"? Do they protest and lambast and defy Islamic theocracy in the name of more agreeable absolutes? (An Iranian filmmaker interviewed on NPR recently was heard to sigh that Scorsese and Woody Allen aren't hit with such queries every time they issue a film.) In fact, Kiarostami's films are as forceful in their moral acuity as they are lyrical in expression, which means: Their politics and their art are one, as they should be. But a better way to counter the American question's presumptions would be to answer: The medieval Iran we get from the evening news is mostly bunk. In reality, beneath the surface orthodoxy imposed by the nation's present regime, there's still Persia—a cosmopolitan culture of longstanding artistic and literary sophistication.

Born in 1940 to a middle-class Tehrani family (his father was a decorative house painter), Kiarostami was fascinated with art as a child, and studied it at university. Movies were an early preoccupation; he has cited *La Dolce vita*, with its heady mix of decadent beauty and moral scrutiny, as the film that spurred an understanding of the director's vision. Working in commercial art after university led him into designing credits sequences, à la Saul Bass, and to making commercials. In 1970, partly due to his work designing children's books, he was invited to help found the cinema department of the Institute for the Intellectual Development of Children and Young Adults, known as Kanoon, which has produced many films besides his own. The organization evidently gave him a stable artistic home. That it also got him into the business of making films about kids proved especially useful after the Revolution; when many other areas of dramatic inquiry were restricted, the child's world remained an open and fertile garden of metaphor.

Kiarostami is the most important filmmaker to appear on the world stage in the 1990s. That view, stated as baldly as possible, comes to us from Europe. It is not impossible to imagine some Iranians cautiously agreeing with the assessment, but it is impossible to imagine them originating it. Iran's film scene ignited in the late 1960s and blazed brilliantly through most of the 1970s; after a few years of post-revolutionary eclipse, in the late 1980s it produced a new brilliance that in part stemmed from film's increased elevation of a form of artistic expression. Kiarostami comes from an extraordinarily vital film culture; as his *Close-Up* shows, serious filmmakers there are revered with a fervency unknown in our culture. That he has been singled out for international lionization must strike some in Iran as odd, disproportionate if not unjust. When I asked him if fame abroad had caused him problems at home, he said it had, until a passionate tribute from Akira Kurosawa arrived to refute suspicions that his renown was a fabrication of "the West."

And yet, to an extent, it had been. The year was 1989, the place the Locarno Film Festival. Filmed two years earlier, *Where Is the Friend's House?*, Kiarostami's third dramatic feature (and first since the revolutionary period), made the kind of European debut that changes things. From then on, he made films that seemed to assume foreign audiences (critics at home would say the work was tainted by that assumption), which returned the interest. The French especially embraced him, and no wonder. Their apprehension of durable cinematic value often outruns other countries', no doubt, but just as surely, Kiarostami fit various agendas at a time when France was beginning to face the Third World in the *banlieues* as well as in the newspapers, and Islam was that world's most menacing face. Plus, the French had the most invested in auteurism. Could there be a more promising Third World auteur than the urbane Kiarostami, whose films combine neorealism's empathetic grit with the Nouvelle Vague's brainy and idiosyncratic formalism?

This is to suggest, mainly, that there were obvious reasons for Kiarostami's European acclaim, and that those have set the terms for the appreciation of his work generally. Yet there are depths beyond the obvious, including two qualities that I haven't seen noted elsewhere. One is his very particular way of "decentering" the narrative by violating the conventions that lead us into and out of stories. Kiarostami films rarely "begin at the beginning" (except, ironically, for *Close-Up*, where the early scenes are fake[iv]); they usually start abruptly, *in media res*, sometimes focused on inconsequential characters or events. Likewise, they end with a jolt, or at the "wrong" place according to expectations set up earlier. The effect of such maneuvers is a kind of challenging dislocation that makes a moral issue of narrative space, obliging the viewer to consider his relation to the

---

iv. This was written when I had seen only the film's first version. Kiarostami later changed the opening after a projectionist in Munich mixed up the film's reels and Kiarostami decided he liked the rearranged version better than the original. The first version showed Sabzian meeting the middle-class lady on the bus; the new one starts with soldiers and the reporter going to arrest Sabzian. Both are reenactments.

story. Their endings, especially, often startle us into a recognition of our own preconceptions and wishes.

The second quality is Kiarostami's playful, yet intently destabilizing, way with binary opposites. Perhaps this is simply the epistemological equivalent of the tendency just noted, but its consistency is striking. In film after film, characters face choices or junctures that seem to be either/or. The right road to take versus the wrong one. The correct decision, or the incorrect. The trustworthy person, the untrustworthy. But such oppositions rarely lead to the expected results. Things change; contraries melt away, switch identities, merge, reappear, vanish. The best example is the end of *Close-Up*, where the filmmaker Mohsen Makhmalbaf and the young man who has criminally impersonated him are asked via intercom to identify themselves. "Makhmalbaf," says Makhmalbaf, answering for them both and thereby erasing the distinction that has dominated the film up until then. Here, literalism and all received knowledge are seen as being at the mercy of two free radicals: human will and chance. Note that this vision is equally inimical to religious fundamentalism and scientific materialism.

What's remarkable is how consistent these qualities, as well as others commonly associated with his work, are from the outset. "Bread and Alley" (1970), his first short, brings a wonderfully sharp monochrome visual style to a deceptively simple tale of a boy returning home through a maze of alleys and encountering a menacing dog. Typical of the decentering just discussed, the film takes a while to locate its subject, then abruptly "loses" the boy who is its protagonist just before the tale's close; the ending also leaves its final "either/or" (good dog or bad?) an abrupt, unanswered question.

The Traveler (1974), Kiarostami's first feature, also comprehends many of the themes and strategies of his later movies. Bearing comparison to *The 400 Blows* and *Bicycle Thieves* for its vivid, masterful depiction of childhood's cruelty, this too-little-known film has a claim to being called Kiarostami's most sophisticated work, since the negatives that in earlier and later films are dramatized as aspects of nature (bad dog, earthquake) or society (oppressive traditions) it presents as functions of the Iranian character.[v] Its analysis of

---

v. Kiarostami later corrected my erroneous interpretation on this point; see "Remembering Abbas Kiarostami" and "Seeking a Home."

that character is singularly devastating. The film's protagonist is a village boy who goes to insane lengths to attend a big soccer match in Tehran, including stealing from his parents and betraying his own soccer team. There's lots of macho nerve in his gambit, but also a pathetic infantilism. Yet the most striking thing about the film is how it insinuates our desires into his designs: The worse the kid acts, the more the viewer identifies with his pursuit of a very unholy grail.

This film was followed by other shorts and, around the time of Iran's revolutionary turmoil, two films (neither of which I've seen) made outside the Institute's auspices: a feature, *The Report* (1977), and the 53-minute "Case No. 1. Case No. 2" (1979). According to Kiarostami, the latter film, which condemns high schoolers who rat on their neighbors, so flummoxed officials of the new Islamic regime that they first gave it an award, then banned it.

Kiarostami did not leave Iran at the time of the Revolution, he told me in a 1994 interview, "because an internal revolution was taking place in my household: I was getting separated from my wife, and was going to take care of my two sons, so it was impossible for me to think of leaving the country." The diaspora he missed divided a generation of Iranian filmmakers. Kiarostami recalled that for a while those who remained behind feared that filmmaking had ended for good in Iran. But history played paradoxical, to the point that "in the past fifteen years we've seen that the filmmakers who left Iran haven't been nearly as successful as the ones who stayed."

As for the origins of that success at the international level, *Where Is the Friend's House?*, rather than comprising any sort of splashy breakthrough, establishes a simple, sturdy paradigm. Set in the rural village of Koker, it begins as second-grader Ahmad sees a classmate harshly chastised by their teacher, who threatens expulsion if the boy does his homework anywhere but in his notebook; after school Ahmad realizes that he's taken his friend's notebook by mistake, and sets off on a long and complicated trek to return it: When the effort fails, he does his friend's homework for him and so prevents him being expelled in a different way than he first intended. Several elements here—the documentary-like realism, the humanist tone, the oblique indictment of harsh authority figures—are so common to Iranian films of the present era as to be virtually archetypal. What distinguishes Kiarostami's approach, besides the unusually fine performances he gets from the cast of non-actors, are the film's lyrical apprehension of the physical spaces traversed by Ahmad, and the sense of a mythic quest theme shrewdly conjoined to a rugged social realism: Both the poetic eye and the knowing narrative suggest a filmmaker of very distinctive gifts and ambitions.

It's worth positing that both the rustic simplicity and the authorial sophistication were essential to the impression the film made in 1989. Other Iranian films of the time tended to boost one quality over the other: There were earnest dramas about poor rural folk, and smart comedies and melodramas about upscale urban Iranians. Only Kiarostami brought an auteur's sensibility to a place that others used mainly for humanitarian pleading, thus creating a fictional world founded in real social difficulty yet unmistakably transmuted by the self-consciousness of the artist's rendering. If this combination of Third World *vérité* and postmodern reflexivity was bound to earn Kiarostami a special form of appreciation in Europe, what he did with the validation is startling nonetheless.

Where Is the Friend's House? became the first in an ongoing series of films that now includes *And Life Goes On* and *Through the Olive Trees*. To my knowledge the cinema presents no obvious parallels to this extraordinary endeavor, which is at once dizzily self-referential and searchingly moral, Pirandello twined with Rossellini. Calling the films sequels is misleading. The whole project—with its recurrent geographic locus recalling Faulkner's Yoknapatawpha—is more accurately described as an evolving palimpsest, with each new film not so much continuing the previous one as springing from it, questioning, emending, reflecting on it.[vi]

In *And Life Goes On*, a film director journeys through a rural area in the aftermath of an earthquake, trying to reach Koker and discover the fate of the children he directed in *Where Is the Friend's House?* An actor plays the director. In *Through the Olive Trees* another actor, playing the director of *And Life Goes On*, and attempting to shoot one of its minor scenes, observes an illiterate bit player trying to persuade a girl he shares a scene with to marry him; the romantic division refracts various problems (poverty, illiteracy, earthquake devastation) registered in the previous films, as well as the auteur's

---

vi. These three films would come to be known as the Koker Trilogy.

Heisenberg-like perspective. Making the assurance of these increasingly intricate fictions even more astonishing, incidentally, is the knowledge that a typical Kiarostami "script" is a 15-page outline; he fills out the story as he proceeds, and writes the dialogue shortly before shooting.

It perhaps needs stressing, especially for those who've never seen these films, that the headiness of their conception never overwhelms their formal pleasures or human concern. The poetry of space and movement of *Friend's House* expands elegantly, and wittily, in the succeeding films, where "being lost" and "searching" leap from dramatic to comic to discreetly metaphysical meanings without ever losing their grounding in sharp-focus observation. And if there is a single value that anchors this mushrooming fictive universe to the ethical, religious and political here-and-now, it is compassion—a word too vague, admittedly, for the impulse far more precisely and vividly registered in a boy's worry over his schoolmate's punishment, a director's difficult attempt to discover the fate of children who acted in his film, another director's bemused inclination to put his art at the service of an unlikely but "real" betrothal.

The word is indeed too easy, since life never lets the value exist in a comfortably pure state but constantly prods and challenges it, leaving it poised dramatically, in so many instances, between noble defeat and equivocal victory. In Kiarostami's script for Jafar Panahi's *The White Balloon*, the quest theme again underpins the headlong efforts of the protagonist, here a 7-year-old girl determined to purchase a special goldfish for her New Year's celebration; the implied success of her enterprise (we never see it actually accomplished) turns on its essential purity and on the compassion of others, the former symbolized by the color white, the latter by a young Afghani balloon seller whose crucial act of assistance stands neither to gain nor to lose him anything. Two other Kiarostami-scripted movies push some of the same ideas in different directions: Ali-Reza Raissian's *The Journey* (1995) finds a family's wartime flight to an idyllic rural refuge undone by an act of cruelty early in the trip; and Ebrahim Forouzesh's *The Key* (1986), about a 3-year-old boy trying to mind things at home while his mom's out shopping, combines the fascinations with space and children's behavior into a comic tour-de-force that suggests Dr. Spock as brought to the screen by Buster Keaton.

Of the two feature-length documentaries Kiarostami has made since *Friend's House?*, *Homework* (which continues the themes of *First Graders*,

1984) is more clearly motivated by straightforward social concerns, ones very much in line with the subjects and emphases of his previous films: The competing claims of compassion and imposed coercion here take the names "encouragement" and "punishment," and the latter dominate a cruel social complex which this lucid, moving, and sometimes surprisingly funny film interrogates. Yet even in this context, questions of cinema and auteurship arise. Kiarostami repeatedly puts himself in the frame, and includes a conversation with a passerby indicating the fame of his films. Moreover, there's that playful deletion of religious chanting noted above, as well as puzzlers such as whether that father with the worldwide experience in educational systems really just happened by during filming.

"We can never get close to the truth except by lying," Kiarostami said to one interviewer. The sentiment is nowhere more brilliantly and provocatively evoked than in *Close-Up* (1990), the film Werner Herzog called "the greatest documentary about filmmaking I have ever seen." It began with a real incident: A poor young man named Sabzian was arrested for impersonating the filmmaker Mohsen Makhmalbaf to a wealthy Tehrani family; though without any evident criminal intent, he had promised the family members parts in his next film, and borrowed money he never returned.

Filming the trial, Kiarostami encounters a real/reel drama of multiple fascinations: Sabzian testifies poignantly to his great admiration for Makhmalbaf, and about the hopelessness of his life before posing as a moviemaker momentarily uplifted him; the family, seething with shame and anger at Sabzian, nevertheless describes the "love of cinema" they shared with him; meanwhile, a turbaned Islamic judge does an admirable job keeping up with increasingly complex arguments about the technical, social and symbolic aspects of the cinema. And just to make things more complex still, Kiarostami wryly taints his documentary with elements of fiction and stage-managing, e.g., persuading the young man and family to reenact certain events that led to the arrest, and arranging for the real Makhmalbaf to meet Sabzian when the latter is released from prison.

This blurring of the line between documentary and fictional filmmaking, a tendency that perhaps begins in technical impoverishment but soon enough has its own philosophical impetus, is one of the hallmarks of recent Iranian cinema. It certainly neither originates with nor belongs to Kiarostami. But he has arguably taken it to more erudite lengths than any of his compatriots, in part by personalizing it—subsequent to *Where Is the Friend's House?*—in ways familiar to the audience he discovered (or did it do that to him?) beyond Iran. This is the "European" Kiarostami, who knows his film history well enough to show others theirs: If *Friend's House?* recaps the ethos of *Bicycle Thieves* (as do so many serious Third World films), the next pages of the palimpsest deftly conjure the shades of, among others, *Journey to Italy, Contempt, Day for Night,* and *Despair*. Yet, in ironically showcasing "the auteur," that figure so crucial to the transition from neorealism to the Nouvelle Vague and beyond, *And Life Goes On, Through the Olive Trees,* and *Close-Up* implicitly question the value of auteurship and the process it represents, wondering if the medium can claim real worth if uprooted from the suffering of the poor and the struggling—the kind of Bazinian moral scruple that would naturally lead Godard to prefer Kiarostami's rugged humanism to Kieslowski's designer mysticism.[vii] At the same time, the "European" Kiarostami retains enough "foreignness" to effect what *Rashomon, Pather Panchali,* and *Red Sorghum* did in years past—escort an unknown cinema into Western art-houses via the right blend of exotic and familiar.

Is there a paradox here? I don't think so. Kiarostami has not become any less a "great Iranian filmmaker" for having become less "purely" Iranian; the reach across cultures can only have strengthened his artistic muscles, and left him more certain than ever of why the filmmakers who stayed in Iran have "succeeded" far more than those who left. Ours is, if anything, the culturally precarious place, since we fail to differentiate between American and European, and European and Iranian. When the sound stops in that scene in *Homework*, I can sense—maybe not accurately, that's not the point—Godard's reaction; I can only wonder about any Iranian's. And wonder I do. Like the best of pedagogues, Kiarostami leaves us aflail in questions.

---

vii. In its 1994 awards, the New York Film Critics Circle voted a special award to Jean-Luc Godard. Godard responded with a message to the group urging that it honor Kiarostami rather than Krzystof Kieslowski, whose *Trois Couleurs: Rouge* won its Best Foreign Language Film award.

Seeking a Home: On Koker, Cannes and *Taste of Cherry*
A version of this was originally published 1998 in Projections 8 *(Faber & Faber)*

JAPANESE TOURISTS, ABBAS KIAROSTAMI tells me, now visit the hill near Koker that appears in his films *Where Is the Friend's House?*, *And Life Goes On* and *Through the Olive Trees*. Most surprising about that is not that the Japanese would revere the Iranian director—much less that their reverence would combine cinemania and landscape worship—but that they would go to such lengths for a glimpse of this sparse knoll, with its zig-zagging path and lone tree at the summit. Koker is a four-hour haul from Tehran, and not even a living place.

It died in the earthquake that hit north-western Iran in June of 1990, on the eve of Kiarostami's 50th birthday. He awoke to the news of its devastation, which claimed 50,000 lives, and set off by car in an effort to discover if the children who had appeared in *Where Is the Friend's House?* were still alive: The journey provided the basis for the documentary-like fiction of *And Life Goes On*.

When we are leaving Tehran for Koker, Kiarostami—who proposed this trip the day before, and tonight, after driving all day long, will fly to the Locarno Film Festival—says something to the effect that we are going to the friend's house. Then he adds, "But the friend is not there." Ahmad and Babak Ahmadpour, brothers who played the friends in *Where is the Friend's House?*, now in their late teens, are away from home doing their military service. They survived the earthquake, though many of their acquaintances, and Koker itself, didn't.

Kiarostami estimates that the village contained perhaps a thousand people when it was struck. I gather that many of the survivors moved down the hill to Rostamabad, a town of many new-looking buildings made with concrete foundations and steel girders, a departure from the mud-brick construction that was blamed for the earthquake's high casualty rate. Hossein Rezai, who started as a tea boy on *And Life Goes On* and won a part co-starring as the lovelorn laborer in *Through the Olive Trees*, works as a taxi driver in Rostamabad. He is happy to see Kiarostami drive up and seems keen for a part in another movie, something that Kiarostami—who clearly likes the unschooled actor's work—says he's considering.

Unlike the character he played, Hossein is married and appears content. Kiarostami smilingly relates that for a long time after *Olive Trees* opened in Tehran, Hossein would hang out at the theatre where it was showing, enjoying the praise that came his way. I'm thus a little surprised that there are no posters or pictures from the movie in his office at the taxi company; instead, there are posters of Imam Khomeini and other religious leaders.

It is mid-August when we visit. That emblematic hill, so green in the films, is now a greyish ochre. There are no tourists about, Japanese or otherwise. Kiarostami says the hill represents friendship, and notes that its image is somewhat artificial; he had the zig-zagging path to the crest created to his specifications.

Koker, a few meters up the road facing the hill, is a sunburnt, mud-brick ghost town dotted with olive trees. Set-dressers revived a couple of its houses for *Olive Trees*, but that, like the evocative zig-zag, was little more than lyrical artifice. The deterioration which has infested the place is striking. It looks like it has been uninhabited for a millennium or more, not less than a decade.

Kiarostami gazes over the village turned undulating hillside ruin and, with a kind of wry ruefulness, says: "My Cinecittà."

On the drive back to Tehran I ask if he endorses the term "Koker Trilogy" to describe the three films set in and near the now-abandoned village. The question reflects both pragmatism and curiosity: The term seems a needed, useful one, yet in interviews Kiarostami has seemed to shy from it. Today he does so again.

Those three films, he says, are united mainly by the accident of place. Wouldn't it be more appropriate to consider as a trilogy his last three films—*And Life Goes On*, *Through the Olive Trees* and the new *Taste of Cherry*—which are united by theme: the struggle of life against death? This response is not only perfectly reasonable, it also shines a sudden, valuable light on the latest film's connection with its immediate predecessors. Yet I'm still intrigued by the reasons Kiarostami might balk at using the T-word to describe the earlier films, which are so evidently interlocked.

It almost seems a little superstitious, as if to pronounce something a trilogy were to seal it off permanently in the hermetic canister of canon (when, in fact, Kiarostami has indicated his interest in perhaps returning someday to the Rostamabad area for a fourth film). More than that, though, his hesitancy suggests to me a roundabout recognition of the combined power of *Where Is the Friend's House?* and its two successors—a strange synergy that seems all the more potent when the films are screened (as they rarely have been) together and in order. Could it happen that this synergy might someday overshadow the man who created it?

It's like the spiraling effect of *Close-Up*, the startling 1990 quasi-documentary that Kiarostami calls his favorite among his films. In 1996 *Close-Up* itself spawned two other films (both shorts): Nanni Moretti's "The Day *Close-Up* Opened," about the Kiarostami film's sparsely attended premiere in Rome, and Mahmoud Chokrollahi and Moslem Mansouri's "Close-Up Long Shot," which probes the personality and subsequent life of the Makhmalbaf impersonator Hossein Sabzian. Is it possible that the world might eventually contain film festivals devoted solely to *Close-Up*—a movie that could be subtitled "Cinema and Its Double"—and an ever-increasing number of films deriving from it, even to the Borgesian point where the proliferating doubles would absorb the original, and its maker?

At the 1996 Turin film festival I introduced Mohsen Makhmalbaf to the director Ning Ying; both had just arrived, were to serve on the festival's main jury, and began talking immediately about the crushing restrictions on filmmakers in China and Iran. Later the talk turned to the much-heralded death of cinema and Ning offered a paradoxical thought. Of course the cinema was approaching its end, she said, but in death it will surely live on: Whatever future audiovisual simulacra might entice the millions in the name of entertainment, there will always be people who love cinema, the cinema of the past century, the way people today love Renaissance painting or the music of Beethoven.

"The Day *Close-Up* Opened" is a minor-key Golgotha. In it, Nanni Moretti the diaristic filmmaker, records Moretti the art-house distributor/exhibitor's droll chagrin as *The Lion King* racks up enormous grosses all across Italy on the same day that *Close-Up* meets a few dozen spectators at his cinema in Rome. Of course, the short exists to register the galling irony that a film of true greatness should be so thoroughly eclipsed by a mass-market cartoon juggernaut. Far more crucial, though, is Moretti's implicit faith that the transforming sublimity of Kiarostami's film will one day be recognized; indeed that it might outlast the commercial empire that now overwhelms it.

Jean-Luc Godard, according to a report which is fitting even if apocryphal, recently defined the cinema as extending from Griffith to Kiarostami; full stop. Does the medium's afterlife—its transmutation into our own private Cinecittà, a virtual ghost town of past glories—begin with the cults forming around the "Koker Trilogy" and *Close-Up*?

If so, no wonder the living filmmaker would be ambivalent (amused at the Japanese tourists, resistant to the idea of a trilogy), or that he would be as absorbed with mortality as *Taste of Cherry* is. *Taste of Cherry* took a long time to complete. Kiarostami reportedly went back and shot the present ending months after shooting the body of the film. He experienced delays due to a car accident while location scouting in the autumn of 1996 (he suffered a broken rib) and others due to officious hardliners who assigned him the graveyard shift in the editing room simply, it seems, as a way of insulting Iran's most celebrated filmmaker.

The film's exit from Iran was precipitous. Until two days before the 50th Cannes festival opened, it was assumed that *Taste of Cherry*, which had been invited but was not listed in the official program, would not make it to France; its last-minute appearance caused some to joke that the Iranians must have stage-managed the whole thing for maximum dramatic impact. In fact, its departure was complicated by several factors: Because it had just been completed, the film had not debuted at February's Fajr festival, as Iranian films are supposed to do (a technicality, but a serious one); it treats a man contemplating suicide, a taboo subject to strict Islamists; and the government was about to change, which left sitting officials nervous about making any decisions that could get them into trouble later. The eleventh-hour decision to let the film leave the country was reportedly made at the highest levels of government. (*Taste of Cherry* will have to be shown at the 1998 edition of Fajr to be eligible for a release in Iran.)

Kiarostami has been climbing the festival ladder since the success of *Where Is the Friend's House?*, his first post-revolutionary feature and quite arguably his last film made in relative innocence of the festival world. It is fascinating to think of him pondering the opportunities he must have recognized in traveling abroad with that film, opportunities that, incidentally, underscore the similar situations of Iranian and Chinese filmmakers in the late 1980s and early 1990s.

Still even more fascinating is to realize the extraordinary way Kiarostami—unlike other directors working in such situations—not only used that cinematic self-consciousness, but made it an implicit subject of his films from then on. In a way, his hesitation about naming a trilogy is well-founded. *Where Is the Friend's House?* is a lovely little film about certain aspects of life, aimed at Iranian audiences. *Close-Up, And Life Goes On* and *Through the Olive Trees*—maybe this is the trilogy?—are about the complex ways cinema interacts with life, and are clearly made in awareness/anticipation of an international audience.

Seen in that light, *Taste of Cherry* is startling in the extreme. Rather than the kind of expansive and embracing work that shows a long-on-the-ascent director reaching out to claim his Palme, rather than a continuance of the lyrical lightness and generous humanism of *And Life Goes On* and *Through the Olive Trees*, the new film is small, severe, and almost overbearingly verbal. It is not even a film that spurns Cannes, in an act of Godardian perversity; more surprisingly, it seems to be made with no essential awareness of Cannes (a film that came from some undeniable private urge) and, simultaneously, to respond to every expectation engendered by Cannes with a willful courting of self-defeat, the artistic equivalent of its protagonist's goal: self-annihilation.

The three films beginning with *Close-Up*, I have suggested, devolve on the question of cinematic *self-consciousness*. In *Taste of Cherry* the "cinematic" portion of that formula is erased (or more accurately, banished to the strata of subtext, where its very invisibility seems to accord it the menacing power of a volcano or an earthquake). What's left, as subject, is consciousness not of the self per se, but of its tenuous, evanescent relations with the world. The film could be called *The Unbearable Beauty of Awareness*. Emphasis on *Unbearable*.

How could a film so cramped, uncomfortable and, in some ways, off-putting, ever hope to win the Palme d'Or? Perhaps it won by not hoping: precisely that. It feels fundamentally at odds with Festival World, even if in certain ways it also gives the impression of being about Festival World. But it clearly refuses the grand gesture, and in doing so reminds us what auteur cinema was like before commodification turned artistic self-consciousness into wariness and calculation. Even the flaw (if it is that) of its ending is significant here: People are willing to forgive the film that, and perhaps would forgive much more, because it is so naked, so uncompromised, so brutally clarifying of the issues that surround the art right now. To paraphrase Cocteau, *Taste of Cherry* shows us cinema's death at work: and thereby brings it momentarily back to life.

Kiarostami seems genuinely surprised to have won the Palme. After the ceremony and his press conference, there's this moment: We are walking along the Croisette toward the banquet for the festival's winners. The place is swarming with tourists and for a while no one recognizes the dignified Iranian. Then we approach the heavily secured area where the festival's post-award banquet will be held. Suddenly Kiarostami is engulfed by lights and attention.

The first time I see him in Iran after Cannes, in late June, is at a party at a friend's country villa celebrating his 57th birthday. The ambiance is upscale, cosmopolitan, festive, with a Rod Stewart song playing when Kiarostami blows out the candles on his cake, which has an inscription reading, in English, "Happy Cherry Day."

He seems very happy in this situation, relaxed and ebullient: at home. There is a generosity about his happiness; he wants you to enjoy the occasion too, as if contentment were consecrated by sharing. His friends are not, in general, filmmakers, but writers, artists, professionals. Hemayoun Ershadi, who plays the lead role in *Taste of Cherry*, is an architect who now hopes to continue acting.

I was driven to the party by Ahmad Kiarostami, the elder of the director's two sons, through hills that are immediately recognizable from *Taste of Cherry*. Rolling and very distinctive in their sinuous contours, in the movie's magic-hour photography they are rendered a hazy gold. "I saw this golden light and decided to take the movie's feeling from that," Kiarostami says later.

A sense of place is crucial to his art. He later tells me that location comprises the motivating foundation of everything that follows in a film. This is manifest even in the first of his shorts, "Bread and Alley." The film tells a story—about a boy following a menacing dog—that is anecdotally slight, but the way it observes and negotiates the Tehran alleyways that are its setting has a vivid particularity that is immediately striking. The same quality of lyrical apprehension anchors all of his work, providing a stylistic consistency that has been much remarked. "Whenever a location doesn't fit my ideas," he says with a smile, "I change my ideas."

The importance of place as aesthetic grounding has a corollary on the emotional and thematic levels: the idea of home. In most Kiarostami films, characters are seen moving away from or toward home; whichever direction they are taking, or even if they are not in motion, home remains the constant reference, the lodestone.

First Graders and *Homework*, documentaries about school children, are ultimately more concerned with the education kids receive at home than what they learn at school. While it begins and ends in the classroom, *Where Is the Friend's House?* remains the most emblematic of Kiarostami films for tracing a boy's journey in search of a schoolmate's home, then back to his own. *And Life Goes On* takes home on the road, as a father and son motor through a ruined landscape. *Through the Olive Trees* stresses that home means marriage and family, and shows how tenuous those are in the midst of poverty, social inequity and natural disaster.

The films that seem to be exceptions to this pattern may be the most suggestive of all. In *Close-Up* the element of home, a slight one, might appear to be the bourgeois household that the Makhmalbaf impersonator cons his way into—until you consider that the real home is cinema itself, a refuge for many dreamers, including one who pursues its beckoning illusions to criminal lengths.

And then there is the extraordinary "Case No. 1, Case No. 2," the only Kiarostami film that Iran has deemed unfit for showing anywhere in the world (four others have been banned within Iran).[viii] He shot it in early 1979, during the heat of revolutionary transformation. Two skits show different solutions to a classroom discipline problem: In one a disruptive student is turned in by classmates, in the other the students maintain solidarity and refuse to inform. After each skit comes a lengthy section of interviews in which prominent Iranians from various fields—government, culture, religion, education—give their views regarding the students' actions. Remarkably, most of the interviewees support the rebellious students over the teacher's efforts to maintain discipline.

Few films, if any, have captured the mentality of revolution at its flashpoint the way "Case No. 1, Case No. 2" does. The film provides a deadpan

---

viii. The film was subsequently released and is now available internationally.

documentary look at a situation it seems to know is highly perishable. Indeed, this is the point: Such anti-authoritarian views coming from the authorities themselves would have been unimaginable a few months before, and would be so again a few months later—a prognosis that, as it turned out, was confirmed by the career of the film. The government first gave it an award, and then, not long after, banned it.

Home, if its figure can be found in "Case No. 1, Case No. 2," is not a house, and not the cinema, but Iran itself. And the question that surrounds it, giving it drama, is, implicitly, how it will be governed. This is what links the film to *Taste of Cherry*, which is just as unusual and, from some angles, anomalous in the totality of Kiarostami's career. Both films are shrewdly, encompassingly political.

Yet not *just* political. At various points in the conversations we have in Tehran, Kiarostami suggests to me that behind every outward intellectual, artistic or otherwise seemingly rational choice that he, or anyone, makes, there are always complex personal dramas unfolding. Earlier, for example, when I asked why he hadn't left Iran during the Revolution, he explained that it was largely due to the fact that his marriage was falling apart, and that he would have to help care for his two young sons.

This is how he put it: "There was a revolution going on in my own house."

Kiarostami wears dark glasses because his eyes are unusually vulnerable to light. Like so much in Iran this simple fact seems felicitously freighted with metaphor; the impression he gives, on so many levels, is of a rare, heightened, remarkably unguarded *sensitivity*.

On several occasions when I see him, he seems almost to be vibrating with happiness, for no evident reason other than what is immediately at hand: life. It is as if he woke up the day after that earthquake, and his fiftieth birthday, and decided that appreciation of existence would be his credo from then on, as a man and an artist. It would be surprising, at least to me, if this kind of jubilation were not one side of a continuum that at its other extreme held much darker moods. Yet his sensitivity also entails an uncommon degree of sympathy for other people, and his love for those close to him, especially his younger son, Bahman, is almost palpable.

He and Bahman, who is 19 and presently studying graphics at university, reside together in the house in northern Tehran where Kiarostami has lived since the 1970s. Set at the end of an alley in a quiet, genteel neighborhood, the home is discreet, substantial and cultured. A basement apartment that serves as his office has walls and shelves that are covered with his awards, including, now, the Palme d'Or.

The house, like most in Iran, seems to face inward, away from the world. House, home, haven: Is the seeking of refuge, protection, not the most undeniable of instincts in one so obviously exposed? He came from a large family and matriculated with, shall we say, consummate deliberation: He grinned broadly, mischievously, in noting that it took him nearly 13 years, from the end of the 1950s till the onset of the 1970s, to finish university. School, of course, had become the second home, one left with obvious reluctance.

Except that he had, by that time, found its replacement. In 1970 Kiarostami was asked to start a filmmaking section for the Center for the Intellectual Development of Children and Young Adults, a government agency that Iranians refer to as Kanoon. The organization remained his professional home for two decades, and the advantages it afforded the development of his art—the security, the shelter, the support—perhaps can't be overstated. Kanoon, he says with a kind of wistfulness, "was like an island in the ocean, a secluded island."

There is this paradox, for those in the West, in a career which has transpired under not one but two "repressive" regimes: that our filmmakers can only envy the creative freedom it has entailed. Kiarostami has sometimes set out to make a feature with only a scant treatment, a 15-page outline; he discovers the film as he makes it, and the result has the bracing, intoxicating feel of that liberty. The films he made under Kanoon's auspices concern children, but, as he has often noted, they are *about*, not necessarily *for*, children. Who, then, is the presumed audience? A benevolent bureaucracy? Critics? Other filmmakers? Future generations of Iranians? Kiarostami himself?

The films seem unusually careless—free—on the question of audience. But perhaps that apparent lack of concern conceals a deeper sense of anxiety and responsibility on the same issue? In the same way, the lifelong search for calm, for safety, for sanctuary, seems to invite, or attract, precisely those troublesome opposites that are required for definition. Earthquake, revolution, divorce. Kiarostami repeatedly remarks on the effects of his unhappiness during the long period surrounding his marriage's breakdown. *The Report*, the second of his two pre-revolutionary features, harrowingly depicts just such a breakdown; and some of the shorts he made during the late 1970s and early 1980s more obliquely refract the same emotional turbulence. The first film made after it had been left behind, he tells me, was *Where Is the Friend's House?*

That feature, then, served not only as a renewal but as a halcyon respite too. Afterwards, when its success began to establish him as the most eminent Iranian director outside of Iran, a different form of turbulence arose. Kiarostami has never been the most popular or highly esteemed director *within* Iran. Many cinephiles and critics have a keener regard for the work of, for example, Bahram Beyzai or Dariush Mehrjui; and of Makhmalbaf, Kiarostami's own *Close-Up* records a form of adulation—so astonishing to foreign eyes—that Kiarostami himself could scarcely dream of.

So his foreign fame rankled, and drew fire from not one direction but several. Among other film people and cultural types on the liberal side, it may have been that envy was at the root of the resentment, but there was also genuine mystification at his singular ascent to international stardom, and suspicion that he had simply found new ways of pandering to fickle foreign tastes in the picturesque and the exotic. On the right, the criticism was considerably fiercer. He was charged with being a tool of "Western" agendas, a vessel for importing the toxic cultural poisons that comprise the most insidious of all threats to the survival of the Revolution.

In Iran, such animosities are fraught with very real peril, which even someone as temperamentally non-political as Kiarostami can scarcely avoid. When the Iran-Iraq War ended, in 1988, rightist hardliners took a deep breath, then found a new arena for their combative energies: the culture wars. The result was that a vengeful wind of self-appointed purification raged through the houses of journalism, literature, the arts and their governmental overseers; one of the most prominent of those blown from office was an urbane, mild-mannered, intellectual cleric named Mohammad Khatami, who, as Minister of Culture and Islamic Guidance, had overseen Iran's state-sponsored cinematic renaissance of the 1980s. The same wind also blew through Kanoon, dislodging Kiarostami from the institutional home he had prized for so long.

He has continued to be buffeted from many ideological directions, and *Taste of Cherry* could hardly make things simpler for him. Indeed, this film, unlike any before—except perhaps "Case No. 1, Case No. 2"—seems nervily willing to be read as a provocation. It is daring, even defiant, and thus doubly surprising coming from an artist who might have been applauded simply for safeguarding the upward arc of his success. And yet the film's greatest risk is that he might not even be thanked for its riskiness: It is too oblique to be a grand gesture, too eccentric to announce its radicalism.

Why did he stop in the midst of his elegantly gradual ascent, to chance a sudden plunge into danger, controversy, taboo? In Tehran I never manage to formulate the question thusly, so it never gets asked. And it is perhaps out of deference to his obvious sensitivity that one avoids, ultimately, alluding to what this season of triumph has become for him—the Summer of the Kiss.

In the most absurd of ironies, the thing that got him into trouble was not any of the brave departures represented by *Taste of Cherry*, but a simple showbiz commonplace. At Cannes, on winning his award, he took the stage and exchanged a polite kiss with its presenter, Catherine Deneuve. This two-second transgression of Islamic propriety instantly set off a polemical firestorm in Iran, one that would singe his steps for months to come. On his return from France a welcoming reception at the airport was derailed by a threatened incursion of angry fundamentalists; Kiarostami was spirited through customs and out a side door. It was entirely possible, of course, that the hardliners' ire in this instance reflected not just fury at Kiarostami but frustration at what happened five days after his Cannes victory: the landslide election to Iran's presidency of the new cinema's erstwhile official patron, Mohammad Khatami—a clear signal that the tide in the culture wars had shifted dramatically.

Dr Khatami was still a few weeks away from assuming office when, in mid-July, the House of Cinema, the umbrella organization for Iran's filmmaking guilds, held its annual awards ceremony at Vahdat Hall, Tehran's former opera house. The evening included special awards given to the outgoing president, Hashemi Rafsanjani, and to Kiarostami.

This time when he took the stage, there was no close encounter with a blonde icon. Instead, Kiarostami was embraced by his peers. The standing ovation he received was long and demonstrative, and he, clearly, was surprised and touched. For once, appreciation came where it counted most: at home.

There is one reason above all why critics should talk with filmmakers, as I have the occasion to do with Kiarostami over the summer: to learn how we are wrong. My most memorable comeuppance occurs one day when we are discussing his first two features.

The Traveler was made in 1974 and is the source of some confusion since its length, 72 minutes, means that some chroniclers don't classify it as a feature. Yet in scope, substance and artistry, it surely is. Telling of a pugnacious provincial boy's desperate quest to reach Tehran and a football match, the movie invites comparison to *Bicycle Thieves* and *The 400 Blows*, without, miraculously, seeming derivative of anything. (Kiarostami tells me that some Iranian critics still consider it his best film, an opinion shared by his son Ahmad.) Its successor, *The Report*, coolly scrutinizes a Tehrani petty bureaucrat whose life is crumbling on two fronts: As charges of corruption ensnarl him at work, his marriage devolves from bickering to violence.

Seen today, these films are brilliant and original enough to suggest that, had the West been paying attention to distant Iran in the 1970s, they might have won Kiarostami a reputation comparable to, say, John Cassavetes or Ken Loach. What remains striking is that the films' central characters, depicted as monumentally selfish and abusive of those around them, seem so precisely symptomatic. Which is what I say to Kiarostami: that while these two protagonists are vastly different in their ages, backgrounds, circumstances, etc., considered in tandem, as a cultural composite of sorts, they comprise *a devastating critique of the Iranian character.*

This he rejects instantly and absolutely. Speaking of his intentions in the films, as well as his method, he says he would never start with such an intellectual formulation, viewing his subject from a clinical distance. Nor would he presume to judge the character of a whole class of people, or even of any person. For him stories begin not in abstractions but in specifics, often very personal. And if the films indict, he says, the indictments have but one target—himself.

In this, I suddenly see that he's speaking not at all rhetorically but quite literally. He sees both protagonists as autocritiques. In *The Traveler's* obsessive young sports fan, who ultimately reaches the football stadium only to fall asleep and miss the match, there's the filmmaker's fear that his own quest is senseless and overwrought, its goal illusory. Even closer to home, the callow, shifty husband in *The Report*—with his expensive aviator glasses and foppish 1970s moustache accentuating a weak chin—is a self-portrait etched in acid, a lacerating description of personal weakness casually destroying a fragile network of work and family ties.

In different ways both characters seem to express self-defeat as a propensity for hurting others, especially the loved ones one should least want to hurt. This they share with no other Kiarostami character until the appearance of Mr. Badii, who spends most of *Taste of Cherry* driving around the outskirts of north-eastern Tehran in his Range Rover trying to find someone to help him commit suicide; specifically, he wants to pay an accomplice to return to the site the next morning and bury him if he's dead, rescue him if he's still alive. His main interlocutors are (in order): a young soldier, who runs away confused and scared; a seminarian, who offers sincere but ineffective religious arguments against suicide; and a ruminative old taxidermist from a natural history museum, who urges the world's glories (the taste of cherries, etc.) as reasons to go on living, but who also, in agreeing to assist Badii, acknowledges that the decision finally belongs to him alone.

Two questions:

1. Why does the man want to kill himself? Answers (of sorts): Why does anyone? Why would we, the individual audience member; or Kiarostami? The film, in refusing to spell out Badii's reasons, thrusts the essential problem back at the spectator, something few current Western art films are bold enough to do. The only hint of a reason in the dialogue is a cryptic comment from Badii about his propensity for hurting other people. This fear, as indicated, connects back to the autocritiques of those earlier features, and thus to Kiarostami's view of his own life.

2. Why does this suicide have to involve another person? Answer (of sorts): Bresson's *The Devil, Probably*, a renowned Western film with a similar premise, uses it to bemoan the degraded state of the modern world. In Bresson's Catholic cosmology the soul is pure, the world hopelessly corrupt and corrupting. Kiarostami effectively reverses this: For him the world is good, the self damaged and damaging. In both films the figure of the accomplice is a device to give dramatic form to an argument which is fore-ordained.

Still, if such explanations perhaps serve as points of departure, they don't carry us very far. Indeed, *Taste of Cherry* is a film to embarrass us with the crimped shallowness of current Western modes of understanding film. At Kiarostami's Cannes press conference some questioners asked about the film's references to Kurds and Afghans, to various wars in the region, and so on; there was an obvious anxiousness to explain the film as a "statement" about geopolitics, or class divisions, or the position of intellectuals in the Islamic Republic, or the issue of suicide, or... etc.

Which is not to suggest that the film's very deliberate pattern of meaning does not encompass these things; it clearly does. But such matters are as interchangeable iron filings drawn into the magnet's force field; seeing only them means missing the defining essentials, the high and the low, the polarities. I was fairly astonished, for example, that at his Cannes press conference no one ever asked Kiarostami the most basic question: Have you grappled with suicide? Does the film come out of *that*?

Only later, in Iran, did it occur to me that in missing the personal, these questions missed the genuinely philosophical, which is also to say what is actually and profoundly political about the film (as opposed to its appearance of treating various "issues"). And here's another question for Monsieur Godard to file under "fin de cinéma": Could it be that the failure to discern the deepest philosophical *and* personal aspects of this movie is related to the increasing inability to understand films in terms of *form*?

Since we reach the topic of his latest film a few days after he has told me categorically how he does *not* see *The Traveler* and *The Report*, I am reluctant to lead with any abstract views of *Taste of Cherry*. (He would surely laugh at that reluctance.) So, as we drive back from Koker, I start by broaching the question that was significantly absent at Cannes. He says, simply, that the film *does* reflect his own wrestling with the suicidal urge, but he won't discuss that further; it is private. Yet there is a link between the private and the public that is still personal.

When he was young, Kiarostami explains, his father fell ill. The illness was protracted and very painful, and at many points his father yearned to die. The fact that he didn't elect to kill himself was not what ended up occupying Kiarostami; what did was the question of his father's right to make the decision. The young man thought long and hard about the taboos surrounding this most crucial of personal choices. What he ultimately decided, he tells me, was that religion did not offer the "higher wisdom" on the subject.

I reply that it seems to me that the film presents us with two subjects, underscoring how the meanings of his films often comprise a double helix of the personal and the philosophical, of eye-level experience and its metaphorical ramifications. Beyond (and essentially separable from) the evident subject of suicidal anguish, the subject of what constitutes and how one determines that "higher wisdom" strikingly recalls the debate that energized Islam for four centuries long ago, and that has some strikingly provocative parallels today. At this, somewhat to my surprise, he smiles—and agrees.

Yet, for once in ten hours of conversation, there's no elaboration. We are entering the city of Qazvin, and shortly he wheels the car over to a streetside sweet shop. We eat our ice cream in the sidewalk's shade, this hot August afternoon, before continuing on to Tehran.

While I am in Tehran an email from a friend notes the success of the re-release of Jean-Luc Godard's *Contempt* in the U.S. Recalling that film brings back a time when "art films" were as personal as diaries, and boasted a combination of playfulness and intellectual seriousness that have become increasingly rare in recent years.

Godard's film risks imposing on the viewer, risks being thought hermetic, inept, pretentious, insupportably self-involved, etc. It is maddening for not giving us a perfect, transcendent aesthetic object while being constantly preoccupied with and suggestive of that possibility. Like the works of literary modernism that are its prototypes, it presupposes not only our knowledge of but also our passionate (and dispassionate) interest in a whole raft of personal and cultural references: everything from Godard's relationship with Anna Karina (and its parallels to Antonioni's with Monica Vitti) to the persona and oeuvre of Fritz Lang, *The Odyssey*, the Lumière brothers, André Bazin, Dante, Brecht, Holderlin, and many others, including countless films.

While less overt in its erudition, *Taste of Cherry* brandishes a similar set of provocations and strategies in its withholding of conventional satisfactions and skirting of viewer alienation, its bruised lyricism, its restive world-weariness, its tension between formal rigor and experimental freedom, its odd blending of personal urgency, contemplative detachment and oblique, sardonic humor. Nor are these similarities merely coincidental; in many ways, the two films inhabit the same tradition.

Though it surely oversimplifies to put it this way, the cinematic modernism that came to the fore in Europe, especially France and Italy, in the 1950s and 1960s eventually spread its seeds to many countries including Iran, where it provided the aesthetic basis for the upsurge in artistic films (the "Iranian New Wave", appropriately) that made a fleeting but decisive mark in the 1970s. That much is a common story, applicable to various national cinemas.

What is uncommon, and peculiar to Iran, is how that aesthetic was preserved virtually intact for future decades via the curious cultural processes that surrounded the Iranian Revolution and the early years of the Islamic Republic. While the rest of the world was swept up in an increasingly globalized and video-dominated media climate, Iran shut off almost everything coming from the outside, and then, circa 1983, encouraged its filmmakers to resume their former preoccupations (albeit with new restrictions on content). Thus did the modernist-cinematic 1960s/1970s survive to enjoy a vital afterlife, two decades later, in a particularly unlikely corner of the globe.

Obviously, this touches on the appeal of Iranian films to Festival World: In some lights, they uncannily reincarnate the auteurist spirit, the *politique* that brought many festivals into being in the first place. Yet the films' real value, apart from this surface appeal, is inevitably more problematic. If they *only* recalled Western art films of eras past, they would strike us as little more than amusing throwbacks, like a place where the men still wear tricorns and knee breeches. Their much more immediate and challenging impact, and their importance, comes from how they evoke not the past but the future, and not *here* but *there*: Their existence forces us toward a world where some of the West's most distinctive cultural expressions are wrenched away from the West, where "Third World" nations can claim the intellectual and artistic lead.

By their *difference*, Iranian films make us realize the extent to which "cinema" has always been defined and controlled by European-American models deriving from Western theatre, fiction, music, painting and so on. Of course European cinema historically offered alternatives to the American (and vice versa), as auteur or artistic filmmaking did to the general commercial rut. But when was there ever an alternative to that closed conversation? Arguably, only Japan in the two decades or so following the storied 1951 breakthrough of *Rashomon* exemplified a full-scale "otherness" challenging and counter defining the Western models. (China, in the 1980s and 1990s, being so circumscribed by political forces, didn't assert itself so much as it donned traditional garb to appear as exotica, *chinoiserie*, in films tailored for Western art houses.)

Iran presents an altogether different case. Unlike Japan, its cinema has not met the West when the West's own artistic cinema was in a period of strength, nor when Iran itself was in a subjugated position, humbly petitioning to rejoin international commerce and culture. On the contrary, the difference of Iranian films owes in large part to Iran's deliberate isolation, its sense of its own cultural separateness and its suspicion of Western influence, a wariness which cuts across the political spectrum: Where hardliners worry about the incursion of anti-religious values, liberals worry about Iranian cinematic culture being molded according to Western viewpoints and prejudices.

Iran's is the first post-colonial cinema to challenge the West on what the West itself defines as the artistic high ground, and given the encroaching obsolescence of the medium and of that definition, it may well be the last. Asking whether that contest will establish new paradigms for the interplay of world cultures beyond the Age of Cinema is, in a crucial sense, to ask if the West will allow itself to see the *Iranianness* of Iranian cinema; and indeed, if Iranians will be allowed the same thing. To return to the example of *Contempt*, imagine if Godard's penchant for referencing were again in vogue, but now the allusions being thrown at audiences were not to Homer and Fritz Lang, et al., but rather to Rhazes and Ibn Arabi and Avicenna, to Ferdowsi and Hafez and Rumi, to Zoroaster and Persian miniatures and the architecture of Isfahan, and to the galaxy of Iranian films cited in Makhmalbaf's *Once Upon a Time, Cinema*, which ends on the zig-zag path of *Where Is the Friend's House?*

Surely the West would be short-sighted in not realizing that such understandings are indeed what is being asked of us—or offered to us? Of course, the analogy is too literalistic, but not by much. The best of the new Iranian films do urge that we learn a new language, when our tendency is to push our own on others. But the films don't force the issue; they can't. We are free to use their reflective surfaces as a mirror, and see only our preconceptions.

Taste of Cherry seems reconciled to the likelihood that it will not be really understood—listened to closely—either abroad or at home, even if its spirit moves those who won't bother with the language. It comes to us from a ghost town that was once a Cinecittà, where there's freedom in resignation and strange comedy in the recognition of futility. *The Traveler*, the alpha to its omega, ends when the obstreperous boy hero, who has gone to mind-numbing lengths to reach a football match, awakens in an empty stadium, having slept through the object of his desires. When we're discussing this film, in August, Kiarostami suddenly recalls his win at Cannes.

He remembered *The Traveler*, he says, when he was standing on the beach with an old friend and colleague, the director Amir Naderi. It was after everything, after the awards, the press conference, the parties and after-parties. Naderi asked finally, sweepingly, what he felt right at that moment, at the end of his evening of triumph.

Kiarostami replied: "Nothing. I feel nothing at all."

How to Read Kiarostami

Originally published in Cineaste, *2000. Revised for Brazilian Kiarostami film festival, 2016.*

AS A CAR SLOWS ON a dusty road in Iran, a man inside asks passersby for directions. Of all the images in Abbas Kiarostami's films, this one must be the most recurrent, the most emblematic. Yet if we project ourselves imaginatively inside it, as a driver or rider seeking a route into the meanings of Kiarostami's latest movie, *The Wind Will Carry Us*, we quickly notice that we can't begin to follow anyone's directions because there's a boulder just feet ahead, blocking the way to the film: Kiarostami's reputation.

Is this cosmopolitan Iranian the era's greatest filmmaker, or one who's been vastly over-hyped by a coterie of critics and festival programmers? The question became unavoidable recently when Kiarostami, who's perhaps still unknown to most art-house filmgoers in the U.S., was voted "Most Important Director of the 1990s" in a decade's-end poll of critics and programmers conducted by *Film Comment*. Impressive though it is, the apparent consensus in that vote conceals a difference of opinion regarding Kiarostami that's been evident among U.S. critics at least since 1997, when *Taste of Cherry* won the Palme d'Or at the Cannes Film Festival.

Kiarostami, recalled Roger Ebert in his review of the film, "received a standing ovation as he entered the [Cannes] theater, and another at the end of his film (although this time mixed with boos).... Back at the Hotel Splendid, standing in the lobby, I found myself in lively disagreement with two critics I respect, Jonathan Rosenbaum of the *Chicago Reader* and Dave Kehr of the *New York Daily News*. Both believed they had seen a masterpiece. I thought I had seen an emperor without any clothes."

That division continued. While Rosenbaum and Kehr joined a critical cheering section that helped net *Taste of Cherry* the National Society of Film Critics' award for Best Foreign Film of 1998, Ebert, David Denby and Andrew Sarris were among the prominent critics whose responses to the film ranged from lukewarm to chilly. While the negative reactions sometimes sounded impatiently anti-elitist, they received some fiercely argued highbrow support in *Artforum* earlier this year when Howard Hampton contrasted critical dismissals of David Lynch's visionary-but-homegrown *The Straight Story* with the genuflections typically awarded foreign auteurs like Kiarostami and Taiwan's Hou Hsiao-hsien. Hampton's polemic, however, only glancingly touched on the king-making role, *vis-à-vis* "international" filmmakers, played by Cannes, which is in the business of celebrating auteurs of a certain type, and will gladly help manufacture reputations that don't arrive full-fledged.

In Iran, an intensely cinephilic society, film lovers have long been puzzled by the extravagant foreign regard for Kiarostami, who's seldom ranked as the best Iranian director at home. Kiarostami's popularity must be a Western thing, Iranians think, without realizing the extent to which it's a festival thing, and even more specifically a Cannes thing with some dubious paternalistic overtones. Distant, politically suspect Third World countries, after all, hardly enjoy the welcome in Cannes that, say, Italy does. In the 1990s Cannes clearly didn't want to fling open the doors to Iran; it strategically wanted to acclaim *one* director (much as it had designated Youssef Chahine its token Egyptian). Bahram Beyzai, Mohsen Makhmalbaf or Dariush Mehrjui might have filled the bill equally well, or not; in any case, it was Kiarostami who got the nod, which came with the immediate leap in global renown that Cannes recognition usually entails.

None of the foregoing relates at all to the quality of Kiarostami's work. Rather, it aims to suggest how factors *other* than quality have contributed to a reputation now so exalted that it may be the worst enemy of any balanced, realistic appreciation of the work. In effect, the way the Great Kiarostami Debate, or Schism, has evolved (i.e., primarily among critics who attend international festivals) not only has largely left the public out in the cold but has driven the two sides into increasingly opposed positions, both of which contain unfortunate elements of stubborn absurdity: While the detractors seem unwilling to consider (or reconsider) Kiarostami's recent work in terms of the films that led to it, the defenders are far better at asserting than at explaining or elucidating his artistic singularity. (Among the critics who voted that *Film Comment* honor, has any written an essay arguing *why* Kiarostami is the era's most important director? If so, I haven't found it.)

Given the unhelpfulness of this stand-off, especially for filmgoers who'd prefer illumination to superlatives-vs.-sniping, following are two suggestions, one each for the debate's two sides:

First, to those who've so far found Kiarostami overrated and/or unappealing: *Realize that the order in which you approach the films is crucial to how you understand them. Above all, view the Koker Trilogy in sequence, as a basis for watching the other films.* This point is so important, if surprisingly little mentioned, that it's easy to believe the anti-Kiarostami camp is composed largely of critics who encountered *Taste of Cherry*, say, without having previously seen the Koker Trilogy and *Close-Up*.

Whatever else one makes of Kiarostami's films, their specific form of *interrelatedness* is unique in cinema, and the more this factor is scrutinized and contemplated, the more important it comes to seem. While it encompasses all of his post-revolutionary features, it's most easily seen in the Koker Trilogy, which begins with a film so delightful and accessible it could be recommended to eight-year-olds. The Trilogy's following two films, though clearly more suited to adult viewers, are easily understood by anyone who's not seen the previous film or films. Yet viewers who *have* seen the previous films know how much—how subtly and pervasively—they influence one's understanding of the movie at hand.

Second, an urging for the pro-Kiarostami faction: *Don't neglect the Iranian context or underestimate its importance.* This applies on two levels. Not only are some critics so hero-hungry they'll ignore a favorite artist's peers in order to have *one* master to acclaim (in my view, Kiarostami is better understood as one of several great Iranian directors than as some kind of "world cinema" super-auteur), but critics are also too often loathe to explore the meaning of the filmmaker's cultural frame of reference, assuming that their own will do just fine. For example, in reviewing *Taste of Cherry* Jonathan Rosenbaum, one of Kiarostami's most fervent and eloquent supporters, draws comparisons to works by Antonioni, Straub-Huillet, Tati, etc., noting that he does so "because those films are part of my world and my vocabulary for understanding it."

That's fine as far as it goes, and it might go a long way if the filmmaker under examination were European, American or even from the Westernized Far East. But beyond the fact that Kiarostami has never evidenced any interest in the filmmakers mentioned above, he comes from a culture whose "vocabulary" is very different from the West's. It's not impenetrable, though: Westerners from Goethe to Emerson to Robert Bly have immersed themselves in Iranian thought and art, and anyone with elbow grease and a library card can embark on the same eye-opening adventure. Ultimately, the more one knows of their context, the more one realizes that Kiarostami and other Iranian directors need to be understood not so much in terms of Antonioni and Tati, say, but of Ferdowsi, Hafez, Sanai, Rumi, Ibn Arabi, Mulla Sadra and other remarkable figures who share and illuminate their cultural lexicon.

In the final analysis, the work of the New Iranian Cinema may prove less significant as a late addition to the waning tradition of auteurist "art" cinema than as a new chapter in a centuries-old drama of cultural contact that has gained new urgency in recent decades. That's the opinion of this article, which attempts to view Kiarostami's work, not from an Iranian perspective, but in terms of some of the cultural, and often non-cinematic, bonds linking the West and Iran. In doing so, it adopts a favorite Iranian symbol, the mirror, to indicate two angles of view: one looking (as it were) from Iran toward the West and modernity, the other gazing east toward Iran and certain of its ancient philosophic legacies.

The Western Mirror

What is Kiarostami up to? How could he evolve from *Where Is the Friend's House?*, a film of patent simplicity and charm, to the rarefied perplexities of *Taste of Cherry* and *The Wind Will Carry Us?* Sometimes, detractors can be as revealing as the artist's supporters. Roger Ebert, again on *Taste of Cherry*: "A case can be made for the movie, but it would involve transforming the experience of viewing the film (which is excruciatingly boring) into something more interesting, a fable about life and death. Just as a bad novel can be made into a good movie, so can a boring movie be made into a fascinating movie review."

Although "excruciatingly" overstates, that's an understandable *vox populi* assessment. Many ordinary moviegoers no doubt would agree that *Taste of Cherry* is "boring" for lacking the kind of dramatic oomph and close emotional identification that we normally associate with cinematic enrapturement; cramped, downbeat and dialogue-heavy, the film even lacks the humanistic warmth and inviting lyricism of previous Kiarostami films. Yet Ebert also provides an inadvertent tribute to Kiarostami's intentions when he suggests that the movie can be transformed from boring to "fascinating" by the viewer's interpretation of its meaning. Here, value comes not in passive experiencing but in an active *reading* of what one has seen, a process in which, by inference, the viewer's intent and understanding are as important as the film itself.

If this sounds like a fundamentally different stance toward cinema than we're accustomed to, it accords with much about Kiarostami, who is openly disdainful toward or entirely uninterested in most movies. It has been observed that there's perhaps no other great director who is less of a cinephile. Indeed, having been an illustrator, a painter, a photographer and a poet, Kiarostami has indicated that he would simply turn his energies to those media if cinema disappeared. As idiosyncratic as such an attitude may sound, it actually reflects an underlying idea in Iranian cinema generally. Where Westerners tend to view cinema as a *fullness*, an art-in-itself composed of and historically supplanting previous forms like novels and theater, much about the Iranian stance seems to posit it as an *emptiness*, a place where those older forms temporarily intersect and display the possibilities of their combination.

Kiarostami's public comments in recent years have repeatedly emphasized cinema's deficiencies and literary-based nature. Asked about the repetition of dialogue in *Taste of Cherry*, he stressed that he wanted the viewer's experience to resemble reading, where certain phrases sink in through being re-read. In discussing *The Wind Will Carry Us* and its sometimes startling way of keeping basic information from the viewer, he elaborated his idea of the "half-made film," whose completion requires the viewer's imaginative (or more accurately: interpretive) participation.

The Wind Will Carry Us certainly outdoes any previous Kiarostami film in the demands it makes on audience collaboration. Its story starts out following a car full of Tehrani men as they approach a remote village in Kurdistan, where their mission appears to involve filming a strange local burial ceremony once a local woman dies. When the woman unexpectedly clings to life, they are effectively stranded. Their leader, Bezhad (Bezhad Dourani), divides his time between interacting with villagers and trying to puzzle out his situation. Five times during the seriocomic story, he's obliged to drive pell-mell to the top of a nearby hill so that his cell phone can pick up his superior, "Mrs. Godarzi," back in Tehran. On the hill, the rather improbable location of a graveyard, he has several conversations with an unseen man who says he's digging a ditch. The digger also receives surreptitious visits from a local girl whom the protagonist later encounters in a subterranean barn, where they discuss poetry and milk.

Although the protagonist's mood mixes curiosity and self-absorbed frustration (the latter strikingly summarized when he petulantly kicks a turtle onto its back), the film itself is droll and playful, with an appreciation of landscape and nature that's pure Kiarostami. Yet its most distinguishing quality is its calculated, multileveled opacity. The Tehran party's purpose in the village, for example, can only be glancingly deduced (if at all) from a few things said halfway through the film; we never see their cameras or any signs of filmmaking activity. In fact, beyond the protagonist, we never see the men themselves. They are among eleven important characters in the film, including the ditch digger, the milk girl and the dying woman, who are heard or referred to but never shown.

Besides leaving numerous such connections to the viewer, the film refers in various oblique ways to the past coordinates of Kiarostami's imaginary universe, references which inevitably separate viewers familiar with that universe from those not. The first scene, for instance, shows the Tehranis' car wending through gorgeous Kurdistan landscapes as the men's voices are heard wondering whether certain trees are the landmarks they're looking for. To anyone who doesn't know Kiarostami this is simply a dryly comic way of introducing the characters and their journey. To initiates, though, the interrogative banter and concern with location, direction, routes and natural signs (trees especially) are rich in associations with the filmmaker's past work.

In offering a welter of such associations while withholding many standard dramatic or explanatory connections, *The Wind Will Carry Us* is worlds away from *Where Is the Friend's House?*, with its seeming transparency and presumption that the viewer knows nothing of the filmmaker. Yet Kiarostami's new movie shares something with the one that launched his post-revolutionary career: Both take their titles from poems. Sohrab Sepheri ("Where Is the Friend's House?") and Forough Farrokhzad ("The Wind Will Carry Us") are two of Iran's most renowned modern poets; and Farrokhzad, who in 1967 died at the age of thirty-two, bears additional distinction as the most famous female author in all of Iranian literature, and as a filmmaker whose one film, "The House is Black" (1962), a short, is credited with exercising a crucial influence on later Iranian filmmakers including Kiarostami.

Indeed, "The House Is Black," with its sonorous, quasi-liturgical narration over images of a leper colony, formulates and advances a very specific idea of *poetic cinema*, one that incorporates both actual verbal poetry and an approach to cinematic construction based on the example of poetry. This double incorporation, in turn, reflects a corresponding duality in the idea of poetry represented, which combines aspects of classical Persian (and Arabic) poetry with aspects belonging to Iranian modernist poetry, a form heavily indebted to Western (especially French and English) modernism. In *The Wind Will Carry Us*, this poetic model with its dual precedents seems more important—it's certainly more explicit—than ever. *Wind* is the first Kiarostami film in which poetry is repeatedly quoted. Not incidentally, the poets most prominently cited are Farrokhzad, the eminent modernist, and Omar Khayyam, a classical poet with a very modern-seeming sensual bent.

If you wanted to reduce Kiarostami to a single idea, you would not be far wrong in saying that he has spent his career developing a cinematic equivalent of Iranian modernist poetry. To suggest why, it's first necessary to note that poetry pervades the educations and consciousnesses of Iranians, from virtually all social strata, to a far greater extent than in the West. When Kiarostami was a university student and fledgling artist in the 1960s, that age-old grounding was in catalytic ferment: The Iranian version of modernist poetry reached a peak of iconoclasm and influence (at least among the young, educated and cosmopolitan) that roughly compares to the impact that the cinema of the Nouvelle Vague and kindred movements had in the West, or that Euro-American modernist poetry had in certain Western circles 30 to 50 years before. For a young Iranian in the 1960s, entering the cinema inspired by and infused with the creative spirit of poets like Forough Farrokhzad was hardly an anomaly; it was an eminently sensible way of approaching an imported medium through the precepts of one's own culture.

Yet—here's the ironic rub—literary modernism was itself largely an import, which gave Kiarostami's cinema a cast that goes a long way toward explaining why it was so readily embraced in the West. (Compare the case of Bahram Beyzai, whom Iranians generally consider their best filmmaker; rooted in *ta'ziyeh*, a native Iranian dramatic form, his masterpieces have found regrettably few champions in the West.) Indeed, if one wanted to explain Kiarostami's basic artistic impulses to educated Westerners who hadn't seen his films, there are fruitful comparisons to be found in the poetry of William Carlos Williams and Marianne Moore (writers whose work Kiarostami has said he admires), or Ezra Pound or Wallace Stevens, as much as in the films of such later, cinematic modernists as Antonioni and Godard. However broadly the (essentially literary, originally Western) sway of modernism is defined, it has an obvious bearing on Kiarostami's insistence on *reading* his films, and, especially, on his notion of the "half-made film," with its implication of a cultured, discerning viewer willing to fill in the blanks of a condensed, allusive, incomplete narrative.

In the West, modernism, with its dedication to idiosyncrasy and experiment, helped negotiate the onslaught of modernity, the vast social and perceptual changes wrought by technology. In the East, it also negotiated, and still does, the onslaught of the West, that protean geopolitical Serpent whose hegemonic charms have been most actively resisted by the Islamic world, especially the Shiite state of Iran: This ongoing struggle helps explain why modernism, which long ago ran out of steam in the West, can retain such currency and vigor in Iran. Yet it should be stressed that Kiarostami didn't cut *his* modernism to fit the anyone's fashion, West or East. He might even resist the use of the *m*-word, which is to say that he took modernism's embrace of idiosyncrasy and personal expression very seriously indeed. In a culture where the modernist struggle to overthrow/recast a looming literary tradition faced heroic difficulties, he found in cinema *his own place*, a parallel arena where he could construct a private world of meaning related to, but not overwhelmed by, the literary cosmos.

The effort to be *outside* yet *attached to*, to create a cine-poetic vernacular that becomes increasingly supple and personal without collapsing into narcissistic unintelligibility: This dynamic has driven the trajectory of his career, and its combination of classical assurance and experimental daring informs his work's most remarkable quality—its sense of being an organic whole in which every film is related to every other, all participating in a pattern that modifies and reconfigures itself with each new work. Yet the meanings thus created aren't open-ended or aleatory; there is an implicit order. And the guiding pattern—or rather, the *way* of patterning—can prove at once alluring and baffling, especially for Westerners, since it connects not only with modernist poetry but also with other, deeper currents in Iranian thought and art.

What does any Kiarostami film mean? Admirers will tell you that his movies are unusual in seeming to mean far more than their face-value, literal contents at first reveal. *Where Is the Friend's House?* appears to be nothing more than the tale of a boy trying to return his pal's notebook after school, yet there's an unmistakable sense—especially for anyone with the patience to allow the film's subtle distinctiveness to take hold over time—that its significance extends to far more profound matters. As close examination will make clear, this is not simply a matter of metaphor and careful ambiguity. Rather, it reflects a Persian understanding of symbolic meaning that differs in crucial ways from our own.

In the West, it's worth recalling, "symbolism" was virtually synonymous with the 1960s apogee of the modernist art film. *Last Year at Marienbad, Knife in the Water, Belle de Jour, Blow-Up, 2001: A Space Odyssey, Persona, The Servant, Woman in the Dunes*: These and countless other films, some estimable, some silly and pretentious, employed an understanding of symbolism much like that used to unravel "The Waste Land" in English classrooms. The relationship was essentially simple and *quid pro quo*: Every event on the narrative's surface was a symbol that relayed the viewer's understanding to another, non-sensible level, where the author had located, somewhat like buried treasure, the event's "real" meaning.

By contrast, in the Persian understanding(s) suggested by Kiarostami's work, the film's surface events themselves are in no sense unreal or insufficient; the symbolic meanings implied aren't confined to one level but occur simultaneously on many (or, if the viewer prefers, on none); and the author doesn't so much *create* these meanings as arrange the spaces and conditions for them—the meanings, *pace* Roger Ebert, are created by the viewer's interpretive powers and inclinations. Unlike the rather mechanistic, and now very out-of-fashion, Western mode of symbolism noted above, the mode described here invites a musical analogy: Each surface event is like a struck chord on a stringed instrument. The artist knows where the other strings lie and their capacities for vibration, but how—and if—they are heard will depend on how "attuned" the auditor is. The symbolic meanings, while real, register not as *the* "real" events but as significant *resonances*.

All of this perhaps helps explain why Kiarostami has found the most favor among Western critics who've followed his work over a period of several years: Not only are such writers likely to have a grasp of the "Western mirror" (modernist poetry) that provides much of his work's conceptual grounding, but their prolonged exposure will mean that they've had the chance to develop a feel for the very personal cinematic idiom and fictional terrain he has constructed on that grounding. Granted, the cultural distance between the West and Iran will cause various meanings to get lost or garbled in the translation. In *Taste of Cherry*, the suicide-prone protagonist has dialogues with three men, who come from Kurdistan, Afghanistan and Turkish-speaking Azerbaijan. At Cannes, some critics tried to derive a political statement from these geographical identifications, much to the puzzlement of Kiarostami, who (as noted) doesn't deal in such literalistic symbol-making or sloganeering. From another angle, Westerners unfamiliar with the intense debates over the relative virtues of philosophy and revealed religion that roiled Islam throughout the Middle Ages would likely miss the hints of a similar dialectic in *Taste of Cherry*, one favoring "wisdom" over dogma.

At the same time, some meanings that critics miss (or at least, don't discuss) are hidden in plain sight, available to the inference of anyone who cares to bother. What is any Kiarostami film about? In part, as the modernist pedigree might suggest, it's about Kiarostami and his place in the world at the time the film is made. After the success of *Where Is the Friend's House?* took him out of Iran and onto the world stage as an increasingly famous film director, cinema, its social operations and film directors became central subjects in his next three films. While Kiarostami himself appeared in *Close-Up*, a film about the symbolic power wielded by film directors, fictional alter egos representing him figured into *And Life Goes On* and *Through the Olive Trees*: Together, these films convey an extraordinarily complex sense of a man reflecting on the evolving relationships among his life, his art and his culture.

Does the current of artistic autobiography end at *Taste of Cherry*? On the contrary, the attuned viewer should sense that it has simply been transmuted by what in Kiarostami's work might be called the law of *ever-increasing implicitness*. As the building rises, one doesn't have to *see* the lower floors to know they're there. Thus it's logical to assume not only that *Taste's* protagonist is in part another projected self-portrait, but also that his reasons for seeking suicide (which of course could be several) include the state that cinema has brought him to. To wit: At the end of *Through the Olive Trees*, the film director character reaches an exalted elevation, like some cinematic Prospero—not a bad correlative for Kiarostami's rapid career ascent. Propelled onto the fast track to Cannes' acclamation, it would be perfectly natural for him to want to run in the opposite direction, into the shadows, to sink downward, to disappear, to die, to bury himself. What could be more human? Success, past or prospective, often triggers an urge for *mortification*. (Of course, whether the man metaphorically dies is left to others—to the viewer or the Cannes jury, as you will. And yes, there's a large element of self-skewering humor to this scenario of drastic overreaction to one's "elevation.")

By the same sort of autobiographical reading, *The Wind Will Carry Us* gives us Kiarostami in a state of querulous frustration. He's been to the top of cinema's mountain, as it were, and now where is he? Stranded in perplexity, it seems. We note that his alter ego this time, Bezhad, both is and is not a filmmaker: We're never told explicitly *what* he is, but the clues suggest he's a member of a TV news crew—a big come-down, in any event, from the earnest and presumably important artists of the previous films. Like *Taste of Cherry's* Mr. Badii, he's also as close to a blank slate as Kiarostami can make him, a screen onto which are projected not only the auteur's feelings but also, if we choose to participate, our own. Will Mr. Ebert find boredom here, too? Well, so be it. Bezhad, beyond spasms of curiosity and activity, himself seems fundamentally bored.

Neither mounting the heights like the director in *Olive Trees* nor sliding toward the abyss like the protagonist of *Cherry*, he's stuck in the grating existential middle, working a job he doesn't seem to care about, waiting for a death that refuses to arrive. With an almost shocking casualness, the film even tosses aside the celebrated "humanism" associated with Kiarostami: Bezhad clearly has no emotional investment in the village (his attitude is one of thoughtless exploitation, so unlike the tender treatment of Koker); even more surprising, he's nasty to Farzad, the boy who serves as his guide. Is this a portrait of the artist as a closet misanthrope? A wry comment on the nature of media, or the yawning chasm between Iran's postmodern professionals and premodern provincials? Or, perchance, another "fable about life and death"?

More than ever before, Kiarostami leaves numerous gaps in the film's surface that invite, even demand, our imaginative participation. Yet *The Wind Will Carry Us* also chafes toward other horizons; as its title suggests, it seems to want to carry us beyond a strictly modernist understanding of Kiarostami's cinematic poetry.

The Eastern Mirror

Films like Kiarostami's give us secular, cosmopolitan Iran: an image we readily identify since it's gratifyingly similar to our own. Yet to assume that such films don't also contain deeper religious and philosophical veins would be to remain fixated on our own reflection. What, in the first place, do we know of Islam? Even the most *au courant* of Westerners, it can be safely assumed, know virtually nothing of Shiism. To suggest to them that this branch of Islamic faith contains a vast, ancient and highly complex system of esoteric thought is to present Iran as it must seem to many a surprised neophyte—a virtual philosophic Atlantis, whose existence remains unsuspected even by many who study philosophy in the West.

Fortunately, there are guides. Seyyed Hossein Nasr, Annemarie Schimmel, William Chittick, Frithjof Schuon and others have explored the philosophic dimensions of Islam in fascinating detail. But for linking Shiism, Iran, aesthetics and Western thought, there's no more eloquent and stimulating Virgil than the great French Iranologist Henry Corbin (1903–78), whose oeuvre comprises that rare thing: seminal scholarship that's also profound spiritual literature. Among Corbin's many works, several with current American editions, are particularly pertinent to this discussion: *Spiritual Body and Celestial Earth: From Mazdean Iran to Shiite Iran* (Princeton/Bollingen), *The Voyage and the Messenger: Iran and Philosophy* (North Atlantic Books), *Alone with the Alone: Creative Imagination in the Sufism of Ibn Arabi* (Princeton/Bollingen), *The Man of Light in Iranian Sufism* (Omega Publications), *History of Islamic Philosophy* (Kegan Paul International) and *Avicenna and the Visionary Recital* (Princeton/Bollingen).

While the Iranian stream of thought explored by Corbin is generally identified with Sufism—the esoteric core of Islam—its sources purportedly extend back to Zoroaster and ancient Persia. And while it has remained a vital current in Shiism and Iran down to the present day, what could be called its key episodes took place in the Middle Ages—not incidentally, near the time when the philosophic/scientific traditions of Islam and the West came to a decisive crossroads, with the latter taking the path that would lead to rationalistic materialism while the former headed into theistic mysticism. These episodes involve the work of two magisterial Persian thinkers. Abu Ali Ibn Sina (d. 1037) was known as Avicenna in the West, where his writings had an impact that lasted throughout the medieval period. Besides his work in medicine and science, Avicenna proposed and initiated the elaboration of an "Oriental philosophy," a project later taken up and brought to fruition by Shihabuddin Suhrawardi (d. 1191), whose relative anonymity in the West Corbin spent his career attempting to redress.

Steeped in Aristotle, Avicenna and Suhrawardi were vastly learned intellectuals and prolific exegetes at a time that simply did not draw sharp lines between study of the body and the soul, of this world and the other. That *other* world, the world of the soul and immaterial beings, was termed the "Imaginal Realm" (or *mundus imaginalis*, from the Arabic *alam al-mithal*) by Corbin, who identifies it as the "interzone" between the realms of pure form and extant matter. As the place where "events of the soul" transpire, it is outside of time, yet isn't the purview merely of the dead and angelic intelligences. In ways that a Blake or a Bunyan would recognize, it comprises the terrain that must be traversed by any living intelligence attempting to return consciously to his or her Source, a journey that inevitably hinges on proper (which is to say esoteric) *orientation*.

Kiarostami's characters discuss their spatial orientation so often that by now it resembles a Sufi joke. Given that his films are called "philosophical," can this parallel with one of Iranian philosophy's most recurrent motifs be mere coincidence? It would hardly seem so, especially when viewed in light of another parallel: Though Avicenna and Suhrawardi both wrote massive philosophical works, they gave their most evocative accounts of "Oriental philosophy" in fictional tales that recount a journey or a quest—a narrative paradigm significantly shared by most of Kiarostami's films. Corbin calls these tales "visionary recitals" (the French *recit* connotes a story rather than a musical performance), and notes that they take place across visionary landscapes that conflate Koranic terrain with Mazdean features such as the cosmic mountain of Qaf.

In this symbolic domain, physical geography undergoes crucial transpositions. West is no longer West but the Occident, the dark place of matter, where the soul is imprisoned (the subject of Suhrawardi's "Recital of Occidental Exile"). And East, where dawn breaks, is the Orient, literally the locus of *orientation* that points from darkness to illumination (Suhrawardi's "philosophy of light" is called Illuminationism). But this is not all. As anyone who senses this schema's roots in Plato and Plotinus will anticipate, the essential journey does not move laterally (although it may seem to at first) but *upwards*, toward the Source of the soul's descent. Thus does East become north. As Corbin says, the true destination "is not on the horizontal but on the vertical. This suprasensory, mystical Orient, the place of the Origin and of the Return, object of the eternal Quest, is at the heavenly pole… the extreme north, so far off that it is the threshold of the dimension 'beyond.'"[1]

Such a shift, or the *desire* for a shift from horizontal to vertical, seems to be at the symbolic heart of *The Wind Will Carry Us*, just as it's at the center of esoteric traditions East and West. To return to the film's opening: Besides providing a droll entree to the story, and resonating with incidents and tropes from previous Kiarostami films, the scene of travelers looking for trees atop barren hills also comprises, in Corbinian terms, a search for *signs of the vertical*.

It is soon rewarded. The Tehranis' car encounters a boy, Farzad, who has been sent to guide them. Bezhad gets out and follows the boy, who leads him up a path that ascends a steep rock face. It's a fine Kiarostamian joke: As Bezhad struggles, Farzad admits there are much easier paths into the village. From a logical standpoint, the climb is absurd. But there's another point: to announce that we've departed the "flatland" and entered the domain of the vertical, where time and other laws governing the logical, everyday world lose their sway and a drama of the soul commences (as he and the boy climb, Bezhad explains the meaning of the term "giving up the ghost"—another hint that entwines spirit and ascent).

From here on, virtually every character and incident in the film is situated by (derives its meaning from) the domain's *vertical axis*. Bezhad and his (unseen) cohorts are lodged in a house of which we see only the wide porch, a decidedly horizontal structure that serves as both the vertical's implicit midpoint and the protagonist's main vantage point. Below, Bezhad sees the signs of poverty, mortality, age and oppression that the blue window of the dying woman represents. Upwards, there's the hilltop where he receives guidance via cell-phone "messages from above." (These generally unhelpful expressions of higher authority emanate from the invisible Mrs. Godarzi, whose name—riffing as it does on God, Godard and even Godot—qualifies as one of the film's drollest touches.)

While Kiarostami is a poet of space par excellence, the way *Wind* articulates its hierarchical domain is exceptionally clever. When Bezhad walks toward the dying woman's house, it barely seems that he's moving downward, just as that hilltop hardly seems higher than the roof of the house where he's staying. The fact that we still understand one locale to be decisively "down" and the other "up" (a direction we begin to anticipate whenever Bezhad's cell phone rings) indicates how such relationships are less a matter of actual physical space than of the mind's *reading* of it—as indeed all directions and compass points are irreducibly symbolic.

This element of transmutation-by-understanding connects us to Islamic *ta'wil*, or spiritual exegesis: a form of reading that, in tracing a term or text back to its (divine) origin, effectively restores it to that higher Meaning. Here again is the sense of a vertical "return"—one that can also take the lateral form, as Corbin puts it, of an *exodus* leading back "to the *Orient* of the original and hidden Idea." In this, *ta'wil* connects us in turn to a pair of complementary terms that seem as essential to Kiarostami's cinema since its inception as they are integral and important to Shiite thought: *zahir* (the outward, the apparent; also, the Koranic text) and *batin* (the inner, the hidden; the esoteric meaning).

Why do eleven of *Wind's* characters (by Kiarostami's count) remain hidden throughout the film? If one pursued this peculiarity's potential symbolic meanings into deep historical terrain, they might inevitably intersect with the "Hidden Imam," and the Lesser and Greater Occultations, concepts that not only have been crucial to Shiite eschatology and ideas of social justice for a millennium, but that also had a profound effect on recent Iranian history. (Is the joke here that, since the Revolution, it's not the Imam but the people who are hidden?) Yet the more immediate point is that such readings aren't necessary, since Kiarostami's "modernist poetry" analogy—the characters' invisibility means to engage the audience's imaginative participation—

provides an explanation that's certainly sufficient, if a bit banal and perhaps purposely incomplete.

In effect, he has covered himself. And yet, ultimately the most striking thing about *Wind's* way with meaning is how it foregrounds *batin*, the hidden. Other Kiarostami films, including *Taste of Cherry*, make use of "poetic" ellipses and such, but that's a far cry from what happens here: Conventions are so disarranged—the insides of things turned out, the outsides turned in— that an esoteric interpretation is not only permitted but tacitly demanded. Moreover, just as it's the first Kiarostami film to make an explicit display of poetry, it's also the first to contain (though this is somewhat less obvious, especially to Westerners) extensive allusions to religion, ones that in context aren't exactly benign.

What makes the allusions often negative? Is it the village's backwards customs? On the contrary, the issue of the primitive burial ritual (in which women scar themselves to gain social status) might be called *Wind's* McGuffin. The village, much unlike Koker, is essentially an abstraction that exists to present the protagonist with a vertical domain beyond the realm of the ordinary. And that it does perfectly well. Yet the story seems to transpire under the signs of *reversal* and *inversion*, negative currents that often find expression in the Engineer's comments and jokes, including (or especially) those with religious connotations. When Farzad is taking a test and asks him for help with the question "What happens on Judgment Day?" Bezhad answers, "The good go to hell and the bad go to heaven." It's mean to the kid, but also a travesty of his own understanding.

Which, indeed, is the crucial factor. In the wilderness far beyond the city, where such dramas of initiation always take place, Bezhad gains sudden access to the vertical and, thus, the chance for a genuine ascent. Yet he is profoundly *disoriented*. Around him are allusions connecting this domain to Abraham and the mystical spring called *zamzam*, Joseph and the well, Jacob and his Ladder, the cosmic crypt or cave (not unlike Plato's) that recurs in Islamic mysticism, and, most important of all, the *Mi'raj*, the Prophet Mohammad's bodily ascent into heaven. But instead of these signs, Bezhad repeatedly heeds only that faulty messenger of the flatland, his cell phone. His recurrent trips to the hilltop are like a stuttering, incomplete mock-*Mi'raj* that must repeat over and over because Bezhad hasn't understood "which way is up" or where the real voice of authority is to be found. In effect, *he* is the tortoise that's upside down, flipped over by his own incognizance.

What we are watching is a drama not only of *understanding* but of *intent*, factors that intermesh crucially throughout. The basic problem: Though Bezhad sees himself as a neutral observer/reporter, he is actually "working for death" in desiring the demise of the old woman (which will complete his assignment and release him from the village); in other words, he hasn't faced his own nature and the significance of his intent. The film's final act brings these issues to a symbolic crescendo. On the last of his trips to the hilltop, Bezhad sees the ditch digger's hole collapse, burying the man inside. Here, in an instant, he realizes that everything *depends on him*, and races to summon people to save the man. Back at the rescue site, he meets an elderly Doctor whom he takes to help the dying woman, thereby confirming the shift of intent brought about by his realization.

This Doctor, though, is himself the true proof and product of that shift. A key figure in the symbolic schema of the visionary recital, as well as myths and folktales the world over, he is the Guide, the Friend, the celestial Self, or in a term that Corbin sees as linking Zoroastrian and Shiite cosmologies, "the angel of one's being." Indeed, he identifies himself in the first bit of poetry he quotes after Bezhad climbs onto his motorbike ("If my guardian angel is the one I know, he'll protect glass from stone"). When the two make their second motorbike trip across a gorgeous landscape, Bezhad remarks that paradise is supposed to be more beautiful. The Doctor retorts that no one has ever returned to confirm that belief, and quotes an Omar Khayyam poem urging the reader to ignore "promises" of the beyond and instead, "prefer the present."

In a way, this moment after Bezhad's realization mirrors a poetry-centered passage that not only precedes that epiphany but seems to prepare the way for it. For a number of scenes Bezhad had been looking for some fresh milk, a quest that seems to combine real thirst with overtones of sexual frustration. Eventually, he gets his milk by going into an underground barn, where the ditch digger's girlfriend (whose face we never see) milks a cow while he recites Farrokhzad poems including the one that provides the film's title, a poem which conflates physical passion and mystical yearning. In this moment, *milk* can obviously stand for sustenance, for sex, for "the milk of human kindness," or even the sense offered by a famous tradition (*hadith*) of the Prophet in which Mohammad, asked the meaning of milk in a dream he's had, replies, "*knowledge*." In Kiarostami's usage, there's no contradiction between "sex" and "knowledge"; rather, comprehended by *poetry*, the sensual and the sacred connotations reflect, reinforce and explicate each other.

A similar multivalence of meaning marks the scene that quotes Khayyam, the Persian poet who perennially excites arguments over whether his rich exhortations to sensual experience contain a mystical dimension or not. Certainly, the poem's sense of "reject belief in the hereafter and enjoy the moment" gives us a clear outward meaning that, like Kiarostami's own "modernist" meanings, doesn't *require* any additional interpretations. Yet anyone familiar with mystical interpretations of Khayyam's work (e.g., Paramahansa Yogananda's) can easily read the Doctor's words to mean: "Look beyond orthodoxies that say paradise lies *out there*—realize that it exists within every soul and every moment." If the first of these readings might be called the *exoteric* and the second the *esoteric*, a third reading, call it *poetic-philosophical*, is one that encompasses both of the preceding meanings, seeing their "higher" truth not as a case of "either/or" but "both/and."

This same understanding, a bridge over many dualisms, has been the epistemological heart of Kiarostami's work since his early shorts. Here, it applies not only to meanings contained within poems (and elsewhere) but also to types of poetry and their cultural ramifications. For anyone who came of age in the 1960s and embraced modernist poetry (and perhaps embraced cinema as a form of same), there would have been a natural tendency to vaunt the new at the expense of older, more traditional forms. If that was ever Kiarostami's inclination, *The Wind Will Carry Us* clearly shows that his position now is not "Farrokhzad *or* Khayyam" but rather "Farrokhzad *and* Khayyam." The two poets' positioning on either side of the story's climactic sequence is eloquently precise. And there's no small significance in the fact that while Farrokhzad's poetry leads to the epiphany, Khayyam's (or an esoteric understanding of it) embodies its outcome, the leap to a superior, more ethical and visionary form of perception.

It must be allowed that all of this amounts to a form of cinema that, though good-humored and sensually appealing, is far more cerebral than emotional. Although it's sure to please a coterie of cine-aesthetes (even those who grasp little of the readings suggested here), *The Wind Will Carry Us* is not a film that touches the heart, and that may well be counted a failing even by viewers who discern in it a deeper, esoteric stream of meaning. In any case, this is clearly Kiarostami's choice. Perhaps one day he'll combine the emotional with the symbolic and make a film that ravishes the heart in the manner of Rumi's poems or Attar's *Conference of the Birds*, that crowning jewel of the visionary-recital tradition. For now, though, his work amounts to an implicit critique and rejection of most cinema, which trades in identification, sensation and catharsis. What Kiarostami's poetic films increasingly seem to propose is a *cinema of contemplation*, like a walled garden of stillness and reflection.

Viewers who grasp that enclosure's value will be those who see that *Wind's* greatest drama of *understanding* and *intent* is not on-screen, nor between the author and his creation, but, potentially, between each viewer and the film. As Roger Ebert indicated, the real action is in the interpretation. Or, as Corbin wrote of Avicenna's visionary recitals: "They are not stories about theoretical truths that could always be expressed differently; they are figures which typify an intimate personal drama, the apprenticeship of an entire lifetime. The symbol is both key and silence; it speaks and does not speak. It can never be explained once and for all. It expands to the degree that each consciousness is progressively summoned by it to unfold—that is to say, to the degree that each consciousness makes the symbol the key to its own transmutation."[2]

Of Experiments and Women: Two Post-Millenium Features

AROUND THE TURN OF THE MILLENNIUM, Abbas Kiarostami's career also seemed to take a turn. In the previous dozen years, he had made seven features—The Koker Trilogy, *Homework*, *Close-Up*, *Taste of Cherry* and *The Wind Will Carry Us*—that took him from being a little-known filmmaker in a virtually invisible national cinema to being one of the world's most celebrated auteurs. What other worlds were there for him to conquer? After the success of *The Wind Will Carry Us* at the 1999 Venice Film Festival, it seemed he was more interested in escaping the image the world had constructed of him. He never made another celluloid feature in Iran.

Instead, he let his creativity run in an array of different directions. Still photography—especially of subjects in nature—was an enduring passion, and he dedicated himself to it increasingly, even saying at one point that he felt more like a photographer than a filmmaker; many of these images went into books and gallery exhibitions. He directed opera. He wrote poetry voluminously; much of it has been published in Iran and translated into other languages. He built furniture and constructed art installations that were shown in museums around the world. He also was an enthusiastic teacher, giving classes on filmmaking in Iran and numerous other countries.

"The Joy of Creating" might be the heading on this fecund phase of Kiarostami's career, which is marked by a spirit of constant experimentation, perhaps especially in the films that he directed after turning away from the type of celluloid Iranian features that had made him famous. In part, the change here had a technological impetus. In 2000, he accepted a commission to make a documentary about AIDS orphans in Africa. He and cinematographer Seifollah Samadian went to Uganda and shot footage with mini-DV cameras, images that were meant to serve as visual notes for the feature that would be made later. But looking at the footage back in Iran, Kiarostami decided that *this* was the movie, that he would never equal its freshness, spontaneity or intimacy if he went back to Uganda with a large crew. So he edited his "notes" into the documentary feature *ABC Africa*, which marked his conversion to digital cinema.

To my knowledge, Kiarostami never engaged in the disputes over the aesthetics of celluloid-versus-digital that were common around this time (and remained in the cultural mix due to the pro-celluloid polemics of directors such as Christopher Nolan and Quentin Tarantino). For Kiarostami, the advantages of digital were practical and tied to an evolving sense of his own artistic practice. If many directors measure their increasing success in terms of greater budgets and larger-scale productions, Kiarostami took the opposite view: Success for him meant leaner budgets, smaller crews and fewer constraints on his creative autonomy. All of which translated into a sense that he could experiment in any way he chose.

This period also saw Kiarostami do something he'd never done before: center films on women. The reasons he hadn't done so earlier have been debated for years and surely are not simple. The films about children he made for Kanoon, including the shorts and documentaries as well as *The Traveler*, his first feature, reflect the male dominance in Iranian society and education at the time, as well as the fact that Kiarostami, who made some of the films out of concern for his own children, had two sons and no daughters. *The Report*, his feature about a crumbling middle-class marriage, was the one film in his early career that had a fully developed female character in a lead role, and it's very likely that Kiarostami might have continued in the direction it indicated had not his work been interrupted by the Iranian Revolution. Under the Islamic Republic, he and others complained, content restrictions made it difficult if not impossible to portray grown women realistically (intimate interactions with male actors were mostly prohibited, and actresses were obliged to cover their hair even in situations where they wouldn't in real life), so filmmakers reacted by focusing mainly on children and male characters. Certainly, there were some memorable women in secondary roles in the Kiarostami films of this period—the mothers in *Where Is the Friend's House?* and *Close-Up*, the assistant in *Through the Olive Trees*, the opinionated shop woman in *The Wind Will Carry Us*—and Kiarostami had planned to extend the Koker Trilogy into a tetralogy with a film that would center on the young actress who says virtually nothing in *Through the Olive Trees*.

But films centered on women would have to await the final phase of his career, when it seemed like he was making up for lost time. The two features discussed below are ones in which Kiarostami put women front and center, a practice intertwined with his concurrent dedication to various forms of experimentation.

Ten

2002's *Ten* opens with one of the most extraordinary scenes in all of Kiarostami's work. We're facing the front seat of a late-model car when 10-year Amin (Amin Maher) gets in. He's wearing the kind of logo-branded t-shirt that boys all over the world now sport. There are two small digital cameras fixed on the car's dashboard, filming the scene, but for roughly its first 16 minutes, we only see the images of the one filming Amin in the passenger seat; we hear but don't see his mother, Mania (Mania Akbari), in the driver's seat. When Amin gets in the car, she offers to buy him ice cream and he expresses concern about getting to his morning swimming date on time; but very soon these innocuous remarks give way to an argument that seems like it may be a frequent occurrence in this volatile parent-child relationship.

The key to the bitter exchange is that Mania divorced Amin's father and doesn't think the boy has accepted her very good reasons for doing that or his new stepfather. The way the boy reacts conveys that he hears such protestations over and over, and is sick of them. He angrily blames her for accusing his father in court of being a drug addict. She hotly replies that "Women have no rights in this country!" and making a charge like being an addict is one of the few ways they have of winning a divorce case. The argument goes on and on, building in acrimony as it does, but what's most riveting about the scene is the sheer intensity of the boy's performance. He is all over the place, physically and emotionally—shouting out the window happily at a friend, bouncing up and down in his seat, screaming at his mom, covering his face with his knapsack in semi-feigned agony, and constantly thinking. The thoughts stream across his face like patches of sunshine and thundershowers, but in fast motion. It's hard to think of another performance by a child actor that has such sustained energy, ferocity and nuance. (Though the scene has a few brief jump cuts, what we see is essentially more than 15 minutes of unbroken acting.)

Many viewers are bound to leave *Ten* wondering about this scene: How could it have possibly been done? Could little Amin have really memorized all the dialogue? Was the scene improvised, scripted, or a combination of the two? What was Kiarostami's part in creating the scene? Was he somehow in the car with the actor(s), as he had been in car-centered scenes in previous films? Such questions are not only necessary to any effort to understand *Ten*, they also invite us to discern which qualities connect the film to Kiarostami's earlier work, and which mark it as a departure.

To be sure, there are numerous evocations of previous films by the director. The focus on a boy protagonist points back to his first short "Bread and Alley," while the headstrong nature of this boy especially recalls the title character of his first feature, *The Traveler*. The remarkable performance by a child actor resembles those of previous films, though this one may well be the most astonishing of all. The theme of divorce as emotionally devastating harkens back to the autobiographical *The Report* (and will be found again in *Certified Copy*). The use of a car as a principal setting continues a practice Kiarostami has employed in every dramatic feature since *And Life Goes On*. And the fact that the scene blurs the line between fiction and documentary invokes what has essentially become a Kiarostami trademark by this point in his career.

The differences with his previous work, however, more clearly reveal the particular qualities which distinguish not only this film but the others in which his concerns with experimentation and women converge. To begin with technical factors that are key to his experimental aims here: The digital cameras used in this scene differ from comparable film cameras in two important ways: 1) They are small enough that they can fit on a car's dash, and 2) They can shoot much longer takes, since film magazines usually hold no more than 12 minutes of celluloid. The second of these assets allows Kiarostami to construct a scene that could last as long as the actors and their emotions take it—which in turn leads him to allow actors even greater control over a scene's content and performance than he has before.

But the other aspect of digital shooting produces results which are arguably even more remarkable. In virtually every film from the celluloid era of cinema, scenes of characters talking in cars were shot in one of two ways: with the camera outside the passenger cabin, often mounted on the car's hood or a camera truck; or with the camera inside the car, either observing the characters from the back seat or taking the place of one in the front seat. (Past Kiarostami films used both techniques.) In *Ten*, however, the camera is inside the car, in front of and very close to the actors, and one of the most significant consequences of this is perhaps registered by most viewers only subliminally: Amin's constantly-in-motion gaze sweeps across the entire visual field, including the space occupied by the camera. Usually, especially in scenes where the camera is so close, an actor must make an effort not to look at the camera, and viewers have grown unconsciously accustomed to the way an actor's eyes "skip" over the place where the camera is. Here, it's like there is no camera. The boy's gaze, unconstrained, seems to belong to him alone, looking right through us while not apparently registering the camera's presence.

This gives the film an unusually intimate feel and, together with the extra length allowed by digital filming, a greater dramatic power and realism than seen in comparable previous scenes by Kiarostami and other directors. To the extent that all this constitutes an experiment, in certain obvious senses it must be considered a success. The question of whether that success is qualified by other factors can be postponed while we consider how the film's experimental aims coincide and interact with Kiarostami's new focus on women.

Although most sources credit Kiarostami with writing and directing *Ten*, significant contributions in both areas were obviously made by Mania Akbari. Their collaboration certainly seems deeper and more integral than those in any of his other films.[ix] Kiarostami's initial idea for the film came from hearing of a psychiatrist whose office had been shut down by authorities but continued to see patients in his car. Using the car would realistically allow most or all of the patients to be female, since in real life they would have kept their head covering on in the automobile's semi-public/semi-private space. When Akbari, then 27, read about Kiarostami making a film about women, she wrote to him offering to work in any capacity. When they met, he thought she was trying to show her ability to act while he just wanted her to be herself. After he told her that, she returned a week later with a videotape showing her knack for appearing natural on camera.

When Kiarostami accepted Akbari as his central performer, it changed the film's premise. The main character is now not a psychiatrist but Mania, a Tehran housewife modeled on but in some senses (according to Akbari) very different from the woman playing her. The film is structured as ten conversations (the film introduces each with numbers on film leader) that Mania has with other

---

ix. After Kiarostami's death, Akbari began claiming she filmed the footage in *Ten*, which Kiarostami took from her, edited and presented as his own. Ahmad Kiarostami and distributor mk2 have refuted the claims, which so far have been issued only on social media.

people in her car. Four of these are with Amin, who is played by Akbari's real-life son. The other six are with women. These include: Mania's sister, with whom she discusses her problems with Amin; a devout older woman, who prays at the Ali Akbar Mausoleum three times daily and talks about her reactions to her husband's death; a prostitute, who gets into Mania's car by accident and talks defiantly about enjoying her job and why wives are like prostitutes; a friend who sobs throughout the conversation because her husband has left her; and another friend, who's so distraught at losing her boyfriend that she removes her head scarf revealing that she's shaved her head.

One very striking aspect of *Ten* is the very up-to-the-minute sense it gives of life in Tehran at the time it was shot. This was something new for the filmmaker. Of the six dramatic features Kiarostami made in the previous phase of his career, four were set and shot in rural or small-town Iran, while the other two, *Close-Up* and *Taste of Cherry*, give only very limited views of the capital. During the time these films were being made, moreover, life in urban Iran was changing rapidly. This writer recalls being in Iran in the late 1990s and hearing a young Tehrani—perhaps one of Kiarostami's sons—telling of a friend who returned after only months away from the city feeling that years' worth of changes had taken place in his absence. Even a visitor could notice the speed of the changes. Sleek foreign cars increasingly replaced the boxy Iranian Paykans on city streets, which themselves were transformed by architectural innovations, constant construction and an aggressive policy of creating green spaces in the city. Illegal satellite dishes brought foreign television channels into Tehran homes, even as black-market videotape dealers delivered Hollywood, European and Asian movies. Once the Internet became pervasive—roughly around the time that Kiarostami made his millennial pivot—it seemed that the Iran of even the early 1990s was a very distant place.

Ten registers many of these changes peripherally, without directly focusing on them. Though the cameras mainly stay close on the characters without taking expansive looks outside Mania's car, we glimpse enough of the streets, buildings, cars and people to sense the city's current energies and textures. Even more important, though, is the human atmosphere registered, for example, in the signs of contemporary discontents such as prostitution and pornography (which Amin says his father watches), subjects which few Iranian films had broached until recently. Though the film has lighter moments and Mania maintains a chipper outlook even when listening to the saddest complaints of her passengers, the pervasive mood is downbeat. And this may be where an oblique political dimension can be discerned. If *Close-Up, And Life Goes On* and *Through the Olive Trees* can be read as reflecting discontent over the fate of the Iranian Revolution in the years following the end of the Iran-Iraq War and Khomeini's death, it's worth considering that *Ten* was made at a time when many Iranians were experiencing disappointment over the Khatami administration's failure to reform the Islamic Republic.

The most Godardian of Kiarostami's features, *Ten* also has a documentary-like feel in how it approaches the subject of women in Iran via a set of vignettes, each narrating a mini-drama that concerns the difficulties the female characters have faced or are facing. All of these difficulties have to do with men (or in one case, a little boy), and it might be asked why Kiarostami didn't focus on one or two women who had other problems, or were carving out lives on their own. Perhaps his point was that women are still so legally dependent on men in Iran—the subject of some of Mania's most acrid remarks in the first scene—that males *are* the primary problem and reference points of most women. Or it could be that these women, most of them acquaintances of Akbari, were actually voicing their own greatest concerns.

In any case, *Ten* stands apart from Kiarostami's previous six dramatic features in lacking their degrees of literary and philosophical allusiveness, their playful wit, tempered lyricism and humanistic warmth. Indeed, it is a colder film than earlier ones and the first thus far to seem so eager to escape the confines of conventional storytelling. In his eloquent book about *Ten*, critic Geoff Andrew discerns a dramatic shape revealed in the film's final scene, which he says shows us that, "Mania has been on a journey, and through her experiences has found for herself a level of calm perfectly expressed by the closing music."[3] That shape, though, is a very slight one if it demands such a close reading of the final moments of a film that otherwise is notably episodic and anecdotal, focused on a protagonist whose stance is mainly reactive. Arguably, in making his cinematic poetry even sparer and less dramatic as he upped the experimental ante, Kiarostami was willing to sacrifice some elements that viewers found appealing in his work. If so, the result was one he must've expected: Critics were divided about the film, which fared less well with audiences than his features of the previous decade.

Ten was nonetheless a bold artistic step, in large part because of the novel working method Kiarostami adopted in trying out new technology, a method that involved an unprecedented collaboration with a single performer. The fruits of his trust in Mania Akbari can best be seen in her scenes with Amin. These duets have an emotional intensity and visceral realism seldom equaled in contemporary cinema, qualities that resulted from Akbari and the boy working out the content of the scenes in advance and then letting themselves loose in front of the cameras, improvising and inventing in a context powerfully connected to their real-life bond. Kiarostami was away from them, in the backseat or outside the car. He saw the results afterwards, and later spoke drolly, and favorably, of "the disappearance of the director."

It is said that when Amin was finished filming, he didn't even realize he'd been making a movie. Where were the actors, the crew?, he asked. As with most experiments, the success of this one was in doubt until its author brought it into the world. After it was premiered at Cannes, Kiarostami said simply, "People seemed to like it. So I realized we'd done it."

Shirin

In the six years between *Ten* and his next film to foreground women, 2008's *Shirin*, Kiarostami made a number of shorts but no dramatic features. The two feature-length works he released during this period might be called experimental documentaries, though no term fits them exactly. *10 on Ten* (2004) was reportedly intended as a DVD extra about the making of *Ten* but evolved into something rather different during its own making. It shows Kiarostami in his car speaking to the camera about his thoughts on various subjects connected to digital filmmaking and his own cinema. While some critics and cinephiles understandably regard the film as the most disposable of Kiarostami's features, since many of the points it makes are either obvious or have been made previously or better in other contexts, it is still valuable and interesting as a more explicit extension of the personal/artistic self-portraiture evident in his work from *Close-Up* on (an element that will continue in the 32-minute "The Roads of Kiarostami," 2005).

The more important of the two features, *Five Dedicated to Ozu* (2003), released between *Ten* and *10 on Ten*, marks the place where Kiarostami's cinema turns from the art-house to the art museum. Filmed on the shores of the Caspian Sea, a favorite vacation spot for Iranians, the 74-minute work contains five shots (each appears unbroken though there are some subtle jump-cuts) averaging just under 15 minutes. In the first, filmed with a handheld camera, a small piece of wood on the beach is reached by the waves and eventually breaks in two, one part floating out to sea while the smaller fragment stays on the beach. The second shot is a fixed-camera view of a seaside promenade where various vacationers stride across the frame from right and left, some clustering into small groups until eventually the last group disperses and the promenade is left empty. The third shot is a distant, fixed-camera view of low figures in front of the ocean who are revealed to be dogs when they get up and begin to move around. The fourth, another strongly horizontal composition, shows ducks quacking as they hurry back and forth on the beach. The fifth shot, the only one set at night, shows the moon's rippling reflection in a dark body of water until it is interrupted by a rainstorm with lightning; when this ends, the moon's reflection returns until it is erased by the brightening of dawn. In the first four segments, the rolling sounds of breaking waves provide the soundtrack, while the fifth includes the sounds of insects and other creatures as well as the noises of the rain storm.

This film and the one that preceded it invite us to consider two different ways that "experimental" is used in cinema. In one, it is a description of unusual technical or aesthetic practices which in principle can be incorporated into conventional narrative features (in this sense, the term can be applied to the work of such idiosyncratic, risk-taking American auteurs as David Lynch and Terrence Malick). *Ten* fits this usage very neatly. The other usage, meanwhile, effectively posits "experimental" as a de facto genre unto itself, one that stands apart from mainstream commercial films by avoiding or greatly distorting standard narrative techniques and focusing instead on "poetic" formal or personal concerns. This thumbnail definition includes a corollary that such experimental films often display connections to other arts such as music, drawing or dance. *Five* obviously fits both parts of this description: Besides the idiosyncratic, non-narrative cinematic vision it presents, the film also evokes kinships to Kiarostami's work in photography, painting and poetry.

If the works that made Kiarostami's name can be attributed in part to their compassionate gaze, *Five* is the first (and perhaps best) feature to exemplify a *contemplative* gaze, one that finds its most congenial subjects in nature. It invites us to stand back, put our narrative expectations aside, and simply ponder the audiovisual flow it presents us with—much as we would a painting or photograph on a museum wall, or the mental images conjured by a haiku. But to leave it at that would be too simple, because *Five*, due to its subtle complexities and sense of discrete illusions, refuses to allow alert viewers to relax into uncritical passivity. Its contemplative gaze also entwines with an intellectual or, perhaps better, an *interrogative* gaze that spurs us to question the film and our experience of watching it. First off: is what we are seeing (and hearing) real, i.e., events simply as they appeared to the camera, or were they mechanically created or manipulated? That is, is Kiarostami asking us to contemplate nature qua nature, or to consider our complicity with the artist in creating an illusory simulacrum of nature? (Or perhaps, both at once?) Beyond that, could such a composite contemplative/interrogative gaze be fully deployed in a film that involved characters and a story?

Shirin almost seems to have been created to provide a positive answer to the latter question. What the film ostensibly shows are scores of women in headscarves (most played by Iranian actresses) apparently watching and reacting emotionally to a dramatic movie. The women are seen in close-ups and medium close-ups that usually frame one, two or three figures, sometimes with men in the background. The women never speak, though their faces are eloquently expressive. The shots showing them linger several seconds, long enough to register one or more shifts of attitude or feeling; the editing is never rushed nor protracted. The movie the characters are watching is not shown. Experienced by the viewer of *Shirin* only via its soundtrack, it is a romantic tragedy based on *Khosrow and Shirin*, a work by the renowned 12th-century poet Nezami Ganjavi, which itself derived from Persian folklore and a previous version recorded in Iran's national epic, the *Shahnameh* by Ferdowsi.

If *Shirin*, like *Five*, invites both contemplative and interrogative responses, the latter begin with questions about how it was actually made. Many viewers will go into the film knowing certain answers; others are supplied by Hamideh Razavi's making-of documentary "Taste of Shirin" (included on the U.S. DVD). As that film shows, the women were all filmed in movie-theater seats in Kiarostami's house. Rather than looking at a movie, they were instructed to gaze at a small drawing of stick figures mounted above the camera as flickering light from reflectors played across their faces; Kiarostami coached them from off-screen, inviting them to think of their own private love stories. Everything was filmed without sound. Reportedly Kiarostami didn't know which story he would use for the unseen movie while shooting the actresses (in a short trial version, he used the soundtrack from Franco Zeffirelli's *Romeo and Juliet*). Once he settled on *Khosrow and Shirin*, he directed actors as they recorded a dramatized version of the poem, and added a lush "historical" score by Morteza Hananeh and Hossein Dehlavi.

Could this be the only time in cinema history that viewers reacted to a drama before it was created? (The deceptions here recall those of the trial in *Close-Up*.) In any case, the film asks us to contemplate two things at once: faces of women (who happen to be watching a film) and faces of movie spectators (who happen to be mostly women). Both women and spectators, moreover, seem to be reacting to a tragic love story, which injects elements of passion, suffering and narrative into our visual contemplation. This whole skein of meaning and potential meaning makes *Shirin* the most complexly conceptual of Kiarostami's films (more than *Five* and *24 Frames*, which focus mainly on nature, it's rich in human concerns). Like other experimental films, it provokes different reactions in different spectators. Speaking personally, I can understand viewers who find it boring or confining, but I found it uniquely entrancing and beautiful, a film that rewards its invitation to contemplate one's own movie spectatorship with an occasion for both self-inspection and reverie. Of course, most (non-Iranian?) viewers will find their minds only intermittently engaged by the story of Khosrow and Shirin on the soundtrack, but Kiarostami often spoke of wanting to allow viewers to dream their own dreams—even to take naps—while watching his films.

For Kiarostami himself, *Shirin* offers an occasion to pay tribute to several things at once: the beauty and character of women; the place of the spectator in the filmic process; and Iranian actresses (very few of whom he used in his films, since he preferred to work with non-professionals). For the women and the actresses, there's an inevitable irony in the way they are presented here: Even more than the young actress at the center of *Through the Olive Trees*, they are seen but not heard. And they're seen in a way that might prompt our interrogative impulses to ask: Why wearing head scarves? If Kiarostami had wanted to pay tribute to the beauty of women without Iran's sartorial restrictions, he could have filmed outside Iran. For that matter, he could have filmed in his own home with women not wearing head scarves (as most don't in private spaces in Iran). That would have meant that *Shirin* could not be shown publicly in Iran, of course, but Kiarostami couldn't have had high hopes for the film's commercial prospects at home. Was he concerned that filming without head scarves would be seen as a political provocation?

The simplest answer here is obvious: He wanted to create the illusion of women watching a film in an Iranian movie theater, a public space where head scarves are obligatory. And this touches on a little-noted quality that distinguishes *Shirin* from other Kiarostami works: It's the film that most decisively separates Iranian from non-Iranian viewers. Rather being a generalized film about female viewers, it is specifically about Iranian women (though one Juliette Binoche makes a guest appearance) reacting to a drama with deep roots in Iranian culture, a drama that Kiarostami said he chose because it's the rare classical text where female passions are recounted by female characters. Surely, Iranian viewers familiar with *Khosrow and Shirin* will experience *Shirin* much differently than viewers who don't know or have an emotional connection to the story. Moreover, behind *Shirin*—and *Khosrow and Shirin*—there's another artwork and tradition that reach even deeper in Iranian culture.

In 2003 in an outdoor theater in Rome, Kiarostami staged his first play, *Ta'ziyeh*. Known as the one indigenous form of drama in Islamic culture, the Persian *ta'ziyeh*, a passion play performed as an open-air pageant in villages all over Iran, depicts the tragic event at the center of Shia Islam: the martyrdom of Iman Hossein, the Prophet's grandson, and his party at Karbala in 680. The actions on stage are bloody and horrific, and among the faithful it generates extreme displays of grief, contrition and ultimate consolation. In Rome, Kiarostami staged his *Ta'ziyeh* (cut from four hours to 90 minutes) underneath six large screens showing films that he shot the previous winter of Iranian villagers' emotional reactions in watching a ta'ziyeh performance. This, almost surely, is where the idea for *Shirin* originated.

Kiarostami said he witnessed a ta'ziyeh long before he saw any film. In effectively linking that experience—primal for him and many Iranians, primal as a dramatic expression of religious feeling—to cinema, the bridge from *Ta'ziyeh* to *Shirin* also encompasses the *Shahnameh* and the great medieval Persian poetic tradition exemplified by Ganjavi. Thus, while the film may well be experimental in a way that would be recognized by Andy Warhol, it is also a subtextual collage of some of the most profound aspects of Iranian culture, sacred and secular. Which, in retrospect, is entirely fitting for the last live-action feature Kiarostami made in Iran.

Certified Copy: At Home and Abroad
First published 2012 for the Criterion Collection's DVD/Blu-ray release of Certified Copy

IN TUSCANY IN JUNE 2009, roughly forty years after the beginning of his filmmaking career, Abbas Kiarostami started shooting his first dramatic feature made outside Iran, a film, moreover, performed in English, French, and Italian, rather than his native Farsi. The same month in Iran, the Ahmadinejad regime brutally suppressed massive protests by the so-called Green Movement over presidential elections that many suspected had been stolen. While the near simultaneity of Iran's leading director decamping and its regime cracking down was clearly coincidental, its symbolism is undeniable. *Certified Copy*, Kiarostami's Tuscan excursion, is a nonpolitical film only if you find no political meaning in its loudest unspoken implication: "I can't work in Iran anymore."

Doubtless Kiarostami could still work in his native land if he was determined to, but since conditions for filmmakers there have grown more difficult in recent years, he has less reason to put himself through that now than ever. I've often heard Iranian directors say that the hardships of working in Iran are worth it because their art is so deeply rooted in their culture; world audiences, they feel, value their films in large part for their Iranian-ness. For Iran's most celebrated director, however, a brand name in Western art houses since the 1990s, maintaining an identification with Iran is evidently not as much of a concern anymore; as an auteur, he now belongs to the world. But perhaps more crucially, this move can be understood in the context of a career that has been remarkable for its continual adventurousness. Every Kiarostami film represents a leap in a new direction, often a very risky one. Viewed from that angle, a film made outside Iran, in foreign languages, was perhaps a creative dare he couldn't resist. But what kind of film would it be: a Kiarostami film that just happened to have foreign backdrops or a Western art film that just happened to be directed by Kiarostami?

Judging from the reviews when *Certified Copy* premiered at the Cannes Film Festival eleven months after its shooting commenced, the consensus on the above question was definitely that the latter was the case. And this may explain why there were notes of reservation, surprise, and sometimes even disdain among the general acclamation. To be sure, the film is recognizably Kiarostamian in many particulars, such as its use of long takes of extended conversations in automobiles and alleyways. But as a type of film, with its desultory chronicling of an implicitly romantic but also querulous and cryptic encounter between two very attractive middle-class intellectuals—an English writer and a French antiques dealer—who discuss art and life and their own peculiar travails against the irrepressibly picturesque stones and vistas of Tuscany, *Certified Copy* looks not only like a European art film but also like a specific subgenre of that form that was proudly exported, especially by France and Italy, from the 1950s through the 1970s.

No wonder some reviewers were restrained in their praise. Critics exist to supply definitions of artists, and the standard definition of Kiarostami has had far more to do with his cerebral Iranian-ness (however that is described) than with an affinity or kinship with any genus of European art cinema, especially one now effectively outmoded. For audiences, on the other hand, that correspondence was no handicap at all; quite the contrary, by all evidence. *Certified Copy* became an art-house hit across the West, Kiarostami's highest-grossing film ever. And if audiences in America, say, were drawn to it by trailers promising a certain kind of Juliette Binoche film rather than any kind of Kiarostami film, what of it? When the box-office results were in, it was clear that Kiarostami had made another nervy leap and landed on his feet. With the advantage of some extra hindsight, it's possible to add that those initial critical reactions had it only half-right: Hidden beneath the alluring surface of a movie that confidently revives the conventions of a certain kind of European art cinema, there's a quintessential Kiarostami film, one of the most deeply personal he has made.

In interviews, both Binoche and Kiarostami, who became friends in the 1990s, have traced the film's genesis to a conversation they had in Tehran, when he first told her the film's story, which he said had actually happened to him. Binoche: "He said, 'Do you believe me?' I said, 'Yes.' And he said, 'It's not true!' I burst out laughing… To this day, I'm sure he lived this story. Just as I'm sure he didn't." For his part, Kiarostami was no doubt being both evasive and truthful in saying that the story began to evolve as he told it to Binoche and watched her reactions; the actress's vulnerability and sensitivity, "what I knew of her soul," became part of his subject.

Like many Kiarostami fictions, *Certified Copy* opens with the matter-of-fact air of a documentary. The camera stares deadpan at a table that stands before an antique stone mantelpiece and contains two microphones, a bottle of water, and a copy of a book titled *Copia conforme*. At length, an Italian man comes in and sets up for the event that is to follow, a lecture before a small crowd in a hall in the town of Arezzo. Running late, the lecturer arrives. James Miller (William Shimell), a handsome, dapper English scholar, apologizes and thanks the crowd for their interest in his book, which he ruefully notes has been more appreciatively received in Italy than in England. From what we can tell of the book by his comments, it challenges conventional thinking about artworks by asserting the value of copies in relation to originals. But we hear no more than the opening of Miller's lecture because our attention is diverted to a woman in the audience, who scribbles something on a piece of paper and hands it to the author's translator, then follows her teenage son out of the hall and to a restaurant.

The interrupted lecture is typical of Kiarostami, whose films follow narrative pathways full of detours, diversions, and interruptions, some felicitous, others more jarring. The same is true of the emotional itineraries of his characters, as we are reminded when Miller, the following day, visits the antiques shop of the woman seen earlier (played by Binoche, she is never named but referred to only as Elle, or "She"). He has only a few hours before he must leave Arezzo. She would like to show him her shop, but he prefers the outdoors, so she offers him an excursion to the nearby town of Lucignano, famous as a site for weddings.

From the first, their conversation evinces an odd mix of attraction and antipathy. She seems dressed and primed to seduce, and has bought six copies of his book, but is also testy, cross, and quick to disagree with him. Cool and a bit distant, Miller remains polite but doesn't refrain from verbally sparring with her. Once they're in Lucignano, however, his greatest displeasure comes not from her but from the sight of young married couples, whose happiness he dismisses as an illusion sure to be cruelly burst in time.

Then, when the couple stop in a trattoria for coffee, something strange happens. After Miller steps outside to take a cell-phone call, She begins a conversation with the woman running the café, who mistakes the two foreigners for a married couple and begins to offer comments and advice about the wisdom and necessity of marriage. In a shot where the woman leans over to whisper something (we never learn what) to She, and completely blocks the camera's view of her, it may be said that the film goes through the looking glass. We become aware of this shift moments later, when the two main characters resume their conversation, and now speak to each other as a couple who have been married fifteen years. For the rest of the film, they maintain this relationship, as they wander through the town, dredging up old differences and disappointments, before ultimately finding their way to the hotel where they spent their wedding night and now make a touching but unsuccessful attempt at re-forming their original bond.

The first effect of this startling *coup de cinéma* is to take us out of the fiction by reminding us that it *is* a fiction. Once this happens, we are less able to relate to the two characters as people we might encounter in life than as artifices created by an artist whose motives can only be called opaque. I once described Kiarostami's work as "a cinema of questions," and the central twist in *Certified Copy* leaves us with many to ask. Which half of the film is "true"? Are these characters playacting in one or the other? Or could it be that the halves are competing falsehoods, or equally true in parallel universes? And how does this connect to all the talk about copies and originals, art and marriage?

In discussing the influence of poetry on his work, Kiarostami has often spoken of leaving gaps or elisions in his stories in order to invite or oblige the viewer to consciously participate in the creation of meaning. *Certified Copy* certainly qualifies as a variation on this technique; ultimately, we must determine what "happens" (or doesn't) in the film, which means that our intentions regarding the characters (do we want them to be strangers or spouses, flirtatious or alienated?) are at least as important as Kiarostami's. As for what he intends, both cinematically and personally, some of that may be discerned by pondering the two films that *Certified Copy* arguably has the most significant relationship to: Roberto Rossellini's *Journey to Italy* (1953) and Kiarostami's own *The Report* (1977).

When Iran's post-revolutionary cinema started getting international attention in the late 1980s, many critics saw it as owing a debt to Italian neorealism. While some of the parallels (shooting on location, using non-actors) can be attributed to exigencies of history and budget, others (social themes, a strong moral sense) no doubt represent actual lines of influence. Others still (the blending of documentary and fiction, the concern for physical environment) specifically link Kiarostami to Rossellini. But *Journey to Italy* does not belong to the neorealist phase of Rossellini's work. It is the third of four films he made with Ingrid Bergman, and was shot when their relationship was disintegrating, a fact that has led many to sense an autobiographical subtext in its story of an English couple (the husband is played by George Sanders) whose marriage comes to the brink of unraveling as they motor through Southern Italy.

Both the matter and the manner of Rossellini's film resemble those of Kiarostami's. The "thin" storyline about unhappily married foreigners in Italy. The chilly husband and sensuous but unmoored wife. The difficulty in communication. The road trip that leads to the contemplation of various artworks. The emphasis on moments, gestures, and textures of place over plot. There's even a religious emblem near the climax of each film (a processional in Rossellini's, a church in Kiarostami's) that seems to change the story's emotional flow. In some senses, it may even be said that Kiarostami has made a "copy" of *Journey to Italy* in *Certified Copy*. If so, could James Miller's defense of copies be intended as a drolly proleptic assertion that the new film shouldn't necessarily be considered inferior to its celebrated model?

Perhaps. But there's also a sense, given the way Kiarostami's films often meditate on cinema itself (an element he's most responsible for introducing to Iranian film), that he's concerned not just with what *Journey to Italy* contains but also with what it represents. Initially derided in Italy, Rossellini's film was later taken up by Éric Rohmer, Jacques Rivette, and other French critics, thereby becoming a foundational text in the Nouvelle Vague's formulation of auteurist cinema. In retrospect, it seems clear that what made the film such a model for young critics aspiring to be filmmakers was both its idiosyncratic emphasis on style over storytelling and the feeling of great personal meaning in Rossellini's account of the torturous relations of men and women (a combination that pointed toward such later masterworks as Antonioni's *L'Avventura* (1960), Godard's *Contempt* (1963), and Bergman's *Scenes from a Marriage* (1973). It is this tradition in which Kiarostami situates himself in transitioning from Iran to Europe. Yet it's also one to which he already belongs.

Prior to Iran's 1979 Revolution, Kiarostami made a number of shorts and two features. The second of these features, *The Report,* is an acidic drama about the collapse of a marriage, and Kiarostami has stated that it was based on the events leading to his own divorce. The film's main characters are a fashionable middle-class Tehrani couple with a young child. While Kiarostami's account of their growing antagonism and estrangement apportions blame to both sides, his portrait of the husband, a vain, foppish, and self-centered bureaucrat, is especially damning. When I asked Kiarostami if this young man was meant to represent a certain type of Iranian, he said that the characterization was a broadside aimed at no one but himself.

At other times, he told me emphatically that he would never make another film about marriage in Iran, since content restrictions in the Islamic Republic effectively bar a realistic depiction of adult intimacies. Given the chance to work outside Iran, it's little wonder that he returned to that very subject. Effectively a companion piece to *The Report, Certified Copy* broods on marriage from the embittered perspective of a wounded survivor (Kiarostami has never remarried). Its divided story very precisely and poetically renders the contradiction at the heart of that perspective: Marriage is essential, yet it is also impossible. In this sense, both halves of the narrative are true. The two people are strangers as well as a couple married for fifteen years. They will always be locked in this pose of thwarted intimacy; nothing can bridge the chasm that both connects and separates them.

As for who gets the blame for the standoff, She is certainly difficult, mercurial, and challenging. Yet She is also given credit for trying to restore the feeling that originally drew them together. When She ducks into the aforementioned church, it's to remove her bra, a gesture that movingly unites the sensual and the spiritual. And it's She who literally tries to return them to their marriage bed. It is he who refuses the gesture, as if unable or unwilling to break through the shell of his intellectual's ego. The last shot of the film, where James Miller stares into a mirror at his own haggard face, not only tells us where the lion's share of the blame belongs but also sums up the candid self-incrimination that makes *Certified Copy* such a remarkable instance of confessional cinema, cleverly cloaked in the raiment of a classic modernist European art film.

Desire's End: *Like Someone in Love*

VIEWED FROM AFTER THE END of Abbas Kiarostami's career, *Like Someone in Love* and the earlier *Certified Copy* seem destined to be forever seen as companion pieces. The last two dramatic features Kiarostami directed prior to his untimely death in 2016, they were made outside Iran due to the difficulties he faced working in his native country: the first in Italy, the second in Japan. While many of the films he made in the previous decade can be described as experimental, these last features were so mainly for taking the leap—a risky one for any Iranian filmmaker—of venturing to plant their dramas in foreign soil. Otherwise, formally, they adhere to the broad stylistic conventions of the international art film. What distinguishes them from other films in that category is their sense of deeply personal meaning, their aura of what I've called confessional cinema.

Kiarostami had great personal affinities for Italy and Japan, had many admirers in both countries, and perhaps felt a closer kinship to their artistic and art-cinema traditions than he did to those of other nations. But the two films were not about Italy and Japan. Their stories could have been made in Iran had the country's content restrictions not been so limiting. Given the freedom to create without such limits, Kiarostami naturally turned to subjects that Iran's Islamic propriety had denied him: desire and coupling, romance and its adult quandaries. In *Like Someone in Love*, he adds another, somewhat less taboo subject: aging.

Visually and dramatically, the opening scene of *Like Someone in Love* reads like a declaration of independence from the strictures of Kiarostami's native cinema. (From the standpoint of Iranian conservatives, of course, the signs of this independence are nothing more than markers of foreign decadence, of "Westoxication" and its moral corruptions.) We are in Bar Rizzo, a dark, sleek, upscale Tokyo drinking establishment. Martinis, beer and wine are being consumed. As jazz tinkles on the PA, some customers smoke or talk on cell phones. The women are dressed skimpily, their hair chicly cut and, sometimes, dyed. But most indicative of the setting's moral character is the main action the scene describes: A call girl gets orders from her procurer (the terms seem more appropriate than "prostitute" and "pimp," given the place's tony ambience) to go to a client who's an hour's drive away.

When the film was first reviewed upon release, this 16-minute scene received copious comments for its style, which is indeed striking in a way that recalls the fixed-camera austerities of Kiarostami's films of the previous decade. In the 14 minutes before one character goes outside to take a phone call, only two camera angles are used. The first, from the POV of the call girl, Akiko (Rin Takanashi), looks across the room toward the bar and a far door to restrooms; to the left, two men and a woman sit at a central table, talking and drinking; to the right, Akiko's friend and fellow call girl, Nagisa (Reika Mari), sits, occasionally turning to talk with Akiko. "I'm not lying," the film's first line, is heard while we are looking from this camera angle, though it comes from Akiko, whom we haven't seen yet. The second camera angle, though, which soon appears and will alternate with the first through the rest of the scene, is a medium close-up focused just on her. She is pretty, and though her frock is low-cut, is dressed and made up fashionably yet rather demurely.

Typical of Kiarostami's way of parceling out dramatic information piecemeal, so as to engage the viewer in constructing the drama's meaning, the nature of the phone conversation Akiko's having as the scene begins is not readily apparent. But thinking back on it later in the film, or watching the film a second time, the viewer will more clearly discern that she's having an argument with her jealous boyfriend. He wants to know where she is and when he can see her. She says she has to study and lies about where she is. She also puts Nagisa on the phone to lie for her, which Nagisa does while signaling that she thinks the boyfriend is crazy. After Akiko hangs up, Hiroshi (Denden), a middle-aged guy with the dress and demeanor of a businessman, comes in, sits at her table and tells her he thinks the boyfriend is bad news and she needs to "break it off." While allowing it's her business, he adds, "It's my business too."

He wants her to go to see a client tonight. She says she can't: She's exhausted, still must study for school and, most importantly, has to go meet her grandmother, who's in Tokyo only for the day. He nevertheless persists, saying he has allowed her to refuse before, but this time is different because the client is someone he greatly respects. He doesn't want to send Nagisa. This one is for Akiko. When she meets the man, he says, she will understand.

She still hasn't said yes when he puts her in a hired car and gives the driver instructions and money.

Set on one night and part of the next day, *Like Someone in Love* has one of the simplest narratives of any Kiarostami movie. Kiarostami said that the script was 35 pages and he wasn't sure that what he shot would add up to a 90-minute feature (the film's running time is 109 minutes). Due to this simplicity, the story's remainder is easily described. After glimpsing her grandmother waiting for her beneath a statue as her car leaves Tokyo—a brief but extraordinarily poignant moment that's also a devastating comment on deteriorating human relationships in the postmodern world—Akiko an hour later arrives in Yokohama and meets the client, Takashi Watanabe (Tadashi Okuno), a mild-mannered elderly writer and retired professor of sociology, the subject Akiko happens to be studying in school. In his cluttered, book-lined living room, they talk, then she moves into the bedroom, begins peeling off clothes and gets into bed saying she's tired. Kiarostami leaves it ambiguous whether the old professor, a widower with an absent daughter, is looking for sex or simply the companionship of a surrogate granddaughter. Either is possible. The scene ends with him talking to her from a chair in the bedroom.

The next day, he drops Akiko off at school and sees her argue with a young man who, after she walks away, comes over and begins talking to him. Lean, intense and worked-up, Noriaki (Ryo Kase) is an obsessive who suspects his girl of vague infidelities while evidently having no idea that she's a prostitute. A mechanic, he admits he wants to get married as a way of possessing and controlling her. Noriaki assumes that Mr. Watanabe is Akiko's grandfather and the old man doesn't correct him. After Akiko returns, the three set off for Noriaki's garage, where the younger man offers some gratis repairs for a problem he has detected in the car. Shifting into his work coveralls, Noriaki is for once relaxed and upbeat. Later, though, Mr. Watanabe goes to pick up Akiko and finds that she's been beaten. He takes her back to his apartment to clean her up. It's there, with a sudden and surprising action, that the film abruptly ends.

That unexpectedness recalls the endings of other Iranian films including some of Kiarostami's, perhaps especially *And Life Goes On*. The film also employs the sort of elisions and ambiguities associated with the director's poetic method. Perhaps the most important resemble those at the center of *Certified Copy*: Rather than asking whether the two main characters are strangers or a long-married couple, here we're left to wonder if Mr. Watanabe and Akiko become lovers or have a platonic relationship that's more like grandfather and granddaughter. Compared to the intricacies and formal bifurcation of *Certified Copy*, though, the newer film appears far more straightforward, as well as lacking obvious cinematic references. Certainly Kiarostami admired both Ozu and Kurosawa, and Mr. Watanabe's surname may be a nod to the protagonist of the latter director's *Ikiru (To Live)*—a very Kiarostamian title—but otherwise the film seems content with avoiding the kinds of tantalizing complexities and resonances of previous Kiarostami films.

What is *Like Someone in Love* about, then? Most reviewers, judging the film by its narrative surface, have seemed inclined to see it as concerning loneliness, alienation and the difficulty of forming genuine relationships amid the exigencies and challenges of contemporary life—a thematic complex that might almost be considered the modern art film's default position. Kiarostami, though, indicated that the film's meaning for him lay elsewhere. In the U.S. DVD's making-of feature, he says, "I don't deny that it's autobiographical. I admit it." He later adds, "In my opinion, an autobiographical work has great merit for a simple reason. At the very least, it represents a real person. An individual."

There has always been an autobiographical element in Kiarostami's work, though its expression varies in different contexts. *And Life Goes On* is the film that most closely matches the standard definition of autobiography since it dramatizes actual events in Kiarostami's life. The earlier *The Traveler* and *The Report*, on the other hand, might be described as emotional autobiographies or self-portraits: Kiarostami very self-critically excavates his own character in the stories of, respectively, a headstrong, duplicitous provincial boy and a vain, dishonest young bureaucrat/husband. *Where Is the Friend's House?* may offer the least clearly autobiographical dimension of any Kiarostami feature centered on males, though its central boy may reflect some of the director's own generosity, fellow-feeling and willingness to explore unknown territory. In *Close-Up* Kiarostami himself appears, yet it may be argued that the self-portrait here is bifurcated if it includes his partial identification with the hapless cine-obsessive Hossein Sabzian. A similar bifurcation also may operate in *Through the Olives Trees* to the extent that Kiarostami identifies both with the director and the lovelorn film extra.

Taste of Cherry is the film where he returns to the two pre-revolutionary features' type of emotional autobiography, a mode that continues in the subsequent *The Wind Will Carry Us*: The former film's portrait of a suicidal middle-class man and the latter's account of a news filmmaker's existential frustrations seem to reflect personal malaises clearly confronted and pointing toward the confessional bent of the two final, foreign-set features. It's worth noting that the earlier films' struggles are essentially matters of the head while those of the later films belong to the heart. And in both *Certified Copy* and *Like Someone in Love*, a kind of bifurcation returns: While there are two versions of James Miller (husband and stranger) in the first film, we must consider the extent to which Kiarostami may identify with both Mr. Watanabe and Noriaki in the second.

Of Tadashi Okuno's understanding of Mr. Watanabe, Kiarostami said, "He, like me, had been young once. He had been jealous, suspicious, in love... now he's old." The identification of youthful love with jealousy and suspicion here of course fits not only the young Okuno, and Kiarostami, but also Noriaki: The raging, obsessive mechanic is the elderly scholar's younger self, as it were. The two mirror each other in a particular, negative way: Both are now involved in types of love that can be considered false. Each is *like* someone in love (the film's title is a 1944 song composed by Jimmy Van Heusen with lyrics by Johnny Burke) rather than the real thing. Noriaki's love is selfish and self-absorbed, the kind that some men experience when they are young and then, if they are lucky, outgrow. Could it be that Mr. Watanabe also experienced that sort of love when he was young but found the genuine, reciprocal variety in his marriage? We don't know enough to say for sure, but it is certainly possible. Now, in any case, he is engaged in another false, if essentially harmless, kind of love, forming a sentimental attachment to Akiko whether or not there's any sex involved. It may be innocent in some senses but it's also self-deluding enough that it virtually invites the fierce interruption that ends the film.

The importance of age in *Like Someone in Love* reflects back on the chronological arc of the autobiographical material in Kiarostami's films. If *Where Is the Friend's House?* recorded aspects of childhood, and *The Traveler* did the same for early adolescence and *The Report* for early adulthood, the main body of his post-revolutionary work—from *Close-Up* through *The Wind*

Will Carry Us—are the films of an adult artist recording at least portions of his emotional states as he moved through life. In the decade between *The Wind Will Carry Us* and *Certified Copy*, though, certain things changed. Kiarostami went from his late fifties to his late sixties. Age now is a factor that affects the story's contents and perspective. Though William Shimell, who played the male lead in *Certified Copy*, was 12 years younger than Kiarostami, he registers as verging on late middle age, and his declining his wife's invitation to rekindle their youthful romance inevitably implies questions of age. Is she no longer attractive to him, due to her age? Or is he incapable of responding to any romantic possibility, due to his?

Kiarostami said that the producers of *Like Someone in Love* urged him to cast an actor in his fifties or sixties in the role of Mr. Watanabe, but he was unable to find one he considered suitable until he saw Tadashi Okuno, a longtime movie extra in his early eighties. Whether or not that account is accurate, it seems fitting that after casting a man who was more than a decade younger than himself as his alter ego in his previous film, Kiarostami cast an actor more than a decade older in the final dramatic film he would make. The move allowed him to go from portraying late middle age to contemplating old age—and his own mortality.

The yin-yang relationship of life and death, a prominent Kiarostami theme, begins with *And Life Goes On*. Prompted by the personal impact on him of an earthquake's massive casualties, the theme at first addressed the fragility of life and its susceptibility to sudden interruption by its opposite, but it came to have deeply personal implications. *Taste of Cherry*, about a man whose attraction to suicide Kiarostami said reflected his own, reads like a proleptic, if obviously only temporary, warding off of the inevitable. Did Kiarostami intuit, at the time of *And Life Goes On* or later, that his own life would be cut short? The question may be impertinent, but it also stems naturally from his last two features. Though he was planning other films, both *Like Someone in Love* and *24 Frames* feel like summings-up, in different ways—the former personal/autobiographical, the latter artistic/philosophical. (Reportedly the working title of *Like Someone in Love* was "The End," a phrase that appears in the last frame of *24 Frames*.)

Poetry was the great model and inspiration for many of Kiarostami's aesthetic values and strategies, and as *The Wind Will Carry Us* indicates, he valued both great periods of Persian verse, classical and modern. While both are noteworthy for their strong personal voices and use of sensual imagery, Sufi-inspired classical poets like Rumi and Hafez (Omar Khayyam may be a significant outlier here) positioned their individual visions as descending from and pointing back toward the divine. Modern poets that influenced Kiarostami, on the other hand, perhaps especially Forough Farrokhzad, described living in modern circumstances as occasionally joyous due to being free from medieval strictures but often feeling like imprisonment due to being cut off from the transcendent. It's this modern tradition, in which the personal becomes confessional, that most informs *Like Someone in Love*.

What's significantly missing in the film, indeed, is any sign of the transcendent, hints of which can be sensed in many previous Kiarostami films, at least up through *The Wind Will Carry Us* (a title that itself signals a vision or hope of transcendence). Without that, what we get is a stark confession in the form of emotional autobiography: *I am an old man. Only fragments of my life remain and those are rapidly dwindling. I still crave the beauty and company of women, especially young ones who remind me of my own youth. Regardless of whether or not I can perform sexually, just being near them gives me comfort, even though I know that grasping at life's straws like this makes me look foolish, even pathetic. Yet this is all I have as I await the inevitable final blow, which may be as sudden as a brick crashing through a window.*

Foolish? Pathetic? Kiarostami said in regard to the film: "It's good to expose yourself. It's the best therapy. Shame yourself. Dishonor is the ultimate form of honor. Nowadays." So it is in the modern world, where many routes to the transcendent have been blocked or forgotten, but where there's still one possible road to a kind of immortality—via art as frank, clear-eyed and masterful as *Like Someone in Love*.

24 Frames

Versions of this piece were published November–December 2017 in Film Comment *and February 1, 2018,* on RogerEbert.com

24 FRAMES WAS NOT MEANT to be Abbas Kiarostami's final feature film. Indeed, it was something of a side project (of which he had many), principally mounted over the last three years of his life, mostly at his home in Tehran but also in the hospital where he spent his final months. (During this time, he was also planning a new feature to be shot in China.)

Like other projects undertaken during the latter phases of his career, *24 Frames* paradoxically seems like an unexpected leap in a new direction yet also deeply connected to other aspects of his work—especially, in this case, his nature photography, to which the film pays cinematic tribute. His main collaborator on the project, Ali Kamali, supervised something that's surprising in a Kiarostami feature yet central to this one: its computer-generated imagery (CGI).

The film's starting point reportedly was Kiarostami's observation that photographs (as well as paintings) show us a split-second in time, leaving us to imagine the seconds and minutes on either side of it. In *24 Frames*, he takes 23 images derived from his photography, plus a Pieter Bruegel painting, and, via computer manipulation, "extends" each temporally to four and a half minutes. The result, a first for Kiarostami, is an animated feature film, one that interweaves reality-based photography with movement-oriented digital interpolations.

Watching *24 Frames*, what we see are still images turned into mini-movies (frames), each comprised of a single, mostly static composition in which various actions play out. Only two frames contain human figures, and none of these speak. Most segments are focused on the natural world and include such favorite subjects as birds, horses, trees, snowy landscapes and seascapes. (The most obvious antecedent here is *Five*, with its abundant natural imagery.) The allure of these moving images stems from their visual compositions (sometimes symmetrical, or semi-abstracted by sea or snow backgrounds) and the suggestion, even when humans aren't visible, that human presence and perspective shape what we see: In one scene, horses frolic in snow but the car window through which they're viewed (and photographed) is also shown.

Kiarostami worked on roughly 40 frames but always intended to have the final film consist of 24. At his death, 30 had been mostly completed. Six of these were based on paintings. When his son Ahmad Kiarostami was faced with the challenge of finishing the film during post-production that was executed in Canada, he elected to eliminate five of the paintings (by Van Gogh, Picasso and others), leaving only Bruegel's "The Hunters in the Snow," which opens the film. (While Ahmad has spoken of the difficulty of making creative decisions in his father's stead, and his fear that he might have gotten some wrong, his reasons for eliminating the paintings strike me as reasoned and understandable.) Other work completed by Ahmad included shortening some of the frames to fit the four-and-a-half-minute length; correcting various technical lapses and problems; and re-recording the film's sound.

That soundtrack is a source of fascination itself, and integral to the film's impact. It's a sensuous aural mix of effects and natural sounds (rain, wind, animal noises and movement) and occasional bits of (Western) music, one song sung by Maria Callas and another penned by Andrew Lloyd Webber. (Though it was re-recorded in post-production, the film's sound was Kiarostami's creation.)

As in many previous Kiarostami features, elements of *24 Frames* are playfully deceptive. Contrary to appearances, most of the frames are not based on a single image but incorporate elements of several, and not just still images: Some contain moving images pulled off the Internet. The latter help give the animated images a curiously dual aspect: Some show animal movements, for example, in ways that are clearly computer-created, while others, usually more natural-seeming, derive from motion photography. In some frames, snow or rain is inserted to cover technical problems. And the film's long list of end credits is a rich Kiarostamian gag: Only a small handful of people worked on the film (some of the end credits' names are jokes in Farsi).

Kiarostami often spoke of wanting to escape the tyranny of "story," yet each of these mini-movies contains a rudimentary narrative with a beginning, middle and end. While those focused on animals sometimes delight in simply following the creatures' movements, there's ultimately no escaping the Disney-like tendency to anthropomorphize, to ascribe human-like intentionality and motives to many such movements. The two most noticeable thematic threads in these little tales are love (mating rituals, grief over a partner's loss) and death (or the threat thereof).

Though the film surely belongs to the experimental phase of Kiarostami's career, and thus will find a natural home in museums, the pleasures of watching it are greater than a simple description can suggest and richly reward repeated viewings. Repetition-with-variations and a sly wit are hallmarks of many Kiarostami films, and these 24 mini-films abound with his visual acuity and dry authorial humor, all of it in very accessible form. While the full two-hour work might be too much for younger viewers, it's easy to imagine portions of it fascinating grade-school audiences.

That accessibility notwithstanding, the film might be called radical in two senses. In the sense of "returning to the root," the elemental simplicity of the 24 stories and the mini-film structure takes us back imaginatively to the beginnings of cinema, to "Workers Leaving the Factory" and other Lumière films, to the Edison shorts and Georges Méliès' earliest cine-magic acts: when narrative was being born rather than dominating cinema. And these Western referents are no doubt complemented by others from the East which may have had a more direct influence on Kiarostami, ranging from Persian miniatures to short poetic forms such as haikus to the example of Kurosawa's *Dreams*.

But *24 Frames* also takes us back to the beginnings of Kiarostami's own cinema and a portion of his career less known to his Western admirers than his post-revolutionary features. Beginning in 1970 Kiarostami directed a number of short films; some were intended as instructional films for school children, while others were, as he put it to me, "films about, but not necessarily for, children"—i.e., a chance to develop his own poetic film language in noncommercial short form. As much as *24 Frames* may have sprung most directly from his interest in photography, it, like these early shorts, also obliquely reflects his interest in illustration, graphic design and animation.

The other sense in which *24 Frames* is radical—the sense of "radical departure"—lies in its use of CGI. Not only is this new in Kiarostami's cinema, it's something that some of his admirers might have assumed was antithetical to his aesthetic. Godard's maxim that "cinema is the truth 24 times a second," after all, is often taken as a prescription of basic Bazinian realism, and much of Iranian cinema is seen, not incorrectly, as descending from that stance and the closely related outlook of the Italian neorealists. Nor is it wrong to think that such realism is at the basis of Kiarostami's cinema.

Yet, at least from the time of *Close-Up*, his most important and influential film, it's been clear that Kiarostami had his own maxim to add to Godard's: "We can only approach the truth through lies." That film's blurring of the line between documentary and fiction, and its elaborate trickery with sound and the staging of events that appear factual, signaled Kiarostami's willingness to violate literal reality in search of a higher, poetic truth. But even here, and through the other four features he made in the 1990s, the basic integrity of the photographic image remained intact.

Once he turned the corner into the new century and the final, experimental phase of his career, however, he left behind any devotion to celluloid. In fact, as he indicated in numerous interviews, he came to regard many of the givens of feature filmmaking—the expense, the large crews, the technological conventions—as so many drags on his creativity, ones he was eager to jettison. He also often said that he could just as easily operate in art forms other than cinema, and he seemed to prefer those that allowed him a meditative solitude, such as nature photography.

It could be that the various manipulations of the basic image practiced by many still photographers suggested to him the possibility of a form of cinema incorporating similar liberties, and CGI allowed him the means to accomplish it. One thing that must be noticed about *24 Frames*: Its artifices, its endless manipulations of the image, are not hidden. Kiarostami openly displays, even underscores, his visual trickery, even if the exact means used to execute it are not always obvious. In effect, the "lies" of this artwork are all on the surface, in plain view. So where, or what, is the truth they point toward?

In most Kiarostami stories, and in the ways they are articulated in space and time, there is a pattern of constraint and release, of dreaming of a goal and then making the effort to attain it, an effort that usually entails a struggle against various barriers or limits. In *24 Frames* any strictly realist aesthetic, any technological restrictions on the artist's creativity, are, like the idea that "nature" can be apprehended apart from human and technical intermediaries, just so many limits to be surpassed. Beyond them lies the artist's great subject and ultimate goal—his freedom to define and explore his own imagination.

Strangely enough, this leaves us in a very unexpected and consummately ironic place. Frame 24 shows a room with a computer monitor, on a table, playing a scene from a Hollywood movie, *The Best Years of Our Lives*. In the movie, a man and a woman kiss, then the letters "The End" appear. So Kiarostami's cinema reaches an end-point with its very first kiss, but one drawn from Hollywood and displayed on a computer? Is this a grand cosmic joke, another self-skewering confession of mortal limits and romantic frustrations à la *Like Someone in Love* or, just possibly, both at once?

Such questions will be of greatest interest to those who followed Kiarostami on his long artistic journey, especially the phases that brought him worldwide renown. In the final phase of his career, his audiences grew smaller as the work became more personal, handcrafted, idiosyncratic and, in some ways, amateurish in the most commendable sense of that term (though his experimental works place him in a category with various Western avant-gardists, they hardly establish him in its front ranks). In this sense, *24 Frames* is not a film for newcomers to begin their approach to Kiarostami's oeuvre. But for those who know the range and overall character of that work, which indeed places him in the front ranks of multi-faceted Iranian and world artists of the past century, this final film offers a fascinating and moving testament precisely for how it draws together, with characteristic wit and passion, so many of his interests and influences—from painting, graphics and photography to poetry, digital technology and, not least of all, cinema.

4.
IRANIAN FILMMAKERS

Dariush Mehrjui:
Revealing an Iran Where the Chadors Are Most Chic
First published November 8, 1998, in the New York Times

IN THE SWEEPSTAKES FOR THE title Most Interesting and Accomplished Filmmaker the United States Has Never Heard Of, Dariush Mehrjui has certain obvious advantages. While still in his twenties, the Iranian director made *The Cow* (1969), a film so powerful that it not only was credited with launching Iran's modern cinema but also, a decade later, made a fan of the Ayatollah Khomeini and thus helped assure that country's cinema of having a post-revolutionary phase. Cosmopolitan and ever-controversial, Mehrjui has had films banned by the Shah's regime and the Islamic Republic, and almost surely is the only filmmaker reared a devout Muslim who counts the novelists J. D. Salinger and Saul Bellow as major influences on his work. He's even made a film of Salinger's *Franny and Zooey*, called *Pari*, set in contemporary Iran.[i]

While the extent of Mr. Mehrjui's career may come as news to American cinephiles, his importance is universally recognized in Iran. In 1997, when the respected Iranian journal *Film Monthly* polled its readers and critics, the results showed that the readers regarded Mehrjui's *Hamoon*, a dark satire of modern Iran, as the best Iranian film in history, ahead of such internationally acclaimed works as Abbas Kiarostami's *Through the Olive Trees* and Mohsen Makhmalbaf's *Gabbeh*. The critics, meanwhile, ranked Mehrjui higher in importance than Kiarostami and Makhmalbaf, and cited *Hamoon* as more significant than any of their films.

So why hasn't his renown traveled as well as others'? Back in 1971, *The Cow* won prizes at film festivals in Chicago and Venice, and even some of his more recent films have captured international awards. Yet in the last decade Mehrjui hasn't been favored by many of the top European film festivals, and the reasons evoke a paradox that goes to the heart of his work and its cultural resonances.

When asked, European festival programmers usually say that they bypass Mehrjui's films because his work is too "Western." That opinion provokes

---

i. See "My Journey with Iranian Cinema," p. 18, for an account of J. D. Salinger's reaction to the news of an Iranian film based on *Franny and Zooey*.

howls of disbelieving laughter in Iran. Iranians feel sure they know why the West doesn't "get" Mehrjui, and they'll gladly tell you: It's that his films are "too Iranian."

Both perceptions stem from the fact that, virtually alone among Iranian directors, Mehrjui deals regularly, knowingly and provocatively with Iran's middle and upper-middle classes. His characters drive BMWs, wear chadors that are distinctly chic, and argue (endlessly) over art, religion, divorce settlements and real-estate deals. At a time when "Iranian cinema" internationally connotes a certain distanced exoticism, views of rug-weaving nomads or impoverished children against crumbling buildings, Mehrjui's sleek, educated, post-modern Tehran is clearly anomalous.

But hardly forbidding. "You see his characters and feel like you could step into their living rooms and be perfectly comfortable," says Richard Peña, the programming director of the Film Society of Lincoln Center, which included Mehrjui films in its two previous Iranian film festivals.

Mehrjui, who lives with his wife, Farial, a Harvard-educated architect, and their two children in genteel northern Tehran, belongs to the world he describes. Born in 1939 to a middle-class family, he describes himself as being intensely interested in music, fiction, religion, philosophy and other subjects as a teenager. Vittorio De Sica's neorealist classic *Bicycle Thieves* was the film that sparked his interest in cinema. After learning English and investigating what was then a very small group of universities abroad that taught film, he selected the University of California at Los Angeles and enrolled in 1959.

The experience proved disillusioning. He was excited by the visions of Antonioni, Fellini and Godard, filmmakers never mentioned by his professors, who, Mehrjui recalled, "were the kind of people who had not been able to make it in Hollywood themselves but would bring the rotten atmosphere of Hollywood to the class and impose it on us." He switched his major to philosophy.

Returning to Iran in 1965, he took an offer to direct a James Bond spoof that set new standards for technical ambition in Iran but was a commercial disappointment. His artistic career began with his second feature.

The Cow remains a dazzling achievement, the most impressive of Mehrjui's pre-revolutionary features. Showing the influence of the neorealist works he admired, the film depicts a poor village thrown into turmoil by the loss of its one cow, whose owner develops a mad identification with the dead animal.

Spare, allusive, featuring starkly beautiful black-and-white photography and an extraordinary lead performance by Ezatollah Entezami, now Iran's most revered actor, *The Cow* had a catalytic effect on Iran's filmmakers and critics. But the Shah's government, which had funded it, bristled at the film's depiction of poverty and suppressed its public display.

Social themes remained at the center of his work through the 1970s. *Mr. Simpleton* (1971), a satire about a bumpkin seduced by Tehran's big-city ways, was his one box-office smash during this period, and the one film not to run afoul of official views. *Postman* (1973), a free adaptation of Georg Büchner's *Woyzeck*, won prizes at the Venice Film Festival but provoked the Shah's censors, while *The Cycle* (1975, released in 1978), a blistering drama about poor people forced to sell their blood, was slapped with a ban that lasted three years.

In the months before the 1979 Revolution, Mehrjui spent time in France filming the Ayatollah Khomeini, whom he supported, and other exiled anti-Shah leaders. Watching *The Cow* reportedly spurred Khomeini to comment approvingly on the cinema's social uses, a statement that proved valuable to progressive officials trying to revive the film industry under the Islamic Republic.

After a sojourn in France, where he made a meditative docudrama about the poet Rimbaud, Mr. Mehrjui returned to Iran and found his post-revolutionary voice in *The Tenants* (1987), an exuberant, brilliantly mounted comedy about a group of apartment dwellers at war with the slick realtor who wants to evict them. The Islamic Republic's first runaway hit, the film, like other Mehrjui works, still amazes with its stingingly direct satire of contemporary social discontents.

Hamoon (1990), which I, like Iranians, consider his best film, tells of a hapless 40-year-old intellectual undergoing a mental meltdown as his marriage unravels. The most autobiographical of his movies, the dark comedy-drama shows a third-world society invaded by Toshiba and Sony, where characters fixate on their connections to Kierkegaard and Salinger as well as to Islamic religious figures, and where the protagonist's artist wife shouts at her beleaguered lawyer, "Women have no rights in this country!"

That accusation leads directly to the four female-centered films Mehrjui made next. *The Lady* (1991), a brooding satire loosely based on Buñuel's *Viridiana*, about a rich woman whose house is invaded by poor people, has been banned since completion. *Sara* (1993) and *Pari* (1995) transfer well-known Western literary works—Ibsen's *A Doll's House* and Salinger's *Franny and Zooey*, respectively—to contemporary Iran with fascinating results. (Both films star the popular young actress Niki Karimi.) And *Leila* (1997), a melodrama about a young wife whose in-laws pressure her to allow her husband to take a second wife, has the distinction of being the first post-revolutionary Mehrjui film picked up for United States distribution, by First Run Features.

His most recent film is *The Pear Tree*. It depicts a writer recalling his adolescence in the idyllic Tehran of decades past. A lyrical, burnished memory film, it occasioned one of the director's slyest end runs around the censor: Unable to show the hair of the teen-age girl who dominates the story's flashbacks, he depicts the character getting her head shaved because of lice, then wearing a "wig" that looks suspiciously like the young actress' hair. The witty ruse typifies the ingenuity of a director who has managed to chronicle the fortunes of Iranians through three decades of shifting political winds.

Mohsen Makhmalbaf:
Gabbeh, Gabbeh, Hey
First published June 18–24, 1997, in New York Press

"SIMPLICITY, HUMANITY, POETRY" WERE the words Mohsen Makhmalbaf used last year in describing to me the qualities he saw as linking the nomad-woven carpets depicted in his film *Gabbeh* and the Iranian cinema itself, at its artistic best. To see how right he was is to realize, with an inevitable mix of astonishment and deep chagrin, how nearly those same qualities are lost to our own cinema.

Regarding *Gabbeh,* superlatives somehow miss the mark. "The most beautiful film I've ever seen," I've heard very different sorts of viewers call it, yet its essential strangeness to Western eyes must be acknowledged. The Iranian cinema has been compared to Italian neorealism for forging an aesthetic of urgent, impassioned humanism out of threadbare technical means and critical historical circumstances. But to say that *Gabbeh* honors the neorealist model while evoking things as disparate as *The Arabian Nights* and the ecstatic verse of Rumi, and also incorporates a political subtext of great immediacy and provocativeness, is inevitably to suggest a film and a filmmaker with little evident claim on the word "simplicity."

Makhmalbaf, admittedly, is an anomaly, but one whom anyone interested in the cinema's—and the world's—dubious future should attend to closely. Born into the slums of south Tehran in 1957, he was a 17-year-old Islamic fundamentalist when he wounded one of the Shah's policemen in an armed action; captured and imprisoned under torture for four years, he was released by Iran's gathering revolution, and became a hardline Muslim writer and broadcaster before discovering the cinema.

In the decade and a half since his first film, he has, as he put it to me, traversed 500 years—moving from a medieval certainty in the Koran to being a visionary humanist who counts among his leading influences Einstein's theory of relativity and Milan Kundera. Quite simply, the history of cinema knows few careers as startling as his—indeed, Makhmalbaf's life and work comprise a pilgrim's progress with few equals anywhere in art—yet it's no less amazing that his films have remained largely unknown in the U.S. until now.

The Museum of Modern Art is hosting the first major Makhmalbaf retrospective. The series is easily one of the two most important cinema events to reach New York this year; and in looking toward the Third World and the future, it provides a symmetrical Janus face to balance that of the European past represented by the spring's Fassbinder series.

It is also, of course, ideally situated to introduce the first Makhmalbaf film to gain U.S. theatrical distribution. Yet *Gabbeh*, the 13th of his 14 features, is not just another Makhmalbaf film more or less like the previous ones. In many ways it is the culmination of all the other works and a huge advance beyond them. Still, ironically, as much as it stands as the omega of his artistic odyssey, its sheer open-heartedness makes it an ideal, welcoming point at which to join that journey's dazzling trajectory.

Rapturous, revelatory, full of breathtaking images and a ceaseless sense of wonder, *Gabbeh* is a miracle in movie form, it seems to me. As basic as a folk song yet with the underlying reach and ambition of philosophy, it teases us by being so direct and obvious that children can enjoy it, while constantly insinuating that adults need to relearn the vernacular of film in order to grasp its elemental truths. The first time I saw it, I thought it easily the best film of the year. The second time, I began to be really awed.

Part of that reaction comes from the sly way the movie invites us to see anew. In every essential sense, *Gabbeh* offers a deliberate answer and antidote to Hollywood's culture of death, technology and narcosis. But how do we interpret its idiosyncratic language when we're so used to hearing another? In retrospect, I realize that some of my first impressions—that *Gabbeh* resembled the films of Paradjanov, or Dovzhenko, or the renowned documentary *Grass*—were conditioned reflexes: the mind's automatic inclination to seek familiarity in the unfamiliar. Seeing the film now, I am amazed at how it looks like nothing but itself, an utter original.

It is a dreamlike story set in the world of Iranian nomads who weave simple but very striking rugs called *gabbehs,* the rustic country cousins of the ornate manufactured carpets Iran is famous for. Just in this, Makhmalbaf announces the film's purposeful balance of simple fact and encompassing metaphor: Much as Persian carpets are the one point of physical contact most of us ever have with Iran, so the "magic carpet" is the first image our culture gives of the entire Middle East. *Gabbeh* itself is a fictional magic carpet ride of the first order, yet one based very much in the real: This duality defines the film's method and appeal throughout.

Its origins were in rejection, and a ruse. Iranian filmmakers must receive official permission to turn their ideas into movies, and Makhmalbaf, because of his controversiality and his combative stance toward the cultural hardliners, in recent years had submitted many proposals for feature films, some fairly innocuous, and had seen them all turned down. So he proposed to make a documentary about gabbeh-weaving nomads. You can imagine the officials shrugging to each other, "Let's get him out of town and our hair all at once—what can a film about rugs hurt, anyway?"

I gather he meant to make a fiction film all along; he went into *Gabbeh* with its story written.[ii] At the same time, he was entirely serious about registering the reality of the nomads, both physical and poetic, and he made their artistic practice the model of his own. He liked that they used only natural dyes, from the plants growing wherever they happened to be; he used only natural light to shoot the film, though sometimes he'd have to wait half a day to get just the right intensity. The film's astonishing language of colors (credit here is due the wizardly cinematographer Mahmoud Kalari) owe nothing to special effects, only to nature and inspiration.

Makhmalbaf also liked that the gabbehs' designs reflect the sights and experiences of the nomads' travels: a range of snow-capped mountains, for example, or a new foal. The images come not just from sight, but from the heart as well. The picture of a child, say, could be a child encountered on the road, or the child the weaver wishes to have: *Gabbeh* follows this dual logic, too.

It opens with a beautiful gabbeh floating down a stream, a simple, concrete, natural image that also is entirely ineffable. A wolf howls, a young nomad woman in blue smiles. Then we are by a spring where an old man and an old woman are arguing about who is going to wash their gabbeh. (Typical of Makhmalbaf's earthy humor is that this exalting film begins with recriminations and complaints over sore feet.) The old woman claims the task and addresses the rug as she washes, asking, "Why are you blue? Why are you silent?"

---

ii. See "Interview with Mahmoud Kalari," p. 241, for a somewhat different account of the film's origins.

Through a simple cut, the rug becomes the young woman in blue seen just before. Standing in the spring with the old woman, she speaks, marveling at the water used to wash her; she says her name is Gabbeh. As the scene continues, the gabbeh is sometimes the rug in the water, sometimes the girl in blue standing in the spring.

The old man asks who her father is. She says: "His name is warp. His name is warp and weft. There he is." We see a man leading a caravan. The girl says: "He is a nomad. We are Qashqais. We can't feel at home anywhere. Even if we did, my father would make us leave. I fell for a loved one, a rider, a strange voice, someone like an illusion, who was following our caravan like a shadow so to take me away with him."

This is only *Gabbeh*'s first few minutes (the scene runs on longer), but it gives an idea. There are no special effects, no lights; the film in many ways retains the aspect of a documentary, yet somehow magic irradiates every color, somehow a girl smiles because a wolf howls, somehow a blue rug turns into that very girl (and vice versa), somehow a rug's "warp and weft" becomes a cruel patriarch leading a caravan away from love. Somehow an old couple glimpses passion again as a gabbeh narrates its own tale of nomadic flights and an elusive lover, saying, in effect: These are the sorrows that art transformed into this beauty, this image of your dreams.

It is something that we even think we understand this—as if film logic were by now infinitely flexible, or we infinitely sophisticated—when of course we actually understand very little. We follow the scene, experience it as some kind of strangely intoxicating magical-realist Iranian fairytale; yet its real strangeness takes hold only when we begin to ponder its way of seeming "perfectly natural" while remaining radically anti-realist.

In every aesthetic move here, there is a poetic philosophy, but also political stances and a courage that may not be readily evident to foreign viewers. In what, for example, is for most viewers probably the film's most striking and memorable scene, Gabbeh's uncle comes into a nomadic tent school and gives the kids a genial lecture on the subject of color. Standing in front of a blackboard, he says that red is the red of poppies and waves his hand; cut to his hand over a field of poppies; cut back to the blackboard scene where his hand now holds a bouquet of red. And so on through blue, yellow, etc.

For us, this is simple delight and amazement (not to mention a happy reversal of an old Godardian trope). For an Iranian audience, though, Makhmalbaf's celebration of color and its natural origins has immediate and unmistakable political force at a time when strict fundamentalists have militated that women wear chadors only in black, navy blue, etc. In fact, while Iranian filmmakers have often resorted to rural settings in order to show women in clothes other than the grim hijab that prevails in cities, Makhmalbaf takes the practice to a pointed extreme here: With a climactic scene that "rhymes" a reprise of the color lesson noted above and a woman (played by Makhmalbaf!) giving birth, the film makes its hymn to color a direct and daring assertion of the natural rights of women.

Yet the film's most truly radical and visionary aspect may well lie in the way it multiplies, fractures and disperses the "rights" implicit in narration. Who tells the tale? It is, of all things, a story told by a carpet. Or by a young woman forever in flight from her patriarchal father, pursuing a lover who never seems to be more than a horse-borne speck atop a distant mountain. Or by an old couple gazing at each other across decades of love and annoyance.

If the presumption of a single, authoritative viewpoint is the first characteristic of conventional Western narrative, including that employed in virtually all our movies, *Gabbeh*, deriving as much from Persian and Eastern poetry as from political thought, implies something altogether different: a multiplicity of voices, a commonwealth of overlapping viewpoints and—not least—a viewer who will help create the story rather than being ruled by it. The liberating possibilities in all of this show that Makhmalbaf now imagines art as a mirror that doesn't simply reflect, entertain and illuminate, but one that can joyously transform what it beholds.

Part of their beguiling fascination is that Makhmalbaf's films never let you off the hook, never let you forget who you are in relation to their images, strategies, values, provocations. In this instance chances are good that you are not a present or former Islamic fundamentalist. For the sake of illustration, let us suppose that you are, instead, an American cinephile willing to ride for a while with a Persian visionary and see where he can take you. But where to start, and how to judge the progress of a journey that, by definition, is guaranteed to be unlike any other?

I pose the questions because I want you to see enough to judge the unusual totality represented by MoMA's Makhmalbaf retrospective, and not be derailed early on by the wrong angle of approach. Getting the whole picture depends, first of all, on figuring out how to situate yourself vis-à-vis a filmmaking enterprise that includes phases that seem staunchly alien to our idea of artistry.

The most comfortable and surely captivating approach, perhaps, would be the one that I experienced fortuitously: See the recent Makhmalbafs first, then follow their threads back through his early work. The magnificence of *Gabbeh*, the courageous humanism of *A Moment of Innocence*, the droll, allegorical reflexiveness of *Salaam Cinema*—the achievements of these three films completed in 1995–96 not only most accord with (and indeed, extend) our own notions of cinematic brilliance, they also provide a persuasive retrospective context for the rough, contentious striving evident in Makhmalbaf's first dozen years as a filmmaker (1982–93).

Looking back to the beginnings of his career, it's impossible not to be struck by the enormous creative distance he's traveled. *Este-aze* (aka *Fleeing from Evil to God*, 1984) is perhaps the closest thing there is to a movie made in the Middle Ages. Mounted with all the creaky, sententious theatricality of an amateur religious pageant, it follows a boat-load of solemn, robed religious seekers to an island where the Devil—i.e., doubt—begins picking them off one by one. At once hootable and riveting (and weirdly cinematic for all its unapologetic archaisms), the film seems half aware that its dark, dogmatic parable can also be read as 1) a purely personal scream of rage at the conditions of existence and 2) an allegory of the unraveling of revolutionary solidarity and certainty.

While those thematic strands would wind throughout Makhmalbaf's films of the 1980s, in terms of style he was already proving an odd combination: primitive experimentalist, aggressive autodidact, quick-change chameleon. (He told me that during this early period he read 400 books about cinema.) Indeed, from *Este-aze* to *Boycott* (1985) he covers a distance roughly akin to that separating 1920s Cecil B. DeMille and 1970s Melvin Van Peebles. Viscerally reflecting Makhmalbaf's own years of prison torture, *Boycott*'s kinetic, queasy, zoom lens–powered prison drama is another tale of the damned leading the damned, yet its implicit recognition of political relativism (which includes a newly understanding attitude toward Iran's anti-Shah communists) led him to a phase where crumbling orthodoxies and simmering existential anguish together fueled an outburst of fervent, daring, no-holds-barred social criticism.

The films of this phase are the output of a fatalist, a disappointed revolutionary and an ideologue slouching toward artistry. In one sense, they are problematic works for Western viewers to encounter first because they lack, by drastic margins, the mollifying polish of our art films as well as the reassuring prescriptiveness of what pass for political films (Miramax and PBS would not like them, in other words; Kafka and Buñuel would). In another sense, though, they introduce Makhmalbaf at his most characteristic: brash, unflinching, ferociously engaged with the Iranian soul's deepest turnings. All are as eye grabbing as recent wounds ripped open. Passionately, purposefully grotesque, *The Peddler* (1987) weaves three short stories—about poor people with deformed children, a mother-dominated young man and a petty criminal doomed by his vicious milieu—into a nightmarish tapestry of powerlessness and desperation. *The Cyclist* (1989), about a man trying to make money in a carny sideshow of ceaseless bike-riding, gives the social jeremiad added psychological pungency as well as a new, blistering economic slant. And in Makhmalbaf's first depiction of middle-class life, *Marriage of the Blessed* (1989), the tale of a professional couple torn asunder by the psychological aftershocks of the Iran-Iraq War becomes a powerful metaphor for a divided, traumatized, ideologically exhausted society.

These films, which greatly increased Makhmalbaf's fame in Iran and drew the attention of international festivals, all still bore the raw, frenetic style of his early period, with its reliance on wide-angle lenses, rapid cutting and overheated acting. They also were all presumed to be the critiques of an insider, a devout fundamentalist tasking his own. Both things changed when Makhmalbaf returned to filmmaking following a reflective respite.

Time of Love (1990), with its cool colors and muted lyricism, is the first of his films that looks like a Western art film. Shot in Istanbul (on the very geographic meeting point of Asia and Europe), it gives three, *Rashomon*-like views of a doomed love triangle, yet the tale's inherent fatalism is offset by an air of heady, intoxicating sensuality. Makhmalbaf sees the film as beginning a new phase where his attention, still seeking the sources of Iran's ills, shifted from society to culture; in various senses it is clearly a departure. Immediately banned, it inaugurated a period where his films would have recurrent troubles with the government (five have now been banned, in some cases temporarily) and where Makhmalbaf increasingly drew down the wrath of his former fundamentalist brethren, who came to see him as a philosophical turncoat.

This was also the period in which he reached the peak of celebrity recorded in *Close-Up*, Abbas Kiarostami's extraordinary meta-documentary about a young man arrested for impersonating Makhmalbaf, his hero. I'm already on record as calling this the most important film of the 1990s to date, a *Citizen Kane* for the meeting of fiction and documentary, and Third World cinema with the West.

With culture the general subject of his investigations, Makhmalbaf honed in on a specific aspect that would predominate in his next few features: cinema. Perhaps oddly for a filmmaker whose mission is so serious, he injected the antic abandon of screwball comedy into two dizzily reflexive films. *Once Upon a Time, Cinema* (1992) constructs a story of hapless artistic effort around an array of film clips from the entire history of Iranian cinema, beginning with the Qajar shah's importation of Iran's first movie camera, in 1900. And *The Actor* (1993) casts roly-poly real-life movie star Akbar Abdi as a star whose fame contributes to his marriage's upheavals; while Makhmalbaf reportedly regards this riotous if uneven film as his least successful of recent years, its warmly affectionate depiction of marriage also feels unusually personal. (*The Actor* is dedicated to Makhmalbaf's wife, who died in an accident around this time; Houshang Golmakani's *Stardust Stricken*, a fascinating documentary portrait of Makhmalbaf, incorporates home-video footage of the distraught filmmaker quoting Tarkovsky at his wife's wake.)

Next came an enormous leap. In *Gabbeh* and the two films that span it Makhmalbaf reaches a level of cinematic intelligence and bravado that leaves him few equals (in the world, not just Iran) apart from Kiarostami. *Salaam Cinema* (1995) and *A Moment of Innocence* (1996) both brilliantly interweave documentary and drama, hilarity and utter seriousness, the political and the personal, issues deeply Iranian and ultimately universal. Both show the filmmaker's former fundamentalist zeal now thoroughly transmuted into a profound and profoundly generous humanism, and both, incidentally, "star" Makhmalbaf.

Salaam Cinema started out when Makhmalbaf announced in the press an open casting call for a film honoring the centenary of moviemaking (said film was, in fact, *A Moment of Innocence* in embryo). More than 5,000 applicants descended on the audition hall and a riot ensued. *Salaam Cinema* begins with that riot, then shifts inside the hall where Makhmalbaf, sitting behind a desk, auditions scores of ordinary Iranians who are all obsessed with the movies and their chances of being a star.

At first the film sees the auditioners as benignly deluded and more than a bit ridiculous; then, gradually, it changes perspective until we see, from their standpoint, the rather cruel power being exercised over them by the director (Makhmalbaf is playing the symbolic heavy here, not his real self) and the medium itself. Like *Gabbeh*, *Salaam Cinema* is a mesmerizing marvel that grows richer and more impressive with repeated viewings. I can think of no other allegory of cinema that's so exacting in evoking the medium's complex meshing of personal identification and social controls; and among political allegories, perhaps only *A Face in the Crowd* so accurately renders the popular appeal of authoritarianism.

Salaam Cinema was a huge hit in Iran, but it was disliked by the government and attacked by fundamentalists. *A Moment of Innocence* so far has not been allowed a theatrical run on home turf, and no wonder: In making an extraordinary statement against violence in life and the movies, it implicitly draws into question that holy of holies, the Iranian Revolution.

In an interview last November in Italy, Makhmalbaf told me that he now sees his work as breaking down into four periods, the first three being the didactic films of the early 1980s, the social-criticism films of the late 1980s, and the culture/cinema films that extend from *A Time for Love* through *A Moment of Innocence*.

Gabbeh, though completed before the latter film, he regards as the first and so far the only film of a new phase. He said, "In the fourth phase of my work I'm looking to pay tribute, to adore, to admire seven things: life... humanity... love... friendship... joy and happiness... hope... and contentment, being satisfied, fulfilled. Because all these things are disappearing from lives in Iran. And not just Iran: I can see them disappearing from the lives of everyone around the world."

Mohsen Makhmalbaf:
Film in the Mirror: *A Moment of Innocence*
First published November 10, 1999, in New York Press

THE 1990S APPROACHES ITS END facing no shortage of uncomfortable ironies at the juncture where history and cinema converge. The day I write this, CNN is running footage showing Iranians massed and burning American flags in the streets of Tehran. The occasion is the 20th anniversary of the takeover of the U.S. Embassy by student militants during the Iranian Revolution, but the image is the same one American television has purveyed for a generation, an image whose chief effect is to disguise, deny or disparage any realities other than its own slightly hysterical oversimplification.

Meanwhile, Iranian cinema has become semi-big among the ever-fewer American cinephiles who still devote serious attention to subtitled films, yet this, too, has entailed simplifications. The greatest reduces an extraordinarily complex artistic and cultural phenomenon to a rudimentary impression based on a handful of films of fairly recent vintage. That's understandable, perhaps, and forgivable until you encounter a review like one I saw a few months back in the *New York Post*, in which the critic spewed erroneous generalities about Iranian films in a breezy "as everyone knows" tone that only made his comprehensive ignorance that much more comical.

The fact is, Iran has had the world's most vital and important national cinema of the 1990s, and has been essentially unrivaled in that since the three corners of China began their slow decline circa mid-decade. Yet several factors have combined to distort the West's understanding of this unlikely renaissance. First, Western prejudices and suspicions regarding Iran and Islam helped keep Iran's post-revolutionary films largely off the world's radar until the mid-1990s, nearly a decade after that renaissance began. The result was that non-Iranians began seeing new films without any knowledge of their artistic context or predecessors; most U.S. critics still evince scant familiarity with the Iranian cinema's complex, amazing progress from 1985–95.

Second, the films the West did see usually arrived via the highly politicized and self-serving agency of international festivals like Cannes, where the desire to create and maintain "star" auteurs—especially one: Kiarostami—

overrides any impetus to present a general and balanced picture of Iran's most significant filmmaking. Third, American distributors gave audiences the chance to encounter Iranian cinema only in a way that was belated, haphazard and inevitably skewed. In part, this was due to the vagaries and difficulties of marketing foreign films in the U.S., but it has left the often-erroneous impression that the really important Iranian films are the ones that somehow make it onto our screens.

There's another obstacle that deserves mention too. Even the most sophisticated, internationally attuned filmgoers tend to expect movies to be obvious or transparent in how they present themselves; the basic grammar of filmmaking, after all, was elaborated some time ago. Yet the Iranian cinema's strongest claim on greatness, it seems to me, lies in the sense that it uses filmic vernacular in ways that are genuinely its own—ways, however, that are also subtle enough to require more attentive, thoughtful and idiomatic viewing than we're now generally accustomed to giving films.

All of this has a bearing on the belated U.S. launch of one of the greatest Iranian films, Mohsen Makhmalbaf's *A Moment of Innocence* (1996). A political and personal statement of extraordinary force and resonance, the film—Iranian title: *The Bread and the Vase*—has its roots in an incident from the filmmaker's youth. Born and reared in Tehran's poor southern district, Makhmalbaf as a teenage Islamic fundamentalist helped form a militant anti-Shah group. In 1974, when he was 17, he attacked a police station and stabbed a young policeman. Shot and wounded in the incident, he was captured and imprisoned under torture for the next four and a half years, until his release by the revolution. (He subsequently became a polemical writer and broadcaster, and turned to filmmaking in the early 1980s.)

A Moment of Innocence is, if you will, a radical reconsideration of the filmmaker's own past and, with it, Iran's. For a project founded on such painful memories and volatile political revisionism, though, the film's most immediately striking aspect is its tone of bemused comic lyricism. It begins with the policeman that Makhmalbaf stabbed years before (Mirhadi Tayebi) arriving in snowy Tehran looking for work—in films. Finding his way to the director's house, he encounters six-year-old Hanna Makhmalbaf, who immediately deduces his purpose; the only people who come to the door that she doesn't know, she says, are would-be actors.

Makhmalbaf has a role for the visitor, it turns out, though not the one he envisioned. The director is planning to recreate for a film the incident when he stabbed the policeman, and he proposes that each of them separately choose and prepare a young actor to play himself in 1974. To play the "young Makhmalbaf" (as he's identified), Makhmalbaf chooses an intense young man (Ali Bakhshi) who says, quite seriously, that he wants "to save mankind"—as Makhmalbaf himself wanted to do at 17. For *his* younger self, the policeman at first selects a handsome, camera-friendly young Tehrani, until Makhmalbaf (acting offscreen through an assistant) imposes another young man (Ammar Tafti), who's much shorter than the policeman but has a provincial accent like his.

In mood halfway between a documentary and a dream, *Moment* seems to glide across the glistening snowscapes of Tehran, through its streets, alleyways and bazaars (the film is gorgeously shot by the great cinematographer Mahmoud Kalari). Makhmalbaf and his former enemy throughout the film remain apart, training and conversing with their "younger selves," although as it turns out, all four are effectively connected by someone else—a girl.

The policeman remembers 1974 this way: For a month before he was stabbed, a girl would approach him every day at his guard's post and ask the time or some other innocuous question. Later he would hate Makhmalbaf for depriving him of the one girl who, he felt sure, loved him. On the day of the attack he brought with him a flower in a vase to give to her, as a way of declaring his love. But instead, stabbed by a young man carrying a loaf of bread that hid a knife, he reached for his gun rather than the vase, and shot the young Makhmalbaf. The policeman has recovered physically but never suspected the truth: The girl he loved was Makhmalbaf's cousin, acting as his decoy.

With the young Makhmalbaf in tow, the director goes to his cousin's to ask if her daughter can play her younger self, but she's now a middle-class householder and wants no part of his film. (We never see her or her daughter, incidentally; the film's use of offscreen characters anticipates the central device in Kiarostami's new *The Wind Will Carry Us*.) Before Makhmalbaf and his younger self go off to enlist the young Makhmalbaf's cousin (Marjam Mohamadamini) to play the girl, he muses that his cousin *used* to want to save mankind—before the revolution, and her own rise in social status.

The provocative implication in that jibe is part of a subtle pattern, one that sometimes tends toward exquisite drollery. When the policeman and his younger self go to get a Shah's-era police uniform made for the young man, the tailor they visit is initially shocked at such a heretical request. But not only does he instantly relent when he's told it's for a film, he also starts chattering away about his own favorite stars and films: e.g., Kirk Douglas in *Spartacus* and *The Vikings*, John Wayne as Genghis Khan in *The Conqueror*. (Just as these vintage references accurately reflect the fondness with which older Iranians recall Hollywood movies of the 1940s and 1950s, they additionally suggest how many epochs in Iran's long history have been brought to cinematic life by American movies.)

As the film approaches its climax, it returns to the scene of the crime(s). Three onscreen actors playing three 1974 characters (the young Makhmalbaf, the young policeman and the girl), who in turn imply three offscreen people (the present-day versions of the same trio), are choreographed in an imaginary "dance of fate" in which fate and history are abruptly, stunningly, reversed. Gun, vase, knife, bread: These implements trade places, as it were, overthrowing violence in the name of tenderness. I will not describe the film's final freeze-frame except to say that it's easily one of the cinema's most breathtaking statements of pacifism.

Nor is that all it is. One of the challenges of discussing Iranian films is that many of the best of them have a surface simplicity and accessibility that are ultimately deceptive. *A Moment of Innocence* is a good example of that. It has what seems to be a completely transparent purpose and method; even its putting filmmaking itself within the frame and story will be familiar to those who've seen other Iranian films do the same. Yet the movie, I think, is far more complex and multivalent than it at first appears.

Realizing that no doubt requires seeing it more than once or twice, and reflecting on the extent to which our ways of reading films depend on standard Western modes of understanding fiction and drama. To be sure, *A Moment of Innocence* is made in full awareness of those modes, even the most modernistic; its echoes of Pirandello, Ionesco, Nabokov, Borges, et al., are hardly accidental. But beneath these understandings are others that underscore the predominance in Iranian art of other influences and aims, especially philosophical argument and poetic allusiveness and symbolism.

One small example: The young policeman places his vase-with-flower in a beam of sunlight. When he comes looking for it later and wonders to a passerby that he can't find it in the beam, the man replies, in effect: Look, dummy, the sun has surely shifted. This incident's transparent meaning is a sight gag worthy of Chaplin. But it can be plumbed for at least three other levels of meaning. 1) Its image is a metaphor that's been famously used by Jalaluddin Rumi and other Persian mystics (the single beam is the individual's portion of God's pervasive light; here we also get a sample of the large Neoplatonic element in Iranian tradition). 2) Further, Makhmalbaf gives that same metaphor a provocative political spin, since it is unmistakably meant to read as a statement that times have changed since the Revolution. 3) In the broadest sense, the image also refers back to what has been a dominant theme in Makhmalbaf's work since about 1990, one that has vast political and, for him, artistic and personal implications: the relativity of truth.

To best understand this film's aims, one needs to examine it in the context of his career, especially the two films preceding it. Its genesis, though, goes back farther than that. According to what Makhmalbaf told me in 1997, the policeman he stabbed in 1974 approached him looking for work as an actor when he was directing *The Cyclist* (1988); he got the idea for *A Moment of Innocence* as a result of that meeting, but didn't act on it for several years.

In September of 1994, as the first stage in making what was intended as *A Moment of Innocence*, he put an open casting call in a Tehran newspaper, intending to use some of those who turned up in the casting scenes of the film's first 10 minutes. Instead, thousands of people showed up, producing a near riot. Makhmalbaf turned this incident and the subsequent casting sessions into the feature *Salaam Cinema* (1995), which combines a hilarious, documentary look at Iranian cinemania with a subtle political allegory deriding the "tyranny" of the film director. The following spring he went to the highlands of central Iran to make *Gabbeh* (1996). He subsequently shot and completed *A Moment of Innocence* over a three-month period in the winter of 1995–96.

This sequence is important, I think, because *Salaam Cinema*, *Gabbeh* and *A Moment of Innocence*—in addition to being, in my opinion, Makhmalbaf's supreme achievements to date—are so unified in their essential concerns as to comprise a de facto trilogy equal to the Kiarostami films critics have dubbed the "Koker Trilogy" (*Where Is the Friend's House?*, *And Life Goes On*, *Through the Olive Trees*). As Makhmalbaf put it to me in 1996, the "essence" of his work in the period that climaxes with these films is "that quote from Rumi that truth is this mirror in the hand of God [that's been] broken into pieces and everyone picks up one piece and says I've got the whole truth, but the whole truth is the mirror."

However: The mirror, in Makhmalbaf's and Iranian films generally, is the great metaphor for cinema itself. Therefore: Any film or filmmaker who pretends to have the whole truth is making the same mistake that repressive ideologues and religious orthodoxies make. Thus *Salaam*, *Gabbeh* and *Moment* share an elaborate program that aims to inscribe multiple viewpoints within each film while also questioning the truth and, above all, the *authority* of each viewpoint, especially that of the one nominally in control: the artist. Like all claims on power, these films imply, the auteur's must be rigorously examined and, if need be, overthrown.

The self-reflexive motif in postrevolutionary Iranian film begins with Kiarostami's *Close-Up* (1990), which, not coincidentally, also inaugurates the theme of questioning the director's public power (the film concerns the trial of a poor man who was arrested for impersonating Makhmalbaf). Makhmalbaf's films, though, bring this idea to its most dazzling and forceful realization. The magisterial *Gabbeh* disperses authorial authority by fragmenting the narrator's perspective into numerous, ever-shifting sub perspectives. *Salaam Cinema* makes an allegorical drama out of its shifting view of the director, who moreover is effectively "doubled": We not only get the tyrannical "bad guy" Makhmalbaf onscreen but the implicit "good guy" Makhmalbaf behind the camera.

A Moment of Innocence likewise deals in doubles and multiple perspectives that ask us to question the relative truths it both presents and re-presents. But perhaps the film's subtlest level is the most personal, where the pattern noted above in *Salaam Cinema* is reversed: Here we get the good guy Makhmalbaf onscreen and the implicit bad guy offscreen. How so? The key thing to realize is that the policeman—whose point of view is subtly derided throughout—is played not by himself but by an actor. Makhmalbaf says he judged the real policeman an incompetent performer.

In Tehran in 1997, I brought up the real-life policeman to Makhmalbaf and—rather impertinently, I admit—asked him, "Weren't you stabbing him a second time in telling him he wasn't good enough to play himself?" He laughed uproariously at that, then turned serious, thought for a moment and said: "The violence that is in our culture is because of ideology and politics. I have ritually washed myself of politics and ideology with art. Right now I am a product of myself and my conditions, where when I was a 17-year-old boy I was a product of my conditions. This relative perspective of mine, and my being kind and human, is not a product of my culture. It is a product of the art that I have mastered."

Samira Makhmalbaf:
The Apple
First published February 17, 1999, in New York Press

WHEN I WAS LIVING IN TEHRAN during the summer of 1997, a friend called one day with the news that Mohsen Makhmalbaf had just decided to make a film and that the shooting would begin almost immediately. I had spent a lot of time with Makhmalbaf in the previous weeks, sometimes seeing or talking by phone with him almost daily, and this news came as a surprise. I knew he was due to go to Tajikistan soon to begin work on a feature he'd been planning for some time. This new film was something out of the blue. It had started, I was told, just a couple of days before, when Makhmalbaf's 17-year-old daughter Samira saw a news report about twin girls, aged 11 or 12, who had been imprisoned by their parents since birth. The idea for the movie was to have the actual family play themselves, and to shoot it quickly, documentary-style. Tehrani pundits soon had their own label for the film: "the Iranian Kaspar Hauser." Makhmalbaf himself called it something else: "Samira's film."

In the U.S., we read about indie filmmakers who plan and gather their resources for years before getting their films before the camera. For better or worse, the richest and the most impecunious American filmmakers have virtually no experience of the kind of cinematic spontaneity that, paradoxically enough, exists in Iran. Samira Makhmalbaf, as I recall, saw that news item on a Tuesday or Wednesday. The film started shooting, in 35mm, on Sunday of the same week, and wrapped 11 days later. The resulting feature, *The Apple*, has been a hit at international film festivals and opens here this week having done solid theatrical business in France, Iran and other countries.

The alacrity with which *The Apple* was made, of course, isn't available to most Iranian filmmakers. Makhmalbaf, who now has the backing of the French art film company mk2, had film stock, a 35mm camera and funding at the ready. Still, it's the rare feature of any sort that goes from brainstorm to wrap in two weeks flat, and that speed and the peculiar freedom it entails surely have a lot to do with the film's unusual appeal, its striking mix of poetic lilt and documentary grit. The question is, whose skill is it at work here?

The film credits Samira Makhmalbaf as director, Mohsen Makhmalbaf as screenwriter and editor. When it debuted at last February's Fajr Film Festival in Iran, the directorial credit drew lots of skeptical and derisory remarks from critics and film buffs who surmised that Mohsen Makhmalbaf had directed the film, or largely so, but gave his daughter the credit in order to launch her career as a filmmaker. When I was with Makhmalbaf one night around the time of Fajr, I suggested that jointly crediting himself and Samira as co-directors when the film went to the world outside Iran was perhaps the best idea, both because I thought this was accurate (which I didn't say) and because it would keep viewers and the press from focusing on the credit at the expense of the film (which I did say).

Though he simply pondered this, and didn't reply, "but the film was directed by Samira," the point was soon moot. The controversy over its directorial credit didn't follow *The Apple* outside Iran; thus Samira, at 18, became the youngest director ever to have a film play in a main section of the Cannes Film Festival. And once the movie returned to Iran bedecked in foreign acclaim, the doubts expressed in February quickly dissipated. Iranians accepted the version given in countless interviews, i.e., that the film was Samira's project and she directed it entirely, while Mohsen, who was absent from the set during shooting, each night helped her sketch out dramatic ideas for the next day's work. The "actors," all non-professionals playing themselves, improvised their dialogue.

The reasons there was skepticism initially over the Makhmalbafs' account of who-did-what have a lot to do with Mohsen Makhmalbaf. In Iran, he has occupied a singular position since emerging as a hero of the Revolution-cum-artist and public figure. There's no American filmmaker remotely comparable. In an Iranian documentary about him he says he identifies at different times with Jesus Christ, Che Guevara and Einstein. Unlike any other filmmaker, he's a fervently admired folk hero among ordinary Iranians, yet intellectuals and other artists, who've seen him go through countless chameleon-like changes in his evolution from Islamic fundamentalist to international art-film hero, regard him with a combination of wary fascination and frank mistrust. There's one good reason to believe him regarding Samira and *The Apple*, though: Samira herself.

When I first met her, at an Italian film festival in 1996, she was an intense but very shy 16-year-old who said she wanted to be a film director. The next summer in Tehran, I saw a couple of shorts she had made on video, which were raw but promising: about what you'd expect from a smart but inexperienced teenager. It was hard to credit the huge, sudden leap in accomplishment that *The Apple* seemed to represent, but only until I encountered Samira at Cannes last May, when she seemed indeed to have undergone a rapid metamorphosis. She had learned English for her press tour, and was giving interviews with extraordinary fluency and poise. Then and since, I've been tremendously impressed by her as a person, and aware of how difficult, hard-won and important such personal transformations are for an Iranian woman, famous father or no.

Difficult transformations, especially those occurring at the father-daughter level, are at the heart of *The Apple* too. The film opens with a view of the petition that neighbors of the central family sent to the municipal government, causing the two young girls to be released from the familial captivity where they'd been kept from birth. Soon it emerges that the situation, though extreme, was not quite as brutal as it first appeared. The parents are poor Turks living in south Tehran. The mother, whose face is always completely shrouded in her chador, speaks no Persian and is blind. She can't watch the children on her own, the father says, explaining why he found it necessary to lock them up whenever he went out.

The movie's action starts at the welfare agency where the girls, Zahra and Massoumeh, have been taken. They've had their hair washed and cut short and been given fresh, modern clothes. After some deliberation, the authorities have decided to let the parents take the girls home, on the condition that they no longer be locked up. The parents, though they agree to the conditions imposed on them, are shamed and angry. The mother curses constantly under her breath, calling the welfare officer "you bitch." The father feels like he's been wronged by his neighbors, handled imperiously by the authorities and tarred by the media. The news reports said the girls had been shackled, he complains, and that's simply not true.

This material is certainly compelling in itself, but what makes the film so striking is the way it provides a structure to contain the material. This structure, which involves having the people play themselves in a "directed" situation, isn't fictional in the usual sense, but it is dramatic: The people create the story by expressing what they really feel. The ultimate effect, though, depends on extremes that no "normal" situation could provide. For example, while Zahra and Massoumeh are entirely transparent to the camera (they seem mentally retarded, but grow noticeably in sureness and awareness during the course of the film), the father adds to the impression that the reason Iranian directors have been so successful in using "nonactors" is that, on some level, all Iranians are actors: Rather than transparency, he presents us with a forceful performance.

The father has been thrust into the public arena willy-nilly, and in his mind, unfairly painted as a villain. Samira Makhmalbaf says she gained his trust, and he certainly had reason to give it: The film and his performance represent an unusual chance to restore his self-image with the media, the neighbors, and who knows, with himself as well, perhaps. Gruff but garrulous, he's astonishingly open, not only crying and singing and pouring out his heart on camera, but also in forthrightly opining that women are made for one thing: marriage. In a sense, your heart can't help but go out to both sides in this battle: the girls because they're so innocent and full of life and have been treated so unfairly, the father because he's done the wrong thing for reasons that he's heartbreakingly convinced are right.

In this case, hardcore fundamentalists (which the father is not) might agree with him, but the state doesn't. One of the film's strongest scenes arrives when a female welfare officer comes to the family's house and firmly, authoritatively, rebukes the father for having locked the girls inside again, as he'd promised not to do; she later locks him in, obliging him to attack the door's bars with a hacksaw. This woman is a wonderful (and wonderfully played) character whose presence offhandedly illustrates the greater social and official status women exercise in Iran compared to other Islamic countries. Her authority is bound to strike many Westerners as paradoxical: While we often equate Iran's government with moldy tradition and repression, its agent here is the instrument of modern openness and liberation from patriarchy's weighty hand.

One reason Iranian films have become so fascinating to Western viewers, I think, is the impression they give of a society where the modern and the medieval coexist in startling proximity. And yet, just when its medieval aspects make Iran seem so "other," we run into the realization that these are *our* Middle Ages, too, they're just closer to the surface in Iran: For the father, the notion that "a man's home is his castle" is only slightly more literal, and more freighted with specific sexual controls regarding women, than it is in the West.

One advantage of proximity to the medieval is a ready grasp of things like symbol and allegory, which the Iranians use with a potency nearly forgotten elsewhere. In *The Apple*, the Makhmalbafs not only discover a situation rich in allegorical associations, they highlight those with their some of their own. Apples, for example, are employed throughout for symbolic purposes, and the main connotation is sexual knowledge, à la Adam and Eve. Plainly, the father keeps his daughters locked up because he doesn't want their purity spoiled by the boys playing in the street, just beyond that barred gate. It's a simple idea, but as so often happens in Iranian films, you emerge astounded that such simple metaphors and images, given adroit handling, can resonate so powerfully.

Unsubtle? Perhaps. Yet its symbolic boldness gives *The Apple* one unquestioned distinction. No other Iranian film so directly identifies as the mainspring of patriarchal oppression (and the multiple religious controls related to it) the male fear of female sexuality.

While that's a profound and necessary perception, *The Apple*, like Majid Majidi's *Children of Heaven*, has the somewhat ambivalent advantage of arriving in U.S. theaters after nearly two decades of brilliant Iranian films that have largely gone unseen in the West. It thus risks being taken as more original than it is, by audiences who haven't encountered important predecessors such as Mohsen Makhmalbaf's *The Peddler* and Abbas Kiarostami's *Close-Up* and *Homework*. It's also a film that raises more questions than it can comfortably answer about the uses made of the two girls (they could not have understood what they were "agreeing" to in signing on as performers) and, finally, about its own metaphorical reach.

Mohsen Makhmalbaf was severely tortured for four years under the Shah's regime, but the central tragedy of his life came in the early 1990s, when his wife (who was also his creative partner and the mother of Samira and two younger kids) died in a freak fire at home. Since then, he has made raising his kids one of his chief projects, and he's pursued it with his customary single-mindedness. He's educated them at home, giving them intensive courses in, for example, the history of all the visual arts. Both girls grew up intending to become directors (the boy, wisely, elected cinematography rather than competition with Dad). In other words: He's made his home his castle, and made of "film directing" a haven for his daughters.

His great film *Salaam Cinema* recognizes the potential for both beneficence and despotism in such creative constructions. *The Apple* deliberately shies away from such recognitions—it nowhere asks us to see the parallels between the family in front of the camera and the one behind it—and in that, it's certainly less self-aware and sophisticated than many Mohsen Makhmalbaf films. Yet that edge of naiveté is what finally convinces me that this is indeed "Samira's film." And a brilliant beginning it is.

Bahman Ghobadi:
Crossing the Border: *A Time for Drunken Horses*
First published November 22, 2000, in the Independent Weekly

My friend David Meyer, the author of the film-noir study *A Girl and a Gun*, sent me an e-mail the other day that began:

"Saw *A Time for Drunken Horses* last night and found it, except for one or two moments, the most moving film I've seen in months. A friend asked me recently when the last time was that I stopped thinking as I watched a film. I could not remember, but this short-circuited the front brain and affected me profoundly. Like Dreiser, but also much like Dickens or *The 400 Blows*. And like the Iranian films I know, it featured astonishing use of naturally occurring color, minimal dialogue, clear visual storytelling and a commitment to the lives of the participants that borders on the saintly... it's still running through my head."

I quote that message not only to provide an opinion of Bahman Ghobadi's film other than that of yours truly, a notoriously biased Iranophile, but also because I think David's words offer a particularly concise yet eloquent summation of a reaction I've now heard many times to *A Time for Drunken Horses*, an Iranian production which dramatizes the lives of Kurdish children who inhabit a perilous region of smugglers along the Iran-Iraq border.

If you've been tuned into this column in recent months, the film may seem like a running theme by now. In September, I reported on its U.S. debut at the Telluride Film Festival, where it drew rapturous praise from filmmakers including Werner Herzog and proved so much the hands-down audience favorite that extra showings had to be scheduled. Later that month in Tehran I saw it awarded the critics' prize for best picture at Iran's equivalent of the Oscars. (This was followed by a further coup: A couple of weeks ago *A Time for Drunken Horses* was named Iran's submission to next spring's U.S. Oscars, a particular honor in a year when a number of strong Iranian films have captured awards at film festivals all over the world.)

For filmgoers who've heard of the current surge in Iranian cinema but have yet to experience it, *A Time for Drunken Horses* is easily one of the best places to start. That's not because it outdoes the intricate and extraordinarily sophisticated cinematic visions found in the movies of Mohsen Makhmalbaf or Abbas Kiarostami. Rather, it's because Ghobadi's film gives us Iranian cinema at its most pure and elemental, with virtues that are as invigorating as spring water.

Ghobadi is a 30-year-old Kurd who grew up near the border his film depicts during the Iran-Iraq War, a horrific, eight-year struggle that left a million dead and regions of both countries littered with bombs and landmines. Such is the landscape into which *A Time for Drunken Horses* plunges us. People in the impoverished area earn money by smuggling goods across the craggy mountains into the opposite country (an endeavor partly stimulated by the international sanctions against Iraq, of course). The perils they face are many: border patrols, bandits, the deadly mines that are sometimes just feet away from the main trail, and the winter snows. It's from the latter that the film gets its title: Smugglers dose the drinking water of their mules with liquor to numb them to the cold.

Ghobadi's tale focuses on siblings who are obliged to fend for themselves since their mother is dead and their father has disappeared on smuggling operations. Ayoub (Ayoub Ahmadi) and his sister Ameneh (Ameneh Ekhtiar-Dini) are able-bodied teens who take care of their brother Madi (Mehdi Ekhtiar-Dini), who's afflicted with dwarfism and other ailments that require constant pills and injections.

The film has a great opening. As Ameneh provides a simple, understated narration, we see the kids in the teeming bazaar of a town near their village. They are wrapping drinking glasses in paper to prevent breakage when they're hauled across the border: the kind of simple job kids can do to pick up some money. The place is chaotic, and every so often the chaos explodes when some man on a truck offers day work to the boys who are milling about. The jobs are so intensely sought that sometimes the clamor to get them provokes fistfights.

The way Ghobadi films this milieu establishes his artistic signature right away. We are tossed into the midst of all the tussling and hustling with very little to orient us either to the place or to the people we're meant to be following. Ghobadi often shoots from low angles, a kid's perspective, which increases our sense of grasping for visual landmarks. There's a documentary feel to the images, yet no documentary has quite the intense-yet-understated eloquence that shapes this dizzying, beautifully photographed sequence, which ends with the kids climbing aboard a truck that will take them out of the city, into the mountains.

The crucial dilemma that animates the story involves Madi. With his large, liquid eyes, he is a speechless teenager trapped in a child's shrunken, wasting body, and his siblings are given to understand that his prospects are bleaker still. Without the operation he needs, he will last only a few weeks. With the operation, he still will live only a matter of months.

For Ayoub and Ameneh, there is no decision: Madi must have the operation. But how to get the money when they have none? One possible solution that comes later in the story involves Ameneh marrying into an Iraqi family. A more immediate and enduring prospect, though, is for Ayoub to join the contraband-laden human and mule caravans that trek across the wintry mountains, into Iraq.

Immediately identifiable by the oversized cap-with-earflaps he always wears, Ayoub has a face that's a great mix of aggressive determination and youthful sensitivity. (One of *Drunken Horses'* marvels is the extraordinary freshness of the performances Ghobadi gets from a nonprofessional cast recruited in the film's actual locations.) The boy here is being pushed into manhood, and Ghobadi captures the moment with great feeling and faultless understatement. Ayoub neither complains nor boasts. He does what he has to do, learning about the smuggling life's many hazards as he goes.

One minor but telling aspect of the film is the way it portrays adults. None has a large part in the story, yet they form a fascinatingly variegated backdrop, from the helpful doctor to a bemused teacher to the much harder types Ayoub encounters along the trail. These characters feel so right, so authentic and believably shaded that it makes you realize that the characters we're accustomed to seeing on screens are invariably movie-tailored fabrications. There's no Ben Affleck or Will Smith or their like here. Ghobadi told me that some of the film's smugglers are the real thing, playing bit parts as a lark.

Granted, many previous Iranian films have used kid-centered stories and nonprofessional actors to equally stunning effect; the way *Drunken Horses* portrays its youngsters has a slight sheen of idealization, and there's more than a hint of old-fashioned melodrama to its premise. Even so, Ghobadi's film emerges as one of the year's best due to a striking combination of artistic assurance, moral vision and sheer conviction that belongs to it alone.

I first met Bahman Ghobadi three years ago at a party in Tehran. He was a shy, bearded, extremely polite young Kurd, apparently not long down from the mountains, yet Mohsen Makhmalbaf and others assured me he was one of Iran's most promising young filmmakers. This says a lot: Ghobadi subsequently worked as Kiarostami's assistant on *The Wind Will Carry Us*, which was shot in Kurdistan, and Kiarostami liked him so much that he offered him a script he'd written. The last time the master scripted a film that was directed by one of his assistants, the result was *The White Balloon*, which became the most successful Iranian film ever released. But Ghobadi politely declined the offer because, he said, he had a story to tell—his own people's story.

The Kurds, an ancient ethnic group, number 20 million and spread across an area that covers parts of Iran, Iraq, Turkey and Syria. They are mainly Sunni Muslims, as opposed to Iran's Shiite majority. Though recent history has been cruel to them, it seems there is little prospect of an independent Kurdistan. Their main hopes depend on the tolerance of their host countries and the understanding of the outside world, regarding which *A Time for Drunken Horses* has a lot to say about the superiority of art—remember art?—to any number of TV news clips or even good documentaries.

In Telluride, I watched Ghobadi speak to a group of high-school kids, including Navajos, who had just seen his film. He told about how his whole family had worked on the production (his mother's tasks included praying for the right weather), about how they hauled the cameras up the mountains by mule, and how he used the prize money he got at Cannes to build a school for his village.

One of these American kids suddenly said, "Mr. Ghobadi, you are such a wonderful person, I think I am going to cry." At that point, pretty much everyone in the room was misty-eyed, and I thought of the word my friend David later used: "saintly." When was the last time you heard that term applied to any young American filmmaker?

Jafar Panahi:
Persian Crack-Up: *Crimson Gold*
First published March 17, 2004, in the Independent Weekly

PONDERING *CRIMSON GOLD*, THE EXTRAORDINARY new film by Iranian master Jafar Panahi, prompted me to recall a moment in the recent Oscar telecast. Accepting her trophy for *Lost in Translation*, Sofia Coppola displayed a charming ingenuousness in thanking several of the filmmakers who had influenced her, including Michelangelo Antonioni. In one sense, the citation was inarguably appropriate, since Coppola's film portrays a latter-day version of the idle rich limned by the great Italian director in films such as *L'Avventura* and *Red Desert*. Yet, as I noted in my review of it, *Lost in Translation* ends up looking more like a vacuous, if beautifully crafted, sitcom than a serious artistic enterprise precisely because it lacks Antonioni's most salient virtue: a moral outlook that comprehends the largest social ramifications of wealth and privilege.

A similar tribute to this filmmaker's vision came in a revealing conversation between two film critics of different generations that appeared in the *New York Times* on February 22. The topic was Antonioni's *Blow-Up*, newly released on DVD. While the younger critic, the *New York Sun's* Nathan Lee, commented on the film's intellectual gamesmanship and enduring formal fascinations, his fifty-something counterpart, Stuart Klawans of *The Nation*, was struck by something he'd missed entirely when seeing the ultra-trendy movie as a teenager: "its social and political critique," the caustic view it offers, for example, of David Hemmings' cool photographer, who turns images of poor people into advertising fodder.

"*Blow-Up* is a bitter diatribe against the hip young characters who go reveling through the movie," avers Klawans, a hip, young wannabe back then who, today, says, "I was blind to the movie then. And watching it now really brought home to me a sense of the wasted possibilities of my own generation, of what we did not achieve because of certain attitudes and issues of temperament that are dealt with in this film... *Blow-Up* became more personal to me this time, in a very disturbing way."

Klawans' bracing auto-critique cuts in two directions, of course. While it takes himself and his generation (which is also mine) to task for not recognizing and building on the moral appraisal at the heart of Antonioni's film, it also implicitly asks where movies of comparable acuity can be found today. The unfortunate answer: In our part of the world, almost nowhere. Its intellectual side is lost in the moral mists of postmodernism, while its commercial side increasingly sacrifices sense to sensation, the West at present is more a culture of moral vacancy than of moral understanding, and its art reflects that at every turn. Billions of dollars are poured into cinema production and consumption annually, yet where is the movie—arty or mainstream, European or American—that probes the widening gap between the rich and the poor in any of the West's individual cultures, or between the West and "the rest"?

To see films that pose such questions in truly illuminating ways, you can look back to cinema of the 1950s, 1960s and 1970s, when art and social scrutiny were not such strangers to each other. Or you can look to the Iranian cinema, which, pretty much alone in the world, has a current reputation for linking artistic vision to social and moral vision.

Crimson Gold opens one morning in a Tehran jewelry store where a robbery is in progress. The camera, looking from inside the darkened showroom toward the front door, keeps a fixed gaze while moving slowly, steadily forward (a movement recalling the famous climactic tracking shot in Antonioni's *The Passenger*) as the store's owner grapples with the robber, a large man in a floppy coat and motorcycle helmet. Amid flailing and shouts, the thief's gun fires. He then moves toward the door and sees that people are closing in outside, trapping him in the store. He raises the gun to his temple, and as the film cuts to black, we hear a shot. What we've just witnessed, evidently, is a murder and a suicide. The film then flashes back to show us what led to the crime.

In praising Iranian cinema for its moral and political dimensions, I don't mean to suggest to the uninitiated that they're in for tidy, pre-packaged polemics in dramatic form. On the contrary, like other great Iranian films, *Crimson Gold*—scripted by the great Abbas Kiarostami for his erstwhile assistant, Panahi—has the carefully inflected, very human richness of a fiction by Tolstoy or Dostoyevsky. Having just seen the film a third time, I'm still marveling at how resonant are many of its smaller details: for example, the woman's purse we encounter in the second scene.

We soon learn that the robber was/is a heavyset guy named Hossein (Hossein Emadeddin) who has a younger, more chipper partner, Ali (Kamyar Sheissi). No one's definition of career criminals, these two work as pizza delivery men, a steady job that in present-day Tehran, alas, doesn't pay anywhere near a living wage; hence their sideline in snatching purses from their motorbikes. When we first see them together, they dump the sparse contents of one such catch onto a café table, suddenly giving us an image that, like an embryo, seems to predict the whole film.

The duo's trifling bounty consists of little more than a couple of tubes of makeup, some candy and a ring. The ring, it seems, has had to be altered because (as that candy suggests) the woman has grown fatter. There's something else in the bag, too: a receipt from a jewelry shop for a necklace costing 75 million rials (nearly $10,000). So there are women walking around Tehran whose very mundane purses one can easily snatch, yet who can afford necklaces worth more than the annual income of most Iranian families? Though Hossein's heavy eyebrows barely arch, he surely reads this bill as a staggering proof of the way things are.

He and Ali take the ring to the jewelry store indicated on the receipt, inventing a little story to explain their presence. They are simply curious, drawn to the sanctum of such wealth. The proprietor, the man Hossein will kill, sees them coming and blocks their entry, telling them to go to south Tehran—the city's low-rent district—to do their business. He can tell by looking at them that they don't belong in his shop. This slighting affront, more than the gold in the man's vault, kindles what is to come.

In the Iranian Revolution of 1978–79 a key slogan was solidarity with "mustaz'afin," meaning "the oppressed." If *Crimson Gold* might be taken as a latter-day defender of that very ideal, it is also, quite clearly, a stinging indictment of Iran's failure to realize its revolutionary promises. In that, this film is hardly alone. After the Islamic Republic acted to revive the nation's cinema in the early 1980s, the Iranian movies that gradually began to attract international attention seemed, in their ethos of compassion and formal lyricism, to reflect both revolutionary idealism and a sense of cultural renewal. Since the election of reformist president Khatami in 1997, however, this remarkable cinema's mood has grown ever darker, more caustic and critical of Iran's fraying social contract.

Kiarostami's suicide-themed *Taste of Cherry* announced the turn toward asperity, and its lead was notably followed by Panahi's *The Circle*, about the plight of poor women in Iran. The latter film and *Crimson Gold* having been banned in Iran, Panahi admits that he is now essentially working for an international audience, and while I've questioned the distortions such an export-only approach can entail, there's no denying that *Crimson Gold* aptly evokes the distress of a country where the middle class is sliding into poverty while a small upper-crust grows ever wealthier, and all efforts at amelioration via politics are blocked by hardliners who control the theocratic government.

The film maps such discontents across the contours of Hossein's bulky person and his sprawling city. He is so bloated, we learn, because of the cortisone he takes to treat injuries he suffered in the Iran-Iraq War. (Note that the U.S. supplied Saddam Hussein, the aggressor in that war, with chemical weapons that were used on the likes of Hossein.) On his nightly deliveries, he gets to witness the contortions other Tehranis must endure. In one striking scene he's held by cops who are arresting people emerging from a swinging party—a common humiliation in a society where the morality police are ever vigilant against ordinary hedonism.

Crimson Gold is beautifully crafted in every particular, from Hossein Jafarian's muted photography to the haunting performance Panahi elicits from the stolid, schizophrenic non-actor who was picked to portray Hossein. One of the most ingeniously captivating things about the film, though, is how it manages to feel episodic and anecdotal up until its penultimate scene, when the story's thematic strands suddenly converge.

It gives away nothing to say that this scene involves Hossein delivering pizzas to the snazzy apartment of a young, rich guy who invites him in for some company and to listen to his complaints about the "bitches" who've recently left. Narrative-wise, not much happens here. What does happen deftly interweaves such formal particulars as decor, music, pacing and camerawork. Notice how, when Hossein enters the apartment, Panahi introduces the use of handheld camera, a very understated way of placing us in the spot that counts most at this juncture: inside Hossein's head, looking through his weary, disillusioned eyes.

Ultimately, this climactic passage strikes me as the subtlest yet most thoroughgoing cinematic coup I've encountered in a movie in recent memory.

And it recalls no one more than Michelangelo Antonioni in its organic way of uniting precise formal expressiveness with both psychological nuance and penetrating moral and political insight.

Given the film's quietly devastating impact, one can easily leave the theater wondering who's worse off: Iranians, who have to deal with the social problems X-rayed here, or Westerners, whose artists seem to have lost the capacity for such brilliant, compassionate engagement.

Jafar Panahi:
Closed Curtain
First published July 9, 2014, on RogerEbert.com

MOST FILMS REQUIRE LITTLE OR NO knowledge on the viewer's part of the filmmaker's likeness or personal history. But folks who walk into *Closed Curtain* unfamiliar with Iranian director Jafar Panahi and his recent travails are sure to find themselves utterly baffled and confounded. A kind of "film à clef," the movie (co-credited to Kambozia Partovi) is essentially a psychological self-portrait that depends on the viewer's knowledge of Panahi's past work and the strange limbo he has existed in since the Iranian government banned him from working for 20 years—and then tacitly allowed him to go on making films "in secret."

With films such as *The White Balloon*, *The Circle* and *Crimson Gold* to his credit, Panahi was one of Iran's most successful and internationally lauded filmmakers when his outspokenness and political activism in the wake of Iran's contested 2009 presidential election got him in trouble with the government. He was arrested and jailed for a time, and has credited international protests with his eventual release. Nonetheless, he was subsequently put on trial, convicted and given a draconian sentence that included being banned from making films for two decades.

Living under house arrest (and barred from leaving the country) since then, he has used digital cameras to make two films that have been smuggled out of Iran and gained acclaim at film festivals and art houses around the world. In the droll *This Is Not a Film* (2011), he showed himself cooped up in his Tehran apartment and dealing with his de facto imprisonment by reflecting on his past work and continuing to film.

Filmed in Panahi's Caspian Sea vacation home, *Closed Curtain* at first seems a very different kind of film. A middle-aged writer (Partovi) arrives at a seaside villa bearing luggage, and immediately begins covering the house's many picture windows with heavy black curtains. One of his bags contains the reason for his secrecy: his dog Boy (played by a personable pooch who gives the best canine performance in recent memory), a pet the man is determined to keep hidden from the authorities who have declared dogs "impure" in Islamic law and therefore subject to confiscation and slaughter.

The solitude of man and dog, though, is short-lived. Going out at night to empty Boy's litter box, the writer leaves the door open just long enough for a young man and woman to rush inside breathlessly. They say they are a brother and sister who were at a party that was broken up by police who are now pursuing them. The writer hears the police as they poke around outside and, thinking the house empty, leave. The young man himself then departs, saying he will get a car and return, and quietly warning the writer that his sister is suicidal.

Something definitely seems amiss with the girl. With her sing-song voice and inexplicable smile, she gets under the writer's skin from the first moments they are together, invading parts of the house that he doesn't want her in and making cryptic, insinuating remarks. At first he suspects she may be a police plant, but then sees that she's too weird for that. After annoying him for a while, she seems to have left the house. Then she reappears and aggressively begins ripping the black curtains from the windows.

At which point, roughly halfway through the film (inevitable spoiler alert here), Panahi himself walks into the frame, and we see that, in addition to baring the windows, the removal of the curtains also reveals Italian and French posters for some of his earlier films. This startling moment recalls a similar one in the middle of Panahi's *The Mirror* when the little girl playing the film's main character suddenly declares she's not acting anymore and runs away from the film location, to be followed by other cameras. That *coup de cinéma*, though, took us from fiction to something closer to documentary, whereas this one transitions to a kind of subjective surrealism—call it a documentary about the inside of Panahi's head in recent years.

What follows resembles a narrative broken into shards. Sometimes the focus stays on Panahi as he moves around the house and interacts with visiting neighbors. Sometimes we return to the writer, his dog and the girl. Sometimes the filmmaker seems aware of these "characters," sometimes not. Occasionally, the tone is gentle and affirming, as when a good-hearted neighbor assures Panahi, "You'll be able to work again," while also counseling, "There are more things to life than work."

Yet there are also darker moments, as when characters are seen walking into the sea to commit suicide, à la Norman Maine in *A Star Is Born* and Roger Wade in *The Long Goodbye*. The girl does this first, yet later reappears.

Then we see Panahi do it, but before the action is completed, the film reverses and he moves out of the sea again—one of several instances where we are reminded of the mechanics of filmmaking.

If the dominant mood of *This Is Not a Film* was defiant, the main feeling here is melancholic. In implicitly confessing to suicidal impulses (as his mentor Abbas Kiarostami did in *Taste of Cherry*), Panahi shows how low his confinement has brought him. He still works in order to stay engaged with life and cinema, and this film's graceful framing, lighting and camera movement testify to his skills as a stylist, yet the movie also raises the question of how many more films he can make about himself and his frustration before hitting a creative wall.

Kiarostami pioneered the Iranian tradition of films about films and filmmakers. After venturing into the same territory with *The Mirror*, Panahi's work grew more political, and politics eventually landed him in a situation where the only ready subjects were a filmmaker (himself) and his work, which has been drastically delimited by the government. He has responded with imaginative films that are invigorating and courageous, yet one wishes that he would soon gain the freedom to make other kinds of movies again.

Asghar Farhadi:
About Elly
First published April 8, 2015, on RogerEbert.com

AT THE END OF ACT ONE IN Asghar Farhadi's gripping *About Elly*, the title character disappears. Elly (Taraneh Alidoosti), a young school teacher, has gone on a weekend vacation with a group of thirtysomething professional couples from Tehran. She's supposed to be looking after three little kids who're playing on a beach, and suddenly she's not there. That this vanishing sets up a mystery that propels the rest of the film has led to understandable critical comparisons to Antonioni's *L'Avventura*.

Yet the scene that immediately follows our last glimpse of Elly reminded me of quite a different movie: Spielberg's *Jaws*. Most of the vacationing adults are playing volleyball behind the villa where they're staying when two of the aforementioned kids appear from the beach and start screaming about the third. It takes the grown-ups several beats to catch on, but when they do, they rush around the house, realize that the third kid, a little boy, is nowhere to be seen, and frantically begin plunging into the Caspian Sea's crashing waves.

I won't reveal how the scene ends, just that I can't help but think Spielberg would admire Farhadi's electrifying direction of it. As the Iranian men dash into the ocean, and their alarmed wives emerge from the house, everything is in motion: the characters, the water, the camera. We seem to be looking in every direction at once, desperately: up and down the beach, back toward the villa, even under the sea as it pounds forward violently. Farhadi's orchestration of all these elements is complex and viscerally kinetic; few viewers will experience it without holding their breath at some point.

So what do we make of an Iranian film whose conceptual parameters are broad enough to span *L'Avventura* and *Jaws*? Perhaps we should begin by venturing that Asghar Farhadi is a new and conspicuously audacious kind of Iranian auteur. When Iranian directors such as Abbas Kiarostami and Mohsen Makhmalbaf began catching the world's eye in the late 1980s and early 1990s, it was for films that had obvious parallels to Euro-style cinematic modernism. Even when newer directors including Jafar Panahi and Majid Majidi gave a more commercial spin to this basic model from the late 1990s onward, their work still spoke the language of the international art film.

Farhadi's *A Separation* (2011) took a different tack, becoming the most successful Iranian film in history, thanks in part to innovations on two fronts. First, Farhadi's Iranian cinematic models were not any of the aforementioned filmmakers but two cinematic masters who are less well known outside Iran: Dariush Mehrjiu (*Leila*), whose films often deal with Iran's middle and upper classes; and Bahram Beyzai (*The Travelers*), whose creative roots are in theater (as are Farhadi's). Second, Farhadi admitted American influences including the likes of Elia Kazan and films such as *A Streetcar Named Desire*.

About Elly represents all the tendencies of Farhadi's mature style as brilliantly as *A Separation*, yet it is not a successor to the latter film. It was made just before it and won the Silver Bear at the Berlin Film Festival in 2009, but, due to complicated rights issues, was not released in the U.S. until now. Its belated appearance should be welcomed by cinephiles, as it offers solid proof of this writer-director's distinctive gifts.

One of those is a way of dramatic structuring that's like peeling an onion: The first layers we see seem familiar and self-evident, but the more layers we reach, the more complex the whole becomes. Here, the starting point is what seems like an entirely happy and carefree outing where three couples—many of whom have been friends since law school—motor out to the Caspian Sea for a holiday weekend. One wife has invited along pretty Elly, her daughter's elementary-school teacher, in obvious hopes of matching her with the excursion's other singleton: Ahmad, a handsome friend who's just returned from Germany after getting divorced.

For Americans who've seen few Iranian films, or only ones centered on the poor or dispossessed, the characters here will be striking. With their BMWs, faded T-shirts and constant joking around, they're like cosmopolitan urbanites anywhere. Sure, we're reminded of their Iranian-ness in their particular styles of music and dance and in the fact that the women all wear head-scarves throughout (something required by law) but even they are casual and stylish.

As in *A Separation*, there's evidence of tension between this class of privileged professionals and the strata of poorer, more pious Iranians beneath them, but this is more peripheral than in the later film: e.g., the Tehranis pretend Elly and Ahmad are newlyweds in order not to offend the religious sensibilities of the rural folks who rent them the villa.

From that little white lie to other similar ones and the uncovering of various personal agendas: The peeling away of the onion skins reveals a continuing succession of hidden realities, and the ones that come after Elly's disappearance are darker and cut deeper than those early on. But when I read that a writer in *Sight & Sound* has said all this constitutes "a critique of the lies and evasions that permeate Iranian society," I can practically hear the groans coming from Farhadi, who has said in interviews that he doesn't want to be one of those filmmakers who is expected "to explain Iran to the West."

The filmmaker has, instead, clearly indicated that his goals in *About Elly* are far less sociopolitical than cinematic, stating that, "[D]irectors can no longer be content with force-feeding [audiences] a set of preconceived ideas. Rather than asserting a world vision, a film must open a space in which the public can involve themselves in a personal reflection, and evolve from consumers to independent thinkers."

"Opening spaces" is precisely what Farhadi's films do, both literally and figuratively. Indeed, the various ways great Iranian directors articulate visual space comprise one of the most fascinating and significant dimensions of Iranian cinema, from the contemplative and symbolic uses in some films to the poetic and documentary-like in others.

Farhadi's way with space is more dynamic and consciously multilayered, as well as technically virtuosic, enough so to recall *Jaws* or indeed *A Streetcar Named Desire*. To anyone going to see *About Elly*, I would say this: Notice the early scene where the four couples and three kids arrive at the villa with the boy whose family is renting it to them. See the way ace cinematographer Hossein Jafarian's gliding hand-held camera takes in the disheveled rooms, glimpses the seascape through the windows and doors, and sets up an enormously complex and involving set of relationships between the characters by continually reframing them.

There are some great little moments here. Two quick shots of the host boy, for instance: In one, he glances out the front door at two kids on the beach, prefiguring the lost-child scene described above; in another, he gives a brief caustic look in reaction to one Tehran man's silly dance—a statement of class differences as eloquent as any dissertation.

Farhadi is a masterful director of actors, and here he gets a range of precise, vivid performances from a cast that also includes Golshifteh Farahani,

Peyman Moadi (*A Separation*), Mani Haghighi and Shahab Hosseini (*The Salesman*). It might be argued that Farhadi doesn't have any grand message, or "world vision" as he puts it. But to me, his way of revivifying cinema, and connecting its spaces to those of human hearts and minds, is vision aplenty.

Asghar Farhadi:
The Salesman
First published January 27, 2017, on RogerEbert.com

For the few Americans fortunate enough to visit Iran, one of the most startling discoveries can be the vitality, diversity and popularity of the arts scene in cities like Tehran. Literary festivals of all sorts abound, as do most varieties of the visual arts. Granted, the government's Islamic restrictions put the damper on all but traditional forms of dance, and public performances of vocal music by women are effectively verboten. Yet, as Bahman Ghobadi's delightful 2009 doc *No One Knows About Persian Cats* showed, pop music including punk and rap thrives in urban undergrounds, the efforts of government censors notwithstanding. Indeed, the chance to defy the regime's thought police seems a prime motivator for many young artists and their fans.

Theater is also a lively center of cultural action. While Iran, uniquely in its region, has not only an indigenous form of traditional theater (*ta'ziyeh*) but also a strong modernist descendant that includes such monumental talents as writer-director (and filmmaker) Bahram Beyzai, Tehran also sees frequent stagings of works by playwrights including Ionesco, Beckett and Pinter. When a friend asked if it was realistic that Asghar Farhadi's new, Oscar-nominated *The Salesman* shows an Iranian company staging Arthur Miller's *Death of a Salesman*—a play by an American Jew—I replied that such things are common, as are presentations of works by Americans such as Tennessee Williams, Edward Albee and Sam Shepard.

Next to Beyzai, Farhadi is the prominent Iranian filmmaker most associated with theater. Arriving in Tehran hoping to study cinema in college, he was instead assigned to the theater school, an apparent misfortune that he has called one of the luckiest things that ever happened to him. Studying the literature of theater—he did his dissertation on Pinter's use of silence—he has said, taught him to write, and that skill has been integral to his career as a filmmaker. *The Salesman*, though, marks the first time he's ever taken us *into* the theater.

The meaning and importance of that move are worthy subjects for discussion, because in no sense does the film seem to be *about* theater. I recently asked Farhadi if he was familiar with theater-themed Jacques Rivette films such as *L'Amour Fou* and *Out 1*, and he said he wasn't. That makes sense, because he's not an experimenter like Rivette. More akin to R. W. Fassbinder, he uses the language of theatrical melodrama to probe social and psychological fissures. Like all but the first two of his features, *The Salesman* tackles what has become his signature subject: middle-class marriage.

The film opens showing us a marriage bed—a startling image in an Iranian film. But the lighting soon signals that this bed is on a theater stage; it will be the bed of Willy and Linda Loman. Next, we are in a suburban apartment building at night where the inhabitants are screaming and running for the exits. A disaster has destroyed the structure's foundations and among the newly homeless are Emad (Shahab Hosseini) and his wife, Rana (Taraneh Alidoosti). They are amateur actors playing the Lomans on the stage we've just witnessed, and that avocation turns out to be fortunate in one sense: One of their fellow performers generously guides them to a vacant apartment he knows about.

A spacious two-bedroom on the top floor of a building, it seems close to perfect, so they move in. Meanwhile, we see Emad in his day job teaching literature to a class of teenage boys. The key reference here will be unfamiliar to American viewers, so it's worth unpacking. Emad is assigning the short story "The Cow" by Gholam Hossein Sa'edi, a leading Persian 20th-century literary figure and political activist. After publishing the story, Sa'edi converted it to a film script that became the basis for Dariush Mehrjui's *The Cow* (which we glimpse in a subsequent scene), the 1969 film that legendarily launched the Iranian New Wave of the 1970s.

In "The Cow," when an impoverished village loses its one cow, its owner goes insane, mooing and eating flowers as he imagines himself to be his beloved animal. "How does a man turn into a cow?" one of Emad's students asks. ("Look in the mirror," another cracks, provoking laughter.) The question, it turns out, prefigures what happens in *The Salesman*, even as the scene also suggests a correlation between the tragic protagonists of "The Cow" and *Death of a Salesman*. Emad names the Miller work when a student asks what play he's rehearsing. He asks the students if they know it; none do. (That many educated adults in Iran undoubtedly would know the play points toward a divide more generational than national: While adults worldwide have grown up in cultures that value literary tradition, young people are more preoccupied with video games and smartphones.)

One night, Rana is taking a shower when the apartment's buzzer sounds. Thinking it's Emad, she hits the buzzer and then returns to the shower. Soon we are in a hospital, where a frantic Emad sees his wife getting stitches in her head, badly injured. As he pieces together what happened, it seems an intruder came upon Rana in the shower, there was a struggle, glass was broken that cut her and left the intruder fleeing with bloodied feet. Neighbors heard the commotion, found Rana and got her to the hospital. She tells Emad she doesn't want the police involved as she doesn't want to tell the story again.

In pursuing his own investigation, Emad finds out that their apartment's previous tenant was a prostitute. It seems that the intruder wasn't a random stranger but a client thinking he was joining her in the shower for some action (he even left some money in the bedroom). Putting the pieces together, Emad first vents his anger on the fellow actor who turned him on to the apartment, snarling improvised insults at him during *Death of a Salesman*. But as this guy is obviously guiltless, the wounded husband becomes more and more obsessed with finding the real guilty party.

The previous film that took Farhadi to the Oscars was *A Separation*. This one could be called *A Violation*. Rana seems to make shaky but real progress in her recovery, even if her return to the stage entails difficulties: She can't complete one performance because she says the eyes of one man in the audience remind her of the intruder's. Increasingly, though, it seems the harshest violation was of Emad—his self-worth, his ego, his manhood.

Some descriptions of *The Salesman* call it a thriller, suggesting a Hollywood-style suspense film. It's not. It's a psychological and moral drama about how one man's anger and damaged self-image drive him to the brink of destroying the very thing he ostensibly most wants to protect: his marriage. Yet Farhadi's stylistic proclivities remind us that he is the most Hollywood-influenced of major Iranian directors. While the shower scene here is just as crucial as (if far less explicit than) the one in *Psycho*, Farhadi's depictions of people ascending or descending stairs recall Hitchcock's, just as his way of moving through rooms (usually shot in smooth hand-held by cinematographer Hossein Jafarian) evokes Kazan's sinuous, stage-influenced sense of mise-en-scène.

Kazan's example may also be felt in the film's strong, finely tuned performances. Though the first post-revolutionary Iranian films to gain international attention often used non-actors, Farhadi's recent films have derived much of their precision and power from the skills of accomplished film and stage actors. Here, Hosseini's work as Emad anchors the film with its deceptively casual gravity: Precisely because he's so modern and hip-urban in demeanor, it's hard to imagine that this guy can collapse into primal vindictiveness, but so he does. Bringing out Rana's combination of disorientation and underlying decency, Alidoosti shows why she's become one of Iran's leading young actresses. Some equally fine performances occur in secondary parts, including ones that come to the fore in the film's tensely suspenseful final act.

When *A Separation* capped its global success by becoming the first Iranian film to win an Oscar, Farhadi effectively became an international director, a fact he implicitly acknowledged by making his next film, *The Past*, in France. With *The Salesman*, he returns not only to Iran but to some deeply Iranian themes, examining an atavistic tendency even in the most modern-seeming men and pitting that against the compassionate humanism at the core of both secular and religious thought in Iran. At the same time, the film finds Farhadi now inhabiting a strangely transnational place in cinema, one where bridging Gholem-Hossein Sa'edi and Arthur Miller is more a playful, aspirational gesture than a purposeful strategy. As impressive as the dramatic facility of *The Salesman* is, it lacks any real urgency or sense of daring, as if a night in the theater (or cinema) was not supposed to signify outside its walls.

Mahmoud Kalari:
Interview with Mahmoud Kalari

A version of this piece was first published November 12, 2018, on FilmComment. com

WHEN ASGHAR FARHADI's *A SEPARATION* became the first Iranian film to win an Oscar, for Best Foreign-Language Film of 2012, it gave the world a look at the work not only of one of Iran's most acclaimed writer-directors but also of an Iranian cinematographer whose skills have contributed to dozens of important films of Iran's post-revolutionary cinema. Born in 1951, Mahmoud Kalari started in the 1970s studying photography, and later became a renowned news photographer whose images of Ayatollah Khomeini and other figures of Iran's revolutionary era appeared in magazines around the world. After turning to cinematography during the mid-1980s revival of Iranian cinema, he collaborated with many of Iran's leading auteurs, including Abbas Kiarostami, Mohsen Makhmalbaf, Dariush Mehrjui, Jafar Panahi, and Farhadi. He is also known for encouraging and working with younger directors such as Mani Haghighi (*Pig*, 2018) and Shahram Mokri (*Fish & Cat*, 2013). In addition to acting in a Mehrjui film, he wrote and directed 1997's *The Cloud and the Rising Sun*. His cinematography has won numerous awards at festivals around the world.

The following interview was conducted mainly in Farsi and translated by Tania Ahmadi.

Godfrey Cheshire: Where in Iran did you grow up, and what was your family like?

Mahmoud Kalari: I was born in Tehran in a very old house in which my father was also born. I was surrounded by a very traditional and religious family. During my childhood, no one I knew had a camera. We led a very simple life. My father sold tea at the bazaar. We lived in that same house until I was seven years old, and then we moved into another house in Tehran that had a great movie theater next to it called Cinema Ramsar. At the age of 15, I got my first photography camera. I have no clue how I became interested in photography. Perhaps it was during that very first encounter with the camera, when I went to the photography studio with my uncle. I spent all my time taking photos.

There was no specific subject or theme in my photos. However, when I later looked through them, I realized that there actually was a theme I had not noticed: People who were alone captured my interest the most. Later, my first photo exhibition was titled "The Story of a Man in Solitude."

During that period, film became more important to me as well. I read reviews and articles on cinema—some film critics, such as Jamsheed Akrami and Parviz Davaie, whom I now know very well, shaped my understanding. Although I really liked cinema, I never thought of becoming a cinematographer. Then, when I was 20 years old, I participated in an experimental cinema institution, where they made 8mm films. I made two 8mm films and, surprisingly, I did not shoot any of them myself. It was Ahmad Amini, a good friend of mine who is now a film director, who shot my films.

How did you begin your career as a photographer?

When I was 20 years old, our neighbor Kambiz Derambakhsh introduced me to Kaveh Golestan who, at that time, was the head of the photography section of a newspaper. When he saw my photos he selected a few and then explained why those photos were more interesting than the rest—he introduced me to the meaning of "concept" and "thought" in photography. Two years before the Revolution of 1979, Golestan had a photo exhibition at Tehran's university, and arranged an exhibition for me right after his. There was where I made my first significant mark. After that I started to think about my themes and subjects more deeply as I knew I had to say something with my pictures. Once I was introduced to the concept of photo-essay I started to work in that field, and the aesthetics of visual creativity became my core concern. I studied the portfolio of famous photographers around the world, including the works of Golestan. Revolution played a great role in my career: I took many photos in the midst of the Revolution, and at that time started to work at the Sygma Agency as a photojournalist. I worked there for four years and my photos were published in many magazines around the world.

What led you to transition from a still photographer to a cinematographer?

I entered the world of cinematography in 1984. I had my fourth photo exhibition and the filmmaker Masoud Jafari Jozani came to see it. At that time, he was making a short film called "Talk to Me" (1984) for Kanoon. Touraj Mansouri was shooting that film and he asked me to come to the set to take pictures. I did this—that was how we got to know each other. When Jozani decided to make *Frosty Roads* (1985), he invited me to collaborate as a cinematographer. I was a bit hesitant, as I had never shot any films before, but Jozani convinced me that I would be able to shoot with a 35mm camera. The shoot took place in the winter and we were shooting in snow. That was actually one of the most difficult projects I have worked on in my entire life. I took the camera home for one week and carefully studied everything about it. So, I really learned the techniques of cinematography while shooting my first film. It was a unique beginning for me, as I did not begin my career as an assistant, but as the main cinematographer. The film was screened at the 4th Fajr Film Festival and I won the prize for best cinematographer! So that was how I became a cinematographer. [Laughs] Then well-known directors such as Mehrjui and [Masoud] Kimiai started to call me, inviting me to collaborate on their films. A fantastic beginning!

The first auteur film director you worked with was Mohsen Makhmalbaf, and you made four films with him. How did you end up working with him? Also, Makhmalbaf did not have a very good reputation within the film industry early in his career. So what was your opinion about his reputation at that time?

Makhmalbaf had two important periods in his early career. In the first period, he made films that were not significant. In the second period, he made *The Cyclist* and *The Marriage of the Blessed*, which were huge hits in Iran. Both had specific visual structures. Makhmalbaf was a really interesting director in my opinion, and changed a lot between his first and second phases.

He had written a short novel called *Time to Love* (or *Time of Love*, 1990), and wanted to make it into a film. It was a strange story that showed his way of thinking was changing. We made that film in Turkey because it was impossible to shoot in Iran. The cast was Turkish and the crew was Iranian.

We shot the film in 17 days. It was never screened in Iran—it was banned. I liked and enjoyed the way he changed both as a person and as a filmmaker over the course of the years, and that was the reason I wanted to work with him. I realized he was completely aware of what he was doing, and that helped me decide to continue our collaboration.

Gabbeh (1996) is a beautiful and unusual film that you had to go to the remote central highlands of Iran to shoot. It was supposed to be a film about nomadic people who were making gabbehs (primitive carpets), but then it ended up being something else.

Yes, *Gabbeh* was supposed to be a documentary. When we went to the Cannes Film Festival with *Salaam Cinema* (1995) and *Time of Love*, we had just finished shooting *Gabbeh*. We just needed to edit it. When we presented those two films at Cannes, Makhmalbaf realized that, although he wanted to send *Gabbeh* to Cannes the following year, he couldn't do so as Cannes didn't accept documentaries. So he decided to change it into a fiction film. On the airplane back to Iran, he started to craft the story on a napkin.

Makhmalbaf had just met a man named Abbas Sayahi, who became the lead actor of the film. His occupation was dying carpet threads using organic pigments extracted from plants. *Gabbeh*'s main plot was centered around this process of dying threads. Thus, the main themes of the film were: plants, colors, threads, and, of course, carpets. For me, color was the most important. We only had two cars, limited equipment, and a very small crew. Today, if we want to make a film in which color plays a dominant role, our vision can easily be achieved in post-production—any color can be added using digital technology. But, at that time, we didn't have that technology, so I had to color the negatives by hand myself. For instance, for long shots, or landscape shots, I added a green gel color, and, for the sky. I added a blue gel color to enhance the shot. I colored all of them in front of the camera lens. In cinema's early days, they used to do the tinting on glass shots. I did the exact same thing, but with filters. It took us nearly forty days to finish filming.

Before you shot Gabbeh, *you and Makhmalbaf set out to make another drama. But first came* Salaam Cinema, *a totally impromptu film that resulted when he published an ad for a casting and thousands of people came. Did that really happen?*

Yes!

Were you surprised?

Very much so! At that time, we didn't know what to do. We were amazed. Makhmalbaf couldn't believe it. Four to five thousand people came for the audition that morning.

Can you tell me how that casting evolved into a feature?

That was one of the most extraordinary experiences of my entire life, and I've had many throughout my career. We intended to make the film that we made afterwards, *A Moment of Innocence*, but before shooting, had decided to call for an audition for the first scene of the film—we intended to start that film with footage of the audition. So we really didn't intend to make *Salaam Cinema* at all. When we saw the huge crowd we were very surprised, and so filmed it. It was such a chaotic situation that we tried to organize, but some people attacked the door to get inside and actually broke it. This moment is in the film. Another issue was time. We didn't want to spend too much time on the audition, but that day we couldn't do anything but test those who had shown up. Makhmalbaf then decided to spend a few more days filming the attendees, because no one would leave until they had a chance to audition. After a few days, Makhmalbaf thought this footage could become its own film. We had to rent another camera in order to film everyone as quickly as possible. At that time we used 400-foot reels, as there was no 1,000-foot film in Iran, so we had to change the reel every four minutes. While my assistant changed the reel I would film with the other camera.

On day six, two girls came for the audition. They were both very good and had to compete against one another. Then an idea came to Makhmalbaf. He decided that one of the girls would test the other. So he brought one of the girls behind the camera and let the audition continue. He realized how differently people behaved when their positions changed. It was then Makhmalbaf felt we had our story. *Salaam Cinema* was made during the audition process and its details were added piece by piece—the ideas came to us during the shoot!

So how long did it take to shoot the entire film?

Seven to eight days!

It seems the film is about power relationships, with Makhmalbaf playing the film director as tyrant. Did he actually say, "I am not being myself, I am playing a character"?

Yes, that was all a show for our film. He's such a sensitive person. And when I was upset at his behavior, he explained everything, that he was just acting. Once a girl who was wearing a chador came to the audition. Makhmalbaf asked what she would do if she was offered the role of a woman who does not wear chador. She panicked because she was married to a religious man. Then Mohsen told her that she was not obliged to answer straight away, giving her time to think about it. Mohsen moved on to the others at the audition, but I kept the camera on the woman while she was thinking. It was such a precious moment. I couldn't make myself cut. Later she came back to the set. Makhmalbaf asked her if she was ready to answer and she said, "If my husband will not let me play the role, I will leave him." Mohsen was so shocked. He asked me if I had heard her response, and I told him that I had recorded everything—he was very happy and excited about this! He couldn't believe it. [Laughs]

In Gabbeh, *color is a main character. In* A Moment of Innocence, *light is a main character. How did you and Mohsen come up with this idea?*

In *Gabbeh*, Mohsen was working closely with Abbas Sayahi, who made colors for carpets. Mohsen wanted to make a film based on colors. Thus, time was very important for us. That is, we had to think about when to film those colors in order to capture their real essence, like those in the sunset and sunrise. For *Moment of Innocence*, the atmosphere and architecture of the set was important to him. Because of this he tried very hard to find a place like the bazaar that you see in the film. That bazaar was not in Tehran. It was in Naeen, a very small town near Isfahan. It was an old bazaar that they kept open for tourists, so the bazaar at that time had no shops or any other businesses.

The architecture of that bazaar was very important to Makhmalbaf. So the difference between these two films is that one of them was based on color and light, whereas the other was based on architecture. After the Revolution, no one had touched the architecture of that bazaar. Some parts of it, such as the main doors, were renovated, but the bazaar was and still is very beautiful and popular with tourists. When we were shooting the film, all the stores were closed. There was a sense of silence and peace that Makhmalbaf loved so much, because his intention was to only showcase characters. He wanted to shoot the film in a quiet place so that the center of attention would remain on these three characters only: the woman and two men.

You worked on three films with Dariush Mehrjui, all significant because of their actors' performances. Leila Hatami in Leila *(1997), Niki Karimi in* Sara *(1993), and Golshifteh Farahani in* The Pear Tree *(1998)—all began their acting careers with Mehrjui. Can you tell me about working with Mehrjui and actresses, particularly when you worked with a new actress?*

For me, Mehrjui was the first director familiar with the language of professional cinema. Every new idea of his is unique—he has all the details in his mind. It's hard for me to imagine how a director could picture an entire film in his mind, but Mehrjui is like that.

He had a special way of working with actors. I think this was not because of any special method but because of his intelligence. It was not about his directorial skills but rather his comprehension and wisdom in understanding the characters and the significance of the actors' expressions. For instance, in *The Cow*, the main character was played by Ezzatolah Entezami. All of his subsequent roles were very close to his character in *The Cow*: the way he talked, the way he expressed emotions, and so on. Later, Mehrjui directed *Mr. Haloo*. The main character was played by Ali Nassirian, who was a professional theater actor. All of Nassirian's later roles were influenced by the way he performed this role. The same thing applies to Khosrow Shakibai and his unforgettable role in *Hamoon*. All the roles Shakibai played after *Hamoon* were deeply influenced by his role in that film. He carried Hamoon's traits within himself at all times: the voice, the motions, the expression, and so on. Mehrjui has an invaluable skill in choosing actors. He chooses people whose own character is nearly 80 percent identical to the characters they play. If Shakibai hadn't had Hamoon's traits, he wouldn't have been chosen for that role. The same thing applied to Leila Hatami, Niki Karimi, and Golshifteh Farahani, who was then 15 years old.

I also acted in one of his films. [Laughs] I played the role of the doctor in *The Lady* (1991, released 1998). I knew nothing about acting. One day, while I was shooting something elsewhere, he called me and invited me to play a role. I asked him hesitantly, "Really? Why do you think that I am able to act"? He said that he was sure about it. I did not give him any response and I told him that I was in the midst of shooting something. I was afraid to act, knowing that it would be especially challenging. In the end Mehrjui insisted that he wanted me to play the role of the doctor and I did end up doing it. We shot most of my parts without rehearsals. I was really stunned that he did not want to have any rehearsals. In the first take, my mind went blank and I literally forgot everything. But in the end I managed to play my part well and he was very satisfied with my performance.

In Sara *and* Leila, *the visual language is distinctive. There is a fading out and fading in of colors. How did that work? What did Mehrjui think about that?*

Yes, Mehrjui thought a lot about those colors and the fading ins and outs. He was thinking about the colors red and yellow for those films, and had something particular in mind for the atmosphere. He gave me a book of photos, but I do not remember the name of the photographer. He was very much influenced by those photos. The colors and details of that book stayed with him and affected him profoundly. He always had some influence in mind—sometimes it came from a photo, sometimes a book, sometimes a painting, and so on.

You first worked with Abbas Kiarostami on The Wind Will Carry Us. *How did you get that job?*

We knew each other and were friends for more than 10 years. I believe we both hesitated to work with each other. I hesitated as I wanted to maintain our friendship, but I don't know his reasons. [Laughs] Working with Kiarostami was difficult. In many ways you had to completely fall under his spell. We went on many journeys together and collaborated on a lot of photography. Before he made *And Life Goes On* we went on a trip and took lots of photos. We had a good relationship. Before making *The Wind Will Carry Us*, he visited the location of *The Pear Tree*, which I was then shooting. He liked our gaffer, my assistant Behzad Dorani. He told me he wanted to test Dorani, as he believed he was suitable for a role in his film. That was how Behzad Dorani got the main role in *The Wind Will Carry Us*. Kiarostami didn't want Dorani to feel like he was an actor. So, as Dorani often worked on my crew, Kiarostami asked me to go to the set, so that Dorani would feel more like a crew member than an actor. Kiarostami never had many people in his crew. He always believed that the entire crew had to fit in two cars. [Laughs] I really think it was because of Behzad Dorani that I worked on that film as a cinematographer. Abbas was very strange and funny. I read him say somewhere that he found Dorani on the street. [Laughing]

Another funny story was that the night before shooting the film Kiarostami called me, saying he thought Behzad was not a good fit for the film. I was very shocked, and I told him that he had to calm himself down because we had no time to bring in another actor. But he insisted that he wanted to test two other guys. I went to his place and he told me to call Behzad, because he wanted to take more videos of him. I said no, because it was very late and we had to be on set early the next morning. But I could not dissuade him, so in the end I called Behzad and asked him to come. Two other guys came as well. One of them was actually Parviz Shahbazi, who is now a well-known director. Kiarostami pointed to Shahbazi and told me that he thought Shahbazi was better than Dorani. I asked him if he was sure about that and he said yes. We spent another three hours shooting videos of Shahbazi, Dorani and the other man, whose name I do not remember. After a couple of hours they left. Then we looked over the videos together and he was not sure which one to choose. I was worried, because the shoot was at 8 a.m. and by then it was 3 a.m. In the end, he came to the conclusion that Behzad Dorani was the best fit for the role. Sometimes, I think maybe he wanted to work with me, and that was the main reason he chose Dorani. The film contained many shots of landscapes and I think he liked my work in *Gabbeh*—that, too, had many landscape scenes.

What was your experience making that film with him in Kurdistan?

It was exactly like making a documentary, because we were working in a school. It was summer and the school was closed. The location was between Kermanshah and Sanandaj. The place that we stayed was far from the shooting location, and every day we drove around two hours to get there. Bahman Ghobadi was our assistant and production manager. He did lots of things for us because he was the only one among us who spoke Kurdish fluently. He prepared almost everything for us. We started early in the morning, let's say at around 4:00, 4:30 a.m., when it was completely dark. We went to the location and worked eight to nine hours every day, and then we went back to the camp.

Was it Bahman Ghobadi who decided the schedule or was it Kiarostami himself?

It was Kiarostami of course! At the time Bahman Ghobadi could not say anything. [Laughs] Everything was decided by Kiarostami. Ghobadi was only an assistant. Kiarostami was self-assertive which is why it was very difficult working with him. He never listened to anyone or to any ideas. Sometimes, he got mad when we suggested things. He constantly asked us to let him do whatever he had in mind. I know that sometimes people stopped working with him because of this. For instance, in the case of *Where Is the Friend's House?*, the cinematographer changed because he and Kiarostami could not work together. That was Kiarostami. No one could intervene in his work. There were some problems between Ghobadi and Kiarostami, and Kiarostami at some point wanted to fire him, but we convinced him that we needed Ghobadi to translate for us and that without him we couldn't finish the film. It was difficult to work with Kiarostami, but it was also really fantastic. He was unique.

Let me tell you something. We were all sitting in the car. We always carried our equipment just in case Kiarostami suddenly wanted to film something. We always had to be ready to shoot. On our route, there were people wandering around the villages or walking along the side of the road. Once he saw someone, stopped the car, and asked us if we were ready. He called out to the person on the road and asked them to come over. It did not really matter if that person was a man or a woman, or even a child, he just wanted to start a simple conversation. Kiarostami asked random questions and we filmed the whole conversation without knowing what the point of those questions was. One of the questions that he asked repeatedly was, "Where is Siyahdareh?" It was the name of a random village that came to his mind. Then he would ask, "Where is Goldareh?" Goldareh was the name of the village where we actually were. Then, the person would say that we were in Goldareh. Surprisingly, Kiarostami asked that person how he knew where Goldareh was, as the name was not mentioned on the map nor was there any sign of its name in the village. He was curious as to how people could find the village. People answered this very wonderful question so differently. Some replied that they knew it by heart, while others replied and pointed out some signs, and so on. But Kiarostami was not satisfied with their answers until one day a man replied: "We never leave the village, so we do not really need to look for it." Kiarostami loved that so much. He always wanted to investigate, to explore. This is what I mean about his uniqueness. He came up with those magnificent questions and was eager to find the best answer.

Kiarostami was a photographer himself. I was wondering, when you made a film like this, did you choose the camera or did he decide on the camera? How did you make those decisions?

Honestly, those decisions were made by both of us. Sometimes we had different visions, but he knew exactly what he wanted. He always chose the perfect location. He knew the lighting and everything else so well. In many cases, we waited three to four hours to get the best lighting for a picture. He had a fantastic vision and a wonderful visual mind. As you know, he was a great painter as well.

Let's talk about Shirin. *I know it was shot without the actresses knowing what film they were supposed to be watching. They were just looking into the camera. What did Kiarostami tell you about the film?*

At first he wanted to put on a film and record the actresses' reactions to it. But the evening of the shooting day, he changed his mind and decided to use voice only. At first he was thinking of using the narrative and music of Zeffirelli's

Romeo and Juliet, which he later changed to the well-known Iranian tragic romance *Khosrow and Shirin*. He wanted to see the actresses' reactions, and told the performers to imagine the film they were watching, anything that would arouse emotions such as grief, sadness, or melancholy. Each performer reacted differently, and Kiarostami decided what to use based on those reactions. I honestly didn't know what he had in mind. He asked some older Iranian actresses, such as Poori Banaei and Iren, who used to be stars before the Revolution of 1979, to be in the film. Those actresses were very excited to perform one more time—they had not appeared on camera for more than twenty years. Being on set after all this time made them exceedingly happy and joyful.

A Separation is a very distinctive-looking film for various reasons. How did that visual language come about for the film?

Farhadi had had experience working with hand-held cameras in some of his films, such as *About Elly* and *Fireworks Wednesday*. In *A Separation*, he wanted to build on this, and have the camera move along with the characters. What I mean is that if in *About Elly* we saw static two shots, three shots, or long shots with characters moving within the shot, in *A Separation* we instead moved the camera along with the characters. Often we started with a close over-the-shoulder shot and then would move to a two-shot or three-shot, and then back to a closer shot.

It was an exceptional experience, especially in filming the shot-reverse shots, which I believe to be exemplary, and could be taught at universities. Those shots were very accurate, perfect, sincere and sensitive; sometimes it made people believe that they were filmed with two cameras. I even heard from a world-famous cinematographer that he thought we had filmed those shots with two cameras. All of the shots were taken with one hand-held camera, which weighed seven kilos. Farhadi never believed in making a film with two cameras. He always wanted to control every shot very attentively. *A Separation* was the most accomplished and perfect version of hand-held camera work that I have ever worked on.

Did you rehearse a lot?

Yes. Too much! Sometimes, we rehearsed a scene more than 12 times.

Did you shoot a lot of takes?

No. We could not shoot many takes because we didn't have much film. That was the problem in Iran. Normally we were given only 100 to 120 rolls. That was the main reason for all the rehearsals.

How did the actors do in that situation? Was it hard for them?

It was very difficult for the actors. Farhadi started the rehearsals 45 days before shooting. So the actors were well-prepared by the first day of shooting. Farhadi had a background in theater, so he trained actors to work on their emotions in the rehearsal process. He wanted to work with Marion Cotillard in *The Past*, but she was unable to come to rehearsals 40 days before the shoot. She could come one week before, but Farhadi wouldn't accept that. So he used Bérénice Bejo instead. Honestly, I don't know any other directors who spend so much time on rehearsals, and that is the key to his success.

What about those things that you were looking through? Those windows? Those barriers?

During the rehearsal process, we tried to find the location. Normally in Iran, we go to people's houses to shoot, so all the locations are real. We never use sets. That is the reason it was very hard for Farhadi to make *The Past* in Paris, because all the locations were made for him. French producers told him it was impossible to search people's houses for locations. [Laughing] Back to *Separation*: After searching lots of houses, we eventually found the apartment. Farhadi asked the art director to take out the doors, and then built them again. For the old man's room, he ordered a door with stained glass. He changed all the colors, and also decided to make changes to the walls. Everything in the apartment was changed completely. He would go back to the location late at night, like at 2 a.m., to think about the shots. He would then call me to consult on his new ideas. The rehearsals were done somewhere else with the actors, but every day he would go back to the location to check, change, and practice. He practiced everything himself, found the best way, and then asked people to do it.

So he figured out all the compositions on his own?

Yes. Exactly!

Mohammad Rasoulof:
Manuscripts Don't Burn
First published June 13, 2014, on RogerEbert.com

WATCHING MOHAMMAD RASOULOF'S RIVETING *Manuscripts Don't Burn*, easily the most daring and politically provocative film yet to emerge from Iran, I was reminded of something I heard when visiting that country to study its cinema in the late 1990s. When I asked an Iranian cinephile the difference between Iran's artistically vital but little-known cinema of the 1970s and its successor, which gradually captured the world's attention following the 1979 Iranian Revolution, he smiled and said, "In the post-revolutionary cinema, there is no bad guy."

The remark was both droll and apt. Films before the Revolution often conveyed a pervasive sense of bitterness and discontent, a mood ultimately—if always implicitly—traceable to one paramount bad guy: the Shah, whose overthrow was supported by the vast majority of Iranians. Iranian films of the 1980s and beyond, by contrast, frequently projected the buoyancy of a culture reinventing itself, even when dealing with harsh social problems or reflecting the content restrictions of the Islamic Republic. When elements of discontent did reemerge, in films such as Abbas Kiarostami's *Taste of Cherry*, Mohsen Makhmalbaf's *A Moment of Innocence* or Jafar Panahi's *The Circle*, the targets were usually—and again, implicitly—cultural structures and the regime generally rather than individual miscreants.

With *Manuscripts Don't Burn*, though, the bad guy returns to Iranian cinema with a vengeance—and in triplicate, no less. Based on real historical events, Rasoulof's drama focuses on two operatives assigned to terrorize, torture and murder dissident writers and intellectuals. These guys go about their dirty business with a methodical, unemotional brutality, but they are simply repression's foot soldiers. Far more chilling is their superior, a young guy who works in an office, wears fashionable clothes, and seems to have no qualms about advancing his career by killing former friends.

The film has the fraught mood if not the adrenaline pace of a thriller. We first see Khosrow and Morteza (no names of cast or crew are given due to the film's perilous political nature) as they are leaving a job. With characteristic subtlety, Rasoulof doesn't show us the killing, only that Khosrow has a man's bloody handprint on his neck—a grisly detail that's somehow more unsettling than explicit violence would be.

Tense and drawn, Khosrow wants their next stop to be an ATM. He needs payment for his mayhem because he has a little boy who requires an operation. But an even greater problem may be his wife, who complains that their son's affliction is punishment for his work. Khosrow's worry over this charge at least shows the flicker of conscience. Morteza, a stolid and unreflective assassin, shrugs it off, saying that their assignments are in accordance with shariah—the very rationale that allows extremist elements in a government supposedly based on religion to slaughter their opponents without compunction, after branding their thought as deviant and foreign-influenced.

Rasoulof interweaves the killers' movements with the actions of certain men who will soon be their targets. They are old and, in one case, infirm, and though they understand their situation well enough to be afraid, their spirits are still defiant. One has a manuscript that recalls an incident some years before when the security apparatus tried to murder a group of writers by driving their bus off a cliff (this is evidently based on an actual incident from 1995). It is this manuscript that is the target of the two killers' superior, a man who seems to combine the worst of medieval theocracy and modern technocracy. The book implicates him, a former dissident turned hardline functionary, so his motives are both nakedly self-serving and cold-bloodedly treacherous.

In his striking earlier films, *Iron Island* and *The White Meadows*, Rasoulof deployed a distinct version of the visual lyricism and quasi-mystical symbolism of other Iranian films. *Manuscripts Don't Burn* offers no such cinematic poetry. It is bluntly literal, almost shockingly so given the context. Rather than other Iranian films, its chilly, muted colors, claustrophobic framings and understated performances by an excellent cast recall 1970s American suspensers such as *The Conversation* and *Klute*.

Like other Iranian directors, however, Rasoulof doesn't care about genre mechanics or conventional narrative arcs. Judged by some standards, the film's last third could use greater dramatic torque and deeper thematic probing. But this is not a standard political thriller. It is an unprecedented statement and damning analysis, an X-ray of not only the toxic political and personal motives that underlie the current regime's murderous assault on dissent, but also of a society polarized between educated cosmopolitans on one side and often illiterate and credulous regime-supporters on the other.

The kinds of killings depicted in the film appear to be based on the "Chain Murders," in which roughly 80 Iranian intellectuals were murdered between the late 1980s and 1998. Rogue hardliners in the security apparatus were supposedly responsible, but though several individuals were tried and convicted of the crimes, their actual provenance and perpetrators remain murky and much-debated.

The film, however, has a contemporary setting, and the anger that fuels it perhaps dates back most directly to 2009, when the Iranian government brutally suppressed protests over a presidential election that many felt was fraudulent. Rasoulof and Panahi were the two most prominent filmmakers associated with the opposition, and both were arrested, tried on trumped-up charges, and given draconian sentences of prison time and banishment from filmmaking for many years. The prison sentences, though, have yet to be carried out, and both filmmakers have gone on making films in secret to be smuggled out of the country. (The exteriors of *Manuscripts Don't Burn* were reportedly shot in Iran, the interiors in Germany, where Rasoulof has been permitted to travel.)

Borrowing his film's title from a famous phrase in *The Master and Margarita* by Soviet dissident Mikhail Bulgakov, Rasoulof no doubt means to encourage a comparison between the dissident artists of the ex-U.S.S.R. and Iran's filmmakers today. But there are also important differences. Under Stalin, artists like Rasoulof and Panahi would have been quickly executed or permanently disappeared to Siberia. In today's Iran, on the other hand, their situation is more like Ai Weiwei's in China: They are too prominent to eradicate completely, yet their continuing obstreperousness makes them targets of constant official harassment and hostility.

In bringing "the bad guy" back into Iranian cinema, Rasoulof has done something that Iranians will instantly recognize: drawn a comparison between the Shah's regime and the present one. Whether he will ever be allowed to work in Iran again, secretly or not, is very much in doubt, but the bravery shown by him and other Iranian artists in recent years will continue to serve as an example to those battling repression the world over.

ENDNOTES

CHAPTER 1

1. "Where Iranian Cinema Is," *Film Comment*, March–April 1993.

2. "Iran So Far Away: Film's New Fertile Crescent," *New York Press*, February 14–21, 1995.

3. "Miramaxed Out," *New York Press*, March 1–7, 1995.

4. "Palme d'Orks: News from Our Man in Cannes," *New York Press*, June 7–13, 1995.

5. Ibid.

6. "The Fraud of Turin," *New York Press*, December 4–10, 1996.

7. "The Death of Film/The Decay of Cinema," *New York Press*, July-August 1999. Reprinted in The Press Gang.

8. *Village Voice*, April 17, 2001.

9. "The Color of God," *The Independent Weekly*, May 17, 2000.

10. "The Circle, Squared," *The Independent Weekly*, July 4, 2001.

11. There Is No Evil, *RogerEbert.com*, May 14, 2021.

12. "Scenes from a Marriage," *Film Comment*, January-February 2012.

CHAPTER 3

1. Henry Corbin, *The Man of Light in Iranian Sufism*, p. 2.

2. Henry Corbin, *History of Islamic Philosophy*, p. 173.

3. Geoff Andrew, *10*, p. 42.

AUTHOR'S WRITINGS ON IRANIAN CINEMA

"Where Iranian Cinema Is," *Film Comment*, March–April 1993.

"Iran So Far Away: Film's New Fertile Crescent" (review of *Through the Olive Trees*), *New York Press*, February 14–21, 1995.

"*Kimia*," *Variety*, September 18, 1995.

"An Iranian Film of Simple Moral Vision" (review of *The White Balloon*), *New York Press*, January 31–February 6, 1996.

"*Gabbeh*," *Variety*, May 14, 1996.

"Abbas Kiarostami: A Cinema of Questions," *Film Comment*, July–August 1996.

"Nights in Tehran," *New York Press*, April 9–15, 1997 (reprinted in *Spectator Magazine*).

"Heart of Palme d'Or" (report on 1997 Cannes Film Festival), *New York Press*, June 4–10, 1997.

"*Gabbeh, Gabbeh*, Hey," *New York Press*, June 18–24, 1997.

"Makhmalbaf: The Figure in the Carpet," *Film Comment*, July–August 1997.

"Journey to the End of Night" (review of *Taste of Cherry*), *Film International*, Vol. 5, No. 1, Fall 1997.

"*Taste of Cherry*," *New York Press*, September 17–23, 1997.

"The Iranian Who Won the World's Attention," *New York Times*, September 28, 1997.

"Seeking a Home," *Projections 9* (published by Faber & Faber), 1998.

"Iran's Fajr Film Festival Closes with *The Glass Agency* Sweeping Top Prizes," *Variety*, February 10, 1998.

"We [Heart] Great Satan," *New York Press*, March 4–10, 1998 (reprinted in *Spectator Magazine*).

"*Taste of Cherry* and *Frozen*," *New York Press*, March 18, 1998.

"*Leila*," *New York Press*, March 25–31, 1998.

"Revealing an Iran Where the Chadors Are Most Chic," *New York Times*, November 8, 1998.

"From Iran, Rising," *New York Press*, November 11, 1998.

"Made in Iran: Films About (Not for) Children," *New York Times*, November 15, 1998.

"The Catcher in the Ire," *New York Press*, November 26, 1998.

"Reeling. Niki to J.D.: Lighten Up," *New York Press*, December 2–8, 1998.

"*Divorce Iranian Style*," *New York Press*, December 9–15, 1998.

"*The Apple*," *New York Press*, February 17, 1999.

"*Birth of a Butterfly*," *New York Press*, March 24–30, 1999.

"Film in the Mirror," *New York Press*, November 10, 1999.

"*Close-Up*," *New York Press*, December 29, 1999–January 4, 2000.

"Confessions of a Sin-ephile: *Close-Up*," *CinemaScope*, Winter 2000 (slightly revised version of *New York Press* article of December 1999).

"*Taste of Cherry*" (liner notes for DVD), The Criterion Collection, 1999.

"*The Color of Paradise* and *Two Women*," *New York Press*, March 29–April 4, 2000.

"The Color of God," *The Independent Weekly*, May 17, 2000.

"*The Wind Will Carry Us*," *New York Press*, July 26–August 1, 2000.

"The Short Films of Abbas Kiarostami," for Cinematexas, 5th Annual Short Film + Video Festival, Austin, Texas, October 16–22, 2000.

"Iran 2000, Part 1," *New York Press*, October 18–24, 2000 (reprinted in *The Independent Weekly* as "Tehran or Not Tehran").

"Iran 2000, Part 2," *New York Press*, October 25–31, 2000 (reprinted in *The Independent Weekly* as "Feast of Cinema").

"How to Read Kiarostami," *Cineaste*, Vol. XXV, November 4, 2000.

"Crossing the Border" (review of *A Time for Drunken Horses*), *The Independent Weekly*, November 22, 2000.

"Poetry and Sufism: A Guide to Understanding Kiarostami's Latest Film," *The Independent Weekly*, December 13, 2000.

"Iran's High-Water Mark," *Village Voice*, April 24, 2001.

"*The Circle*, Squared," *The Independent Weekly*, July 4–10, 2001.

"So Fajr Away," *Village Voice*, February 26, 2002.

"Axis of Cinema," *The Independent Weekly*, February 27, 2002.

The Wind Will Carry Us (article in book *The Hidden God: Film and Faith*, Mary Lea Bandy and Antonio Monda, eds.), The Museum of Modern Art, New York, 2003.

"Why We Should Care About Iranian Films," *newsweekonline.com*, May 2003.

"Present Ten(se)" (reviews of *Ten* and *Divine Intervention*), *The Independent Weekly*, June 18, 2003.

"Persian Crack-up," *The Independent Weekly*, March 17, 2004.

"A Carpet of Light: *Gabbeh*" (DVD booklet essay), New Yorker Films, 2005.

"*A Moment of Innocence*," (DVD booklet essay), New Yorker Films, 2005.

"Forbidden Games," *The Independent Weekly*, May 25, 2005.

"The Elemental Poetics of *Iron Island*" (essay for pressbook), Kino International, 2006.

"Parallel Lives" (obits of Fereydoun Hoveyda and Farrokh Ghaffari), *Film Comment*, March–April, 2007.

"An Iranian Coming-of-Age Tale in *Persepolis*," *The Independent Weekly*, February 6, 2008.

"*Makhmalbaf at Large: The Making of a Rebel Filmmaker*," *Sight & Sound*, October 2008.

"*Close-Up*: Prison and Escape" (DVD booklet essay), The Criterion Collection, 2010.

"The Power and Fascination of Persian Cats" (review of *No One Knows About*

Persian Cats), *Metro Magazine*, May 2010.

"Iranian Director Gets Freedom and Moral Victory," *Salon.com*, May 25, 2010.

"*Of Gods and Me*n and *Certified Copy*," *Metro Magazine*, April 2011.

"*Certified Copy*: At Home and Abroad" (DVD booklet essay), The Criterion Collection, 2012.

"Scenes from a Marriage" (about Asghar Farhadi and *A Separation*), *Film Comment*, January–February, 2012.

"A Must-See New Film Crosses Boundaries" (review of *A Separation*), *Metro Magazine*, February 2012.

"Iran's Cinematic Spring" (includes discussions of Farhadi's *A Separation* and Panahi's *This Is Not Film*), *Dissent*, Spring 2012.

"*The Past*," *RogerEbert.com*, December 20, 2013.

"*Manuscripts Don't Burn*," *RogerEbert.com*, June 13, 2014.

"*Closed Curtain*," *RogerEbert.com*, July 9, 2014.

"*Fifi Howls from Happiness*," *RogerEbert.com*, August 8, 2014.

"*About Elly*," *RogerEbert.com*, April 8, 2015.

"*Fireworks Wednesday*," *RogerEbert.com*, March 16, 2016.

"*The President*," *RogerEbert.com*, June 3, 2016.

"Godfrey Cheshire on Knowing Abbas Kiarostami Through His Films and Friendship," *RogerEbert.com*, July 5, 2016.

"*The Salesman*," *RogerEbert.com*, January 27, 2017

"How Abbas Kiarostami Changed My Life," *IndieWire*, July 4, 2017.

"City of Abbas," *Film Comment*, November–December 2017

"*24 Frames*," *Film Comment*, November–December 2017

"*24 Frames*," *RogerEbert.com,* February 1, 2018

"Tehran Taboo," *RogerEbert.com*, Feb. 14, 2018

"Oliver Stone to Iranian Government: Let Jafar Panahi Attend the Cannes Film Festival," *IndieWire*, April 25, 2018.

"*No Date, No Signature*," *RogerEbert.com*, Aug. 1, 2018.

"Interview with Mahmoud Kalari," *FilmComment.com*, November 12, 2018

"The Charmer," *RogerEbert.com*, Dec. 5, 2018.

"Iranian Cinema is Finally Getting a NYC Festival, and Cinephiles Should Pay Attention, *IndieWire*, Jan. 10, 2019.

"*Pig*," *RogerEbert.com*, Feb. 1, 2019.

"*There Is No Evil*," *RogerEbert.com*, May 14, 2021.

"*Chess of the Wind*," *RogerEbert.com*, Oct. 29, 2021.

"*Atabai*," *RogerEbert.com*, June 2, 2022.

"*A Man of Integrity*," *RogerEbert.com*, June 17. 2022.

ACKNOWLEDGMENTS

As noted in the Preface, my work on Iranian cinema over the past three decades has benefited from the kindness, help and expertise of many people, including Iranians, Iranian-Americans and others of the Iranian diaspora, as well as friends and colleagues of various sorts, including editors, fellow journalists and members of the international film community. Many of these are named in the text, and I extend my thanks to all of them.

Of those not named, I also thank the following: Gabriel Motta Thimoteo, for his love and support; Katherine Dieckmann, for suggesting the book's title; Tania Ahmadi, for help on many fronts; Deborah Young; Steve Levitas; John Rosenthal; Jonathan Steven Lee; Fatemeh Motamed-arya; Alireza Shoja-noori; Amir Soltani; Azar Nafisi; Maani Petgar; Houshang Golmakani; Aurelia Thiérrée; Rob Williams; Miguel Gesso Rodriguez; Sophie Gluck; Susan Norget; Nariman Hamed; Fereshteh Taerpour; Shamil Idriss; Nicholas Elliott; Isil Baghdadi; Ahmad Nadalizadeh; Parviz Kalantari; Seyyed Hossein Nasr; Iraj Anvar; Scott Kiernan; Michael Galinsky; Sujewa Ekanayake; Shahen Bazil; Dorna Khazeni; Olga Davidson and the Ilex Foundation; plus my mother, sister, brother and their families in North Carolina.

My profound gratitude also goes to the 247 people who contributed to an Indiegogo campaign that provided great assistance in the completion of this book. Special thanks go to Gus Gusler and Diana Takata for their help. And to Todd Phillips, the auteur of *The Hangover* and *Joker*, for his timely generosity.

Finally, as I was at the completion of *Conversations with Kiarostami*, I am enormously indebted to Jim Colvill, for his extraordinarily intelligent, painstaking and patient skills in editing this book, as well as in publishing and releasing it. Thank you, Jim!

INDEX

3 Faces/Se Rokh (Jafar Panahi), 61, 67, 100fn
10 on Ten/Dah ruye Dah (Abbas Kiarostami), 169, 170
24 Frames/24 Ghāb (Abbas Kiarostami), **188–192**
    as "experimental," 94, 190–91
    method of animation, 188–89
    natural world as focus, 188–90
    as reflecting Kiarostami's artistic journey, 191–92
    use of computer-generated imagery (CGI), 188–90, 190–91
76 Minutes and 15 Seconds with Abbas Kiarostami/Haftādo Shesh Daghighe va Pānzdah Sāniye bā Abbas Kiārostami (Seifollah Samadian), 66, 93
400 Blows, The (Francois Truffaut), 38, 119, 136, 221
2001: A Space Odyssey (Stanley Kubrick), 27, 151

Abadan (city), 42, 61fn
Abadan/Abādān (Mani Haghighi), 66, 95
ABC Africa/Ey Bi Ci Afrighā (Abbas Kiarostami), 54–55, 93, 94, 107, 162
Abdi, Akbar, 206
About Elly/Darbāreye Elly (Asghar Farhadi), **233–236**
    and comparisons to *L'Avventura* (Antonioni)
    and *Jaws* (Spielberg), 233
    Mani Haghighi on, 97
    middle and upper classes as focus, 234
    as "opening space" for audience reflection, 235
    structure of, 234–35
    U.S. release of, 64
Academy Awards, 60, 65, 82
Actor, The/Honarpishe (Mohsen Makhmalbaf), 206
Affleck, Ben, 223
Afkami, Beyrouz (Film) *The Bride/Arus*, 20
Agha-Soltan, Neda, 58, 99
Ahmadinejad, Mahmoud (President)
    contested election, 58, 230
    repression under, 56, 175
Ahmadi, Tania, 241
Ahmad, Jalal Al-e, 42

Ahmadpour, Ahmad, 125
Ahmadpour, Babak, 95, 125
Ahura Mazda, 77
Ai Weiwei, 257
Akbari, Mania, 164, 166, 167, 168, 169
Akrami, Jamsheed, 14, 27, 42, 54, 55, 58, 60, 66, 242
Albee, Edward, 237
Alexander the Great, 32, 76
Alidoosti, Taraneh, 66, 97, 233, 238, 240
Almereyda, Michael, 50, 51
Altman, Robert, 31
Amenabar, Alejandro, 85
American Tragedy, An (Theodore Dreiser), 41
Amini, Abbas (Films), *Hendi and Hormoz/Hendi va Hormoz*, 67
Amini, Ahmad, 242
Amour Fou, L' (Jacques Rivette), 238
Anderson, Laurie, 75
And Life Goes On/Zendegi va Digar Hich (Abbas Kiarostami)
    auteur cinema questioned, 124
    autobiographical dimension in, 15, 107, 184, 152
    humanism of, 129
    and idea of home, 131
    as Koker Trilogy film, 121
    life-death relationship as motif, 186
    and Masterworks period, 107
    and Revolution's failures, 106
    self-reflexive element, 25–26, 109
Andrew, Geoff, 15, 93, 168
Antonioni, Michelangelo, 38, 139, 145, 146, 150, 179, 196, 225–26, 229, 233
Apple, The/Sib (Samira Makhmalbaf), **215–220**
    alacrity of production, 47, 215
    directorial credit questioned, 216
    and female status in Iran, 49, 218–19
    international acclaim for, 49–50
    as "Samira's film," 220
    symbolism in, 219
    use of non-professional actors, 216, 217–18

Arabian Nights, The, 199
Aristotle, 155
Aslani, Mohammed Reza, 39
Atebbai, Mohammad, 93, 95
At Five in the Afternoon/Panj-e Asr (Samira Makhmalbaf), 56
Attar, 161
auteur cinema
    connection with literary culture, 23, 77–78, 139–41
    and Iranian films (1985-2000), 19–21, 25, 31, 140
    questioned, 123–24, 213
    and *Journey to Italy* (Roberto Rossellini), 179
    See also Iranian New Wave cinema
Avicenna (Ibn Sina), 141, 155
Avventura, L' (Michelangelo Antonioni), 179, 225, 233
Azadi Stadium, 58

Bahari, Maziar, 55fn
Bahrani, Ramin, 63
Ballad of Tara, The/Cherike-ye Tārā (Bahram Beyzai), 40
Banaei, Poori, 252
Bani-Etemad, Rakhshan, 44
Bani-Etemad, Rakhshan (Films)
    May Lady, The/Bānuye Ordibehesht, 49
    Under the Skin of the City/Zir-e Pust-e Shahr, 56
Baran/Bārān (Majid Majidi), 56
Beautiful City, The/Shahr-e Zibā (Asghar Farhadi), 64, 96
Bashu, the Little Stranger/Bāshu, Gharibeye Kuchak (Bahram Beyzai), 20, 21, 68
Bazin, André, 139
Beckett, Samuel, 237
Beheshti, Seyyed Mohammad, 43–44
Bejo, Berenice, 253
Belle de Jour (Luis Buñuel), 151
Bellow, Saul, 51, 83, 195
Bergman, Ingmar, 95, 179
Bergman, Ingrid, 179
Berlin Film Festival, 58, 60, 61, 234
Best Years of Our Lives, The (William Wyler), 192

Beyzai, Bahram
    background in theater, 39, 149–50, 234, 237
    depiction of women, 22
    deviation from "Iranian" cinema aesthetic, 65
    exploration of myth, 39–40
    influence on Asghar Farhadi, 65, 234
    post-revolution career resurrection, 43–44
    reputation, 65, 92, 134, 149
Beyzai, Bahram (Films)
    Ballad of Tara, The/Cherike-ye Tārā, (1978), 40
    Bashu, the Little Stranger/Bāshu, Gharibeye Kuchak, 20, 21, 68
    Downpour/Ragbār, 40
    Stranger and the Fog, The/Gharibe va Meh, 40
    Travelers, The/Mosāferān, 65, 234
Bicycle Thieves (Vittorio De Sica), 119, 124, 136, 196
Binoche, Juliette, 93, 173, 176, 177
Blackboards/Takhte Siyāh (Samira Makhmalbaf), 52, 53
Blake, William, 155
Blow-Up (Michelangelo Antonioni), 151, 225
Bly, Robert, 145
Borges, Jorge Luis, 211
Boycott/Bāycot (Mohsen Makhmalbaf)
    autobiographical dimension in, 204
    and political relativism, 204–5
    Brandão, Rodrigo, 62
"Bread and Alley"/"Nān va Kuche" (Abbas Kiarostami)
    decentered narrative, 119
    and Kanoon period, 40, 107
    spatial orientation as motif, 130–31
Breathless (Jean-Luc Godard), 38, 41
Brecht, Bertolt, 139
Bresson, Robert, 137
Brick and the Mirror, The/Khesht va Ayne, (Ebrahim Golestan)
    as film noir, 37–38
    use of direct sound, 38
Bride, The/Arus (Beyrouz Afkami), 20
Brighter Summer Day, A (Edward Yang), 104

Brooks, Richard, 41
Brother (Takeshi Kitano), 85
Bruegel, Pieter, 188, 189
Büchner, Georg, 197
Bulgakov, Mikhail, 257
Bullets Over Broadway (Woody Allen), 29
Buñuel, Luis, 37, 83, 198, 205
Bunyan, John, 155
Bush, George W. and "axis of evil" remarks, 55, 56, 67, 85–86

Cahiers du cinéma, 14, 26, 35
Callas, Maria, 189
Canaan/Kan'ān (Mani Haghighi), 98
Cannes Film Festival
    as author's *Variety* assignment, 29–30
    influence of, 25–26, 144, 208–9
    Iranian prizewinners, 25, 26, 30, 31, 52, 60
    as venue for bridge-building, 50–51
Carter, Jimmy, 47
"Case No. 1, Case No. 2"/"Ghaziye Shekl-e Aval, Shekl-e Dovom" (Abbas Kiarostami)
    and idea of home, 132
    mentality of revolution in, 131–32
Cassavetes, John, 79, 136
Castaneda, Carlos, 44
"Castle, The"/"Ghal'e"(Kamran Shirdel), 36
Center for the Intellectual Development of Children and Young Adults (Kanoon), 40, 53, 107, 108, 117, 133, 134, 163, 243
Certified Copy/Copy Barābar-e Asl (Abbas Kiarostami), **175–180**
    autobiographical dimension in, 107, 114
    blurring of truth and fiction, 178
    as companion to *The Report*, 180
    as European art film, 175–76
    as female-centered, 176–79
    genesis of, 176
    as "half-made" film, 178
    interrupted journeys in, 177

link to *Journey to Italy* (Roberto Rossellini), 178–79
made outside Iran, 175
mixed responses to, 175–76
woman as central figure in, 176–79
Chahine, Youssef, 144
"Chain Murders," 257
Chaplin, Charlie, 46, 212
Chazelle, Damien, 91
Chekhov, Anton, 41
Children of Heaven/Bache-hāye Asemān (Majid Majidi)
Fajr Festival award winner, 82
grade school audience response to, 53
vs. U.S. news image of Iran, 85
U.S release of, 49
Chittick, William, 154
Chomsky, Noam, 75
Christ, Jesus, 216
Cinémathèque Française, 14, 35
cinematic modernism
and Kiarostami, 139, 149–51, 233
See also French New Wave cinema; Iranian New Wave cinema
Circle, The/Dāyere (Jafar Panahi)
anti-regime stance, 100
oppression of women in, 57, 228
Venice Film Festival award winner, 52
Citizen Kane (Orson Welles), 27, 206
Closed Curtain/Parde (Jafar Panahi), **230–232**
banning of, 99, 230
compared with *This Is Not a Film*, 60
as reflection on effects of confinement, 230–32
Close-Up (Abbas Kiarostami)
at 1992 Lincoln Center film festival, 20
anticipated by *Haji Agha, Cinema Actor*, 34
auteur cinema questioned, 124
autobiographical dimension in, 184
blurring of truth and fiction, 123–24
cinephilia reflected by, 23–24, 117
and "Close-Up Long Shot," 32

and "The Day *Close-Up* Opened," 127
director as hero in, 24
films derived from, 127–28
Hossein Sabzian character in, 23–24, 32
and idea of home, 131
international impact, 24–25
and Masterworks period, 107
New York theatrical opening, 52
and Revolution's failures, 106
self-reflexive element, 25, 109
use of binary opposites, 119
"Close-Up Long Shot"/"Close-Up Namāye Dur" (Mamhoud Chokrallahi and Moslem Mansouri), 32, 127
commercial cinema
    features of, 34–35
    and *filmfarsi*, 35, 39, 44
    and Iranian New Wave, 38, 41–42
    and *The Lor Girl*, 34–35
Conference of the Birds, The (Attar), 161
Conqueror, The (Dick Powell), 211
Constitutional Revolution (1906-11), 33
Contempt (Jean-Luc Godard), 124, 139, 141, 179
Conversation, The (Francis Ford Coppola), 256
Conversations with Kiarostami (Godfrey Cheshire), 45, 47, 106fn
Coppola, Francis Ford, 59, 99
Coppola, Sofia, 225
Corbin, Henry, 44, 154–56, 157, 159, 161
Cotillard, Marion, 253
Council for Foreign Relations, 50
Cow, The/Gāv (Dariush Mehrjui)
    and 1971 Venice Film Festival award, 38
    as art film, 38–39, 83, 92
    Ayatollah Khomeini's admiration of, 43, 83, 92, 195, 197
    banning of, 48–49, 197
    and Gholem-Hossein Sa'edi's poem, 238
    Ezzatolah Entezami in, 247
    as launching Iranian New Wave cinema, 83, 92, 238

neorealist influence on, 196–97
   referenced in *The Salesman*, 238
Crimson Gold/Talāye Sorkh (Jafar Panahi), **225–229**
   anti-regime stance, 100
   artistic and moral vision linked, 226–29
   as indictment of Revolution's failures, 227–28
   social realities in, 57–58
   use of non-professional actors, 228
Cronin, Paul, *Lessons with Kiarostami*, 94
Cycle, The/Dāyere-ye Minā (Dariush Mehrjui)
   banning of, 197
   as social criticism, 205
   U.S. art house release, 39
Cyclist, The/Bicycle-rān (Mohsen Makhmalbaf)
   influence on Asghar Farhadi, 96
   as social criticism, 24, 80, 96

Dabashi, Hamid, 14, 27, 47–48
Dances with Wolves (Kevin Costner), 78
Dante, 139
D'Arcy, William Knox, 40
Dariush, Hajir, 39
Davaie, Parviz, 242
Davudnezhad, Alireza, 20, 41
Davudnezhad, Alireza (Films), *Need, The/Niyāz* , 20
"Day *Close-Up* Opened, The" (Nanni Moretti), 127
Day for Night (Francois Truffaut), 124
Day I Became a Woman, The/Ruzi ke Zan Shodam (Marziyeh Meshkini), 52, 53
"Day My Aunt Was Ill, The"/"Ruzi ke Khāle-am Mariz Bud" (Hana Makhmalbaf), 47
Dead End (Parvis Sayyad), 41–42
Dead Man (Jim Jarmusch), 75
Death of a Salesman (Arthur Miller), 237, 238, 239
"Death of Film/The Decay of Cinema" (Godfrey Cheshire essay), 52
Dehlavi, Hossein, 172
Deliverance (James Dickey novel), 50
DeMille, Cecil B., 204

Demme, Jonathan, 59, 99
Denby, David, 143
Denden, 182
Deneuve, Catherine, 105, 135
De Niro, Robert, 59, 99
Derambakhsh, Kambiz 242
De Sica, Vittorio, 95, 196
Despair (R. W. Fassbinder), 124
Devil, Probably, The (Robert Bresson), 137
Dickens, Charles, 77, 221
Dickey, Christopher, 50
Dickey, James, 50
digital technology
    Kiarostami's conversion to, 52, 56, 60, 94, 107, 162–63, 165–66, 188–90, 190–91
    Panahi's use of, 60, 230
Djomeh (Hassan Yektapanah), 52, 53
Doll's House, A (Henrik Ibsen), 83, 198
Dorani, Behzad, 249
Dormishian, Reza, 91, 101
Dostoyevsky, Fyodor, 226
Double Take Documentary Film Festival (Durham, North Carolina), 54–55
Douglas, Kirk, 46, 211
Dovzhenko, Alexander, 200
Downpour/Ragbār (Bahram Beyzai), 40
Dreams (Akira Kurosawa), 190
Dreiser, Theodore, 41, 221

Ebert, Chaz, 53
Ebert, Roger, 53, 143, 146–47, 151, 153, 161
Ebrahimifar, Sa'ied (Films), *Pomegranate and Cane/Nār va Ney*, 20
Edison, Thomas, 190
Eel, The (Shohei Imamura), 45
Eidizadeh, Hossein, 98
Einstein, Albert, 199, 216
Emadeddin, Hossein, 227
Emerson, R. W., 145

Entezami, Ezatollah, 38, 197, 247
Erice, Victor, 93
Ershadi, Hemayoun, 130
Ershad (Ministry of Culture and Islamic Guidance), 21–22
Esfandiari, Amir, 45
Esfandiari, Vahid, 45
Este-aze (Fleeing from Evil to God) (Mohsen Makhmalbaf), 204
Evin Prison, 58, 59fn

Face in the Crowd, A (Elia Kazan), 67, 207
Fajr Film Festival (1985), 243
Fajr Film Festival (1990), 25
Fajr Film Festival (1997-2002), 32–33, 49–50, 52, 55, 58, 63–65, 66, 67, 74–75, 82–83, 85–88, 128, 216
Fajr Film Festival and Fajr International Film Festival (2017), 63–65, 89–94, 95
Farabi Cinema Foundation, 43–44, 64, 78–79
Farahani, Golshifteh, 49, 99, 235, 247, 248
Farhadi, Asghar
    biographical background, 237, 253
    deviation from "Iranian" film aesthetic, 65–66, 95–98, 234
    influences on, 65, 96, 234, 237–38, 239
    films winning Academy Awards, 20
    Mahmoud Kalari on, 252–54
    Mani Haghighi on, 95–98
    middle class marriage as signature subject, 238
    on "opening spaces" for audience reflection, 235
    use of professional actors, 235–36, 240, 253
Farhadi, Asghar (Films)
    About Elly/Darbāreye Elly, 64, 66, 68, 95, 97, 98, **233–36**, 252
    Fireworks Wednesday/Chāhārshanbe Suri, 66, 96, 97, 252
    Beautiful City, The/Shahr-e Zibā, 64, 96
    Past, The/Gozashte, 97, 240, 253–54
    Salesman, The/Forushande, 22, 65, 66, 68, 97, 98, 236, **237–40**
    Separation, A/Jodāie Nāder az Simin, 22, 64–65, 66, 68, 97, 98, 99, 234, 236, 239, 240, 241, 252–254
Farmanara, Bahman (Films)
    House Built on Water, A/Khāne ie Ruye Ab, 88

I Want to Dance/Delam Mikhād, 66
Prince Ehtejab/Shāzde Ehtejāb, 40
Smell of Camphor, Fragrance of Jasmine/Buye Kāfur Atr-e Yās, 52
Tale of the Sea/Hekāyat-e Daryā, 66
Tall Shadows of the Wind/Sāye-hāye Boland-e Bād, 40
Farrokhzad, Forough
    collaboration with Ebrahim Golestan, 36–37
    death of, 37
    and poetic cinema, 37, 113, 148–49
    and *The Wind Will Carry Us*, 37, 148–49, 159, 187
Farrokhzad, Forough (Films), "The House is Black," 39, 68, 149
Fassbinder, R. W., 40, 238
Father, The/Pedar, (Majid Majidi), 32
Fellini, Federico, 95, 196
Ferdowsi, 141, 146, 171
Film Actors School, 34
Film Comment, 19, 20, 143
Film Monthly, 195
filmfarsi, 35, 39, 44
filmmaker/critic relationship
    benefits of friendship, 104, 135–36
    and objectivity, 103–4
film noir
    Brick and the Mirror, The (Ebrahim Golestan) as, 37–38
    Night of the Hunchback (Farrokh Gaffary) as, 37
FIPRESCI (international critics) prize, 38, 52
Fireworks Wednesday/Chāhārshanbe Suri (Asghar Farhadi)
    as new model, 66, 96
    as remake of *The Report*, 97
    Mani Haghighi on, 97
First Graders/Avali-hā (Abbas Kiarostami)
    as critique of educational system, 47
    and idea of home, 131
    as Kanoon period film, 107
First Run Features, 198
Fish & Cat/Māhi va Gorbe (Shahram Mokri), 101
Fitzgerald, Edward, translation of *The Rubaiyat of Omar Khayyam*, 77

Five Dedicated to Ozu/Panj (Abbas Kiarostami)
    contemplative/interrogative responses invited by, 170–71
    as experimental, 94, 170
    natural world as focus, 170, 188
    Seifollah Samadian as cinematographer, 93
Forouzesh, Ebrahim (Films)
    Key, The/Kelid, 20
Franny and Zooey (J. D. Salinger), 195, 198
French New Wave cinema
    and Fereydoun Hoveyda, 35
    and Iranian post-revolutionary cinema, 25, 38, 139–40
Fridricksson, Fridrick Thor, 93
Frosty Roads/Jāde-hāye Sard (Masoud Jafari Jozani), 243

Gabbeh (Mohsen Makhmalbaf), **199–203**
    as antidote to Hollywood culture, 200
    auteur cinema questioned, 213
    author's response to, 31
    color as symbol in, 203, 246
    Mahmoud Kalari as cinematographer, 201
    Mahmoud Kalari on, 244
    multiplicity of voices in, 203, 213
    as New York Film Festival feature, 49
    nomadic artistic practice as model, 201
    as poetic cinema, 80–81, 200–202
    self-reflexive element, 213
    as tribute to disappearing things, 207
Gaffary, Farrokh
    influence on Iranian cinema culture, 35, 39
    and neorealism, 35–36
    post-revolutionary emigration, 43
Gaffary, Farrokh (Films)
    Night of the Hunchback/Shab-e Ghuzi, 37
    South of the City, The/Jonub-e Shahr, 35–36
Ganjavi, Nezami, 171
Game of Thrones (TV series), 91
Get Out (Jordan Peele), 91

gharbzadegi ("Westoxication"), 42
Gharib, Shapour, 41
Ghobadi, Bahman
    biographical background, 54, 222, 224
    and Kiarostami, 224, 250
    and Telluride Film Festival, 54, 224
Ghobadi, Bahman (Films)
    Marooned in Iraq/Avāz hāye Sarzamin-e Mādari-am, 56
    No One Knows About Persian Cats/Kasi az Gorbe-hāye Irāni Khabar Nadāre, 56
    Time for Drunken Horses, A/Zamāni Barāye Masti-e Asb-hā, 52, 54, 221–24
    Turtles Can Fly/Lākposht hā ham Parvāz Mikonand, 56
Golmakani, Houshang, 40, 206
Gilmore, Geoffrey, 50
Godard, Jean-Luc, 14, 35, 36, 38, 41, 77, 124, 128, 139, 150, 157, 179, 191, 196
Goethe, J. W. v., 145
Gogoosh, 41
Goleh, Fereydoun, 41
Golestan, Ebrahim
    collaboration with Forough Farrokhzad, 36–37
    interest in Iranian culture, 39
Golestan, Ebrahim (Films), *Brick and the Mirror, The/Khesht va Ayne*, 37–38
Golestan Film Studio, 36
Golestan, Kaveh, 242
Golshiri, Houshang, 40
Goodbye, Friend/Khodāhafez Rafigh (Amir Naderi), 41
Goodbye/Be Omid-e Didār (Mohammad Rasoulof), 61
Grass (Merian C. Cooper, Ernest B. Schoedsack), 200
Green Movement and Jafar Panahi, 58–59, 100
    as response to Ahmadinejad's re-election, 58, 98, 175
Griffith, D. W., 77–78
Guevara, Che, 216
Guillemet, Nicole, 50

Hafez, 95, 141, 146, 187
Haghighi, Mani
    and *About Elly*, 235–36
    collaboration with Farhadi, 65–66, 97, 98

on Farhadi, 95–98
perspective on Iranian film, 95–98
rejection of "Kiarostami-Makhmalbaf" model, 65–66, 96–97
Haghighi, Mani (Films)
Abadan/Abādān, 65, 95
Canaan/Kan'ān, 98
Fireworks Wednesday/Chāhārshanbe Suri (co-writer with Farhadi), 66, 97
Pig/Khuk, 66–67
Haji Agha, Cinema Actor/Hāji Aghā, Actor-e Cinemā (Ovanes Ohanian), 34
Hamid-Nezhad, Azizollah (Films) *Hoor on Fire/Hur dar Ātāsh*, 20
Hamoon/Hāmoon (Dariush Mehrjui)
autobiographical dimension in, 197
critical acclaim in Iran, 195
depiction of women in, 65
feminist protest in, 197
Khosrow Shakibai in, 21, 247–48
Hamlet (Michael Almereyda), 50
Hampton, Howard, 143-144
Hananeh, Morteza, 172
Haritash, Khosrow, 41
Hatami, Ali, 41
Hatamikia, Ebrahim (Films), *Low Heights/Ertefā'-e Past*, 88
Hatami, Leila, 247, 248
Hauser, Kaspar, 215
Hawke, Ethan, 50
Hayward, Susan, 46
Hekmat, Manijeh (Films), *Women's Prison/Zendān-e Zanān*, 86
Hendi and Hormoz/Hendi va Hormoz (Abbas Amini), 67
Herzog, Werner, 80, 123, 221
Hitchcock, Alfred, 37, 98, 239
Hölderlin, Friedrich, 139
Home, The/Khāne (Asghar Yousefinejad), 67
Homer, 141
Homework/Mashgh-e Shab (Abbas Kiarostami)
as critique of educational system, 47, 115–16
and idea of home, 131
and Masterworks period, 107, 108

Hoor on Fire/*Hur dar Ātāsh* (Azizollah Hamid-Nezhad), 20
Hope, Ted, 59
Hosseini, Shahab, 98, 235–36, 238, 240
Hotel Naderi, Tehran, 74–75
Hou Hsiao-hsien, 31, 109, 144
House Built on Water, A/*Khāne ie Ruye Ab* (Bahman Farmanara), 88
"House is Black, The"/"Khāne Siyāh Ast" (Forough Farrokhzad)
    influence of, 37, 39, 148–49
    as poetic cinema, 37, 149
Hoveyda, Fereydoun, 14, 35
"Hunters in the Snow, The" (Pieter Bruegel), 189
Hussein, Saddam, 72, 228

Ibn Arabi, 141, 146
Ibsen, Henrik, 83, 198
Ikiru (Akira Kurosawa), 184
Imamura, Shohei, 45
I'm Not Angry/*Asabāni Nistam* (Reza Dormishian), 101
Impasse/*Tangnā* (Amir Naderi), 41
Independence Day (Roland Emmerich), 78
In the Alleys of Love/*Dar Kuche-hāye Eshgh* (Khosro Sinaie), 20
Ionesco, Eugene, 211, 237
Iranian cinema (1900-1978)
    artistic cinema roots, 35–38
    cinematograph introduced, 33
    commercial cinema, 34–35
    documentaries, 36–37
    dramatic films, 37–38
    early films spoofed in *Once Upon a Time, Cinema* (Mohsen Makhmalbaf), 34
    and government policy, 36, 42
    Shah as target of discontent, 265
    and Western cultural influence, 34, 42
    See also Iranian New Wave cinema
Iranian cinema (1978-82)
    Ayatollah Khomeini's support of, 43, 92, 197
    disarray of, 42–43
Iranian cinema (1985-2000)
    approach to political issues, 22–23

auteur voices in, 25
as challenge to Western models, 140–41
cinephilia reflected by, 23–24
depiction of women, 22, 65
factors in Western perception of, 208–9
government policy toward, 19, 21–22, 78–79, 99
humanism of, 20, 25, 85, 199
international reputation, 85, 92–95
and literary culture, 23, 77–78
low-budget ingenuity, 21, 22, 25
prize winners, 25, 26, 30, 31, 52
and production code, 21–22, 65–66, 81–82, 163
reconstruction under Farabi Cinema Foundation, 43–44, 64, 78–79
and Search for Common Ground effort, 50–51
self-reflexive element, 25–26, 109, 204, 213
social realism in, 22–23, 25, 96, 255
and "the Khatami wave," 53
use of children as characters, 22, 53, 163
use of non-professional actors, 21, 65, 97, 239–40
Iranian cinema (2000s)
artistic and moral vision linked, 226
dominance of Jafar Panahi films, 57
effects of Ahmadinejad election on, 56, 59
Fireworks Wednesday as new film model, 66
oppositional tone of, 56–58
social and political events reflected by, 56
Iranian cinema (2010s)
commercial vs. art films, 91
government repression, filmmakers' responses to, 61–62
and Jafar Panahi, 59–61, 62
and Mohammad Rasoulof, 61–62
Iranian Film Festival New York (2019)
author as co-founder, 66
cinema self-renewal illustrated in, 66–67
historical format, 66–67
Iranian New Wave cinema (1969–1979)
art film directors, 38–40

artistic/commercial paradigm established in, 38–39
commercial film directors, 38, 41–42
defined, 38
and French New Wave, 25, 35, 77–78, 139–40
Iranian culture as central to, 39–40
and Italian neorealism, 25, 35, 77
and post-revolutionary cinema revival, 25, 43–44
social criticism in, 41–42
See also auteur cinema
Iranians, The (Sandra Mackey), 78
Iren, 252
Iron Island/Jazireye Ahani (Mohammad Rasoulof), 56, 256
Isfahan, 46, 141, 246
Islamic Republic
attempt to impede foreign cultural intrusions, 78–79
Ayatollah Khomeini's support of cinema, 43, 92, 197
"brain drain," 87
cinema as image booster, 73, 78–79
conservative obstructionism, 87, 134, 228
cultural liberalization under Khatami, 53, 56, 86–87
and film industry reconstruction, 43–44, 78–79
paradoxical relationship with film industry, 19, 21–22, 42–43, 48–49
post-Khatami repression, 56, 58–59, 61, 175
production code, 21–22, 65–66, 81–82, 163
Italian neorealism
and Fereydoun Hoveyda, 35
and Iranian New Wave, 25, 35–36, 77
and Iranian post-revolutionary cinema, 25, 35
I Want to Dance/Delam Mikhād (Bahman Farmanara), 66

Jafarian, Hossein, 228, 235, 239
Jarmusch, Jim, 63, 104
Jaws (Steven Spielberg), 233, 235
JFK (Oliver Stone), 78
Johnson, Lyndon Baines, 84
Jones, Kent, 59
Journey, The/Safar (Ali-Reza Raissian)

Kiarostami's script for, 122
Kalari, Mahmoud
   on, Abbas Kiarostami, 248–52
   on Asghar Farhadi, 252–54
   biographical background, 241–43
   on Dariush Mehrjui, 247–48
   as *Gabbeh* cinematographer, 201, 204
   on *Gabbeh*, 244
   on Mohsen Makhmalbaf, 243–44
   as *Moment of Innocence* cinematographer, 210
   on *Salaam Cinema*, 244–47
   as *A Separation* cinematographer, 241
   on *The Wind Will Carry Us*, 248–51
Journey to Italy (Roberto Rossellini), 124, 178-179
Jozani, Masoud Jafari, 243
Jung, Carl, 44

Kafka, Franz, 205
Kamali, Ali, 188
Kandahar/Safar-e Ghandehār (Mohsen Makhmalbaf), 56
Kanoon (Center for the Intellectual Development of Children and Young Adults), 40, 53, 107, 117, 133, 134, 163
Kaplanoglu, Semih, 93
Karimi, Niki, 198, 247, 248
Karim-Masihi, Varuzh (Films), *Last Act, The/Parde-y Ākhar*, 20
Karina, Anna, 139
Kase, Ryo, 183
Kaufman, Anthony, 59
Kazan, Elia, 234, 239
Keaton, Buster, 104, 122
Kehr, Dave, 143
Key, The/Kelid (Ebrahim Forouzesh), 20, 122
Khamenei, Ali (Ayatollah), 32, 80, 197
Khaneh Cinema, 50
Khatami, Mohammad (President)
   cultural liberalization under, 53, 56, 86–87
   dissatisfaction with, 87–88, 168, 227

as Minister of Culture and Islamic Guidance (1980s), 84, 134
   obstruction by conservative clerics, 87, 134, 228
Khayyam, Omar, 77, 149, 159, 160, 187
Khazeni, Dorna, 62
Khomeini, Ruhollah (Ayatollah), 24, 33, 43, 72, 83, 92, 168, 185, 195, 197
Khosrow and Shirin (Nezami Ganjavi), 171, 172
Kiarostami, Abbas
   activity beyond filmmaking, 94–95, 112, 162
   and Akira Kurosawa, 79, 117–18, 184
   apolitical stance, 62, 105–6
   author's friendship with, 27, 45, 47
   biographical background, 117, 120, 128, 129
   and cinematic modernism, 139, 149–51, 233
   on "Close-Up Long Shot," 32
   conversion to digital technology, 52, 56, 60, 94, 107, 162–63, 165–66, 188–90, 190–91
   death of, 62, 92
   Experimental period films, 94, 107, 108, 112, 162–74
   films as "cinema of questions," 116–17
   how to approach, 112–14, 145–46, 160–61
   influence on Iranian filmmakers, 53, 89, 91
   insistence on "reading" the film, 147, 150, 157
   as Kanoon film division director, 40, 133
   Kanoon period films, 107, 133
   Mahmoud Kalari on, 248–52
   Masterworks period films, 107–8
   mode of "symbolism," 151–52, 156–61
   personal characteristics, 105, 109, 132–33, 248–49, 250–51
   and poetic cinema, 37, 39, 52, 148–49, 158, 159, 159–60, 187
   reputation, 79, 85, 92–95, 108–9, 117–18, 134, 143, 150, 152
   shift to female-centered films, 163, 166–67, 171–73, 176–79, 180, 181–83
   and Shiism, 157–58, 159
   and Sufism, 111–12, 155–61
   tributes to, 62–63, 92–94
   use of children as central characters, 40, 133, 163, 165
   use of non-professional actors, 65
   visual acuity of, 103, 190, 251

Kiarostami, Abbas (Film Features)
  autobiographical dimension, 106–7, 112, 114, 115, 152–54, 165, 180, 184–87, 188–90, 191–92
  blurring of truth and fiction, 123–24, 165, 178, 191
  connections among films, 121–22, 126, 145, 148, 150–51
  "decentering" the narrative, 118–19
  the "half-made" film, 147–48, 150, 157–58, 161, 178, 183–84
  idea of home as motif, 131–34
  interrupted journeys as motif, 177
  life-death relationship as motif, 186
  quest theme, 122
  self-reflexive element, 25–26, 109, 152, 153
  spatial orientation as motif, 130–31, 155–59
  use of binary opposites, 119, 133–34
Kiarostami, Abbas (Films)
  24 Frames/24 Ghāb, 94, 188–192
  ABC Africa/Ey Bi Ci Afrighā, 54–55, 93, 94, 162
  And Life Goes On/Zendegi va Digar Hich, 25–26, 106, 107, 109, 121, 124, 129, 131, 152
  "Bread and Alley"/"Nān va Kuche," 40, 107, 119, 130–31
  "Case No. 1, Case No. 2"/"Ghaziye Shekl-e Aval, Shekl-e Dovom," 131–32
  Certified Copy/Copy Barābar-e Asl, 107, 114, 175–80
  Close-Up, 23–25, 32, 52, 106, 107, 109, 119, 120, 124, 127–28
  First Graders/Avali-hā, 47, 107, 131
  Five Dedicated to Ozu/Panj, 93, 94, 170–71, 188
  Homework/Mashgh-e Shab, 47, 107, 108, 115–16
  Like Someone in Love, 62, 94, 181–87
  Report, The/Gozāresh, 40, 97, 107, 114, 133–34, 163, 180, 184
  Roads of Kiarostami/Jāde-hāye Kiārostami, 93
  Seven Trees (art installation), 94
  Shirin, 94, 171–74, 251–52
  "Take Me Home"/"Mara be Khāne Bebar," 66
  Taste of Cherry/Ta'ame Gilās, 26, 44–45, 48, 49, 57, 107, 110–11, 114, 128, 129–30, 132, 134–35, 137–39, 141–44, 148, 152, 185
  Ten/Dah, 55nviii, 56, 94, 112, 164–69
  Through the Olive Trees/Zir-e Derākhtān-e Zeytun, 26, 27, 28–29, 85, 106, 107, 109, 121, 124, 129, 131, 152, 153

Traveler, The/Mosāfer, 40, 107, 114, 119–20, 136–37, 141–42
Where Is the Friend's House?/Khāneye Dust Kojāst?, 107, 118, 120–22, 122–24, 131, 148
Wind Will Carry Us,The/Bād Mā Rā Khāhad Bord, 37, 52, 59, 99, 107, 111–12, 147–48, 148–49, 153–54, 156–61, 248–51
Kiarostami, Ahmad, 47, 54, 62, 63, 93, 189
Kiarostami, Bahman, 47, 54, 93, 132–33
Kiarostami Foundation, 93
"Kiarostami-Makhmalbaf" model, 21–22, 65–66, 97
Kierkegaard, Soren, 197
Kimiai, Masoud (Films), *Qeysar/Gheysar*, 38
Kimiavi, Parviz (Films)
    Mongols/Moghol-hā (1973), 40
    Okay Mister/OK MR, 40
Kitano, Takeshi, 85
Klawans, Stuart, 225
Klute (Alan J. Pakula), 256
Knife in the Water (Roman Polanski), 151
Koker Trilogy (*Where Is the Friend's House?*, *And Life Goes On*, *Through the Olive Trees*) (Abbas Kiarostami)
    compassion as anchoring value, 122
    connections among films, 121–22, 126
    films included in, 121
    historical background, 125–26
    Makhmalbaf films compared to, 31–32
    poetry combined with realism in, 120–22
    use of non-professional actors, 125–26
Kubrick, Stanley, 27
Kundera, Milan, 199
Kurosawa, Akira
    and *Dreams*, 190
    as multiple Oscar winner, 95
    on Kiarostami, 79
    Kiarostami's admiration of, 184
    and Kiarostami's reputation in Iran, 79, 117–18
Kushan, Ismail and *filmfarsi*, 35
Kusturica, Emir, 30

Lady, The/*Bānu* (Dariush Mehrjui)
    as female-centered, 198
    Mahmoud Kalari as actor in, 248
    and *Viridiana* (Luis Buñuel), 198
La La Land (Damien Chazelle), 91
Lang, Fritz, 139, 141
Langlois, Henri, 14, 35
Last Act, The/*Parde-y Ākhār* (Varuzh Karim-Masihi), 20
Last Year at Marienbad (Alain Resnais), 151
Lee, Ang, 59
Lee, Nathan, 225
Leigh, Mike, 31
Leila/*Leilā* (Dariush Mehrjui)
    depiction of sexual mores, 82–83, 198
    depiction of women in, 65
    Fajr Festival prize winner, 49
Lessons with Kiarostami (Paul Cronin), 94
Like Someone in Love (Abbas Kiarostami), **181–187**
    autobiographical dimension in, 184–87
    bleak views reflected in, 114
    as female-centered, 181–83
    filmed in Japan, 62, 94, 181
    as "half-made" film, 183–84
    use of digital technology, 107
Lincoln Center Festival of Iranian cinema, 19–20, 51
Lipsky, Jeff, 30
Loach, Ken, 136
Locarno Film Festival, 31, 49, 118, 125
Long Goodbye, The (Robert Altman), 231
Lor Girl, The/*Dokhtar-e Lor* (Abdolhossein Sepanta), 34–35
Lost in Translation (Sofia Coppola), 225
Low Heights/*Ertefā'-e Past* (Ebrahim Hatamikia), 88
Luddy, Tom, 93
Lumière brothers, 139
Lynch, David, 91, 143, 170

McCarthy, Todd, 30
Mackey, Sandra, 78
Maghsoudlou, Bahman, 27, 42
Maher, Amin, 164, 169
Majidi, Majid, 44
Majidi, Majid (Films)
    Baran/Bārān, 56
    Children of Heaven/Bache-hāye Asemān, 49, 53, 82, 85
    Father, The/Pedar, 32
Makhmalbaf, Hana (Films), "The Day My Aunt Was Ill"/"Ruzi ke Khāle-am Mariz Bud," 47
Makhmalbaf, Mohsen
    on Abbas Kiarostami, 63
    biographical background, 24, 47–48, 80, 81, 199, 206, 214, 219–20
    career phases, 204–7
    conversion from fundamentalism, 24, 80, 205–6, 214
    depiction of women, 22, 65–66
    films compared to Koker Trilogy, 31–32
    as hero in *Close-Up*, 23–24
    Houshang Golmakani's documentary about, 206
    how to approach, 203–4
    influence on Iranian filmmakers, 53, 96
    Mahmoud Kalari on, 243–44
    multiplicity of voices as film feature, 203, 213, 272
    personality, 31, 32, 80–81
    and poetic cinema, 80–81, 200–202
    relationship with his children, 47, 219–20
    relations with Islamic Republic, 24, 48, 201, 206
    reputation, 24, 80, 206–7, 216
    and self-reflexive element, 204, 213
    as social critic, 24, 80–81, 96, 205
    on *Still Life*, 39
    as target of ideological attacks, 80
Makhmalbaf, Mohsen (Films)
    Actor, The/Honarpishe, 206
    Cyclist, The/Bicycle-rān, 24, 80, 96
    Este-aze (Fleeing from Evil to God), 204

Gabbeh, 31, 49, 80–81, 199–207, 213, 244, 246
Marriage of the Blessed/Arusi-e Khubān, 24, 80, 205
Moment of Innocence, A/Nun va Goldun, 31, 204, 206–7, 208–14
Once Upon a Time, Cinema/Nāser al-din Shāh, Actor-e Cinemā, 34, 38, 206
Peddler, The/Dastforush, 24, 80, 205
Salaam Cinema/Salām Cinemā, 30–31, 204, 206, 207, 212, 213, 244–46
Makhmalbaf, Samira, biographical background, 47, 216–17
Makhmalbaf, Samira (Films)
    Apple, The/Sib, 47, 49–50, 215–20
    At Five in the Afternoon/Panj-e Asr, 56
    Blackboards/Takhte Siyāh, 52, 53
Malick, Terrence, 59, 170
Manhattan By Numbers/Manhattan az ruye Shomāre (Amir Naderi), 26–27
Manicheism, 78
Man of Integrity/Lerd, A (Mohammad Rasoulof), 61
Mansouri, Touraj, 243
Mantle of the Prophet, The (Roy Mottahedeh), 27
Manuscripts Don't Burn/Dastneveshte-hā Nemisuzand (Mohammad Rasoulof), **255–257**
    evocation of "Chain Murders", 61, 257
    and *The Master and Margarita* (Mikhail Bulgakov), 257
    Shah's regime likened to current government, 255–57
Mari, Reika, 182
Marks, John, 50
Marooned in Iraq/Avāz hāye Sarzamin-e Mādari-am (Bahman Ghobadi), 56
Marriage of the Blessed/Arusi-e Khubān (Mohsen Makhmalbaf)
    middle class life depicted, 205
    and Makhmalbaf's reputation, 80
    as social criticism, 24, 205
Master and Margarita, The (Mikhail Bulgakov), 257
Mature, Victor, 46
May Lady, The/Bānuye Ordibehesht, (Rakhshan Bani-Etemad), 49
Mehrjui, Dariush
    and Ayatollah Khomeini, 33, 43, 83, 197
    biographical background, 83, 196, 247
    comment on government restrictions, 49, 83
    deviation from "Kiarostami-Makhmalbaf" model, 22, 65–66, 196

female-centered films, 198
films banned, 48–49, 83, 195, 197–98
focus on upper and middle classes, 196
influence on Asghar Farhadi, 234
J. D. Salinger as influence, 51, 83, 195
Mahmoud Kalari on, 247–48
outburst at Kiarostami's funeral, 92
reception in Iran vs. the West, 195–96
response to government restrictions, 62, 198
Saul Bellow as influence, 51, 83, 195
Mehrjui, Dariush (Films)
    Cow, The/Gāv, 38–39, 43, 48–49, 83, 92, 196–97, 238, 247
    Hamoon/Hāmoon, 21, 65, 195, 197, 247–48
    Lady, The/Bānu, 198, 248
    Leila/Leilā, 49, 65, 82–83, 198
    Mr. Simpleton/Aghāye Hālu, 197, 247
    Pari (remake of J. D. Salinger's *Franny and Zooey*), 51, 65, 83, 198
    Pear Tree, The/Derakht-e Golābi, 49, 198
    Postman/Postchi, 197, 198
    Sara/Sārā, 198
    Tenants, The/Ejāre Neshin-hā, 197
    Cycle, The/Dāyere-ye Minā, 39, 197, 205
Méliès, Georges, 190
Meshkini, Marziyeh (Films), *The Day I Became a Woman/Ruzi ke Zan Shodam*, 52
Meyer, David, 221
Miladi, Armin, 66
Milani, Tahmineh 44
Miller, Arthur, 237, 238
Mina Cycle, The/Dāyere-ye Minā (Dariush Mehrjui). See *The Cycle*
Ministry of Culture and Islamic Guidance (Ershad), 21–22, 90–91
Miramax Films, 205
    and *Through the Olive Trees*, 28–29
Mirror, The/Dāyere (Jafar Panahi)
    and *Closed Curtain*, 231
    as Kiarostami-like, 57, 100, 232
    as Locarno award winner, 49
Moadi, Peyman, 235–36

Mirtahmasb Mojtaba, 59
Moadi, Peyman, 98
Mokri, Shahram, 91, 101
Moment of Innocence, A/Nun va Goldun (Mohsen Makhmalbaf), **208–214**
    architecture as important in, 246–47
    auteur cinema questioned, 213
    autobiographical roots of, 31, 209–10
    and genesis of *Salaam Cinema*, 207, 212, 244–45
    history reversed in, 210–11
    humanism of, 204, 206–7
    influence of Iranian culture in, 211–12
    Mahmoud Kalari as cinematographer, 210
    multiplicity of voices in, 213
    self-reflexive element, 213
    as statement against violence, 207, 211
Mongols/Moghol-hā (Parviz Kimiavi), 14, 40
Montreal World Film Festival, 32, 49
Moore, Marianne, 104, 113, 150
Moore, Michael, 59
Moqaddam, Jalal (Filmo), *The Window/Panjere* (1970), 41
Moretti, Nanni, "The Day *Close-Up* Opened", 127
Mossadegh, Mohammed, 33–34
Mottahedeh, Roy, 27
Mousavi, Mirhossein, 98
Moving Midway (Godfrey Cheshire), 56
Mr. Simpleton/Aghāye Hālu, 197, 247
Mulla Sadra, 146
Museum of Modern Art (New York), 200
Muzzafer al-Din Shah, 33

Nabili, Marva, 39
Nabokov, Vladimir, 211
Naderi, Amir
    and film industry reconstruction, 43
    and Kiarostami, 142
    Iranian New Wave commercial films by, 41
    relocation to New York, 26, 54, 61

use of children as characters, 22
Naderi, Amir (Films)
   Goodbye, Friend/Khodāhāfez Rafigh, 41
   Impasse/Tangnā, 41
   Manhattan by Numbers/Manhattan az ruye Shomāre, 26–27
   Runner, The/Davande, 68
   Tangsir, 41
   Water, Wind, Dust/Ab, Bād, Khāk, 26
Nasr, Seyyed Hossein, 143
Nassirian, Ali, 247
National Society of Film Critics (U.S.), 143
Navel/Nāf (Mohammad Shirvani), 95
Need, The/Niyāz (Alireza Davudnezhad), 20
Neshat, Shirin, 63
New Iranian Cinema
   defined, 38
   See also post-1979 Iranian cinema entries
New Yorker Films, 31
New York Film Festival, 28, 31, 49–50, 64
Niami, Ramin, 27
Night of the Hunchback/Shab-e Ghuzi (Farrokh Gaffary), 37
Ning Ying, 127
Nolan, Christopher, 163
No One Knows About Persian Cats/Kasi az Gorbe-hāye Irāni Khabar Nadāre
   (Bahman Ghobadi), 56, 237

October Films, 30
Odyssey, The, 139
Offside (Jafar Panahi)
   anti-regime stance, 100
   concerns of women in, 58
   Mahmoud Kalari as cinematographer, 99
   success of, 58
Ohanian, Ovanes, 34
Ohanian, Ovanes (Films), *Haji Agha, Cinema Actor/Hāji Aghā, Actor-e Cinemā*, 34
Okay Mister/OK MR (Parviz Kimiavi), 40
Okuno, Tadashi, 183, 185, 186

Once Upon a Time, Cinema/Nāser al-din Shāh, Actor-e Cinemā (Mohsen Makhmalbaf), 34, 38, 206
Others, The (Alejandro Amenabar), 85
Out 1 (Jacques Rivette), 238
Ovanesian, Arbi, 39
Overlooked Film Festival, 53
Ozu, Yasujirō, 170, 184

Pahlavi dynasty, 33–34
Panahi, Jafar
  American filmmakers support of, 59, 99
  depictions of women, 57, 58
  domination as film director post-2000, 56–58
  on filmmaking, 99–100, 101
  on his current situation, 100
  international acclaim for "unofficial" films, 59–61
  and Kiarostami, 60, 226
  relations with Islamic Republic, 58–60, 98–101, 230, 257
  use of digital technology, 60, 230
Panahi, Jafar (Films)
  3 Faces/Se Rokh, 60, 66
  Circle, The/Dāyere, 52, 57, 100, 228
  Closed Curtain/Parde, 60, 99, 230–32
  Crimson Gold/Tālaye Sorkh, 57–58, 100, 225–29
  Mirror, The/Ayne, 49, 57, 100, 231, 232
  Offside, 58, 99, 100
  Taxi/Tāxi, 60, 99
  This Is Not a Film/In Yek Film Nist, 60, 99
  White Balloon, The/Bādkonak-e Sefid, 26, 30, 57, 85, 100, 122
Paradjanov, Sergei, 200
Pari (Dariush Mehrjui)
  as female-centered, 198
  as remake of *Fanny and Zooey* (J. D. Salinger), 51, 65, 83, 198
Partovi, Kambozia, 230
Passenger, The (Michelangelo Antonioni), 226
Past, The/Gozashte (Asghar Farhadi), 97, 240, 253–54
Pather Panchali (Satyajit Ray), 124

Pear Tree, The/Derakht-e Golābi (Dariush Mehrjui), 49, 198
Peddler, The/Dastforush (Mohsen Makhmalbaf)
    and Makhmalbaf's reputation in Iran, 80
    as social criticism, 24, 80, 205
Peele, Jordan, 91
Peña, Richard, 28, 50, 196
Persona (Ingmar Bergman), 151
Piano, The (Jane Campion), 29
Picasso, Pablo, 189
Pig/Khuk (Mani Haghighi), 66–67
Pinter, Harold, 237
Pirandello, Luigi, 211
Plato, 156
Plotinus, 156
poetic cinema
    and Abbas Kiarostami, 37, 39, 52, 59, 148–49, 158, 159–66, 187
    and Forough Farrokhzad, 37, 149
    and Mohsen Makhmalbaf, 80–81, 200–202
Pomegranate and Cane/Nār va Ney (Sa'ied Ebrahimifar), 20
pop culture, American vs. Iranian, 81
Portishead, 75
Portrait of a Lady (Jane Campion), 82
Positif, 35
Pound, Ezra, 104, 150
Postman/Postchi (Dariush Mehrjui), 197
Prince Ehtejab/Shāzde Ehtejāb (Bahman Farmanara), 40
production code, 21–22, 65–66, 81–82, 163
Professionals, The (Richard Brooks), 41
Psycho (Alfred Hitchcock), 239
Pulp Fiction (Quentin Tarantino), 29
Qajar dynasty, 33
Qazvin (city), 139
Qashqais (nomadic tribe), 202
Qeysar/Gheysar (Masoud Kimiai)
    as commercial hit, 38
    Hollywood-style production values, 38–39

Rafsanjani, Hashemi, 72, 84, 135
Rashomon (Akira Kurosawa), 124, 140
Rasoulof, Mohammad
　　Islamic Republic's persecution of, 61, 257
　　response to government repression, 61–62, 256–57
Rasoulof, Mohammad (Films)
　　Goodbye/Be Omid-e Didār, 61
　　Iron Island/Jazireye Ahani, 56, 256
　　Man of Integrity, A/Lerd, 61
　　Manuscripts Don't Burn/Dastneveshte-hā Nemisuzand, 61, 255–57
　　There Is No Evil/Sheytān Vojud Nadārad, 61
　　White Meadow, The/Keshtzār-hāye Sepid, 256
Ray, Bingham, 30
Ray, Satyijit, 79
Red Desert (Michelangelo Antonioni), 225
Redford, Robert, 59
Red Sorghum (Zhang Yimou), 124
Reed, Lou, 83
Report, The/Gozāresh (Abbas Kiarostami)
　　autobiographical dimension, 40, 97, 107, 114, 133–34, 180, 184
　　as female-centered, 163, 180
Rezai, Hossein, 125–26
Rex Cinema, 42
Rhazes, 141
Rimbaud, Arthur, 197
Rivette, Jacques, 179, 237
Roads of Kiarostami (Abbas Kiarostami), 93
Rohmer, Éric, 179
Romeo and Juliet (Franco Zeffirelli), 172, 252
Ronde, La (Max Ophuls), 116
Rosenbaum, Jonathan, 10, 15, 93, 143, 145
Rossellini, Roberto, 35, 178, 179
Roud, Richard, 28
Rouhani, Hassan (President), 67, 90
Rubaiyat of Omar Khayyam, The (trans. by Edward Fitzgerald), 77
Rumi, Jelaluddin, 77, 80, 146, 187, 199, 212, 213
Runner, The/Davande (Amir Naderi), 68

Russian Ark (Alexander Sokurov), 101

Saasani, Arsalan, 39
Sabzian, Hossein, 23, 24, 25, 46, 127
Sa'edi, Gholem-Hossein, 41, 238, 240
Sahhafbashi, Mirza Ebrahim, 34
Salaam Cinema/Salām Cinemā (Mohsen Makhmalbaf)
    auteur cinema questioned, 213
    genesis of, 207, 212, 244–45
    humanism of, 206
    Iranian cinephilia reflected in, 30
    multiplicity of voices in, 213, 272
    reception of, 207
    self-reflexive element, 204, 213
    tyranny of film director in, 30–31, 207, 212, 246
    as "unintended" film, 245–46
Salesman, The/Forushande (Asghar Farhadi), **237–240**
    The Cow (Mehrjui) referenced in, 238
    Death of a Salesman (Miller) referenced in, 237, 238–39
    focus on middle class marriage, 238
    Mani Haghighi on, 97
    as Oscar winner, 65
    use of professional actors, 240
Salinger, J. D., 195, 197, 198
Samadian, Seifollah, 66, 92–93
Sanai, 146
Sanders, George, 178
Sara/Sārā (Dariush Mehrjui), 198
Sarris, Andrew, 143
Sartre, Jean-Paul, 44
SAVAK, 42
Sayahi, Abbas, 244
Sayyad, Parviz (Films)
    Dead End/Bonbast, 41–42
    In the Course of the Night/Dar Emtedād-e Shab, 41
Scenes from a Marriage (Ingmar Bergman), 179
Schimmel, Annemarie, 154

Schrader, Paul, 64
Schuon, Frithjof, 154
Scorsese, Martin, 59, 63
Search for Common Ground, 50–51
Sepanta, Abdolhossein, 34
Sepanta, Abdolhossein (Films), *Lor Girl, The/Dokhtar-e Lor*, 34
Separation, A/Jodāie Nāder az Simin (Asghar Farhadi)
    depiction of women in, 65
    Hossein Eidizadeh's analysis of, 98
    innovations in, 65, 234
    Mahmoud Kalari as cinematographer for, 99, 241
    Mahmoud Kalari on, 252–54
    Mani Haghghi on, 97
    as Oscar prizewinner, 64, 240–41
    use of hand-held camera, 252
Sepheri, Sohrab, 114, 148
Servant, The (Joseph Losey), 151
Seven Samurai (Akira Kurosawa), 41
Seven Trees (Abbas Kiarostami art installation), 94
sexual content of film and government production code, 21–22, 65–66, 81–82, 163
Seyyedi, Houman (Films), *Sheeple/Maghz-hāye Kuchak-e Zang-zade*, 66
Shah Muzzafer al-Din, 33
Shahid-Saless, Sohrab (Films), *Still Life/Tabi'at-e Bi-jān*, 39
Shakibai, Khosrow, 21, 247–48
Shahnameh (Book of Kings, The) (Ferdowsi), 171
Sheeple/Maghz-hāye Kuchak-e Zang-zade (Houman Seyyedi), 66
Sheissi, Kamyar, 227
Shepard, Sam, 237
Shiism, influence on Kiarostami, 157
Shimell, William, 177, 186
Shiraz, 46
Shirdel, Kamran (Films)
    Morning of the Fourth Day, The/Sobh-e Ruz-e Chāhārom, 41
    "Castle, The"/"Ghal'e," 36
    "Night it Rained, The," 14
    "Women's Prison, The"/"Nedāmatgāh," 36

Shirin (Abbas Kiarostami), **171–174**
    contemplative/interrogative responses invited by, 171–72
    as experimental, 94
    as female-centered, 169, 171–73
    and *Khosrow and Shirin* (Ganjavi), 171–72, 173, 252
    Mahmoud Kalari on, 251–52
    and Persian passion play *ta'ziyeh*, 173–74
    and "Taste of Shirin" (Tazavi), 171–72
    use of professional actors, 252
    women as central figures in, 171–73
Shirvani, Mohammad, 95
Sight & Sound, 235
Sinaie, Khosro (Films), *In the Alleys of Love/Dar Kuche-hāye Eshgh*, 20
Sly/Mārmuz (Kamal Tabrizi), 67
Smell of Camphor, Fragrance of Jasmine/Buye Kāfur Atr-e Yās (Bahman Farmanara), 52
Smith, Gavin, 19
Smith, Will, 223
Soderbergh, Steven, 31, 85
Sokurov, Alexander, 101
South of the City, The/Jonub-e Shahr (Farrokh Gaffary)
    government suppression of, 36
    neorealism in, 35–36
Spectator magazine, 28
Spielberg, Steven, 59, 233
Stardust Stricken/Gong-e Khāb-dide (Houshang Golmakani), 206
Star is Born, A (George Cukor), 231
Stardust Stricken/Gong-e Khāb-dide (Houshang Golmakani), 206
Stevens, Wallace, 150
Stevenson, Adlai, 84
Stewart, Rod, 130
Still Life/Tabi'at-e Bi-jān (Sohrab Shahid-Saless), 39, 41
Stone, Oliver, 59, 64, 66
Stone, Sharon, 73
Straight Story, The (David Lynch), 144
Stranger and the Fog, The/Gharibe va Meh (Bahram Beyzai), 40
Straub-Huillet, 40, 145
Streetcar Named Desire, A (Elia Kazan), 234, 235

Sufism
    and Avicenna (Ibn Sina), 155
    influence on Kiarostami, 111–12, 155–61
    and Shihabuddin Suhrawardi, 155–56
Suhrawardi, Shihabuddin, 155
suicide, and *Taste of Cherry*, 45, 57, 128, 137–39, 228
Sundance Film Festival, 50
"symbolism," in modernist art films vs. Kiarostami's films, 151–52, 156–61

Tabrizi, Kamal (Films), *Sly/Mārmuz*, 67
Taghvai, Naser (Films), *Tranquility in the Presence of Others/Arāmesh dar Hozur-e Digarān* (1969), 41
Takanashi, Rin, 182
"Take Me Home"/"Mara be Khāne Bebar" (Abbas Kiarostami), 66, 93
Tale of the Sea/Hekāyat-e Daryā (Bahman Farmanara), 66
Tall Shadows of the Wind/Sāye-haye Boland-e Bād (Bahman Farmanara), 40
Tangsir (Amir Naderi), 41
Tarantino, Quentin, 91, 163
Tarkovsky, Andrei, 79
Tarr, Béla, 91
Taslimi, Susan, 21
Taste of Cherry/Ta'ame Gilās (Abbas Kiarostami)
    1997 Palme d'Or winner, 26, 31, 44, 49, 128–30, 134–35, 141–42
    autobiographical dimension in, 110, 114, 137–39, 152, 185
    as Cannes entry, government opposition to, 44–45, 48, 105, 128
    as cinematic gamble, 110–11, 134–35, 139, 141
    and cinematic modernism, 139
    cinematic self-consciousness in, 129–30
    connections with past work, 148
    divided reception by critics, 143–44
    life-death relationship as motif, 186
    and Masterworks period, 107
    as New York Film Festival feature, 49
    philosophical aspects of, 138–39
    "reading" the film, 147
    and suicide, 45, 57, 128, 137–39, 228
"Taste of Shirin" (Hamideh Razavi), 171–72

Tati, Jacques, 145, 146
Taubman, Philip, 49
Taxi/Tāxi (Jafar Panahi), 60, 99
ta'ziyeh, 149, 173–74
Ta'ziyeh/Ta'ziye (Abbas Kiarostami), 173
Tehran (1997)
    anti-Americanism as proforma, 72–73
    class differences in, 74
    Hotel Naderi, 74–75
    interactions with Kiarostami and Makhmalbaf, 47–49
    Iranians response to Americans, 46, 71–72
    similarities to Los Angeles, 73–74
    visa difficulties, 45–46
Tehran (2017)
    absence of "morality police," 90
    diversity of art scene, 56, 237
    north section development, 90
Telluride Film Festival, 54, 221
Tehrani, Hedieh, 66
Telluride Film Festival, 224
Ten/Dah (Abbas Kiarostami), **164–169**
    blurring of truth and fiction, 165
    as career turning point, 56, 112
    divided reception by critics, 168
    downbeat atmosphere, 166–67
    evocations of previous work, 165
    as female-centered, 166–67
    feminist theme in, 56, 112, 164, 168
    modern Tehran as setting, 167
    use of child actor, 164–65
    use of digital technology, 165–66, 94
Tenants, The/Ejāre Neshin-hā (Dariush Mehrjui), 197
There Is No Evil/Sheytān Vojud Nadārad (Mohammad Rasoulof), 61
Thiérrée, James, 46
This Is Not a Film/In Yek Film Nist (Jafar Panahi)
    banning of, 99
    cinephilia in, 60

    self-reflexive element, 60
    use of digital technology, 60, 230
Through the Olive Trees/Zir-e Derākhtān-e Zeytun (Abbas Kiarostami)
    auteur cinema questioned, 124
    autobiographical dimension in, 184
    humanism of, 129
    and idea of home, 131
    as Koker Trilogy film, 121
    and Masterworks period, 107
    Miramax Films bungled release of, 28–29
    and Revolution's failures, 106
    self-reflexive element, 27, 109, 152, 153
    vs. U.S news image of Iran, 85
Time for Drunken Horses, Al Zamāni Barāye Masti-e Asb-hā (Bahman Ghobadi), **221–224**
    autobiographical dimension in, 222
    as Cannes 2000 Camera d'Or prize winner, 52, 224
    critical acclaim for, 221
    David Meyer on, 221
    as family production, 224
    Ghobadi's artistic signature in, 222–23
    as kid-centered, 223
    Telluride audience response to, 54, 224
    use of non-professional actors, 223
Time of Love/Nobat-e Asheghi (Mohsen Makhmalbaf)
    culture as focus, 205–6
    and Mahmoud Kalari, 243–44
Tolstoy, Leo, 226
Toronto International Film Festival, 63
Traffic (Steven Soderbergh), 85
Tranquility in the Presence of Others/Arāmesh dar Hozur-e Digarān (Naser Taghvai), 41
Traveler, The/Mosāfer (Abbas Kiarostami)
    as analysis of character, 114, 119–20
    autobiographical dimension in, 136–37, 184
    future cinematic strategies in, 119
    and Kanoon period, 40, 107

and Kiarostami's reaction to Palme d'Or prize, 141–42
Travelers, The/Mosāferān (Bahram Beyzai), 65, 234
Trouble with Harry, The (Alfred Hitchcock), 37
Truffaut, Francois, 14, 35, 36, 38
Trump, Donald and "Muslim travel ban," 67, 90–91
Turin Film Festival, 32
Turtles Can Fly/Lākposht hā ham Parvāz Mikonand (Bahman Ghobadi), 56
Twister (Jan de Bont), 78

Underground (Emir Kusturica), 30
Under the Skin of the City/Zir- e Pust-e Shahr (Rakhshan Bani-Etemad), 56

Van Gogh, Vincent, 189
Van Peebles, Melvin, 204
Variety, 29–30
Venice Film Festival, 38, 52, 162, 195, 197
Vikings, The (Richard Fleischer), 211
Viridiana (Luis Buñuel), 83, 197
Vitti, Monica, 139
Vossoughi, Behrouz, 38, 41

"Walk with Kiarostami, A"/*"Ghadam Zadan bā Kiārostami"* (Jamsheed Akrami), 66
Warhol, Andy, 174
"Waste Land, The" (T. S. Eliot), 151
Water, Wind, Dust/Ab, Bād, Khāk (Amir Naderi), 26
Wayne, John, 211
Webber, Andrew Lloyd, 189
Weinstein, Harvey, 28–29
"Westoxication" (*gharbzadegi*), 42
Where Is the Friend's House/Khāneye Dust Kojāst?, (Abbas Kiarostami)
    auteur cinema questioned, 123–24
    as European debut film, 118
    and idea of home, 131
    as Koker Trilogy film, 121
    and Masterworks period, 107
    social realism joined with poetry in, 120–22, 122–24

and Sohrab Sepheri's poem, 148
use of non-professional actors, 120
"Where Is the Friend's House" (Sohrab Sepheri), 148
White Balloon, The/Bādkonak-e Sefid (Jafar Panahi)
    as child-centered, 57, 100
    as international art house hit, 26
    Kiarostami's script for, 122
    October Films release of, 30
    vs. U.S. news image of Iran, 85
White Meadow, The/Keshtzār-hāye Sepid (Mohammad Rasoulof), 256
Williams, Tennessee, 237
Williams, William Carlos, 104, 113, 150
Window, The/Panjere (Jalal Moqaddam), 33–34
"Wind Will Carry Us, The" (Forough Farrokhzad), as model for Kiarostami, 37, 148–49, 159, 187
Wind Will Carry Us, The/Bād Mā Rā Khāhad Bord, (Abbas Kiarostami)
    autobiographical dimension in, 111–12, 153–54, 185
    connections with past work, 148
    and Forough Farrokhzad poem, 37, 148–49, 159, 187
    as "half-made" film, 147–48, 153–54, 157–58, 161
    influence of Shiism on, 157–58, 159
    influence of Sufism on, 111–12, 156–57, 159
    Mahmoud Kalari as cinematographer, 99, 248–49
    Mahmoud Kalari on, 248–51
    and Masterworks period, 107
    and Omar Khayyam, 149, 159, 160
    as poetic cinema, 52, 59, 148–49, 158, 159–61
    "reading" the film, 157
    spatial orientation as symbolic, 156–59
    symbolism in, 156–61 women, depiction of, and production code, 22, 65–66, 81–82, 163
Woman in the Dunes (Hiroshi Teshigahara), 151
"Women's Prison, The"/"Nedāmatgāh" (Kamran Shirdel), 36
Women's Prison/Zendān-e Zanān (Manijeh Hekmat), 86
"Workers Leaving the Factory" (Lumière brothers), 190

Yang, Edward, 104

Yektapanah, Hasan (Films), *Djomeh*, 52
Yogananda, Paramahansa, 161
Yousefinejad, Asghar (Films), *The Home*, 67

Zeffirelli, Franco, 172, 252
Zeitgeist Films, 52
Zero de conduite (Jean Vigo), 115
Zoroaster/Zoroastrianism, 77, 78, 141, 155, 159

ABOUT THE AUTHOR

Godfrey Cheshire is an award-winning film critic, journalist, filmmaker and teacher based in New York City. His writings on Iranian cinema have appeared in publications including the *New York Times*, *Variety*, the *Village Voice*, *Cineaste*, *Sight & Sound*, *Cinemascope*, *Film International* and *Dissent*. He is a member of the National Society of Film Critics and a former chairman of the New York Film Critics Circle. His book *Conversations with Kiarostami* was published in 2019.